Android Application Development

(with KitKat Support)

Black Book™

DT Editorial Services

&

Pradeep Kothari

Published by:

dreamtech PRESS

ISBN: 978-93-5119-409-5

Edition: 2023

Reprint: 2024

Printed at: Nisha Enterprises

Dedication

I would like to dedicate this book to my parents
Mr Radha Krishan Kothari and Mrs Vijay Laxmi,
without whom my life would not have any meaning. Thank you so much for all your unconditional support, love, and education.
Everything I am, I owe to my parents.

About the Author

Pradeep Kothari holds the B.E. degree in Electronics and Communication and has about 9 years of industry experience in developing, architecting, and deploying enterprise-level mobile technological product and solutions for Windows mobile, J2ME, Android, and iOS-based devices while working in some top technology companies in the domain of Telecom, Gaming, Mobile content solutions, and Education technology.

Pradeep started his software career writing Mobile apps for Pocket PC 2003 (early version of windows mobile) in the early days of evolution of smart phones. He then progressed to Android and iOS programming for handled devices.

He also provided consulting to some top technology companies like Lionbridge Inc. and Microsoft.

Currently, he is a Ph.D. researcher in the field of mobility and a Technical Manager with a technology company, where he is leading a team in designing and developing cutting edge enterprise mobile products for mobile phones as well as tablets.

DT Editorial Services

DT Editorial Services has seized the market of computer books, bringing excellent content in software development to the fore. The team is committed to excellence—excellence in quality of content, excellence in the dedication of its authors and editors, excellence in the attention to detail, and excellence in understanding the needs of its readers.

Contents at a Glance

Introduction xv

Chapter 1: Fundamentals of Java for Android Application Development 1

Chapter 2: Getting an Overview of Android 49

Chapter 3: Working with the Activities and Intents in Android 79

Chapter 4: Working with the User Interface Using Views and ViewGroups 135

Chapter 5: Handling Pictures and Menus with Views 205

Chapter 6: Storing the Data Persistently 229

Chapter 7: Networking and E-mailing in Android 279

Chapter 8: Working with Location Services and Maps 303

Chapter 9: Working with Graphics and Animation 329

Chapter 10: Audio, Video, and Using the Camera 361

Chapter 11: Thread and Services 395

Chapter 12: Bluetooth, NFC, and Wi-Fi 417

Chapter 13: Telephony and SMS 449

Chapter 14: Hardware Sensors 473

Chapter 15: Widgets and Live Wallpapers in Android 487

Chapter 16: Developing NDK Applications 507

Chapter 17: Developing, Monetizing, Promoting, and Publishing Android Applications 527

Glossary 551

Index 555

Online Resource Available with the Book 561

Bonus Chapters Available with the Book

Appendix A: Getting Started with Android Studio – New IDE for Development by Google

Appendix B: Introducing Tasker

Table of Contents

Introduction .... **xv**

Chapter 1: Fundamentals of Java for Android Application Development **1**

Introduction to Java 2
Need for Java for Android Application Development 2
Features of Java 3
Introducing Java Dalvik Virtual Machine 5
Developing a Simple Java Program 5
Writing the Java Program 5
Compiling and Executing the Java Program 9
Working with Java Tokens 10
Keywords 10
Identifiers 11
Literals 11
Constants 15
Knowledge Check—1 16
Operators 16
Explaining Data Types 27
Integer Data Types 27
Floating-Point Data Types 27
Character Data Type 28
The boolean Data Type 29
Declaring Variables 29
Declaring the Instance Variables 30
Declaring the Class Variables 30
Declaring the Local Variables 31
Declaring Classes 32
Inner Classes 33
Declaring Methods 34
Methods Returning a Value 35
Passing Arguments to Methods 35
Creating Objects 36
Explaining Access Specifiers 36
Interfaces 37
Inheritance 39
Implementing Flow Control Statements 39

Using Selection Statements 40
Using Iteration Statements 42
Using Jump Statements 45
Summary 47
Quick Revise 47

Chapter 2: Getting an Overview of Android 49

Introducing Android 50
Listing the Version History of Android Platform 50
Discussing Android APIs 51
Describing the Android Architecture 52
Application Framework 53
Exploring the Features of Android 54
Discussing about Android Applications 54
The Application Components 54
The Manifest File 55
Downloading and Installing Android 55
Downloading and Installing the Android SDK 55
Setting up Android Virtual Device 59
Setting up Android Physical Device 61
Exploring the Development Environment 63
The Java Perspective Using Eclipse 63
The DDMS Perspective 63
The Command-Line Tools 63
Developing and Executing the First Android Application 66
Using Eclipse IDE to Create an Application 66
Running Your Application 68
Exploring the Application 70
Using Command-Line Tools 74
Summary 75
Quick Revise 75

Chapter 3: Using Activities, Fragments, and Intents in Android 79

Working with Activities 80
Creating an Activity 80
Starting an Activity 82
Managing the Lifecycle of an Activity 87
Applying Themes and Styles to an Activity 90
Displaying a Dialog in the Activity 92
Hiding the Title of the Activity 104
Using Intents 105
Exploring Intent Objects 105
Exploring Intent Resolution 108
Exploring Intent Filters 109
Resolving Intent Filter Collision 109
Linking the Activities Using Intent 110
Obtaining Results from Intent 114
Passing Data Using an Intent Object 119
Fragments 123

Fragment Implementation ... 124
Finding Fragments ... 125
Adding, Removing, and Replacing Fragments ... 126
Finding Activity Using Fragment ... 126
Using the Intent Object to Invoke Built-in Application ... 126
Summary ... 129
Quick Revise ... 129

Chapter 4: Working with the User Interface Using Views and ViewGroups ... 135

Working with View Groups ... 136
The LinearLayout Layout ... 139
The RelativeLayout Layout ... 143
The ScrollView Layout ... 145
The TableLayout Layout ... 147
The FrameLayout Layout ... 149
The TabLayout Using the Action Bar ... 150
Working with Views ... 154
Using the TextView ... 159
Using the EditText View ... 160
Using the Button View ... 161
Using the RadioButton View ... 163
Using the CheckBox View ... 166
Using the ImageButton View ... 168
Using the ToggleButton View ... 170
Using the RatingBar View ... 172
Binding Data with the AdapterView Class ... 174
Using the ListView Class ... 174
Using the Spinner ... 175
Using the Gallery View ... 178
Designing the AutoTextCompleteView ... 179
Implementing Screen Orientation ... 181
Anchoring the Views of the Current Activity ... 182
Customizing the Size and Position of the Views ... 182
Designing the Views Programmatically ... 182
Handling UI Events ... 184
Handling User Interaction with Activities ... 184
Handling User Interaction with the Views ... 186
Specialized Fragments ... 187
ListFragment ... 187
DialogFragment ... 189
PreferenceFragment ... 191
Creating Menus ... 193
The Options Menu ... 193
The Context Menu ... 195
The SubMenus ... 198
Summary ... 198
Quick Revise ... 199

Chapter 5: Handling Pictures and Menus with Views 205
Working with Image Views 206
Displaying Images in the Gallery View 206
Displaying Images in the Grid View 212
Using the `ImageSwitcher` View 214
Designing Context Menu for Image View 216
Using the `AnalogClock` and `DigitalClock` Views 219
Embedding Web Browser in an Activity 222
Notifying the User 224
Creating the Toast Notification 224
Creating the Status Bar Notification 225
Creating the Dialog Notification 226
Summary 226
Quick Revise 226

Chapter 6: Storing the Data Persistently 229
Introducing the Data Storage Options 230
Using Preferences 230
Using the Internal Storage 233
Exploring the Methods Used for Internal Storage 234
Developing an Application to Save User Data Persistently in File 235
Using the External Storage 239
Exploring the Methods Used for External Storage 239
Developing Application to Save File in SD Card 240
Using the SQLite Database 243
Creating the Database Helper Class 243
Creating the Layout and Main Activity Class 246
Creating the Layout and Activity for the Insert Operation 249
Creating the Layout and Activity to Search a Record 250
Creating the Activity Class to Fetch All Records 252
Creating the Layout and Activity for the Update Operation 253
Creating the Layout and Activity for the Delete Operation 255
Executing the Database Operations 257
Working with Content Providers 262
Exploring the android.provider Package 263
Creating User-Defined Content Provider 266
Consuming User-Defined Content Provider 271
Summary 274
Quick Revise 274

Chapter 7: Emailing and Networking in Android 279
Building an Application to Send Email 280
Networking in Android 283
Getting an Overview of Networking Fundamentals 283
Checking Network Availability 283
Accessing Web Services Using HTTP Post 284
Accessing Web Services Using the GET Method 287
Working with Binary Data and Text Files 290

Consuming JSON Services ... 293
Sockets Programming ... 296
Summary ... 301
Quick Revise ... 301

Chapter 8: Working with Location Services and Maps ... 303

Working with Google Maps ... 304
Exploring Google Maps External Library ... 304
Creating an Application Using Google Maps Android API ... 304
Disabling the Zoom Control Button ... 312
Changing the Map Type ... 313
Displaying the Specific Location and Adding Markers ... 315
Handling Map Gestures Interaction ... 318
Getting the Current Location of a User ... 318
Working with Geocoding and Reverse Geocoding ... 322
Summary ... 326
Quick Revise ... 326

Chapter 9: Working with Graphics and Animation ... 329

Working with Graphics ... 330
Drawing Graphics to Canvas ... 330
Using the Drawable Object ... 336
Referencing an Image File ... 337
Defining Drawable in XML ... 338
Using the `ShapeDrawable` Object ... 340
Working with the `NinePatchDrawable` Graphics ... 343
Understanding the Concept of Hardware Acceleration ... 345
Working with Animations ... 346
The Property Animation ... 346
View Animation ... 349
Drawable Animation ... 351
Summary ... 352
Quick Revise ... 352

Chapter 10: Audio, Video, and Camera ... 361

Role of Media Playback ... 362
Using Media Player ... 362
Media Formats Supported by Media Player ... 362
Preparing Audio for Playback ... 363
Preparing Video for Playback ... 364
Creating Application to Play Audio and Video Using MediaPlayer ... 365
Recording and Playing Sound ... 374
Use of Media Store ... 375
Audio Recording Application ... 375
Creating a Sound Pool ... 380
Using Camera for Taking Pictures ... 382
Recording Video ... 386
Creating Video Recording Application ... 387

Summary ... 391
Quick Revise ... 391

Chapter 11: Threads and Services ... 395

Introducing Threads ... 396
Worker Threads ... 396
Using AsyncTask ... 398
Introducing Services ... 401
Exploring Services Essentials ... 401
Understanding the Lifecycle of a Service ... 402
Exploring the `Service Class` ... 403
Introducing the `Service Class` ... 403
Creating a Bound Service ... 409
Summary ... 414
Quick Revise ... 414

Chapter 12: Bluetooth, NFC, and Wi-Fi ... 417

Working with Bluetooth ... 418
Exploring the Android Bluetooth APIs ... 418
Permissions Required to Access Bluetooth ... 420
Setting Up the Bluetooth for an Application ... 420
Identifying the Bluetooth-Enabled Devices ... 421
Querying the Paired Devices ... 421
Discovering Devices ... 421
Creating an Application Using Bluetooth Functionality ... 422
Connecting the Devices Using Bluetooth for Data Transfer ... 428
Connecting as a Server ... 428
Connecting as a Client ... 430
Working with Bluetooth Low Energy ... 433
Working with NFC ... 434
Exploring the Basics of NFC ... 434
Developing an Application Using NFC ... 436
Working with Wi-Fi ... 439
Exploring the Wi-Fi APIs ... 440
Creating an Application Using Wi-Fi ... 441
Summary ... 446
Quick Revise ... 446

Chapter 13: Telephony and SMS ... 449

Handling Telephony ... 450
Displaying Phone Information Application ... 453
Receiving Phone Calls Application ... 455
Making Outgoing Phone Calls Application ... 457
Handling SMS ... 460
Sending SMS Using SmsManager ... 460
Sending SMS Using Intent ... 463
Receiving SMS Using the BroadcastReceiver Object ... 467
Role of Default SMS Providers ... 468

Summary 470
Quick Revise 470

Chapter 14: Hardware Sensors 473

Introducing Sensors 474
Exploring the Sensor Framework 475
Managing Various Sensor Configurations 478
Understanding the Sensor Coordinate System 479
Using Sensors 479
Summary 485
Quick Revise 485

Chapter 15: Widgets and Live Wallpapers in Android 487

Home Screen Widgets 488
Adding the Broadcast Receiver Class to an Android Manifest 489
Using the RemoteViews and AppWidgetManager Classes 490
Creating a Customized Clock Widget 490
Collection View Widgets 494
Collection View Widget Layouts 495
Creating the Remote Views Service Class 495
Creating a Remote Views Factory Interface 496
Populating Collection View Widgets 497
Live Wallpaper 497
Creating Live Wallpaper Resource and Service 497
Configuring Wallpaper Service 498
Creating Live Wallpaper Application 498
Summary 503
Quick Revise 503

Chapter 16: Working with NDK 507

Introducing NDK 508
When to Use NDK? 508
Benefits of NDK 508
Communication between Java and Native Code 508
Installing the NDK 509
Installing C/C++ Support on Eclipse 509
Installing NDK Plugin through ADT 511
Installing Cygwin 512
Installing Android NDK 515
Configuring Eclipse for NDK Programming 516
Setting the Environment Variable 517
Building the Basic NDK Application 519
Summary 524
Quick Revise 524

Chapter 17: Publishing, Monetizing, and Distributing Android Applications 527

Signing the Android Application 528
Exploring the Strategies for Signing the Application 528
Obtaining the Appropriate Private Key 529
Preparing the Application for Release 532
Aligning the APK Package 532
Signing and Aligning APK Using the Eclipse IDE 533
Versioning the Android Application 535
Setting the Application Version 535
Specifying API Requirements of an Android Application 536
Publishing the Android Application 536
Releasing Applications on Google Play 537
Releasing Applications through Email 541
Releasing Applications through a Website 541
Monetizing Applications 541
Monetizing an Application through Advertising Platform 542
Integrating the Google AdMob SDK with an Application 543
Summary 547
Quick Revise 547

Glossary 551

Index 555

Online Resource Available with the Book 561

Bonus Chapters Available with the Book

Appendix A: Getting Started with Android Studio – New IDE for Development by Google

Appendix B: Introducing Tasker

Introduction

Congratulations on buying *Android Application Development Black Book*! This book is designed to provide a one-stop reference for your entire Android programming, which includes Android architecture; activities and intents; user interface using Views and ViewGroups; storing data persistently; network and emailing in Android; location services and maps; graphics and animation; audio, video, and using the Camera; threads and services; sending data through wireless networking technologies; telephony and SMS; hardware sensors; widgets and live wallpapers in Android; and **Native Development Kit** (**NDK**) programming. Google Play is the premier marketplace for selling and distributing Android applications. The pace of technological enhancements is getting faster day by day, leading to the extensive use of the Android platform. Nowadays, most of the companies are using Android **Software Development Kit (SDK)** to develop their day-to-day mobile applications.

The Audience

You must be wondering about the aims and objectives behind the release of Android edition. This has been released focusing on the developer or programmer working with Android SDK. Therefore, *Android Application Development Black Book* will serve you as an excellent guide in true sense—introducing the fast-changing world of today's Android SDK and various programming concepts related to it. The release of this book also offers one of the best available resources on the current version of the Android development used in mobile application development.

This book is equally beneficial for people who want to learn mobile application development using Android from scratch, or who are already involved in developing applications in Android mobile application development.

About this Book

Android Application Development Black Book provides a greater emphasis on application development using Android up to Android 4.4, the KitKat version.

This book mainly covers the following topics:

- Fundamentals of Java including its features, the concepts of interfaces, Java tokens, keywords, identifiers, literals, constants, operators, data types, variables, classes, methods, objects, access specifiers, inheritance, and control flow statements.
- Android architecture, application components, and how to develop the basic Android application using the Eclipse **Integrated Development Environment** (**IDE**).
- Activities and their life cycle, fragments, and intents in Android.
- View groups comprising linear layout, relative layout, scroll view, table layout, frame layout, and tab layout.

- Views comprising `TextView`, `EditText`, `Button`, `RadioButton`, `CheckBox`, `ImageButton`, `ToggleButton`, and `Rating Bar`.
- Data binding with `AdapterView` using `ListView`, `Spinner`, and `Gallery`.
- Handling user-interface events with `Activities` and `Views`.
- Specialized fragments, such as `ListFragment`, `DialogFragment`, and `PreferenceFragment`.
- The `ImageSwitcher` view, `Gallery` view, and `ImageView` used for displaying images on Android-supported devices.
- Custom application to send emails through Android-supported devices.
- Basic networking concepts, such as using the GET method, the POST method, JSON Web services, and downloading binary or text data.
- Google Maps external library comprising classes such as `GoogleMap`, `MapView`, `MapFragment`, `Marker`, and `UiSettings`.
- Operations that can be performed on Google Maps, such as disabling zoom control button, changing the Map type, adding markers, displaying specific user locations, managing map gestures, and geocoding as well as reverse geocoding.
- The `SurfaceView` and `ShapeDrawable` classes used for working with graphics and animation.
- Nine patch drawable image and hardware acceleration.
- The `MediaPlayer`, `AudioManager`, and `MediaRecorder` classes to play media stored in application resources, local files, content providers, and streamed from a network **Uniform Resource Locator** (URL).
- Use camera to capture still images and record videos using a media recorder.
- The concept of threads to perform multiple processes and explore the different types of services, such as start service, bound service, and intent service with their life cycles.
- Data transfer through wireless technologies such as Bluetooth, **Near Field Communication** (**NFC**), and Wi-Fi.
- Classes used to handle telephony and messaging features in mobile devices.
- Motion, environmental, and position sensors of Android-supported devices using the `SensorManager` class.
- Own home screen widgets developed using the `AppWidgetManager` and `AppWidgetProvider` classes.
- Live wallpaper developed for the home screen of Android-supported devices.
- NDK programming by adding native support to an Android application.
- Publish, monetize, and distribute the Android applications

Our sole intent has been to provide a book with a depth sufficient knowledge to make more than one reading rewarding to most programmers. Enjoy reading!

How to Use This Book

In this book, most of the code is tested with Android 4.4 SDK and the Eclipse IDE providing support for the Android platform. The Java programming language is used to develop the Android applications. In Chapter 15 of the book, the NDK programming is done using C/C++ programming language and you will learn to add native support to an Android application.

Conventions

We have used standard conventions throughout this book. This section helps you get acquainted with these conventions to ensure a superior learning experience.

Replace the code of the activity_main.xml file of the NFC application with the code shown in Listing 1:

Listing 1: Showing the Code to Design the Layout for the NFC Application

```
<?xml version="1.0" encoding="utf-8"?>
<LinearLayout xmlns:android="http://schemas.android.com/apk/res/android"
    android:layout_width="fill_parent"
    android:layout_height="fill_parent"
```

```
        android:orientation="vertical" >

        <TextView
        android:id="@+id/textView1"
        android:layout_width="fill_parent"
        android:layout_height="wrap_content"
        android:text="Ensure that Android Beam is enabled by turning it on in
            the system Settings (select the setting icon above), then place this device up
            against another Android device that supports Android Beam to send a
            message"
        android:padding="10dp"
        android:textSize="18sp"
        />
    </LinearLayout>
```

The reserved words, properties, methods, events, classes, interfaces, namespaces (used in the code snippets), exceptions, etc. are shown distinctly using a different font within the text.

Each figure has a caption to help you understand the figure better, as illustrated in the following figure:

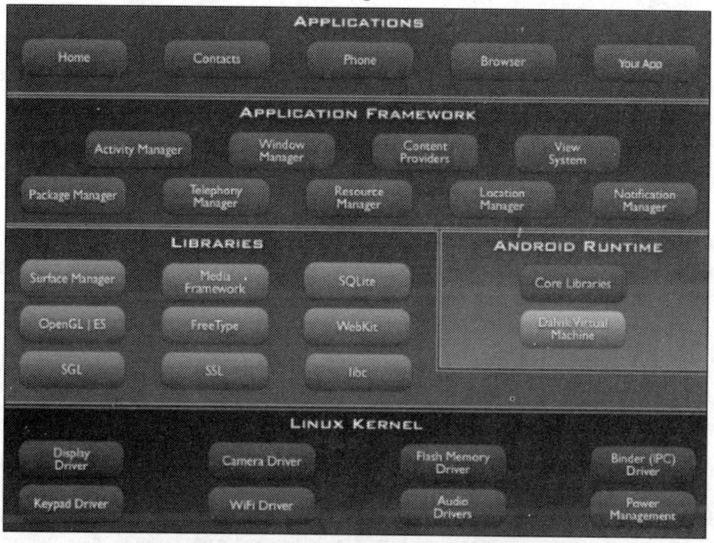

Figure 1: Displaying Android Architecture

Notes are represented in the following format:

NOTE

If you have images of different resolutions, you can put these images in drawable–ldpi, drawable–mdpi, drawable–hdpi, drawable–xhdpi, or drawable–xxhdpi folder.

The tables are numbered and are placed just below their references in the chapters, as shown in the following:

Table 1: Noteworthy Constants Required for Implementing Wi-Fi Functionality through the `WifiManager` Class

Constants	Description
ACTION_PICK_WIFI_NETWORK	Allows to select a Wi-Fi network to establish a connection
ACTION_REQUEST_SCAN_ALWAYS_AVAILABLE	Allows a user to enable scans even if the Wi-Fi is disabled
ERROR_AUTHENTICATING	Depicts the error code if there exists a problem in authentication
EXTRA_BSSID	Refers to the lookup key that gives the Basic Service Set Identification (BSSID) of the access point to which the connection is established

Table 1: Noteworthy Constants Required for Implementing Wi-Fi Functionality through the `WifiManager` Class	
Constants	**Description**
EXTRA_NETWORK_INFO	Refers to the lookup key for the NetworkInfo object related with the Wi-Fi network
WIFI_STATE_DISABLED	Specifies that the Wi-Fi is disabled
WIFI_STATE_DISABLING	Specifies that the Wi-Fi is in the process of disabling
WIFI_ENABLED	Specifies that the Wi-Fi is enabled
WIFI_STATE_ENABLING	Specifies that the Wi-Fi is in the process of enabling
WIFI_MODE_SCAN_ONLY	Locks the Wi-Fi mode; the Wi-Fi will be activated, but will perform only the scanning process and reporting of the scanning results

Other Resources

Android comes with an immense amount of documentation—hundreds of books worth referring to. The documentations are hosted online, and you can access them using a Web browser. Of course, there are plenty of Web pages out there on Android 4, some of which are as follows:

- Android SDK, https://developer.android.com/sdk/index.html?hl=sk
- Building Your First App, https://developer.android.com/training/basics/firstapp/index.html?hl=it
- Android tutorial, `http://www.tutorialspoint.com/android/`

The code provided in the book will run on the machine supporting Android SDK. For some of the examples like Bluetooth and NFC we need real Android devices having these capabilities as simulator do not offer these features.

The Black Book Philosophy

"Complexity kills. It sucks the life out of developers, it makes products difficult to plan, build and test, it introduces security challenges, and it causes end-user and administrator frustration."

Ray Ozzie - Chief Software Architect at Microsoft Corporation

Whichever language or platform you might be learning or working on, being a prolific programmer and administrator is fraught with challenges, complications, complexities, and frustrations. We at Dreamtech Press realize this veracity seamlessly and ensure that our **Black Book** series comes as an accomplished and dexterous solution to these complexities. The unique structure of Black Books ensures that complex topics are chunked into appropriate sections and presented in a more comprehensible manner, employing diagrams, code, and real-life examples for further simplicity. In addition, Black Books ensure a learning path replete with adequate practice avenues of the concepts learned by means of code examples, listings, executable programs, and applications. Each Black Book is designed to grow with its readers, providing all the guidance and reference material they need as they move toward software proficiency. In summation, the Black Book philosophy extends beyond simple pedagogy and seeks to decipher the practical challenges imbibed in the professional roles of its readers, whether students or professionals - that is why we call it an "Comprehensive Problem Solver"!

1

Fundamentals of Java for Android Application Development

If you need an information on:	See page:
Introduction to Java	2
Introducing Java Dalvik Virtual Machine	5
Developing a Simple Java Program	5
Working with Java Tokens	10
Knowledge Check—1	16
Explaining Data Types	27
Declaring Variables	29
Declaring Classes	32
Declaring Methods	34
Creating Objects	36
Explaining Access Specifiers	36
Interfaces	37
Inheritance	39
Implementing Flow Control Statements	39

Until the mid-2000s, the word Android represented a mechanical, humanlike creature and then in 2005, Google purchased Android, Inc.— a 22-month old company creating software for mobile phones. That move brought a revolution in the mobile market.

In 2007, a group of 34 companies formed the **Open Handset Alliance**. Its task is to accelerate innovation in mobile and offer consumers a richer, less expensive, and better mobile experience. Its primary project is Android, an open, free operating system based on the Linux operating system kernel.

Though HTC released the first commercially available Android phone near the end of 2008, public's awareness of Android and its potential didn't surface until early 2010 in the United States.

Now, Mobile Marketing Watch reports more than 50 billion downloads from the Google Play app store. Android developers earned more from their applications in the first half of 2013 than in all of 2012. According to Forbes, Google paid approximately $900 million to Android developers during the 12-month period starting in mid-2012. The pace is accelerating.

For developing mobile devices, Google uses the Android software stack, which consists of the following elements:

- Applications (native applications for mobile devices)
- A virtual machine (an environment in which programs or applications run)
- Middleware (a software that is located above the operating system in the stack and offers different services to the virtual machine and its applications)
- Linux-based operating system

Java is used to develop Android applications and therefore this session provides an overview of the Java language fundamentals.

Introduction to Java

Java is a platform-independent, object-oriented programming language originally developed by Sun Microsystems and now owned by Oracle. It is a programming language, which inherits its object-oriented features from C++. Java language was created by a software developer, James Gosling, at Sun Microsystems in 1991. It was first called Oak, which got changed to Java in 1995, when it was first released for public use. Java was basically created to act as a platform independent and object-oriented language that could run on any operating system. Java has a slogan that is 'write once, compile once, and run anywhere'. This slogan means once a program is compiled and run successfully on a platform then that program can easily be executed on any other operating system.

The sections that follow will discuss the need for using the Java language for android application development and the key features of Java.

Need for Java for Android Application Development

The Java programming language is used to develop native applications for the Android platform. The following are some of the reasons why Java has been chosen to develop Android applications:

- Java is a very popular language so most of the developers must be familiar with it and need not put any extra efforts to learn a new language.
- It provides security features such as protection from memory leaks and bad pointer usage.
- Android runs on different hardware platforms which means that the native code also known as machine code must be compiled and optimized according to each of these platforms. However, if using the Java language, the Java code runs in a virtual machine and requires no interaction with the inner hardware of a device. A virtual machine safely manages the execution of the code within its virtual environment. In case of Android applications, these applications run in a virtual machine called **Dalvik Virtual Machine (DVM)** and therefore it is not required to recompile the code for every phone.
- Java provides huge open source support by offering many libraries and tools for creating applications in Java.

Features of Java

Java is a simple, robust, platform independent, and portable programming language. It is designed to meet the real world requirements with its key features, as illustrated in **Figure 1.1**:

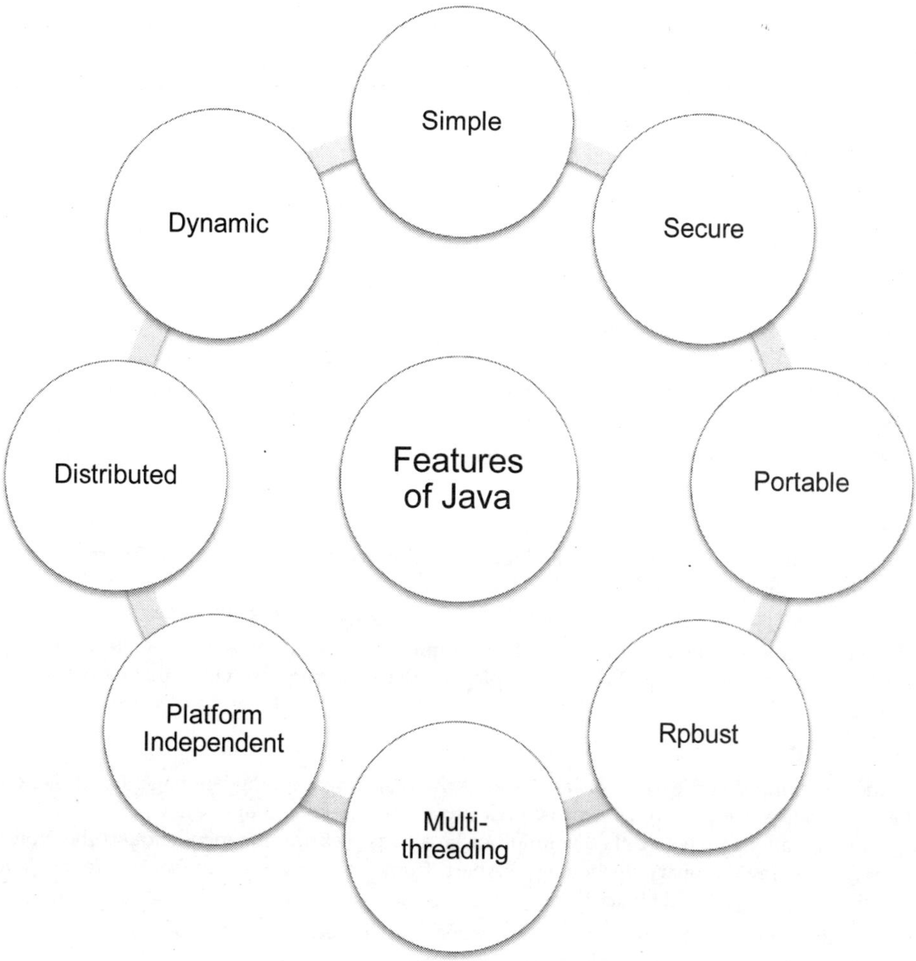

Figure 1.1: Characteristics of Java

Simple

Java is simple to learn and use. Java programs are easy to write and debug because it does not use pointers. Moreover, Java provides bug free system due to strong memory management and also has automatic memory allocation and deallocation system. Unlike other programming languages, which provide dozens of complicated ways to perform a simple task, Java provides a simple and clear approach. If a programmer understands the basic concepts of OOP, it becomes easier for the programmer to learn Java.

Secure

In today's world, everybody needs safety and security while performing online transactions. In order to overcome such threats, Java provides the safety and security features.

With the help of the Java compatible browser, Java applets can be easily and safely downloaded over the Internet. As the Java programs are confined to the Java runtime environment, the hackers can only access that part of your computer which is required for program execution. The data outside the Java runtime environment cannot be accessed by Java programs, and therefore downloading a Java application through Internet will not harm your computer. That's why Java is a secure language.

Portable

In the distributed world of Internet, an application developed with the help of a programming language might be accessed on various computers having different kinds of operating systems. But, it's not guaranteed that the application is portable, that is the application runs successfully on all operating systems. To overcome this portability issue, Java introduces a concept of what is known as bytecode.

So, in order to run your Java program, you should have only JVM installed. JVM is also considered as the Interpreter of bytecode. In this way, Java has solved the problem of portability.

Robust

Generally, programs fail for the following two reasons:

- Lack of Memory management devices for allocating and deallocating memory for objects.
- Occurrence of Unexpected, Exceptional conditions

Considering the preceding reasons, Java was designed to create robust programs. Java compels its programmers to resolve the mistakes during compilation. Moreover, it also frees the programmers from the common causes of programming errors as the program code is verified during compilation.

Java also eradicates the problem of memory management by performing automatic garbage collection. It manages the memory allocation and deallocation for unused objects.

Multi-threading

Java is a programming language that is designed for the distributed environment of the Internet and for that the concept of multithreading is implemented. This feature helps to write interactive programs wherein multiple tasks can be performed simultaneously; thus making it a robust programming language.

Java is inherently multi-threaded as there can be multiple executing threads in a single Java program. For example, a Java programmer can run three Java applets on the same page, provided that each applet gets equal time from the CPU.

Platform Independent

It is one of the most important features of Java. Java is the first programming language, which is not bound to any specific operating system. In other words, Java programs can be executed anywhere on any system. No other programming language, before the evolution of Java, was platform independent and therefore, it can be said that Java is a revolutionary technology. Apart from cross-platform in source form, Java is also platform-independent in compiled binary form.

A Java program does not execute natively on the host machine, instead Java interpreter reads the bytecode and executes the corresponding native machine instructions. Java interpreter is a special naïve program, which reads the bytecode, an intermediate form after compilation. Therefore, in order to port a Java program to a new platform, you need the interpreter and some of the library routines. Moreover, the Java compiler is also written in Java and the bytecodes are precisely defined, which remain same on all platforms.

Distributed

Java is a distributed language as it can be used to create applications to communicate over the network. Java can communicate over the network because it supports Transmission Control Protocol/Internet Protocol (TCP/IP).

Dynamic

During runtime of a Java program, the relevant information is required to verify and resolve access to objects. This concept of providing runtime information is referred to as dynamically linking the code. This feature of Java adds strength to the applet environment, in which small fragments of bytecode are dynamically updated on a running system.

Introducing Java Dalvik Virtual Machine

Dalvik virtual machine is used in Android system similarly as the JVM is used in Java. However, Dalvik VM is optimized for the low power CPUs and low memory modules. Unlike the JVM, the Dalvik VM doesn't recognize files with `.class` extension; instead it executes the files with `.dex` extension. In fact, `.dex` files are generated implicitly from `.class` file and are highly optimized for where memory and processing power is a constraint. Using Dalvik over JVM has the following advantages:

- It is optimized for small platform where memory and processing power is a constraint.
- It recognizes its exclusively designed APIs along with some useful APIs of Java.

At a time, many instances can be created simultaneously that benefit in security, isolation, memory management, and multithreading.

Developing a Simple Java Program

You need to create a simple program, which displays a Hello message. In this session, we will use the **Eclipse Integrated Development Environment (IDE)** to develop Java programs. Perform the following steps to develop a simple Java program:

- Writing the Java Program
- Compiling and executing the Java Program

Writing the Java Program

You need to create a Java source file by using the Eclipse IDE. The vi or pico editors are used to type programs in Unix system whereas in Windows, the notepad, DOS editor, or the Eclipse IDE is used. Follow these steps to create a simple Java program:

1. *Open* the Eclipse IDE.
2. *Select* **File→New→Java Project**, as shown in Figure 1.2:

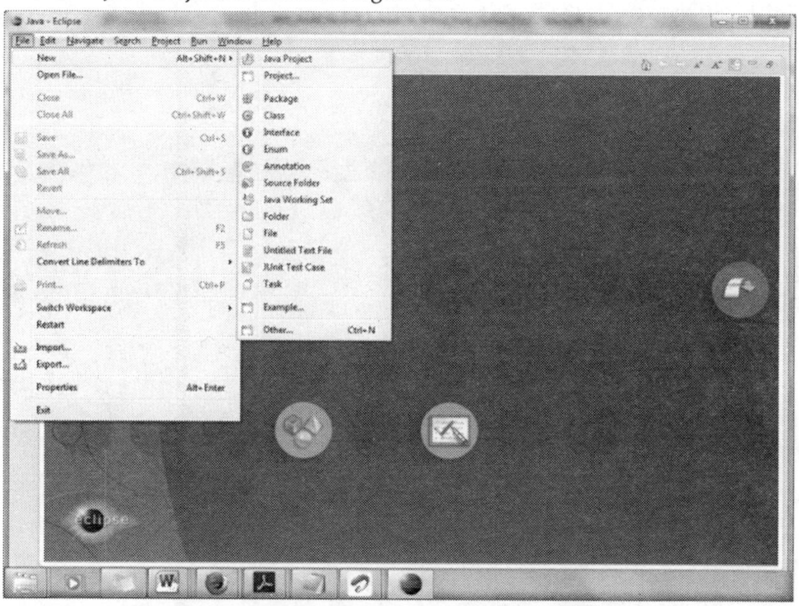

Figure 1.2: Selecting the Java Project Option

The **New Java Project** dialog box appears (Figure 1.3).

3. Enter the name of the project in the Project name text box. In this case, enter Java Samples (Figure 1.3).
4. *Click* the Next button, as shown in Figure 1.3:

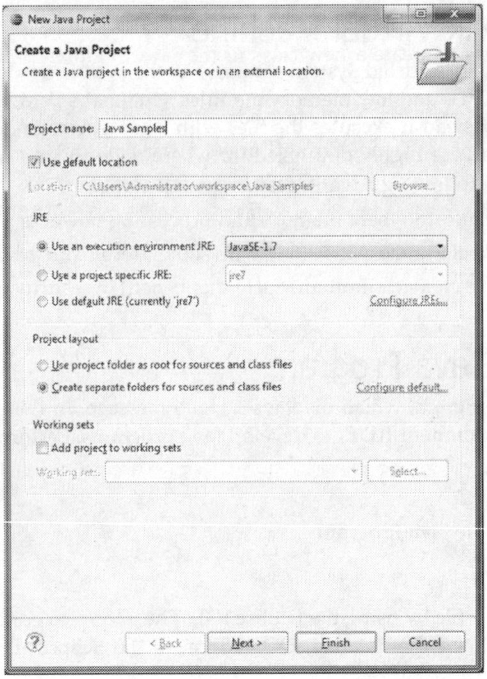

Figure 1.3: The New Java Project Dialog Box

The Java Settings page of the New Java Project dialog box appears **Figure 1.4.**

5. *Click* the **Finish** button to create the project, as shown in Figure 1.4:

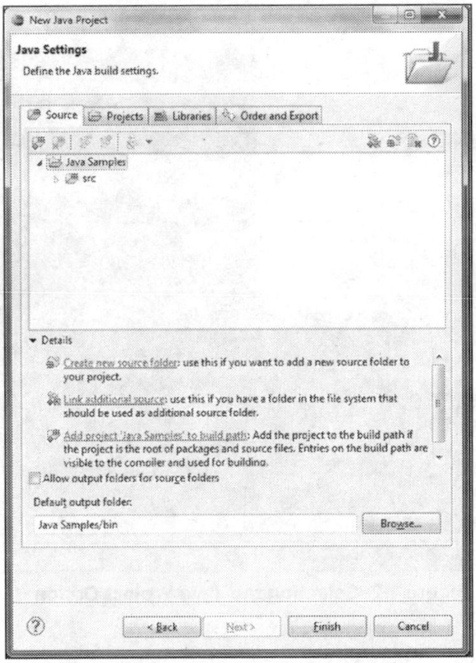

Figure 1.4: The Java Settings Page

The **Java Samples** project is created.

6. *Select* **File→New Class** to create a new class in the **Java Samples** project. The **New Java Class** dialog box appears (Figure 1.5).
7. *Enter* the name of the class in the **Name** text box. In this case, enter the name as `Hello` (Figure 1.5).
8. *Select* the public static void main (String[] args) check box and deselect the **Inherited abstract methods** check box and select the **Generate comments** check box (Figure 1.5).
9. *Click* the **Finish** button to create the `Hello` class, as shown in Figure 1.5:

Figure 1.5: The New Java Class Dialog Box

A file named `Hello.java` is added to the Java Samples project (Figure 1.6).

Now, add the following code within the `main()` method, declared in the `Hello` class, as shown in the following code snippet:

```
System.out.println("Welcome to the world of programming");
```

The preceding code snippet is used to print the string "Welcome to the world of programming", followed by a new line on the screen. As Java is an object oriented language, thereby every method must be part of an object. Here, `println()` method is a member of the out object, which is a static data member of the `System` class. It is a predefined class that provides access to system and out is the output stream that is connected to the console.

The `Hello.java` file appears, as shown in Figure 1.6:

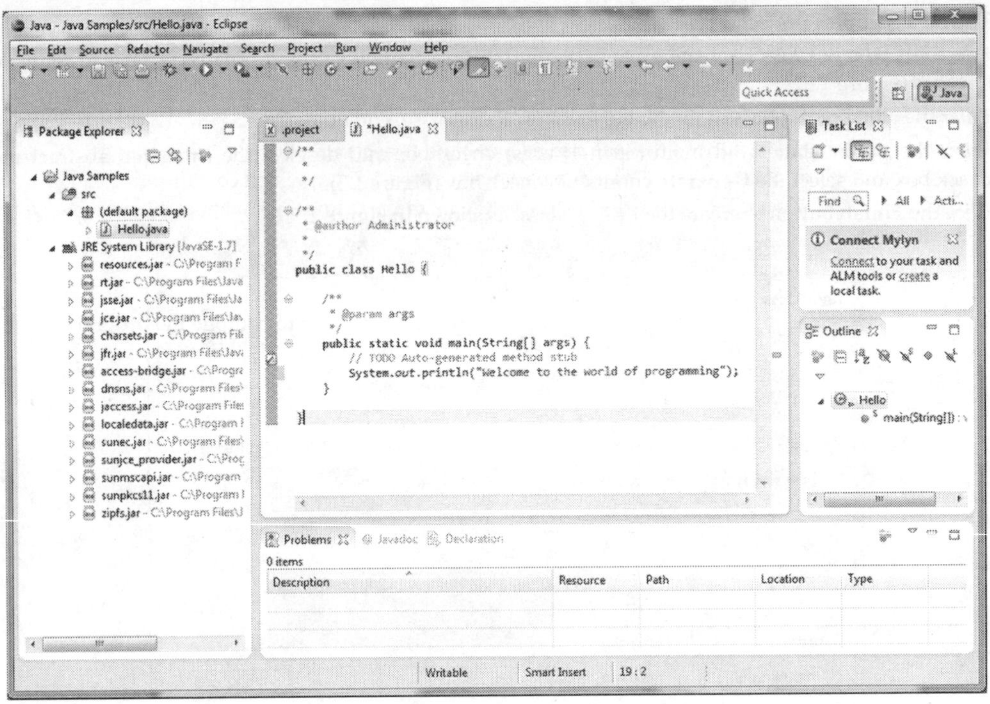

Figure 1.6: Displaying the Hello.java File

In Figure 1.6, you can see that the text enclosed within the /** */ symbols indicates a comment in Java. The contents of comments are ignored by the Java compiler as comments only describe the operation of a Java program. Java permits both single line and multiple line comments. The single line comments begins with // and multiple line comments begins with /** and ends with */.

The following code snippet is used to declare the Java class:

```
public class Hello {
}
```

The preceding code snippet declares the Hello class. The keyword class is used to declare a new class followed by the name of the class to be declared. As Java is an object-oriented programming language, therefore everything must be placed within the class. You must also note that in Java every class definition begins with an opening brace { and ends with the matching closing brace}. This is similar to C++ class construct except a semicolon, which is provided towards the end in the C++ class declaration.

Then, the main() method within the Hello class is declared, as shown in the following code snippet:

```
public static void main(String args[]) {
}
```

In the preceding code snippet, the `main()` method is declared, which is similar to the `main()` function in C++. In Java, every program must include the `main()` method as it is the starting point for the Java interpreter to start the execution of a program. A Java application can have numerous classes but the `main()` method must be declared in only one of the classes to initiate the execution.

In the preceding code snippet, it is important to understand the **public, static,** and **void** keywords. The explanation of these keywords is as follows:

- **`public`**—It is an access specifier that allows Java programmers to control the visibility of class members. The public access specifier used before a class member implies that the class member may be accessed outside the class in which it is declared. Here, the `main()` method is declared as public implying that it can be called outside a class, when a program is started.

- **`static`**—It allows the main() method to be invoked without creating an instance of the class. It is essential to use the static keyword before the `main()` method as it is invoked by the Java interpreter before objects are created.
- **`void`**—It implies that the `main()` method does not return any value.

  Moreover, you must have noticed that the `main()` method is declared with the parameters provided within the parenthesis. Here, String args[] declares a parameter named `args`, which contains an array of objects of the `String` class. The args parameter receives the command-line arguments, when the program is executed.

Compiling and Executing the Java Program

In order to see the desired output of the simple Java program, you first need to compile the program. Firstly, the javac compiler translates the source code to bytecode, then java interpreter reads the bytecode and displays the desired output. Perform the following steps to compile and execute the Hello.java source file in the Eclipse IDE:

1. *Select* **Run→Run** to compile and execute the Java program.

   The Save and Launch dialog box appears (Figure 1.7).

2. *Click* the **OK** button to save the Hello.Java file, as shown in Figure 1.7:

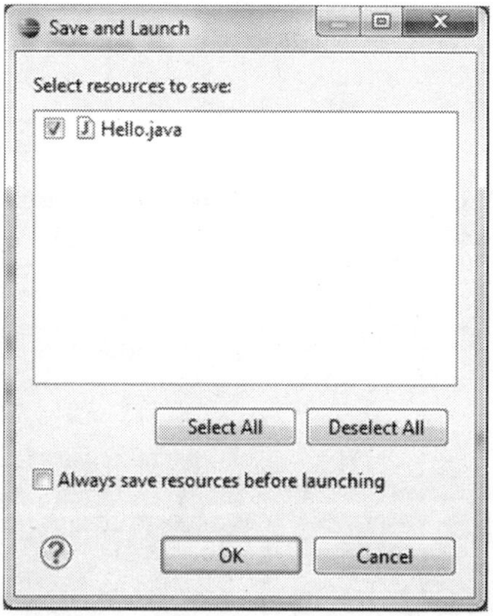

Figure 1.7: The Save and Launch Dialog Box

The output of the Hello.java class appears, as shown in Figure 1.8:

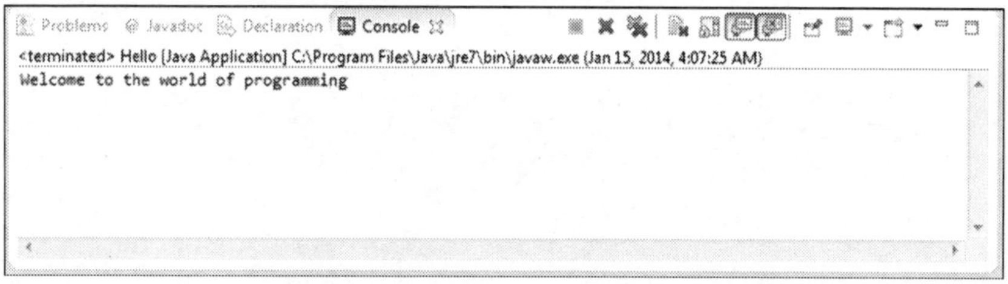

Figure 1.8: Displaying the Welcome Message

Internally within the Java environment, the Java compiler executes the following command to compile the `Hello.java` file:

```
javac Hello.java
```

In the preceding command `javac` is a compiler followed by the name of the Java source file, `Hello.java`. After executing the preceding command, the `Hello.class` file is created in the current directory.

The `javac` compiler has translated the source code of the Hello.java file into the bytecode. Now, the java interpreter helps in executing the Java program with the help of the following command:

```
java Hello
```

In the preceding command, java is an interpreter followed by the name of the bytecode file, `Hello` and then the output is displayed.

Now, let's discuss the Java tokens comprising of keywords, identifiers, literals, and operators.

Working with Java Tokens

The smallest individual element in a Java program is known as token. A Java program is a collection of classes which include a set of declaration statements and methods containing executable statements. Most of the statements contain expressions, which describe the actions performed on data. The compiler recognizes tokens for building up expressions and statements. The Java programming language provides the following tokens:

- Keywords
- Identifiers
- Literals
- Constants
- Operators

Keywords

Keywords are reserved words that cannot be used while naming a variable or method. The keywords in Java are:

- `abstract`
- `assert`
- `boolean`
- `break`
- `byte`
- `byvalue`
- `case`
- `cast`
- `catch`
- `char`
- `class`
- `const`
- `continue`
- `default`
- `do`
- `double`
- `else`
- `extends`
- `enum`
- `final`
- `finally`
- `float`
- `for`
- `goto`
- `if`

- `implements`
- `import`
- `instanceof`
- `int`
- `interface`
- `long`
- `native`
- `new`
- `package`
- `private`
- `protected`
- `public`
- `return`
- `short`
- `static`
- `strictfp`
- `super`
- `switch`
- `synchronized`
- `this`
- `throw`
- `throws`
- `transient`
- `try`
- `var`
- `void`
- `volatile`
- `while`

These keywords should not be used as identifiers in Java. The following section explains what are identifiers and rules for legal identifiers.

Identifiers

An identifier is a symbolic name that refers to variables, methods, classes, packages, or interfaces in a Java program. Each variable is identified by its name. The variable name should relate to its purpose. Similarly, in case of a method, the name of the method should relate to the method's functionality. Java identifiers consist of alphabets, numbers, underscore (_), and the dollar sign ($).

Literals

In a Java program, you can assign a literal value to a variable. Literal refers to the constant values that can be changed depending on the program requirement. The source code representations of the values of primitive data types in a Java program are known as *primitive literals*. These primitive literals can be an integer number, floating-point number, a boolean value, or a character that you use in your program. Some examples of the primitive literals are:

```
24          // an int literal
124.543     // a double literal
true        // a boolean literal
'v'         // a char literal
```

In the preceding example, 24 is an *integer value*, 124.543 is a *floating point number*, true is the *boolean literal*, and v is a *character value*. Literals can be of different types as illustrated in Figure 1.9:

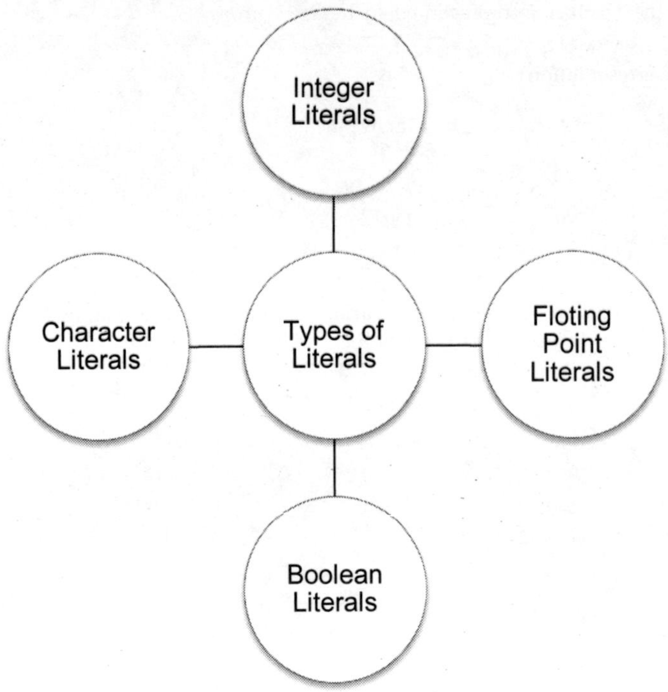

Figure 1.9: Categories of Literals

Integer Literals

Based on the requirement of the program, an integer number can be represented in the following three ways:

- Decimal (base 10)
- Octal (base 8)
- Hexadecimal (base 16)

Decimal Literals

The decimal literals are commonly used to represent numbers in real life. They have base 10 and use digits between 0-9 to represent all numbers. The decimal representation of an integer number does not use any prefix as compared to other forms of representing integers.

Listing 1.1 shows representation of the decimal literal:

Listing 1.1: Decimal Representation

```
class DecimalRep {
  public static void main(String args[]) {
        int sixteen=16;
        System.out.println("Decimal Sixteen="+sixteen);
  }
}
```

In Listing 1.1, an integer value (16) is represented in decimal notation, which is assigned to an int type of variable sixteen. Here, you can notice that no prefix is used with (16); however, in the case of *octal* and *hexadecimal* *literals*, the prefix is used.

Octal Literals

The other way of representing integer numbers is octal representation, which has base 8. It uses only 8 digits, from 0 to 7, to represent all the numbers. In Java, the octal numbers are preceded with a prefix 0, which notifies the compiler that the number is represented in the octal form. Listing 1.2 shows representation of the octal literals:

Listing 1.2: Octal Representation

```
class OctalRep {
  public static void main(String args[]) {
  int five=05;              // value of five is equal to decimal 5
  int eight=010;     // value of eight is equal to decimal 8
  int ten=012;     // value of ten is equal to decimal 10
  System.out.println("Octal value 012 is equivalent to
  "+ten+" in decimal");
  }
}
```

In Listing 1.2, five, eight, and ten are integer variables, which are being assigned with octal literals. Notice a prefix 0 (zero) in all the octal numbers, which intimates the JVM that the numbers assigned are in octal representation.

Hexadecimal Literals

The hexadecimal representation of an integer number has base 16. It uses 10 digits and 6 special symbols/characters to represent numbers. The digits used by hexadecimal notation are 0 to 9 and the special symbols used are a, b, c, d, e, and f. The representation of 0-9 in the hexadecimal notation is the same as in the decimal notation and the remaining 6 are represented by characters a to f. The respective representations of 10 to 15 in the hexadecimal notation are:

- 10 – a or A
- 11 – b or B
- 12 – c or C
- 13 – d or D
- 14 – e or E
- 15 – f or F

Listing 1.3 shows representation of the integer numbers in the hexadecimal notation:

Listing 1.3: Hexadecimal Representation

```
class HexaDecimalRep {
public static void main(String ar[]) {
  int a=0x5;       // value of a is equivalent to decimal 5
  int b=0XF;       // value of b is equivalent to decimal 15
  int c= 0xd;      // value of c is equivalent to decimal 13
  System.out.println("Decimal five= "+a);
  System.out.println("Decimal fifteen= "+b);
  System.out.println("Decimal thirteen="+c);
  }
}
```

By default, all the three integer types (decimal, octal, and hexadecimal) are considered to be of int type, but we can also assign these integer literals to long type of variables with a trailing l or L, as shown in the following code snippet:

```
long distance=65347L;    // a decimal integer literal is assigned
long length=0xCCCCl;     //a hexadecimal integer literal is assigned
```

Now, after discussing all the three forms of representing integer literals, let's discuss the floating-point literals, which provide fractional values to variables.

Floating-Point Literals

In a Java program, the whole numbers are represented as integers but a fractional number is represented and assigned using floating-point values. The source code representation of floating-point values in a Java program is called floating-point literals. A floating point number consists of integer numbers and a decimal point. Consider the following example:

```
double distance=43213.13245;
```

Here, we have represented a floating-point literal as 43213.13245 in which the first part is 43213, followed by a decimal point (.), and the second part is 13245.

In Java programming language, by default, the floating-point literals are defined as double that has a width of 64 bits. You can assign a floating-point literal in a float type of variable but it will generate compilation error. The error states the possible loss of precision as the width of float data type is 32 bits.

To avoid such compilation errors, you can explicitly take the responsibility of loss of precision in your program, which means that you can add F or f at the end of floating-point literal assigned. When the compiler comes across the floating-point literal with a postfix F or f, it concludes that the programmer is aware of the possible loss of precision and therefore the compiler does not show any error. Listing 1.4 shows the correct implementation of the floating-point literals through float data type:

Listing 1.4: Floating-Point Representation through Float Data Type

```
class FloatingPointRep {
   public static void main(String ar[]) {
          float height=6.45f;
          System.out.println("Height= "+height);
   }
}
```

The code provided in Listing 1.4 displays no compilation error. In Listing 1.4, f is added at the end of the floating-point literal 6.45 to explicitly intimate the compiler that the programmer is aware of the possible loss of precision, so that it does not generate any compilation error.

Similarly, you can also specify D or d to a floating-point literal while assigning it to a double data type, but it is optional because by default the floating-point literals are double values. The following code snippet shows an example, in which D is added while assigning a double value to the height variable:

```
double height=67582.4545D;
double height=67582.4545;
```

In the preceding code snippet, both the representations are same and correct, although D has not been used in the second representation.

Apart from integer and floating-point literals, we also have boolean literals which can have either true or false as their value. Now, let's discuss the boolean literals in detail.

Boolean Literals

In Java, `boolean` values are the result of conditions, which return either true or false. The source code representation of the `boolean` values is called boolean literals. The two possible `boolean` literals are true and false. You must know that unlike C and C++ programming languages, in Java, the `boolean` literals cannot be represented in the form of numbers as 0 for false and 1 or any other number for true. In other words, the Java programming language does not support any number for true and false `boolean` literals. Consider the following code snippet:

```
boolean status=true;       // no error
boolean status=1;          // will generate compilation error
```

In the preceding code snippet, the first representation of the `boolean` literal is correct and executes without any compilation error. However, the second representation of `boolean` literal is incorrect as 1 is assigned to a boolean data type leading to a compilation error. Listing 1.5 shows an example where a compilation error is generated due to incorrect representation of `boolean` literal:

Listing 1.5: Boolean Literal Representation

```
class BooleanRep
{
   public static void main(String ar[]) {
   boolean status=1;      // this statement will generate error
   if(status) {
          System.out.println("Here Status= "+status);
   }
   }
}
```

Save Listing 1.5 as BooleanRep.java file and during compilation, it generates a compilation error. The error states that instead of assigning a boolean value to a boolean type variable, an integer value is assigned. Such an error is incompatible types error.

To represent characters in a program, Java provides us with character literals. Let's now study about character literals in detail.

Character Literals

In Java, the source code representation of a single character value is called character literal. The character literals in Java are represented by a single character or an escape sequence character enclosed within single quotes. Consider the following code snippet:

```
char letter='A';
char value='y';
char newline='\n';
```

Here, the character literals A, y, and \n (escape sequence character for a new line) are represented. It is essential to understand that the character literals can also be represented using their Unicode values. These Unicode values are prefixed with \u. Consider the following code snippet:

```
char character J='\u004A';
```

Here, you can see that character J is represented as a Unicode character. You must know that the characters are 16-bit unsigned integers and you must assign only those number literals for characters that fit into the unsigned 16-bit range, that is, 65535. Consider the following code snippet:

```
char characterA=65;// an integer literal representation of character A
char characterB=0102     // an octal literal representation of character B
char characterC=0x43;    // a hexadecimal representation of character C
```

In the preceding code snippet, different values of integer literals are assigned to character literals and all are legal as they are written in unsigned 16-bit range. However, if you assign an integer literal which is out of unsigned 16-bit range, then the compiler generates error, provided that you have not explicitly typecast its value.

Apart from all the primitive literals discussed so far in this session, sometimes you may also come across String literals. Although String is not a primitive data type in Java, String values can be represented as literals. Let's now discuss String literals in detail.

Strings Literals

Unlike C++, in Java programming language, String is considered as a class instead of a primitive data type and thereby all the string literals are the values of the String class objects. The source code representation of a value of a String object is called String literal. The String literal is a collection of characters enclosed within double quotes. The following code snippet represents the String literals:

```
String msg="Welcome to Java Programming";
System.out.println(msg);
```

In the preceding code snippet, first, a `String` literal is assigned as a value to the String object `msg` and then the literal assigned is displayed on the standard output console.

Constants

Sometimes the values assigned to variables change throughout the execution of a program; however, it may be possible that you want to lock the assigned value to a variable. In other words, if you want a value to remain fixed throughout the execution of a program, then it is known as `constant`.

Let's consider an example where you want to calculate the area of a circle in your program. While calculating the area of a circle, the value of pi remains same irrespective of the change in radius. Therefore, you need to assign a fixed value, 3.14, as shown in the following code snippet:

```
final double pi = 3.14;
```

Here, in the preceding code snippet, the `pi` variable is assigned a fixed value 3.14. You must note that the final keyword is used to avoid the modifications in the value of pi variable. The final keyword in Java is similar to const in C/C++.

Knowledge Check—1

1. While creating a Human Resource Management application, Annie needed a salary variable to store the salary of employees. Out of the following options, which one is not a legal identifier?
   a. $salary
   b. 9 salary
   c. salary
   d. _salary
2. What will be the output of the following program?

```
class Ques2 {
   public static void main(String args[]) {
            int i = 50;
            String str = (i > 50) ? "Hello" : (i < 50) ?
            "World" : "Java";
            System.out.println(str);
   }
}
```

Operators

An operator is a symbol that allows a programmer to perform certain arithmetic or logical operations on data and variables. Figure 1.10 shows the operators in Java:

Figure 1.10: Java Operators

Now, let's discuss all these operators and their implementation in detail.

The Arithmetic Operators

The operators that are used to perform arithmetic operations are called arithmetic operators, such as addition (+), subtraction (-), and multiplication (*). Table 1.1 lists the arithmetic operators supported in Java:

Table 1.1: Arithmetic Operators in Java

Arithmetic operator	Description
+	Addition
-	Subtraction
*	Multiplication
/	Division
%	Modulus

The arithmetic operators are used to perform mathematical operations as in algebra. You can perform the addition and subtraction operations on either integers or double numbers. Listing 1.6 shows the addition and subtraction of integers:

Listing 1.6: Addition and Subtraction on Integers

```
/* Adding and Subtracting Integer numbers in this program
*/
class IntAddSub {
  public static void main(String args[]) {
        int a = 50;
        int b = 30;
        System.out.println("First Number is:" +a);
        System.out.println("Second Number is:" +b);
        int c = a + b;
        System.out.println("Addition of two numbers is:" +c);
        c = a-b;
        System.out.println("Subtraction of two numbers is:" +c);
  }
}
```

In Listing 1.6, the two integer numbers a and b are added and the resultant value is displayed. Similarly, these two numbers are subtracted and their output is displayed.

In the second command, the java interpreter displays the output on the console, as shown in Figure 1.11:

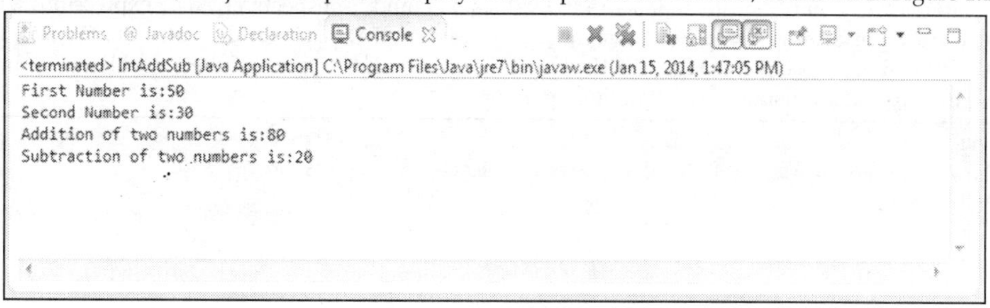

Figure 1.11: Displaying Output of the IntAddSub Class

Apart from the arithmetic operations, you also need to understand the arithmetic assignment operator, which is discussed in the following section.

The Arithmetic Assignment Operator

The equal (=) symbol is known as the assignment operator. The assignment (=) operator is used to store or assign a value to a variable. For example, in expression, i=10, we are assigning a value 10 to the variable i. Remember that in expression i=10, we are not comparing the variable i with 10; rather we are assigning the value 10 to the i variable.

In Java, assignment operators can be used in two ways—simple and compound. In simple assignment, we use the equal (=) operator for assigning a value to a variable. The following code snippet shows an example of simple assignment:

```
x = 10;             //x stores 10
x = x + 10;         //x stores 20
x = x + 5 * 15;     //x stores 95
```

In compound assignment, we use the +=, -=, *=, /=, and %= operators. The following code snippet shows an example of compound assignment:

```
i = 10;             // i is initialized with the value 10
i += 15;            // i is compound assigned with 25
i -= 5;             //i is compound assigned with 20
```

In the preceding code snippet, the variable i is assigned with the value 10. In the expression i+=15, the value 15 is added to the value already contained in the variable i and the total value is reassigned to i, so i will contain 25. In the expression i-=5, the value 5 is subtracted from the value already contained in the variable i and then the resultant value is reassigned to i, so in this case the variable i will contain 20. Listing 1.7 shows an example of compound assignment:

Listing 1.7: Example of Compound Assignment

```
public class AssignmentOpt
{
  public static void main(String args[])
  {
        int x = 3;
        int y = 4;
        int z = 5;
        x += 5;
        y *= 4;
        z += x * y;
        System.out.println("x = " + x);
        System.out.println("y = " + y);
        System.out.println("z = " + z);
  }
}
```

In Listing 1.7, the `AssignmentOpt` class is defined. Within the `main()` method of the `AssignmentOpt` class, the three variables x, y, and z of int type store the values 3, 4, and 5, respectively. The expressions x+=5, y*=4, and z += x*y are performing compound assignment operations that reassign the values 8, 16, and 133 to the variables x, y, and z, respectively. Figure 1.12 shows the final values stored in the variables x, y, and z, after evaluating the expressions using the assignment operator:

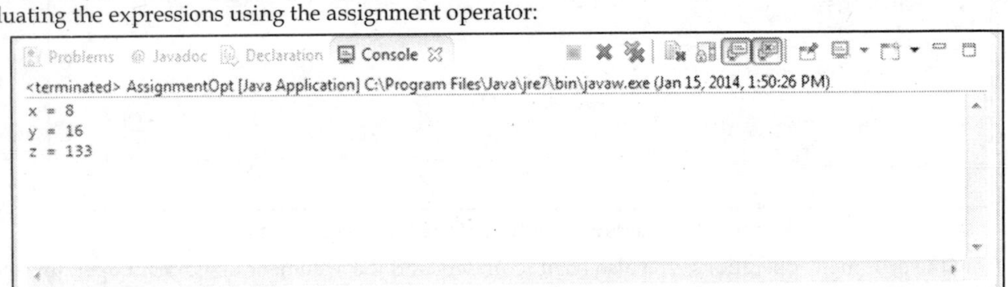

Figure 1.12: Displaying Result of Compound Assignment

Now, after understanding the implementation of the arithmetic operators, let's discuss the relational operators.

The Relational Operators

Operators that are used to determine the relationship between two operands are known as relational operators. The expressions that contain relational operators always return a boolean value, which is either true or false. There are six relational operators that can be used to compare any value of integers, floats, or characters. Table 1.2 lists relational operators:

Table 1.2: Relational Operators

Relational Operators	Description
==	Equal to
!=	Not equal to
<	Less than
>	Greater than
<=	Less than or equal to
>=	Greater than or equal to

All relational operators are binary operators. The relational operators can be used as given in the following code snippet:

```
int x = 5;
int y = 8;
int z = 10;
boolean valid = x >= y;            // false.
boolean valid1 = x >= y && y >= z;          // false.
```

In the preceding code snippet, the expression x >= y returns a false value, which is stored in the valid variable of boolean type. Similarly, the expression x >= y && y >= z is evaluated as (x >= y) && (y >= z), which returns a false value. This false value is stored in the valid1 variable of boolean type. Listing 1.8 shows the use relational operators:

Listing 1.8: Usage of Relational Operators

```
/* Program implementing the Relational Operators */
class RelationalOperator
{
   static int value1 = 10;
   static int value2 = 8;
   public static void main(String args[])
   {
          float a = 3.6f;
          float b = 5.1f;
          float c = 1.1f;
          System.out.println("First Number is:" +a);
          System.out.println("Second Number is:" +b);
          System.out.println("Third Number is:" +c);
          System.out.println("a < b is:" + (a<b));
          System.out.println("a > b is:" + (a<b));
          System.out.println("b == c is:" + (b==c));
          System.out.println("a <= b is:" + (a<=b));
          System.out.println("a >= b is:" + (a>=b));
          System.out.println("a != c is:" + (a!=c));
          System.out.println("b == a + c is:" + (b == a + c));
   }
}
```

Listing 1.8 declares the `RelationalOperator` class. Within the `main()` method of the `RelationalOperator` class, three float type variables `a`, `b`, and `c` are initialized with the values 3.6f, 5.1f, and 1.1f, respectively. Next, the values of the a, b, and c variables are compared by using the relational operators ==, !=, <, and >, and then the result is displayed accordingly. Figure 1.13 shows the output of Listing 1.8:

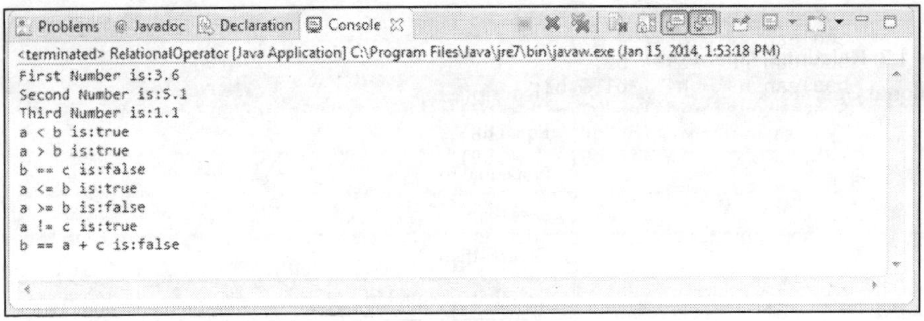

Figure 1.13: Usage of Relational Operators

From Figure 1.13, it is clear that the values contained in the variables a, b, and c are not equal and also depending upon the comparison, the boolean value is displayed.

Now after understanding the relational operators, let's study the boolean logical operators.

The Boolean Logical Operators

These operators operate only on the boolean operands. All of the binary logical operators combine two boolean values and provide the resultant boolean value. Table 1.3 lists the boolean logical operators:

Table 1.3: The Boolean Logical Operators

Operator	Its Meaning
&	Logical AND
|	Logical OR
^	Logical XOR (Exclusive OR)
||	Short-circuit OR
&&	Short-circuit AND
!	Logical Unary NOT
&=	AND assignment
|=	OR assignment
^=	XOR assignment
==	Equal to
!=	Not Equal to

In order to understand implementation of the boolean logical operators provided in Table 1.3, let's create a simple program. Listing 1.9 shows the implementation of the boolean logical operators:

Listing 1.9: The BooleanLogicApp.java File

```
/* Program implementing the boolean logical operators */
class BooleanLogicApp
{
  public static void main(String args[])
  {
        boolean b1 = false;
        boolean b2 = true;
        boolean b3 = b1 & b2;
        boolean b4 = b1 | b2;
        boolean b5 = b1 ^ b2;
        boolean b6 = !b2;
        System.out.println("b1 = " + b1);                // false
        System.out.println("b2 = " + b2);                // true
        System.out.println("b1 & b2 = " + b3);  // false
        System.out.println("b1 | b2 = " + b4);  // true
        System.out.println("b1 ^ b2 = " + b5);  // true
        System.out.println("!b2 = " + b6);               //false
```

```
            int i = 10;
            boolean b7 = 6 == 4 & i < 4;                    // false
            boolean b8 = b3 ^ b2;                           // true
            boolean b9 = b4 | b1 & b2;                      // true
            System.out.println("b7 = " + b7);
            System.out.println("b8 = " + b8);
            System.out.println("b9 = " + b9);
        }
    }
```

In Listing 1.9, the boolean logical operators, such as !, ^, &, and ! are used. Depending upon the boolean logical comparison, the boolean value is returned and displayed as output. Figure 1.14 shows output of the `BooleanLogicApp` class:

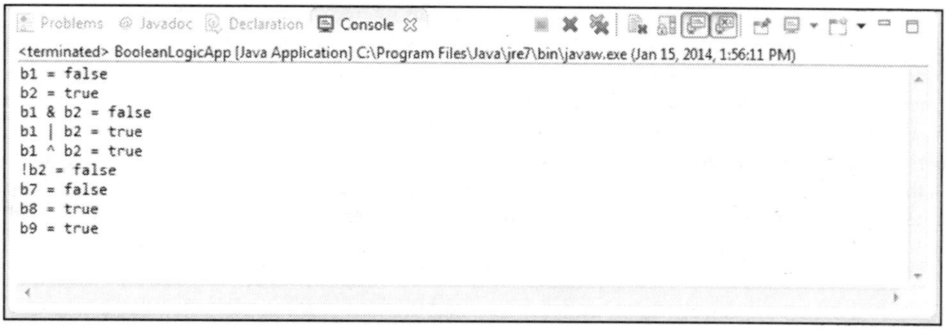

Figure 1.14: Displaying Output of the BooleanLogicApp Class

Figure 1.14 shows the boolean values returned on the basis of the boolean logical operators.

The Increment and Decrement Operators

The increment and decrement operators can be used in two ways: either before or after an operand. Depending on the placement of these operators, they can be classified as prefix or postfix. The difference between prefix and postfix notations is that in the prefix notation, the value of the operand is incremented or decremented before assigning it to another variable, while in the postfix notation, the value of the operand is incremented or decremented after assigning it to another variable.

Consider the following code snippet:

```
int x=10;
int y=20;
++x;
   //Prefix notation of increment operator
--y;
   // Prefix notation of decrement operator
x++;
   //Postfix notation of increment operator
y--;
   // Postfix notation of decrement operator
```

In the preceding code snippet, ++x is the prefix notation of the increment operator and --y is the prefix notation of decrement operator. On the other hand, x++ is the postfix notation of the increment operator and y-- is the postfix notation of the decrement operator. Listing 1.10 shows how to use the prefix and postfix notations of the increment (++) operator:

Listing 1.10: Usage of the Increment (++) Operator

```
/* Program implementing the Increment operator */

class IncrementApp
{
   public static void main(String args[])
   {
         int i, j, k;
         i = 10;
```

```
            j = i++;  // using postfix increment operator j = 10
            System.out.println("After postfix increment");
            System.out.println("i = " + i);
            System.out.println("j = " + j);
            i = 10;
            j = 0;
            j = ++i;   // using prefix increment operator j = 11
            System.out.println("After prefix increment");
            System.out.println("i = " + i);
            System.out.println("j = " + j);
    }
}
```

In Listing 1.10, the `IncrementApp` class is defined. Within its `main()` method, the two variables i and j of int type are declared. The variable `i` is initialized with number 10. The number that is stored in the i variable is incremented by one when the `i` variable is post-incremented (i++). It means that the value of the i variable will be 11; however, the variable `j` still stores the number 10, because in the postfix notation, the value of the operand is incremented or decremented after assigning it to another variable. Next, the i and j variables are reassigned numbers 10 and 0, respectively. When the i variable is pre-incremented (++i), its value is incremented by one. It means that the value of the i variable will be 11; however, the variable j also stores the number 11, because in the prefix notation, the value of the operand is incremented or decremented before assigning it to another variable. Figure 1.15 displays the output of Listing 1.10:

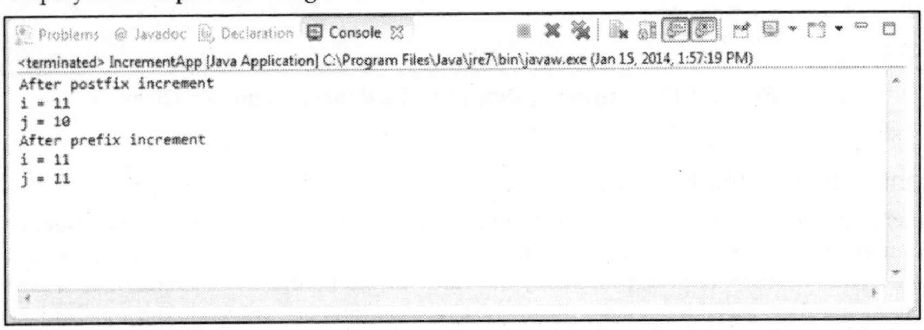

Figure 1.15: Difference Between Post-Increment and Pre-Increment Operators

The Conditional Operator

The conditional (?:) operator is a ternary operator that takes three operands. It works similar to an if-else statement. The conditional (?:) operator evaluates a boolean expression and gives the result based on this boolean expression. The conditional operator is constructed using a question mark (?) and a colon (:) symbol. The syntax to declare a conditional operator is:

```
operand1? operand2 : operand3
```

In this syntax, operand1 is any valid boolean expression, such as 10>5. If operand1 is true, then operand2 is evaluated; otherwise, operand3 is evaluated. For example:

```
a = (x < y) ? x : y;
```

Listing 1.11 shows use of the conditional operator:

Listing 1.11: Usage of the Conditional (?:) Operator

```
/* Program implementing the Conditional Operator */
class ConditionalOpt
 {
  public static void main(String args[]) {
          int i=20, j=15 ;
          boolean test=false;
          test = i > j ?  true :  false;
          System.out.println("The value of test =" +test);
  }
}
```

In Listing 1.11, a class `ConditionalOpt` is defined. Within the `main()` method of the `ConditionalOpt` class, two variables i and j store the values 20 and 15, respectively. The boolean variable `test` stores the result of the conditional (?:) operator. In the expression i > j ? true : false, the value contained in the variable i is greater than that of the variable j; therefore, the?:operator returns true and the value is then assigned to the test variable. Figure 1.16 shows the result of using the conditional (?:) operator.

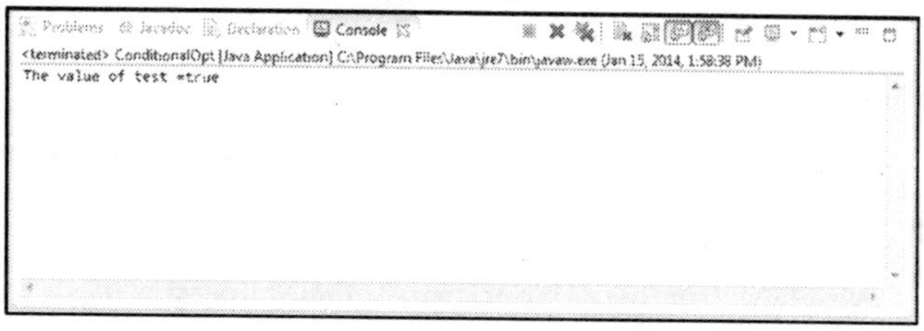

Figure 1.16: Usage of Conditional Operator

The Bitwise Operators

These operators perform on the individual bits (0 and 1) of their operands. They can be applied only on integer types such as long, int, short, and byte. Bitwise operators should be used where memory savings are needed, such as for system programming. Table 1.4 lists the bitwise operators:

Table 1.4: Bitwise Operators

<table>
<tr><th>Operator</th><th>Meaning</th></tr>
<tr><td>&</td><td>AND</td></tr>
<tr><td>|</td><td>OR</td></tr>
<tr><td>^</td><td>Exclusive OR</td></tr>
<tr><td>>></td><td>Right Shift</td></tr>
<tr><td><<</td><td>Left Shift</td></tr>
</table>

Let's now discuss the operators listed in Table 1.4.

The AND Operator

This operator produces 1 bit in case the corresponding bits in both the operands are 1; otherwise, it produces zero, as shown in Table 1.5:

Table 1.5: Outcomes with AND operator

A	B	A & B
0	0	0
1	0	0
0	1	0
1	1	1

The OR Operator

This operator produces 1 if one or both of the corresponding bits in its operands are 1, and produces 0 if both of the corresponding bits are 0. In other words, OR (|) operator returns one in all cases except in a situation where the corresponding bits of both operands are zero, as shown in Table 1.6:

Table 1.6: Outcomes with OR operator

<table>
<tr><th>A</th><th>B</th><th>A | B</th></tr>
<tr><td>0</td><td>0</td><td>0</td></tr>
<tr><td>1</td><td>0</td><td>1</td></tr>
<tr><td>0</td><td>1</td><td>1</td></tr>
<tr><td>1</td><td>1</td><td>1</td></tr>
</table>

The Exclusive OR Operator

This operator produces 1 where the corresponding bits in its operands are different and produces 0 if they are the same as shown in Table 1.7:

Table 1.7: Outcomes with Exclusive OR

A	B	A ^ B
0	0	0
1	0	1
0	1	1
1	1	0

Let's now discuss shift operators. Before that, we must understand what exactly does shifting mean. Shifting means moving bits left or right depending upon the kind of shift operator used. Here, one bit moves forward making space for the next bit to take its place.

The Right Shift Operator

This operator >> shifts the bits to the right by a specified number of positions. The number of positions upto which the shifting should occur depends on the value given after the operator. When shifting right >>, the lost bits are filled in with previous leftmost bits.

To understand right shift operator more clearly, let's see an example:

- Consider 78 whose binary equivalent is:

  00000000 00000000 00000000 01001110

- By shifting it right >> 2 times, the output we get is:

  00000000 00000000 00000000 00010011 (= 19)

The Left Shift Operator

This operator shifts the bits to the left by a specified number of positions. When you shift left <<, the void left behind by the shift is filled by zeros and the lost bits are filled in with previous rightmost bits.

To understand the left shift operator more clearly, let's see an example:

- Consider 78 again whose binary equivalent is:

  00000000 00000000 00000000 01001110

- By shifting it left << 3 times, the output we get is:

  00000000 00000000 00000010 01110000 (= 624)

Now let's create a simple program to demonstrate the bitwise logical operators.

Using the Bitwise Logical Operator

Here, let's create a simple program which explains the implementation of the bitwise logical operator. Listing 1.12 shows the use of bitwise logical operator:

Listing 1.12: The BitLogicApp.java File

```
/* Program implementing bitwise logical operators */
class BitLogicApp
{
    public static void main(String args[])
    {
            int a = 30;
            int b = 10;
            int c = 3;
            System.out.println("First Number: "+ a);
            System.out.println("First Number: " + a);
            System.out.println("A|B is:" + (a | b));
            System.out.println("A & B is:" + (a & b));
            System.out.println("A ^ B is:" + (a ^ b));
            int d = ~c & 0x0f;
            System.out.println("~c is :" + d);
    }
}
```

In Listing 1.12, the bitwise logical operators, such as |, ^, and &. Figure 1.17 shows output of the `BitLogicApp` class:

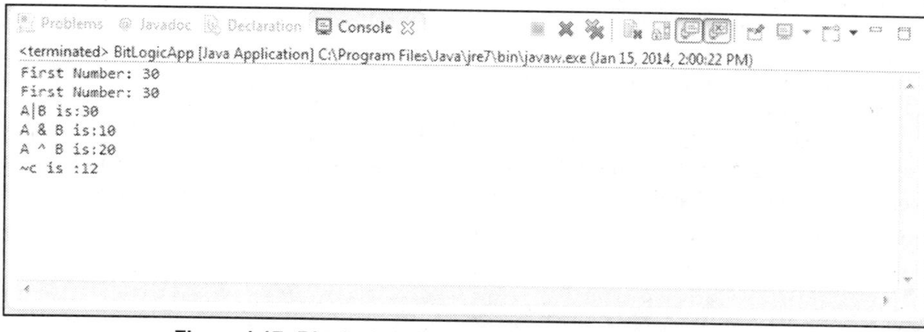

Figure 1.17: Displaying Output of the BitLogicApp.java File

Now, after understanding the implementation of the bitwise operators, let's discuss the implementation of the bitwise shift, i.e. left or right shift operators.

Using the Bitwise Shift Operators

Here, let's create a simple program to understand implementation of the bitwise shift operator. Listing 1.13 shows the usage of the left and right shift bitwise operator:

Listing 1.13: The BitShiftApp.java File

```
/*Program implementing the bitwise shift operators */
class BitShiftApp
{
  public static void main(String args[])
  {
        int x=6;
        int y = -6;
        System.out.println("First Number:" +x);
        System.out.println("Second Number:" +y);
        System. out.println("X >> 2" +(x>>2));
        System.out.println("X << 1" +(x<<1));
        System.out.println("X >>> 1" +(x>>>1));
        System.out.println("y >> 1" +(y>>1));
        System.out.println("y >>> 2" +(y>>>2));
  }
}
```

In Listing 1.13, implementation of the left and right shift bitwise operators is shown in the `BitShiftApp` class. Figure 1.18 shows output of the `BitShiftApp` class, after compilation and execution:

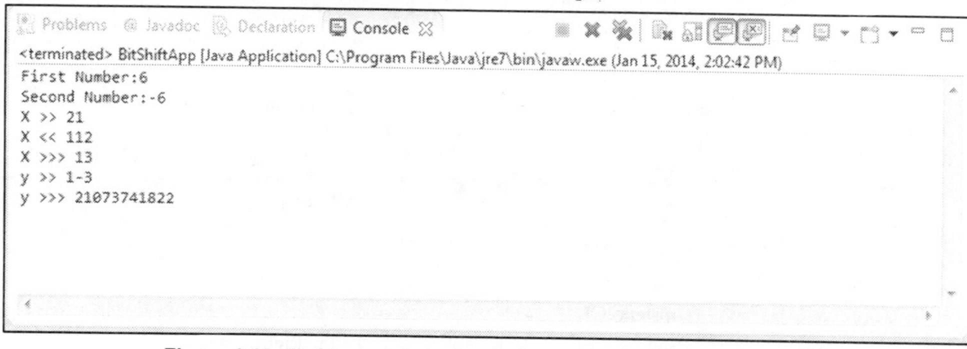

Figure 1.18: Displaying Output After Using Bitwise Shift Operators

Special Operators

Here, we discuss the `instanceof` and dot operators. The `instanceof` operator is a binary operator that checks whether an object is of a particular type (here, type can be a class, interface, or an array). It is used for object reference variables only. The syntax to use the `instanceof` operator is:

```
<objectReference> instanceof <XxxType>
```

Here, the left-hand operand of the `instanceof` operator is object Reference, which must be an instance (or we can say an object) of a class while the right-hand operand (`XxxType`) can be a class, interface, or an array type. The `instanceof` operator returns true if the object mentioned on the left-hand side is an instance of the type that is mentioned at the right-hand side of this operator; otherwise, it (`instanceof` operator) returns false.

Apart from the `instanceof` operator, in Java we also use the dot (.) operator as shown in the following code snippet:

```
X x;
x.go();
```

In the preceding code snippet, the x instance of the X class is followed by a dot (.) operator to invoke the method, i.e. member of the X class.

Now after understanding all types of operators in detail, let's discuss the precedence of operators and their associativity.

Operator Precedence and Associativity

In Java, each operator has an associated precedence which helps in determining how an expression is evaluated if more than one operator is used. On the basis of operator precedence, the evaluation of an operator depends. In other words, the operators at the higher level of precedence are evaluated first and operators of same precedence are evaluated either from left to right or vice-versa. Such a property of an operator is known as associativity. Table 1.8 describes the operator precedence and its associativity:

Table 1.8: Operator Precedence and its Associativity

Order	Operator	Associativity
1	() []	Left to Right
2	(Unary Minus) ++ -- ! ~	Right to Left
3	* / %	Left to Right
4	+ (Subtraction)	Left to Right
5	<< >> >>>	Left to Right
6	< <= > >= instanceOf	Left to Right
7	== !=	Left to Right
8	&	Left to Right

Table 1.8: Operator Precedence and its Associativity

Order	Operator	Associativity
9	^	Left to Right
10	|	Left to Right
11	&&	Left to Right
12	||	Left to Right
13	>:	Right to Left
14	=	Right to Left

Explaining Data Types

Java is a strongly typed language, therefore it is important to understand the data types available in Java. You cannot even declare a variable without specifying its data type in Java program. The data types available in Java can be divided into four broad categories:

- `Integer` – Represents integers using byte, short, int, and long
- `Floating-point` – Represents fractional numbers using float and double data types
- `Character` – Represents `char`, which is used to store characters
- `Boolean` – Represents logical values using `boolean` data type

Let's start discussion with Integer data types first.

Integer Data Types

Integer data types are used to store integer data items. Java provides four integer data types to store the integer values – *`byte`*, *`short`*, *`int`*, and *`long`*. As Java only supports the signed integers, these integers types have `-ve` and `+ve` values. Among all, byte is the smallest integer data type while long is the largest `integer` data type. Table 1.9 lists the width and range of the `integer` types:

Table 1.9: Width and Range of Integer Data Types

Data Type Representation	Width (bytes)	Range
byte	1	-128 to 127
short	2	-32, 768 to 32, 767
int	4	-2,147,483,648 to 2, 147,483,647
long	8	-9,223,372,036,854,775,808 to 9,223,372,036,854,775,807

Few examples of integer data types are:

```
byte x;
short sum;
int age;
long milliseconds;
```

Here, x, sum, age, and milliseconds are variables of `byte`, `short`, `int`, and `long` data type respectively. As shown in Table 1.9, the width of different types are different, therefore you must take care while using these data types. If you need to store a small data, for example, 25, you must use the `byte` data type as it is sufficient to store 25. If you use any other data type than `byte`, it allocates extra memory space unnecessarily which leads to increased execution time.

Floating-Point Data Types

In Java, to manipulate the real numbers, the `floating-point` data type is used. Java provides two floating-point data types – *float* and *double*. The float data type is used to store the single precision numbers whereas the double data type is used to store the double precision numbers. The float and double data types are used to represent numbers along with decimal values. The `float` data type can represent a maximum of 7 digits after decimal while the double data type can represent 15 digits. Table 1.10 lists the width and range of the `floating-point` data types:

Table 1.10: Width and Range of Floating-point Data Types

Data Type	Width (bytes)	Range
float	4	--3.4e38 to -1.4e-45 for negative values and 1.4e-45 to 3.4e to 3.4e38 for positive value
double	8	-1.8e308 to -4.9e-324 for negative values and 4.9e-324 to 1.8e308 for positive values

An example of floating-point data types is as follows:

- float x=3.458f;
- double d=3.24;

In the preceding code snippet, x is declared and initialized as float data type, whereas d is declared as double type. Let's discuss these two data types in the following sections.

The float Data Type

The `float` data type is used to represent the `single-precision` values, which use 32 bits (4 byte) of the memory space. You are suggested to use `float` data type when you don't need to store a large degree of precesion. A `float` data type can store maximum 7 digits after the decimal point. While declaring and using `float` data type, you must add the `f` or `F` postfix to the data. If you declare and initialize a `float` data type variable without the `f` or `F` postfix, it causes the compilation error. As all the floating-point numbers are considered as double in Java. For example, consider the code snippet:

```
float height=6.1;    //incorrect
float height=6.1f;  //correct
```

In the preceding code snippet, the first declaration is incorrect as `f` postfix is not added at the end of data, therefore it is considered as double.

The double Data Type

The double data type is used to represent the `double-precision` values, which use 64 bits (8 bytes) of the memory space. You are suggested to use double data type when you need to deal with iterative calculations, which results in a value of larger width. Although in Java all the floating-point numbers are considered as double, you can use the d or D postfix with double type of data. It does not make any difference whether you are using the d or D postfix or not with the double data type. For example, consider the following code snippet:

```
double pi=3.14;
double pi=3.14d;
```

In the preceding code snippet, both the declarations are correct and represent the same double value. After discussing the two types of floating-point data types, let's discuss the character data type in the next section.

Character Data Type

The character data type is used to represent and store the character constants in Java programs. The character data type available in Java is `char`. This data type follows the Unicode character set to represent the characters that can be uniquely identified by the processor. Unicode is a standard character set that supports all the international characters of various languages, such as American, Latin, and so on. Table 1.11 lists the width and range of the character data type:

Table 1.11: Width and Range of Character Data Type

Data Type Representation	Width (bytes)	Range
char	2	0 to 65535

An example of `char` data types is as follows:

```
char grade='A';
```

In the preceding code snippet, the `grade` variable is declared and initialized with data `'A'`. You must remember to enclose any character within single quotes, while initializing a character data type.

The boolean Data Type

The `boolean` data type represents two logical values denoted by true or false. Let's see the following code snippet to initialize and use boolean data type:

```
boolean x = true;
```

In the preceding code snippet, the `x` variable of boolean data type is declared and initialized as true. You can also initialize it with false. All the data types discussed here may not always be initialized when they are declared. If you do not initialize a variable it takes its default value according to its data type. Table 1.12 lists the default value of all the data types:

Table 1.12: Default Values of Data Types

Data Type	Default value
byte	0
short	0
int	0
long	0L
float	0.0f
double	0.0d
char	'\u0000'
boolean	false

All data types have their default values until some other value is not assigned to them.

You have learned different data types and their default values available in Java. Now, let's discuss about the variables in the following section.

Declaring Variables

Java provides us containers or placeholders to store data within a program. These containers are called variables since the values stored in them can be changed during the course of execution of a program. To declare a variable in a Java program, you need to use the combination of a data type and an identifier. An identifier is the name given to the variable and it must be a logical name. A variable must be declared before it is used in the program. The syntax for declaring a variable is:

```
dataType variable;// declaring variable
```

In the preceding syntax, `dataType` specifies a valid Java data type, such as `int`, char, and so on. `Variable` can have any name that follows some specified naming conventions, which are discussed later in this topic.

Apart from declaring a single variable in a declaration statement, you can also declare more than one variable of a particular data type. The syntax for declaring more than one variable in a declaration statement is given here:

```
dataType variable1, variable2,....variableN;// declaring more than one variable
```

As shown in the preceding syntax, if you declare more than one variable at a time, they must be separated by comma (,). You must always remember to terminate a variable declaration by semicolon (;). After declaring the variable, let's now see how to initialize it in the following syntax:

```
dataType variable = val;// initializing a variable
```

In the preceding syntax, `val` represents the value that is used to initialize the variable. Apart from initializing a variable at the time of its declaration, it can also be initialized later after its declaration. The following syntax shows how a variable is initialized after its declaration:

```
dataType variable;
.
.
variable=val;
```

In the preceding syntax, the variable is declared first and initialized later.

Variables in Java are categorized into the following three main types:

- Instance Variables
- Class Variables
- Local Variables

Let's discuss all these variables in detail in the following sections.

Declaring the Instance Variables

Instance variables are declared inside a class as its member and created when the objects of the class are instantiated. The instance variables are associated with objects and can take different values for each object. The instance variable allocates separate memory space for each object. Instance variables are available in the program till their associated objects are available. Once the associated object goes out of scope, the associated instance variable is no longer accessible. The following code snippet declares the instance variables:

```
class InstanceVar
{
    int var1;
    .
    .
    public static void main(String ar[])
    {
            InstanceVar obj1=new InstanceVar();
            InstanceVar obj2=new InstanceVar();
    }
}
```

In the preceding code snippet, the `var1` variable is an instance variable. When the `obj1` and `obj2` objects are instantiated, separate memory space is allocated to `var1` for each object.

Declaring the Class Variables

Class variables are also declared inside the class as its member, but with the `static` keyword. Class variables are associated with that class and they allocate only one memory space for all the objects of that class. In other words, the same value of the class variable is shared by all the objects of that class. Class variables are available in the program till the existence of their associated class. The following code snippet declares the class variables:

```
class ClassVar
{
    int var1;
    static int var2;
    .
    .
    public static void main(String ar[])
    {
            ClassVar obj1=new ClassVar();
            ClassVar obj2=new ClassVar();
    }
}
```

In the preceding code snippet, `var1` is the instance variable, whereas `var2` is the class variable. Figure 1.19 shows the difference between instance variable and class variable:

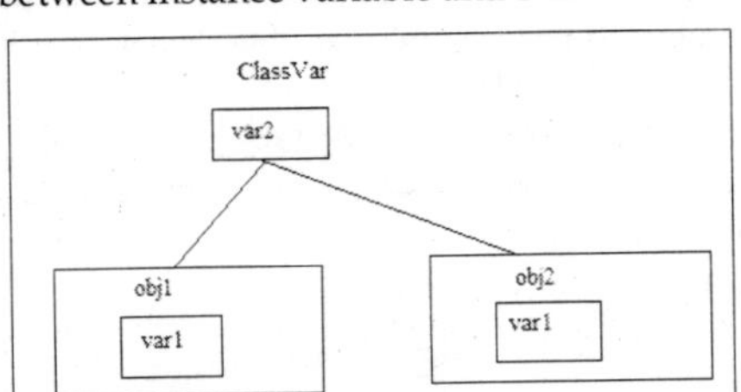

Figure 1.19: Difference between Instance and Class Variables

In Figure 1.19, the `var1` variable allocates separate memory spaces for `obj1` and `obj2`, whereas the `var2` variable allocates single memory space for both the objects. The `ob1` and `obj2` objects have their separate copy of the `var1` instance variable whereas both the objects share the same copy of the `var2` class variable.

Declaring the Local Variables

Apart from declaring instance variables and class variables, you can also declare local variables in a class. Local variables are declared inside a block or a method. The local variable declared in a block or method is only visible to that block or method. It cannot be accessed outside the block or method. Local variables are alive till the execution of their respective block of declaration. The following code snippet declares the local variables inside a method:

```
class LocalVar {
   int var1;
   static int var2;
   .
   .
   void method1(){
           int lclvar=10;
           .
           .
   }
}
```

In the preceding code snippet, the `lclvar` variable is declared inside the `method1()` method. The `lclvar` variable can only be used inside the `method1()` method. Similarly, local variables can also be declared inside a block defined between a opening brace, {, and closing brace, }. The variables declared inside a block are visible only inside that program block. The following code snippet declares the local variables inside a program block:

```
class LocalVar {
   int var1;
   static int var2;
   .
   .
   {
           int localvar=10;
           .
           .
   }
}
```

In the preceding code snippet, the `localvar` variable is a local variable declared inside a program block. The `localvar` variable is not accessible outside the block where it is declared. Apart from having a single block, you can have nested blocks also in your program. These nested blocks can have their local variable declarations. You must not declare a local variable in inner block with the name same as the variable name declared in the outer block, in case of nested blocks. The following code snippet shows how variables are declared in nested blocks:

```
class LocalVar {
   int var1;
   static int var2;
   .
   .
   {
           int localvar=10;
           .
           .
           {
                   char grade='A';
                   .
                   .
           }
           {
                   int roll=1;
                   .
                   .
           }
   }
}
```

In the preceding code snippet, the `localvar`, `grade`, and `roll` local variables are declared in nested program blocks. The variables (`localvar`) declared in outer block are accessible inside the inner block, whereas the variables inside the inner blocks (`grade`, `roll`) are not accessible inside the outer block.

Declaring Classes

Java is pure object-oriented programming language, which implies that all the instructions in a Java program must be written inside the class. Class is a template to create Java programs consisting of attributes and methods. Attributes are the data member of the class, which are manipulated and accessed by the methods of the class. Unlike C and C++, methods in normal Java classes are defined at the time of its declaration. The `class` keyword is used to declare a class. Following syntax declares a class in Java:

```
class <class_name> // Class declaration
{
// declaring variables
   datatype <var_name1>;
   datatype <var_name2>;
// defining methods
   return_type method_name (parameters)
   {
          //Method body
   }
}
```

In the preceding code snippet, only two variables are declared but you can create as many as required. In the same way, number of methods that need to be used in a class depends on the requirement of the program. A Java class, which is the starting class of your program must contain the `main()` method as you need to call the class containing `main()` method, to execute the Java program.

Listing 1.14 shows an example to understand how to create a class:

Listing 1.14: Creating a Sample Java Class

```
class Sample {
   public static void main (String args[])
   {
          // variable declaration
          String fname;
          String sname;
          int age;

          // Assigning values to the variables declared
          fname = "Vikash";
          sname = "Suman";
          age = 24;

          //Displaying the values assigned
          System.out.println ("First name of the person is =" +  fname);
          System.out.println ("Last name of the person is =" +  sname);
          System.out.println ("Age of the person is =" + age);
   }
}
```

In Listing 1.14, the `Sample` class is created. This class contains the `main()` method, which is the very first method called during the execution of a Java program. In Listing 1.14, first we have declared some variables such as `fname`, `sname`, and `age`, which are then followed by some values assigned to those variables. At last, we have displayed the value assigned to those variables. Figure 1.20 shows the output of the Listing 1.14:

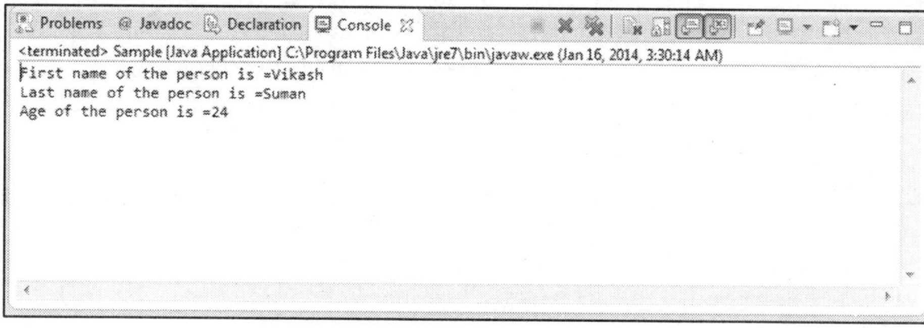

Figure 1.20: Output of the Sample Program

In Figure 1.20, you can see that the values assigned to the variables are displayed along with the statements specified within the `System.out.println()` statement. Apart from simple classes, you can also create classes within classes in Java.

You can also declare a class within another class, which is known as inner or nested classes.

Inner Classes

In Java, it is possible to create a class inside another class. The class that is created inside the other class is known as inner class, and the class in which the inner class resides is called outer class. An inner class has full access to the member variables of its outer class.

The benefit of using inner class is that inner class is visible to its outer class only. Therefore, no other class can use the code written inside the inner class. The object of an inner class can only be created in the context of its outer class. You can use inner class to implement security features when you are writing some important code, such as password checking in an application, and do not want to grant access of this code to other classes except its outer class. Let's create an inner class named `in_cls` within an outer class named `out_cls`. The following code snippet shows the code of the outer class `out_cls`:

```
class out_cls // outer class
{
   int[] a ={2,4,5,7,10}; // Array of numbers
   class in_cls    //  creating inner class
   {
          public void odd_even() // inner class method to segregate odd and even values
          {
                   for (int i=0; i<a.length; i++)
                   {
                            if (a[i]%2 == 0)
                     {
                        System.out.println("The value at the position " + a[i] + " is even");
                      }
                            else
                   {
                        System.out.println("The value at the position " +  a[i] + " is odd");
                   }
                   }
          }
   } // ending inner class

   public void cal_inr()  // outer class method to call inner class members
   {
          in_cls val = new in_cls(); // creating object of inner class
          val.odd_even(); // calling method of inner class
   }

   public static void main(String args[])
   {
```

```
        out_cls show = new out_cls(); // creating object of outer class
        show.cal_inr(); // calling method of outer class
    }
}
```

In preceding code, an outer class named out_cls is created, wherein another class called `in_cls` is created, which is the inner class. In the `in_cls` class, you have created a method called `odd_even()` to segregate odd and even values from the values stored in the array a.

A method called cal_inr() is created in which you have created the object of the inner class. The method odd_even() of the inner class are called from the outer class method `cal_inr()`.

In the main method, an object of the outer class is created, which is then followed by calling the outer class method. As soon as the outer class method is called, the control transfers to the `cal_inr` method, which in turn performs its functioning.

Declaring Methods

A Java class consists of attributes and methods. Methods are considered as functions that are used to perform some specific task in an application. A method can have any name, such as `disp`, `vol`, and so on. Depending on the requirement of the program, many methods can be created in a program. The syntax to create a method is as follows:

```
<return_type> <method_name> ([para_list])
{
    // method body;
}
```

In the preceding syntax, `return_type` can be any data type depending on the type of values that a method is returning. If the method is not returning any value, then the data type is replaced with void. A method returns the value to calling routine through the return statement. The `method_name` is the name of the method. The `para_list` represents a list of parameters that are passed in a method. It may happen that there is no need to use parameters in a method. In that case, the `para_list` is not used and brackets remain empty. Within the curly braces, the body of the method is written.

Listing 1.15 shows how to create and use methods:

Listing 1.15: Creating and Using Methods

```
class MethodDemo {
    void no_para()
    {
            int j=5;
            int k=6;
            int s= j + k;
            System.out.println("sum of the two numbers in a method without
            parameters are = " + s);
    }
    public static void main(String args[])
    {
            MethodDemo get_sum = new MethodDemo();
            get_sum.no_para(); //  Invoking  the no_para method
    }
}
```

In Listing 1.15, the `MethodDemo` class is created with the `no_para()` method. The `no_para()` method is used to calculate the sum of two numbers. In the `no_para()` method, two variables are declared and initialized with some value. After that, we have used '+' operator to calculate their sum, which is then followed by assigning the sum into a third variable. Finally, the sum assigned in the third variable is displayed along with the statement written within '`System.out.println()` statement'.

Inside the `main()` method, the `get_sum` instance of the `MethodDemo` class is created. Then this object is used to invoke the `no_para()` method. The `no_para()` method is invoked with no parameter values because it is a non-parameterized method. (The method defined without any parameter is known as non-parameterized method). As a result, the sum of the number is displayed.

This is how methods are created and used. The `no_para()` method in the `MethodDemo` class does not return any value.

You can also create methods, which return some value. Also, you can pass arguments to the methods. Let's discuss these activities performed with methods in the following sections.

Methods Returning a Value

Apart from creating methods which does not return any value to the caller, you can also create methods returning some value to the caller. For example, instead of printing the value of sum of the numbers provided in the `no_para()` method, you can return the sum to the caller. Listing 1.16 shows how methods returning values are created and used:

Listing 1.16: Creating and Using Method Returning a Value

```
class MethodReturnDemo {
    int no_para()
    {
            int j=5;
            int k=6;
            int s= j+k;
            return s;
    }
    public static void main(String args[])
    {
            MethodReturnDemo get_sum = new MethodReturnDemo();

            int sum=get_sum.no_para();
            System.out.println("The Sum returned from the no_para() method is "+ sum);
    }
}
```

In Listing 1.16, the `MethodReturnDemo` class is created with the `no_para()` method. The `no_para()` method calculates the sum of two numbers and returns the sum to the caller block. As this method is called from the `main()` method, the sum is returned in the `main()` method. Finally, the sum is displayed inside the `main()` method.

The sum of 5 and 6 is displayed to the standard output. The `no_para()` method in the `MethodReturnDemo` class has no parameter. You can also pass parameters to the methods. Let's discuss how methods with arguments are created and used in the following section.

Passing Arguments to Methods

In Java, you can create methods, which accept argument. The methods with arguments are called *parameterized methods*. These methods can accept all the data type available in Java. The parameter is passed at both the places, when the method is invoked and when the method is defined. The parameters passed at the time of invocation of method are called *actual parameter*, and the parameter passed at the time of its definition is called *dummy parameter*. Listing 1.17 shows how to create and use methods with parameter:

Listing 1.17: Creating and Using Method with Arguments

```
class MethodParaDemo {
    int with_para(int j, int k)
    {
            int s= j+k;
            return s;
    }
    public static void main(String args[])
    {
            MethodParaDemo get_sum = new MethodParaDemo();
            int sum=get_sum.with_para(7,8);
            System.out.println("The Sum returned from the with_para() method is "+ sum);
    }
}
```

In Listing 1.17, the `MethodParaDemo` class is created with the `with_para()` method. This method accepts two integer arguments and returns the sum of those two arguments. Sum is retrieved inside the `main()` method and displayed there. The parameters 7 and 8 are actual parameter, which is passed when the method is called. The parameters `j` and `k` are dummy parameters, which are passed when the method is defined.

Sum of 7 and 8 is calculated inside the `with_para()` method and displayed in the main() method.

The parameters passed to the `with_para()` method inside the `main()` method are constant values, you can also pass variables containing those values.

Let's discuss the effects of passing values and object references to the methods in the following sections.

Creating Objects

Instances of a class are known as objects and the process of creating objects from a class is known as *instantiation*. While creating an instance of a class, the class works as a data type. To create an object, you have to declare a variable of class type to store the object reference. For example, if you have to create an object of the Sample class (Listing 1.14), then you first have to declare a variable of the Sample class type. You can create the variable of the sample class as follows:

```
Sample info;
```

Now, you can create the object of the class. To create an object, the `new` operator is used that dynamically allocates memory to an object and returns a reference to it. This reference is then stored in the variable declared. Let's see how to create an object of the Sample class (Listing 1.14):

```
info = new Sample();
```

You can also combine both the steps to create an object, as follows:

```
Sample info = new Sample();
```

Each object has its own copy of the instance variables declared in the class definition. Listing 1.18 shows how the objects are created:

Listing 1.18: Creating Objects Example

```
class ObjectDemo {
void show()
   {
        System.out.println("An Example of Object Creation");
   }
   public static void main(String ar[])
   {
        ObjectDemo obj1,obj2;
        obj1=new ObjectDemo();
        obj2=new ObjectDemo();
        obj1.show();
        obj2.show();
   }
}
```

In Listing 1.18, the `ObjectDemo` class is created with the `show()` method. Inside the `main()` method, the objects of the `ObjectDemo` class are created. First two reference variables `obj1` and `obj2` are created and then using the `new` keyword, the objects are instantiated and assigned to these reference variables. Finally, the `show()` method is invoked using the `obj1` and `obj2` objects.

The `show()` method is invoked two times and the message is displayed twice. The members of a class, such as method and fields and even the class itself can have a level of protection, so that they cannot be misused. Let's discuss the how the class members and the class can be protected in the following section.

Explaining Access Specifiers

The members of a class have its visibility in the same class or other classes. Even the classes have their associated accessibility. How and where a member of a class is accessed is determined by access specifiers. In Java programming language, `public`, `protected`, `private`, and `default` are the available access specifiers. The access specifiers available in Java are described as follows:

- `public`—When a class member is declared with the public access specifiers, it can be accessed from anywhere in the program. You can access public classes, methods, and fields from everywhere. The public classes, methods, or fields are used only if you explicitly want to offer access to these members and if this access cannot do any harm.

- `protected`—You can have access protected methods and fields from within the same class to which the methods and fields belong, within its subclasses, and within classes of the same package, but not from other packages. The protected access specifier cannot be used with class declaration.
- `private`—You can access the private methods and fields only within the same class to which the methods and fields belong. When you declare a method or field as private, it is not visible within subclasses and is not inherited by subclasses. The private access specifier works opposite to the public access specifier. The concept of encapsulation, in which, data are hidden within the class and accessor methods are provided, is implemented through the use of private access specifier.
- `default`—If you do not specify any access specifier while declaring class, method, or field, then they are considered with default access specifier. The class, method or field with default access specifier can be accessed from within the same package to which the class, method or field belongs. These are not accessible outside the package they belong to.

Interfaces

In Java, an interface is a collection of various methods without definition. It is similar to a Java class, except that unlike an interface, a class may contain method definition. An interface can be implemented by one or more classes using the implements keyword in the class definition. A class that implements an interface is known as the implementation class.

An advantage of using interfaces is that they support multiple inheritances, as a class can implement more than one interface. The only requirement is that the implementation class must define all the methods declared in the interface which the class implements.

Let's consider a situation where you have to write a Java program to connect to a database. For this purpose, you write the ABC class that provides connectivity to the Oracle database and another class XYZ that provides connectivity to the SQL Server database, as shown in the following code snippet:

```
// Class to connect to the Oracle
class ABC {
   void connect()
   {
         // code to connect to the Oracle database
   }
}
// Class to connect to the SQL Server
class XYZ {
   void connect(){
         // code to connect to the SQL Server database
   }
}
```

In the preceding code snippet, both the classes ABC and XYZ have limitations. The ABC class can only connect to the Oracle database and the XYZ class can only connect to the SQL Server database. In other words, you cannot use these classes to connect to any other database. To do that, you have to either change the definition of these classes or create other classes.

Creating several different classes, each with code to connect to different databases, takes a lot of time and effort. However, let's suppose you manage to do this. Now, suppose that by the time you finish creating the classes, the versions of the databases you want to connect to the classes have changed. What would do you do then? You are left with no choice but to rewrite the classes and connect them to the new versions of the databases.

To solve this problem, you can create an interface and declare methods in it. The definition of a method declared in an interface is provided within the class that implements the interface. The following code snippet shows how to create an interface:

```
interface MyInterface {
   //All the methods of an interface are by default public
   void connect();
}
```

The preceding code snippet creates the MyInterface interface, which declares the connect() method. However, you cannot instantiate an interface in Java because an interface does not contain method definition. Therefore, to use an interface, you have to implement it in a class. The following code snippet shows how to implement an interface:

```
class OracleImp implements MyInterface {
  public void connect()
  {
  // code to connect to the Oracle server database
  }
}
```

In the preceding code snippet, the `OracleImp` class implements the `MyInterface` interface, which is created to connect to the Oracle database. Similarly, if you want to connect to the SQL server database, you can use another implementation class `SQLImp`, which contains the code to connect to the SQL `Server` database. The following code snippet shows how to create a class that connects to the SQL `Server` database:

```
class SQLImp implements MyInterface {
  public void connect()
  {
  // code to connect to the SQL server database
  }
}
```

In both the `OracleImp` and `SQLImp` classes, the `connect()` method can be defined according to the statements required to connect to the respective databases. To connect to a database, database vendors provide drivers. These drivers vary from database to database; therefore, the types of drivers used to connect to the Oracle database are quite different from the drivers specified for SQL Server database. The method definition also varies according to the driver's implementation. The `connect()` method of the `OracleImp` class provides implementation to connect to Oracle database according to the database drivers of Oracle. Similarly, the `connect()` method of the `SQLImp` class provides implementation to connect to the SQL Server database according to the database drivers of SQL Server. Now, both the classes have the same method but different implementation. In this way, you can create other classes and connect them to other databases. All you have to do is to define the `connect()` method in the class according to the specifications of the driver.

Now, to connect to a database, you need to create an instance of the implementation class whose connect() method you want to use. The following code snippet shows how to create and use the `MyInterface` interface:

```
interface MyInterface {
  void connect();
}
class OracleImp implements MyInterface {
  public void connect()
  {
        System.out.println("Successfully connected to Oracle database");
  }
}
class SQLImp implements MyInterface {
  public void connect(){
        System.out.println("Successfully connected to SQL Server
        database");
  }
}
public class DemoInterface {
  public static void main(String args[]) throws Exception {
        Class c=Class.forName(args[0]);
        MyInterface obj=(MyInterface)c.newInstance();
        obj.connect();
  }
}
```

The preceding code snippet accepts the name of a class at runtime to connect to a database. The name is then accepted by the forName() method that belongs to the Class class, which is present in the java.lang package. The forName() method returns the name of the Class object, which is passed at runtime. The Class object is then used to access the connect() method of the class.

In the preceding code snippet, the connect() method is declared in the MyInterface interface. The OracleImp and SQLImp classes implement the MyInterface interface and provide the definition of the connect() method in their own terms. In short, an interface provides empty methods, which are defined in the implementation classes according to the user's requirements.

Inheritance

The feature by which one class acquires the characteristics of an existing class is known as inheritance. In Java, a class that is inherited is called a superclass and the class that inherits the superclass is called a subclass. For example, the BallPointPen class is a subclass of the Pen class. In terms of OOP, this means that BallPointPen is a subclass derived from its superclass Pen. The principle behind inheritance is that each derived class acquires all the characteristics of its superclass, thereby ensuring reusability of the code.

NOTE

Multiple inheritance is not supported in Java, which means a subclass can extend only one superclass in Java.

In Java, the extends keyword is used in the subclass definition to inherit a superclass. Let's understand inheritance with the help of an example. The following code snippet declares two classes, Person and Sportsperson, to help you understand the concept of inheritance:

```
class Person {
   private String name;
   public void setName(String n) {
           name = n;
   }
   public void getName(){
           System.out.println("Name :" + name);
   }
}
public class SportsPerson extends Person {
   private String sport;
   public void setSport(String sp) {
           sport = sp;
   }
   public void getSport(){
           System.out.println("Sport:" + sport);
   }
   public static void main(String[] args) {
           SportsPerson sp = new SportsPerson();
           sp.setName("Jim Johnson");
           sp.setSport("Soccer");
           sp.getName();
           sp.getSport();
   }
}
```

In preceding code snippet, the SportsPerson class has inherited the Person class, which means that the Person class is a superclass of the SportsPerson class. In the Person class, two methods named setName() and getName() are defined. The setName() method sets the name of a player and the getName() method displays the name of the player. Next, two methods named setSport() and getSport() are defined in the SportsPerson class. The setSport() method sets the value for the sport variable and the getSport() method displays the value of the sport variable.

You have also created an object sp of the SportsPerson class. Since the SportsPerson class extends the Person class, it has accessed to the members of both the SportsPerson and Person classes.

Implementing Flow Control Statements

In a Java program, to achieve certain results, some specific operations need to be performed repeatedly. The execution of these operations is based upon the fulfillment of certain conditions. These conditions are placed in various control flow statements, such as *conditional statements*, *iteration statements*, and *jump statements*. The operation to be performed is provided in the block of control flow statements. A conditional statement is a control statement that allows choosing between two or more execution paths in a program. Iteration statements repeatedly execute the code block on the basis of the conditional statement. Once the conditional statement evaluates to false, the loop exits. After that, the control transfers to the next statement that follows the loop. Jump statements explicitly redirect the flow of program execution.

Let's discuss these flow control statements in detail in the following sections.

Using Selection Statements

Selection statements, as the name itself suggests, cause a program to execute a block of code on evaluating a conditional expression and selecting code for execution. If the conditional expression comes out to be true, the accompanying block of code is executed and if it is false, the accompanying block of code is bypassed. Following are the selection statements available in Java:

- `if` statement
- `if-else` statement
- `switch` statement

Let's discuss these selection statements in detail.

Using if Statement

The `If` statement is a conditional construct that is used to evaluate an expression for a `boolean` value. In case, the expression returns true, the statements following the conditional expression will be executed but in case, it returns false, the code following the conditional expression would not be executed and the program would just move along to the next statement. Following is the general syntax for the `if` statement:

```
if (conditional expression)
   <Statements to be executed when conditional expression evaluated to true>;
```

In the preceding syntax, `if` is the keyword and inside the parenthesis, the conditional expression is provided.

Listing 1.19 shows how to use the `if` statement:

Listing 1.19: Using `if` Statement

```
class IfDemo {
   public static void main(String args[])
   {
         int age;
         age=16;
         if (age<18)
         System.out.println("Not eligible to vote");
   }
}
```

In Listing 1.19, `if` statement is used to test a condition that is whether age specified in the program is less than 18 or not. The value for `age` variable is set to 16 in the program. Since, 16 is less than 18, the condition set in the `if` statement becomes automatically true. Therefore, the statement following the if condition is displayed, because the condition is `true`. Apart from executing statements when the statement is `true`, you can also write code to execute statements when the condition is `false`. Let's discuss how it can be achieved in the following section.

Using if-else Statement

The `if-else` statement is used in situations where we can provide an alternative course of action, in case, the `if` clause returns false. For example, when the conditional expression for the `if` clause evaluates to false, the statements coded in else clause gets executed.

Following is the general syntax for 'if-else' statement:

```
if (conditional expression)
   <Statement1 to be executed in case it's true>;
   else
         <Statement2 to be executed in case it's false>;
```

In the preceding syntax, the condition is written inside the parenthesis (). According to the preceding syntax, if the condition specified after 'if' is true, then statement1 is executed; else, statement2 is executed. Listing 1.20 shows how to use if-else statement:

Listing 1.20: Using if-else Statement

```
class IfElseDemo {
    public static void main(String[] args) {
            int a = 10, b = 20;
            if (a > b) {
                    System.out.println("a > b");
            } else {
                    System.out.println("b > a");
            }
    }
}
```

In Listing 1.20, the 'if' statement is used to test a condition that whether value stored in variable 'a' is greater than the value stored in variable 'b' or not. Since the value stored in variable 'a' is set to 10 and that of 'b' to 20, the condition automatically evaluates to false and the statement immediately following the condition does not get executed. Then, the statement after the else construct gets executed as the condition in if statement is false. In both the preceding examples, only one if statement is used, you can use multiple if in your program also.

Using switch Statement

When there are several options and we have to choose only one option from them, we can use switch statement. Depending on the selected option, a particular task is performed. Task here represents one or more statements. Following is the general syntax for using switch statement:

```
switch (variable)
{
    case value 1: statements 1;
    case value 2: statements 2;
    case value 3: statements 3;
    :
    case value n : statements n;
    [default : default_statements;]
}
```

In the preceding syntax, depending on the value of the variable, a particular task (statement) is executed. If the variable value is equal to value1, statements1 will be executed. If the variable value is value2, statements2 will be executed, and so on. If the variable value is not equal to value1, value2, ... then none of the statements will execute. In that case, control comes to the default clause and the set of default_statements gets executed. In the preceding syntax, the default statement is enclosed in square bracket, [ ] because it is optional. It should be remembered that you cannot use all data types with switch statement. We can use char, int, byte, and short types only. Listing 1.21 shows how to use switch statement in your program:

Listing 1.21: Using switch Statement

```
class SwitchDemo {
    public static void main(String args[])
    {
            char country='i'; // country is set to 'i'
            switch(country)
            {
                    case 'a': System.out.println("America");
                    case 'c': System.out.println("Canada");
                    case 'i': System.out.println("India");
                    case 'e': System.out.println("England");
                    default: System.out.println("No Country");
            }
    }
}
```

In Listing 1.21, a variable of char type named country is declared and is initialized to i. Depending on the value stored in the variable country, America is displayed when the value is a; Canada is displayed when the value is c; India is displayed when the value is i; and England is displayed when the value is e. If the value of a country is neither of the specified values–a, c, i, or e, then the value in the default statement is displayed.

We expected that it would display India, but it is displaying every statement from India onwards. The question here is what could possibly be the reason? The value of variable country is set to 'i', so India should get displayed but we found that it has executed the rest of the statements following India. The reason for this problem is that once India is displayed, the control was not able to come out of the switch statement. For this purpose, break statement should be used in the program (Listing 1.21), which allows the program to come out of the switch statement after displaying India, as shown in Listing 1.22:

Listing 1.22: Using switch break Statement

```
class SwitchBreakDemo {
   public static void main(String args[])
   {
          char country='i';// country is set to 'i'
          switch(country)
          {
                 case 'a': System.out.println("America");
                        break;
                 case 'c': System.out.println("Canada");
                        break;
                 case 'i': System.out.println("India");
                        break;
                 case 'e': System.out.println("England");
                        break;
                 default: System.out.println("No Country");
          }
   }
}
```

In Listing 1.22, 'i' becomes true and hence, JVM displays India and then executes break, which terminates the switch block:

- Only India is displayed this time. It is because of the use of break statement.

So far, we have learned various selection statements. Let's now take a look on another category of control flow statements used to execute a block of statements repeatedly. These types of control flow statements are known as iteration statements. Let's discuss iteration statements in the following section.

Using Iteration Statements

Repeating the execution of same code fragment several times is called iteration. The basic logic behind iteration is that a sequence of statements is repeated until a certain condition is met. When this condition is false, the iteration terminates, and the loop is completed. There are various types of iteration statements available in Java. The iteration statements are also known as loops in Java. Following are the iteration statements that discussed in this section:

- while loop
- do-while loop
- for loop
- for each loop

Let's discuss types of iteration statements in detail now.

Using while Loop

The function of the while loop is to execute a specific block of statements until a condition evaluates to be true. Once the condition becomes false, the loop gets terminated. Following is the general syntax for using while loop:

```
while (conditional expression is true) {
   Statements to be executed;
}
```

In the preceding syntax, the condition is first tested. If the condition is true, the statements following it will go on executing repeatedly till it continues to be true. Once the condition becomes false, the loop terminates. There must be an increment/decrement statement inside the while block that should make the evaluation result to return false; otherwise, an infinite loop is created. Listing 1.23 shows how to use while loop in your program:

Listing 1.23: Using while loop Statement

```
class WhileDemo {
   public static void main(String args[]){
        int i=1;// setting the value to 1
        while(i<=20) {
                  System.out.println(i);// display i
                  i=i+2; // increment the value by 2
        }
   }
}
```

In Listing 1.23, first ten odd numbers are displayed using while loop. Firstly, variable 'i' is set to 1. To display odd numbers, 'i' gets incremented by 2 in each iteration. When the evaluation becomes false, that is once the value of 'i' exceeds 20, the loop terminates.

Odd numbers from 1 to 20 is displayed using the while loop. Let's now take a look on another loop called do-while loop, which is almost like a while loop but with a slight difference. Unlike while loop, the statement code will always be executed at least once by the do-while loop as the conditional expression is evaluated at the end of the loop.

Using do-while Loop

The do-while loop works like a while loop where a group of statements is executed as long as the condition is true. If the condition becomes false, the flow of execution comes out of the do-while loop. Following is the general syntax for using while loop:

```
do{
   statements;
} while(condition);
```

In the preceding syntax, the statement code is followed by the while keyword and a test expression. In case the evaluation returns true, the control goes back to the do keyword and continues until the evaluation becomes false. Listing 1.24 shows how you can use the do-while loop in your program:

Listing 1.24: Using do-while loop Statement

```
class DoWhileDemo {
   public static void main(String args[]){
        int i=2;// setting the value to 2
        do{
                  System.out.println(i);// displaxy i
                  i=i+2; // increment the value by 2
        }
        while(i<=20);
   }
}
```

In Listing 1.24, first ten even numbers are displayed using do-while loop in the same way as that of while loop. The difference, however, comes in the manner in which they are implemented. Here, in Listing 1.24, the value of i gets displayed before evaluating the conditional expression unlike while loop where the condition is checked first and only then the statements are executed further.

Firstly, variable i is set to 2. To display even numbers, i get incremented by 2 in each iteration. The loop gets terminated when the evaluation becomes false, that is once the value of i exceeds 20.

The do-while loop is used to display even numbers up to 20. After learning the basic difference between while and do-while loop, let's now discuss yet another type of iteration statement called for loop.

Using for Loop

The for loop is also like a while loop, but is syntactically more compact. The for loop executes a group of statements as long as a condition is true. Following is the general syntax of the for loop:

```
for (initializer; condition; increment)  {
   Statements;
}
```

In the preceding syntax, initializer is used to set the initial value for the counter to control the iteration. For this purpose, a variable may be declared. A boolean condition is evaluated at each pass of the loop to check whether the loop will continue to run or not. In case the condition evaluates to true, the loop will continue; otherwise, it will terminate. Listing 1.25 shows how you can use for loop in your program:

Listing 1.25: Using for loop Statement

```
class ForDemo {
   public static void main(String args[])
   {
          int i=1;
          //setting the value to 1
          for(i=1;i<=20;i=i+2)
          {
                 System.out.println(i);
          }
   }
}
```

In Listing 1.25, the first ten odd numbers are displayed with the help of for loop. Firstly, variable i is set to 1. To display odd numbers, i gets incremented by 2 in each iteration. The evaluation becomes false once the value of i exceeds 20 and the loop terminates.

The odd numbers up to 20 is displayed with the help of for loop. The next type of iteration statement that we are going to discuss is for-each loop. This loop executes statements for each element of the collection.

Using for-each Loop

The for-each loop is specifically designed to handle the elements of a collection. A collection is represented by a group of objects. Array is an example of collection since it stores a group of objects, such as integer values or strings. Similarly, the classes of java.util package are also developed to handle a group of objects. The for-each loop repeatedly executes a group of statements for each element of the collection. Following is the general syntax for using for-each loop:

```
for(var:collection) {
   Statements:
}
```

In the preceding syntax, var represents each element of the collection one by one. For instance, there is a collection of 5 elements then this loop will execute 5 times and the var will represent these elements one by one. Let's understand the use of for-each loop with the help of an example shown in Listing 1.26:

Listing 1.26: Using for-each Loop

```
class ForEachDemo {
   public static void main(String args[])
   {
   int arr[]={1,3,5,7,9,11,13,15,17,19}; //declare an array with 10 elements
   System.out.println("First 10 odd numbers are as follows:");
   for(int i:arr) // use for each to retrieve elements from an array
   {
          System.out.println(i); // i represents each element of array
   }
   }
}
```

In Listing 1.26, the for-each loop is used to display each element of an array. Here, there is a collection of array type containing ten elements. The for-each loop will execute 10 times and i will represent these elements thereby executing statements for each of these elements.

The numbers in the array are displayed using the for-each loop. Apart from using single loops in your program, you can also use nested loops in you program.

So far, we have discussed about control flow statements, such as selection statements and iteration statements. In the next section, we study another kind of control flow statements known as jump statements.

Using Jump Statements

Jump statements are the statements that transfer control from one part of the program to another. The jump statements supported by Java are as follows:

- break
- continue
- return

Let's discuss the types of jump statements in detail now.

Using break Statement

One of the important purposes of `break` statement is to exit from `switch` statement. At times, we need to break out of a loop before the whole thing gets executed. The `break` statement allows us to get out of a loop even before it is completely executed. This statement is written in the form of a simple `break` keyword followed by a semicolon. Let's understand the use of `break` statement with the help of an example shown in Listing 1.27:

Listing 1.27: Using break Statement

```
class BreakDemo {
   public static void main(String[] args)
   {
           int i = 0;
           while (true) // loop will execute infinitely
           {
                     i=i+2;
                     if (i >10)
                     {
                               break;    // when the condition becomes true break
                               will get execute
                     }
                     System.out.println(i);
           }
   }
}
```

In Listing 1.27, an infinite loop is shown to display even numbers up to infinity. In order to avoid infinity situation, a `break` statement is used within a condition stating that if the value of the `i` variable exceeds `10`, then the control comes out of the `while` loop. If the control comes out of the loop, then the first 5 even numbers are displayed.

Because of execution of the `break` statement even numbers up to 10 are displayed and loop comes out of infinite loop.

The `break` statement can also be used as an alternative to the `goto` statement. Java does not support `goto` statements directly but indirectly the same can be implemented with the help of a `labeled break` statement.

The `break` statement, without a label, transfers control out of the nearest enclosing `for`, `while`, `do`, or `switch` statement. If the `break` keyword is followed by a label of an enclosing statement, execution transfers out of that enclosing statement. Let's understand the use of a labeled break statement with the help of an example shown in Listing 1.28:

Listing 1.28: Using labeled break Statement

```
class LabelBreakDemo {
   public static void main(String[] args)
   {
           int i = 1;
           breaking:while (true) // loop will execute infinitely
           {
                     if (i >10)
                     {
                               break breaking;
                     }
                     System.out.println(i);
```

```
                    i=i+2;
            }
        }
    }
```

In Listing 1.28, an infinite loop is shown to display odd numbers up to infinity. In order to avoid this situation, a `labeled break` statement is used within a condition stating that if the value of `i` variable exceeds `10`, the control comes out of the `while` loop and only first `5` odd numbers will get displayed.

Because of execution of the `break` statement, the `while` loop terminates and the odd number up to 9 is displayed only.

Using continue Statement

The `continue` statement is used to quit the current iteration of the loop and begin the execution of the next iteration of the loop. When `continue` is used without a label, it starts a new iteration of the innermost loop. When it is used with a label, which represents the name of the containing loop, it starts a new iteration of the named loop. Let's understand the use of `continue` statement with the help of an example shown in Listing 1.29:

Listing 1.29: Using continue Statement

```
class ContinueDemo {
  public static void main(String[] args)
  {
  for (int i=2;i<=20;i=i+2)
  {
  if (i == 12) // if i becomes 12 then continue statement will get execute
  {
        continue;
  }
  System.out.println(i);
  }
  }
}
```

In Listing 1.29, first ten even numbers are shown excluding `12` from the result. This is done with the help of `continue` statement inside the `if` condition, which gets executed in case, the value of `i` variable becomes 12. Here, even numbers are shown successfully until the value of `i` becomes 12. When the value of `i` becomes 12, the control of execution quits from the current loop and returns back to the `for` loop. The next iteration then begins to display the remaining even numbers till the value of `i` exceeds 20.

Because of execution of the continue statement 12 is not displayed and the next iteration of the loop starts.

That was all about the `continue` statement. Let's now discuss about another kind of jump statement available in Java called `return` statement.

Using return Statement

The `return` statement causes the control of execution to return back to the caller of the method. Let's understand the use of `continue` statement with the help of an example shown in Listing 1.30:

Listing 1.30: Using return Statement

```
class ReturnDemo {
  public static void main(String args[])
  {
        int input=Integer.parseInt(args[0]);
        int result=square(input);
        System.out.println(result);
  }
  public static int square(int x)        {
        return x*x;
  }
}
```

In Listing 1.30, the `square()method` accepts an integer value, calculates its square value, and returns that value to the `main()` method, which is its calling method. In the `main()` method, we are calling the `square()` method and passing the input that is supplied by the user at run time. Here, we are directly calling the `square`

`()` method since it is a static method as static methods can be called directly inside a static context. The value 4 is entered at run time, which is passed to the `square()` method. Therefore, the `square()` method returns 16 as output.

To get more details about the Java programming concepts, refer Java 7 in Simple Steps, Kogent Learning Solutions Inc.

Summary

In this chapter, you are introduced to Java programming language and its features such as simple, secure, portable, robust, multi-threading, platform independent, distributed, and dynamic. You learned about Java Dalvik Virtual Machine and developed a simple Java program. You also explored Java tokens such as keywords, identifiers, literals, constants, and operators. The chapter also helped you to learn about data types, variables, classes, methods, objects, access specifiers, interfaces, inheritance, and control flow statements.

Quick Revise

Q1. Which of the following features allow Java to be used to create applications to communicate over the network?

a. Simple

b. Distributed

c. Dynamic

d. Platform Independent

Ans. The correct option is b.

Q2. Which of the following operators is used to store or assign a value to a variable?

a. Arithmetic assignment operator

b. Arithmetic operator

c. Relational operator

d. Boolean logical operator

Ans. The correct option is a.

Q3. Which of the following are the reserved words that cannot be used while naming a variable or method?

a. abstract

b. keywords

c. constants

d. operators

Ans. The correct option is a.

Q4. Which of the following statements is used to quit the current iteration of the loop and begin the execution of the next iteration of the loop?

a. break

b. continue

c. return

d. while

Ans. The correct option is a.

Q5. Which of the following statement allows you to exit from the `switch` statement?

a. break

b. continue

c. return

d. while

Ans. The correct option is a.

Q6. Which of the following access specifier allows you to access from within the same package to which the class, method or field belongs?

a. **public**

b. **protected**

c. **default**

d. **private**

Ans. The correct option is a.

Q7. Which of the following allows one class to acquire the characteristics of an existing class?

a. **Inheritance**

b. **Interafce**

c. **Polymorphism**

d. **None of the above**

Ans. The correct option is a.

Q8. Which of the following operators are used to determine the relationship between two operands?

a. **Relational**

b. **Arithmetic**

c. **Arithmetic Assignment**

d. **None of the above**

Ans. The correct option is a.

Q9. Which of the following is a symbolic name that refers to variables, methods, classes, packages, or interfaces in a Java program?

a. **Keywords**

b. **Identifiers**

c. **Literals**

d. **None of the above**

Ans. The correct option is a.

Q10. Which of the following is known as instance of a class?

a. **Object**

b. **Interface**

c. **Class**

d. **Access Specifier**

Ans. The correct option is a.

2

Getting an Overview of Android

If you need an information on:	See page:
Introducing Android	50
Discussing about Android Applications	54
The Manifest File	55
Downloading and Installing Android	55
Exploring the Development Environment	63
Developing and Executing the First Android Application	66

The process of developing application software that is specifically designed for low-power handheld or mobile devices is termed as mobile application development. A mobile phone is the most common device that comes under the mobile application development category. Other devices are Personal Digital Assistants (PDAs), enterprise digital assistants, and digital cameras. The applications developed for mobile application development can be either preinstalled on devices during their manufacturing, or offered by Operating Systems (OSs) platform (such as Android) to download for users, or offered as a client-server model, which provides access through a Web browser. The size of applications can vary and they can possess lengthy array of screens, hardware configurations, and specifications due to competitive mobile market.

This chapter introduces you to a mobile OS called Android, which is a leading brand in mobile application development as it has a very large customer span. Next, it discusses about Android applications, wherein you learn about application components and broadcast receivers. Then you learn about manifest file and how to download and install Android. Toward the end, the chapter explains development environment and development and execution of the first Android application.

Introducing Android

Mobile phones are very common today among people of various age groups. The era of mobile phone has changed dramatically in the last few decades with increased demand of mobile phones. The mobile phones used today are more than just phones. Although basic phones are still in use, smartphones are widely used and appreciated. The versatility that makes a phone powerful relies heavily on its OS. There are many OS to power the mobile phones, though we will focus on the Android OS in this chapter, which is a product of Google Inc. Android is primarily designed for touchscreen mobile phones.

Android is based on Linux family of OSs and written in C, C++, and Java programming languages. Java lies on the top of its all development layers and therefore its applications are primarily written in Java. To develop an Android application, Android Software Development Kit (Android SDK) is available with all essential tools. The Android SDK includes a compiler, debugger, a device emulator, and its own virtual machine to run Android programs. The emulator is a virtual device that is used to test or run the application without the availability of hardware.

Listing the Version History of Android Platform

In November 2007, Android beta was released as the first version of Android. After its beta version, it was launched commercially in September 2008 as Android 1.0. The evolution is still continuing with the launch version at regular intervals. The Android versions available till date are tabulated in Table 2.1:

Table 2.1: Different Versions of Android

Version	Code Name	Released On	Remarks
Beta	----	November 5, 2007	The Android SDK was released on November 12, 2007.
Android 1.0	----	September 23, 2008	The first commercial version.
Android 1.1	----	February 9, 2009	Also known as "Petit Four"; however, this name was not used official.
Android 1.5	Cupcake	April 30, 2009	First release to officially use a name based on a dessert. This fashion of naming the version based on a dessert would be used for all releases hereafter.
Android 1.6	Donut	September 15, 2009	Lots of new features.
Android 2.0 and 2.1	éclair	October 26, 2009	Based on Linux kernel 2.6.29.
Android 2.2.x (where x represents sub versions)	Froyo	May 20, 2010	Code name derived from "Frozen Yogurt."

Table 2.1: Different Versions of Android			
Version	**Code Name**	**Released On**	**Remarks**
Android 2.3.x	Gingerbread	December 6, 2010	Updated User Interface (UI) design with increased simplicity and speed.
Android 3.x	Honeycomb	February 22, 2011	The first tablet-only Android update.
Android 4.0.x	Ice Cream Sandwich (ICS)	October 19, 2011	Compatible with any Android 2.3.x device.
Android 4.1	Jelly Bean	June 27, 2012	Improved performance of the UI.
Android 4.2	Jelly Bean	October 29, 2012	Called as a new flavor of Jelly Bean.
Android 4.3	Jelly Bean	July 24, 2013	Called as an even sweeter Jelly Bean.
Android 4.4	KitKat	October 31, 2013	Enhanced to run on a greater range of devices.

NOTE

The latest release of Android is 4.4.2 KitKat. In this book, all the applications are compiled and developed using this version.

Discussing Android APIs

API stands for application programming interface, which, as a portion of code, acts as an interface for communication among different software. An API contains specifications to develop a program by means of all the building blocks. These building blocks are then joined by a programmer.

The applications developed for Android are also called Android apps. Many new features have been added for users and application developers. Let's discuss the most noteworthy and useful new APIs for developers. API levels available up to Android 4.4 are tabulated in Table 2.2:

Table 2.2: Description of the Android API Levels	
Version	**API Level**
1.5	3
1.6	4
2.1	7
2.2	8
2.3 - 2.3.2	9
2.3.3 - 2.3.7	10
3.1	12
3.2	13
4.0	14
4.1	16
4.2	17
4.3	18
4.4	19

API level provides the API review offered by a version of the Android platform. The platform provides a framework API, which allows the applications to communicate with the underlying Android system. The API level for Android consists of packages, classes, Extensible Markup Language (XML) element and attributes, intents, and a set of permissions. All the terms identified above will be discussed comprehensively in the forthcoming sections and chapters.

The API designers always keep in the mind the backward compatibility with the lower API levels. For example, the API level 14 has compatibility with the API level 3. When a new API level is introduced, there are always additions of new or replacement functionality. Instead of removing older parts of old APIs, they are declared as deprecated to offer an advantage for existing applications. However, occasionally, a few parts of old APIs can be removed to make the current API robust and for the sake of system security. The explicit support of older APIs is not available for the current API; however, they can be used implicitly. Each version of Android platform supports exactly one API. For instance, Android KitKat 4.4 supports only level 19 API.

Describing the Android Architecture

The only thing that an Android developer should know is the architecture of Android OS. It is required that a developer must have the knowledge of all the nut and bolts of the Android system. An Android user can make calls, send text message, share photos, and alter the settings. While seeing from a developer's perspective, much more information is required besides such basic operations. All the key concepts have to be grasped if one wants to develop applications for Android.

The architecture of an Android system consists of a software stack of different layers. Each layer contains a group of various program components. The software stack of architecture works in a way that each underneath layer provides services to the layer just above it. Together, it includes OS, middleware, and important applications. Putting all layers together comprises an architecture called Android architecture, as shown in Figure 2.1:

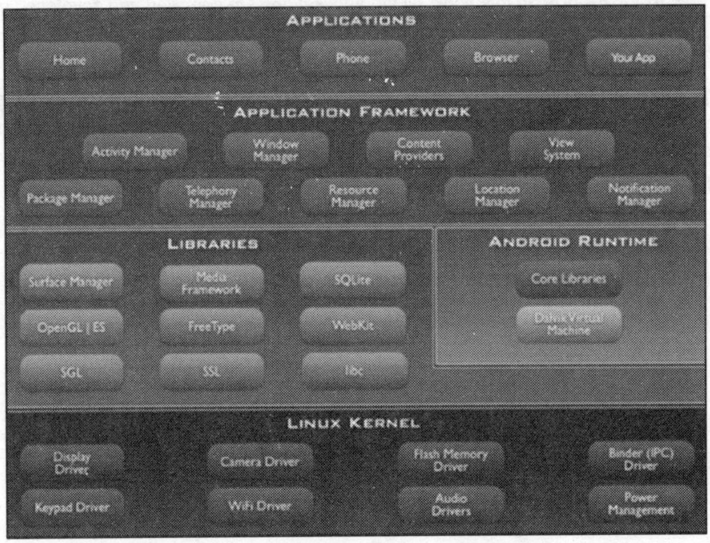

Figure 2.1: Displaying Android Architecture

As the Android architecture is a software stack of different layers, let's discuss the components of each layer one by one.

Linux Kernel

Linux kernel is the chief component in the Android architecture. The interaction of the hardware with the software is provided by means of Linux. All the hardware drivers are handled by this kernel. Drivers are the small programs written specifically to communicate with the hardware. It can be seen in Figure 2.1 that the lowest layer is the Linux kernel, which is the closest to the hardware. It has all the major hardware drivers such as display driver, camera driver, power management driver, and so forth. For example, the Linux kernel has the camera driver. On installing the Android OS in a compatible device, the Linux kernel will search the camera and then make it available to the system by using camera driver.

The Linux kernel not only contains hardware drivers, but also serves as the abstraction layer for other layers. Since the core of the Android system lies in the Linux kernel, all the main functionality of the system is based on Linux. The foundation of Android is Linux, which is a much powerful system; therefore, it provides a great versatility to the Android OS to work it on multiple devices without any (or few) glitches.

Libraries

The layer next to the Linux kernel layer is the Android's native libraries. This layer provides the device, which has the capability to handle different types of data and information. These libraries are coded in C and C++ languages for fast procedural transactions of data. A brief description of some of the native Android libraries is as follows:

- **WebKit**—Refers to the browser engine used to render and display HyperText Markup Language (HTML) content.
- **Media Framework**—Refers to a library that handles the entire multimedia feature by deploying media codecs.
- **Surface Manager**—Refers to the surface manipulations performed on the screen of the device. To do so, Window manager is combined with off-screen buffering. An off-screen buffering is a technique to draw the image in the buffer and then copy them on the original screen. The off-screen buffer is also responsible for the transparency of windows.
- **SQLite**—Refers to the database engine used in Android for data storage purposes.
- **OpenGL**—Refers to as a rendering engine, which is used to render graphics to the screen.

Android Runtime

Dalvik Virtual machine and the Core Java libraries are the part of Android runtime environment. For those who are familiar with Java may realize that there is no Java Virtual Machine (JVM). In Android runtime, Dalvik virtual machine is present instead of JVM. Let's have a glimpse of the Dalvik virtual machine.

Dalvik Virtual Machine

It has been aforementioned that Dalvik virtual machine is used in Android system similar to the usage of JVM in Java. However, Dalvik virtual machine is optimized for low-power Central Processing Units (CPUs) and low-memory modules. Unlike the JVM, the Dalvik virtual machine does not recognize files with the .class extension; instead, it executes the files with the `.dex` extension. In fact, .dex files are generated implicitly from the .class file and are highly optimized where memory and processing power are constraints. Using Dalvik over JVM has the following advantages:

- It is optimized for small platform where memory and processing power are constraints.
- It recognizes its exclusively designed APIs along with some useful APIs of Java.
- At times, many instances can be created simultaneously, giving benefit in security, isolation, memory management, and multithreading.

Core Java Libraries

Core Java Libraries are the exclusively designed Java libraries for Android rather than Java SE and Java ME libraries. However, most of the functionality of these libraries is similar to the Java SE libraries.

Application Framework

Application framework is of utmost importance for developer as the blocks inside this layer directly communicate with Android applications. The basic and much needed functionalities such as resource management and voice call management are provided by this layer. From the developer's perspective, this layer provides basic building blocks for Android applications. The important blocks of Application framework are as follows:

- **Activity Manager**—Manages the activity life cycle of applications.
- **Content Providers**—Provide data sharing between applications.
- **Telephony Manager**—Manages all voice calls. This management can be considered as optional. If your application is meant to use the voice calls, then telephony manager is used.
- **Location Manager**—Manages the activities related with location in your application.
- **Resource Manager**—Manages the different kinds of resources in an application.

Application

Application layer is the top layer in the Android architecture. This is the place where your application is finally deployed over a device. Some applications are installed by default in a device, such as SMS client app, dialer, Web browser, and contact manager.

Pre-installed applications can be replaced by newly written applications. This is the fact which makes Android OS so flexible. Many device vendors modify the pure Android applications with their own applications for the sake of different feel and look. In other words, Android has much flexibility for a developer to explore endless opportunities.

Exploring the Features of Android

Android is one of the most used OS in the world. It is so popular that more than one million new Android devices are activated every day. Some of its features are as follows:

- It is a world-class platform for creating applications for Android users.
- There is an open marketplace for distributing the created applications.
- More than 1.5 billion applications and games are downloaded on Android; hence, it is the best platform for selling the created application.
- The power of hardware can be utilized at its best by using the exclusive APIs.
- A single application binary can be created, which can be used for both devices-phone and tablet.
- It has the largest user base in the world and is growing rapidly.
- The marketplace for selling and distributing Android applications is called Google Play. Once your application is ready, you can distribute it over the Google Play.
- The applications are intelligently differentiated on the basis of different versions of Android.
- Applications can be developed by using either a Java IDE (such as Eclipse) or a tool like Apace Ant.

Besides these features, there is much more to explore in Android. Its popularity explains why this platform is so much popular among the users as well as developers.

Discussing about Android Applications

Android applications are developed in Java. Although the full blend of Java is not used, it can be considered as a part of Java. The Java part used in Android application development does not include the classes that are not important for mobile devices. Therefore, it is prerequisite to have a basic knowledge of Java to start development of Android applications. If you do not have any knowledge of Java programming language, any good book can be referred to learn the basics.

As the full blend of Java is used, it is the XML and Apache Ant scripting that fills the remaining gap of programming. So, you should have some knowledge of XML too.

In essence, if you know the basics of Java and XML, then you are ready to develop Android applications. Let's discuss the basic components used for application development.

The Application Components

The major components associated with an Android application are activity, service, content provider, and broadcast receiver. Each component is discussed in brief in the following subsections.

Activity

The screen of an application with which a user interacts is provided by an application component called activity. For example, if there is a media player application, then the screen that plays, pauses, and forwards the song is an activity. It is a kind of interface drawn inside a window of an activity. A window can either fully fit on the screen or it can float over other windows.

It is evident that an application can have multiple activities which can be loosely coupled. The main or the very first screen (as soon as you launch an application) of the application is known as `MainActivity`. When you switch for the next activity (screen), the previous activity is halted and stored in a stack called as back-stack. As stack is a data structure with the last-in-first-out property, on pressing the `Back` button by user, the previous activity is activated. Consequently, the current activity (from where the `Back` button was pressed) gets demolished as it was popped out from the back stack.

Services

An application component in the working process that does not use UI is called a service. For example, a service that is playing music, providing contents, etc., from the background but not appearing on the screen.

A service is an application component that can perform long-running operations in the background and does not provide a UI. Even on switching to another application, the services of the previously activated application cannot be stopped.

Content Providers

Accessing of contents from the central data warehouse is managed by a content provider. Being a part of Android application, the content provider empowers its UI for working with the data.

Broadcast Receivers

Many system-generated notifications, such as battery low, downloading starts, or file received, are broadcasted by broadcast receivers. However, some applications can also stimulate broadcast receivers. For example, an application informs the other application that data has been downloaded for them to use. The broadcast receivers do not have a UI; however, they send a notification to the status bar to alert the user. In essence, a broadcast receiver is a component that alerts a user by sending a notification, which is intended to do a very little work (just notify). It just acts as a gateway for other components.

The Manifest File

The manifest file is the core of Android development. It is an XML file and is so important to Android application that sometimes it is also known as the heart of the Android application. It is named as `AndroidManifest.xml` file. A careless attempt to modify the `AndroidManifest.xml` file may not let you develop your application and reuse of Android platform and its services. You need to dedicate some time to get familiar with the Android manifest file, as if you do not understand the content of this file, it may lead you to obscure understanding of the association between life cycle of an Android application and its (Android) platform. We will discuss this file deeply in the upcoming sections when we use it.

Downloading and Installing Android

In this section, you will learn how to set the environment to develop Android applications. This comprises downloading, configuring, and installing of several software components required to make the IDE complete and ready for developing purpose. The prerequisite components to setup your Android IDE are as follows:

- Java Development Kit or JDK since Android applications are developed in Java
- Android Software Development Kit (SDK)
- Eclipse IDE

Lets' start from downloading and installing the Android SDK

Downloading and Installing the Android SDK

The Android SDK is a complete set of API libraries and developer tools. By configuring these tools and libraries with Eclipse, an Android-specific development environment will be ready. The link to download the latest Android SDK from the Android developer's website is as follows:

http://developer.android.com/sdk/index.html

The Android SDK is a kit, which helps in building, testing, and debugging applications for Android. On accessing the preceding link, you will be directed to the Android developer's site, where you will find the `Download the SDK` button. This button will provide Android SDK as an ADT Bundle that includes everything you need to begin developing Android applications. This bundle includes the following items:

- Eclipse + ADT plugin

- ❑ Android SDK tools
- ❑ Android Platform tools
- ❑ The latest Android platform
- ❑ The latest Android system image for the emulator

You need to click on it and then select the check box to accept its terms and conditions. Finally, the Android SDK pack will be downloaded as a zip folder.

Now, perform the following steps to install Android SDK:

1. Unzip the ZIP file named adt-bundle-<os_platform>.zip and save it to an appropriate location, such as D:\Development.
2. Open the adt-bundle-<os_platform>/eclipse/ directory and launch Eclipse. The Java - ADT window opens as shown in Figure 2.2:

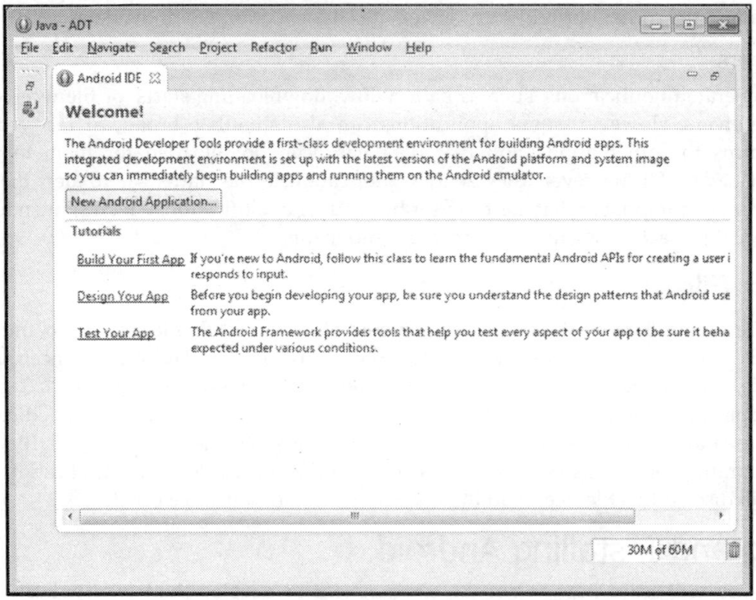

Figure 2.2: Showing the Java – ADT Window

You should not move any of the files or directories from the adt-bundle-<os_platform> directory; otherwise, ADT will not be able to locate the SDK and you will be required to manually update the ADT preferences.

NOTE

You can also use an existing version of Eclipse or another IDE for Android applications development. For this, you need to set up a new SDK by downloading the SDK tools and then select the additional Android SDK packages to install (such as the Android platform and system image). You can download the SDK tools from the Android developer's website by clicking the `Download the SDK Tools for Windows` *button. Moreover, if you are using an existing version of Eclipse, then you need to add the ADT plugin to it.*

ADT is an extension to increase the capabilities of Eclipse to create Android projects, create an application UI, add packages of Android API, and debug the Android applications. The steps to download the ADT plugin are as follows:

1. *Start* the Eclipse from the location you have installed earlier.
2. Select Help→Install **New Software,** as shown in Figure 2.3:

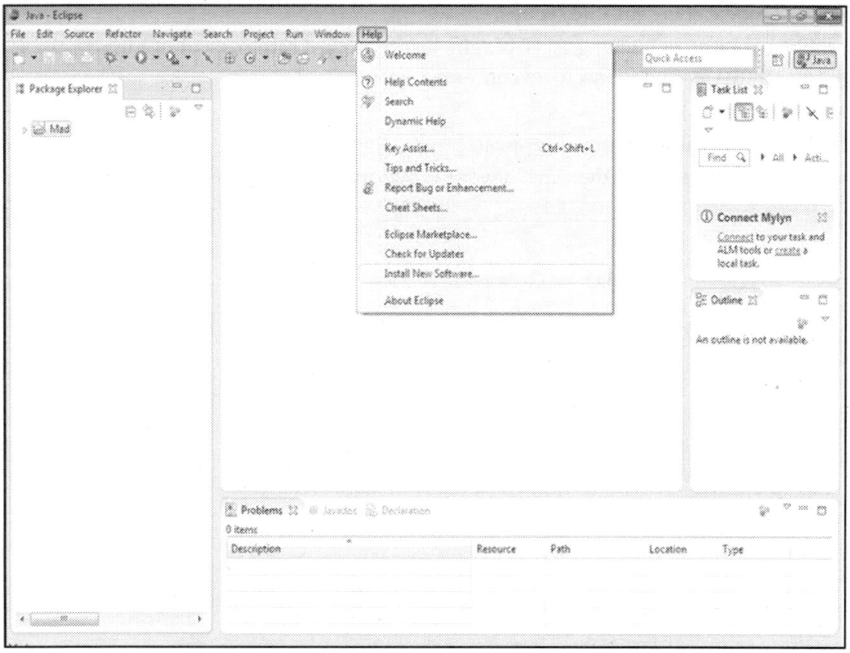

Figure 2.3: Installing a New Software in Eclipse IDE

3. *Click* the **Add** button from the top-right corner, as shown in Figure 2.4:

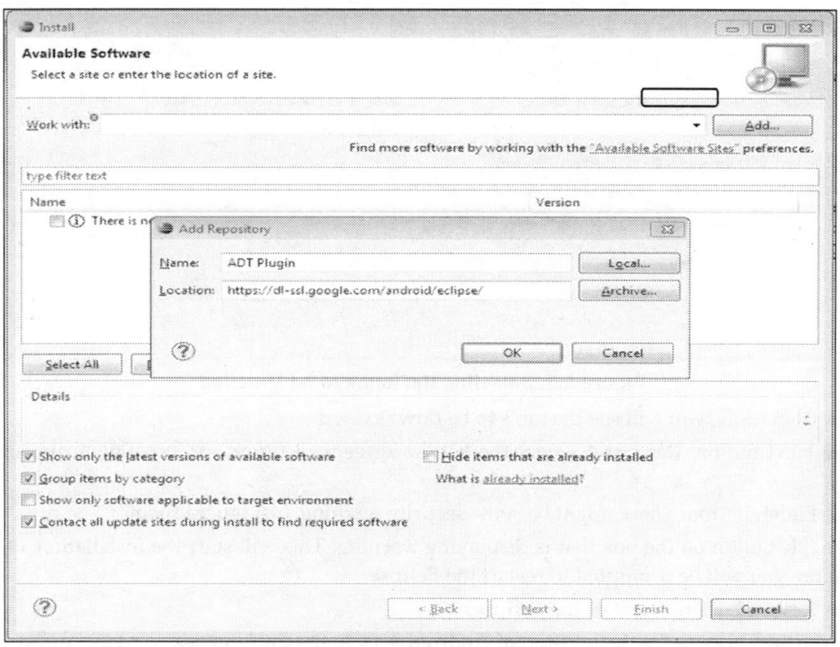

Figure 2.4: Adding Repository

A diagonal box named **Add Repository** appears, showing name and location in the text boxes.

4. *Enter* **ADT Plugin** as name and enter the following location in the location box:

https://dl-ssl.google.com/android/eclipse/

If any problem persists in fetching ADT plugin, just try to use http instead of https in the *Uniform Resource Locator (URL)* (https is used for security concerns).

5. *Click* the **OK** button.

   The **Add Repository** diagonal box disappears.

6. *Click* the **Select All** button and then click the **Next** button, as shown in Figure 2.5:

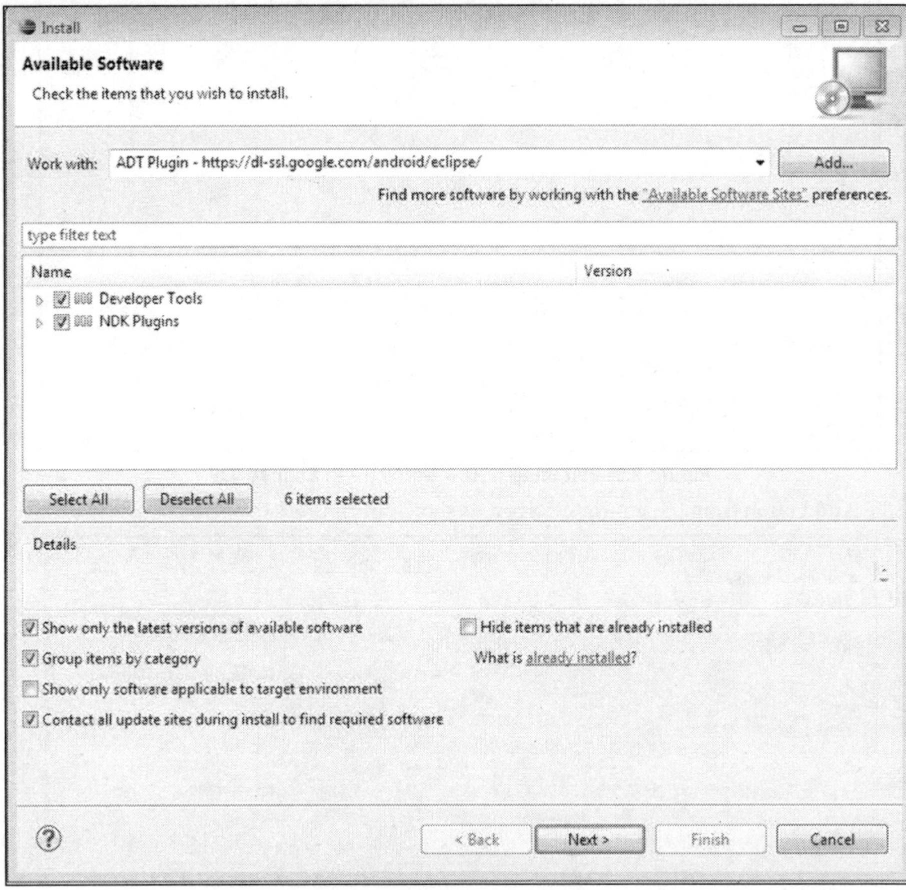

Figure 2.5: Selecting the Items to be Installed

In the next window, you will see the tools to be downloaded.

7. *Click* the **Next** button. Read and accept the license agreement terms and conditions appearing in the next page.
8. *Click* the **Finish** button. There might be some security warning, just ignore them.
9. *Click* the **OK** button on the box that is displaying warning. This will start the installation. On completion of installation, you will be prompted to restart the **Eclipse**.
10. *Click* the **Restart** button to restart the **Eclipse**.

    After restarting, browse for the location of Android SDK in the **Preferences** window, as shown in Figure 2.6:

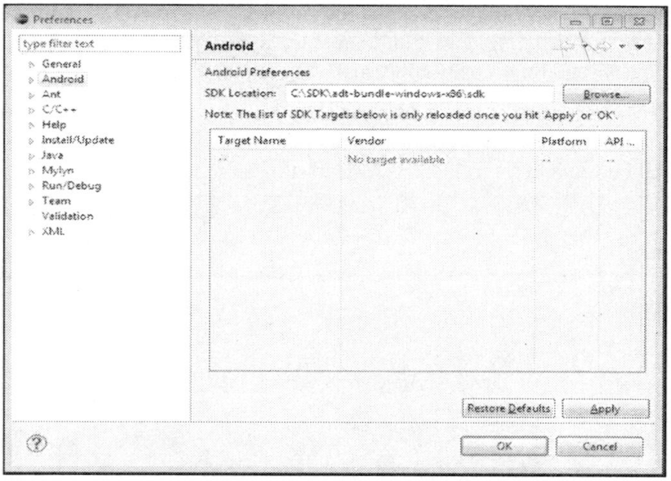

Figure 2.6: Setting Android Preferences

You can choose any location to extract SDK, but provide the same path in the preferences. In this case, the location where Android SDK has been unpacked is:

```
C:\SDK\adt-bundle-windows-x86\sdk
```

Your Eclipse IDE is now ready to develop Android applications. However, some configuration is still required, which will be discussed in the next section.

It is obvious that there is no particular device to run the created Android applications. Therefore, we have emulator to do all the application run experiments that eliminate the requirement of a real device. This emulator is also known as Android Virtual Device (AVD). Let's learn how to configure it.

Setting up Android Virtual Device

An AVD can be used as a replacement for any Android device available in the market. You can create as many AVDs as you need with different configurations. By default, the `AVD_for_Nexus_S_by_Google` AVD is provided by the AVD Manager.

The steps for creating and configuring AVD for Android 4.4.2 are as follows:

1. Launch **Eclipse** and select the **Window→Android Virtual Device Manager** option, as shown in Figure 2.7:

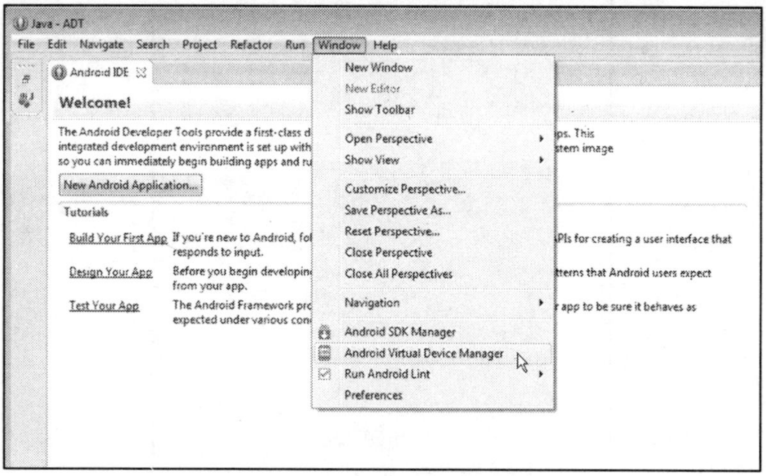

Figure 2.7: Clicking the AVD Manager

The **Android Virtual Device Manager** diagonal box appears, as shown in Figure 2.8:

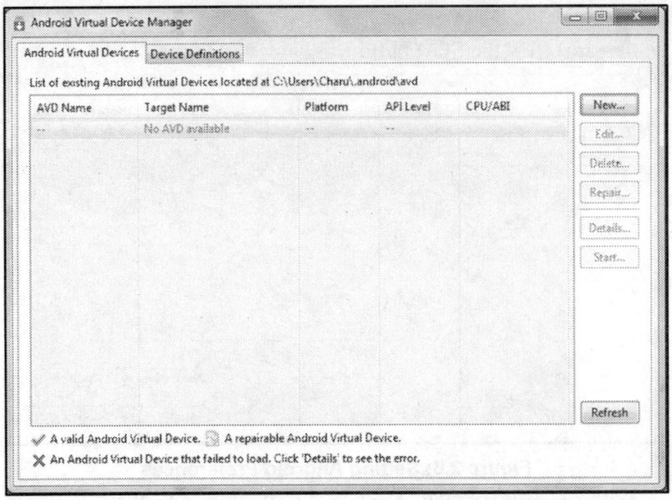

Figure 2.8: Displaying the Android Virtual Device Manager Diagonal Box

2. *Click* the New button. The **Create new Android Virtual Device (AVD)** diagonal box appears.
3. *Type* a name, the device type, and the target API. In this case, the target API is **Android 4.4.2-API Level 19**, and leave other fields as default, as shown in Figure 2.9:

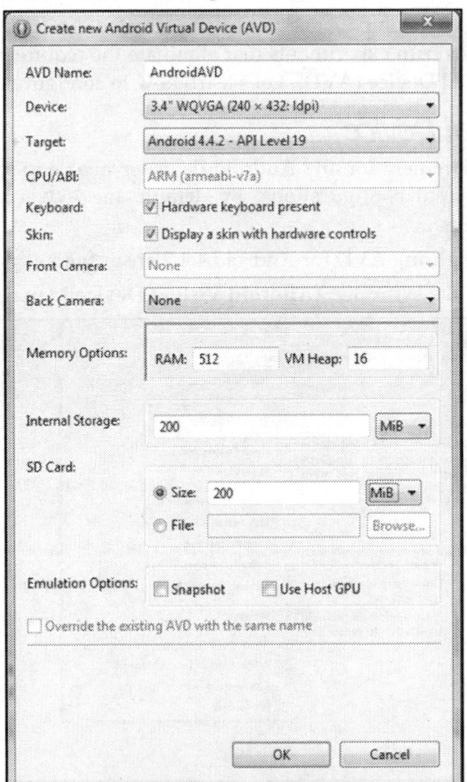

Figure 2.9: Creating a New AVD Device

4. *Click* the **OK** button to create **AVD**.

   Now your **AVD** appears in the list of AVDs.

5. *Select* the **AVD** option and click the **Start** button, as shown in Figure 2.10:

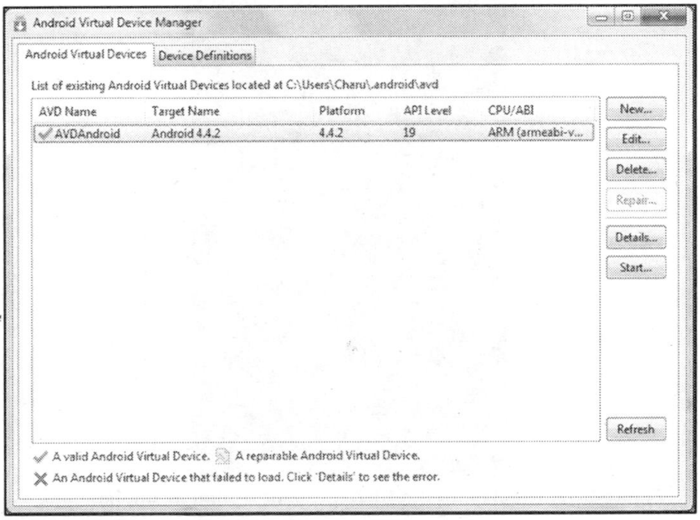

Figure 2.10: Starting an AVD Device

While staring AVD, it takes several minutes to boot and load for the first time. As soon as it loads, the home screen appears. Finally, there is a complete setup of Android application development. You can now start creating Android applications and then check them on Android Emulator.

Setting up Android Physical Device

Sometimes you need to execute your application on a real mobile device to view the actual functioning of it. For example, if you create an application that needs to capture a picture, you need to test it on a physical mobile device. For this, you require an Android-based mobile device and enable the **USB debugging** and **Allow mock locations** options in the development section of phone settings.

Let's perform the following steps to configure an Android based mobile phone for development purpose:

1. *Select* the **Settings** or **Phone Settings** option in a mobile device.
2. *Select* the **Applications** option, as shown in Figure 2.11:

Figure 2.11: Displaying the Applications Option in Phone Settings

3. *Select* the **Development** option, as shown in Figure 2.12:

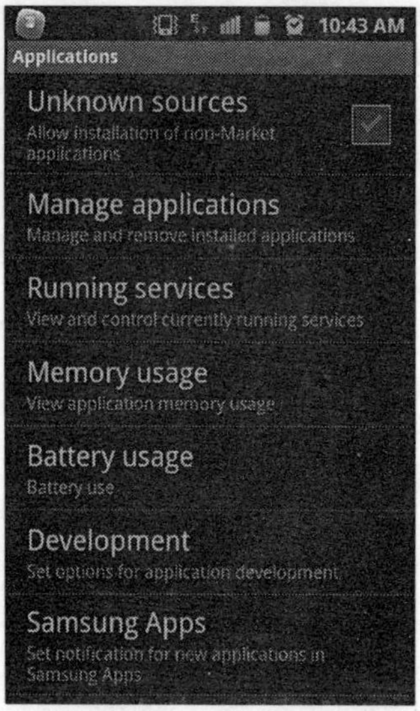

Figure 2.12: Displaying the Development Option in Applications

4. *Enable* the **USB debugging** and **Allow mock locations** options in **Development**, as shown in Figure 2.13:

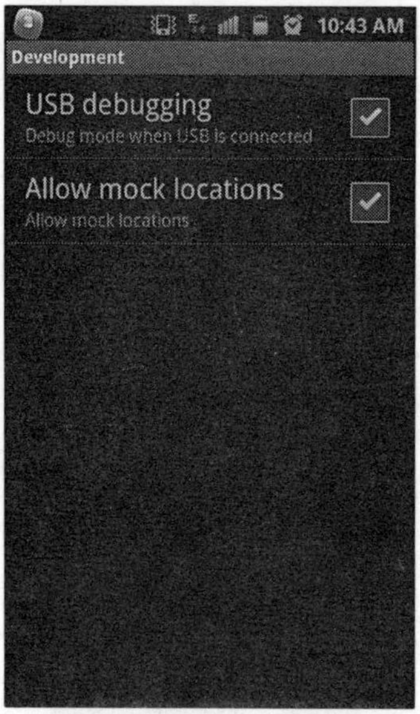

Figure 2.13: Enabling the Required Options for Development

NOTE

In these days various companies have launched Android based phones. In these phones, the location and name of development section in the phone setting may vary from mobile to mobile.

Exploring the Development Environment

The functionality to develop and run Android application in Eclipse is a result of not only Java, but also the inclusion of ADT plugin in it. Several tools and features are available in Eclipse after the ADT plugin. The Graphical UI (GUI) accessibility of command line tools and designing of UI are provided by this ADT.

The Java Perspective Using Eclipse

The Java perspective in Eclipse lets you access the associated Java libraries, which are to be used with Android applications in Eclipse IDE. The sections of Java perspective in Eclipse IDE are as follows:

- **Package Explorer**—Shows the full view of the project in a hierarchy
- **Task List**—Shows the available tasks associated with the project
- **Java Class Pane**—Shows the body of the Java class
- **Outline**—Shows the internal outline of files such as Java and XML

In essence, Java perspective is the interface where you can make Android application by using some of the Java's native libraries. However, Dalvik Debug Monitor Server (DDMS) has much more functionalities powered by ADT.

Let's see the DDMS perspective of Eclipse in the next section.

The DDMS Perspective

The DDMS perspective in Eclipse provides you the full functionality of the DDMS features inside the Eclipse IDE. The following features of DDMS are present in Eclipse:

- **Devices**—Refer to the list of devices and AVDs
- **Emulator Control**—Refers to the control of replica of original device
- **LogCat**—Refers to a view system in which log messages are displayed in real time
- **Threads**—Refer to the currently running thread in virtual machine
- **Heap**—Represents the heap structure of virtual machine
- **Allocation Tracker**—Portrays the memory allocation of an object
- **File Explorer**— Explores the file system of device

To enable the DDMS perspective in Eclipse, select **Window→Open Perspective→DDMS** option, or select **Window→Open Perspective→Other option→DDMS** option.

The Command-Line Tools

Command-line tool is an alternative to Eclipse IDE for Android application development. For using this tool, you require Android SDK and the applicable API.

Let's first set the environment to work with command-line tools.

Setting the Environment Variable

The steps to set up the environment variable to access the SDK are as follows:

1. *Open* **Control Panel** and *select* **System→Advanced system** setting option. The **System Properties** dialog box opens.
2. In the **System Properties** dialog box, under the **Advanced** tab, *click* the **Environment Variables** button. The **Environment Variable** diagonal box opens.
3. *Select* the **Path** variable and *click* the **Edit** button for the user variable in the **Environment Variable** diagonal box, as shown in Figure 2.14:

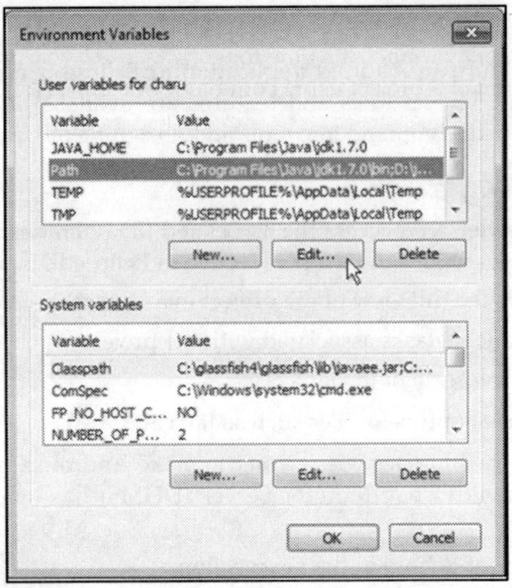

Figure 2.14: Setting the Environment Variable

The **Edit User Variable** diagonal box appears.

4. *Add* the location of **platform-tools** as well as the **tools** directories of Android SDK in the value of the **Path** variable. Both path addresses must be separated by a semicolon.
5. *Click* the **OK** button, as shown in Figure 2.15:

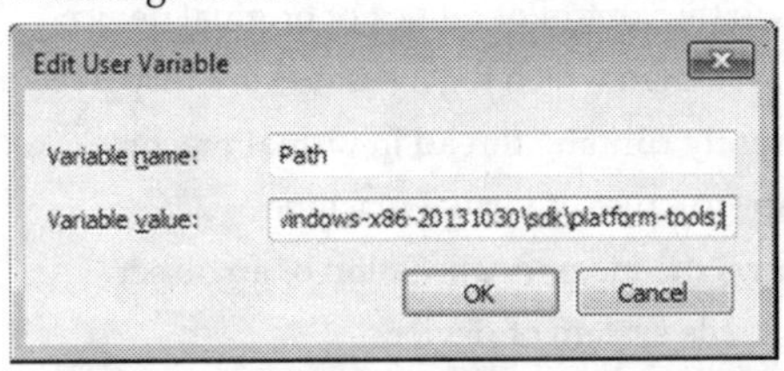

Figure 2.15: Editing a User Variable

6. *Click* the **New** button in **Environment Variable** diagonal box (Figure 2.14).
7. *Enter* the variable name as **Home** and variable value as the path up to the **sdk** folder in Android SDK. Figure 2.16 shows the setting of **Home** variable:

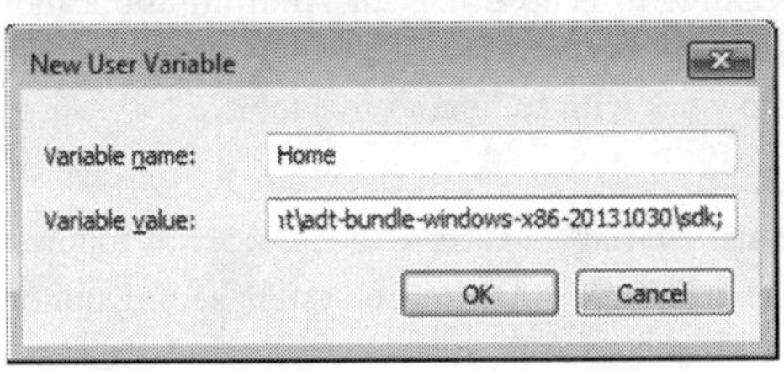

Figure 2.16: Setting the HOME Variable

8. *Click* the OK button to close the New User Variable dialog box.
9. *Click* the OK button to close the Environment Variable dialog box.
10. *Click* the OK button to close the System Properties dialog box.

Creating a Project

After setting up the environment variable, it's time to work with the command-line tool using Android SDK. The steps that elaborate the creation of a project using command line are as follows:

1. *Open* the **Command Prompt**.
2. *Go* to the directory where you want to create the project.
3. *Execute* the command, **android list targets**, as shown in Figure 2.17:

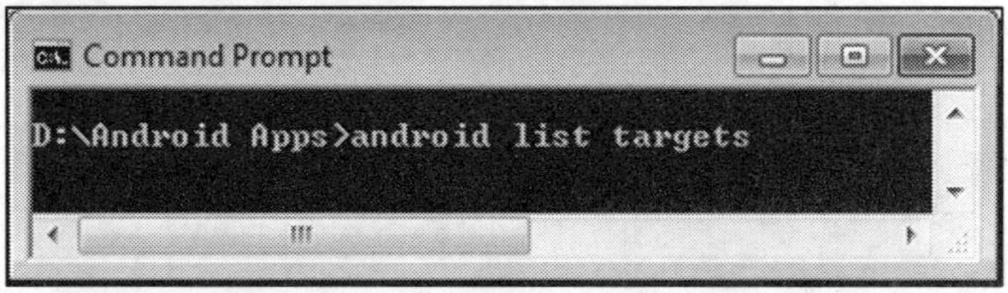

Figure 2.17: Showing the Command to List the Android Targets

This command will show you the existing Android platforms. Since we are developing with Android 4.4.2 API 19, note down the target id, which is required in the next command. If your command is not working, again check with your environment variable setup. The result of the command is shown in Figure 2.18:

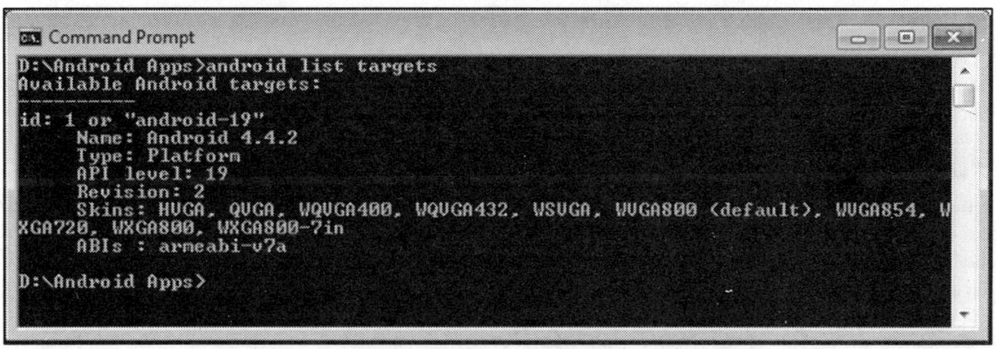

Figure 2.18: Displaying Available Android Targets

4. *Execute* the command: android create project --target <target-id> --name AndroidProject --path <path-to-workspace>\FirstAndroidApp --activity MainActivity --package com.kogent. The modified command is shown in Figure 2.19:

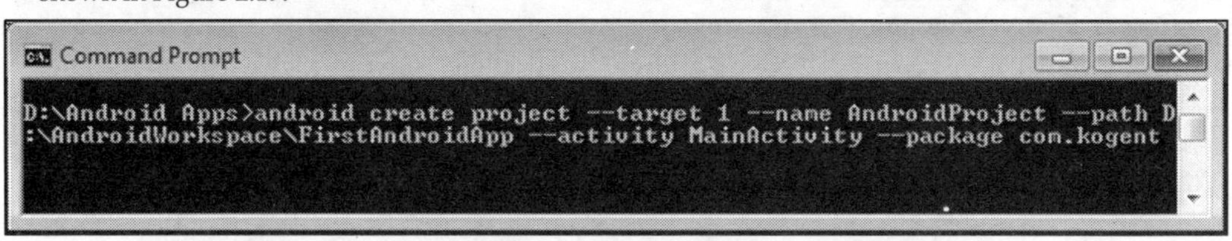

Figure 2.19: Showing the Command to Create an Android Project

Note that we have changed the `<target-id>` to **1** and then replaced the `<path-to-workspace>` with **D:\AndroidWorkspace**. The rest of the syntax remains unaltered. On pressing the **Enter** key, the project along with its artifacts will be created. The execution of the command is shown in Figure 2.20:

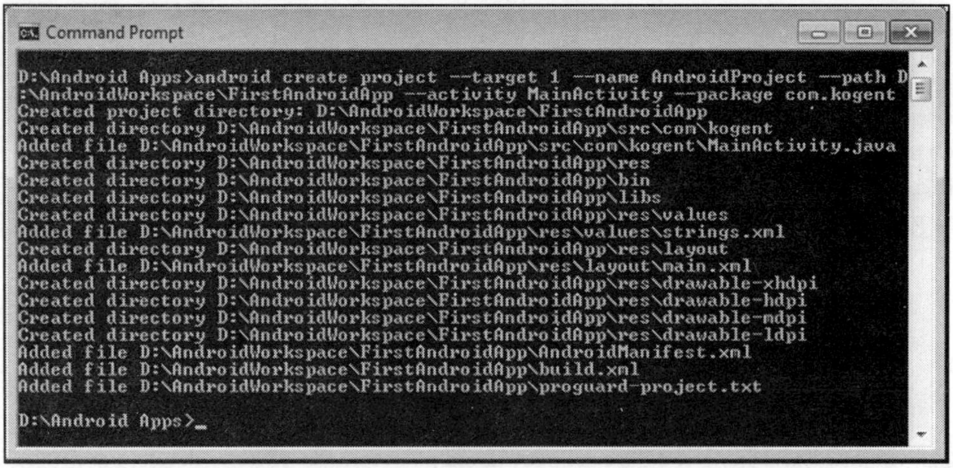

Figure 2.20: Showing the Output of the Command

The `<target-id>` is set to **1** since it is given 1 for API 19 when we have executed the **android list targets** command earlier (see Figure 2.18). The workspace address is based on your choice. Whatever the address you choose, provide that full qualified address.

As of now, your Android project is ready with some default configurations. You can now start developing your applications.

Developing and Executing the First Android Application

You have seen that whenever you learn new programming languages, the first program always displays hello world on the screen. The same trend continues with Android here; yet, we will write somewhat comprehensive "hello world" application. It is very easy and practically no coding is required. However, to make this application interesting, we will add some extra coding in it.

Using Eclipse IDE to Create an Application

The use of an IDE is recommended for the Android application development. In this section, you learn the basic steps to create an Android application using the Eclipse IDE. We are using the Eclipse IDE, which is bundled with Android SDK 4.4.2. In this IDE, you need to use the New Android Application wizard to start creating an Android application. Let's discuss the development of first Android application, named `MyFirstApp`. The steps to create a new project in Eclipse IDE are as follows:

1. *Open* **Eclipse** IDE and go to **File→New→Android Application Project**, as shown in Figure 2.21:

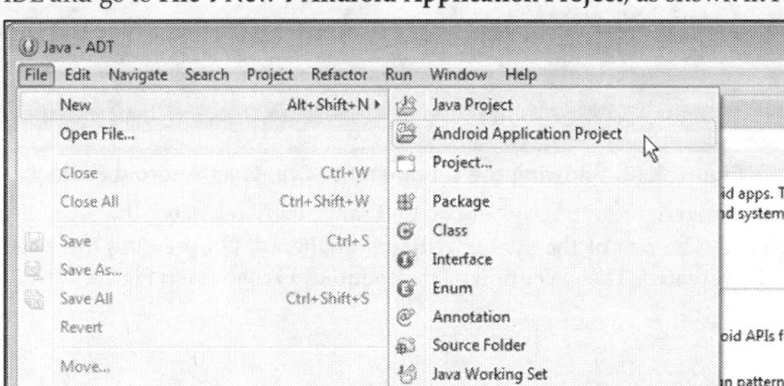

Figure 2.21: Creating Android Application Project in Eclipse

The New Android Application window appears.

2. *Enter* the following details in the **New Android Application** window:
   - **Application name**—The name you want to choose for your application. For example, we have selected `MyFirstApp` as our application name.
   - **Project name**—This is the name of your Project. It should be self-expressive so that if you need to identify it later, you can do it easily. It is a directory that will be created in the Eclipse workspace and will contain all the files associated with the project.
   - **Package name**—It is the organization of code according to the convention of Java. It is helpful to manage the Java classes as modules. The naming convention followed is `com.maindomain.subdomain`. For instance, in our project, we are using `com.kogent.android.myfirstapp` package.
   - **Minimum required SDK**—This is the minimum level of Android version (API) with which your application will be compatible. For instance, we have selected the API 14: Android 4.0 (IceCreamSandwich) option. The reason to use the lower level API is that it gives the advantage of backward compatibility with Android devices. In other words, our application is still compatible with the lower version of Android rather than only the API 19: Android (4.4.2).
   - **Target SDK**—The target SDK is related to the API level, which we are going to use in the application development. Since we are dealing with Android (4.4.2), we will select API level 19.
   - **Compile with**—It also represents the level of Android API to compile the application. This should be the latest API; therefore, select level API 19: Android (4.4.2).
   - **Theme**—Let it be the default theme.

   Figure 2.22 shows the **New Android Application** window filled with the details:

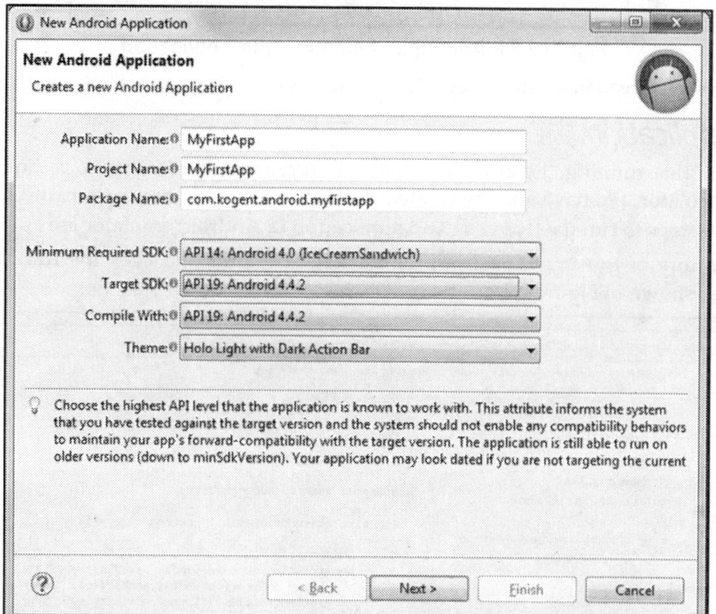

Figure 2.22: Showing the Details For the New Android Application

3. *Click* the **Next** button (Figure 2.22). The **Configure Project** page appears, where you need to keep the default settings.
4. *Click* the **Next** button. The next window that opens is to set the launcher icon for your applications. Since it is a beginner level of development, keep the default setting.

5. *Click* the **Next** button. The **Create Activity** page appears. *Ensure* that the **Create Activity** check box is selected and **Blank Activity** is by default selected.
6. *Click* the **Next** button. The **Blank Activity** page appears. Retain the default settings in this page.
7. *Click* the **Finish** button, as shown in Figure 2.23:

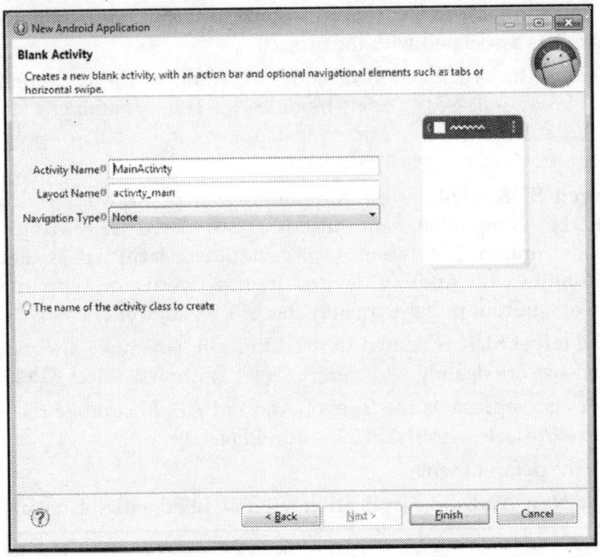

Figure 2.23: Adding an Activity to the Application

Note that no changes have been made from steps 3 to 6. In this way, your project is ready with all the necessary files.

Running Your Application

It is aforementioned that running "hello world" application practically requires no coding. Let's prove this fact by running it on emulator. We have already created an Android AVD or emulator named, `AndroidAVD`, to run the application. The steps to run the `MyFirstApp` application in Android emulator are as follows:

1. *Open* any directory of `MyFirstApp` from the **Package** explorer and click the **Run** icon in the toolbar of **Eclipse IDE**, as shown in Figure 2.24:

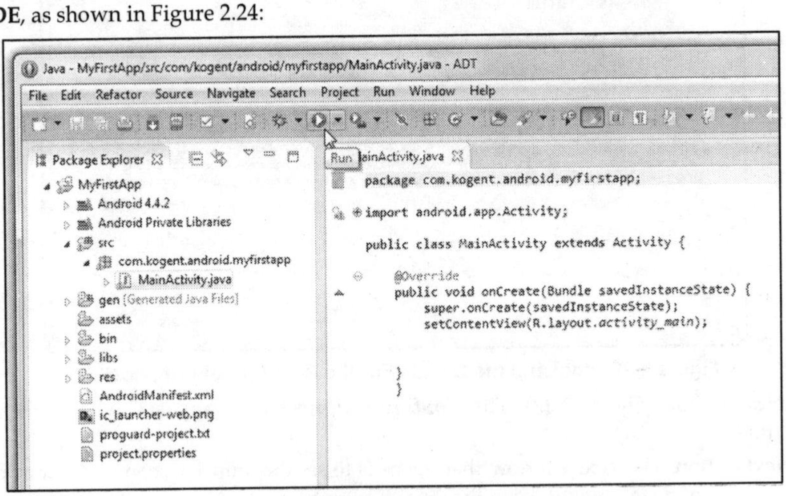

Figure 2.24: Running the Application

You can also run your application by selecting application and clicking the `Run→Run` option in the menu bar. You can also select the `Run→Run As→Android Application` option, as shown in Figure 2.25:

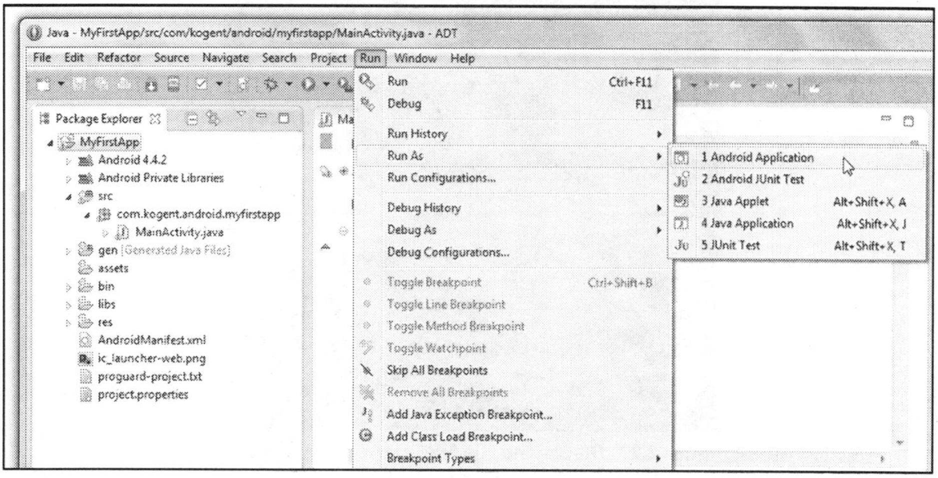

Figure 2.25: Selecting the Run As Option

The **emulator** will appear as the next window. It will take some time to boot up and then the home screen will be displayed.

2. *Click* the applications icon on the home screen of the emulator. The icon is shown enclosed in circle, as shown in Figure 2.26:

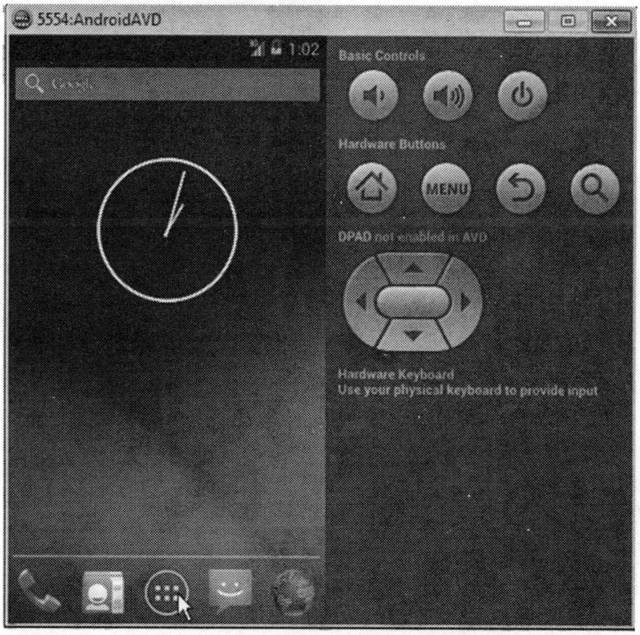

Figure 2.26: Displaying the Home Screen

The next screen shows the applications. You will see your application named as `MyFirstApp`, as shown in the Figure 2.27:

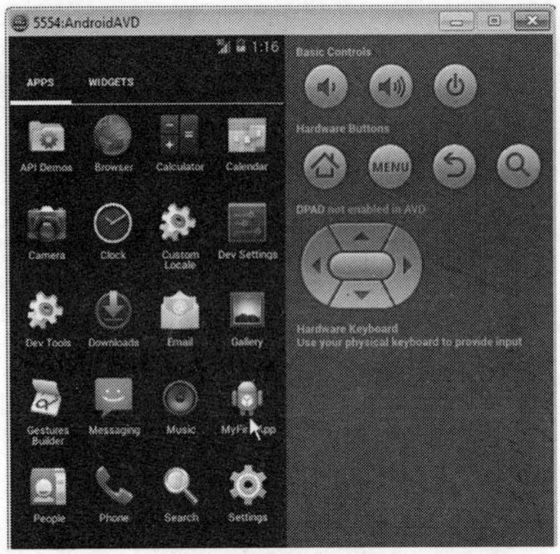

Figure 2.27: Displaying the MyFirstApp Application

3. *Click* on the icon of your application; the screen will show you the output as "**Hello world!**" The output screen is as shown in Figure 2.28:

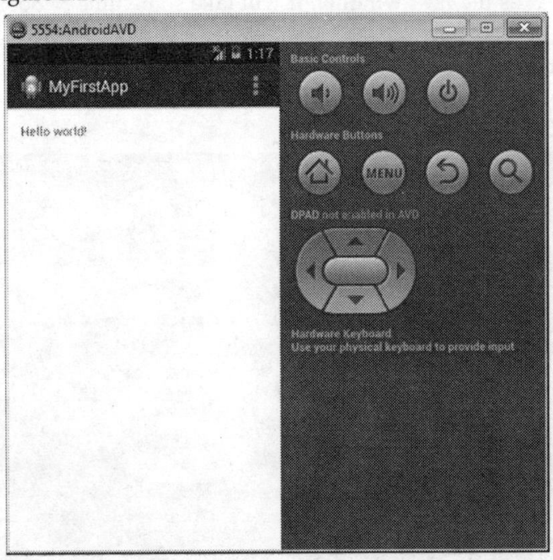

Figure 2.28: Showing the Output of the MyFirstApp Application

In this way, you learn how to create and run an Android application. Interestingly, it is not so easy. We are still not aware with the *anatomy* of the `MyFirstApp` application.

Exploring the Application

The purpose of exploring the application is to know how the hello world text message has been displayed by the `MyFirstApp` application.

To explore the internal structure of the application, let's get familiar with some important directories of the `MyFirstApp` application.

AndroidManifest.xml

This is the manifest file, which we have discussed earlier by acknowledging it as the heart of the Android application. However, every file has importance in an Android project. The `AndroidManifest.xml` file is the most important file. All the components of the application are managed by this file. We will make some changes in the file of the `MyFirstApp` application to understand it.

Open my eclipse and expand the `MyFirstApp` project. You will see the `AndroidManifest.xml` file. To open the file, double click on it. The code of the file is shown in Figure 2.29:

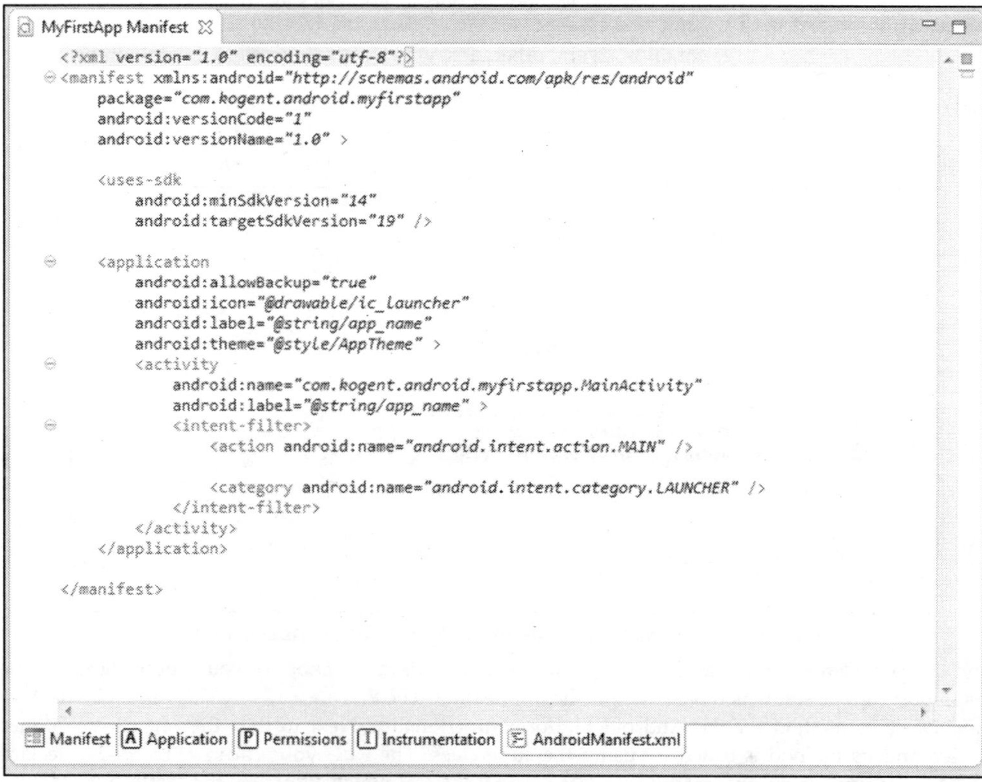

Figure 2.29: Showing the Code of the Android Manifest File

This file describes the components such as activities, services, broadcast receivers, and content providers. Some of the components of the `AndroidManifest.xml` file are tabulated in Table 2.3:

Table 2.3: Description of the AndroidManifest.xml Components

Component Declaration	Description
`<manifest>`	The main element in which whole structure of the manifest file is enclosed. It is the root element of the file.
`<uses-sdk>`	This element shows the compatibility of the created application. It contains the minimum and maximum version (API level) of the Android application platform.
`<application>`	This element is the major part of the manifest element as it contains declaration of the components and attribute.
`<activity>`	This element is declared inside the application element. It is responsible for the visual UI of the application.

Table 2.3: Description of the AndroidManifest.xml Components

Component Declaration	Description
`<intent-filter>`	Activities, services, and broadcast receivers are activated through messages called intents. This declaration ensures the responding of activities, services, and broadcast receivers through the intent types.
`<action>`	This element helps in adding actions to an intent filter.
`<category>`	This element adds category names to an intent filter.

The `AndroidManifest.xml` file contains several other tags, which are discussed in the upcoming chapters.

MainActivity.java

The next file to explore is `MainActivity.java`, which lies in the \src folder under the package name, `com.kogent.android.myfirstapp`. The code of this file is shown in Figure 2.30:

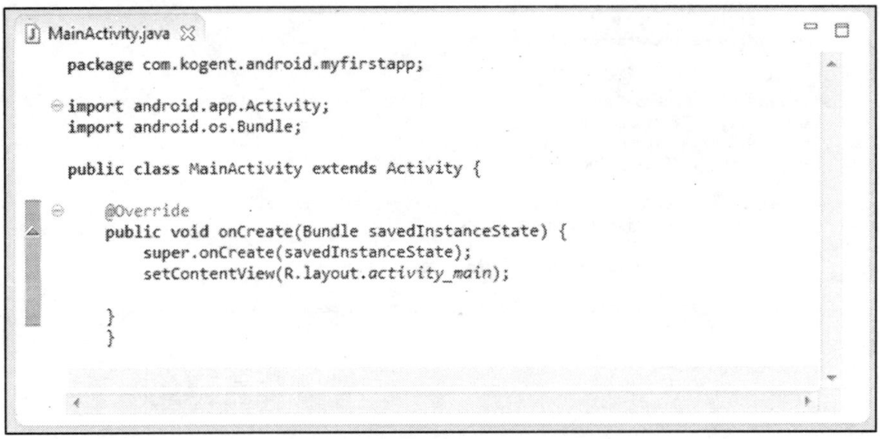

Figure 2.30: Showing the Code of the Activity of the Application

The first line represents the package, `com.kogent.android.myfirstapp`, of your application. The next line or lines import the classes, which required for the application. The `MainActivity` class extends the `Activity` class to inherit its method for the Android platform functionality. Next to this, the `onCreate()` method is overridden and its method is called by using the superclass. The `R.layout.activity_main` declaration is passed as a parameter in the method `setContentView()`, which contains the definition of UI of the `MyFirstApp` application. The `R.layout.activity_main` declaration shows that the `activity_main.xml` file is contained in the **layout** directory of the **res** folder. This shows the way how you can access a file in Java.

activity_main.xml

To know how the UI works, let's focus on the `R.layout.activity_main` declaration. The steps to view the code of the `activity_main.xml` file are as follows:

1. *Open* the `activity_main.xml` file under the **res→layout** directory.
2. *Double* click to open the file. By default, the graphical interface of the file is visible.
3. *Switch* the tab at the bottom of the file.

   The code of the `activity_main.xml` file is shown in Figure 2.31:

Figure 2.31: Showing the Code of the `activity_main.xml` File

Relative layout in the `activity_main.xml` file is the widget containers used in Android. The management of widgets depends on this file. The `layout_width` and `layout_height` attributes correspond to the filling of screen. The `TextView` element represents the widget used in an application. It is the only widget for this application. The text displayed by the `TextView` attribute is associated with the `strings.xml` file.

strings.xml

To know how the texts are displayed, open the `strings.xml` file by performing the following steps:

1. *Expand* the `MyFirstApp` project in the **Package Explorer** pane.
2. *Click* the **res** directory and then the **values** directory. A file named, `strings.xml`, will appear.
3. *Double*-click to open it. The structure of the `strings.xml` file is shown in Figure 2.32:

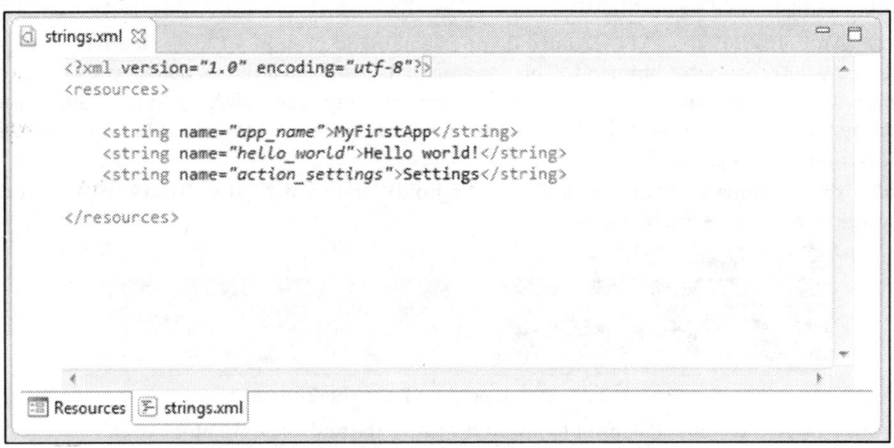

Figure 2.32: Showing the Code of the strings.xml File

In this file, you can see the three strings attributes, namely, `app_name`, `hello_world`, and `action_settings`. The `app_name` string is used as the label of application in the `AndroidMannifest.xml` file, and the `hello_world` string is used as `TextView` in the `strings.xml` file. The `action_settings` string is the default setting for menu.

So, ultimately, this is how an Android program can be made. Since "**Hello world!**" is the default text in the `strings.xml` file.

Using Command-Line Tools

You have already created an Android application under the project name, `AndroidProject` using the command-line tool. You also know that we have created it in the D:**\AndroidWorkspace\FirstAndroidApp** directory. Now, we will run that project using the `command-line` tool. The steps to run the project from the `command-line` tool are as follows:

1. *Install* **Apache ant** first, which is a tool to build the Android application. You can download it from **http://ant.apache.org/**. *Extract* ant in your preferred directory and set the class path to **\bin** directory in the environment variables. For example, in this case, the **PATH** variable for Ant is set as **C:\Ant\apache-ant-1.9.3\bin;** in the environment variables. This will give accessibility of "ant" anywhere in the command-line tool.
2. *Run* the emulator to see the output of the `FirstAndroidApp` application. For this, go to the SDK's tool directory and execute the `android avd` command, as shown in Figure 2.33:

Figure 2.33: Starting the Emulator Using the Command-Line Tools

On executing the command of step 2, the **AVD Manager** appears. You can see here an already created Android emulator (AVD) named, `AndroidAVD`, which we have created while running the application with Eclipse IDE. You can use this emulator or you can create new one to run your application from command line. The procedure for creating a new emulator has been explained in detail earlier. In this application, we are using the same `AndroidAVD` emulator.

3. *Select* the `AndroidAVD` emulator and *click* the **Start** button. The Emulator first boots up and then starts. You can also start the emulator from command line by navigating to SDK's /tools directory and then by executing emulator avd AndroidAVD.
4. *Go to* **D:\AndroidWorkspace\FirstAndroidApp** in command prompt (or the root directory of your project) and execute `ant debug` command. This command is used to build a debug package project, and it compiles the essential dependencies. On execution of the command, navigate to the **\bin** directory of your project by using GUI. You will find the `AndroidProject-debug.apk` file. On this file, we will execute the next command as given in step 5.
5. *Execute* the command adb install D:\AndroidWorkspace\FirstAndroidApp\bin\AndroidProject-debug.apk after a successful build, as shown in Figure 2.34:

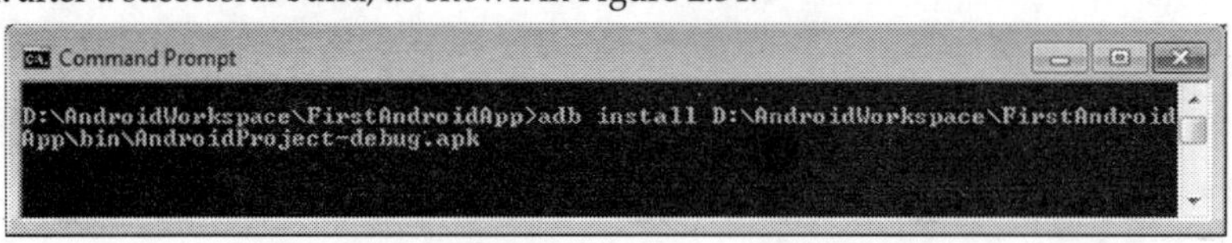

Figure 2.34: Installing the File to the Emulator

The `adb install` command is used to install the file to the android emulator.

6. Locate the `MainActivity` icon on the emulator and then click on it. The output screen appears with the text "**Hello World, Main Activity.**" To change the texts, navigate to the directory **C:\Workspace\FirstAndroidApp\res\layout** through GUI. Here, you will find the activity_`main.xml` file. Open this file in Notepad and replace the string "**Hello World**" with "**Hello Android!**" under the `TextView` attribute. Save the file and execute the following two commands again at the root directory ("**FirstAndroidApp**" in this case) to recompile the project:

   a. ant debug

   b. ant installd

The `ant installd` command is used to install an already compiled debug package and is applicable only if the **.apk** file is in the bin directory.

In this way, we can run a project from command line. It is possible that more than one emulator is opened. To overcome this situation or to run it over a particular emulator, you can use the following command:

adb -s emulator-5554 install D:\AndroidWorkspace\FirstAndroidApp\bin\AndroidProject- debug.apk

where 5554 is the serial number of the emulator that can be found on the top left of the window of the emulator.

Now, let's summarize the main topics discussed in this chapter.

Summary

In this chapter, you have learned about the mobile device applications based on Android OS. The chapter has introduced you to Android. Then, you have explored its history, API levels, architecture, and components of Android. Next, the chapter has explained how to create a project using Eclipse IDE or the command-line tool. Finally, you have executed the Hello android project on Eclipse IDE and learned to execute it using the `command-line` tool.

Quick Revise

Q1. Which of the following is the code name assigned to Android 4.0?

a. **Froyo**

b. **Gingerbread**

c. **Honeycomb**

d. **Ice Cream Sandwich (ICS)**

Ans. The correct option is d.

Q2. Which of the following Android versions use API level 12?

a. **1.6**

b. **2.2**

c. **3.1**

d. **4.0**

Ans. The correct option is c.

Q3. Which of the following API levels is used for Android 4.4?

a. **12**

b. **13**

c. **19**

d. **15**

Ans. The correct option is c.

Q4. Which of the following is the lowest layer in Android architecture?

a. **Linux kernel**

b. **Dalvik virtual machine**

c. **SQLite**

d. **Application Framework**

Ans. The correct option is a.

Q5. Which of the following is a component of applications in the Android architecture?

a. **Activity**

b. **Home**

c. **App**

d. **Phone**

Ans. The correct option is a.

Q6. ________ specifies a library that handles the entire multimedia feature by deploying media codecs.

a. **WebKit**

b. **Media Framework**

c. **Surface Manager**

d. **OpenGL**

Ans. The correct option is b.

Q7. Which of the following is an inbuilt database engine used in Android?

a. **SQLite**

b. **MySQL**

c. **Oracle**

d. **SQL Server**

Ans. The correct option is a.

Q8. Which of the following blocks of Application framework provides data sharing between the applications?

a. **Activity Manager**

b. **Content Providers**

c. **Telephony Manager**

d. **Location Manager**

Ans. The correct option is b.

Q9. The screen of an application with which a user interacts is provided by an application component called:

a. **Intent**

b. **Activity**

c. **Broadcast receivers**

d. **Main.xml file**

Ans. The correct option is b.

Q10. Which of the following command lists all the "available Android target platforms"?

a. **List targets**

b. **Lists target**

c. **Android list targets**

d. **Android lists target**

Ans. The correct option is c.

Q11. What is Android?

Ans. Android is an operating system, which is a product of Google Inc. It is primarily designed for touchscreen mobile phones and based on Linux family of operating systems. It is written in C, C++, and Java programming languages. Java lies on the top of its all development layers and therefore its applications are primarily written in Java. To develop an Android application, Android Software Development Kit (Android SDK) is available with all essential tools. The Android SDK includes a compiler, debugger, a device emulator, and its own virtual machine to run Android programs. The emulator is a virtual device that is used to test or run the application without the availability of hardware.

Q12. Explain the role of Linux kernel in Android architecture.

Ans. Linux kernel is the chief component in the Android architecture. The interaction of the hardware with software is provided by means of Linux. All the hardware drivers are handled by this kernel. It also serves as the abstraction layer for other layers. Since the core of the Android system lies in the Linux kernel, all the main functionality of the system is based on Linux. The foundation of Android is Linux, which is a much powerful system and therefore provides a great versatility to the Android OS to work it on multiple devices without any (or few) glitches.

Q13. Enlist some native Android libraries used in Android architecture.

Ans. A brief description of some of the native Android libraries is as follows:

- **WebKit**—Refers to the browser engine used to render and display HTML content.
- **Media Framework**—Refers to a library that handles the entire multimedia feature by deploying media codecs.
- **Surface Manager**—Refers to the surface manipulations performed on the screen of the device. To do so, Window manager is amalgamated with off-screen buffering. An off-screen buffering is the technique for drawing the image in the buffer and then copying them on the original screen. The off-screen buffer is also responsible for the transparency of windows.
- **SQLite**—Refers to the database engine used in Android for data storage purposes.
- **OpenGL**—Refers to as a rendering engine, which is used to render graphics to the screen.

Q14. Describe the role of Dalvik virtual machine.

Ans. Dalvik virtual machine is used in Android system similar to the JVM is used in Java. However, Dalvik VM is optimized for low-power CPUs and low memory modules. Unlike the JVM, the Dalvik VM does not recognize files with the .class extension; instead, it executes the files with the .dex extension. In fact, .dex files are generated implicitly from the .class file and are highly optimized where memory and processing power are constraint.

Q15. Enlist the features of Android OS.

Ans. Android is one of the most used OS in the world. It is so popular that more than one million new Android devices are activated every day. Some of its features are as follows:

- It is a world-class platform for creating applications for Android users.
- There is an open marketplace for distributing the created applications.
- More than 1.5 billion applications and games are downloaded on Android; hence, it is the best platform for selling the created application.
- The power of hardware can be utilized at its best by using the exclusive APIs.
- A single application binary can be created, which can be used for both devices-phone and tablet.
- It has the largest user base in the word and is growing rapidly.
- The marketplace for selling and distributing Android applications is called Google Play. Once your application is ready, you can distribute it over the Google Play.
- The applications are intelligently differentiated on the basis of different versions of Android.
- Applications can be developed by using either a Java IDE (such as Eclipse) or a tool like Apace Ant.

Q16. Discuss the major Android application components.

Ans. The major components associated with an Android application are as follows:

- **Activity**—The screen of an application with which a user interacts is provided by an application component called activity. The main or the very first screen (as soon you launch an application) of the application is known as main activity. When you switch for the next activity (screen), the previous activity is halted and stored in a stack called as back-stack. As stack is a data structure with the last-in-first-out property, the previous activity is activated on pressing the back button by user. Consequently, the current activity (from where the back button was pressed) gets demolished as it was popped out from the back stack.
- **Services**—An application component in the working process that does not use a user interface is called a service. For example, a service that is playing music, providing contents, etc., from the background but not appearing on screen. A service is an application component that can perform long-running operations in the background and does not provide a user interface. Even on switching to another application, the services of the previously activated application cannot be stopped.

- **Content Providers** – Accessing of contents from the central data warehouse is managed by content provider. Being a part of Android application, the content provider empowers its user interface for working with the data.
- **Broadcast Receivers** – Many system-generated notifications, such as battery low, downloading starts, or file received, are broadcasted by broadcast receivers. However, some applications can also stimulate broadcast receivers. For example, an application informs the other applications that data has been downloaded for them to use. The broadcast receivers do not have a UI; however, they send a notification to the status bar to alert the user. In essence, a broadcast receiver is a component that alerts a user by sending a notification, which is intended to do a very little work (just notify). It just acts as a gateway for other components.

Q17. What is API level and why it is very important?

Ans. API level provides the API review offered by a version of the Android platform. The platform provides a framework API, which allows the applications to communicate with the underlying Android system. The API designers always keep in the mind the backward compatibility with the lower API levels. For example, the API level 14 has compatibility with the API level 3. When a new API level is introduced, there are always additions of new or replacement functionality. Instead of removing older parts of old APIs, they are declared as deprecated to offer an advantage for existing applications. However, occasionally, a few parts of old APIs can be removed to make the current API robust and for the sake of system security. The explicit support of older APIs is not available for the current API; however, they can be used implicitly. Each version of Android platform supports exactly one API.

Q18. Create an Android application that displays the "Welcome to the world of Android" message.

Ans. Follow the steps given in this chapter to create the required Android application. Modify the code of the Java file as follows:

```
package com.kogent.hello;

import android.app.Activity;
import android.os.Bundle;
import android.widget.TextView;

public class HelloWorld extends Activity {
    /** Called when the activity is first created. */
    @Override
    public void onCreate(Bundle savedInstanceState)     {
        super.onCreate(savedInstanceState);
        TextView message = new TextView(this);
        message.setText("Welcome to the world of Android");
        setContentView(message);
    }
}
```

3

Using Activities, Fragments, and Intents in Android

If you need an information on:	*See page:*
Working with Activities	80
Using Intents	105
Fragments	123
Using the Intent Object to Invoke Built-in Application	126

An activity is an application component that allows a user to perform an operation. Generally, a user performs various operations, such as making a call, capturing a photo, sending a message, or viewing a map. For each such operation, an activity is being defined. An application is a collection of these activities. The main objective of an activity is to interact with users; therefore, each activity provides a window in which the user interface is being created. You should note that in a single application, there can be one or more activities. However, there is a main activity displayed to the users. In other words, during the launch of an application, the main activity provides an interface to the users and further invokes the other activity depending upon the request of the user. Whenever the other activity is invoked, the previous activity is stopped; however, the system preserves the stopped activity in a stack. Therefore, the invocation of the new activity is being pushed onto the back stack and the user focus lies on it. An important concept related to activities is fragments. A fragment represents a behaviour or a portion of the user interface in an activity. It is always embedded in an activity and its lifecycle is directly affected by its host activity's lifecycle.

Another important concept is intent that allows the different activities of different applications to work together in such a manner that they all belong to a single application. In other words, you can say that three of the basic components of an Android application, i.e., activities, services, and broadcast receivers, are activated with the help of messages known as intents.

In this chapter, you learn about the use of activities, intents, and fragments in Android programming. The chapter explains the use of intent object to invoke built-in application. It discusses about fragments. Finally, the chapter concludes with a discussion on using the intent object to invoke built-in application.

Let's start with activities.

Working with Activities

Activities play a crucial role in an Android application because they are used to make up the screens for users. Therefore, it is very essential to learn how to start, stop, suspend, and resume an Android activity. An activity is composed of views that handle the layout and provide text elements, button, forms, and graphics to a device screen. In this section, you learn how to work with activities by performing the following actions:

- Creating an activity
- Starting an activity
- Managing the lifecycle of an activity
- Applying themes and styles to an activity
- Displaying dialogs in the activity
- Hiding the title of the activity

Let's perform each of them one by one.

Creating an Activity

You can create an activity by creating a Java class that extends the `Activity` class. Note that each activity needs to create a window in which its user interface components can be loaded. For this, the `setContentView(View)` method is invoked. Generally, the activities are displayed as a full-screen window to the users. You can also set them in different views, such as floating or embedded in the other activity. You can set the floating windows by using the theme with the `windowIsFloating` attribute, and you can embed an activity into another by using the `ActivityGroup` class (deprecated in API level 13). You should note that all the activities (or subclasses of the `Activity` base class) generally implement the two methods, namely, `onCreate(Bundle)` and `onPause()`. Apart from these methods, the base `Activity` class provides various other methods that serve as events to manage the lifecycle of the activity. Table 3.1 describes the methods of the `Activity` class that governs its lifecycle:

Table 3.1: Description of the Lifecycle Callback Methods of an Activity

Method	Description
`onCreate()`	Invokes when an activity is created for the first time. In this method, you should provide the basic static set up, such as creating views or binding data, to the lists. This method is invoked with null

Table 3.1: Description of the Lifecycle Callback Methods of an Activity

Method	Description
	Bundle `savedInstanceState` parameter during the first time creation of the activity. However, if the activity is either be stopped by the user or destroyed by the system, then this method is invoked with its previous state held by the Bundle `savedInstanceState` parameter. Even when you change the orientation of the device, i.e., landscape or portrait, the activity is recreated and this method is invoked. The execution of this method is followed by the `onStart()` method.
`onRestart()`	Invokes when an activity has been stopped and is being started again. This method is always invoked after the `onStart()` method.
`onStart()`	Invokes when an activity is displayed to the users. When the activity is either launched for the first time or brought back to the foreground, the execution of the `onStart()` method is followed by the `onResume()` method. However, if the activity becomes hidden, then the invocation of this method is followed by the `onStop()` method.
`onResume()`	Invokes when an activity starts interacting with a user. When this method of an activity is being invoked, the activity is at the top of the activity stack. The execution of this method is always followed by the `onPause()` method.
`onPause()`	Invokes when the system is going to resume the previous activity. If the activity is returned to the front, then the execution of this method is followed by the `onResume()` method. However, if the activity has become invisible to the users, then this method is invoked followed by the `onStop()` method.
`onStop()`	Invokes when the activity is not visible to the users, which is possible due to two reasons. First, if the activity has been destroyed, and second, when the processing of the other activity has been resumed. In the first case, the invocation of this method is followed by the `onDestroy()` method. However, in the other case, this method is invoked followed by the `onResume()` method.
`onDestroy()`	Invokes when the activity has been destroyed. In other words, this method would be executed either when the finish() method has been invoked on the activity or temporarily; the instance of the activity has been destroyed by the system.

As you have the overview of the methods of the `Activity` base class, let's now move ahead to understand how to create an activity. The following code snippet shows how to create the activity Java class that extends the `Activity` base class:

```
//defining the activity in the com.kogent.android package
package com.kogent.android;
//importing the required packages
import android.os.Bundle;
import android.app.Activity;
import android.view.Menu;

public class MainActivity extends Activity {
//Invoked when the activity is created for the first time
   @Override
   protected void onCreate(Bundle savedInstanceState) {
         super.onCreate(savedInstanceState);
         setContentView(R.layout.main);
   }

   @Override
   public boolean onCreateOptionsMenu(Menu menu) {
// Inflate the menu; this adds items to the action bar if it is present.
         getMenuInflater().inflate(R.menu.main, menu);
         return true;
   }

}
```

In the preceding code snippet, the `SampleActivity` class has been defined within the `com.kogent.android` package. Moreover, the `SampleActivity` class extends the `Activity` base class and provides the implementation of the `onCreate()`and `onCreateOptionsMenu()` methods. You should note that in the preceding code snippet, the `setContentView()` method has been invoked so that the activity class can load its user interface components from the `activity_main.xml` file.

Each activity that has been declared in an Android application should be declared in the `AndroidManifest.xml` file also. The following code snippet shows how the `SampleActivity` class is declared in the `AndroidManifest.xml` file:

```
<application

    android:allowBackup="true"
    android:icon="@drawable/ic_launcher"
    android:label="@string/app_name"
    android:theme="@style/AppTheme" >
    <activity
        android:name="com.kogent.android.MainActivity"
        android:label="@string/app_name" >
        <intent-filter>
            <action android:name="android.intent.action.MAIN" />
           <category android:name="android.intent.category.LAUNCHER" />
        </intent-filter>
    </activity>
</application>
```

In the preceding code snippet, it can be seen that the `SampleActivity` class has been declared by using the `<activity>` tag.

Let's now learn how to start an activity.

Starting an Activity

The Android API provides the `startActivity(Intent)` method to start a new activity. When a new activity is invoked, this activity is placed at the top of the activity stack by pushing the other activities. The `startActivity()` method accepts the single argument of the `Intent` type that describes the activity to be executed. Sometimes, it is possible that you need to invoke an activity from an existing activity and return to the previous activity. In such a case, the `startActivityForResult(Intent, int)` method is invoked and the result would be returned to the `onActivityResult(int, int, Intent)` method. In this section, let's perform the following steps to learn how to start an activity:

- Create the StartActivityDemo application
- Run the StartActivityDemo application

Creating the `StartActivityDemo` Application

Let's create a simple Android application, `StartActivityDemo`, using Eclipse IDE. In this application, we would create the `MainActivity` class, which would call the other in-built activity, `Contacts`. In other words, during the execution of the `MainActivity` class, when you touch the mobile screen, the Contact in-built activity is invoked, displaying the list of contacts stored in the device. You can pick up an appropriate contact and press the `OK` button on the device, which would take you back to the `MainActivity` activity.

Perform the following steps to create the `StartActivityDemo` application:

1. *Open* Eclipse IDE. The **Java - ADT** window displays.
2. *Select* the **File→New→Android Application Project** option, as shown in Figure 3.1:

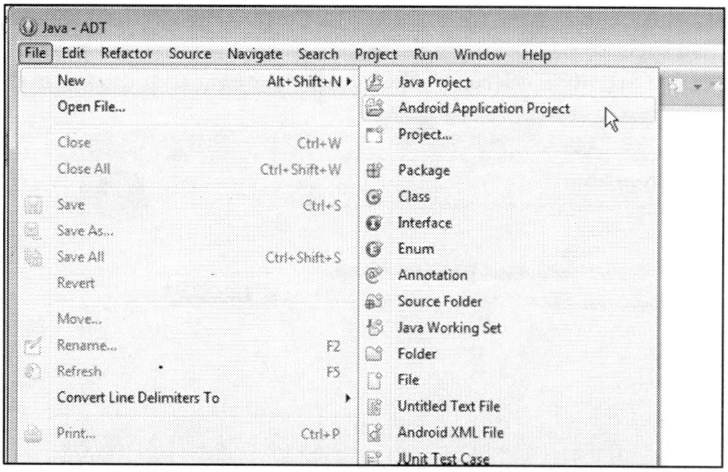

Figure 3.1: Selecting the Android Application Project Option

The **New Android Application** wizard starts (Figure 3.2).

3. *Enter* a name in the **Application Name** and **Project Name** fields; for instance, in our case, the name is `StartActivityDemo`. Enter a package in the `Package Name` field; for instance, `com.kogent.android`. Specify the android version in the **Minimum Required SDK**, **Target SDK**, and **Compile With** fields. In our case, the **Minimum Required SDK** is API 14: Android 4.0 (IceCreamSandwich), and **Target SDK** and **Compile With** are set to API 19:Android 4.4.2. Keep the **Theme** field as default, as shown in Figure 3.2:

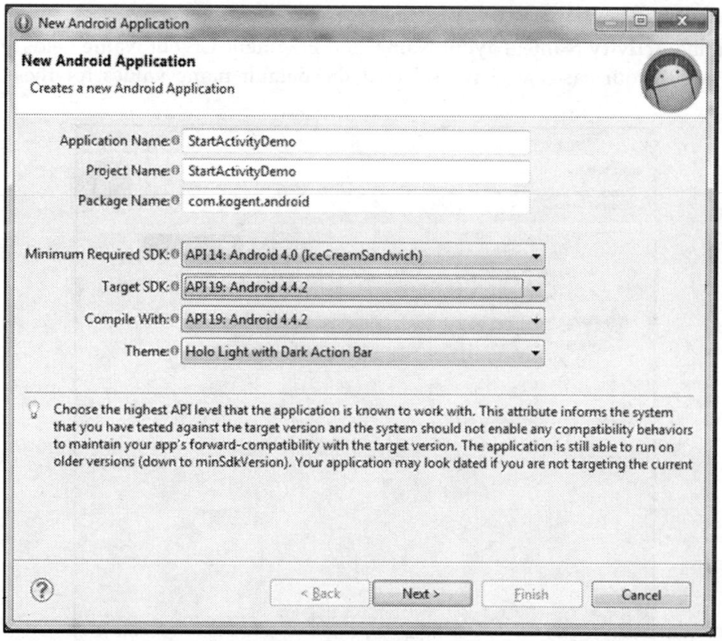

Figure 3.2: Showing the New Android Application Wizard

4. *Click* the **Next** button.The **Configure Project** screen appears.
5. *Keep* the default settings and *click* the **Next** button.The **Configure launcher Icon** screen appreas. It helps in configuring the attributes of the icon set.

6. *Keep* the default settings and *click* the **Next** button. The **Create Activity** screen appreas. It helps in creating activity in Android application.
7. *Ensure* that the **Create Activity** check box is selected. *Select* the `Blank Activity` in the provided activities list, as shown in Figure 3.3:

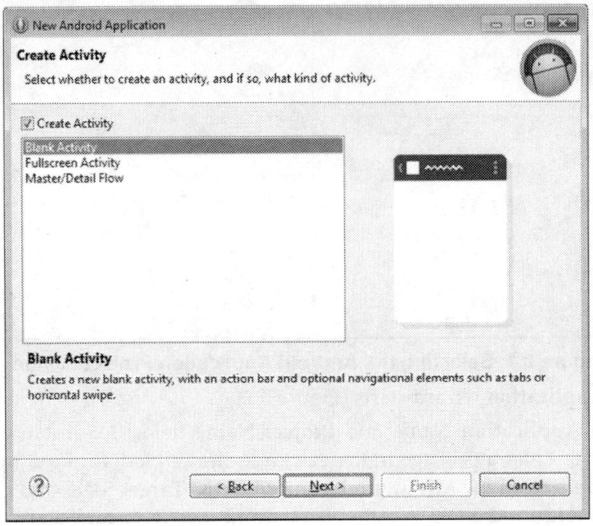

Figure 3.3: Showing the Create Activity Screen

8. *Click* the Next button. The **Blank Activity** screen appears.
9. *Enter* values in the **Activity Name**, **Layout Name**, and **Fragment Layout Name** fields and in the **Navigation Type** combo box. In our case, we have selected the default name values for these fields, as shown in Figure 3.4:

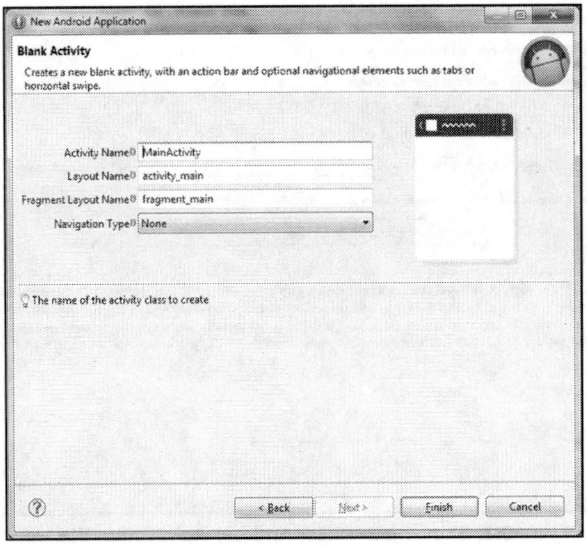

Figure 3.4: Showing the Blank Activity Screen

10. *Replace* the code of the `MainActivity.java` file, located in the **/src/com/kogent/android** folder, with the code shown in Listing 3.1:

Listing 3.1: Showing the Code of the `MainActivity.java` File in the `StartActivityDemo` Application

```
package com.kogent.android;

import android.net.Uri;
import android.os.Bundle;
import android.provider.ContactsContract;
import android.app.Activity;
import android.content.Intent;
import android.view.MotionEvent;

public class MainActivity extends Activity {
  /** Called when the activity is first created. */
   static final int PICK_CONTACT_REQUEST = 0;
  @Override
   public void onCreate(Bundle savedInstanceState) {
       super.onCreate(savedInstanceState);
       setContentView(R.layout.activity_main);
   }
public boolean onTouchEvent(MotionEvent motionEvent)
  {
   if (motionEvent.getAction() ==MotionEvent.ACTION_DOWN)
     {
                      // This is invoked when  user touches the screen
         startActivityForResult(new Intent(Intent.ACTION_PICK,
                      ContactsContract.Contacts.CONTENT_URI),
                      PICK_CONTACT_REQUEST);
        return true;
     }
  return false;

  }
 protected void onActivityResult(int requestCode, int resultCode,Intent data)
 {
  if (requestCode == PICK_CONTACT_REQUEST)
  {
        if (resultCode == RESULT_OK)
        {
              // The picked contact would be displayed to the user.
              Uri uri = data.getData();
           Intent intent = new Intent(Intent.ACTION_VIEW, uri);
              startActivity(intent);
              }
        }
 }
}
```

In Listing 3.1, the `onTouchEvent()` event would be raised when a user touch down anywhere at the screen. This event invokes the `startActivityForResult()` method, which accepts three arguments, namely, `Intent` object, and URI of the `Contacts` activity, and the `int` type value. The `startActivityForResult()` method returns true if the appropriate action has been performed by the user; otherwise, it returns false. Further, the `onActivityResult()` method is invoked, which displays the contact picked up by the user.

Let's now run the application.

Running the StartActivityDemo Application

Once you have created the `StartActivityDemo` application, you can execute the application to view its output. *Right-click* the `StartActivityDemo` application in the **Package Explorer** and *select* the **Run As→Android Application** option. The output of the `StartActivityDemo` application is shown in Figure 3.5:

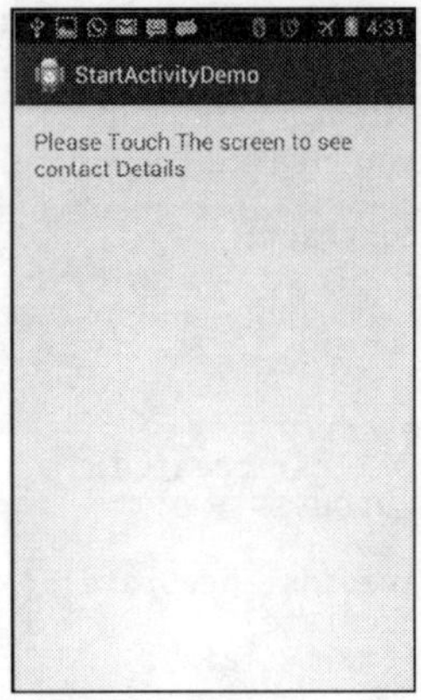

Figure 3.5: Showing the Output of the StartActivityDemo Application

Touch the mobile screen to call the `Contacts` activity, as shown in Figure 3.6:

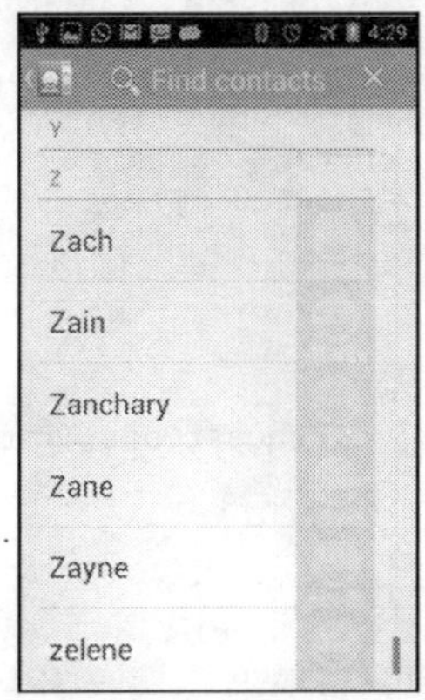

Figure 3.6: Showing the Contacts Activity

Select a contact whose details you want to display on your screen. In our case, we have selected, Zane, and the corresponding contact detail is displayed as shown in Figure 3.7:

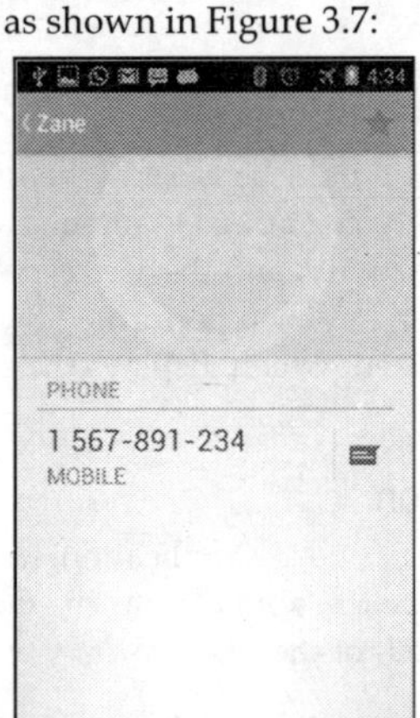

Figure 3.7: Displaying the Details of the Contact

Let's now move ahead and explore how to manage the lifecycle of an activity.

Managing the Lifecycle of an Activity

You have already learned that an activity has various lifecycle callback methods, which have been explored in detail in Table 3.1. By default, when you create an activity, the `onCreate()` method is being provided. This method provides the code used to display the user interface elements of the application. Let's now look at the stages from which an activity goes through.

Figure 3.8 shows the stages with which an activity goes through:

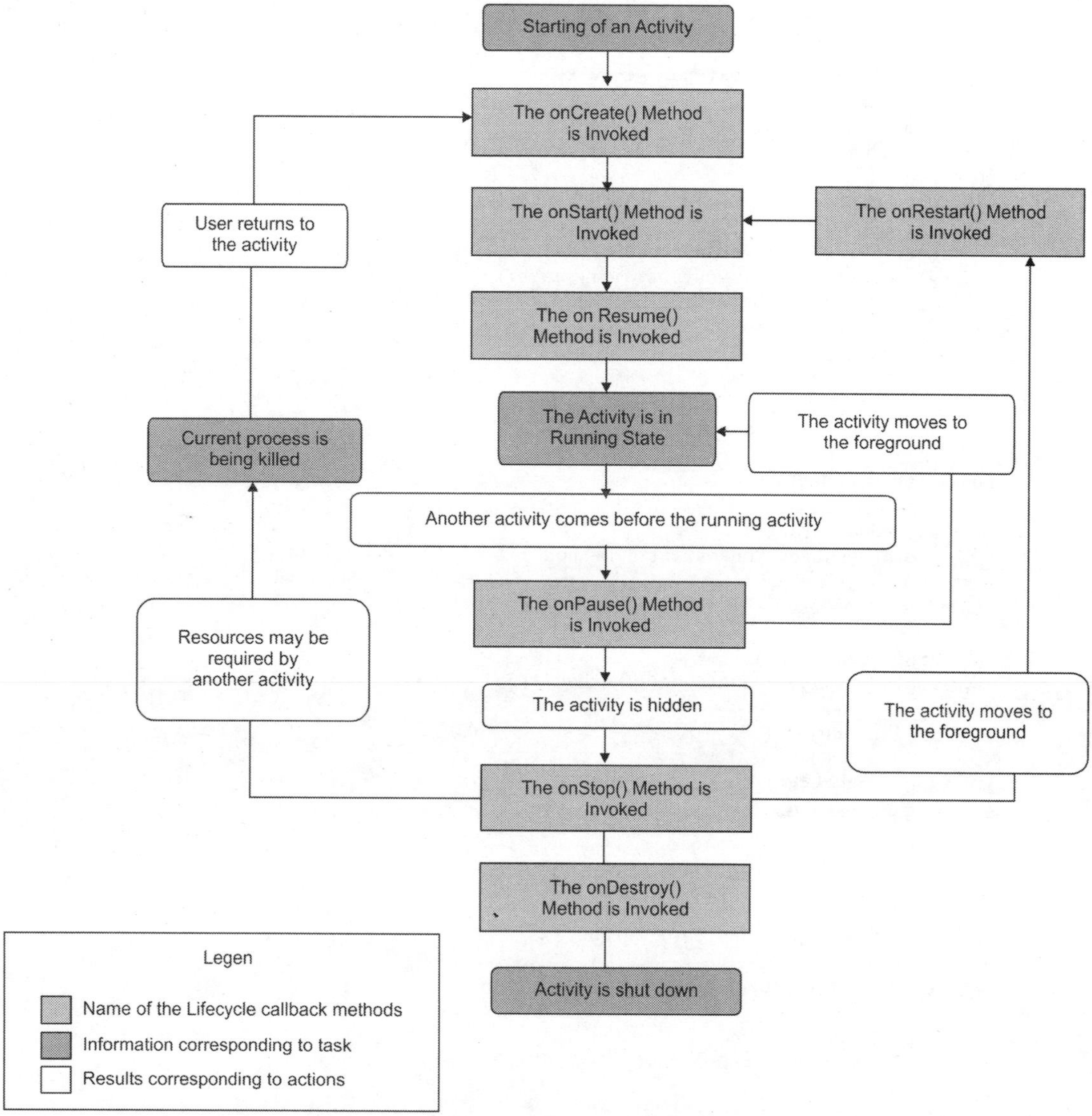

Figure 3.8: Showing the Lifecycle of an Activity

You can have a better understanding of the flowchart shown in Figure 3.8 by creating a simple Android application and noting the events that are raised.

Let's create the `ManageActivityCycle` application that would display the appropriate message according to the event being raised. Perform the following steps to create and run the `ManageActivityCycle` application:

1. *Create* the `ManageActivityCycle` application in the Eclipse IDE under the `com.kogent.android` package.
2. *Replace* the code of the `MainActivity.java` file, located in the **/src/com/kogent/android** folder, with the code shown in Listing 3.2:

Listing 3.2: Displaying the Code of the `MainActivity.java` File in the `ManageActivityCycle` Application

```
package com.kogent.android;
import android.app.Activity;
import android.os.Bundle;
import android.util.Log;
public class MainActivity extends Activity
{
    String message="Event being invoked";
  /** Called when the activity is first created. */
    @Override
    public void onCreate(Bundle savedInstanceState)
    {
        super.onCreate(savedInstanceState);
        setContentView(R.layout.activity_main);
        Log.d(message, "onCreate() Method");
    }
    public void onStart()
    {
        super.onStart();
        Log.d(message, "onStart() Method");
    }
    public void onRestart()
    {
        super.onRestart();
        Log.d(message, "onRestart() Method");
    }
    public void onResume()
    {
        super.onResume();
        Log.d(message, "onResume() Method");
    }
    public void onPause()
    {
        super.onPause();
        Log.d(message, "onPause() Method");
    }
    public void onStop()
    {
        super.onStop();
        Log.d(message, "onStop() Method");
    }
    public void onDestroy()
    {
        super.onDestroy();
        Log.d(message, "onDestroy() Method");
    }
}
```

Listing 3.2 provides the implementation of all the lifecycle callback methods of an activity, such as `onStart()`, `onResume()`, `onPause()`, and `onStop()`.

3. *Save* the changes in the `ManageActivityCycle` application. *Select* the application folder in the **Package Explorer** pane and *click* the **Run** button from the toolbar of Eclipse IDE. The application is executed as shown in Figure 3.9:

Figure 3.9: Showing the Output of the `ManageActivityCycle` Application

Once the application starts, the `onCreate()`, `onStart()`, and `onResume()` events are raised. You can view the messages in the **LogCat** window of the **Debug** perspective, as shown in Figure 3.10:

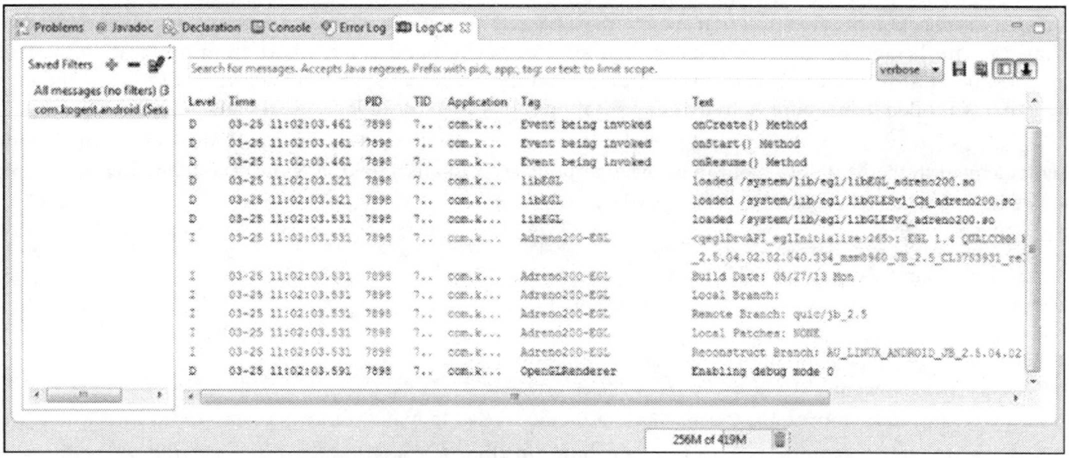

Figure 3.10: Showing the LogCat Window of the Debug Perspective

4. *Press* the **Back** button on the mobile device; the `onPause()`, `onStop()`, and `onDestroy()` events are raised, which you can see in the **LogCat** window of the **Debug** Perspective. Figure 3.11 shows the raising of these methods in the **LogCat** window:

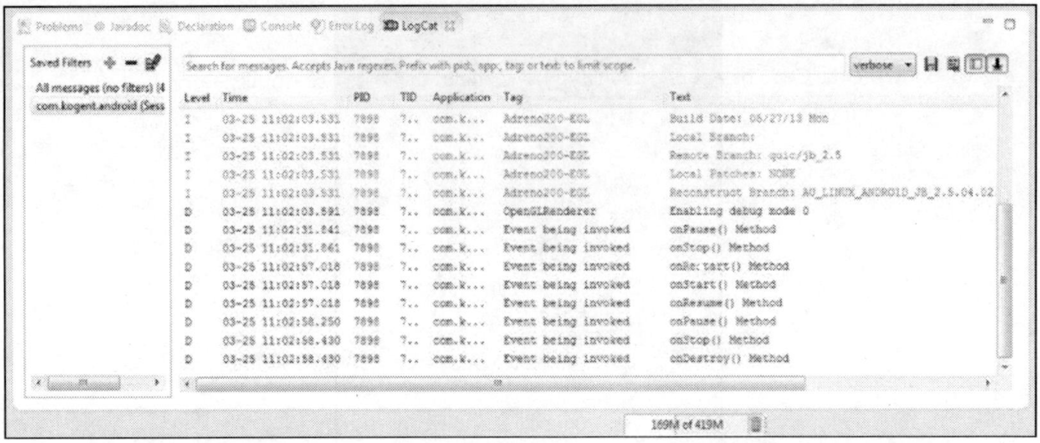

Figure 3.11: Displaying the Events Raised during the Execution of Application

5. *Click* the **Home** button on the mobile device; the Android activities icon appears. Click the `ManageActivityCycle` icon.

You can again observe in the **LogCat** window that the `onCreate()`, `onStart()`, and `onResume()` events are being triggered.

Moreover, when you click the F3 key from the keyboard to make a call, the `ManageActivityCycle` activity is being pushed to the background and the `onPause()` and `onResume()` events are being raised.

You should note that the `onDestroy()` method would be invoked only when the `ManageActivityCycle` activity is not visible.

Applying Themes and Styles to an Activity

A style is a collection of properties that specify the look and format of a view or window. Some examples of such properties are height, padding, font color, font size, or background color. In Android application, a style is specified in an XML resource, which is separated from the XML that specifies the layout. However, theme is a style that is applied to an entire Activity or application rather than on an individual view.

There are two ways to set themes and styles in Android applications. First is to add the `style` attribute to a `View` element in the XML for layout in order to apply a style to an individual view. The following code snippet shows how to set a style for a `View` in the XML layout:

```
<TextView
style="@style/CodeFont"
android:text="@string/hello" />
```

Another is to add the `android:theme` attribute to the `<activity>` or `<application>` element in the Android manifest in order to apply the theme to an entire `Activity` or application. The following code snippet shows how to set a theme for all the activities of your application:

```
<application android:theme="@style/CustomTheme">
```

In the preceding code snippet, the `CustomTheme` theme is used to make your customize application.

You have to set the `android:theme` attribute in the `AndroidManifest.xml` file by editing the `<application>` tag. However, if you want a theme applied to just one `Activity` in your application, then add the `android:theme` attribute to the `<activity>` tag, as shown in the following code snippet:

```
<activity android:theme="@android:style/Theme.Dialog">
```

In the preceding code snippet, the `Dialog` theme is used to make your `Activity` appear like a dialog box.

Let's create an application named `Themes` to learn how to set themes in Android applications. Perform the following steps to create the `Themes` application:

1. *Create* the `Themes` application in Eclipse IDE under the `com.kogent.android` package.

2. *Replace* the code of the `MainActivity.java` file, located in the **/src/com/kogent/android** folder, with the code shown in Listing 3.3:

Listing 3.3: Showing the Code of `MainActivity.java` File in the `Themes` Application

```
package com.kogent.android;

import android.os.Bundle;
import android.app.Activity;
import android.view.Menu;

public class MainActivity extends Activity {
   @Override
   protected void onCreate(Bundle savedInstanceState) {
         super.onCreate(savedInstanceState);
         setContentView(R.layout.activity_main);
   }
   @Override
   public boolean onCreateOptionsMenu(Menu menu) {
         // Inflate the menu; this adds items to the action bar if it is present.
         getMenuInflater().inflate(R.menu.main, menu);
         return true;
   }
}
```

3. *Replace* the code of the `strings.xml` file, which is located in the **/res/values** folder, with the code shown in Listing 3.4:

Listing 3.4: Showing the Code of the `strings.xml` File in the `Themes` Application

```
<?xml version="1.0" encoding="utf-8"?>
<resources>
    <string name="app_name">Themes</string>
    <string name="action_settings">Settings</string>
     <string name="hello_world">We use themes to override the default look and feel of an
Android application. A theme is a set of styles. Android theme was inspired by CSS styles.
We normally separate the styles to CSS file in our web
applications, in the same way we are separating Android styles to themes.
</string>
</resources>
```

4. *Add* a new XML file `Blackbook_style.xml` file, which is located in the **/res/values** folder, as shown in Listing 3.5:

Listing 3.5: Showing the Code of the `Blackbook_style.xml` File in the `Themes` Application

```
<?xml version="1.0" encoding="utf-8"?>
<resources>
    <style name="new_style" parent="@android:style/TextAppearance.Small">
        <item name="android:textColor">#008000 </item>
        <item name="android:typeface">sans</item>
        <item name="android:textSize">20sp</item>
    </style>
</resources>
```

5. *Replace* the code of the `activity_main.xml` file, which is located in the **/res/layout** folder, with the code shown in Listing 3.6:

Listing 3.6: Showing the Code of the `activity_main.xml` File in the `Themes` Application

```
<RelativeLayout xmlns:android="http://schemas.android.com/apk/res/android"
    xmlns:tools="http://schemas.android.com/tools"
    android:layout_width="match_parent"
    android:layout_height="match_parent"
    android:paddingBottom="@dimen/activity_vertical_margin"
    android:paddingLeft="@dimen/activity_horizontal_margin"
    android:paddingRight="@dimen/activity_horizontal_margin"
    android:paddingTop="@dimen/activity_vertical_margin"
    tools:context=".MainActivity" >
    <TextView
        android:id="@+id/textView2"
```

```
        style="@style/new_style"
        android:layout_width="wrap_content"
        android:layout_height="wrap_content"
        android:layout_alignParentLeft="true"
        android:layout_alignParentTop="true"
        android:text="@string/hello_world" />
</RelativeLayout>
```

6. *Click* the **Save All** button to save all the changes. *Select* the application folder, **Themes**, in the **Package Explorer** and *select* the Run→Run As→Android Application option from the menu.

Figure 3.12 shows the output of the `Themes` application:

Figure 3.12: Displaying the Output of the `Themes` Application

Displaying a Dialog in the Activity

A dialog is a small window that may appear in front of an activity in various forms. For example, if you want to display an alert message to the users, then you can design the `AlertDialog` class. However, to display the progress of a process, you can design the `ProcessDialog` class. When a dialog box is displayed, the focus of the current activity is lost and the user can interact with the dialog being displayed. In Android, the `Dialog` class is used as the base class to create the dialog window. The most important thing to be noted here is that you cannot directly create the instance of the `Dialog` class; instead, you need to use either of the following subclasses:

- `AlertDialog`
- `ProgressDialog`
- `DatePickerDialog`
- `TimePickerDialog`

Apart from creating the instances of the preceding subclasses, you can also create a custom dialog box.

Let's learn how to work with these subclasses and design a custom dialog box.

Using the `AlertDialog` Class

The `AlertDialog` class is capable of displaying zero or more buttons along with the list of selectable items, which can contain check boxes or radio buttons. `It` is the extension class of the `Dialog` class. You can create the `AlertDialog` class by using the `AlertDialog.Builder` subclass. In other words, you can create an instance of the `AlertDialog.Builder`(Context) class. Further, by using this instance, you can define all the properties of the `AlertDialog class`, such as text message, title, and buttons. Finally, you can retrieve the object of the `AlertDialog` class by invoking the `create()` method. The following code snippet shows how to create the `AlertDialog` with two buttons, Yes and No:

```
    //Get the Builder to create the AlertDialog
```

```
AlertDialog.Builder demoBuilder = new AlertDialog.Builder(this);

//Set the properties of the AlertDialog
demoBuilder.setMessage("Do you want to exit from the application?");
demoBuilder.setCancelable(false);
demoBuilder.setPositiveButton("Yes", new DialogInterface.OnClickListener()
{
        public void onClick(DialogInterface dialog, int id)
        {
                CreateDialogActivity.this.finish();
        }
  });
  demoBuilder.setNegativeButton("No", new DialogInterface.OnClickListener()
  {
        public void onClick(DialogInterface dialog, int id)
        {
                dialog.cancel();
        }
  });
//Create the AlertDialog
AlertDialog alert = demoBuilder.create();

//Display the AlertDialog
alert.show();
```

In the preceding code snippet, the `demoBuilder` instance created is of the `AlertDialog.Builder` type by passing the current activity as the argument of the `Context` type. Next, the `setMessage()` method has been invoked on the `demoBuilder` instance to set the message to be displayed on the `AlertDialog` class. Further, the positive button of the `AlertDialog` class has been set along with the implementation of its `OnClickListener()` event. Similarly, the negative button of the `AlertDialog class` has been set along with the implementation of its event. The `create()` method has been invoked on the `demoBuilder` instance to create the `AlertDialog class`. You should note that the `create()` method returns the object of the `AlertDialog` type. Finally, the `show()` method has been invoked to display the `AlertDialog`.

Apart from adding buttons, you can also add a list containing check boxes or radio buttons on the `AlertDialog class`. Let's now move ahead to learn how to create a progress dialog.

Using the `ProgressDialog` Class

The `ProgressDialog` class is the extension of the `AlertDialog` class, which is used to display the progress of a task in the form of a spinning wheel or in the display format being set by you. You simply have to create the instance of the `ProgressDialog` class and invoke the `show()` method to display the `ProgressDialog` class. You can also display the animated progress bar by creating the instance of the `ProgressDialog` class using the class constructor `ProgressDialog(Context)`. Further, you can set the progress style as well as its other properties, such as the message that you want to display. Finally, you can invoke the `show()` method to display the `ProgressDialog` class. The following code snippet shows how to create the `ProgressDialog` class:

```
//Creating the instance of the ProgressDialog
ProgressDialog progressDialog;

//Instantiating the ProgressDialog using the Constructor class
progressDialog = new ProgressDialog(CreateDialogActivity.this);

//Setting the properties of ProgressDialog
progressDialog.setProgressStyle(ProgressDialog.THEME_TRADITIONAL);
progressDialog.setMessage("Loading...");
progressDialog.setCancelable(false);
progressDialog.incrementProgressBy(50);

//Adding a button to the ProgressDialog
```

```
progressDialog.setButton("Stop Progress", new DialogInterface.OnClickListener()
{
        public void onClick(DialogInterface dialog, int id)
        {
                progressDialog.dismiss();
        }
});
//Displaying the ProgressDialog
progressDialog.show();
```

In the preceding code snippet, the instance of the `ProgressDialog` class is created and then the properties of the `ProgressDialog` have been set. Next, a button has been added to the `ProgressDialog` class. Finally, the `show()` method has been invoked to display the `ProgressDialog` class.

Using the `DatePickerDialog` Class

The `DatePickerDialog` class displays a widget that allows you to select the month, day, and year. In this section, let's learn how to create a `DatePickerDialog` class. Consider the following code snippet to understand how to create the `DatePickerDialog` class to display the current date:

```
//Defining a textView to display date
TextView mDateDisplay = (TextView) findViewById(R.id.dateDisplay);

//Creating the instance of the DatePickerDialog class
DatePickerDialog dateDialog;

//Creating the instance of the Calendar class to get current date
final Calendar c = Calendar.getInstance();
mYear = c.get(Calendar.YEAR);
mMonth = c.get(Calendar.MONTH);
mDay = c.get(Calendar.DAY_OF_MONTH);

//Defining the listener for the DatePickerDialog
DatePickerDialog.OnDateSetListener mDateSetListener =  new
DatePickerDialog.OnDateSetListener() {
public void onDateSet(DatePicker view, int year, int monthOfYear, int dayOfMonth)
{
mYear = year;
mMonth = monthOfYear;
mDay = dayOfMonth;
mDateDisplay.setText(new StringBuilder().append(mMonth + 1).append("-
").append(mDay).append("-").append(mYear).append(" "));
}};
//Instantiating the DatePickerDialog
dateDialog = new DatePickerDialog(CreateDialogActivity.this,mDateSetListener,
mYear, mMonth, mDay);

//Displaying the DatePickerDialog
dateDialog.show();
```

In the preceding code snippet, an instance of the `TextView` class is created to display current date, which is provided with the help of using the calendar class and its methods. A listener is defined by using the `OnDateSetListener()` method of the `DatePickerDialog` class. Then, an instance, `dateDialog`, of the `DatePickerDialog` class is instantiated to display the current date with the help of using the `show()` method.

Let's now move ahead to understand how to work with the `TimePickerDialog` class.

Using the `TimePickerDialog` Class

Similar to the `DatePickerDialog` class, the `TimePickerDialog` class shows a widget that allows you to select hour and minute. In this section, let's learn how to create a `TimePickerDialog` class. Consider the following code snippet in which the `TimePickerDialog` class has been created that displays the current time:

```
//Defining a TextView to display the current time
TextView mTimeDisplay = (TextView) findViewById(R.id.timeDisplay);

//Creating the instance of the TimePickerDialog class
TimePickerDialog timeDialog;

// Creating the instance of the Calendar class
final Calendar c = Calendar.getInstance();

//Retrieving the hour and minute details
mHour = c.get(Calendar.HOUR_OF_DAY);
mMinute = c.get(Calendar.MINUTE);

//Defining the listener for the TimePickerDialog
TimePickerDialog.OnTimeSetListener mTimeSetListener =  new
TimePickerDialog.OnTimeSetListener() {
public void onTimeSet(TimePicker view, int hourOfDay, int minute)
{
        mHour = hourOfDay;
        mMinute = minute;
        mTimeDisplay.setText(new
StringBuilder().append(mHour).append(":").append(mMinute));
};
//Instantiating the TimePickerDialog
timeDialog = new TimePickerDialog(CreateDialogActivity.this,mTimeSetListener,
mHour, mMinute, false);

//Displaying the TimePickerDialog
timeDialog.show();
```

In the preceding code snippet, an instance of the `TextView` class is created to display current time, which is provided with the help of using the calendar class and its methods. A listener is defined by using the `OnTimeSetListener()` method of the `TimePickerDialog` class. Then, an instance, `timeDialog`, of the `TimePickerDialog` class is instantiated to display the current time with the help of using the `show()` method.

Let's now create a sample application that would provide implementation of all the types of dialogs discussed earlier and also help you to create a custom dialog.

Developing and Executing the `CreateDialog` Application

Let's create the `CreateDialog` application in which we would create different buttons, and a new dialog displays as each button is clicked. Perform the following steps to create the `CreateDialog` application:

1. Create the `CreateDialog` Android application in Eclipse IDE under the `com.kogent.android` package.
2. *Replace* the code of the `activity_main.xml` file, which is located in the **\res\layout** folder of the application, with the code shown in Listing 3.7:

Listing 3.7: Showing the Code of the `activity_main.xml` File in the `CreateDialog` Application

```
<?xml version="1.0" encoding="utf-8"?>
<LinearLayout xmlns:android="http://schemas.android.com/apk/res/android"
    android:orientation="vertical"
    android:layout_width="fill_parent"
    android:layout_height="fill_parent"
    >
<TextView
```

```
    android:layout_width="fill_parent"
    android:layout_height="wrap_content" />
<Button
  android:layout_width="wrap_content"
  android:layout_height="wrap_content"
  android:text="@string/show_alert"
  android:id="@+id/alertbtn"></Button>
<Button
  android:layout_width="wrap_content"
  android:layout_height="wrap_content"
  android:text="@string/show_progress"
  android:id="@+id/progressbtn"></Button>
<Button
  android:layout_width="wrap_content"
  android:layout_height="wrap_content"
  android:text="Show Custom Dialog Box"
  android:id="@+id/custombtn"></Button>
<Button
  android:layout_width="wrap_content"
  android:layout_height="wrap_content"
  android:text="Show DatePicker"
  android:id="@+id/datepickerbtn"></Button>
<Button
  android:layout_width="wrap_content"
  android:layout_height="wrap_content"
  android:text="Show TimePicker"
  android:id="@+id/timepickerbtn"></Button>
<TextView
  android:id="@+id/timeDisplay"
  android:layout_width="wrap_content"
  android:layout_height="wrap_content"
  android:text=""/>
<TextView
  android:id="@+id/dateDisplay"
  android:layout_width="wrap_content"
  android:layout_height="wrap_content"
  android:text=""/>
</LinearLayout>
```

In Listing 3.7, various components, such as buttons and textviews, have been defined, which would be used in the application. In the `CreateDialog` application, we have created 4 buttons and 3 textviews. You should note that in the activity of this application, we would be fetching these components and initializing them.

3. *Replace* the code of the `MainActivity.java` file, located in the **/src/com/kogent/android** folder with the code shown in Listing 3.8:

Listing 3.8: Displaying the Code of the `MainActivity.java` File in the `CreateDialog` Application

```
package com.kogent.android;

import java.util.Calendar;
import android.app.Activity;
import android.app.AlertDialog;
import android.app.DatePickerDialog;
import android.app.Dialog;
import android.app.ProgressDialog;
import android.app.TimePickerDialog;
import android.content.DialogInterface;
import android.view.View.OnClickListener;
import android.os.Bundle;
import android.view.View;
```

```
import android.widget.Button;
import android.widget.DatePicker;
import android.widget.ImageView;
import android.widget.TextView;
import android.widget.TimePicker;

public class MainActivity extends Activity implements OnClickListener {
   int mHour;
   int mMinute;
         int mYear;
         int mMonth;
         int mDay;
   /** Called when the activity is first created. */
   @Override
   public void onCreate(Bundle savedInstanceState)
   {
        super.onCreate(savedInstanceState);
        setContentView(R.layout.activity_main);
        Button alertbtn = (Button) findViewById(R.id.alertbtn);
        alertbtn.setOnClickListener(this);
        Button progressbtn = (Button) findViewById(R.id.progressbtn);
        progressbtn.setOnClickListener(this);
        Button custombtn = (Button) findViewById(R.id.custombtn);
        custombtn.setOnClickListener(this);
        Button datepickerbtn = (Button) findViewById(R.id.datepickerbtn);
        datepickerbtn.setOnClickListener(this);
        Button timepickerbtn = (Button) findViewById(R.id.timepickerbtn);
        timepickerbtn.setOnClickListener(this);
   }
   public void onClick(View v)
   {
           if(v== findViewById(R.id.alertbtn))
           {
                     //Get the Builder to create the AlertDialog
                     AlertDialog.Builder demoBuilder = new AlertDialog.Builder(this);
                     //Set the properties of the AlertDialog
                demoBuilder.setMessage("Do you want to exit from the application?");
                demoBuilder.setCancelable(false);
                demoBuilder.setPositiveButton("Yes", new DialogInterface.OnClickListener()
                {
                     public void onClick(DialogInterface dialog, int id)
                     {
                               MainActivity.this.finish();
                               }
                     });
                demoBuilder.setNegativeButton("No", new DialogInterface.OnClickListener()
                     {
                     public void onClick(DialogInterface dialog, int id)
                     {
                               dialog.cancel();
                     }
                     });
                //Create the AlertDialog
                AlertDialog alert = demoBuilder.create();
                //Display the AlertDialog
                alert.show();
           }
           if(v== findViewById(R.id.progressbtn))
           {
                     final ProgressDialog progressDialog;
                     progressDialog = new ProgressDialog(MainActivity.this);
                     progressDialog.setProgressStyle(ProgressDialog.THEME_TRADITIONAL);
                     progressDialog.setMessage("Loading...");
                     progressDialog.setCancelable(false);
                     progressDialog.incrementProgressBy(50);
```

```
                progressDialog.setButton("Stop Progress", new
                DialogInterface.OnClickListener()
                {
                public void onClick(DialogInterface dialog, int id)
                {
                        progressDialog.dismiss();
                }
                });
                progressDialog.show();
                }
        if(v== findViewById(R.id.custombtn))
        {
                Dialog dialog = new Dialog(MainActivity.this);
                dialog.setContentView(R.layout.custom_dialog);
                dialog.setTitle("Custom Dialog");
                TextView text = (TextView) dialog.findViewById(R.id.text);
                text.setText("Here is your custom dialog");
                ImageView image = (ImageView) dialog.findViewById(R.id.image);
                image.setImageResource(R.drawable.ic_launcher);
                dialog.show();
        }
        if(v== findViewById(R.id.datepickerbtn))
        {
                final TextView mDateDisplay = (TextView) findViewById(R.id.dateDisplay);
                final DatePickerDialog dateDialog;
                final Calendar c = Calendar.getInstance();
                mYear = c.get(Calendar.YEAR);
                mMonth = c.get(Calendar.MONTH);
                mDay = c.get(Calendar.DAY_OF_MONTH);
                DatePickerDialog.OnDateSetListener mDateSetListener =  new
                DatePickerDialog.OnDateSetListener() {
                public void onDateSet(DatePicker view, int year, int monthOfYear, int
                dayOfMonth) {
                mYear = year;
                mMonth = monthOfYear;
                mDay = dayOfMonth;
                mDateDisplay.setText(new StringBuilder().append(mMonth + 1).append("-
                ").append(mDay).append("-").append(mYear).append(" "));
         }};
         dateDialog = new
    DatePickerDialog(MainActivity.this,mDateSetListener, mYear, mMonth, mDay);
          dateDialog.show();
        }
        if(v== findViewById(R.id.timepickerbtn))
        {
                final TextView mTimeDisplay = (TextView) findViewById(R.id.timeDisplay);
                final TimePickerDialog timeDialog;
                final Calendar c = Calendar.getInstance();
                mHour = c.get(Calendar.HOUR_OF_DAY);
                mMinute = c.get(Calendar.MINUTE);
                TimePickerDialog.OnTimeSetListener mTimeSetListener =  new
                TimePickerDialog.OnTimeSetListener() {
                public void onTimeSet(TimePicker view, int hourOfDay, int minute) {
                mHour = hourOfDay;
                mMinute = minute;
                mTimeDisplay.setText(new
                StringBuilder().append(mHour).append(":").append(mMinute));
         }};
         timeDialog = new
        TimePickerDialog(MainActivity.this,mTimeSetListener, mHour, mMinute,
        false);
         timeDialog.show();
       }
        }
    }
```

In Listing 3.8, we have verified the button that has been clicked, and accordingly, the action has been performed. For example, if we have clicked the **Show Alert** button, then the `AlertDialog` is being displayed.

Creating the Android XML File

Note that in Listing 3.8, we have created a custom dialog box in which a text message and an image are being displayed. For the custom dialog box, you need to create an Android XML file, `custom_dialog`. Perform the following steps to create the `custom_dialog.xml` file:

1. *Right-click* the **/res/layout** folder of the application (Figure 3.13).
2. *Select* **New→Other** from the context menu, as shown in Figure 3.13:

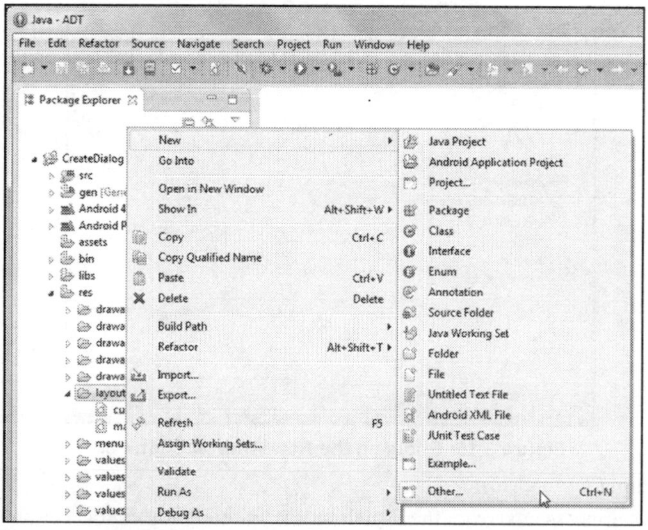

Figure 3.13: Creating the Android XML File

The **New** wizard opens (**Figure 3.14**).

3. *Select* the Android XML File and *click* the **Next** button, as shown in Figure 3.14:

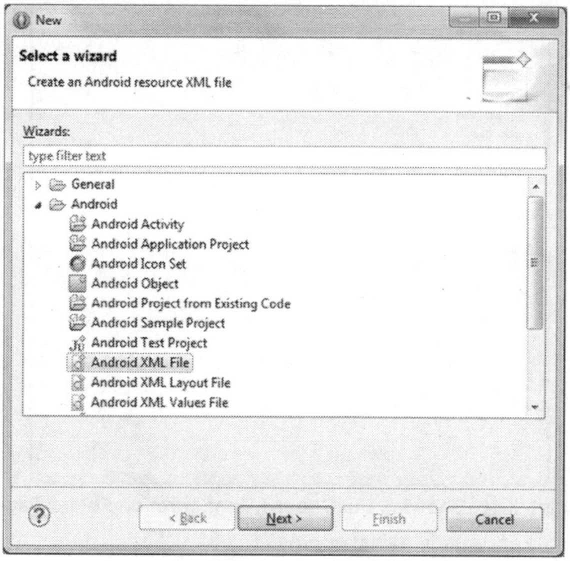

Figure 3.14: Showing the New Wizard

The **New Android XML File** dialog box opens (Figure 3.15).

4. *Enter* the name of the XML file in the dialog box. In our case, we have entered `custom_dialog` (Figure 3.15).

Figure 3.15: Showing the New Android XML File

5. *Click* the **Next** button (Figure 3.15).
6. In the window that appears next, *click* the **Finish** button without any change, as shown in Figure 3.16:

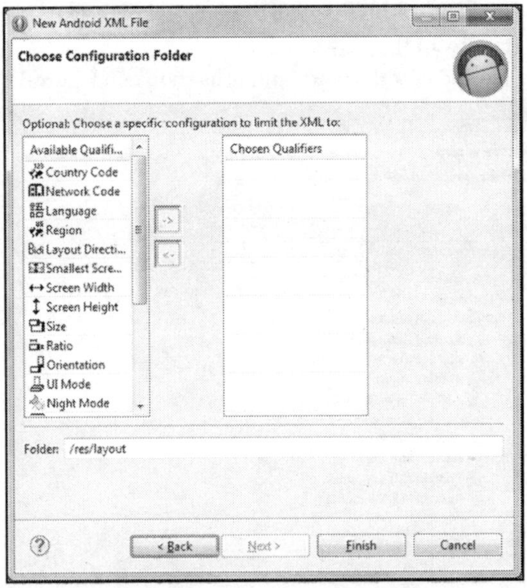

Figure 3.16: Showing the Choose Configuration Folder Page

The `custom_dialog` file appears in the layout folder.

7. Open and add the code shown in Listing 3.9 in the `custom_dialog.xml` file:

Listing 3.9: Displaying the Code of the `custom_dialog.xml` File in the `CreateDialog` Application

```
<?xml version="1.0" encoding="utf-8"?>
<LinearLayout
  xmlns:android="http://schemas.android.com/apk/res/android"
  android:orientation="horizontal"
   android:background="@android:color/black"
  android:layout_width="match_parent"
  android:layout_height="match_parent">
 <ImageView android:id="@+id/image"
   android:layout_width="wrap_content"
   android:layout_height="fill_parent"
   android:layout_marginRight="10dp" />
<TextView
   android:id="@+id/text"
   android:layout_width="wrap_content"
   android:layout_height="fill_parent"
   android:textColor="@android:color/white" />
</LinearLayout>
```

In Listing 3.9, an `ImageView` view is defined with the id as image and the `TextView` view with the `id` text.

8. *Replace* the code of the `strings.xml` file, located under the **\res\values** folder of the application, with the code shown in Listing 3.10:

Listing 3.10: Displaying the Code of the `strings.xml` File in the `CreateDialog` Application

```
<?xml version="1.0" encoding="utf-8"?>
<resources>

    <string name="app_name">CreateDialog</string>
    <string name="action_settings">Settings</string>
    <string name="hello_world">Hello world!</string>
     <string name="show_alert">Show Alert</string>
    <string name="show_progress">Show Progress</string>

</resources>
```

In Listing 3.10, the `show_alert` and `show_progress` strings are added, which are referred in the `activity_main.xml` file in the **\res\layout** folder.

Let's now run the application.

Running the `CreateDialog` Application

When you execute the `CreateDialog` application, the output is displayed as shown in Figure 3.17:

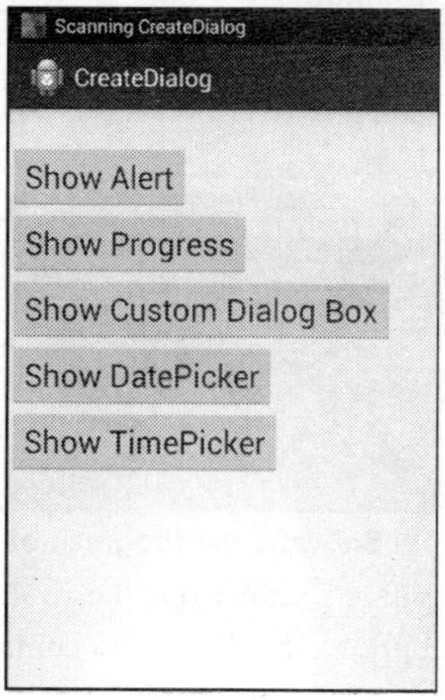

Figure 3.17: Showing the Output of the CreateDialog Application

Let's understand the execution of the `CreateDialog` application in the following steps:

1. *Click* the **Show Alert** button. The `AlertDialog` is displayed, as shown in Figure 3.18:

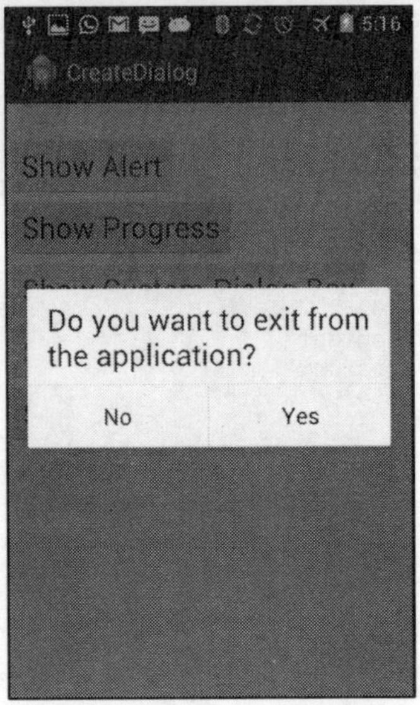

Figure 3.18: Showing the AlertDialog Message

2. *Click* the **Yes** button. The application is closed. However, if you click the **No** button, you are redirected to the application.
3. *Click* the **Show Progress** button. The `ProgressDialog` will be displayed as shown in Figure 3.19:

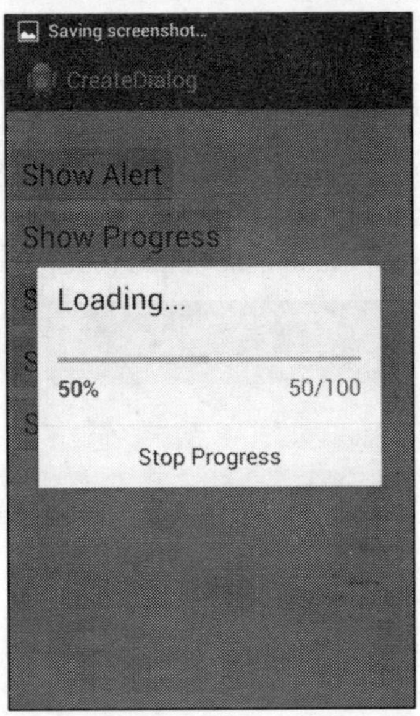

Figure 3.19: Showing the Progress of a Task

4. *Click* the **Stop Progress** button. You will be redirected to the application.
5. *Click* the **Show Custom Dialog Box** button. The dialog box containing a text message and an image will be displayed, as shown in Figure 3.20:

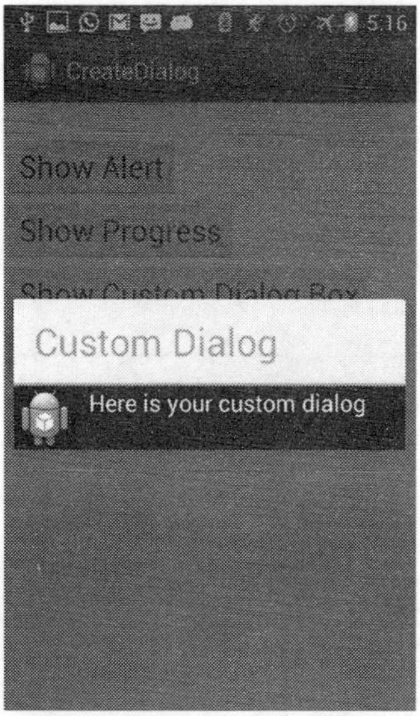

Figure 3.20: Showing the Custom Dialog Box

Further, to move back to the application, you need to press the **Esc** key from the keyboard.

6. *Click* the **Show DatePicker** button. A `date picker dialog box` will be displayed, as shown in Figure 3.21:

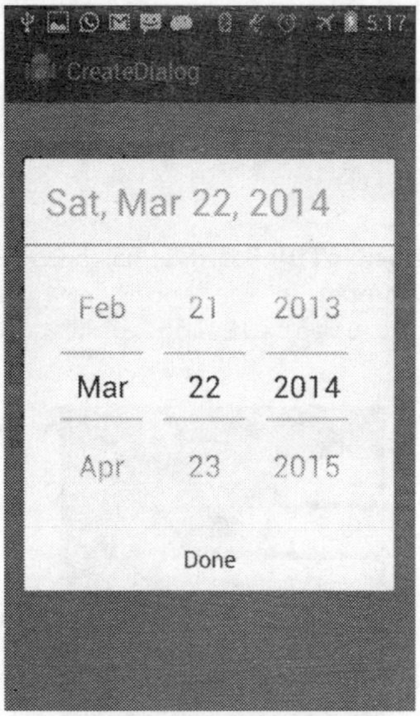

Figure 3.21: Displaying the Date

You can be redirected to the application by clicking the **Cancel** button. Moreover, if you pick a date from the `DatePickerDialog` class and click the **Set** button, you would notice that the date chosen by you is displayed below the **Show TimePicker** button.

7. *Click* the **Show TimePicker** button; a time picker dialog box will be displayed, as shown in Figure 3.22:

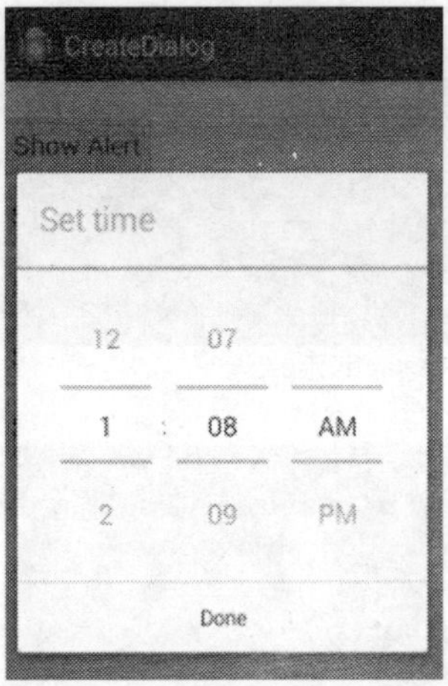

Figure 3.22: Displaying the Time as a Dialog Box

Similar to the `DatePickerDialog class`, you can set the time of your choice and click the **Set** button, the time would be displayed below the **Show TimePicker** button. However, if you click the **Cancel** button, you will be redirected to the application.

Let's now learn how to hide the title of an activity.

Hiding the Title of the Activity

By default, the Android title bar will be displayed for every activity (Figure 3.23). Sometimes, you may wish to hide the title of the activity. There are two ways in which you can hide the title bar. The first way is to set the theme of no title bar (in our case) in the `AndroidManifest.xml` file, as shown in the following code snippet:

```
<activity android:name="com.kogent.android"
        android:theme="@android:style/Theme.NoTitleBar" >
   <intent-filter> </ intent-filter>
</activity>
```

In the preceding code snippet, the **Theme.NoTitleBar** style has been set as the Android theme. In our case, we have provided the preceding code snippet in the `AndroidManifest.xml` file of the `CreateDialog` application. Now, when we execute the `CreateDialog` application, the output is displayed as shown in Figure 3.23:

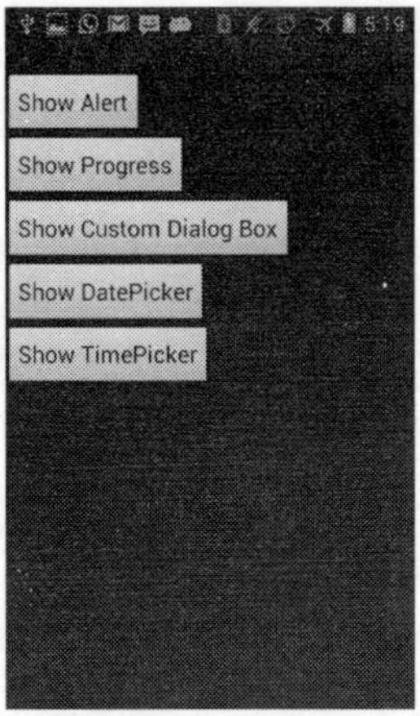

Figure 3.23: Hiding the Title Bar

You can also hide the title bar of the activity by providing the following code snippet within the `onCreate()` method of the activity class:

```
public void onCreate(Bundle savedInstanceState)
{
...
requestWindowFeature(Window.FEATURE_NO_TITLE);
}
```

In the preceding code snippet, the `FEATURE_NO_TITLE` field of the `Window` class can be used to hide the title.

Let's now understand how *intents* link up the activities.

Using Intents

In Android programming, you can bind one or more activities defined in an application by using intent. Apart from binding the activities of the same application, an Intent object also allows you to bind the activities of two different applications. The `Intent` object is a passive data structure that stores the abstract description of the task that needs to be performed. Moreover, an `Intent` object also holds the description of what has happened and what needs to be announced.

You should note that the mechanism of passing the intent varies from one component to another. For example, in case of launching a new activity or performing a new task by using the existing activity, the `Intent` object is passed either to the `Context.startActivity()` or `Activity.startActivityForResult()` method. However, in case of initiating a new service or providing a new set of instructions to the running service, the Intent object is passed to the `startService()` method. In addition, to establish the connection between the calling component and the target service, the Intent object is passed to the `Context.bindService()` method. Lastly, in case of broadcast receivers, the Intent objects are passed through various broadcast methods, such as `sendStickyBroadcast()`, `sendOrderedBroadcast()`, and `sendBroadcast()`.

The Android system identifies the appropriate components activity, service, or broadcast receivers that would respond to the intent and then instantiate them according to the requirements. In this section, you would learn about intent in detail under the following subsections:

- Exploring Intent Objects
- Exploring Intent Resolution
- Exploring Intent Filters
- Resolving Intent Filter Collision
- Linking the Activities Using Intent
- Obtaining Results from an Intent
- Passing Data Using an Intent Object

Exploring Intent Objects

An `Intent` object contains the information that is required by the component that receives the *intent* and the information that would be required by the Android system. In case of the component that is receiving the intent, the `Intent` object contains the information related to the action or task to be performed and the data on which the operation would be performed. For the Android system, the `Intent` object can hold the information as to how the target activity needs to be launched or the category of component that needs to manage the intent. In brief, an `Intent` object contains the following types of information:

- Name of the component
- Action to be performed
- URI of the data on which the operation is to be performed
- Category of the component used to handle intent
- Key-value pairs to be delivered to the component that is handling the intent
- Set of instructions for the Android system for launching an activity

Let's explore each of these in detail.

Component Name

The Intent object specifies the name of the component that would handle the *intent*. This field is of the ComponentName type, whose constructor accepts two arguments, i.e., name of the package where the target component is available and the fully qualified name of the target component. You should note that the package name specified for the ComponentName class type object should be the same as provided in the manifest file of the application.

NOTE

The term "fully qualified" implies the name of the target component along with the package name.

Suppose the target component is the MainActivity activity of the CreateDialog application. In this case, the fully qualified name of the target component would be com.kogent.android.MainActivity and the package name provided in the manifest file is com.kogent.android. It is not essential that the package name specified in the manifest file should be the same as that of the package part of the target component.

It is optional to provide the component name. If the component name has been specified, then the intent would be delivered to the specified component. Otherwise, the other information would be used by the Android system to identify the appropriate target component. You can set the name of the component by using either of the following methods:

- setComponent()
- setClass()
- setClassName()

The getComponent() method is used to retrieve the name of the component.

Action to be Performed

The Intent class provides various action strings defining the actions that can be performed. However, in case of broadcast receivers, the Intent object contains the information related to the action that has taken place.

Table 3.2 describes noteworthy standard activity action constants provided by the Intent class:

Table 3.2: Noteworthy Standard Activity Action Constants of the Intent Class

Name of the Action	Description
ACTION_MAIN	Indicates the activity as the main entry point and no data is received. The constant value of this action is android.intent.action.MAIN.
ACTION_VIEW	Displays the required data to the users. For example, if this action is being used on the contacts entry, then the entry would be displayed to the user. The constant value of this action is android.intent.action.VIEW. The information that needs to be displayed can be retrieved by the getData() method.
ACTION_ATTACH_DATA	Specifies that a piece of information or data needs to be attached to other data. For example, the image type data can be attached to either mail or contact. The constant value of this action is android.intent.action.ATTACH_DATA.
ACTION_EDIT	Allows the user to edit the given data. The constant value of this action is android.intent.action.EDIT.
ACTION_PICK	Selects a particular item from the data and returns the selected item. The constant value of this action is android.intent.action.PICK.
ACTION_CHOOSER	Displays activity chooser from which a user can select what needs to be performed before proceeding with the other activity. Generally, this action is used when the user is expected to choose an activity in the order in which the actions would proceed. For example, if a user clicks on **Add a contact** option, then it is obvious that the contacts application should be directly started. However, if the user wishes to add some more details of a contact, such as birthday or address, then the user is expected to choose the appropriate option for the type of information that needs to be added. In this case, the activity chooser needs to be displayed, which

Table 3.2: Noteworthy Standard Activity Action Constants of the Intent Class

Name of the Action	Description
	would be listing the various types of information that the user can add. The constant value of this action is `android.intent.action.CHOOSER`.
`ACTION_DIAL`	Dials the number being specified by the data. This action displays a user interface containing the numbers to be dialled and allows the user to explicitly make the call. The constant value of this action is `android.intent.action.DIAL`.
`ACTION_SEND`	Delivers the data. In this action, the target to which the data needs to be delivered is not specified. In other words, the receiver of this action needs to ask the user the target where the data is to be sent. The constant value of this action is `android.intent.action.SEND`.
`ACTION_SENDTO`	Delivers a message to the target specified by the data. The constant value of this action is `android.intent.action.SENDTO`.
`ACTION_ANSWER`	Handles the incoming phone call. The constant value of this action is `android.intent.action.ANSWER`.
`ACTION_INSERT`	Adds an empty item into the directory specified by the `getData()` method. The constant value of this action is `android.intent.action.INSERT`.
`ACTION_DELETE`	Deletes the data from the URI specified by the `getData()` method. The constant value of this action is `android.intent.action.DELETE`.

The `setAction()` method is used to set an action in the Intent object, and the `getAction()` method is used to read the action that has been set.

URI of the Data

URI refers to the unique resource identifier that specifies a unique location at which a resource is available. With the help of this unique resource identifier, a user can easily access the resource in the application.

Each action is associated with different types of data specifications. For example, if the action field is `ACTION_VIEW`, then the data field would contain the URI of the view to be displayed. However, if the action field is `ACTION_EDIT`, then the data field would contain the URI of the document that needs to be edited. It is the responsibility of the receiving activity to download and display the data referred by the URI.

Apart from the URI of the data to be acted upon, it is very important to know the type of the data that a component is capable of handling. For example, an audio file should not be called to display an image. Generally, the type of the data can be interpreted from the URI. However, it is better to explicitly set the type of the data in the Intent object by using the `setType()` method.

You can set the URI of the data by using the `setData()` method. However, if you want to set both the URI and the type of the data, then you can use the `setDataAndType()` method. In addition, the `getData()` and `getType()` methods are used to read the URI and type of the data, respectively.

Category

The category field allows you to provide additional information about the type of component that should handle the *intent*. The `Intent` class provides the following category constants:

- **`CATEGORY_HOME`** – Helps to display the home screen to the users. The home screen is the first screen that is being displayed to the users when the device is turned on. You can also view the home screen by pressing the Home key from the keyboard.
- **`CATEGORY_BROWSABLE`**–Invokes the browser so that the user can view the data being referenced by a link. The data can be an image or an email message.
- **`CATEGORY_GADGET`**–Embeds the activity within the other activity that hosts the gadgets.
- **`CATEGORY_LAUNCHER`**–Indicates the initial activity of the application and is placed at the top level in the application.
- **`CATEGORY_PREFERENCE`**–Represents the target activity as the preference panel.

You can define the category for the `Intent` object by using the `addCategory()` method. The `removeCategory()` method is used to remove the category. You can also retrieve all the set of categories associated with the current `Intent` object by using the `getCategories()` method.

Extras

The extras field presents the key-value pairs that are provided to the component managing the *intent*. You have already learned that some actions are being paired with the data URI; similarly, some actions are being paired with extras. For example, if you use an action to send an e-mail, then you need to provide some extra information, such as subject and body. In such cases, you need to use the extras field. Let's consider another example of the `ACTION_HEADSET_PLUG` action in which you need to provide some extra information, such as the state of the headset, i.e., whether or not it is plugged. You can set the extra information for the actions by using the `putExtras()` method that accepts the instance of the `Bundle` type. You can retrieve the extra information associated with an `Intent` object by using the `getExtras()` method.

Flags

The flags field is used to specify various instructions for the Android system, which is used while launching an activity. This field is also used to provide the information related to how the activity would be treated once it has been launched, that is, whether or not the launched activity would be added to the list of recent activities.

Exploring Intent Resolution

Intent is basically a message, which contains the intention of doing an action. Depending on an intent, the applications react accordingly. Android supports two types of intents, explicit and implicit. In case of explicit intents you have to specify an activity that is required to respond to the intent. In other words, you explicitly designate a target component, which is used for an application for internal messages as the developers of the other applications would not be aware of the name of the component. The following code snippet shows how to define an explicit intent:

```
Intent intentObj = new Intent(this, Target.class);
startActivity(intentObj);
```

In case of the explicit intent, the Android system provides the `Intent` object to the instance of the specified target class. The object of the explicit `Intent` object contains no other information, except the name of the component used to identify the component that should handle the intent.

On the other hand, in case of an implicit intent, you just declare an intent and leave it to the platform to find an activity, which respond to the intent. Here, you do not require declaring the target component, so that the intent is used for activating components of other applications easily, as shown in the following code snippet:

```
Intent intentObj = new Intent(ACTION_VIEW,  Uri.parse("http://www.google.com");
startActivity(intentObj);

// Create a text message with a string
Intent sendIntent = new Intent();
sendIntent.setAction(Intent.ACTION_SEND);
sendIntent.putExtra(Intent.EXTRA_TEXT, textMessage);
sendIntent.setType(HTTP.PLAIN_TEXT_TYPE);

// Verify that the intent will resolve to an activity
if (sendIntent.resolveActivity(getPackageManager()) != null) {
    startActivity(sendIntent);
}
```

In case of using implicit intents, the Android system is required to identify the appropriate component to handle the intent for a single activity or service that is used to perform the requested action or the set of broadcast receivers. The component is identified by mapping the contents of the `Intent` object with that specified in the intent filters. The following three fields are considered while comparing the `Intent` object with the intent filter:

- `action`
- `data`
- `category`

Note that the extras and flags fields are not used to resolve the component for an implicit intent.

Let's now learn about intent filters.

Exploring Intent Filters

As mentioned that using implicit intent, we can open other application and get some task done using action, categories, data scheme, which are associated with intent. In the same way, intent filters allow other applications to use our application. An intent filter is used to provide the capabilities of a component and the type of intents that the component can receive. The intent filters, defined for the components, inform the Android system about the type of intents that the components can handle. You should note that for each task or job of a component, new filters are defined. The important part to be noted is that the Android system should be aware of the capabilities of the components that would be launched. In other words, the system should know the types of intents that can be handled by the component before launching the component.

The instance of the `IntentFilter` class represents an intent filter. Also, the intent filters are not configured in the Java code; instead, they are configured in the `AndroidManifest.xml` file. You can define the capabilities of a component in the manifest file by using the `<intent-filter>` element. A filter provides the appropriate fields for action, data, and category.

The following code snippet shows how the `<intent-filter>` element lists the actions of the component:

```
<intent-filter>
   <action android:name = "android.intent.action.MAIN"/>
   <action android:name = "android.intent.action.VIEW"/>
   <action android:name = "android.intent.action.EDIT"/>
      ….
</intent-filter>
```

In the preceding code snippet, the intent filter lists more than one action by using the `<action>` sub element. Note that at least one action must be specified for the intent filter; otherwise, the filter would block all intents.

Similar to action, let's now look at the following code snippet to specify the category:

```
<intent-filter>
   <category android:name = "android.intent.category.DEFAULT"/>
   <category android:name = "android.intent.category.BROWSABLE"/>
         ….
</intent-filter>
```

Note that in the preceding code snippet, the complete string values have been provided for action and category. For example, we have not used the `CATEGORY_DEFAULT value`; instead, the string value `android.intent.category.DEFAULT` has been used. Every category specified for the `Intent` object must match the category in the filter. You can specify the data for the intent filter as shown in the following code snippet:

```
<intent-filter>
   <data android:mimeType = "image/*" android:scheme ="…." />
   <data android:mimeType = "video/*" android:scheme= "…" />
   ….
</intent-filter>
```

In the preceding code snippet, the `mimeType` data type for data has been set for the intent filter. Each `<data>` element accepts the data type (`mimeType`) and URI. For each part of the URI, separate attributes have been specified, such as scheme, host, and port. For example, in the content://com.kogent.android:8080/res/layout URI, the scheme is content, host is `com.kogent.android`, the port number is 8080, and the path is **/res/layout**.

Resolving Intent Filter Collision

In the previous section, you have learned that the `<intent-filter>` element defines how an activity can invoke another activity. Now, what will happen if another activity has the same filter name? For example, suppose your application has two activities, which have the following entry in the `AndroidManifest.xml` file:

```
<application
...
...
<activity
```

```
android:label="Second Activity"
android:name=".SecondActivity" >
<intent-filter >
<action android:name="example.SecondActivity" />
<category android:name="android.intent.category.DEFAULT" />
</intent-filter>
</activity>
<activity
android:label="Third Activity"
android:name=".ThirdActivity" >
<intent-filter >
<action android:name="example.SecondActivity" />
<category android:name="android.intent.category.DEFAULT" />
</intent-filter>
</activity>
</application>
```

Now, if you call the `startActivity()` method, the Android emulator will display a selection of activities. In such a case, you need to click the `Settings` application in the Android emulator and select the **Apps→Manage** applications option. Now, select the application name, and when the details of the application are shown, scroll down to the bottom and click the **Clear defaults** button.

Let's now learn how to connect two or more activities using the Intent object.

Linking the Activities Using Intent

In an Android application, there may be more than one activity and one activity would be calling the other activity to perform the required task. Consider the scenario of the e-mail application installed on your device. In the e-mail application, various tasks need to be performed, such as composing e-mail, searching an e-mail address, and reading an incoming e-mail. For all these tasks, separate activities have been defined, which are invoked according to the task to be performed. In the e-mail application, all these activities are linked in such a manner that appropriate activity is initiated according to the user requirement.

Let's first understand how a new activity is initiated from the current activity. Suppose you want to develop an Android application in which the user details are displayed when the user clicks the button shown on the interface. For this, let's consider that there are two activities, namely, `MainActivity` and `UserDetails`. The `MainActivity` activity displays a button, which when clicked triggers another activity, that is, `UserDetails`. Now, at this stage, you need to understand how the `MainActivity` activity calls or links the `UserDetails` activity. The following code snippet shows new activity is started from the existing activity:

```
//Create the Intent Object
Intent i = new Intent(this, UserDetails.class);

//Start the new activity
startActivity(i);
```

In the preceding code snippet, the `i` object contains the target component, i.e., `UserDetails`. Now, when the `startActivity()` method is applied, the target component would be displayed to the user.

Let's now learn how to link two or more activities and then we would discuss how intent returns the result to the activity.

Linking the Activities

Let's create the `LinkingActivities` application that contains the `MainActivity` and `UserDetails` activities. Perform the following steps to create the `LinkingActivities` Android 4.4 application:

1. Create the `LinkingActivities` application in the Eclipse IDE under the `com.kogent.android` package.
2. *Replace* the code of the `activity_main.xml` file located in the **/res/layout** folder of the `LinkingActivities` application, with the code given in Listing 3.11:

Listing 3.11: Displaying the Code of the `activity_main.xml` File in the `LinkingActivities` Application

```
<RelativeLayout xmlns:android="http://schemas.android.com/apk/res/android"
    xmlns:tools="http://schemas.android.com/tools"
```

```
    android:layout_width="match_parent"
    android:layout_height="match_parent"
    android:paddingBottom="@dimen/activity_vertical_margin"
    android:paddingLeft="@dimen/activity_horizontal_margin"
    android:paddingRight="@dimen/activity_horizontal_margin"
    android:paddingTop="@dimen/activity_vertical_margin"
    tools:context=".MainActivity" >

   <Button android:text="@string/user_details"
android:id="@+id/button1"
android:layout_width="wrap_content"
android:layout_height="wrap_content" android:layout_gravity="top"></Button>
   </RelativeLayout>
```

In Listing 3.11, the button of button1 id has been created.

3. *Replace* the code of the `strings.xml` file located in the **/res/values** folder of the `LinkingActivities` application, with the code given in Listing 3.12:

Listing 3.12: Displaying the Code of the `strings.xml File` in the `LinkingActivities` Application

```
<?xml version="1.0" encoding="utf-8"?>
<resources>

    <string name="app_name">LinkingActivities</string>
    <string name="action_settings">Settings</string>
    <string name="user_details">User Details</string>

</resources>
```

4. *Replace* the code of the `MainActivity.java` file, located in the **/src/com/kogent/android** folder, with the code shown in Listing 3.13:

Listing 3.13: Displaying the Code of the `MainActivity.java` File in the `LinkingActivities` Application

```
package com.kogent.android;

import android.app.Activity;
import android.content.Intent;
import android.os.Bundle;
import android.view.View;
import android.view.View.OnClickListener;
import android.widget.Button;

public class MainActivity extends Activity implements OnClickListener
{
    /** Called when the activity is first created. */
    @Override
    public void onCreate(Bundle savedInstanceState) {
        super.onCreate(savedInstanceState);
        setContentView(R.layout.activity_main);
        Button btn = (Button) findViewById(R.id.button1);
        btn.setOnClickListener(this);
        }
    @Override
  public void onClick(View v) {
         Intent i = new Intent(this, UserDetails.class);
         startActivity(i);
  }
}
```

In Listing 3.13, the `button1` View (created in main.xml) has been retrieved and stored by creating the instance of the `Button` class `btn`. Further, the `setOnClickListener()` event is set on the `btn` instance and the implementation of the `onClick()` has been provided. In the `onClick()` method, the `Intent` object has been created to link the other activity, that is, `UserDetails`. Finally, the `startActivity()` method has been invoked to start the `UserDetails` activity.

Note that Listing 3.13 calls another activity named `UserDetails`; therefore, in the next section, let's learn how to create it. Also, you would be creating the view named `userdetails.xml` for the `UserDetails` activity.

Creating the `UserDetails` Activity and Its View

Let's now create the other activity `UserDetails` that would be linked with the `MainActivity` activity. The `UserDetails` activity would simply display name, address, and phone number details of a user. Perform the following steps to create the `UserDetails` activity class:

1. *Right-click* the `LinkingActivities` application and select the **New→Class** option.

   The **New Java Class** dialog box opens (Figure 3.24).
2. *Enter* the package name as `com.kogent.android` in the **Package** text box (Figure 3.24).
3. *Enter* `UserDetails` as the class name in the **Name** text box (Figure 3.24).
4. *Click* the **Finish** button, as shown in Figure 3.24:

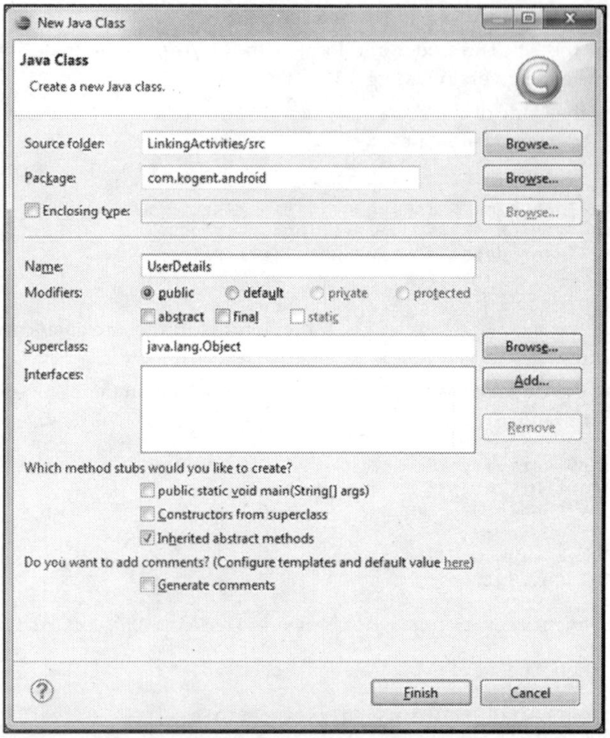

Figure 3.24: Showing the New Java Class Dialog Box

   The **Source Code** window of the `UserDetails` class is displayed.

5. *Add* the code shown in Listing 3.14 in the `UserDetails` class:

Listing 3.14: Showing the Code of the `UserDetails` Class in the `LinkingActivities` Application

```
package com.kogent.android;

import android.app.Activity;
import android.os.Bundle;
import android.widget.EditText;

public class UserDetails extends Activity {
  EditText uname;
  EditText uaddress;
  EditText uphone;
   @Override
     public void onCreate(Bundle savedInstanceState) {
       super.onCreate(savedInstanceState);
         setContentView(R.layout.userdetails);
```

```
        uname= (EditText) findViewById(R.id.uname);
        uname.setText("Charu");
        uaddress= (EditText) findViewById(R.id.uaddress);
        uaddress.setText("Delhi");
        uphone= (EditText) findViewById(R.id.uphone);
        uphone.setText("123456789");
    }
}
```

In Listing 3.14, three edit text boxes have been created and the appropriate values have been set for these text boxes. You should note that in the `UserDetails` class, the `userdetails` view has been used instead of `activity_main.xml`. Therefore, you need to create the `userdetails.xml` file.

6. *Add* an Android XML file named `userdetails.xml` in the **/res/layout** folder of the `LinkingActivities` application, as shown in Listing 3.15:

Listing 3.15: Showing the Code of the `userdetails.xml` File in the `LinkingActivities` Application

```
<?xml version="1.0" encoding="utf-8"?>
<LinearLayout
  xmlns:android="http://schemas.android.com/apk/res/android"
  android:orientation="horizontal"
  android:layout_width="match_parent"
  android:layout_height="match_parent">
<EditText android:layout_width="wrap_content"
android:layout_height="wrap_content"
android:id="@+id/uname">
</EditText>
<EditText android:layout_width="wrap_content"
android:layout_height="wrap_content"
android:id="@+id/uaddress">
</EditText>
<EditText android:layout_width="wrap_content"
android:layout_height="wrap_content"
android:id="@+id/uphone">
</EditText>
</LinearLayout>
```

In Listing 3.15, three editable text boxes have been defined by using the `<EditText>` element.

7. *Edit* the `AndroidManifest.xml` file to add the `UserDetails` activity by using the following code snippet:

```
<activity android:name=".UserDetails" android:label="UserDetails">
   <intent-filter>
         <action android:name="com.kogent.android.UserDetails" />
         <category android:name="android.intent.category.DEFAULT" />
   </intent-filter>
</activity>
```

In the preceding code snippet, the intent filter has been defined for the `UserDetails` activity. The `<action>` element has been used to set the action as fully qualified name of the `UserDetails` activity class. Moreover, the `android.intent.category.DEFAULT` string value has been set for the category field.

Running the `LinkingActivities` Application

Once you have created the required files for the `LinkingActivities` application, let's now run the application. First, select the application that you want to execute. In our case, we have selected the `LinkingActivities` application and then select **Run→Run As→Android Application.** The output of the application is displayed as shown in Figure 3.25:

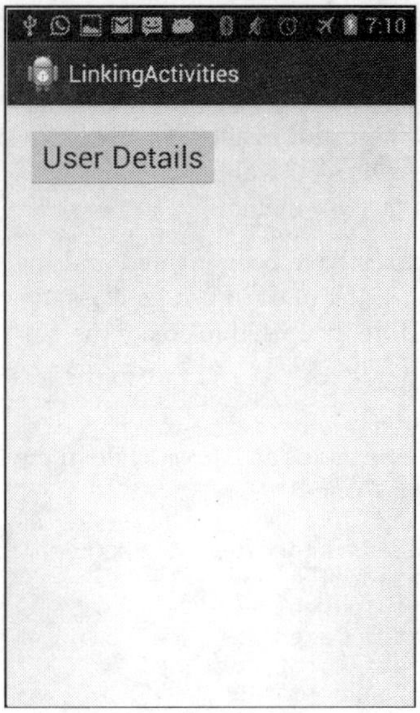

Figure 3.25: Showing the Output of the LinkingActivities Application

Now, when you click the **User Details** button, the `UserDetails` activity will be displayed as shown in Figure 3.26:

Figure 3.26: Displaying Details of a User

In Figure 3.26, the values set for the user, such as name, address, and phone number.

Obtaining Results from Intent

You have learned that one activity can invoke another activity just by using the `startActivity()` method and passing the `Intent` object of the target component. However, when you invoke the `startActivity()` method, the new activity being invoked does not return a result to the main activity. Now, re-consider our example in which the `UserDetails` activity is displaying the details of a user. In this example, it is possible that a user edits the details in the `UserDetails` activity. Therefore, once the edited details are submitted by the user, they should be displayed on the `MainActivity` class.

In this section, you would learn how the result of the `UserDetails` activity is displayed on `MainActivity` class. You should remember that whenever you want to obtain the results from a new activity, you should use the `startActivityForResult()` method. Let's create a new application, `LinkingActivitiesForResults`, which is the copy of the `LinkingActivities` application. Replace the code of the `activity_main.xml` file, located in the **/res/layout** folder, with the code shown in Listing 3.16:

Listing 3.16: Showing the Modified Code of the `activity_main.xml File in the` `LinkingActivitiesForResults` Application

```
<RelativeLayout xmlns:android="http://schemas.android.com/apk/res/android"
    xmlns:tools="http://schemas.android.com/tools"
    android:layout_width="match_parent"
    android:layout_height="match_parent"
    android:paddingBottom="@dimen/activity_vertical_margin"
    android:paddingLeft="@dimen/activity_horizontal_margin"
    android:paddingRight="@dimen/activity_horizontal_margin"
    android:paddingTop="@dimen/activity_vertical_margin"
    tools:context=".MainActivity" >

<TextView
    android:id="@+id/result"
     android:layout_height="wrap_content"
     android:layout_width="wrap_content" android:textSize="30sp"/>

<Button
    android:id="@+id/button1"
    android:layout_width="wrap_content"
    android:layout_height="wrap_content"
    android:layout_below="@+id/result"
    android:layout_centerHorizontal="true"
    android:layout_marginTop="30dp"
    android:text="@string/user_details" />
</RelativeLayout>
```

In Listing 3.16, a `Button` and a `TextView` controls are added. When a user clicks the button, the details are displayed in the `TextView` control.

Next, you need to replace the code of the `MainActivity` class with the code shown in Listing 3.17:

Listing 3.17: Showing the Modified Code of the `MainActivity` Class in the `LinkingActivitiesForResults` Application

```
package com.kogent.android;

import android.app.Activity;
import android.content.Intent;
import android.os.Bundle;
import android.view.View;
import android.view.View.OnClickListener;
import android.widget.Button;
import android.widget.TextView;


public class MainActivity extends Activity implements OnClickListener
{

   int request_Code=1;
   /** Called when the activity is first created. */
     @Override
     public void onCreate(Bundle savedInstanceState) {
         super.onCreate(savedInstanceState);
         setContentView(R.layout.activity_main);
         Button btn = (Button) findViewById(R.id.button1);
         btn.setOnClickListener(this);
```

```
    }
        @Override
            public void onClick(View v) {
                Intent i = new Intent(this, UserDetails.class);
                startActivityForResult(i,request_Code);
            }
        public void onActivityResult(int requestCode, int resultCode, Intent data)
        {
            if(requestCode == request_Code)
            {
                if(resultCode ==  RESULT_OK)
                {
                    TextView t1 = (TextView) findViewById(R.id.result);
                    t1.setText(data.getData().toString());
                }
            }
        }
}
```

In Listing 3.17, we have used the `startActivityForResult()` method to start the `UserDetails` activity. When this method is invoked, consequently, the `onActivityResult()` method is being invoked, provided the invoked activity is ready to return the result. In the `onActivityResult()`method, we have verified the request code as well as the result code and finally used the `getData()` method to obtain the result of the `Intent` object.

Now, add a button in the `userdetails.xml` file. When the user clicks this button, the result is displayed on the main activity. In our case, we have used the code given in Listing 3.18 to add a button to the view:

Listing 3.18: Displaying the Modified Code of the `userdetails.xml` File in the `LinkingActivitiesForResults` Application

```
<?xml version="1.0" encoding="utf-8"?>
<LinearLayout
  xmlns:android="http://schemas.android.com/apk/res/android"
  android:orientation="vertical"
  android:layout_width="match_parent"
  android:layout_height="match_parent">
<EditText android:id="@+id/uname"
android:layout_width="wrap_content"
android:layout_height="wrap_content"
android:inputType="text" >
</EditText>
<EditText android:layout_width="wrap_content"
android:layout_height="wrap_content"
android:id="@+id/uaddress"
android:inputType="text" >
</EditText>
<EditText android:layout_width="wrap_content"
android:layout_height="wrap_content"
android:id="@+id/uphone"
android:inputType="phone" >
</EditText>
<Button android:layout_width="wrap_content"
android:layout_height="wrap_content"
 android:id="@+id/OK"
 android:text="Edit User Details ">
 </Button>
</LinearLayout>
```

Finally, replace the code of the `UserDetails` activity class, with the code shown in Listing 3.19:

Listing 3.19: Displaying the Modified Code of the `UserDetails` Activity in the `LinkingActivitiesForResults` Application

```
package com.kogent.android;

import android.app.Activity;
```

```
import android.content.Intent;
import android.net.Uri;
import android.os.Bundle;
import android.view.View;
import android.view.View.OnClickListener;
import android.widget.Button;
import android.widget.EditText;

public class UserDetails extends Activity implements OnClickListener {
   EditText uname;
   EditText uaddress;
   EditText uphone;
   @Override
   public void onCreate(Bundle savedInstanceState) {
          super.onCreate(savedInstanceState);
          setContentView(R.layout.userdetails);
          uname= (EditText) findViewById(R.id.uname);
          uname.setText("Charu");
          uaddress= (EditText) findViewById(R.id.uaddress);
          uaddress.setText("Delhi");
          uphone= (EditText) findViewById(R.id.uphone);
          uphone.setText("123456789");
          Button btn = (Button) findViewById(R.id.OK);
          btn.setOnClickListener(this);
   }
   public void onClick(View view) {
           Intent data = new Intent();
           data.setData(Uri.parse(uname.getText().toString()));
           setResult(RESULT_OK,data);
           finish();
    }
}
```

In Listing 3.19, the `setData()` method has been invoked on the `Intent` object to set the username to be returned to the main activity `MainActivity`.

Now, execute the `LinkingActivitiesForResults` application, initially the `MainActivity` class is displayed as shown in Figure 3.27:

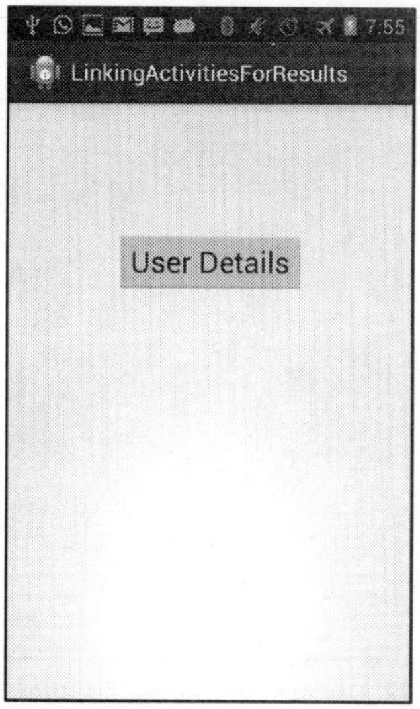

Figure 3.27: Displaying the Output of the `LinkingActivitiesForResults` Application

Click the **User Details** button; the `UserDetails` activity is displayed as shown in Figure 3.28:

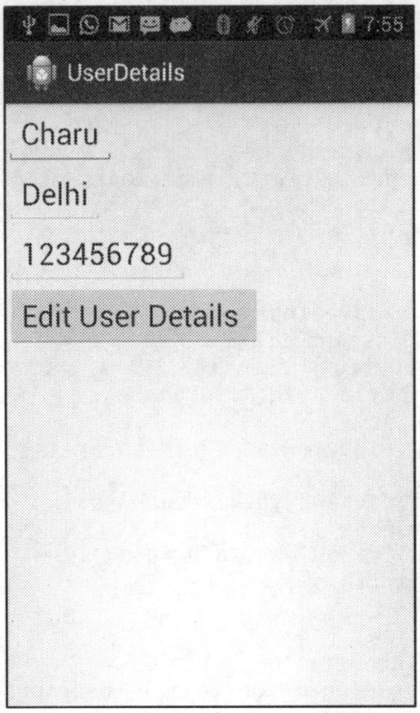

Figure 3.28: Allowing to Edit User Details

Next, edit the user name; in our case, we have edited it to `Suchita` and click the **Edit User Details** button. The edited user name is returned to the `MainActivity` class, which displays the result, as shown in Figure 3.29:

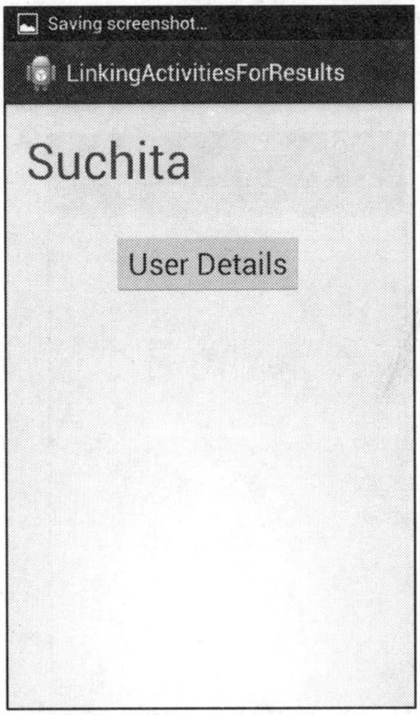

Figure 3.29: Displaying the Edited User Name

Till now, you have learned how to link the user-created activities. Let us now understand how to invoke the built-in applications using the `Intent` object.

Passing Data Using an Intent Object

In an Android application, you can also pass data from one activity to another using an intent object. To do this, you need to create a `Bundle` object and then attach it using the `putExtras()` method. The `putExtras()` method of an `Intent` object is used to add a name/value pair. A `Bundle` object acts as a dictionary object that contains a set of name/value pairs. Now, in the second activity, to obtain the data sent using the `Intent` object, you need to obtain the `Intent` object using the `getIntent()` method. Then, call its `getExtras()` method to get the name/value pair.

Let's create an application named `PassingDataIntent` to learn how to pass data using an intent object.

Perform the following steps to create the `PassingDataIntent` application:

1. *Create* the `PassingDataIntent` application in the Eclipse IDE under the `com.kogent.android` package.
2. *Replace* the code of the `MainActivity.java` file, located in the **/src/com/kogent/android** location, with the code shown in Listing 3.20:

Listing 3.20: Showing the Code of the `MainActivity.java` File in the `PassingDataIntent` Application

```
package com.kogent.android;

import android.os.Bundle;
import android.app.Activity;
import android.content.Intent;
import android.view.View;
import android.widget.Button;
import android.widget.EditText;


public class MainActivity extends Activity {

   @Override
   protected void onCreate(Bundle savedInstanceState) {
         super.onCreate(savedInstanceState);
         setContentView(R.layout.activity_main);

    Button b1 = (Button) findViewById(R.id.btOk);

      b1.setOnClickListener(new View.OnClickListener() {

          @Override
          public void onClick(View v) {
               // TODO Auto-generated method stub

               EditText etName = (EditText) findViewById(R.id.etName);

               String Data = etName.getText().toString();

               Intent i = new Intent("com.kogent.android.layout2");
               Bundle extras = new Bundle();
               extras.putString("Name", Data);
               i.putExtras(extras);
               startActivityForResult(i, 1);

          }
      });
  }
}
```

3. *Add* a new Java file named `layout2.java` file located in the **/src** folder and under the `com.kogent.android` folder, as given in Listing 3.21:

Listing 3.21: Showing the Code of the `layout2.java` File in the `PassingDataIntent` Application

```
package com.kogent.android;

import android.app.Activity;
import android.os.Bundle;
import android.widget.TextView;

public class layout2 extends Activity{

   @Override
     public void onCreate(Bundle savedInstanceState) {
         super.onCreate(savedInstanceState);
         setContentView(R.layout.layout2);

         String myName = null;
         Bundle extras = getIntent().getExtras();
         if(extras != null)
         {
             myName = extras.getString("Name");
         }


         TextView tvData = (TextView) findViewById(R.id.tvData);
         tvData.setText(myName);

     }
}
```

4. *Add* a new XML file named `layout2.xml` file located in the **/res/layout** folder, as given in Listing 3.22:

Listing 3.22: Showing the Code of the `layout2.xml` File in the `PassingDataIntent` Application

```
<?xml version="1.0" encoding="utf-8"?>
<LinearLayout xmlns:android="http://schemas.android.com/apk/res/android"
    android:layout_width="match_parent"
    android:layout_height="match_parent"
    android:orientation="vertical" >

    <TextView
        android:id="@+id/tvData"
        android:layout_marginTop="15dp"
        android:layout_width="wrap_content"
        android:layout_height="wrap_content" />
</LinearLayout>
```

5. *Replace* the code of the `activity_main.xml` file, which is located in the **/res/layout** folder, with the code shown in Listing 3.23:

Listing 3.23: Showing the Code of the `activity_main.xml` File in the `PassingDataIntent` Application

```
<?xml version="1.0" encoding="utf-8"?>
<LinearLayout xmlns:android="http://schemas.android.com/apk/res/android"
    android:layout_width="fill_parent"
    android:layout_height="fill_parent"
    android:paddingLeft="16dp"
    android:paddingRight="16dp"
    android:orientation="vertical" >


  <TextView
        android:layout_width="fill_parent"
        android:layout_height="wrap_content"
        android:text="Enter your Name:" />
```

```
    <EditText
        android:id="@+id/etName"
        android:layout_width="fill_parent"
        android:layout_height="wrap_content" />

    <Button
        android:id="@+id/btOk"
        android:layout_width="fill_parent"
        android:layout_height="wrap_content"
        android:text="OK" />
</LinearLayout>
```

6. *Replace* the code of the `AndroidManifest.xml` file, with the code shown in Listing 3.24:

Listing 3.24: Showing the Code of the `AndroidManifest.xml` File in the `PassingDataIntent` Application

```
<?xml version="1.0" encoding="utf-8"?>

<manifest xmlns:android="http://schemas.android.com/apk/res/android"
    package="com.kogent.android"
    android:versionCode="1"
    android:versionName="1.0" >
    <uses-sdk
        android:minSdkVersion="8"
        android:targetSdkVersion="18" />
    <application
        android:allowBackup="true"
        android:icon="@drawable/ic_launcher"
        android:label="@string/app_name"
        android:theme="@style/AppTheme" >
        <activity
            android:name="com.kogent.android.MainActivity"
            android:label="@string/app_name" >
            <intent-filter>
                <action android:name="android.intent.action.MAIN" />

                <category android:name="android.intent.category.LAUNCHER" />
            </intent-filter>
        </activity>

        <activity
            android:name=".layout2"
            android:label="@string/app_name" >
            <intent-filter>
              <action android:name="com.kogent.android.layout2" />
               <category android:name="android.intent.category.DEFAULT" />
            </intent-filter>
        </activity>
        </application>
</manifest>
```

7. *Click* the **Save All** button to save all the changes. *Select* the application folder **PassingDataIntent** in the **Package Explorer** and click the **Run→Run As→Android Application** option.

Figure 3.30 shows the output of the `PassingDataIntent` application:

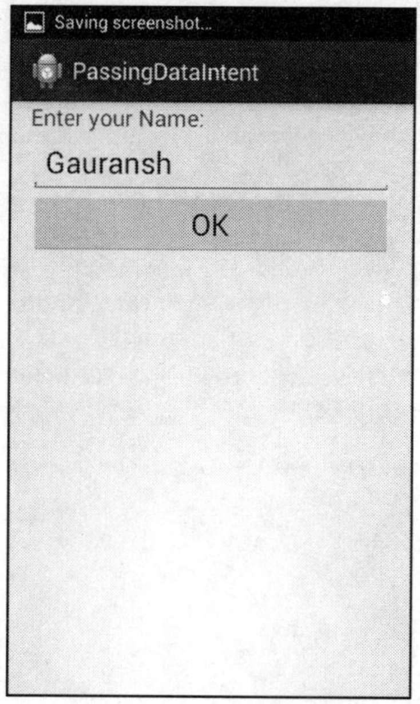

Figure 3.30: Displaying the Output of the PassingDataIntent Application

You need to enter a name; for instance, we have provided Gauransh; then you will see the entered name in another activity, as shown in Figure 3.31:

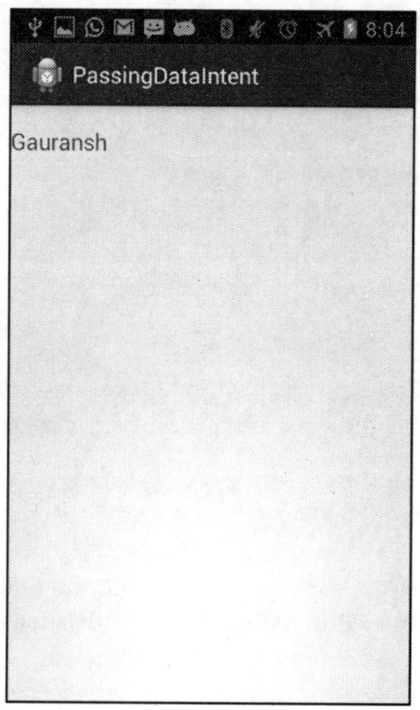

Figure 3.31: Passing Data Using the Intent object

Let's now learn about fragments.

Fragments

In these days, you see a variety of Android devices available in market, which have different resolution and screen density. And it is a challenge for Android application developers to develop applications that support all types of devices. In such a case, fragments come into picture. Fragments allow you to arrange and combine together to provide different layouts.

`Fragment` is a class or component that is used by an activity. It encapsulates functionality, which can be reused within activities and layouts. The concept of fragment is introduced after Android 3.0. A fragment runs in the context of an activity, but has its own lifecycle and user interface. It is also possible to define fragments without any user interface, which are also called headless fragments. Android 4.4 automatically creates class and methods for fragments.

Fragments can be added statically or dynamically to an activity. In fact, a single activity can contain multiple fragments. To add, remove, or replace fragments dynamically at runtime from an activity, you need to use the methods of the `FragmentManager` class.

Figure 3.32 shows the lifecycle of a fragment:

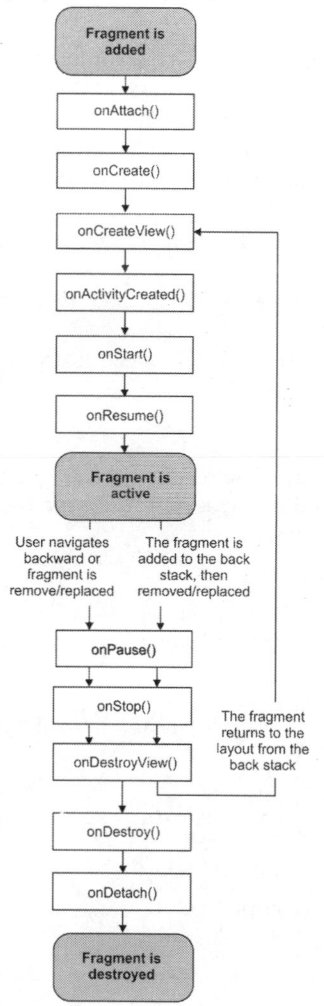

Figure 3.32: Showing the Lifecycle of a Fragment

In Figure 3.32, you see the following stages in the lifecycle of a fragment in a running activity:

- **Fragment Creation**—Refers to the stage in which a fragment gets created by going through the following states:
  - **The `onAttach()` method**—Refers to the method that is invoked after the fragment is associated with its activity
  - **The `onCreate()` method**—Creates a fragment
  - The **`onCreateView()`** method—Creates and returns the view hierarchy associated with the created fragment
  - **The `onActivityCreated()` method**—Informs the fragment that its activity has been created
- **Fragment Visible**—Refers to the stage in which a fragment becomes visible by going through the following states:
  - **The `onStart()` method**—Refers to the method that makes the fragment visible to the user
  - **The `onResume()` method**—Refers to the method that makes the fragment interacting with the user
- **Fragment goes in Background**—Refers to the stage in which a fragment goes into the background mode by going through the following states:
  - **The `onPaused()` Method**—Refers to the fragment that is no longer interacting with the user because either its activity is being paused or a fragment operation is modifying it in the activity
  - **The `onStop()` Method**—Refers to the fragment that is no longer visible to the user because its activity is being stopped or a fragment operation is modifying it in the activity
- **Fragment Destroyed**: Refers to the stage in which a fragment gets destroyed by going through the following states:
  - **The `onDestroyView()` Method**—Refers to the method that allows the fragment to clean up resources associated with its `View`.
  - **The `onDestroy()` Method**—Refers to the method that is called to do final cleanup of the fragment's state.
  - **The `onDetach()` Method**—Refers to the method that is called immediately prior to the fragment no longer being associated with its activity.

Fragment Implementation

A fragment exists only inside an Activity; therefore, it is necessary to define a fragment first. Then, you can add a fragment to an activity statically. Another way is to instantiate a fragment and add it to an activity at runtime. Let's learn about these in the next sections.

Calling Fragment Statically from XML

To call a fragment statically in an activity, create an XML file in the **res/layout** location. In our case, the `new_fragment.xml` file is created as shown in Listing 3.25:

Listing 3.25: Showing the Code of the `new_fragment.xml` File

```
<?xml version="1.0" encoding="utf-8"?>
<LinearLayout xmlns:android="http://schemas.android.com/apk/res/android"
android:orientation="horizontal"
android:layout_width="match_parent"
android:layout_height="match_parent">
<fragment android:name="com.kogent.android.news.ArticleListFragment"
android:id="@+id/list"
android:layout_weight="1"
android:layout_width="0dp"
android:layout_height="match_parent" />
<fragment android:name="com.kogent.android.news.ArticleReaderFragment"
android:id="@+id/viewer"
android:layout_weight="2"
android:layout_width="0dp"
android:layout_height="match_parent" />
</LinearLayout>
```

Now, initialize your fragment's layout, as shown in the following code snippet:

```
public class FirstFragment extends Fragment implements OnClickListener {
@Override
public View onCreateView(LayoutInflater inflater, ViewGroup container,
Bundle savedInstanceState) {
View view = inflater.inflate(R.layout.new_fragment, container, false);
Button nextButton = (Button) view.findViewById(R.id.button_first);
nextButton.setOnClickListener(this);
return view;
}
// ...
}
```

In the preceding code snippet, `inflater` is used to create a view by passing three parameters. The first parameter is resource id of the layout which we need to inflate; the second parameter is the `viewgroup`; and the third parameter is providing a `Boolean` value specifying that only inflate the layout and do not attach to parent.

Implementing Fragment Dynamically

In case of calling fragments statically inside the XML layout file, we don't have much freedom to modify the fragments. To modify the fragments later, you need to opt for implementing fragments dynamically. Perform the following steps to implement the fragments dynamically:

1. *Ensure* that an activity is running so that you can add fragments to your activity layout.
2. *Use* the `Activity.getFragmentManager()` method to get a reference to the `FragmentManager` class. The `FragmentManager` provides the methods that are used to add, remove, or replace from activities.
3. *Invoke* the `FragmentManager.beginTransaction()` method to get an instance of the `FragmentTransaction` class.
4. *Instantiate* an instance of your fragment.
5. *Use* the `FragmentTransaction.add()` method to add the fragment to a `ViewGroup` in the activity, specified by its ID. Optionally, you can also provide a String tag to identify the fragment.
6. *Commit* the transaction using `FragmentTransaction.commit()`, as shown in the following code snippet:

```
FragmentManager fragmentManager = getFragmentManager()
// Or: FragmentManager fragmentManager = getSupportFragmentManager()
FragmentTransaction fragmentTransaction = FragmentManager.beginTransaction();
ExampleFragment fragment = new ExampleFragment();
FragmentTransaction.add(R.id.fragment_container, fragment);
FragmentTransaction.commit();
```

NOTE

Each fragment requires a unique identifier that the system can use to restore the fragment if the activity is restarted. There are three ways to provide an ID for a fragment:

- *Using the `android:id` attribute with a unique ID*
- *Using the `android:tag` attribute with a unique string*
- *Using the ID of the fragment's container view*

Let's learn how to find fragments.

Finding Fragments

You can use the `findFragmentById()` or `findfragmentbytag()` methods of the `FragmentManager` interface to search fragments within an activity. The following code snippet shows how to use the `findFragmentById()` method:

```
MyFragment myFragment = (MyFragment)fragmentManager.findFragmentById(R.id.MyFragment);
```

Let's learn how to add, remove, or replace fragments.

Adding, Removing, and Replacing Fragments

The `FragmentManager` class and its object also allow you to add, remove, and replace the fragments dynamically from an activity. For example, the following code snippet shows how to add a fragment dynamically to an activity:

```
FragmentTransaction fragmentTransaction = fragmentManager.beginTransaction();
fragmentTransaction.add(R.id.add_fragment, new fragment());
fragmentTransaction.commit();
```

The following code snippet shows how to remove a fragment dynamically from an activity:

```
FragmentTransaction fragmentTransaction = fragmentManager.beginTransaction();
Fragment fragment = fragmentManager.findFragmentById(R.id.add_fragment);
fragmentTransaction.remove(fragment);
fragmentTransaction.commit();
```

Similarly, the following code snippet shows how to replace a fragment dynamically in an activity:

```
FragmentTransaction fragmentTransaction = fragmentManager.beginTransaction();
fragmentTransaction.replace(R.id.add_fragment,
new DetailFragment(selected_index));
fragmentTransaction.commit();
```

Let's learn how to find activity using fragments.

Finding Activity Using Fragment

Earlier, you have learned how to find a particular fragment using `FragmentManager` and its `findFragmentById()` or `findFragmentByTag()` method. But you can also search an activity using a fragment. To do this, you need to use the `fragment.getActivity()` method, as shown in the following code snippet:

```
View listView = getActivity().findViewById(R.id.list);
```

Let's learn about how to use the intent object to invoke built-in application.

Using the Intent Object to Invoke Built-in Application

Once you have understood how to call your own activities, you should also know that the `Intent` objects can also be used to call built-in applications, such as Contacts, Messaging, and Phone Call. For example, imagine your application needs to send a message to a particular person whose details have been saved in the `Contacts` application. In this example, you need not create an application to completely load all your contacts. Instead, you can simply select the person by calling the `Contacts` application. Let us develop a simple application, `BuiltAppsIntent`, to invoke various built-in applications on the click of buttons.

Perform the following steps to create and run the `BuiltAppsIntent` application:

1. *Create* the `BuiltAppsIntent` application in the Eclipse IDE and under the com.kogent.android package.
2. *Add* the code shown in Listing 3.26 in the `activity_main.xml` file, located in the **/res/layout** folder:

Listing 3.26: Displaying the Code of the `activity_main.xml` File in the `BuiltAppsIntent` Application

```
<?xml version="1.0" encoding="utf-8"?>
<LinearLayout xmlns:android="http://schemas.android.com/apk/res/android"
    android:orientation="vertical"
    android:layout_width="fill_parent"
    android:layout_height="fill_parent"
    >
<TextView
    android:layout_width="fill_parent"
    android:layout_height="wrap_content"
    android:text="@string/hello"
    android:textSize="30sp"/>
<Button android:id="@+id/button_showBrowser"
    android:layout_width="wrap_content"
    android:layout_height="wrap_content"
    android:text="@string/show_browser"
    ></Button>
    <Button android:id="@+id/button_dialNumber"
```

```
        android:layout_width="wrap_content"
        android:layout_height="wrap_content"
        android:text="@string/dial_number"
        ></Button>
</LinearLayout>
```

In Listing 3.26, two buttons have been designed to perform the following tasks:

- Display a Web page on browser
- Dial the specified number

3. *Replace* the code of the `strings.xml` file, located in the **/res/values** folder, with the code shown in Listing 3.27:

Listing 3.27: Displaying the Code of the `strings.xml` File in the `BuiltAppsIntent` Application

```
<?xml version="1.0" encoding="utf-8"?>
<resources>

    <string name="app_name">BuiltAppsIntent</string>
    <string name="action_settings">Settings</string>
    <string name="hello">Hello world!</string>
    <string name="show_browser">Show Browser</string>
    <string name="dial_number">Dial a Number</string>

</resources>
```

4. *Replace* the code of the `MainActivity` class, located in the **/src/com/kogent/android** folder, with the code shown in Listing 3.28:

Listing 3.28: Showing the Code of the `MainActivity.java File` in the `BuiltAppsIntent` Application

```
package com.kogent.android;

import android.app.Activity;
import android.content.Intent;
import android.net.Uri;
import android.os.Bundle;
import android.view.View;
import android.view.View.OnClickListener;
import android.widget.Button;


public class MainActivity extends Activity {

  Button button_editcontact, button_showBrowser, button_dialNumber;
    int request_Code=1;
    String selectedImagePath;
        /** Called when the activity is first created. */
      @Override
      public void onCreate(Bundle savedInstanceState) {
          super.onCreate(savedInstanceState);
          setContentView(R.layout.activity_main);
      Button button_showBrowser = (Button) findViewById(R.id.button_showBrowser);
      button_showBrowser.setOnClickListener(new OnClickListener(){
        public void onClick(View v)
        {
                Intent i = new Intent(android.content.Intent.ACTION_VIEW,
                Uri.parse("http://www.dreamtechpress.com"));
                startActivity(i);
        }
      });
      Button button_dialNumber = (Button) findViewById(R.id.button_dialNumber);
      button_dialNumber.setOnClickListener(new OnClickListener(){
        public void onClick(View v)
        {
                Intent i = new Intent(android.content.Intent.ACTION_DIAL,
                Uri.parse("tel:+12345678"));
                startActivity(i);
```

```
            }
        });

    }
}
```

In Listing 3.28, the code has been provided for the click events of all the two buttons defined in Listing 3.27. You should note that in order to display the browser, the action field specified is `ACTION_VIEW`. In addition, to dial the specified number, the `ACTION_DIAL` action field has been set for the Intent object.

5. *Run* the `BuiltAppsIntent` application by selecting **Run→Run As→ Android Application** option from the main menu. The output of the application has been displayed in Figure 3.33:

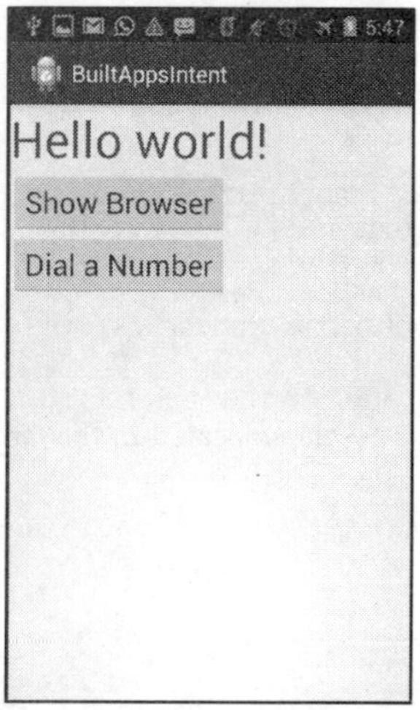

Figure 3.33: Displaying the Output of the BuiltAppsIntent Application

When you click the **Dial a Number** button, a dialog box will be displayed, prompting you to either add the number in the contacts list or close the dialog box.

When you click the **Close** button, you will be redirected to the `BuiltAppsIntentActivity` activity.

Figure 3.34:

Figure 3.34: Editing the Details of a Contact

Now, click the **Show Browser** button, the http://www.dreamtechpress.com Web page would be displayed.

When you close the browser, you will be again redirected to the `BuiltAppsIntentActivity` activity.

This brings us to the end of the chapter.

Summary

In this chapter, you have learned about the activities that serve as application components. You have also learned to manage the lifecycle of an activity with the help of an application. While understanding the lifecycle of an activity, you have learned about different methods, such as `onStart()`, `onRestart()`, `onResume()`, `onPause()`, `onStop()`, and `onDestroy()`. Next, the focus was on displaying different types of dialogs in an activity. For example, to display the progress of an activity, the `ProgressDialog` is used. To set the date and time, the `DatePickerDialog` and `TimePickerDialog` classes are displayed on the mobile screen. The chapter has explained how to hide the title of the activity and use intents in an Android application. The use of different types of intent resolution and intent filters in an Android application has also been the part of learning of the chapter. Then, you have learned about fragments. Toward the end, you learned to invoke built-in application using the intent object.

Quick Revise

Q1. A small window that may appear in front of an activity in various forms is called:

a. Dialog
b. Box
c. Intent
d. Activity

Ans. The correct option is a.

Q2. A dialogue window with not a single button can be created by which of the following class?

a. AlertDialog
b. ProgressDialog
c. DatePickerDialog
d TimePickerDialog

Ans. The correct option is a.

Q3. Which of the following class is used to show a spinning wheel in an Android application?

a. AlertDialog
b. ProgressDialog
c. DatePickerDialog
d. TimePickerDialog

Ans. The correct option is b.

Q4. Which of the following attribute is used to hide the title of an activity in the manifest.xml file?

a. android:theme
b. android:title
c. android:text
d. android:hidetexts

Ans. The correct option is b.

Q5. Which of the following can be used to bind activities?

a. Intents
b. Manifests
c. Layouts
d. Strings

Ans. The correct option is a.

Q6. Which of the following methods is used to retrieve the name of component to be accessed by intent?

a. setComponent()

b. getComponent()

c. setClass()

d. getClass

Ans. The correct option is b.

Q7. What is an activity? How is it created?

Ans. An activity is an application component that allows a user to perform an operation. Generally, a user performs various operations, such as making a call, capturing a photo, sending a message, or viewing a map. For each such operation, an activity is defined, where an application is a collection of these activities. The main objective of an activity is to interact with the users; therefore, each activity provides a window in which the user interface is created. In a single application, there can be one or more activities. However, there is a main activity that is displayed to the users. In other words, during the launch of the application, the main activity provides an interface to the users, and further, the main activity can invoke the other activity depending upon the request of the user.

You can create an activity by creating a Java class that extends the `Activity` class. Each activity needs to create a window in which its user interface components can be loaded. For this, the `setContentView(View)` method is invoked. Generally, the activities are displayed as a full-screen window to the users. You can also set them in different views, such as floating or embedded in the other activity. You can set the floating windows by using the theme with the `windowIsFloating` attribute, and you can embed an activity into another by using the `ActivityGroup` class. Generally, all the activities (or subclasses of the `Activity` base class) implement two methods, namely, `onCreate(Bundle)` and `onPause()`.

Q8. Define style and theme. How are they applied to an activity?

Ans. A style is a collection of properties that specify the look and format of a view or window. Some examples of such properties are height, padding, font color, font size, or background color. In an Android application, a style is specified in an XML resource, which is separated from the XML that specifies the layout. However, theme is a style that applied to an entire activity or application, rather than on an individual view.

There are two ways to set themes and styles in Android applications. First is to add the `style` attribute to a View element in the XML for layout in order to apply a style to an individual view. Another is to add the `android:theme` attribute to the `<activity>` or `<application>` element in the Android manifest in order to apply the theme to an entire activity or application. You have to set the `android:theme` attribute in the `AndroidManifest.xml` file by editing the `<application>` tag. However, if you want a theme applied to just one `Activity` in your application, then add the `android:theme` attribute to the `<activity>` tag.

Q9. What is the use of the `Dialog` and `AlertDialog` classes?

Ans. A dialog is a small window that may appear in front of an activity in various forms. For example, if you want to display an alert message to the users, then you can design the `AlertDialog` class. In Android, the `Dialog` class is used as the base class to create the dialog window. The `AlertDialog` class is capable of displaying zero or more buttons along with the list of selectable items, which can contain check boxes or radio buttons. The `AlertDialog` class is the extension class of the `Dialog` class. You can create the `AlertDialog` class by using the `AlertDialog.Builder` subclass. In other words, you can create an instance of the `AlertDialog.Builder(Context)` class. Further, by using this instance, you can define all the properties of the `AlertDialog` class, such as text message, title, and buttons. Finally, you can retrieve the object of the `AlertDialog` class by invoking the `create()` method.

Q10. Describe the role of intent in Android programming.

Ans. In the Android programming, you can bind one or more activities defined in an application by using intent. Apart from binding the activities of the same application, an Intent object also allows you to bind the activities of two different applications. The `Intent` object is a passive data structure that stores the abstract description of the task that needs to be performed. Moreover, an Intent object also holds the description of what has happened and what needs to be announced.

Q11. Explain fragments in Android programming.

Ans. In these days, you see a variety of Android devices available in the market, which have different resolution and screen density. It is a challenge for Android application developers to develop applications that support all types of devices. In such a case, fragments come into picture. Fragments allow you to arrange and combine together to provide different layouts.

`Fragment` is a class or component that is used by an activity. It encapsulates functionality, which can be reused within activities and layouts. The concept of fragment is introduced after Android 3.0. A fragment runs in the context of an activity, but has its own lifecycle and user interface. It is also possible to define fragments without any user interface, which are also called headless fragments. Fragments can be added statically or dynamically to an activity. In fact, a single activity can contain multiple fragments. To add, remove, or replace fragments dynamically at runtime from an activity, you need to use the methods of the `FragmentManager` class.

Q12. Create an Android application, which pops up an Alert Dialog with three buttons.

Ans. Create application with name `AlertDialog`. Replace the code of the `MainActivity.java` file with the code shown below:

```
package com.kogent.android.alertdialog;

import android.app.Activity;
import android.app.AlertDialog;
import android.content.DialogInterface;
import android.os.Bundle;
import android.widget.TextView;

public class MainActivity extends Activity
{
    /** Called when the activity is first created. */
    @Override
    public void onCreate(Bundle savedInstanceState)
    {
        super.onCreate(savedInstanceState);
        final TextView message = new TextView(this);
        message.setText("");
        AlertDialog.Builder builder = new AlertDialog.Builder(this);
        builder.setMessage(R.string.AlertBoxMessage);
        builder.setPositiveButton(R.string.Yes, new DialogInterface.OnClickListener() {
            public void onClick(DialogInterface dialog, int id) {
                message.setText("Your Answer is Yes" );

            }
        });
        builder.setNegativeButton(R.string.No, new DialogInterface.OnClickListener() {
            public void onClick(DialogInterface dialog, int id) {
                message.setText("Your Answer is No");

            }

        });
        builder.setNeutralButton(R.string.CanNotSay, new
        DialogInterface.OnClickListener() {
            public void onClick(DialogInterface dialog, int id) {
                message.setText("Your Answer is Can Not Say");

            }

        });


        builder.show();
```

```
        setContentView(message);

    }
}
Replace the code of the strings.xml file with the code shown below:
<?xml version="1.0" encoding="utf-8"?>
<resources>
    <string name="action_settings">Settings</string>
    <string name="app_name">HelloWorld</string>
    <color name="BackgroundColor">#337700</color>
    <string name="AlertBoxMessage">Do You Like Icecream</string>
    <string name="Yes">Yes</string>
    <string name="No">No</string>
    <string name="CanNotSay">Cant Say</string>
</resources>
```

Q13. Create an Android application using intents and two activities. On the first activity, user can add name and then on pressing the OK button, the second activity should be started. The second activity must greet the user by using the text that entered on Activity one (e.g., Hi User).

Ans. Create an application named, `HiUser`. The `MainActivity.java` file shown in the following code:

```
package com.kogent.android.hiuser;
import android.os.Bundle;
import android.app.Activity;
import android.content.Intent;
import android.view.View;
import android.widget.Button;
import android.widget.EditText;

public class MainActivity extends Activity  {

   @Override
   protected void onCreate(Bundle savedInstanceState) {
         super.onCreate(savedInstanceState);
         setContentView(R.layout.activity_main);
         final EditText  Name  = (EditText) findViewById(R.id.TextBox);
         Button btnValidate = (Button)findViewById(R.id.Submit);
         btnValidate.setOnClickListener(new View.OnClickListener() {
                @Override
                public void onClick(View v) {
                       Intent intent = new Intent(MainActivity.this,Activity2.class);
               intent.putExtra("Name",Name.getText().toString());
               startActivity(intent);

                }
         });

   }
}
```

Add the `Activity2.java` file shown in the following code:

```
package com.kogent.android.hiuser;
import android.app.Activity;
import android.os.Bundle;
import android.widget.TextView;

public class Activity2 extends Activity {

   protected void onCreate(Bundle savedInstanceState)
     {
          // TODO Auto-generated method stub
          super.onCreate(savedInstanceState);
          final TextView message = new TextView(this);
```

```
            message.setText("Welcome ,"+getIntent().getExtras().getString("Name"));
            setContentView(message);
    }

}
```

Replace the code of the `activity_main.xml` file with the code shown below:

```
<RelativeLayout xmlns:android="http://schemas.android.com/apk/res/android"
    xmlns:tools="http://schemas.android.com/tools"
    android:layout_width="match_parent"
    android:layout_height="match_parent"
    tools:context=".MainActivity" >
    <TextView
        android:id="@+id/textView1"
        android:layout_width="wrap_content"
        android:layout_height="wrap_content"
        android:layout_alignParentLeft="true"
        android:layout_alignParentTop="true"
        android:layout_marginTop="20dp"
        android:text="Enter Your Name " />
    <EditText
        android:id="@+id/TextBox"
        android:layout_width="wrap_content"
        android:layout_height="wrap_content"
        android:layout_alignBaseline="@+id/textView1"
        android:layout_alignBottom="@+id/textView1"
        android:layout_alignParentRight="true"
        android:ems="10" />
    <Button
        android:id="@+id/Submit"
        android:layout_width="wrap_content"
        android:layout_height="wrap_content"
        android:layout_alignLeft="@+id/TextBox"
        android:layout_below="@+id/TextBox"
        android:layout_marginTop="21dp"
        android:text="Submit" />
</RelativeLayout>
```

Replace the code of the `AndroidManifest.xml` file with the code shown below:

```
<?xml version="1.0" encoding="utf-8"?>
<manifest xmlns:android="http://schemas.android.com/apk/res/android"
    package="com.kogent.android"
    android:versionCode="1"
    android:versionName="1.0" >
    <uses-sdk
        android:minSdkVersion="14"
        android:targetSdkVersion="19" />
    <application
        android:allowBackup="true"
        android:icon="@drawable/ic_launcher"
        android:label="@string/app_name"
        android:theme="@style/AppTheme" >
        <activity
            android:name="com.kogent.android.hiuser.MainActivity"
            android:label="@string/app_name" >
            <intent-filter>
                <action android:name="android.intent.action.MAIN" />

                <category android:name="android.intent.category.LAUNCHER" />
            </intent-filter>
        </activity>
        <activity android:name="com.kogent.android.hiuser.Activity2"
              android:label="UserDetails">
            <intent-filter>
                <action android:name="com.kogent.android.hiuser.Activity2" />
                <category android:name="android.intent.category.DEFAULT" />
```

```
            </intent-filter>
        </activity>
        </application>

</manifest>
```

Q14. Make an Android Application using the intent object to invoke the built-in browser and open google.com in it.

Ans. Create application with name, `BuiltInBrowser`. Replace the code of the `MainActivity.java` file with the code shown below:

```
package com.kogent.android.builtinbrowser;
import android.net.Uri;
import android.os.Bundle;
import android.app.Activity;
import android.content.Intent;
import android.view.View;
import android.widget.Button;

public class MainActivity extends Activity  {

   @Override
   protected void onCreate(Bundle savedInstanceState) {
         super.onCreate(savedInstanceState);
         setContentView(R.layout.activity_main);
         Button btnValidate = (Button)findViewById(R.id.Submit);
         btnValidate.setOnClickListener(new View.OnClickListener() {

                @Override
                public void onClick(View v) {
                       Intent viewIntent = new Intent("android.intent.action.VIEW",
                                     Uri.parse("http://www.google.com"));
                       startActivity(viewIntent);

                }
         });
   }
}
```

Replace the code of the `activity_main.xml` file with the code shown below:

```
<RelativeLayout xmlns:android="http://schemas.android.com/apk/res/android"
    xmlns:tools="http://schemas.android.com/tools"
    android:layout_width="match_parent"
    android:layout_height="match_parent"
    tools:context=".MainActivity" >
    <TextView
        android:id="@+id/textView1"
        android:layout_width="wrap_content"
        android:layout_height="wrap_content"
        android:layout_alignParentLeft="true"
        android:layout_alignParentTop="true"
        android:layout_marginTop="20dp"
        android:text="Press Submit to open Google.com" />
    <Button
        android:id="@+id/Submit"
        android:layout_width="wrap_content"
        android:layout_height="wrap_content"
        android:layout_alignLeft="@+id/textView1"
        android:layout_below="@+id/textView1"
        android:layout_marginTop="21dp"
        android:text="Submit" />
</RelativeLayout>
```

4

Working with the User Interface Using Views and ViewGroups

If you need an information on:	*See page:*
Working with View Groups	136
Binding Data with the AdapterView Class	174
Designing the AutoTextCompleteView	179
Implementing Screen Orientation	181
Designing the Views Programmatically	182
Handling UI Events	184
Specialized Fragments	187
Creating Menus	193

Developers of Android applications design the User Interface (UI) of the applications by using the Views and ViewGroups objects. There are various types of views and view groups, which are based on the View class. This class serves as the basis for designing interactive UI components, such as buttons, text fields, and check boxes. A View is a rectangular area on a user's screen on which the components are drawn as well as the events associated with these components are handled.

You can add views programmatically by providing the appropriate code in the Activity class. You can also provide the tree of views in the Extensible Markup Language (XML) layout files. Apart from defining the tree of views, you can also set the properties, listeners, focus, and visibility of the views. A specific view can be identified from the tree of views with the help of the ids that are defined in the XML layout files.

In this chapter, you learn about various types of ViewGroups, such as LinearLayout and ScrollView. Next, you learn how to work with Views and bind data using the AdapterView view. Then the chapter discusses about the AutoCompleteTextView view. It explains how to manage screen orientation and design UI programmatically. Further, the chapter explains how to handle events in Android and special fragments use. Finally, you learn to create various menus, such as context menu and options menu.

Let us learn how to create different layouts.

Working with View Groups

Generally, an activity contains views and view groups in different styles and arrangements. A view is a widget that is displayed on the screen of the users, such as buttons, text boxes, check boxes, and radio buttons. The base class of a view is `android.view.View`. The grouping of one or more views is known as `ViewGroup`. A `ViewGroup` helps you in specifying the layout according to which the views can be placed and arranged. Some of the layouts that can be defined for the views are `LinearLayout`, `RelativeLayout`, and `TableLayout`. A `ViewGroup` is derived from the `android.view.ViewGroup` base class.

Let us create an Android application, named Layouts, in which each layout is added by defining the Android XML file. For example, the linear_layout.xml file would be created for the `LinearLayout` layout and tree of views defined in this file would be set in an Activity class by invoking the `setContentView()` method. You need to create the Layouts application in the Eclipse IDE within the com.kogent.android package. While creating the Layouts application, by default, an activity class, the activity_main.xml file, and the Androidmanifest.xml file are created. You need to define the buttons for each layout so that when the user clicks a button, the appropriate layout is displayed. In our case, we have defined five buttons for each layout, i.e., `LinearLayout`, `RelativeLayout`, `TableLayout`, `ScrollingView`, and `TableLayout`. Listing 4.1 shows the code of the `activity_main.xml` file located in the /res/layout folder:

Listing 4.1: Showing the Code of the `activity_main.xml`File in the Layouts Application

```
<LinearLayout xmlns:android="http://schemas.android.com/apk/res/android"
    android:layout_width="fill_parent"
    android:layout_height="fill_parent"
    android:orientation="vertical" >
    <TextView
        android:layout_width="fill_parent"
        android:layout_height="wrap_content" />
    <Button
        android:id="@+id/linearlayout"
        android:layout_width="fill_parent"
        android:layout_height="wrap_content"
        android:gravity="left"
        android:text="Linear Layout" />
    <Button
        android:id="@+id/relativelayout"
        android:layout_width="fill_parent"
        android:layout_height="wrap_content"
        android:gravity="left"
        android:text="Relative Layout" />
    <Button
```

```
        android:id="@+id/scrollingview"
        android:layout_width="fill_parent"
        android:layout_height="wrap_content"
        android:gravity="left"
        android:text="Scroll View" />
    <Button
        android:id="@+id/tablelayout"
        android:layout_width="fill_parent"
        android:layout_height="wrap_content"
        android:gravity="left"
        android:text="Table Layout" />
    <Button
        android:id="@+id/framelayout"
        android:layout_width="fill_parent"
        android:layout_height="wrap_content"
        android:gravity="left"
        android:text="Frame Layout" />
</LinearLayout>
```

After you have defined all the required views in the `activity_main.xml` file, as shown in Listing 4.1, you can use these views in the activity class of the `Layouts` application. In our case, we have accessed these views (defined in Listing 4.1) in the `Layouts` activity class through their ids. Listing 4.2 shows the code of the `Layouts` activity class:

Listing 4.2: Showing the Code of the `Layouts` Activity Class in the Layouts Application

```
package com.kogent.android;
import android.app.Activity;
import android.content.Intent;
import android.os.Bundle;
import android.view.View;
import android.view.View.OnClickListener;
import android.widget.Button;
public class Layouts extends Activity implements OnClickListener {
   Button button_linearlayout, button_relativelayout, button_scrollview,
              button_tablelayout, button_framelayout;
   /** Called when the activity is first created. */
   @Override
   public void onCreate(Bundle savedInstanceState) {
         super.onCreate(savedInstanceState);
         setContentView(R.layout.activity_main);

         // Initializing the buttons declared as view components
         button_linearlayout = (Button) findViewById(R.id.linearlayout);
         button_relativelayout = (Button) findViewById(R.id.relativelayout);
         button_scrollview = (Button) findViewById(R.id.scrollingview);
         button_tablelayout = (Button) findViewById(R.id.tablelayout);
         button_framelayout = (Button) findViewById(R.id.framelayout);

         // Setting the click event for layout button
         button_linearlayout.setOnClickListener(this);
         button_relativelayout.setOnClickListener(this);
         button_scrollview.setOnClickListener(this);
         button_tablelayout.setOnClickListener(this);
         button_framelayout.setOnClickListener(this);
   }

   // Verifying which button has been clicked and accordingly the Activity is
   // being started
   public void onClick(View view) {
         if (view == findViewById(R.id.linearlayout)) {
```

```
                Intent i = new Intent(this, SampleLinearLayout.class);
                startActivity(i);
            }
            if (view == findViewById(R.id.relativelayout)) {
                Intent i = new Intent(this, SampleRelativeLayout.class);
                startActivity(i);
            }
            if (view == findViewById(R.id.scrollingview)) {
                Intent i = new Intent(this, SampleScrollingLayout.class);
                startActivity(i);
            }
            if (view == findViewById(R.id.tablelayout)) {
                Intent i = new Intent(this, SampleTableLayout.class);
                startActivity(i);
            }
            if (view == findViewById(R.id.framelayout)) {
                Intent i = new Intent(this, SampleFrameLayout.class);
                startActivity(i);
            }
        }
    }
```

In Listing 4.2, the views are identified through their ids by using the `findViewById()` method. The click event has been set for all the buttons through the `setOnClickListener()` method. Further, according to the button clicked, the appropriate activity is initiated. For example, if the linearlayout button has been clicked, then the `SampleLinearLayout` activity is started. Similarly, if the relativelayout button is clicked, then the `SampleRelativeLayout` activity is invoked.

When you add the code shown in Listing 4.2 in your activity class, the code may display some errors as you may not have defined the activity classes in the `AndroidManifest.xml` file. Moreover, you may not have created these activity classes. Ensure that you have defined all the activity classes in the `AndroidManifest.xml` file by using the <activity> element, as shown in Listing 4.3:

Listing 4.3: Showing the Code of the `AndroidManifest.xml` File in the Layouts Application

```
<?xml version="1.0" encoding="utf-8"?>
<manifest xmlns:android="http://schemas.android.com/apk/res/android"
    package="com.kogent.android"
    android:versionCode="1"
    android:versionName="1.0" >

    <uses-sdk
        android:minSdkVersion="14"
        android:targetSdkVersion="19" />

    <application
        android:allowBackup="true"
        android:icon="@drawable/ic_launcher"
        android:label="@string/app_name"
        android:theme="@style/AppTheme" >
        <activity
            android:name="com.kogent.android.Layouts"
            android:label="@string/app_name" >
            <intent-filter>
                <action android:name="android.intent.action.MAIN" />

                <category android:name="android.intent.category.LAUNCHER" />
            </intent-filter>
        </activity>
         <activity
            android:name=".SampleFrameLayout"
            android:label="Frame Layout" >
        </activity>
        <activity
```

```
            android:name=".SampleLinearLayout"
            android:label="Linear Layout" >
        </activity>
        <activity
            android:name=".SampleRelativeLayout"
            android:label="Relative Layout" >
        </activity>
        <activity
            android:name=".SampleScrollingLayout"
            android:label="Scrolling Layout" >
        </activity>
        <activity
            android:name=".SampleTableLayout"
            android:label="Table Layout" >
        </activity>

    </application>

</manifest>
```

In Listing 4.3, all the activities are defined by using the <activity> element.

Let us move ahead to create the activity classes and the Android XML file for each layout.

The LinearLayout Layout

LinearLayout aligns all the views in a single direction, either horizontal or vertical. You can set the direction by using the orientation attribute of the `<LinearLayout>` element. In this type of layout, all the views are placed one after the other; therefore, in case you have set the orientation as vertical, then only one view would be displayed in one row. You can set the LinearLayout either by using the `<LinearLayout>` element in the Android XML file or by using the `LinearLayout` class, which is the subclass of the `ViewGroup` class. If you are using the Android XML file, then you need to set this XML file as the argument for the `setContentView()` method in the `Activity` class. However, if you are using the `LinearLayout` class, then you need to create its instance and invoke the appropriate methods.

Table 4.1 lists the noteworthy attributes of the `<LinearLayout>` element:

Table 4.1: Noteworthy Attributes of the <LinearLayout> Element

Attribute	Description
`orientation`	Allows you to define the layout which can be either in row or column format. You can set the orientation as horizontal for row format and vertical for column format.
`gravity`	Allows you to arrange the content of an object corresponding to the specific x- and y-axes within the object.
`id`	Allows you to specify a unique id that can be used to identify the view group in the Activity class.
`layoutAnimation`	Defines the layout animation that can be used when the ViewGroup class is defined for the first time.
`background`	Allows you to define the resource that can be used as the background for the layout.
`focusable`	Specifies whether or not a View can accept focus. The Boolean type value can be assigned to this attribute.
`layout_width`	Allows you to provide the width of a View or ViewGroup.
`layout_height`	Allows you to provide the height of a View or ViewGroup.
`layout_marginTop`	Allows you to specify the margin area on the top side of a View or ViewGroup.

Table 4.1: Noteworthy Attributes of the <LinearLayout> Element	
Attribute	**Description**
layout_marginBottom	Allows you to specify the margin area of the bottom side of a View or ViewGroup.
layout_marginLeft	Allows you to specify the margin area on the left-side of a View or ViewGroup.
layout_marginRight	Allows you to specify the margin area on the right side of a View or ViewGroup.
layout_x	Allows you to provide the value for the x coordinate of the View or ViewGroup.
layout_y	Allows you to provide the value for the y coordinate of the View or ViewGroup.

After getting an overview of the XML attributes, let us move ahead and create the `linear_layout` XML file for the Layouts application. Listing 4.4 shows the code for the `linear_layout.xml` file that defines the LinearLayout class for the `Layouts` application:

Listing 4.4: Displaying the Code of the `linear_layout.xml` File in the Layouts Application

```
<?xml version="1.0" encoding="utf-8"?>
<LinearLayout
 xmlns:android="http://schemas.android.com/apk/res/android"
 android:orientation="vertical"
 android:layout_width="fill_parent"
 android:layout_height="fill_parent">
  <LinearLayout
        android:orientation="horizontal"
        android:layout_width="fill_parent"
        android:layout_height="fill_parent"
        android:layout_weight="1">
  <TextView
        android:text="Enter User Name"
        android:gravity="center_horizontal"
        android:layout_width="wrap_content"
        android:layout_height="fill_parent"
        android:background="#0000aa"
        android:textSize="30dp"
        android:layout_weight="1"/>
  <EditText
        android:gravity="center_horizontal"
        android:text="Your text"
        android:layout_width="wrap_content"
        android:layout_height="fill_parent"
        android:textSize="30dp"
        android:background="#00aa00"
        android:layout_weight="1"/>
  <TextView
        android:text="Enter Email Address"
        android:gravity="center_horizontal"
        android:layout_width="wrap_content"
        android:layout_height="fill_parent"
        android:textSize="30dp"
        android:background="#0000aa"
        android:layout_weight="1"/>
  <EditText
        android:text="Your text"
        android:gravity="center_horizontal"
        android:layout_width="wrap_content"
        android:layout_height="fill_parent"
        android:textSize="30dp"
        android:background="#00aa00"
        android:layout_weight="1"/>
  <Button
```

```
        android:layout_width="wrap_content"
        android:layout_height="wrap_content"
        android:layout_alignParentTop="true"
        android:layout_toRightOf="@+id/label_uname"
        android:text="Your Text" />
    <TextView
        android:id="@+id/label_uemail"
        android:layout_width="wrap_content"
        android:layout_height="wrap_content"
        android:layout_alignParentLeft="true"
        android:layout_below="@+id/label_uname"
        android:layout_marginTop="26dp"
        android:text="Enter User Email" />
    <EditText
        android:id="@+id/text_uemail"
        android:layout_width="wrap_content"
        android:layout_height="wrap_content"
        android:layout_alignLeft="@+id/text_uname"
        android:layout_alignTop="@+id/label_uemail"
        android:text="Your Text" />
    <Button
        android:id="@+id/login"
        android:layout_width="wrap_content"
        android:layout_height="wrap_content"
        android:layout_alignParentLeft="true"
        android:layout_below="@+id/label_uemail"
        android:layout_marginTop="28sp"
        android:text="Login" />
</RelativeLayout>
```

In Listing 4.6, the `<RelativeLayout>` element has been used to define the RelativeLayout for the Layouts application. Firstly, the TextView has been placed at the top and left of the View area. Note that the values of the `layout_alignParentTop` and `layout_alignParentLeft` attributes have been set to true. You should also remember that the id set for the TextView is `label_uname`. Next, the EditText view has been defined in the `relative_layout.xml` file. It is set on the right of the `label_uname` view. Note that the value of the `layout_toRightOf` attribute has been set to the `label_uname` TextView. Similarly, the other views have been defined in relation to each other.

Now, create the `SampleRelativeLayout` Activity in which the relative_layout view would be set. The code of the `SampleRelativeLayout` Activity class is same as provided for the `SampleLinearLayout` class in Listing 4.5. The only difference is that instead of the linear_layout.xml file, you need to set the relative_layout.xml file.

Let us now execute the Layouts application to view the RelativeLayout. The first screen of the application is the same as shown in Figure 4.1. Now, when you click the Relative Layout button to find, the output is displayed as shown in Figure 4.3:

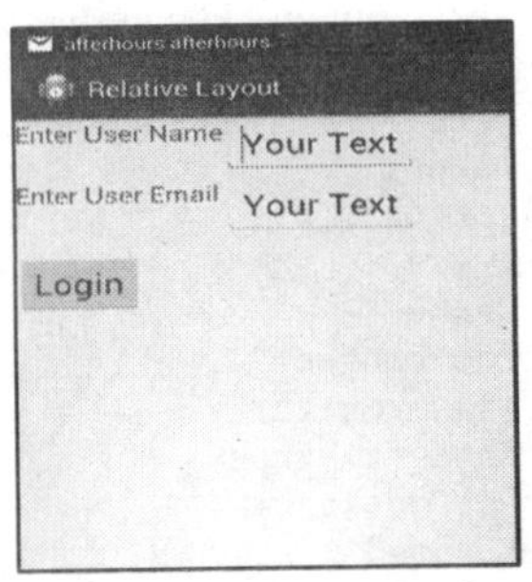

Figure 4.3: Showing the Relative Layout View


```
            android:text="Login"
            android:textSize="30dp"
            android:gravity="center_horizontal"
            android:layout_width="wrap_content"
            android:layout_height="fill_parent"
            android:background="#0000aa"
            android:layout_weight="1"/>
    </LinearLayout>
    <LinearLayout
            android:orientation="vertical"
            android:layout_width="fill_parent"
            android:layout_height="fill_parent"
            android:layout_weight="1">
    <TextView
            android:text="Enter User Name"
            android:gravity="center_horizontal"
            android:layout_width="fill_parent"
            android:layout_height="wrap_content"
            android:background="#aa0000"
            android:textSize="30dp"
            android:layout_weight="1"/>
    <EditText
            android:gravity="center_horizontal"
            android:text="Your text"
            android:layout_width="fill_parent"
            android:layout_height="wrap_content"
            android:textSize="30dp"
            android:background="#aaaa00"
            android:layout_weight="1"/>
    <TextView
            android:text="Enter Email Address"
            android:gravity="center_horizontal"
            android:layout_width="fill_parent"
            android:layout_height="wrap_content"
            android:textSize="30dp"
            android:background="#aa0000"
            android:layout_weight="1"/>
    <EditText
            android:text="Your text"
            android:gravity="center_horizontal"
            android:layout_width="fill_parent"
            android:layout_height="wrap_content"
            android:textSize="30dp"
            android:background="#aaaa00"
            android:layout_weight="1"/>
    <Button
            android:text="Login"
            android:textSize="30dp"
            android:gravity="center_horizontal"
            android:layout_width="fill_parent"
            android:layout_height="wrap_content"
            android:background="#aa0000"
            android:layout_weight="1"/>
    </LinearLayout>
</LinearLayout>
```

In Listing 4.4, the nested `LinearLayout` is defined in which the orientation of one layout has been set as horizontal while that of the other is set as vertical. After creating the XML file, let us create the Java class `SampleLinearLayout` and add the code shown in Listing 4.5:

Listing 4.5: Showing the Code of the SampleLinearLayout.java File in the Layouts Application

```
package com.kogent.android;
import android.app.Activity;
import android.os.Bundle;

public class SampleLinearLayout extends Activity {
   @Override
     public void onCreate(Bundle savedInstanceState)  {
```

```
        super.onCreate(savedInstanceState);
        setContentView(R.layout.linear_layout);

    }
}
```

In Listing 4.5, the linear_layout XML file is set as the View by invoking the setContentView() method. Now, execute the Layouts application, by right-clicking the application folder in the Package Explorer and selecting the Run As→Android Application. Figure 4.1 shows the output of the Layouts application:

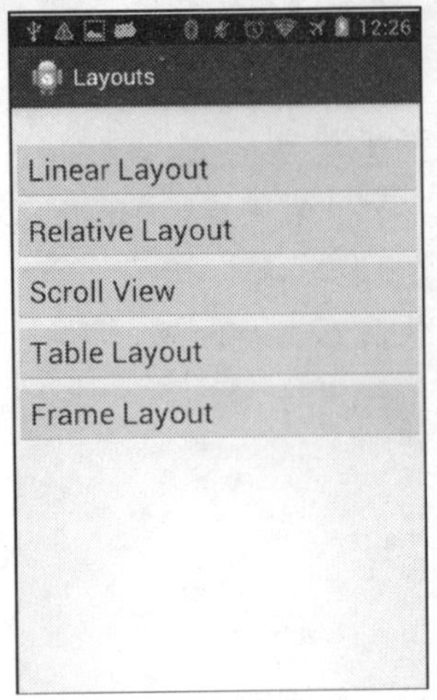

Figure 4.1: Displaying the Various Layouts in the Layouts Application

Now, click the **Linear Layout** button to view the linear layout, as shown in Figure 4.2:

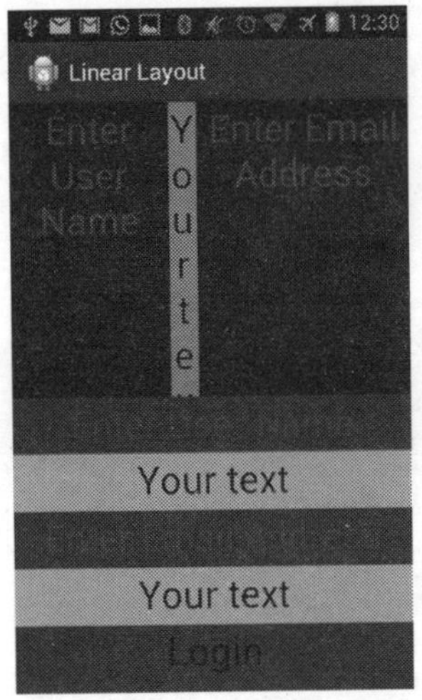

Figure 4.2: Showing the Linear Layout View

Figure 4.2 shows the horizontal and vertical layouts in the rows and columns formats, respectively. Note that these are the LinearLayout, whose display direction has been changed due to varied value set for the orientation attribute.

Let us now move ahead to learn about the other layout, i.e., RelativeLayout.

The RelativeLayout Layout

The RelativeLayout layout allows you to position the child views in relation to either each other parent. For example, if you have placed a TextView control at some place in the layout, th RelativeLayout, you can arrange the Button (or any other View) to the left, right, or below the TextView words, you can position the next View in relation to the previous View or the View defined earlier. describes the XML attributes that are used to refer the other view in the RelativeLayout:

Table 4.2: Description of the XML Attributes to Refer the Other View

Attribute	Description
android:layout_alignParentTop	Allows you to align the parent View at the top of the lay
android:layout_alignParentLeft	Allows you to left align the parent View
android:layout_alignParentRight	Allows you to right align the parent View
android:layout_alignParentBottom	Allows you to align the parent View at the bottom of the l
android:layout_alignLeft	Allows you to left align a View in the layout
android:layout_alignRight	Allows you to right align a View in the layout
android:layout_alignTop	Allows you to align a View at the top of the layout
android:layout_alignBottom	Allows you to align a View at the bottom of the layout
android:layout_below	Allows you to position a View below the other view th already been placed in the layout
android:layout_above	Allows you to place a View above the other view tha already been placed in the layout
android:layout_centerHorizontal	Allows you to position a View at the center horizontally in layout
android:layout_centerInParent	Allows you to position a View at the center of the parent V in the layout
android:layout_centerVertical	Allows you to position a View at the center vertically in layout
android:layout_toRightOf	Allows you to position a View on the right side of the ot View that has already been placed in the layout
android:layout_toLeftOf	Allows you to position a View on the left side of the other Vie that has already been placed in the layout

Let us now create the relative_layout XML file to define the RelativeLayout for the Layouts applicatio Listing 4.6 shows the code of the relative_layout.xml file:

Listing 4.6: Showing the Code of the relative_layout.xml File in the Layouts Application

```
<?xml version="1.0" encoding="utf-8"?>
<RelativeLayout xmlns:android="http://schemas.android.com/apk/res/android"
    android:layout_width="fill_parent"
    android:layout_height="fill_parent" >
    <TextView
        android:id="@+id/label_uname"
        android:layout_width="wrap_content"
        android:layout_height="wrap_content"
        android:layout_alignParentLeft="true"
        android:layout_alignParentTop="true"
        android:text="Enter User Name" />
    <EditText
        android:id="@+id/text_uname"
```

In Figure 4.3, you can see that the views have been arranged in relation to each other. Note that the text that can be edited is displayed on the right of the labels and the Button is displayed just below the `label_uemail` TextView.

The ScrollView Layout

The ScrollView is a layout container in which the users can scroll through the tree of views that are displayed. It occupies more space than the physical display. Generally, the child views are displayed in the LinearLayout within the vertical orientation. In this type of layout, the views are displayed in the form of vertical array through which a user can scroll.

Let us create the ScrollView layout in the Layouts application, containing a number of buttons displayed in the vertical orientation. This type of the ScrollView layout would be defined in the scrolling_layout XML file. Once the scrolling_layout XML file (view layout) is created, you need to create an Activity class in which this view layout should be set by invoking the setContentView() method.

Listing 4.7 shows the code of the scrolling_layout.xml file:

Listing 4.7: Displaying of the Code of the scrolling_layout.xml File in the Layouts Application

```
<?xml version="1.0" encoding="utf-8"?>
<ScrollView xmlns:android="http://schemas.android.com/apk/res/android"
    android:layout_width="match_parent"
    android:layout_height="match_parent" >
    <LinearLayout
        android:layout_width="fill_parent"
        android:layout_height="wrap_content"
        android:orientation="vertical" >

        <Button
            android:layout_width="fill_parent"
            android:layout_height="wrap_content"
            android:text="Button1" />

        <Button
            android:layout_width="fill_parent"
            android:layout_height="wrap_content"
            android:text="Button2" />

        <Button
            android:layout_width="fill_parent"
            android:layout_height="wrap_content"
            android:text="Button3" />

        <Button
            android:layout_width="fill_parent"
            android:layout_height="wrap_content"
            android:text="Button4" />

        <Button
            android:layout_width="fill_parent"
            android:layout_height="wrap_content"
            android:text="Button5" />

        <Button
            android:layout_width="fill_parent"
            android:layout_height="wrap_content"
            android:text="Button6" />

        <Button
            android:layout_width="fill_parent"
```

```
            android:layout_height="wrap_content"
            android:text="Button7" />

        <Button
            android:layout_width="fill_parent"
            android:layout_height="wrap_content"
            android:text="Button8" />

        <Button
            android:layout_width="fill_parent"
            android:layout_height="wrap_content"
            android:text="Button9" />

        <Button
            android:layout_width="fill_parent"
            android:layout_height="wrap_content"
            android:text="Button10" />

        <Button
            android:layout_width="fill_parent"
            android:layout_height="wrap_content"
            android:text="Button11" />

        <Button
            android:layout_width="fill_parent"
            android:layout_height="wrap_content"
            android:text="Button12" />
        <Button
            android:layout_width="fill_parent"
            android:layout_height="wrap_content"
            android:text="Button13" />

        <Button
            android:layout_width="fill_parent"
            android:layout_height="wrap_content"
            android:text="Button14" />

        <Button
            android:layout_width="fill_parent"
            android:layout_height="wrap_content"
            android:text="Button15" />

        <Button
            android:layout_width="fill_parent"
            android:layout_height="wrap_content"
            android:text="Button16" />

        <Button
            android:layout_width="fill_parent"
            android:layout_height="wrap_content"
            android:text="Button17" />

        <Button
            android:layout_width="fill_parent"
            android:layout_height="wrap_content"
            android:text="Button18" />
        <Button
            android:layout_width="fill_parent"
            android:layout_height="wrap_content"
```

```
            android:text="Button19" />

        <Button
            android:layout_width="fill_parent"
            android:layout_height="wrap_content"
            android:text="Button20" />
    </LinearLayout>

</ScrollView>
```

In Listing 4.7, 20 buttons have been created which can be viewed by the user by scrolling through. Now, you can create the SampleScrollingLayout Activity class in which the R.layout.scrolling_layout value has been passed as an argument to the setContentView() method.

After creating all the required files, let us execute the Layouts application, which would display Figure 4.1 as the welcome screen. Click the Scroll View button to find the output displayed, as shown in Figure 4.4:

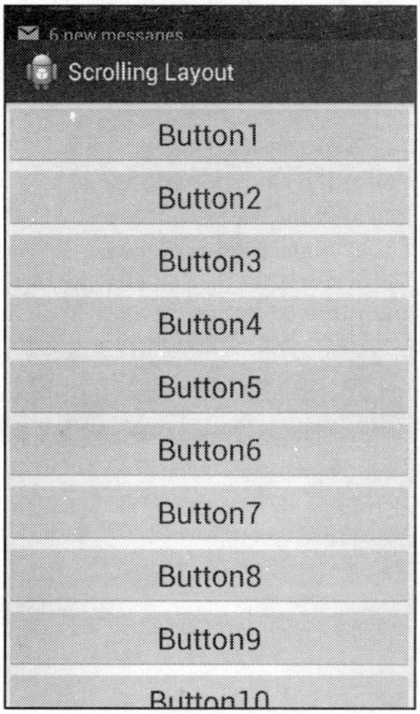

Figure 4.4: Showing the Scroll View

To view the 20 buttons, you need to scroll the view hierarchy. Initially, you might be able to view up to 10 buttons at a time, and to view further, you need to scroll the hierarchy.

Let us now discuss about the other layout known as the TableLayout.

The TableLayout Layout

In the TableLayout layout, the views are arranged in rows and columns. For this, you need to use the <TableRow> element and define the views that you want to be displayed in a row of the table. You can arrange each view as a cell of the row so that a row would contain multiple views. In the Layouts application, let us create the table_layout Android XML file in which the views are arranged to be displayed in the table format. Further, you need to set this layout (table_layout) in the Activity class to be defined for the TableLayout.

Listing 4.8 shows the code of the table_layout XML file:

Listing 4.8: Displaying the Code of the table_layout XML File in the Layouts Application

```
<?xml version="1.0" encoding="utf-8"?>
<TableLayout xmlns:android="http://schemas.android.com/apk/res/android"
```

```
        android:layout_width="match_parent"
        android:layout_height="match_parent" >
        <TableRow>
            <TextView
                android:text="Enter User Name" android:width="300px" />
            <EditText
                android:id="@+id/text_uname" android:width="200px" />
        </TableRow>
        <TableRow>
            <TextView
                android:text="Enter Email" android:width="300px" />
            <EditText
                android:id="@+id/text_uemail" android:width="200px" />
        </TableRow>
        <TableRow>
            <TextView />
            <Button
                android:id="@+id/login" android:text="Login" />
        </TableRow>
    </TableLayout>
```

In Listing 4.8, the <TableLayout> element has been used to define the TableLayout in which the rows are defined by using the <TableRow> subelement. Within a row, various views have been defined, such as the TextView and EditText views.

After creating the table_layout XML file, you can set it as the layout for the SampleTableLayout Activity class. Let us now execute the Layouts application to view the TableLayout. When you click the Table Layout button on the first screen of the Layouts application, the output displayed is as shown in Figure 4.5:

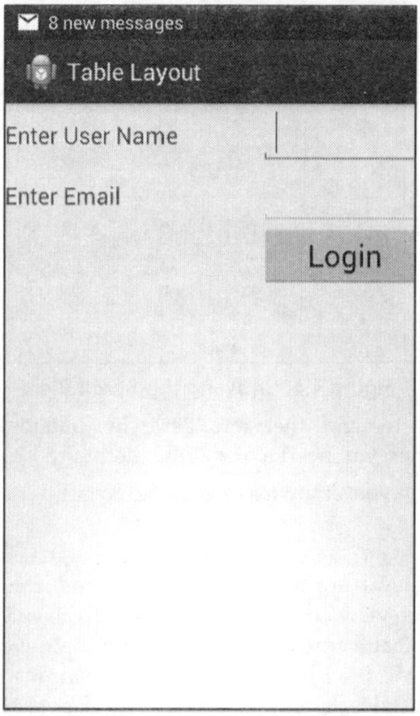

Figure 4.5: Displaying the Output of the SampleTableLayout Activity

Let us now learn how to work with the FrameLayout.

The FrameLayout Layout

The layout in which an area is used to display a single child view is known as FrameLayout. Generally, in different sizes of the screen, it is possible that the child elements or views of the layout may overlap each other. In this case, the FrameLayout layout is the suitable layout that can hold a single child view and allows you to control the positions of the various children views to be displayed. You can handle the positions of the child views by using the android:layout_gravity attribute.

In this section, you would learn how to design the FrameLayout. Let us create the frame_layout XML file in the Layouts application. Listing 4.9 shows the code of the frame_layout.xml file:

Listing 4.9: Displaying the Code of the frame_layout.xml File in the Layouts Application

```
<?xml version="1.0" encoding="utf-8"?>
<FrameLayout xmlns:android="http://schemas.android.com/apk/res/android"
    android:id="@+id/FrameLayout01"
    android:layout_width="fill_parent"
    android:layout_height="fill_parent" >
    <Button
        android:id="@+id/Button01"
        android:layout_width="wrap_content"
        android:layout_height="wrap_content"
        android:text="Register Now"
        android:textColor="#FF0000" >
    </Button>
    <Button
        android:id="@+id/Button02"
        android:layout_width="wrap_content"
        android:layout_height="wrap_content"
        android:text="Hello"
        android:textColor="#FF0000" >
    </Button>
</FrameLayout>
```

In Listing 4.9, the <FrameLayout> element has been used to define the FrameLayout in which two buttons are added as the view.

After creating the frame_layout.xml file, you can set it as the layout for the SampleFrameLayout Activity class. Let us now execute the Layouts application to view the FrameLayout. When you click the Frame Layout button on the first screen of the Layouts application, the output is displayed as shown in Figure 4.6:

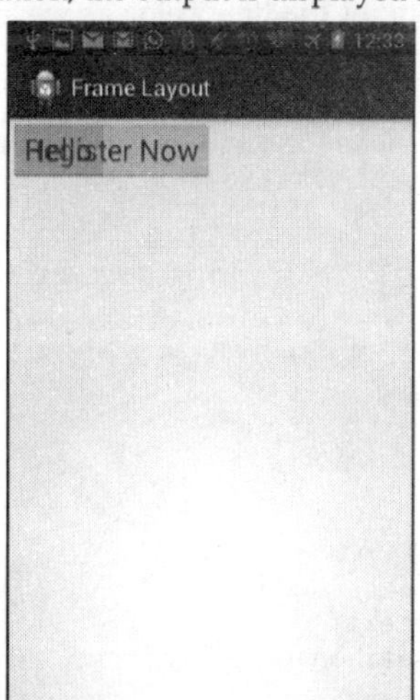

Figure 4.6: Showing the Frame Layout

Let us now move ahead and learn to design the TabLayout.

The TabLayout Using the Action Bar

The TabActivity class has been deprecated in Android 4.0, and the new concept called action bar is used. Prior to API 4.0, the action bar did not have tabbed view facility.

The action bar pertains to the UI of application in Android 4.4 in an enhanced manner. The basic intention to employ action bar is to:

i. Identify the application and user location

ii. Assist in user actions and navigation modes

In best practices, a developer should use the action bar in the activity, which is associated with more user actions or navigations. The use of action bar ensures that you have as much dedicated space on the screen as you want. The dedicated space can be generated through the different tabs. The ActionBar APIs fulfill all the requirements of a developer to develop a powerful and efficient action bar. Some primary goals behind the adoption of action bar in an application are as follows:

- Action bar provides the way to identify the user location and application brand through a dedicated space.
- It provides easy navigation across multiple applications.
- Action empowers the user with some of the most frequently used activities, such as share, create, and search. This can be done by plugging an option menu into the action bar.

Prior to Android 4.0, there was not much flexibility in the action bar. The action bar with tabs is the new feature in Android 4.0. The setNavigationmode() method of the ActionBar class is used to create tabs on the action bar. The following code snippet shows the way to set the navigation mode for tabs:

```
ActionBar actionbar = getActionBar();
actionbar.setNavigationMode(ActionBar.NAVIGATION_MODE_TABS);
```

Besides this, fragments are also used to empower the action bar. A fragment is used to display a distinct working set for an activity in a specified portion. A collection of fragments can be employed in an activity for multipanel user interfaces, and one can also reuse the code of a fragment across multiple activities. It follows a modular approach and can be taken as a module of an activity.

To get more insight into the working of the action bar, let us make an application, named ActionBar. Create a new project named ActionBar inside the com.kogent.android package using Android 4.4 (API level 19). Name the main activity class as the ActionBarActivity class and continue with the other default settings. Add the code shown in Listing 4.10 in the ActionBarActivity class. When you execute this code, you will find some errors due to some unavailable classes. Ignore them for the time being as we are going to create them in the forthcoming steps. All the errors will disappear at the end of all the steps. Now let us write the code for the ActionBarActivity class as shown in Listing 4.10:

Listing 4.10: Displaying the Code of the ActionBarActivity Class in the ActionBar Application

```
package com.kogent.android;

import android.app.ActionBar;
import android.app.ActionBar.Tab;
import android.app.Activity;
import android.app.Fragment;
import android.content.Context;
import android.os.Bundle;
import android.util.Log;

public class ActionBarActivity extends Activity {

   public static Context myContext;
   /** Called on first time creation of of activity */
   @Override
   public void onCreate(Bundle savedInstanceState) {
          super.onCreate(savedInstanceState);
          setContentView(R.layout.activity_main);
          myContext = getApplicationContext();
```

```
        try {
            /*
             *  ActionBar   for   the   current   navigation   mode   The   tabs   are
                 navigating
             * within the activity
             */
            ActionBar actionbar = getActionBar();
            actionbar.setNavigationMode(ActionBar.NAVIGATION_MODE_TABS);

            // Tab creation
            Tab tab1 = actionbar.newTab().setText("Tab 1");
            Tab tab2 = actionbar.newTab().setText("Tab 2");
            Tab tab3 = actionbar.newTab().setText("Tab 3");
            Tab tab4 = actionbar.newTab().setText("Tab 4");

            /*
             *  Fragment  creation.  A  fragment  is  the  space  under  the  activity
                 to
             * display the tab contents
             */
            Fragment fragment1 = new FirstFragment();
            Fragment fragment2 = new SecondFragment();
            Fragment fragment3 = new ThirdFragment();
            Fragment fragment4 = new FourthFragment();

            // listening for tapping on tabs
            tab1.setTabListener(new MyTabsListner(fragment1));
            tab2.setTabListener(new MyTabsListner(fragment2));
            tab3.setTabListener(new MyTabsListner(fragment3));
            tab4.setTabListener(new MyTabsListner(fragment4));

            // Addition of tabs to UI
            actionbar.addTab(tab1);
            actionbar.addTab(tab2);
            actionbar.addTab(tab3);
            actionbar.addTab(tab4);
        } catch (Exception ex) {
            Log.e("error from onCreate", ex.toString());
            Log.e("error from onCreate", ex.getStackTrace().toString());
            // TODO: handle exception
        }
    }
}
```

Since the listener method will be invoked each time a tab is clicked, we have to create a class that listens the tab when they are being invoked. Note that we have already implemented this class in the preceding step. Let us create the MyTabsListner Java class whose code is given in Listing 4.11:

Listing 4.11: Showing the Code of the MyTabsListner Class in the ActionBar Application

```
package com.kogent.android;

import android.annotation.SuppressLint;
import android.app.ActionBar;
import android.app.ActionBar.Tab;
import android.app.Fragment;
import android.app.FragmentTransaction;
import android.widget.Toast;

// This class is invoked when an action is performed on tabs
```

```
@SuppressLint("NewApi") public class MyTabsListner implements ActionBar.TabListener {
   public Fragment fragment;

   // Creating fragment for activity
   public MyTabsListner(Fragment fragment) {
         this.fragment = fragment;
   }
   // On successive tapping or clicking of tabs
   @Override
   public void onTabReselected(Tab tab, FragmentTransaction transaction) {
         Toast.makeText(ActionBarActivity.myContext, "You have clicked again!",
                        Toast.LENGTH_LONG).show();
   }
   // On first time tapping or clicking of tabs
   @Override
   public void onTabSelected(Tab tab, FragmentTransaction transaction) {
         transaction.replace(R.id.actionbar, fragment);
   }
   // When tabs are not selected
   @Override
   public void onTabUnselected(Tab tab, FragmentTransaction transaction) {
         transaction.remove(fragment);
   }
}
```

Now we can write the code for each of the fragment or tab. A much simple code is given for these classes, and here, we have provided the code of only one class, which is the FirstFragment java class. You can create the remaining three classes easily by replacing "firstfragment" with secondfragment, thirdfragment, and fourthfragment in the SecondFragment, ThirdFragment, and FourthFragment classes, respectively. Actually, these are the xml classes residing in the res/layout folder of the project. We will create them in the forthcoming steps. The code for the FirstFragment class is given in Listing 4.12:

Listing 4.12: Displaying the Code of the FirstFragment Class in the ActionBar Application

```
package com.kogent.android;
import android.annotation.SuppressLint;
import android.app.Fragment;
import android.os.Bundle;
import android.view.LayoutInflater;
import android.view.View;
import android.view.ViewGroup;

@SuppressLint("NewApi") public class FirstFragment extends Fragment {
   @Override
   public View onCreateView(LayoutInflater inflater, ViewGroup container,
               Bundle savedInstanceState) {
         // Inflate the layout for this fragment
   return inflater.inflate(R.layout.firstfragment, container, false);
   }
}
```

Let us now create the xml classes in the res/layout folder, which are the firstfragment, secondfragment, thirdfragment, and fourthfragment xml files. Listing 4.13 shows the code for the firstfragment.xml file:

Listing 4.13: Displaying the Code of the firstfragment.xml File in the ActionBar Application

```
<?xml version="1.0" encoding="utf-8"?>
<LinearLayout xmlns:android="http://schemas.android.com/apk/res/android"
    android:layout_width="match_parent"
    android:layout_height="match_parent"
    android:orientation="vertical" >
    <TextView
```

```
            android:id="@+id/textView1"
            android:layout_width="wrap_content"
            android:layout_height="wrap_content"
            android:text="This is First Tab"
            android:textSize="20sp" />
    </LinearLayout>
```

You can easily create the remaining three xml files by replacing the id and text attributes. The following code snippet shows the applicable changes for the secongfragment.xml file:

```
    android:id="@+id/textView2"
    ...
    ...
    android:text="This is Second Tab"
```

Similarly, by changing these attributes, other files can be created. Finally, the code for the activity_main.xml file is given in Listing 4.14:

Listing 4.14: Displaying the Code of the activity_main.xml File in the ActionBar Application

```
    <?xml version="1.0" encoding="utf-8"?>
    <LinearLayout xmlns:android="http://schemas.android.com/apk/res/android"
        android:layout_width="fill_parent"
        android:layout_height="fill_parent"
        android:layout_gravity="center"
        android:orientation="vertical" >
     <LinearLayout
            android:id="@+id/actionbar"
            android:layout_width="match_parent"
            android:layout_height="match_parent"
               android:orientation="vertical">
       </LinearLayout>
    </LinearLayout>
```

Figure 4.7 shows the complete directory structure created so far:

Figure 4.7: Showing the Directory Structure of the ActionBar Application

Now, the creation of the ActionBar application is complete, so let us execute it. When we execute this application, it will look like in device, as shown in Figure 4.8:

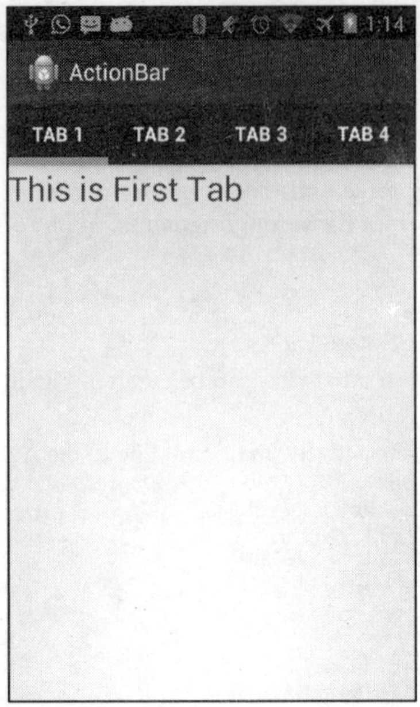

Figure 4.8: Showing the Execution of the ActionBar Application

Now, if you click Tab 2, Tab 3, and Tab 4, then the message written in their respective XML file will be displayed.

Working with Views

In an Android application, an activity contains various views, such as TextView, Button, RadioButton, and CheckBox, which are used to design an UI. Generally, there are three types of views, namely, basic views, picker views, and list views. The basic views are the general views, such as TextView, EditText, and Button. The picker views allow the users to choose from a view, such as TimePicker and DatePicker. The TimePicker and DatePicker views are used to select the desired time and date, respectively. The list views display the list of items. Some examples of the list views are ListView and SpinnerView. Let us create an Android application, InputControl, which will display different types of views.

Perform the following steps to create the InputControl application:

1. Create the InputControl application in the Eclipse IDE under the com.kogent.android package.
2. Modify the code of the activity_main.xml file, located in the /res/layout folder, as shown in Listing 4.15:

Listing 4.15: Displaying the Code of the activity_main.xml File in the InputControl Application

```
<LinearLayout xmlns:android="http://schemas.android.com/apk/res/android"
    android:layout_width="fill_parent"
    android:layout_height="fill_parent"
    android:orientation="vertical" >
    <TextView
        android:layout_width="fill_parent"
        android:layout_height="wrap_content" />

    <Button
        android:id="@+id/textview"
        android:layout_width="fill_parent"
        android:layout_height="wrap_content"
        android:gravity="left"
        android:text="Text View" />

    <Button
        android:id="@+id/edittext "
```

```
        android:layout_width="fill_parent"
        android:layout_height="wrap_content"
        android:gravity="left"
        android:text="Edit Text " />

    <Button
        android:id="@+id/buttonview"
        android:layout_width="fill_parent"
        android:layout_height="wrap_content"
        android:gravity="left"
        android:text="Button View" />

    <Button
        android:id="@+id/radiobuttonview"
        android:layout_width="fill_parent"
        android:layout_height="wrap_content"
        android:gravity="left"
        android:text="RadioButton View" />

    <Button
        android:id="@+id/checkboxview"
        android:layout_width="fill_parent"
        android:layout_height="wrap_content"
        android:gravity="left"
        android:text="CheckBox View" />

    <Button
        android:id="@+id/imagebuttonview"
        android:layout_width="fill_parent"
        android:layout_height="wrap_content"
        android:gravity="left"
        android:text="ImageButton View" />

    <Button
        android:id="@+id/togglebuttonview"
        android:layout_width="fill_parent"
        android:layout_height="wrap_content"
        android:gravity="left"
        android:text="ToggleButton View" />

    <Button
        android:id="@+id/ratingbarview"
        android:layout_width="fill_parent"
        android:layout_height="wrap_content"
        android:gravity="left"
        android:text="RatingBar View" />
</LinearLayout>
```

In Listing 4.15, eight buttons are added to display different views in a linear layout.

3. Add the following XML files in the /res/layout folder:
   - textview_layout.xml
   - edittext_layout.xml
   - buttonview_layout.xml
   - radiobuttonview_layout.xml
   - checkboxview_layout.xml
   - imagebuttonview_layout.xml
   - togglebuttonview_layout.xml
   - ratingbarview_layout.xml

NOTE

The codes of preceding listed files are explained later.

4. Create the following Java files in the /src folder within the com.kogent.android package:
   - TextView.java
   - EditTextView.java
   - ButtonView.java
   - RadioButtonView.java
   - CheckBoxView.java
   - ImageButtonView.java
   - ToggleButtonView.java
   - RatingBarView.java

NOTE

The codes of preceding listed files are explained later.

5. Modify the code of the MainActivity.java file, located in the /src/com/kogent/android folder, as shown in Listing 4.16:

Listing 4.16: Displaying the Code of the MainActivity.java File in the InputControl Application

```
package com.kogent.android;

import android.app.Activity;
import android.content.Intent;
import android.os.Bundle;
import android.view.View;
import android.view.View.OnClickListener;
import android.widget.Button;

public class MainActivity extends Activity implements OnClickListener {
   Button button_textview, button_edittext, button_buttonview,
   button_radiobuttonview, button_checkboxview,button_imagebuttonview,
   button_togglebuttonview, button_ratingbarview;

   /** Called when the activity is first created. */
   @Override
   public void onCreate(Bundle savedInstanceState) {
         super.onCreate(savedInstanceState);
         setContentView(R.layout.activity_main);

         // Initializing the buttons declared as view components
         button_textview = (Button) findViewById(R.id.textview);
         button_edittext = (Button) findViewById(R.id.edittext);
         button_buttonview = (Button) findViewById(R.id.buttonview);
         button_radiobuttonview = (Button) findViewById(R.id.radiobuttonview);
         button_checkboxview = (Button) findViewById(R.id.checkboxview);
         button_imagebuttonview = (Button) findViewById(R.id.imagebuttonview);
         button_togglebuttonview = (Button) findViewById(R.id.togglebuttonview);
         button_ratingbarview = (Button) findViewById(R.id.ratingbarview);


         // Setting the click event for layout button
         button_textview.setOnClickListener(this);
         button_edittext.setOnClickListener(this);
         button_buttonview.setOnClickListener(this);
         button_radiobuttonview.setOnClickListener(this);
         button_checkboxview.setOnClickListener(this);
         button_imagebuttonview.setOnClickListener(this);
         button_togglebuttonview.setOnClickListener(this);
         button_ratingbarview.setOnClickListener(this);
```

```
    }

    // Verifying which button has been clicked and accordingly the Activity is
    // being started
    public void onClick(View view) {
            if (view == findViewById(R.id.textview)) {
                    Intent i = new Intent(this, TextView.class);
                    startActivity(i);
            }
            if (view == findViewById(R.id.edittext)) {
                    Intent i = new Intent(this, EditTextView.class);
                    startActivity(i);
            }
            if (view == findViewById(R.id.buttonview)) {
                    Intent i = new Intent(this, ButtonView.class);
                    startActivity(i);
            }
            if (view == findViewById(R.id.radiobuttonview)) {
                    Intent i = new Intent(this, RadioButtonView.class);
                    startActivity(i);
            }
            if (view == findViewById(R.id.checkboxview)) {
                    Intent i = new Intent(this, CheckBoxView.class);
                    startActivity(i);
            }
            if (view == findViewById(R.id.imagebuttonview)) {
                    Intent i = new Intent(this, ImageButtonView.class);
                    startActivity(i);
            }
            if (view == findViewById(R.id.togglebuttonview)) {
                    Intent i = new Intent(this, ToggleButtonView.class);
                    startActivity(i);
            }
            if (view == findViewById(R.id.ratingbarview)) {
                    Intent i = new Intent(this, RatingBarView.class);
                    startActivity(i);
            }

    }
}
```

In Listing 4.16, all the previously created Java classes are called and their respective activity will be start if the user selects any of these.

6. Modify the code of the AndroidManifest.xml file, as shown in Listing 4.17:

Listing 4.17: Displaying the Code of the AndroidManifest.xml File in the InputControl Application

```
<?xml version="1.0" encoding="utf-8"?>
<manifest xmlns:android="http://schemas.android.com/apk/res/android"
    package="com.kogent.android"
    android:versionCode="1"
    android:versionName="1.0" >

    <uses-sdk
        android:minSdkVersion="8"
        android:targetSdkVersion="19" />

    <application
        android:allowBackup="true"
        android:icon="@drawable/ic_launcher"
        android:label="@string/app_name"
        android:theme="@style/AppTheme" >
        <activity
            android:name="com.kogent.android.MainActivity"
            android:label="@string/app_name" >
            <intent-filter>
                <action android:name="android.intent.action.MAIN" />
```

```
                <category android:name="android.intent.category.LAUNCHER" />
            </intent-filter>
        </activity>
        <activity
            android:name=".TextView"
            android:label="TextView" >
        </activity>
        <activity
            android:name=".EditTextView"
            android:label="EditTextView" >
        </activity>
        <activity
            android:name=".ButtonView"
            android:label="ButtonView" >
        </activity>
        <activity
            android:name=".CheckBoxView"
            android:label="CheckBoxView" >
        </activity>
        <activity
            android:name=".ImageButtonView"
            android:label="ImageButtonView" >
        </activity>
        <activity
            android:name=".ToggleButtonView"
            android:label="ToggleButtonView" >
        </activity>
        <activity
            android:name=".RadioButtonView"
            android:label="RadioButtonView" >
        </activity>
        <activity
            android:name=".RatingBarView"
            android:label="RatingBarView" >
        </activity>
    </application>

</manifest>
```

In Listing 4.17, all the activities classes are configured.

7. Execute the InputControl application by selecting the Run→Run As→Android Application. Figure 4.9 shows the output of the InputControl application:

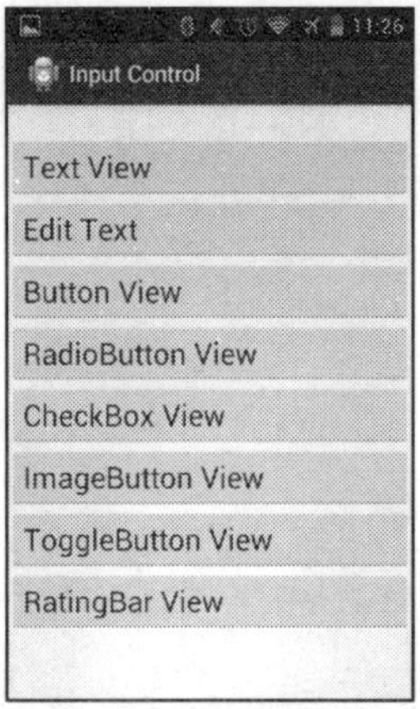

Figure 4.9: Displaying the Output of the InputControl Application

In Figure 4.9, you see various buttons displaying the names of different views. Let's learn about these views in the following sections along with the different Java and XML files created in the InputControl application.

Using the TextView

The TextView view is used to display the texts that are used frequently in the Android applications. You can create the TextView view by using the <TextView> element in an Android XML file, which is located in the res/layout folder of the application. Table 4.3 shows the noteworthy XML attributes of the <TextView> element:

Table 4.3: Description of the Noteworthy XML Attributes of the <TextView> Element

Attribute	Description
`android:gravity`	Allows you to align the text according to the x- or y-axis of the view, provided the text to be displayed is smaller than the view.
`android:height`	Allows you to set the height of the TextView view. You should ensure that the value of this attribute is being provided in pixels.
`android:hint`	Allows you to set the hint text to be displayed if no text has been specified.
`android:lines`	Allows you to set the number of lines you want the text that can be displayed in the TextView view.
`android:text`	Allows you to set the text to be displayed.
`android:textSize`	Allows you to set the size of the text to be displayed. You should ensure that the text size should be in dp.
`android:textAppearance`	Allows you to set the text color, typeface, size, and style.

In the InputControl application, the textview_layout.xml file is created in the /res/layout location, which dispiays the use of the <TextView> element. Listing 4.18 shows the code of the textview_layout.xml file:

Listing 4.18: Displaying the Code of the textview_layout.xml File in the InputControl Application

```
<LinearLayout xmlns:android="http://schemas.android.com/apk/res/android"
    android:layout_width="fill_parent"
    android:layout_height="fill_parent"
    android:orientation="vertical" >

    <TextView
        android:id="@+id/sampletextview"
        android:layout_width="fill_parent"
        android:layout_height="wrap_content"
        android:text="This is sample text view"
        android:textSize="30dp" >
    </TextView>

</LinearLayout>
```

In Listing 4.18, a TextView control is added by using the <TextView> tag to display the text, "This is sample text view". Corresponding to the textview_layout.xml file, the TextView Java class is created in the InputControl application to display the use of text view. Listing 4.19 shows the code of the TextView.java file:

Listing 4.19: Displaying the Code of the TextView.java File in the InputControl Application

```
package com.kogent.android;
import android.app.Activity;
import android.os.Bundle;
import android.widget.Button;
public class TextView extends Activity {
  @Override
  public void onCreate(Bundle savedInstanceState) {
        super.onCreate(savedInstanceState);
        setContentView(R.layout.textview_layout);
        Button button_textview = (Button) findViewById(R.id.textview);
  }
}
```

In Listing 4.19, a text view is attached with a button, and the name of the textview_layout.xml file is specified within the setContentView() method.

When you execute the InputControl application and click the Text View button, you see a text view, as shown in Figure 4.10:

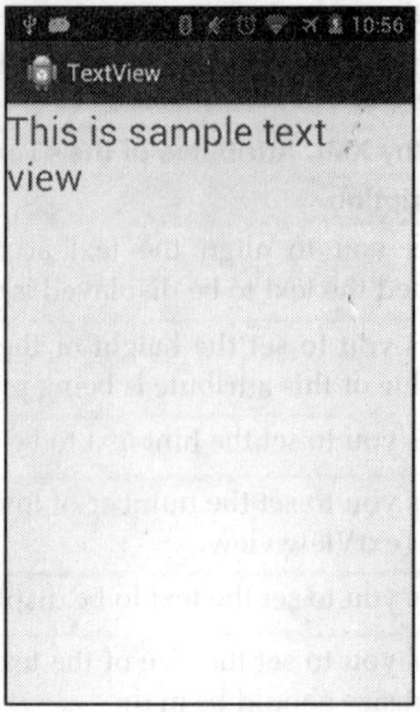

Figure 4.10: Displaying the Output of the TextView Activity

If you want an editable text field, then instead of using the TextView view, you should use the EditText view.

Next, let us discuss about the EditText view.

Using the EditText View

The EditText view is the editable TextView, which implies that the users are allowed to edit the text of the EditText view. The EditText view can be set in the Android XML file by using the <EditText> element or by creating the instance of the android.widget.EditText class in the Activity class. The EditText class is the subclass of the TextView class; therefore, the XML attributes are the same.

In the InputControl application, the edittext_layout.xml file is created in the /res/layout location, which displays the use of the <EditText> element. Listing 4.20 shows the code of the edittext_layout.xml file:

Listing 4.20: Displaying the Code of the edittext_layout.xml File in the InputControl Application

```
<LinearLayout xmlns:android="http://schemas.android.com/apk/res/android"
    android:layout_width="fill_parent"
    android:layout_height="fill_parent"
    android:orientation="vertical" >

    <EditText
        android:id="@+id/sampleeditview"
        android:layout_width="fill_parent"
        android:layout_height="wrap_content"
        android:text="This is sample text view"
        android:textSize="30dp" >
    </EditText>

</LinearLayout>
```

In Listing 4.20, an EditText control is added by using the <EditText> tag to display the editable text, "This is sample text view". Corresponding to the edittext_layout.xml file, the EditTextView Java class is created in the InputControl application to display the use of editable text view. Listing 4.21 shows the code of the EditTextView.java file:

Listing 4.21: Displaying the Code of the EditTextView.java File in the InputControl Application

```
package com.kogent.android;
```

```
import android.app.Activity;
import android.os.Bundle;
import android.widget.EditText;

public class EditTextView extends Activity {
   @Override
   public void onCreate(Bundle savedInstanceState) {
          super.onCreate(savedInstanceState);
          setContentView(R.layout.edittext_layout);
          final EditText edit = (EditText) findViewById(R.id.sampleeditview);

   }
}
```

In Listing 4.21, an editable text view is attached with a button, and the name of the edittext_layout.xml file is specified within the setContentView() method.

When you execute the InputControl application and click the Edit Text button, you see an editable text view, as shown in Figure 4.11:

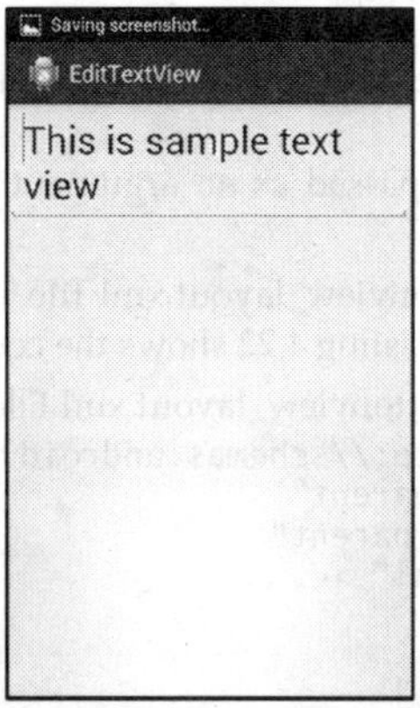

Figure 4.11: Displaying the Output of the EditTextView Activity

Let us now learn how to create a button in an Activity class.

Using the Button View

The Button view is a push button widget that can be either clicked or pressed, and accordingly, the events can be set, such as click event. Generally, you can declare or define a button in the Android XML file by using the following code snippet:

```
<Button
   android:id="@+id/button1"
   android:text="Click Me"
   android:textSize="30dp"
   android:layout_width="wrap_content"
   android:layout_height="wrap_content"
   android:background="#0000aa">
</Button>
```

Once you have defined the Button view, let us now look at the code to set the click listener. The following code snippet shows the implementation of the OnClickListener interface:

```
Button button1 = (Button) findViewById(R.id.button1);
button1.setOnClickListener(new View.OnClickListener() {
public void onClick(View v) {
// Provide the code to implement the click operation
}
});
```

Instead of providing the preceding code in the Activity class, you can also specify in the XML file, the method to be invoked the onClick() operation. The following code snippet shows how to set the method for the click operation in the Android XML file:

```
<Button
   android:id="@+id/button1"
   android:text="Click Me"
   android:textSize="30dp"
   android:layout_width="wrap_content"
   android:layout_height="wrap_content"
   android:background="#0000aa"
   android:onClick="method1">
</Button>
```

Now, if a user clicks the "button1" button, then the Android system invokes the method1(View) method of the Activity class. For this, you need to declare the method1 method in the Activity class, which accepts View as a parameter, as shown in the following code snippet:

```
public void method1(View v) {
// Provide the code to implement the click operation
}
```

In the preceding code snippet, the View passed as an argument is the reference of the widget that has been clicked by the user.

In the InputControl application, the buttonview_layout.xml file is created in the /res/layout location, which displays the use of the <Button> element. Listing 4.22 shows the code of the buttonview_layout.xml file:

Listing 4.22: Displaying the Code of the buttonview_layout.xml File in the InputControl Application

```
<LinearLayout xmlns:android="http://schemas.android.com/apk/res/android"
    android:layout_width="fill_parent"
    android:layout_height="fill_parent"
    android:orientation="vertical" >

    <Button
        android:id="@+id/button1"
        android:layout_width="wrap_content"
        android:layout_height="wrap_content"
        android:background="#0000aa"
        android:text="Click Me"
        android:textSize="30dp" >
    </Button>

</LinearLayout>
```

In Listing 4.22, the <Button> tag is used to display a button, which is having the Click Me text. Corresponding to the buttonview_layout.xml file, the ButtonView Java class is created in the InputControl application to display the use of a button view. Listing 4.23 shows the code of the ButtonView.java file:

Listing 4.23: Displaying the Code of the ButtonView.java File in the InputControl Application

```
package com.kogent.android;

import android.app.Activity;
import android.os.Bundle;
import android.view.View;
import android.widget.Button;
import android.widget.Toast;

public class ButtonView extends Activity {
   @Override
   public void onCreate(Bundle savedInstanceState) {
          super.onCreate(savedInstanceState);
          setContentView(R.layout.buttonview_layout);
          Button button1 = (Button) findViewById(R.id.button1);
          button1.setOnClickListener(new View.OnClickListener() {
```

```
                public void onClick(View v) {
        // Provide the code to implement the click operation
                        Toast.makeText(ButtonView.this, "ButtonView is clicked!",
                                        Toast.LENGTH_SHORT).show();
                }
        });
    }
}
```

In Listing 4.23, the ButtonView class extends the Activity class and displays a button, "Click Me". When a user clicks this button, the "ButtonView is clicked!" message is displayed, as shown in Figure 4.12:

Figure 4.12: Displaying the Output of the ButtonView Activity

Let us now create the RadioButton view.

Using the RadioButton View

The RadioButton view has two states, i.e., either checked or unchecked. A user can click the unchecked radio button to change its state. However, you should note that the RadioButton view cannot be unchecked by re-clicking it; you need to click the other RadioButton view. Generally, the radio buttons are grouped together in a RadioGroup. The following code snippet allows you to create the RadioButton view:

```
<RadioGroup
  android:layout_width="fill_parent"
  android:layout_height="wrap_content"
  android:orientation="vertical">
<RadioButton android:id="@+id/radio_male"
  android:layout_width="wrap_content"
  android:layout_height="wrap_content"
  android:text="Male"
android:textSize="30dp"/>
<RadioButton android:id="@+id/radio_female"
  android:layout_width="wrap_content"
  android:layout_height="wrap_content"
  android:text="Female"
android:textSize="30dp"/>
</RadioGroup>
```

In the preceding code snippet, a RadioGroup view has been defined with two RadioButton views, namely, radio_male and radio_female. To provide some action that would be performed on clicking of either of the radio buttons, you can provide the following code snippet:

```
    protected void onCreate(Bundle savedInstanceState) {
            super.onCreate(savedInstanceState);
            setContentView(R.layout.activity_main);
            RadioButton radio_male = (RadioButton) findViewById(R.id.radio_male);
           RadioButton radio_female = (RadioButton) findViewById(R.id.radio_female);
           radio_male.setOnClickListener(radiolistener);
           radio_female.setOnClickListener(radiolistener);

    }
      private OnClickListener radiolistener = new OnClickListener()
      {
      public void onClick(View view)
      {
            RadioButton radiobutton = (RadioButton) view;
            Toast.makeText(MainActivity.this, radiobutton.getText(),
    Toast.LENGTH_LONG).show();
            }
      };
```

In the InputControl application, the radiobuttonview_layout.xml file is created in the /res/layout location, which displays the use of radio buttons. Listing 4.24 shows the code of the radiobuttonview_layout.xml file:

Listing 4.24: Displaying the Code of the radiobuttonview_layout.xml File in the InputControl Application

```
   <LinearLayout xmlns:android="http://schemas.android.com/apk/res/android"
       android:layout_width="fill_parent"
       android:layout_height="fill_parent"
       android:orientation="vertical" >
    //Defining the RadioGroup to hold RadioButtons

       <RadioGroup
           android:layout_width="fill_parent"
           android:layout_height="wrap_content"
           android:orientation="vertical" >
   //Defining the First RadioButton

           <RadioButton
               android:id="@+id/radio_male"
               android:layout_width="wrap_content"
               android:layout_height="wrap_content"
               android:text="Male"
               android:textSize="30dp" />
   //Defining the Second RadioButton

           <RadioButton
               android:id="@+id/radio_female"
               android:layout_width="wrap_content"
               android:layout_height="wrap_content"
               android:text="Female"
               android:textSize="30dp" />
       </RadioGroup>

   </LinearLayout>
```

In Listing 4.24, a radio group is created with two radio buttons displaying, Male and Female, texts. Corresponding to the radiobuttonview_layout.xml file, the RadioButtonView Java class is created in the InputControl application to display the use of radio buttons. Listing 4.25 shows the code of the RadioButtonView.java file:

Listing 4.25: Displaying the Code of the RadioButtonView.java File in the InputControl Application

```
   package com.kogent.android;

   import android.app.Activity;
   import android.os.Bundle;
   import android.view.View;
```

```
import android.view.View.OnClickListener;
import android.widget.Button;
import android.widget.RadioButton;
import android.widget.Toast;

public class RadioButtonView extends Activity {
  @Override
  protected void onCreate(Bundle savedInstanceState) {
        super.onCreate(savedInstanceState);
        setContentView(R.layout.radiobuttonview_layout);
        RadioButton radio_male = (RadioButton) findViewById(R.id.radio_male);
        RadioButton radio_female = (RadioButton) findViewById(R.id.radio_female);
        radio_male.setOnClickListener(radiolistener);
        radio_female.setOnClickListener(radiolistener);

  }

  private OnClickListener radiolistener = new OnClickListener() {
        @Override
        public void onClick(View view) {
                RadioButton radiobutton = (RadioButton) view;
                Toast.makeText(RadioButtonView.this, radiobutton.getText(),
                                Toast.LENGTH_LONG).show();
        }

  };
}
```

In Listing 4.25, two radio buttons, radio_male and radio_female, are initialized. They display either Male or Female message, respectively, whenever a user selects any one of these.

When you execute the InputControl application and click the RadioButton View button, you see two radio buttons, as shown in Figure 4.13:

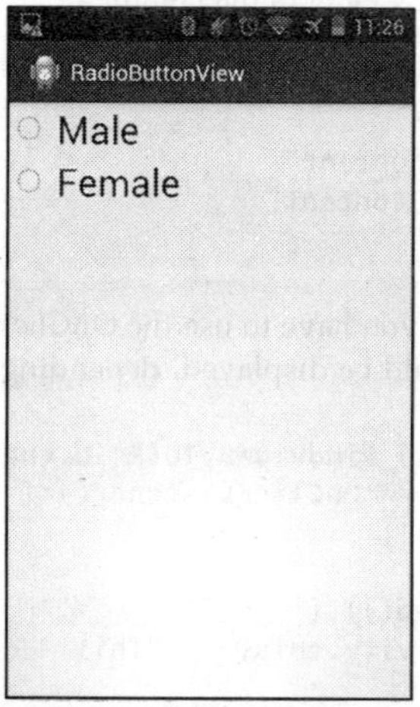

Figure 4.13: Showing the RadioButton View

When you select either of the radio buttons, the corresponding text is displayed. In our case, we have selected the Male radio button and the text is displayed, as shown in Figure 4.14:

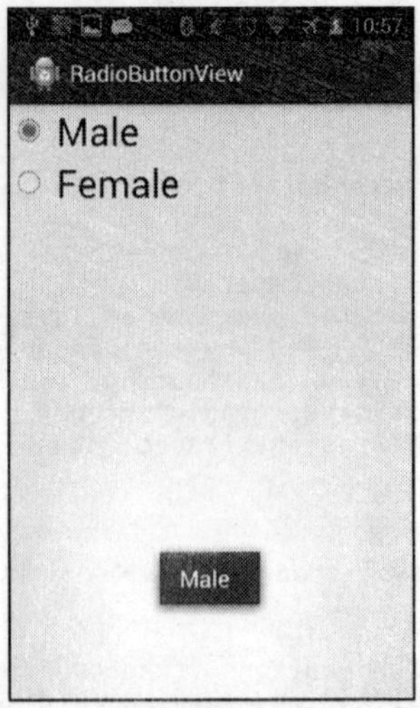

Figure 4.14: Selecting a Radio Button

Let us now understand how to create the CheckBox view.

Using the CheckBox View

Similar to the RadioButton view, the CheckBox view is also two-state button that can be selected or unselected by the user. However, unlike RadioButton view, you can clear the selected CheckBox view by re-clicking the view. You need to define the CheckBox view in the layout XML file first and then implement View.onClickListener interface for the CheckBox view that would be checked by the user. The following code snippet shows how to create the CheckBox view in the layout:

```
<CheckBox

    android:id="@+id/checkbox1"
    android:layout_width="wrap_content"
    android:layout_height="wrap_content"
    android:text="Qualification"
    android:textSize="30dp" />
```

To perform some action by check boxes, you have to use the OnClickListener interface for the CheckBox view. In the following code snippet, the text would be displayed, depending upon whether or not the CheckBox view is selected:

```
CheckBox checkbox1 = (CheckBox) findViewById(R.id.checkbox1);
checkbox1.setOnClickListener(new OnClickListener() {
public void onClick(View view) {

if (((CheckBox) view).isChecked()) {
Toast.makeText(FormDisplayActivity.this,    "This    CheckBox    has    been    Selected",
  Toast.LENGTH_LONG).show();
}
else {
Toast.makeText(FormDisplayActivity.this,   "This   CheckBox   has   not   been   selected",
  Toast.LENGTH_LONG).show();
}
}});
```

In the InputControl application, the checkboxview_layout.xml file is created in the /res/layout location, which displays the use of the <CheckBox> element. Listing 4.26 shows the code of the checkboxview_layout.xml file:

Listing 4.26: Displaying the Code of the checkboxview_layout.xml File in the InputControl Application

```
<LinearLayout xmlns:android="http://schemas.android.com/apk/res/android"
    android:layout_width="fill_parent"
    android:layout_height="fill_parent"
    android:orientation="vertical" >

    <CheckBox
        android:id="@+id/checkbox1"
        android:layout_width="wrap_content"
        android:layout_height="wrap_content"
        android:text="Qualification"
        android:textSize="30dp" />

</LinearLayout>
```

In Listing 4.26, a CheckBox control is added, which displays the text, Qualification. Corresponding to the checkboxview_layout.xml file, the CheckBoxView Java class is created in the InputControl application to display the use of a check box view. Listing 4.27 shows the code of the CheckBoxView.java file:

Listing 4.27: Displaying the Code of the CheckBoxView.java File in the InputControl Application

```
package com.kogent.android;

import android.app.Activity;
import android.os.Bundle;
import android.view.View;
import android.view.View.OnClickListener;
import android.widget.CheckBox;
import android.widget.Toast;

public class CheckBoxView extends Activity {

   @Override
   public void onCreate(Bundle savedInstanceState) {
         super.onCreate(savedInstanceState);
         setContentView(R.layout.checkboxview_layout);
         CheckBox checkbox1 = (CheckBox) findViewById(R.id.checkbox1);
         checkbox1.setOnClickListener(new OnClickListener() {
                public void onClick(View view) {
                      if (((CheckBox) view).isChecked()) {
                            Toast.makeText(CheckBoxView.this,
                                         "This CheckBox has been Selected",
                                         Toast.LENGTH_LONG).show();
                      } else {
                            Toast.makeText(CheckBoxView.this,
                                         "This CheckBox has not been selected",
                                         Toast.LENGTH_LONG).show();
                      }
                }
         });

   }
}
```

In Listing 4.27, an object of CheckBox class is created. This object will display a message with the help of the OnClickListener interface, whenever a user checks or unchecks the check box.

When you execute the InputControl application and click the CheckBox View button, you see a check box view, as shown in Figure 4.15:

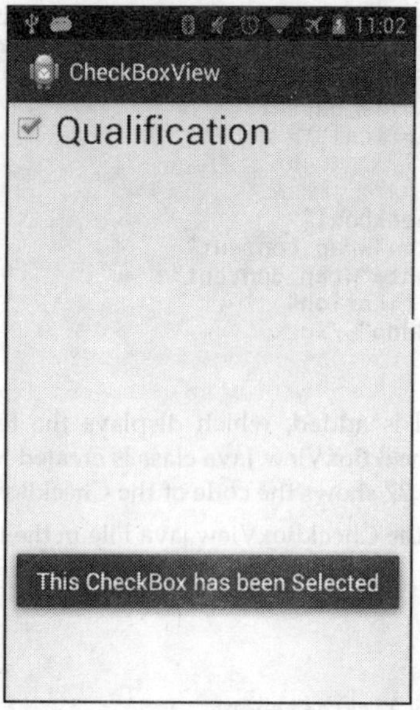

Figure 4.15: Displaying the Output of the CheckBoxView Activity

If you check the Qualification CheckBox view, the message is displayed that this checkbox has been selected.

Using the ImageButton View

The ImageButton view is similar to the Button view, but it displays an image instead of the text. Generally, the background of the ImageButton view changes during the various states of a button, such as clicked or focused. The following code snippet shows how to create an image button:

```
<ImageButton
        android:id="@+id/imageButton1"
        android:layout_width="wrap_content"
        android:layout_height="wrap_content"
        android:src="@drawable/android_icon"
      android:contentDescription="@string/image_description"/>
```

In the preceding code snippet, android_icon is the name of the image file placed in the drawable folder. The contentDescription attribute provides the description about the image. This description can be set by defining a string text in the string.xml file. The src attribute provides the location of the image.

If you want that the image button do some action when you click it, use the OnClickListener interface, as shown in the following code snippet:

```
super.onCreate(savedInstanceState);
        setContentView(R.layout.activity_main);
        final ImageButton      imageButton= (ImageButton)
findViewById(R.id.imageButton1);
                                    imageButton.setOnClickListener(new
OnClickListener() {
                               public void onClick(View v) {
                               Toast.makeText(FormDisplayActivity.this,"ImageButton is
clicked!", Toast.LENGTH_SHORT).show();
                               }
        });
```

In the preceding code snippet, an object of the ImageButton class is created. Then, the OnClickListener interface provides the onClick() method, which displays a message when a user click the image button.

In the InputControl application, create a folder, named drawable, in the /res location and add an image file in it. In our case the file is android_icon.jpeg. Then, add the code in the imagebuttonview_layout.xml file, located in the /res/layout folder, which displays the use of the <ImageButton> element. Listing 4.28 shows the code of the imagebuttonview_layout.xml file:

Listing 4.28: Displaying the Code of the imagebuttonview_layout.xml File in the InputControl Application

```
<LinearLayout xmlns:android="http://schemas.android.com/apk/res/android"
    android:layout_width="fill_parent"
    android:layout_height="fill_parent"
    android:orientation="vertical" >
    <ImageButton
        android:id="@+id/imageButton1"
        android:layout_width="wrap_content"
        android:layout_height="wrap_content"
        android:contentDescription="image_description"
        android:src="@drawable/android_icon" />
</LinearLayout>
```

In Listing 4.28, an ImageButton control is added, which displays an image. Corresponding to the imagebuttonview_layout.xml file, the ImageButtonView Java class is created in the InputControl application to display the use of an image button view. Listing 4.29 shows the code of the ImageButtonView.java file:

Listing 4.29: Displaying the Code of the ImageButtonView.java File in the InputControl Application

```
package com.kogent.android;
import android.app.Activity;
import android.os.Bundle;
import android.view.View;
import android.view.View.OnClickListener;
import android.widget.ImageButton;
import android.widget.Toast;
public class ImageButtonView extends Activity {
   @Override
   public void onCreate(Bundle savedInstanceState) {
        super.onCreate(savedInstanceState);
        setContentView(R.layout.imagebuttonview_layout);
        final ImageButton imageButton = (ImageButton) findViewById(R.id.imageButton1);
        imageButton.setOnClickListener(new OnClickListener() {
                 @Override
                 public void onClick(View v) {
                           Toast.makeText(ImageButtonView.this, "ImageButton is clicked!",
                                    Toast.LENGTH_SHORT).show();
                 }
        });
   }
}
```

In Listing 4.29, an instance of the ImageButton is created, which displays the "ImageButton is clicked!" message when a user clicks it.

When you execute the InputControl application and click the ImageButton View button, you see an image button, as shown in Figure 4.16:

Figure 4.16: Showing the Image Button

When the user clicks the given icon, the floating view -"ImageButton is clicked!" appears. Next, let us create the ToggleButton view.

Using the ToggleButton View

The ToggleButton view shows whether or not the state of the button has been changed (checked/unchecked) with the help of the light indicator. Also, you can set the ON and OFF text to be displayed when the state of the ToggleButton view changes. You can use the following code snippet to define the ToggleButton view in the XML file:

```
<ToggleButton
   android:id="@+id/toggle_button"
   android:layout_width="wrap_content"
   android:layout_height="wrap_content"
   android:textOn="Silent Mode on"
   android:textOff="Silent Mode off"
   android:textSize="30dp"/>
```

Then, you need to implement the OnClickListener interface in an activity class, as shown in the following code snippet:

```
protected void onCreate(Bundle savedInstanceState) {
        super.onCreate(savedInstanceState);
        setContentView(R.layout.activity_main);
        final ToggleButton      toggle_button = (ToggleButton)
findViewById(R.id.toggle_button);
        toggle_button.setOnClickListener(new OnClickListener() {
        public void onClick(View v) {
        if (toggle_button.isChecked()) {
                Toast.makeText(FormDisplayActivity.this,"ToggleButton is On",
Toast.LENGTH_LONG).show();
                                }
        else {
                Toast.makeText(FormDisplayActivity.this,"ToggleButton is Off",
Toast.LENGTH_LONG).show();
                                }
                        }
                });
        }
```

In the InputControl application, the togglebuttonview_layout.xml file is created in the /res/layout location, which displays the use of the <ToggleButton> element. Listing 4.30 shows the code of the togglebuttonview_layout.xml file:

Listing 4.30: Displaying the Code of the togglebuttonview_layout.xml File in the InputControl Application

```
<LinearLayout xmlns:android="http://schemas.android.com/apk/res/android"
    android:layout_width="fill_parent"
    android:layout_height="fill_parent"
    android:orientation="vertical" >

    <ToggleButton
        android:id="@+id/toggle_button"
        android:layout_width="wrap_content"
        android:layout_height="wrap_content"
        android:textOff="Silent Mode off"
        android:textOn="Silent Mode on"
        android:textSize="30dp" />

</LinearLayout>
```

In Listing 4.30, a ToggleButton control is added with different attributes. Corresponding to the togglebuttonview_layout.xml file, the ToggleButtonView Java class is created in the InputControl application to display the use of a toggle button view. Listing 4.31 shows the code of the ToggleButtonView.java file:

Listing 4.31: Displaying the Code of the ToggleButtonView.java File in the InputControl Application

```
package com.kogent.android;
```

```
import android.app.Activity;
import android.os.Bundle;
import android.view.View;
import android.view.View.OnClickListener;
import android.widget.Toast;
import android.widget.ToggleButton;

public class ToggleButtonView extends Activity {
   @Override
   public void onCreate(Bundle savedInstanceState) {
           super.onCreate(savedInstanceState);
           setContentView(R.layout.togglebuttonview_layout);
           final ToggleButton toggle_button = (ToggleButton)
findViewById(R.id.toggle_button);
           toggle_button.setOnClickListener(new OnClickListener() {
                       @Override
                       public void onClick(View v) {
                                   if (toggle_button.isChecked()) {
                                              Toast.makeText(ToggleButtonView.this, "ToggleButton is
On",
                                                                   Toast.LENGTH_LONG).show();
                                   } else {
                                              Toast.makeText(ToggleButtonView.this,
                                                                   "ToggleButton is Off",
Toast.LENGTH_LONG).show();
                                   }
                       }

           });
   }

}
```

In Listing 4.31, a ToggleButton is created, which displays the text on the basis of whether it is checked or not.

When you execute the InputControl application and click the ToggleButton View button, you see a toggle button, displaying the "Silent Mode off" text, as shown in Figure 4.17:

Figure 4.17: Showing the Toggle Button

Now, when you click the toggle button, the text changes as the state of the view has been changed to checked. You can see the light indicator in Figure 4.18, depicting that the ToggleButton view is checked:

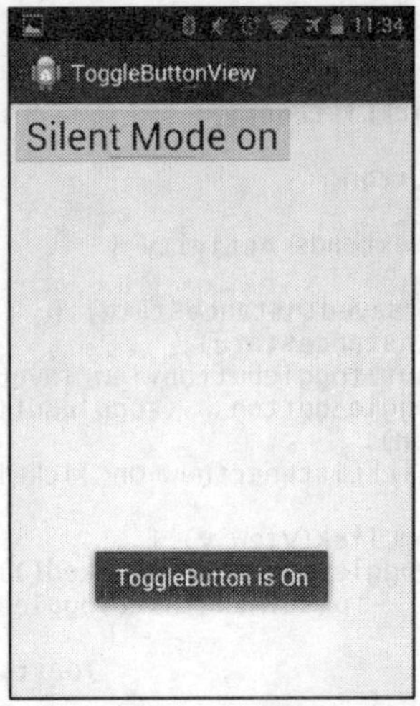

Figure 4.18: Switching On the Toggle Button

Let us move ahead to underStand how to create the rating bar.

Using the RatingBar View

The RatingBar view is used to display rating in the form of stars, which can be set by a user by touching, dragging, or using arrow keys. You can set the number of stars to be displayed by using the setNumStars(int) method in the Activity class or by using the android:numStars XML attribute in the XML layout. You must ensure that the layout_width of the RatingBar view should be set to wrap_content to display the number of stars being set. However, if another layout_width is being set, then the output may be unpredictable.

You can define the RatingBar view in the XML layout file by using the following code snippet:

```
<RatingBar
   android:id="@+id/ratingbar"
   android:layout_width="wrap_content"
   android:layout_height="wrap_content"
   android:numStars="7"
   android:stepSize="1.0"/>
```

Then, you need to implement the setOnRatingBarChangeListener() method for the RatingBar view in an Activity class, as shown in the following code snippet:

```
protected void onCreate(Bundle savedInstanceState) {
        super.onCreate(savedInstanceState);
        setContentView(R.layout.activity_main);
          RatingBar rating_bar = (RatingBar) findViewById(R.id.ratingbar);
         rating_bar.setOnRatingBarChangeListener(new OnRatingBarChangeListener() {
         public void onRatingChanged(RatingBar ratingBar, float rating, boolean
fromUser) {
         Toast.makeText(FormDisplayActivity.this, "User Rating is:" + rating,
Toast.LENGTH_LONG).show();
         }});
    }
```

In the InputControl application, the ratingbarview_layout.xml file is created in the /res/layout location, which displays the use of the <RatingBar> element. Listing 4.32 shows the code of the ratingbarview_layout.xml file:

Listing 4.32: Displaying the Code of the ratingbarview_layout.xml File in the InputControl Application

```
<LinearLayout xmlns:android="http://schemas.android.com/apk/res/android"
    android:layout_width="fill_parent"
    android:layout_height="fill_parent"
    android:orientation="vertical" >
```

```
    <RatingBar
        android:id="@+id/ratingbar"
        android:layout_width="wrap_content"
        android:layout_height="wrap_content"
        android:numStars="7"
        android:stepSize="1.0" />

</LinearLayout>
```

In Listing 4.32, a RatingBar control is added with various attributes. Corresponding to the ratingbarview_layout.xml file, the RatingBarView Java class is created in the InputControl application to display the use of a rating bar view. Listing 4.33 shows the code of the RatingBarView.java file:

Listing 4.33: Displaying the Code of the RatingBarView.java File in the InputControl Application

```
package com.kogent.android;

import android.app.Activity;
import android.os.Bundle;
import android.widget.RatingBar;
import android.widget.RatingBar.OnRatingBarChangeListener;
import android.widget.Toast;

public class RatingBarView extends Activity {
   @Override
   public void onCreate(Bundle savedInstanceState) {
         super.onCreate(savedInstanceState);
         setContentView(R.layout.ratingbarview_layout);
         RatingBar rating_bar = (RatingBar) findViewById(R.id.ratingbar);
         rating_bar.setOnRatingBarChangeListener(new OnRatingBarChangeListener() {
   public void onRatingChanged(RatingBar ratingBar,
                                          float rating, boolean fromUser) {
                                  Toast.makeText(RatingBarView.this,
                                          "User Rating is:" + rating,
Toast.LENGTH_LONG)
                                                .show();
                                          }
                                  });
   }
}
```

In Listing 4.33, an object of the RatingBar class is created. Then, the OnRatingBarChangeListener interface is used to display a message when a user gives rates. When you execute the InputControl application and click the Ratingbar View button, you see a rating bar with seven stars, as shown in Figure 4.19:

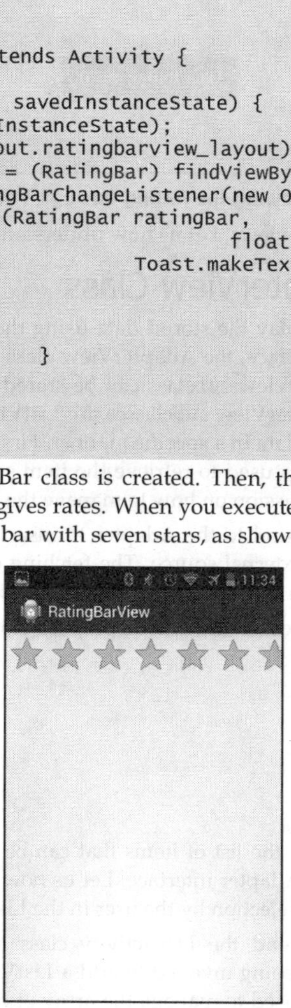

Figure 4.19: Showing the Rating Bar in the FormDisplay Application

Now, click or drag over the stars, the user rating is displayed as the message. Moreover, the stars are being focused, as shown in Figure 4.20:

Figure 4.20: Showing the Rating through Toast Notification

This ends up the discussion on the basic views. Let us now understand how to bind the data to the list views.

Binding Data with the AdapterView Class

In Android programming, you can display the stored data using the AdapterView subclass of the ViewGroup class. With the help of the Adapter interface, the AdapterView class can bind the data to a particular view. The data to be displayed using the AdapterView subclass can be stored in an external resource, such as strings or drawables. Some examples of the AdapterView subclasses are ListView, Spinner, and Gallery, which allow you to bind the stored data and display the data in a specific manner. Firstly, the AdapterView object needs to fill the data in the layout and then this object is used to retrieve the item selected by the user. Let us first understand how to fill the data followed by the discussion on how to manage the item being selected by a user.

Generally, the AdapterView class is bound to the Adapter to insert the data in the layout and the Adapter is responsible to fetch the data from an external source. The fetching of data can be done either from the list or array of string defined in the application or by querying the device database.

You can use either of the following classes to bind and display the stored data:

- ListView
- Spinner
- Gallery

Let us explore each of them in detail.

Using the ListView Class

The ListView class allows you to create the list of items that can be scrolled by the users. You can add the list items to the ListView by using the ListAdapter interface. Let us now look at the code to understand the process of data binding and managing the item selection by the user in the ListView class.

Firstly, your Activity class should extend the ListActivity class instead of the Activity class. Further, the setListAdapter(ListAdapter) method is being invoked to add a ListView class to occupy the entire screen of the Activity class. The ArrayAdapter class used to manage the array of list of items is passed as an argument to the setListAdapter() method. This array of list of items would be displayed into the ListView class. The following code snippet shows the list of parameters that are passed to the setListAdapter() method:

```
public class ListViewActivity extends ListActivity{
....
@Override
public void onCreate(Bundle savedInstanceState) {
super.onCreate(savedInstanceState);
setListAdapter(new ArrayAdapter<String>(this, R.layout.list_item, FOODMENU));
....
}
}
```

In the preceding code snippet, the setListAdapter() method accepts the ArrayAdapter object as an argument, which in turn accepts the following three arguments:

- **this**—Refers to the instance of the current application Context
- **R.layout.list_item**—Provides the layout description for each item
- **FOODMENU**—Provides the list of objects that need to be added in the ListView class

Now, you need to define a ListView class and further invoke the setTextFilterEnabled(boolean) method to filter the text as a user type. You also need to implement the setOnItemClickListener(OnItemClickListener) method to create a listener for each item that would the onItemClick() method as the user clicks an item. The following code snippet shows the implementation of the onItemClick() method, which displays the item selected by the user as a message:

```
//Declaring and Instantiating the ListView object
ListView list_view = getListView();
list_view.setTextFilterEnabled(true);

//Defining a Listener for the ListView
list_view.setOnItemClickListener(new OnItemClickListener()
{
public void onItemClick(AdapterView<?> parent, View v, int pos, long id)
{
//Provide code for the task to be performed when a user clicks an item in the   ListView
}
});
```

You can use the preceding code snippets to create an application and view how the long list of items can be displayed. However, you need to ensure that you have defined the array string containing the data to be displayed.

Using the Spinner

In Android programming, Spinner is a widget that displays the list of items as a drop-down list. Let us understand how to create a spinner to which an array is bound using the ArrayAdapter class. In the following code snippet, we first create the instance of the Spinner class and then that of the ArrayAdapter class:

```
//Creating the instance of the Spinner class
Spinner spinner1 = (Spinner) findViewById(R.id.spinner);

//Create the instance of the ArrayAdapter class to bind the data
ArrayAdapter       array_adapter        =        ArrayAdapter.createFromResource(this,
  R.array.sevenwonders, android.R.layout.simple_spinner_item);
```

In the preceding code snippet, the spinner1 is the instance of the Spinner class that has been initialized by retrieving the spinner View being defined in the XML layout. Moreover, the instance of the ArrayAdapter class has been created and initialized by using the createFromResource() method. Let us now set the array_adapter ArrayAdapter for the Spinner object and also set how the drop-down list would appear. The following code snippet shows the use of the setDropDownViewResource() method to set the display of the drop-down view resources:

```
//Setting the Drop-down View of the Resources
array_adapter.setDropDownViewResource(android.R.layout.simple_spinner_dropdown_item)     ;

//Setting the ArrayAdapter to the Spinner object
spinner1.setAdapter(array_adapter);
```

Now, you have understood how to set or bind the data. We shall explain how to handle the item that has been selected by the user. For this, you need to use the AdapterView.OnItemSelectedListener interface, as shown in the following code snippet:

```
spinner1.setOnItemSelectedListener(new OnItemSelectedListener()
{
public void onItemSelected(AdapterView<?> parent, View view, int pos, long id)
{
  Toast.makeText(parent.getContext(),   "The   food   item   selected   by   you   is   "
  +parent.getItemAtPosition(pos).toString(), Toast.LENGTH_LONG).show();
}
public void onNothingSelected(AdapterView<?> parent) {
                // Do nothing.
}
});
```

In the preceding code snippet, the onItemSelected() method has been implemented to fetch the position of the item being selected by the user.

Let us create an application in which the list of food menu is displayed to the user, and when the user selects a menu, the message is displayed along with the item being selected by the user.

Perform the following steps to create and execute the BindingData application:

1. Create the BindingData application in the Eclipse IDE under the com.kogent.android.bindingdata package.
2. Modify the code shown in Listing 4.34 in the activity_main.xml file located in the res/layout folder of the application:

Listing 4.34: Displaying the Code of the activity_main.xml File in the BindingData Application

```
<RelativeLayout xmlns:android="http://schemas.android.com/apk/res/android"
    xmlns:tools="http://schemas.android.com/tools"
    android:layout_width="match_parent"
    android:layout_height="match_parent"
    tools:context=".MainActivity" >

    <TextView
  android:id="@+id/hello"
        android:layout_width="fill_parent"
        android:layout_height="wrap_content"
        android:text="@string/hello"
        android:textSize="30sp" />

    <Spinner
        android:id="@+id/spinner_button"
        android:layout_width="wrap_content"
        android:layout_height="wrap_content"
         android:layout_alignParentLeft="true"
android:layout_below="@id/hello"
android:entries="@array/menu_items"
android:prompt="@string/food_menu_items"
        android:textSize="30sp" />

</RelativeLayout>
```

In Listing 4.34, a Spinner has been created by using the <Spinner> element, whose id is spinner and the value of the android:prompt attribute has been set to food_menu_items, which needs to be defined in the strings.xml file.

3. Modify the code shown in Listing 4.35 in the strings.xml file located in the res/value folder of the application:

Listing 4.35: Displaying the Code of the strings.xml File in the BindingData Application

```
<?xml version="1.0" encoding="utf-8"?>
<resources>

    <string name="app_name">BindingData</string>
```

```
    <string name="hello">BindingData</string>
    <string name="action_settings">Settings</string>
    <string name="food_menu_items">Select an item</string>
    <string-array name="menu_items">
        <item >South Indian</item>
        <item >North Indian</item>
        <item >Chinese</item>
        <item >Italian</item>
        <item >Thai</item>
        <item >Snacks</item>
        <item >Continental</item>
    </string-array>

</resources>
```

In Listing 4.35, the string array menu_items has been defined, which contains the list of items to be displayed in the Spinner View.

4. Modify the code shown in Listing 4.36 in the MainActivity class:

Listing 4.36: Displaying the Code of the MainActivity Class in the BindingData Application

```
package com.kogent.android;

import android.app.Activity;
import android.os.Bundle;
import android.view.View;
import android.widget.AdapterView;
import android.widget.AdapterView.OnItemSelectedListener;
import android.widget.ArrayAdapter;
import android.widget.Spinner;
import android.widget.Toast;

public class MainActivity extends Activity {
  /** Called when the activity is first created. */
    @Override
    public void onCreate(Bundle savedInstanceState) {
        super.onCreate(savedInstanceState);
        setContentView(R.layout.activity_main);
        Spinner spinner1 = (Spinner) findViewById(R.id.spinner_button);
        ArrayAdapter<CharSequence> array_adapter =
         ArrayAdapter.createFromResource(this, R.array.menu_items,
         android.R.layout.simple_spinner_item);

  array_adapter.setDropDownViewResource(android.R.layout.simple_spinner_dropdown_item);
      spinner1.setAdapter(array_adapter);
         spinner1.setOnItemSelectedListener(new OnItemSelectedListener()
        {
  public void onItemSelected(AdapterView<?> parent, View view, int pos, long id)
        {
         Toast.makeText(parent.getContext(), "The food item selected by you is "
        +parent.getItemAtPosition(pos).toString(), Toast.LENGTH_LONG).show();
        }
        public void onNothingSelected(AdapterView<?> parent) {
                    // Do nothing.
        }
        });

    }
}
```

In Listing 4.36, the Spinner object has been created and the data provided in the strings.xml file has been bind with the object by using the ArrayAdapter class.

5. *Right-click* the application and select Run As→Android Application. The output of the application is displayed as shown in Figure 4.21:

Figure 4.21: Displaying the Output of the BindingData Application

When you click the drop-down list, the items would be displayed, as shown in Figure 4.22:

Figure 4.22: Displaying the Drop-Down List

When you click an item from the Spinner view, the message would be displayed.

Let us now understand how the Gallery view is created and the position of the picture selected by a user is tracked.

Using the Gallery View

The Gallery view displays the images horizontally as a scrolling list. To display the images in this view, you first need to ensure that the images have been saved in the res/drawable folder of the application. Next, you need to define the Gallery View in the activity_main.xml (Android XML layout file), as shown in the following code snippet:

```
<Gallery xmlns:android="http://schemas.android.com/apk/res/android"
   android:id="@+id/gallery_view"
   android:layout_width="fill_parent"
   android:layout_height="wrap_content"/>
```

Next, you need to create an Adapter class that would manage and bind the images to be displayed in the Gallery view. Further, in the Activity class, you need to retrieve the reference of the Gallery View defined in the activity_main.xml file. Then, similar to Spinner and ListView, you need to set the Adapter class (you have created) by using the setAdapter() method on the instance of the Gallery class. In the following code snippet, we have created the instance of the Gallery class and set the customized Adapter class:

```
Gallery gallery_view = (Gallery) findViewById(R.id.gallery_view);
gallery_view.setAdapter(new PictureAdapter(this));
```

In the preceding code snippet, the gallery_view instance has been created for the Gallery class and then the setAdapter() method has been invoked by passing the PictureAdapter class as an argument.

Let us now understand how to manage user selection by defining a listener, which would invoke the onItemClick() method when an item (image) is clicked by a user. The following code snippet shows how the position of the user-selected image is managed:

```
gallery_view.setOnItemClickListener(new OnItemClickListener() {
public void onItemClick(AdapterView parent, View view, int pos, long id) {
Toast.makeText(BindingDataActivity.this, "" + pos, Toast.LENGTH_LONG).show();
}
});
```

Let us now move ahead and understand how to create the AutoTextComplete View.

Designing the AutoTextCompleteView

In Android, AutoTextCompleteView is a class that provides an editable text view, which also displays the list of suggestions that are prompted when the user is typing the text in the view. You can create the AutoTextCompleteView view by using the <AutoTextCompleteView> element in the Android XML file. Further, in the Activity class, you need to create an array of the values that you want to be displayed as suggestions to the user. Let us create the AutoTextComplete Android application in which we would create the AutoTextCompleteView view, which would provide suggestions for the name of the books as the user types the first three alphabets of the book name.

Perform the following steps to create and execute the AutoTextComplete application:

1. *Create* an Android application, named AutoTextComplete, in the Eclipse IDE under the com.kogent.android package.
2. *Modify* the activity_main.xml file located in the res/layout folder by adding the code shown in Listing 4.37:

Listing 4.37: Displaying the Code of the activity_main.xml File of the AutoTextComplete Application

```
<?xml version="1.0" encoding="utf-8"?>
<RelativeLayout xmlns:android="http://schemas.android.com/apk/res/android"
    xmlns:tools="http://schemas.android.com/tools"
    android:layout_width="match_parent"
    android:layout_height="match_parent"
    tools:context=".MainActivity" >

    <TextView
        android:id="@+id/textView1"
        android:layout_width="wrap_content"
        android:layout_height="wrap_content"
        android:text="@string/hello"
        android:textSize="30sp" />

    <AutoCompleteTextView
        android:id="@+id/bookSearch"
        android:layout_width="fill_parent"
        android:layout_height="wrap_content"
        android:layout_alignParentLeft="true"
        android:layout_below="@+id/textView1"
        android:ems="10" />
</RelativeLayout>
```

3. *Add* a variable, hello, in the strings.xml file, as shown in the following code snippet:

```
<string name="hello">Name of the Book</string>
```

4. Modify the code of the MainActivity class by providing the code shown in Listing 4.38:

Listing 4.38: Displaying the Code of the MainActivity Class

```
package com.kogent.android;

import android.app.Activity;
import android.os.Bundle;
import android.widget.ArrayAdapter;
import android.widget.AutoCompleteTextView;

public class MainActivity extends Activity {
   String[] books = {
                "Java 7 in Simple Steps","AutoCAD 2011 in Simple
Steps","Entrepreneurship","Advance      .NET Technology",
                "Sun Certified Programmer for Java 6 SCJP","WPF 4.0 in Simple Steps","SQL
& PL/SQL        for Oracle 11g Black Book",
                "Advance Database Management System","Advance Computing
Technology","Concepts of       Programming and OOPs",
                "Basic Computer Engineering","Spring 3.0 in Action","Java Server
Programming Java EE      6 (J2EE 1.6)",
                "Excel 2010 in Simple Steps","Excel 2007 in Simple Steps","Access 2010 in
Simple   Steps"
                };
                    /** Called when the activity is first created. */
                @Override
                public void onCreate(Bundle savedInstanceState) {
                super.onCreate(savedInstanceState);
                setContentView(R.layout.activity_main);
                ArrayAdapter<String> array_adapter = new
                ArrayAdapter<String>(this,android.R.layout.simple_dropdown_item_1line,
                books);
                AutoCompleteTextView auto_view =
                (AutoCompleteTextView)findViewById(R.id.bookSearch);
                auto_view.setThreshold(3);
                auto_view.setAdapter(array_adapter);
                }

}
```

In Listing 4.38, a class, MainActivity, extends the Activity class. In this class, an array of String type is defined with a list of various books details. Next, in the onCreate() method, the ArrayAdapter class is initalized and the created String array is attached to it. The auto_view object is created and initialized of the AutoCompleteTextView class. Then, the findViewById() method is used to search a book on the basis of provided ID. The setThreshold() method is used to provide the number of characters must be typed by a user, so that the application will provide the suggestion of words. The setAdapter() method is used to bind the object of the ArrayAdapter class with the auto_view object.

5. Execute the AutoTextComplete application by right-clicking the application and selecting Run As→Android Application option. The output would be displayed as shown in Figure 4.23:

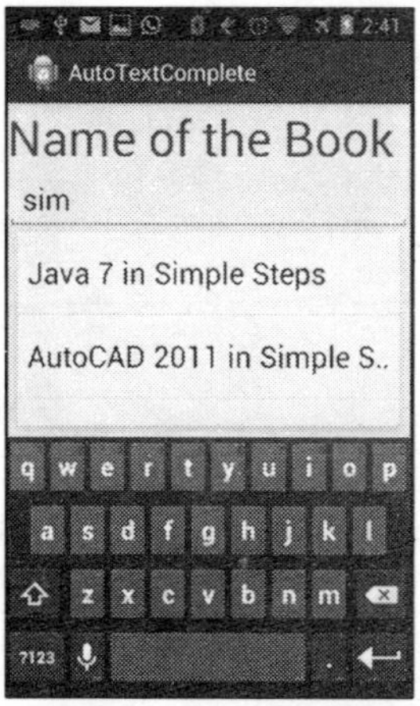

Figure 4.23: Displaying the Output of the AutoTextComplete Application

Let us now understand how the screen orientation is being managed in the Android-based gadgets or devices.

Implementing Screen Orientation

The most important feature of the tablets, Ipads, and smartphones is the switching of the screen orientation, i.e., from landscape to portrait and vice versa. By default, when the orientation changes, the content of the current activity is redrawn automatically according to the new orientation. For example, Figure 4.24 shows the portrait orientation of the browser:

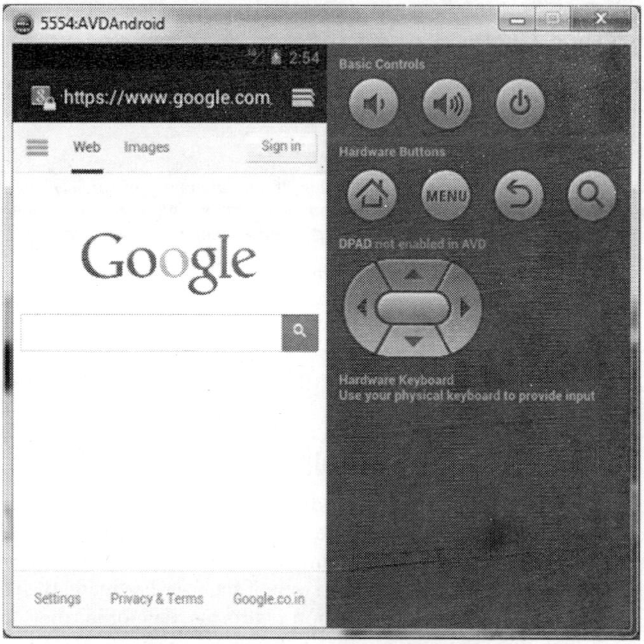

Figure 4.24: Showing the Portrait Orientation

Now, when you click the Ctrl+F11 keys from the keyboard on your emulator (in MAC system, use FN +control+F11 keys), the orientation changes to landscape, as shown in Figure 4.25:

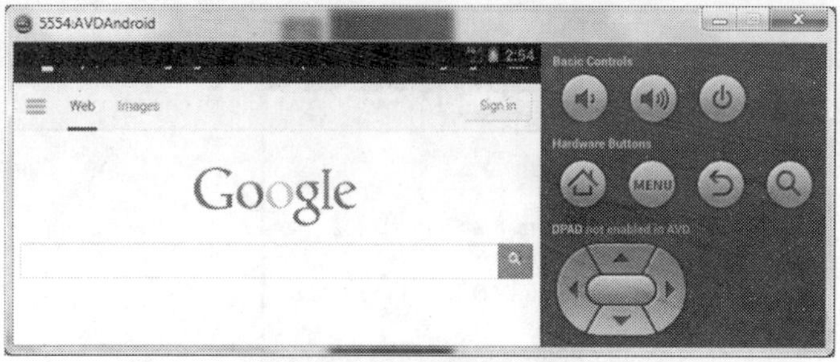

Figure 4.25: Showing the Landscape Orientation

When the content of the activity is redrawn, due to change in the orientation, it is possible that some views of the activity may not be positioned appropriately. Therefore, you need to manage the change in the screen orientation. For this, you can use either of the following ways:

- Anchoring the views of the current activity
- Customizing the size and position of the views

Let us explore each of them in detail.

Anchoring the Views of the Current Activity

Generally, it has been observed that when the orientation of a screen changes, the extra space could be found on the right side or bottom of the screen. To manage it, you can anchor your views to the four edges of the screen. This can be implemented easily by using the RelativeLayout. In the RelativeLayout, you can position the views to the left, right, top, and bottom of the parent view. In this case, when the orientation of the screen changes, the views located at the center gets stretched across its width fully.

Customizing the Size and Position of the Views

The other technique of managing the change in the screen orientation is to design a separate layout folder containing the Android XML files for the UI of each orientation.

NOTE

When a user changes the orientation of a view, portrait or landscape, the main activity is actually restarted. To avoid such a restart of the main activity in your application, by configuring the configChanges attribute in the activity element in the AndroidManifest.xml file of the application. The following code snippet shows how to configure the configChanges attribute in the activity element:

```
<activity android:name=".ActivityName" android:label="@string/name"
android:configChanges="orientation|keyboardHidden|keyboard">

</activity>
```

Till now, you have drawn the views in the Android XML file by using the XML elements and attributes. Let us now learn how to design the views programmatically.

Designing the Views Programmatically

Apart from creating the UI (Views) by using the Android XML file, you can also create the UI components dynamically, which are generated during runtime. The need for dynamic creation of UI occurs when you want to design the UI based on the user selection. For example, if you are creating the railways ticket reservation application, the availability of seats would be displayed only if the user has made the required selection. In other words, if the user has selected the source and destination platforms, date of journey, and the class (i.e., sleeper, 1st AC class, 2nd AC class), then only the availability of the seats can be displayed. Let us create an Android application, DynamicUI, with the DynamicUIActivity class, which displays a DatePicker control on the click event of a button. Perform the following steps to create and execute the DynamicUI application:

1. *Create* the DynamicUI Android application in the Eclipse IDE within the com.kogent.android package.

2. *Modify* the code of the DynamicUIActivity Java class, located in the /src/com/kogent/android folder, as shown in Listing 4.39:

Listing 4.39: Displaying the Code of the DynamicUIActivity.java File in the DynamicUI Application

```
package com.kogent.android;
import android.app.Activity;
import android.os.Bundle;
import android.view.View;
import android.view.View.OnClickListener;
import android.view.ViewGroup.LayoutParams;
import android.widget.Button;
import android.widget.DatePicker;
import android.widget.LinearLayout;
import android.widget.RelativeLayout;
public class DynamicUIActivity extends Activity {
  /** Called when the activity is first created. */
  @Override
  public void onCreate(Bundle savedInstanceState) {
        super.onCreate(savedInstanceState);
        // setContentView(R.layout.activity_main);
        LayoutParams layout_params = new LinearLayout.LayoutParams(
                    LayoutParams.WRAP_CONTENT, LayoutParams.WRAP_CONTENT);
        final LinearLayout layout = new LinearLayout(this);
        final DatePicker dt = new DatePicker(this);
        dt.setLayoutParams(layout_params);
        Button button1 = new Button(this);
        button1.setText("Click Me to display date");
        button1.setTextSize(10);
        button1.setLayoutParams(layout_params);
        layout.addView(button1);
        button1.setOnClickListener(new OnClickListener() {
              public void onClick(View v) {
                    layout.addView(dt);
              }
        });
        LinearLayout.LayoutParams layout_param = new LinearLayout.LayoutParams(
                    LayoutParams.FILL_PARENT, LayoutParams.WRAP_CONTENT);
        this.addContentView(layout, layout_param);
  }
}
```

In Listing 4.39, we have created the LinearLayout view for the Button and DatePicker controls. Further, the instance of the Button and DatePicker classes have been created as well as initialized. Finally, the text and layout for the button1 instance have been set. Moreover, the addView() method has been invoked to add the button1 instance to the layout.

You can also find that the instance of the DatePicker class has also been initialized and added to the layout in the onClick event of the button.

3. *Right-click* the DynamicUI application and select Run As→Android Application option to execute it. The output is displayed as shown in Figure 4.26:

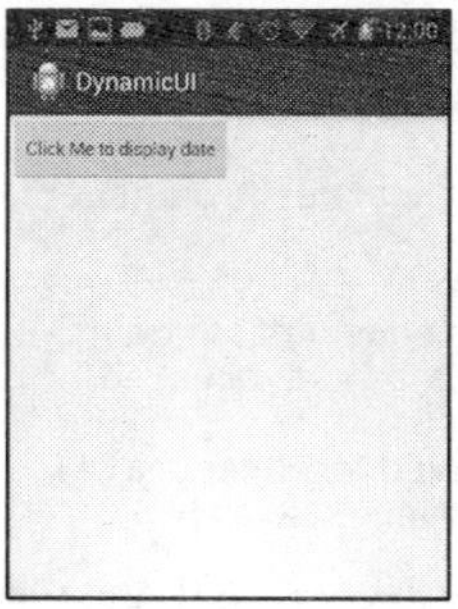

Figure 4.26: Displaying the Output of the DynamicUI Application

Now, when you click the button shown in Figure 4.26, the DatePicker control is displayed, as shown in Figure 4.27:

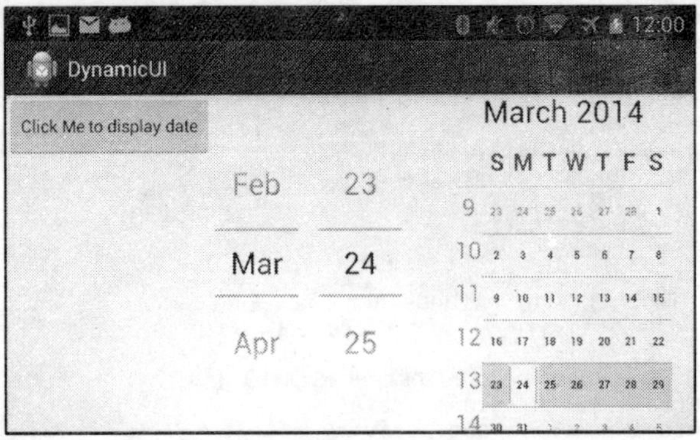

Figure 4.27: Showing the DatePicker View of the DynamicUI Application

You should have noticed that the creation of UI dynamically contains a lot of code to be provided in the activity class.

Let us now discuss how the events that are raised by the views or activities are handled. For example, the onKeyDown() and onClick() events can be raised.

Handling UI Events

Generally, a user can have the interaction in an Android application at either the activity level or the view level. In other words, the events can be raised either from the view that has been created in the activity class or by any key of the device. The key events are not handled by any of the view within the activity.

Let us learn how the events are handled at both the levels.

Handling User Interaction with Activities

The user interaction with the activities can be handled by overriding some of the activity methods, such as onKeyDown() and onKeyUp(). Let's create the UIEvents application in which the UIEventsActivity class would be created. In this class, the appropriate message would be displayed depending upon the key being pressed by the user.

Perform the following steps to create and execute the UIEvents application:

1. *Create* the UIEvents application in the Eclipse IDE with in the com.kogent.android package.
2. *Modify* the code of the UIEventsActivity Java class, as shown in Listing 4.40:

Listing 4.40: Displaying the Code of the UIEventsActivity Class in the UIEvents Application

```
package com.kogent.android;
import android.app.Activity;
import android.content.Context;
import android.os.Bundle;
import android.view.KeyEvent;
import android.view.inputmethod.InputMethodManager;
import android.widget.Toast;

public class UIEventsActivity extends Activity {
   /** Called when the activity is first created. */
   @Override
   public void onCreate(Bundle savedInstanceState) {
        super.onCreate(savedInstanceState);

   ((InputMethodManager)getSystemService(Context.INPUT_METHOD_SERVICE)).toggleSoftInput(In
   putMethodManager.SHOW_FORCED, InputMethodManager.HIDE_IMPLICIT_ONLY);

   }
```

```
    @Override
    public boolean onKeyDown(int keyCode, KeyEvent event) {
            switch (keyCode) {
            case KeyEvent.KEYCODE_1:
                    Toast.makeText(getBaseContext(), "The key 1 was clicked",
                                    Toast.LENGTH_LONG).show();
                    break;
            case KeyEvent.KEYCODE_2:
                    Toast.makeText(getBaseContext(), "The key 2 was clicked",
                                    Toast.LENGTH_LONG).show();
                    break;
            case KeyEvent.KEYCODE_3:
                    Toast.makeText(getBaseContext(), "The key 3 was clicked",
                                    Toast.LENGTH_LONG).show();
                    break;
            case KeyEvent.KEYCODE_4:
                    Toast.makeText(getBaseContext(), "The key 4 was clicked",
                                    Toast.LENGTH_LONG).show();
                    break;
            case KeyEvent.KEYCODE_5:
                    Toast.makeText(getBaseContext(), "The key 5 was clicked",
                                    Toast.LENGTH_LONG).show();
                    break;
            }
            return false;
    }
}
```

In Listing 4.40, the keyCode variable has been created to maintain the records for the key that has been pressed. According to the key that has been pressed, the appropriate switch case would be invoked and the message would be displayed.

3. Execute the UIEvents application. Now, press a number key from 1 to 5 from the keypad of the mobile device, the respective message is displayed, as shown in Figure 4.28:

Figure 4.28: Displaying the Output of the UIEvents Application

After understanding how to handle the events in the activity, we shall now explain how to handle the events that are raised by the views defined in the activity class.

Handling User Interaction with the Views

Users can fire events through various views, such as Button or RadioButton. For example, when a user touches the Button, the onClick() event is fired. Let's create a new application UIEventsButton with UIEventsButton as Activity class, which displays a message when the user touches (clicks) a button.

Perform the following steps to create and execute the UIEventsButton application:

1. *Create* the UIEventsButton application in the Eclipse IDE under the com.kogent.android package.
2. *Modify* the code of the UIEventsButton.java file, located in the /src/com/kogent/android folder, as shown in Listing 4.41:

Listing 4.41: Displaying the Code of the UIEventsButton.java File in the UIEventsButton Application

```
package com.kogent.android;

import android.app.Activity;
import android.os.Bundle;
import android.view.View;
import android.view.View.OnClickListener;
import android.view.ViewGroup.LayoutParams;
import android.widget.Button;
import android.widget.LinearLayout;
import android.widget.Toast;


public class UIEventsButton extends Activity {
  /** Called when the activity is first created. */
  @Override
  public void onCreate(Bundle savedInstanceState) {
        super.onCreate(savedInstanceState);
        // setContentView(R.layout.activity_main);
        LayoutParams layout_params = new LinearLayout.LayoutParams(
                      LayoutParams.WRAP_CONTENT, LayoutParams.WRAP_CONTENT);
        final LinearLayout layout = new LinearLayout(this);
        layout.setOrientation(LinearLayout.VERTICAL);
        Button button1 = new Button(this);
        button1.setText("Click Me");
        button1.setTextSize(30);
        button1.setLayoutParams(layout_params);
        layout.addView(button1);
        button1.setOnClickListener(new OnClickListener() {
               public void onClick(View v) {
                      Toast.makeText(getBaseContext(),
                                    ((Button) v).getText() + " button was clicked",
                                    Toast.LENGTH_LONG).show();
               }
        });
        LinearLayout.LayoutParams layout_param = new LinearLayout.LayoutParams(
                      LayoutParams.FILL_PARENT, LayoutParams.WRAP_CONTENT);
        this.addContentView(layout, layout_param);
  }
}
```

In Listing 4.41, the Button has been created dynamically, and when the button is clicked, the appropriate message is clicked.

3. Execute the UIEventsButton application. The UIEventsButton activity is displayed with a Button, and when the button is clicked, the message displayed is shown in Figure 4.29:

Figure 4.29: Displaying the Output of the UIEventsButton Application

Let us now learn how to create various types of specialized fragments in Android.

Specialized Fragments

In Chapter 2, Using Activities, Fragments, and Intents in Android, you have already learned that fragments allow you to customize UIs of Android application both statically and dynamically. Fragments allow you to build applications that run on devices with different screen sizes. To create a fragment, you need to create a class that extends the Fragment base class. Besides the Fragment base class, there are three subclasses of it, namely, ListFragment, DialogFragment, and PreferenceFragment. These classes also allow you to create fragments.

ListFragment

A fragment that contains a ListView is called a list fragment. It displays a list of items from a data source, such as an array or a cursor displays. To create a list fragment, you need to extend the ListFragment base class, as shown in the following code snippet:

```
public class Fragment1 extends ListFragment {
}
```

Let's create an application named listfragment to understand the use of ListView. Perform the following steps to create the listfragment application:

1. *Create* the listfragment application in the Open Eclipse IDE within the com.kogent.android.listfragment package.
2. *Modify* the code of the activity_main.xml file, located in the /res/layout folder, as shown in Listing 4.42:

Listing 4.42: Displaying the Code of the activity_main.xml File in the listfragment Application

```
<RelativeLayout xmlns:android="http://schemas.android.com/apk/res/android"
    xmlns:tools="http://schemas.android.com/tools"
    android:layout_width="match_parent"
    android:layout_height="match_parent"
    android:paddingBottom="@dimen/activity_vertical_margin"
    android:paddingLeft="@dimen/activity_horizontal_margin"
    android:paddingRight="@dimen/activity_horizontal_margin"
    android:paddingTop="@dimen/activity_vertical_margin"
    tools:context=".MainActivity" >

    <TextView
        android:layout_width="wrap_content"
        android:layout_height="wrap_content"
```

```
        android:text="@string/hello_world" />

</RelativeLayout>
```

In Listing 4.42, layout-related changes are implemented.

3. *Modify* the code of the MainActivity.java file, located in the /src/com/kogent/android/listfragment folder, as shown in Listing 4.43:

Listing 4.43: Displaying the Code of the MainActivity.java File in the listfragment Application

```
package com.kogent.android.listfragment;

import android.os.Bundle;
import android.app.Activity;
import android.app.FragmentManager;
import android.app.ListFragment;
import android.view.LayoutInflater;
import android.view.View;
import android.view.ViewGroup;
import android.widget.ArrayAdapter;
import android.widget.ListView;
import android.widget.Toast;

public class MainActivity extends Activity {

  @Override
  protected void onCreate(Bundle savedInstanceState) {
        super.onCreate(savedInstanceState);
        FragmentManager fm = getFragmentManager();

          if (fm.findFragmentById(android.R.id.content) == null) {
           SimpleListFragment list = new SimpleListFragment();
           fm.beginTransaction().add(android.R.id.content, list).commit();
          }
         }

         public static class SimpleListFragment extends ListFragment
         {

          String[] numbers_text = new String[] { "one", "two", "three", "four",
            "five", "six", "seven", "eight", "nine", "ten", "eleven",
            "twelve", "thirteen", "fourteen", "fifteen" };
          String[] numbers_digits = new String[] { "1", "2", "3", "4", "5", "6", "7",
            "8", "9", "10", "11", "12", "13", "14", "15" };

          @Override
          public void onListItemClick(ListView l, View v, int position, long id) {
         Toast.makeText(getActivity(), numbers_digits[(int)
        id].toString(),Toast.LENGTH_LONG).show();
          }

          @Override
          public View onCreateView(LayoutInflater inflater, ViewGroup container,
            Bundle savedInstanceState) {
           ArrayAdapter<String> adapter = new ArrayAdapter<String>(
             inflater.getContext(), android.R.layout.simple_list_item_1,
             numbers_text);
           setListAdapter(adapter);
           return super.onCreateView(inflater, container, savedInstanceState);
          }
         }
        }
```

In Listing 4.43, the StringListFragment class is extended from the ListFragment class. Then two string arrays are initialized lists of data. Now, in the onCreateView() event, the setListAdapter() method is used programmatically to fill the ListView object with the content of the array. The ArrayAdapter object is used to manage the array of strings that will be displayed by the ListView object. Then, you set the ListView view to display in the simple_list_item_1 mode. Finally, the onListItemClick() method is fired whenever an item in the ListView is clicked.

4. Execute the listfragment application. Figure 4.30 shows the output of the listfragment application:

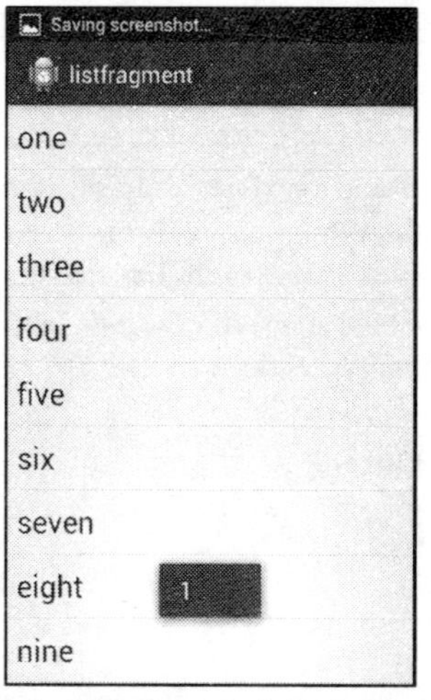

Figure 4.30: Displaying the Output of the listfragment Application

DialogFragment

A dialog fragment works in an activity and is displayed modally. Dialog fragments are required when you need to obtain the user's response before continuing with execution. To create a dialog fragment, you need to extend a class from the DialogFragment base class, as shown in the following code snippet:

```
public class Fragment1 extends DialogFragment {
}
```

Let's create an application, DialogFragment, to understand the use of dialog fragment. Perform the following steps to create the DialogFragment application:

1. *Create* the DialogFragment application in the Eclipse IDE within the com.kogent.android.dialogfragment.
2. *Modify* the code of the activity_main.xml file, located in the /res/layout folder, as shown in Listing 4.44:

Listing 4.44: Showing the Code of the activity_main.xml File in the DialogFragment Application

```
<RelativeLayout xmlns:android="http://schemas.android.com/apk/res/android"
    xmlns:tools="http://schemas.android.com/tools"
    android:layout_width="match_parent"
    android:layout_height="match_parent"
    tools:context=".MainActivity" >

    <TextView
        android:layout_width="wrap_content"
        android:layout_height="wrap_content"
        android:layout_centerHorizontal="true"
        android:layout_centerVertical="true"
        android:text="@string/hello_world" />

</RelativeLayout>
```

In Listing 4.44, layout-related changes are implemented.

3. Add an XML file, alertdialogfragment.xml file, in the /res/layout location, as shown in Listing 4.45:

Listing 4.45: Displaying the Code of the alertdialogfragment.xml File in the DialogFragment Application

```
<LinearLayout xmlns:android="http://schemas.android.com/apk/res/android"
    android:id="@+id/edit_name"
    android:layout_width="wrap_content"
    android:layout_height="wrap_content"
```

```
    android:orientation="vertical" >

    <TextView
        android:id="@+id/lbl_your_name"
        android:layout_width="wrap_content"
        android:layout_height="wrap_content"
        android:text="Simple example of Dialog fragment " />

</LinearLayout>
```

In Listing 4.45, linear layout is used, and a textview is implemented to display a string message.

4. Add a Java file, MyDialogWindow.java file, in the /src folder with in the com.kogent.android.dialogfragment package, as shown in Listing 4.46:

Listing 4.46: Displaying the Code of the MyDialogWindow.java File in the DialogFragment Application

```
package com.kogent.android.dialogfragment;

import android.os.Bundle;
import android.view.LayoutInflater;
import android.view.View;
import android.view.ViewGroup;
import android.app.DialogFragment;

public class MyDialogWindow extends DialogFragment {

   @Override
   public View onCreateView(LayoutInflater inflater, ViewGroup container,
                Bundle savedInstanceState) {
          View view = inflater.inflate(R.layout.alertdialogfragment, container);
          return view;
   }

}
```

In Listing 4.46, the MyDialogWindow class is a dialog fragment class as it extends the DialogFragment class. This fragment will display a simple string message in message box format. The string message is stored in the alertdialogfragment.xml file.

5. Modify the code of the MainActivity.java file, located in the /src/com/kogent/android/dialogfragment folder, as shown in Listing 4.47:

Listing 4.47: Showing the Code of the MainActivity.java File in the DialogFragment Application

```
package com.kogent.android.dialogfragment;

import android.os.Bundle;
import android.app.Activity;
import android.app.FragmentManager;

public class MainActivity extends Activity {

   @Override
   protected void onCreate(Bundle savedInstanceState) {
          super.onCreate(savedInstanceState);
          setContentView(R.layout.activity_main);

          FragmentManager fm = getFragmentManager();
          MyDialogWindow testDialog = new MyDialogWindow();
          testDialog.setRetainInstance(true);
          testDialog.show(fm, "fragment_name");
   }
}
```

In Listing 4.47, an instance of the MyDialogWindow class is created. Then, its setRetainInstance() and show() methods are invoked to display a string message in the created fragment.

6. Execute the DialogFragment application. Figure 4.31 shows the output of DialogFragment application:

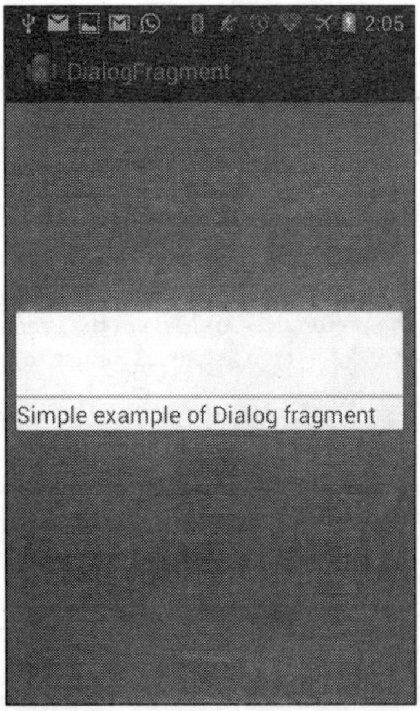

Figure 4.31: Displaying the Output of the DialogFragment Application

PreferenceFragment

Preference fragment allows you to set preferences in your Android applications. Preferences means some settings related to a user's choice concerning the using of applications. For example, some users like and allow saving the login credentials that they need to access their Web resources. In Android, the PreferenceActivity base class allows you to display an activity for editing preferences. However, from Android 3.0 version onwards, you can use the PreferenceFragment class to do the same thing.

To create a list of preferences in your Android application, you first need to create an XML file and populate it with the various XML elements. This XML file defines the various items that you want to set in your application. Then, you create the fragment class by extending the PreferenceFragment base class, and use the addPreferencesFromResource() method to load the XML file of preferences in the preference fragment. Let's create an application, PreferenceFragments, in order to understand the use of dialog fragment.

Perform the following steps to create the PreferenceFragments application:

1. *Create* the PreferenceFragments application in the Eclipse IDE within the com.kogent.android.preferencefragments package.
2. *Modify* the code of the activity_main.xml file, located in the /res/layout folder, as shown in Listing 4.48:

Listing 4.48: Displaying the Code of the activity_main.xml File in the PreferenceFragments Application

```
<LinearLayout xmlns:android="http://schemas.android.com/apk/res/android"
    xmlns:tools="http://schemas.android.com/tools"
    android:layout_width="match_parent"
    android:layout_height="match_parent"
    android:orientation="vertical"
    android:paddingBottom="@dimen/activity_vertical_margin"
    android:paddingLeft="@dimen/activity_horizontal_margin"
    android:paddingRight="@dimen/activity_horizontal_margin"
    android:paddingTop="@dimen/activity_vertical_margin"
    tools:context=".MainActivity" >

    <Button
        android:id="@+id/setpreference"
        android:layout_width="match_parent"
```

```
            android:layout_height="wrap_content"
            android:text="Set Preference" />

        <TextView
            android:id="@+id/setting_checkbox"
            android:layout_width="match_parent"
            android:layout_height="wrap_content" />

</LinearLayout>
```

In Listing 4.48, a button view and a text view are set.

3. Add an XML file, preferences.xml file, in the /res/layout location, as shown in Listing 4.49:

Listing 4.49: Displaying the Code of the preferences.xml File in the PreferenceFragments Application

```
<PreferenceScreen xmlns:android="http://schemas.android.com/apk/res/android">

    <PreferenceCategory
        android:title="PreferenceCategory A">
        <CheckBoxPreference
            android:key="PREF_CHECKBOX"
            android:title="Title"
            android:summary="summary" />
    </PreferenceCategory>
  </PreferenceScreen>
```

In Listing 4.49, preferences are set by using the PreferenceScreen, PreferenceCategory, and CheckBoxPreference elements.

4. Add a Java file, PrefFragment.java file, in the /src folder within the com.kogent.android.preferencefragments package, as shown in Listing 4.50:

Listing 4.50: Showing the Code of the PrefFragment.java File in the PreferenceFragments Application

```
package com.kogent.android.preferencefragments;

import android.os.Bundle;
import android.preference.PreferenceFragment;

public class PrefFragment extends PreferenceFragment {

   @Override
   public void onCreate(Bundle savedInstanceState) {
         super.onCreate(savedInstanceState);
         addPreferencesFromResource(R.layout.preferences);
   }
}
```

In Listing 4.50, a class PrefFragment is created by extending the PreferenceFragment class. Then, its addPreferencesFromResource() method is invoked to apply the preferences specified in the preferences.xml file.

5. Modify the code of the MainActivity.java file, located in the /src/com/kogent/android folder, as shown in Listing 4.51:

Listing 4.51: Displaying the Code of the MainActivity.java File in the DialogFragment Application

```
package com.kogent.android.preferencefragments;

import android.os.Bundle;
import android.widget.Toast;
import android.app.Activity;
import android.app.FragmentManager;
import android.app.FragmentTransaction;


public class MainActivity extends Activity {

   @Override
   protected void onCreate(Bundle savedInstanceState) {
         super.onCreate(savedInstanceState);
```

```
            PrefFragment prefFragment = new PrefFragment();
             FragmentManager fragmentManager = getFragmentManager();
             FragmentTransaction fragmentTransaction = fragmentManager.beginTransaction();
             fragmentTransaction.replace(android.R.id.content, prefFragment);
             fragmentTransaction.addToBackStack(null);
             fragmentTransaction.commit();

            }
    }
```

In Listing 4.51, the FragmentManager and the FragmentTransaction classes are used to display the preference fragment in an activity. The addToBackStack() method is used to add the preference fragment to the back stack so that the user can dismiss the fragment by clicking the back button.

6. *Execute* the PreferenceFragments application. Figure 4.32 shows the output of the PreferenceFragments application:

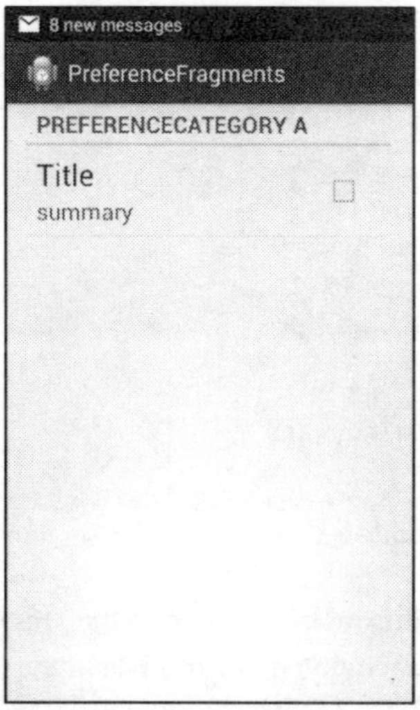

Figure 4.32: Displaying the Output of the PreferenceFragments Application

Let us now learn how to create various types of menus in Android.

Creating Menus

Note that in the devices based on Android 4 platform, there are different types of menus, such as options menu or context menu. The Android SDK provides the simple framework to add different types of menus to your applications. In this section, you would learn how to create the following types of menus:

- The Options menu
- The Context menu
- The Submenus

The Options Menu

Generally, the options menu is created for the applications, such as email, in which a user should have various options to be performed. For example, in the email application, a user can compose an email, reply to the email, or forward the e-mail. Let us create the OptionsMenu application in which the MainActivity class would be displaying the options menu by creating the instance of the Menulnflater class.

Perform the following steps to create and execute the OptionsMenu application:

1. *Create* the OptionsMenu application in Eclipse IDE within the com.kogent.android package.
2. *Modify* the code of the strings.xml file, located in the /res/values folder, as shown in Listing 4.52:

Listing 4.52: Displaying the Code of the strings.xml File in the OptionsMenu Application

```
<?xml version="1.0" encoding="utf-8"?>
<resources>
    <string name="app_name">OptionsMenu</string>
    <string name="hello_world">Hello world!</string>
    <string name="action_settings">Settings</string>
    <string name="new_mail">Compose</string>
    <string name="reply">Reply</string>
    <string name="forward">Forward</string>
</resources>
```

In Listing 4.52, some new strings are defined, which will be required in the application. These are new_mail, reply, and forward.

3. *Add* the code of the options_menu.xml file, located in the /res/menu folder, as shown in Listing 4.53:

Listing 4.53: Displaying the Code of the options_menu.xml File in the OptionsMenu Application

```
<?xml version="1.0" encoding="utf-8"?>
<menu xmlns:android="http://schemas.android.com/apk/res/android"
    xmlns:tools="http://schemas.android.com/tools"
    tools:context="com.kogent.android.MainActivity" >

    <item
        android:id="@+id/new_mail"
        android:title="@string/new_mail"/>
    <item
        android:id="@+id/reply"
        android:title="@string/reply"/>
    <item
        android:id="@+id/forward"
        android:title="@string/forward"/>

</menu>
```

In Listing 4.53, three items are added in a menu. These items display text, which are defined in the strings.xml file.

4. Modify the code of the activity_main.xml file, located in the /res/layout folder, as shown in Listing 4.54:

Listing 4.54: Displaying the Code of the activity_main.xml File in the OptionsMenu Application

```
<FrameLayout xmlns:android="http://schemas.android.com/apk/res/android"
    xmlns:tools="http://schemas.android.com/tools"
    android:id="@+id/container"
    android:layout_width="match_parent"
    android:layout_height="match_parent"
    tools:context="com.kogent.android.MainActivity"
    tools:ignore="MergeRootFrame" />
```

In Listing 4.54, a frame layout is set to display an options menu.

5. Modify the code of the MainActivity class, located in the /src/com/kogent/android folder, as shown in Listing 4.55:

Listing 4.55: Displaying the Code of the MainActivity.java File in the OptionsMenu Application

```
package com.kogent.android;

import android.app.Activity;
import android.os.Bundle;
import android.view.Menu;
import android.view.MenuInflater;
import android.view.MenuItem;
import android.widget.Toast;


public class MainActivity extends Activity {
    /** Called when the activity is first created. */
    @Override
    public void onCreate(Bundle savedInstanceState) {
        super.onCreate(savedInstanceState);
```

```
        setContentView(R.layout.activity_main);
    }
    @Override
    public boolean onCreateOptionsMenu(Menu menu) {
        MenuInflater inflater = getMenuInflater();
        inflater.inflate(R.menu.options_menu, menu);
        return true;
    }
    @Override
    public boolean onOptionsItemSelected(MenuItem item) {
        switch (item.getItemId()) {
            case R.id.new_mail:     Toast.makeText(this, "A new mail is composed!",
                Toast.LENGTH_LONG).show();
                            break;
            case R.id.reply:     Toast.makeText(this, "Reply to the mail sender!",
                Toast.LENGTH_LONG).show();
                            break;
            case R.id.forward: Toast.makeText(this, "Forward your mail!",
                Toast.LENGTH_LONG).show();
                            break;
        }
        return true;
    }
}
```

In Listing 4.55, the instance of the MenuInflater class has been created and the options_main.xml file of the res/menu folder is set as the menu to be inflated by invoking the inflate() method on the instance. Note that we have overridden the onCreateOptionsMenu() method to create the options menu. Further, if you want to perform any action on the click of the option displayed in the options menu, then you need to override the onOptionsItemSelected() method.

6. Execute the OptionsMenu application. The options menu is displayed, when you click the Menu button on the mobile device, as shown in Figure 4.33:

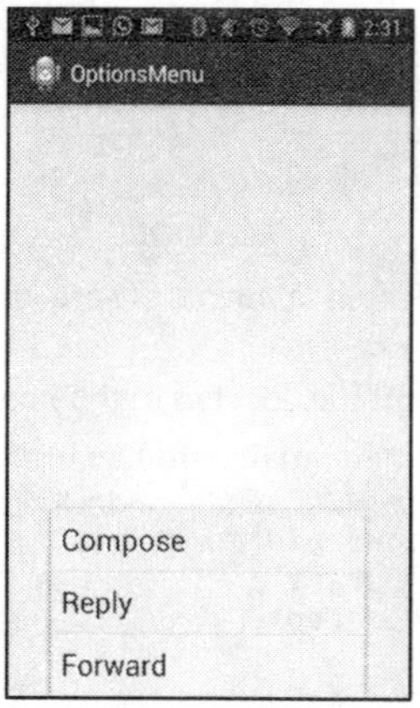

Figure 4.33: Displaying the OptionsMenu Application

Whenever you click an option from the options menu, shown in Figure 4.33, the appropriate message is displayed.

Let us now learn how to create the context menu.

The Context Menu

In the Android devices, a context menu is similar to the menu displayed when a user performs a right-click on the computer. Generally, the context menu is used in devices to display various options related to an item in UI. On Android devices, a context menu is displayed when a user presses and holds an item for a long time.

Let us create a new application ContextMenu with activity class, named ContextMenuActivity. The ContextMenuActivity class would display the context menu options when the button is clicked for a long time.

Perform the following steps to create and execute the ContextMenu application:

1. *Create* the ContextMenu application in Eclipse IDE within the com.kogent.android package.
2. *Modify* the code of the strings.xml file, located in the /res/values folder, as shown in Listing 4.56:

Listing 4.56: Displaying the Code of the strings.xml File in the ContextMenu Application

```
<?xml version="1.0" encoding="utf-8"?>
<resources>

    <string name="app_name">ContextMenu</string>
    <string name="hello_world">Hello world!</string>
    <string name="action_settings">Settings</string>
    <string name="new_mail">Compose</string>
    <string name="reply">Reply</string>
    <string name="forward">Forward</string>

</resources>
```

In Listing 4.56, some new strings are defined, which will be required in the application. These are new_mail, reply, and forward.

3. Modify the code of the context_menu.xml file, located in the /res/menu folder, as shown in Listing 4.57:

Listing 4.57: Displaying the Code of the context_menu.xml File in the ContextMenu Application

```
<menu xmlns:android="http://schemas.android.com/apk/res/android"
    xmlns:tools="http://schemas.android.com/tools"
    tools:context="com.kogent.android.ContextMenuActivity" >

    <item
        android:id="@+id/new_mail"
        android:title="@string/new_mail"/>
    <item
        android:id="@+id/reply"
        android:title="@string/reply"/>
    <item
        android:id="@+id/forward"
        android:title="@string/forward"/>

</menu>
```

In Listing 4.57, three items are added in a menu. These items display text, which are defined in the strings.xml file.

4. *Modify* the code of the activity_main.xml file, located in the /res/layout folder, as shown in Listing 4.58:

Listing 4.58: Displaying the Code of the activity_main.xml File in the ContextMenu Application

```
<LinearLayout xmlns:android="http://schemas.android.com/apk/res/android"
    xmlns:tools="http://schemas.android.com/tools"
    android:layout_width="match_parent"
    android:layout_height="match_parent"
    android:orientation="vertical" >
  <Button
    android:id="@+id/button1"
    android:layout_width="wrap_content"
    android:layout_height="wrap_content"
    android:text="Click Me" />
 </LinearLayout>
```

In Listing 4.58, a linear layout is set with a Button control, which will display the Click Me text.

5. Modify the code of the ContextMenuActivity class, located in the /src/com/kogent/android folder, as shown in Listing 4.59:

Listing 4.59: Displaying the Code of the ContextMenuActivity.java File in the ContextMenu Application

```
package com.kogent.android;
import android.app.Activity;
```

```
import android.os.Bundle;
import android.view.ContextMenu;
import android.view.ContextMenu.ContextMenuInfo;
import android.view.MenuInflater;
import android.view.MenuItem;
import android.view.View;
import android.widget.AdapterView.AdapterContextMenuInfo;
import android.widget.Button;
import android.widget.Toast;

public class ContextMenuActivity extends Activity
{
    /** Called when the activity is first created. */
    @Override
    public void onCreate(Bundle savedInstanceState)
  {
        super.onCreate(savedInstanceState);
        setContentView(R.layout.activity_main);
        Button button1 = (Button) findViewById(R.id.button1);
        button1.setOnCreateContextMenuListener(this);
       }

    @Override
    public void onCreateContextMenu(ContextMenu menu, View v, ContextMenuInfo    menuInfo)
    {
         super.onCreateContextMenu(menu, v, menuInfo);
         MenuInflater inflater = getMenuInflater();
         inflater.inflate(R.menu.context_menu, menu);
         }

    @Override
    public boolean onContextItemSelected(MenuItem item)
    {
         AdapterContextMenuInfo info = (AdapterContextMenuInfo) item.getMenuInfo();
         switch (item.getItemId()) {
           case R.id.new_mail:
                  Toast.makeText(this, "A new mail is composed!",
               Toast.LENGTH_LONG).show();
          break;

           case R.id.reply:
                      Toast.makeText(this, "Reply to the mail sender!" ,
               Toast.LENGTH_LONG).show();
          break;

           case R.id.forward:
                      Toast.makeText(this, "Forward your mail!" ,
               Toast.LENGTH_LONG).show();
          break;

         }
         return true;
         }
}
```

In Listing 4.59, we have created the context menu by overriding the onCreateContextMenu() method in which the instance of the MenuInflater class has been created. Moreover, to implement the clicking of an option from the context menu, we have overridden the onContextItemSelected() method.

6. Execute the ContextMenu application. In the output, you see a button with the text, "Click Me". When you press the button for a long time, the context menu appears, as shown in Figure 4.34:

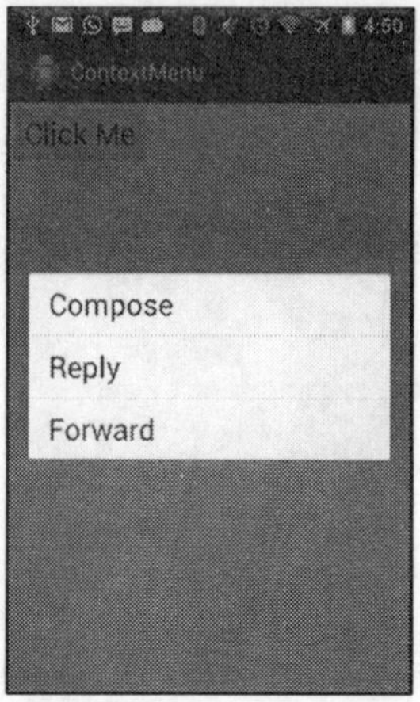

Figure 4.34: Displaying the Output of the ContextMenu Application

Finally, let us discuss how to create submenus.

The SubMenus

As the name suggests, a submenu is a menu that appears when a user selects an item from an existing menu. The submenu is similar to that displayed when the user clicks the File or Edit menu from the Notepad application in the computer. You can create a submenu by simply adding a menu under an existing menu item. For example, we have already created the Reply menu in the preceding section. Let us assume that you want to create the submenus Reply to All and Reply to Sender for the Reply menu. For this, you can edit the activity_main.xml file of the menu folder by providing the code shown in the following code snippet:

```
<?xml version="1.0" encoding="utf-8"?>
<menu xmlns:android="http://schemas.android.com/apk/res/android">
   <item android:id="@+id/new_mail"
          android:title="@string/new_mail" />
     <item android:id="@+id/reply"
          android:title="@string/reply" />

//Creating the Submenu
<menu>
<item android:id="@+id/reply_to_all"
          android:title="reply_to_all" />
<item android:id="@+id/reply_to_sender"
          android:title="reply_to_sender" />
</menu>
     <item android:id="@+id/forward"
          android:title="@string/forward" />
</menu>
```

After editing the code of the activity_main.xml file in the Menus application, you should ensure that you have provided the appropriate values to the string types in the strings.xml file.

Let us now recapitulate what has been explored in the chapter.

Summary

In this chapter, you have learned how to design different types of layouts, such as linear, relative, and table. To create these layouts, the ViewGroup object is used. Further, you have learned how to create various views, such as RadioButton, CheckBox, TextView, and Button. The chapter has also helped you to learn how to change the orientation from landscape to portrait and vice versa. When you need to change the orientation of a view, the readability of the text and other controls displayed on the screen are also required to be managed. You have also learned to change the size and positions of the components of an application. Next, you have learned the process of handling events of the views. Moreover, you have learned about some special fragments in Android development. The chapter has explained how to create different types of menus, such as context menu, submenus, and options menu. Finally, you have learned how to apply the theme and styles along with the discussion on the notifications to be provided to the users.

Quick Revise

Q1 The Click event is invoked by using which of the following method?

a. **setOnClickListener()**
b. **getOnClickListener()**
c. **setOnClick()**
d. **getOnClick()**

Ans. The correct option is a.

Q2. Which of the following attribute allows you to arrange the content of an object corresponding to the specific x and y ax-s within the object?

a. **gravity**
b. **layout_marginRight**
c. **layout_x**
d. **layout_y**

Ans. The correct option is a.

Q3. Which of the following attributes allows you to right align a View in the relative layout?

a. **android:layout_alignParentRight**
b. **android:layout_alignRight**
c. **android:layout_toRightOf**
d. **android:layout_Right**

Ans. The correct option is b.

Q4. Which of the following layouts is used to display the single child view?

a. **Linear**
b. **Relative**
c. **Table**
d. **Frame**

Ans. The correct option is d.

Q5. Which of the following classes is used to make modules in an activity?

a. **ActionBar**
b. **ActionListner**
c. **Fragment**
d. **TabListner**

Ans. The correct option is c.

Q6. Which of the following XML attributes of the TextView element allows you to set the text?

a. **android:lines**
b. **android:text**
c. **android:textSize**
d. **android:textAppearance**

Ans. The correct option is b.

Q7. Which of the following XML attributes of the TextView element is useful if no text has been specified?

a. **android:gravity**
b. **android:height**

c. **android:hint**

d. **android:lines**

Ans. The correct option is c.

Q8. Which of the following bears most resemblance with the button view?

a. **Image button**

b. **Radio Button**

c. **Toogle Button**

d. **Checkbox**

Ans. The correct option is a.

Q9. Which of the following classes is used to insert and fetch the data in an Android application?

a. **ListView**

b. **Spinner**

c. **Gallery**

d. **AdapterView**

Ans. The correct option is d.

Q10. Which of the following views displays the images horizontally as a scrolling list?

a. **Spinner View**

b. **Gallery View**

c. **Adapter View**

d. **List View**

Ans. The correct option is b.

Q11. What are View and ViewGroup?

Ans. A view is a widget that is displayed on the screen of users, such as buttons, text boxes, check boxes, and radio buttons. The base class of a view is android.view.View. The grouping of one or more views is known as ViewGroup. A ViewGroup helps you in specifying the layout according to which the views can be placed and arranged. Some of the layouts that can be defined for the views are LinearLayout, RelativeLayout, and TableLayout. A ViewGroup is derived from the android.view.ViewGroup base class.

Q12. Describe the LinearLayout in Android.

Ans. LinearLayout aligns all the views in a single direction, either horizontal or vertical. You can set the direction by using the orientation attribute of the <LinearLayout> element. In this type of layout, all the views are placed one after the other; therefore, in case you have set the orientation as vertical, then only one view would be displayed in one row. You can set the LinearLayout either by using the <LinearLayout> element in the Android XML file or by using the LinearLayout class, which is the subclass of the ViewGroup class.

Q13. What is the difference between RelativeLayout and FrameLayout?

Ans. The RelativeLayout allows you to position the child views in relation to either each other or to their parent. For example, if you have placed a TextView at some place in the layout, then in the RelativeLayout, you can arrange the Button (or any other View) to the left, right, or below the TextView. In other words, you can position the next View in relation to the previous View or the View defined earlier.

On the other hand, the layout in which an area is used to display a single child view is known as FrameLayout. Generally, in different sizes of the screen, it is possible that the child elements or views of the layout may overlap each other. In this case, FrameLayout is the suitable layout that can hold a single child view and allows you to control the positions of the various children views to be displayed. You can handle the positions of the child views by using the android:layout_gravity attribute.

Q14. Describe the role of the AdapterView class.

Ans. In Android programming, you can display the stored data using the AdapterView subclass of the ViewGroup class. With the help of the Adapter interface, the AdapterView class can bind the data to a particular view. The data to be displayed using the AdapterView class can be stored in an external resource, such as strings or drawables. Some examples of the AdapterView subclasses are ListView, Spinner, and Gallery, that allow you to bind the stored data and display the data in a specific manner.

Q15. Explain about preference fragment.

Ans. Preference fragment allows you to set preferences in your Android applications. Preferences means some settings related to a user's choice concerning the using of applications. For example, some users like and allow saving the login credentials that they need to access their Web resources. In Android, the PreferenceActivity base class allows you to display an activity for editing preferences. However, from Android 3.0 version onwards, you can use the PreferenceFragment class to do the same thing.

To create a list of preferences in your Android application, you first need to create an XML file and populate it with the various XML elements. This XML file defines the various items that you want to set in your application. Then, you create the fragment class by extending the PreferenceFragment base class. Use the addPreferencesFromResource() method to load the XML file of preferences in the preference fragment.

Q16: Create an Android application with three toggle buttons named toggle 1, toggle2, and toggle 3. Use an extra button called states, which on tapping shows the current states (i.e., ON or OFF) of three toggle buttons through a toast notification.

Ans. Create an application, FormDisplay. Modify the code of the strings.xml file in the \res\values folder as follows:

```
<?xml version="1.0" encoding="utf-8"?>
<resources>

    <string name="app_name">FormDisplay</string>
    <string name="hello_world">Hello world!</string>
    <string name="menu_settings">Settings</string>
    <string name="editText">This is simple edit text view</string>
    <string name="clickHere">Click Here</string>
    <string name="maleDisplay">This might be displayed for male</string>
    <string name="Android_Image">This is an image button</string>
    <drawable name="button_pressed">#FF3300</drawable>
    <drawable name="button_focused">#FF0000</drawable>

</resources>
```

Modify the code of the activity_main.xml file in the \res\layout folder as follows:

```
<LinearLayout xmlns:android="http://schemas.android.com/apk/res/android"
    xmlns:tools="http://schemas.android.com/tools"
    android:layout_width="fill_parent"
    android:layout_height="fill_parent"
    android:orientation="vertical" >

<ToggleButton
   android:id="@+id/toggle_button1"
   android:layout_width="wrap_content"
   android:layout_height="wrap_content"
   android:textOn="Silent Mode on"
   android:textOff="Silent Mode off"
   android:textSize="30dp"/>

<ToggleButton
   android:id="@+id/toggle_button2"
   android:layout_width="wrap_content"
   android:layout_height="wrap_content"
```

```
    android:textOn="Silent Mode on"
    android:textOff="Silent Mode off"
    android:textSize="30dp"/>

<ToggleButton
    android:id="@+id/toggle_button3"
    android:layout_width="wrap_content"
    android:layout_height="wrap_content"
    android:textOn="Silent Mode on"
    android:textOff="Silent Mode off"
    android:textSize="30dp"/>

<Button
        android:id="@+id/btnDisplay"
        android:layout_width="wrap_content"
        android:layout_height="wrap_content"
        android:text="@string/clickHere" />

</LinearLayout>
```

Create the FormDisplayActivity.java file as follows:

```
package com.kogent.android;

import android.app.Activity;
import android.os.Bundle;
import android.view.View;
import android.view.View.OnClickListener;
import android.widget.Button;
import android.widget.CheckBox;
import android.widget.ImageButton;
import android.widget.RadioButton;
import android.widget.RatingBar;
import android.widget.RatingBar.OnRatingBarChangeListener;
import android.widget.Toast;
import android.widget.ToggleButton;

public class FormDisplayActivity extends Activity {
private ToggleButton toggle_button1, toggle_button2, toggle_button3;
    @Override
    protected void onCreate(Bundle savedInstanceState) {
         super.onCreate(savedInstanceState);
         setContentView(R.layout.activity_main);
         onClickButton();

    }

    public void onClickButton() {


          toggle_button1 = (ToggleButton) findViewById(R.id.toggle_button1);
          toggle_button2 = (ToggleButton) findViewById(R.id.toggle_button2);
          toggle_button3 = (ToggleButton) findViewById(R.id.toggle_button3);
         Button btnDisplay = (Button) findViewById(R.id.btnDisplay);

         //final ToggleButton toggle_button = (ToggleButton)
    findViewById(R.id.toggle_button);
         btnDisplay.setOnClickListener(new OnClickListener() {

                public void onClick(View v) {
```

```
                        StringBuffer result = new StringBuffer();
                            result.append("ToggleButton1 :
    ").append(toggle_button1.getText());
                            result.append("\nToggleButton2 :
    ").append(toggle_button2.getText());
                            result.append("\nToggleButton3 :
    ").append(toggle_button3.getText());

                            Toast.makeText(FormDisplayActivity.this, result.toString(),
                                            Toast.LENGTH_SHORT).show();
                    }
            });
    }

}
```

Q17. Write an Android application using the multiple radio buttons in Alert Dialog.

Ans. Create an application, alertdialogbox. Modify the code of the activity_main.xml file in the \res\layout folder as follows:

```
<RelativeLayout xmlns:android="http://schemas.android.com/apk/res/android"
    xmlns:tools="http://schemas.android.com/tools"
    android:layout_width="match_parent"
    android:layout_height="match_parent">

    <TextView
        android:layout_width="wrap_content"
        android:layout_height="wrap_content"
        android:layout_centerHorizontal="true"
        android:layout_centerVertical="true"
        android:text="@string/hello_world" />

</RelativeLayout>
```

Create the MainActivity.java file as follows:

```
package com.Kogent.android.alertdialogbox;

import android.os.Bundle;
import android.app.Activity;
import android.app.AlertDialog;
import android.content.DialogInterface;
import android.view.Menu;
import android.widget.Toast;


public class MainActivity extends Activity {
    private  String gen;
  @Override
  protected void onCreate(Bundle savedInstanceState) {
        super.onCreate(savedInstanceState);

         final CharSequence[] gender = {"Male","Female"};
            AlertDialog.Builder alert = new AlertDialog.Builder(this);
            alert.setTitle("Select Gender");
            alert.setSingleChoiceItems(gender,-1, new DialogInterface.OnClickListener()
            {
                @Override
                public void onClick(DialogInterface dialog, int which)
                {
                                Toast.makeText(
```

```
                                        MainActivity.this,
                        gender[which]+"Select ",
                        Toast.LENGTH_SHORT
                        )
                        .show();
                }
            });
    //   AlertDialog alert = builder.create();
        alert.show();

    }}
```

5

Handling Pictures and Menus with Views

If you need an information on:	See page:
Working with Image Views	206
Designing Context Menu for Image View	216
Using the `AnalogClock` and `DigitalClock` Views	219
Embedding Web Browser in an Activity	222
Notifying the User	224

Generally, in mobile phones or tablets, users prefer to save, edit, move, delete, or rename their personal images. These options can be provided to the users by designing the context or options menu. You might have noticed that the images appear either in the gallery or grid view. By gallery view, we mean that the images are displayed as a horizontally scrolling view, and when a user clicks an image, the selected image is displayed in enlarged form. However, in the grid view, the images are displayed as thumbnails. In this chapter, you will learn how to create both the views. Moreover, the images are displayed or changed at the click of a button by using the `ImageSwitcher` view.

Even clocks can be displayed in different views, such as analog or digital view. In the analog view, the hour and minute hands of a clock are displayed, whereas in the digital view, the clock displays the time in the hh:mm:ss format. Generally, in small-screen devices, users have to define various activities to perform a single task. However, in large-screen devices, such as tablets, the user has the flexibility to access different views simultaneously in the single screen. This type of view has been made possible in Android 4.4 supported devices by introducing the use of `Fragment` class. While designing the different clock views, you will also learn how to work with `Fragment` class.

This chapter discusses about working with Image views. Then, it explains how to design context menu for Image views. Further, you learn about the use of `AnalogClock` and `DigitalClock` views. Next, you learn about embedding Web browser in the activity. Finally, the chapter helps you to learn how to display notifications to the users in different ways, such as toast notification, status bar notification, and dialog notification.

Working with Image Views

In Android, views are used to display various components, such as text box, buttons, and labels, to the users. Apart from the general components, you may also need to display an image to the users through your Android application. Android SDK provides various views, such as `ImageView`, `Gallery`, `ImageSwitcher`, and `GridView`, to display images on the screen of Android-supported devices. The `ImageView` view is used to simply display an image to the users. However, if you want to display more than one image to the users, you can either create the `Gallery` view of the `Grid` view of the images. In the `Gallery` view, the images are being displayed in the form of horizontal scrolling list. When the user selects an image from the list, the selected image is displayed in enlarged view. In case of the `Grid` view, the thumbnail view of multiple images is displayed as a collection.

In this section, you will learn how to create the Gallery and Grid views of the images and the use of `ImageSwitcher` view.

Displaying Images in the Gallery View

In the Gallery view, the images are displayed as center locked and in the horizontal scrolling list. You must have seen in various mobile phones or tablets that the thumbnail views of images are displayed as a scrolling list. This type of view is known as the Gallery view. In Android APIs, `Gallery` is a class (deprecated in API level 16) used to provide a view to display items in a horizontal scrolling view.

Suppose you want to create an application in which the images of cakes are displayed to the users in the horizontal scrolling list. When the user selects an image, the enlarged view of the image is displayed at the center of the screen. Moreover, the `Toast` notification of the details of the selected item is displayed to the users. Perform the following steps to create and run such an Android application:

1. *Open* **Eclipse IDE**. The **Java - ADT** window displays.
2. *Select* the File→New→Android Application Project option. The New Android Application wizard starts.
3. Enter a name in the **Application Name** and **Project Name** fields; for instance, in our case, we have given the `GalleryView` name in both fields. *Enter* a package in the **Package Name** field; for instance, `com.kogent.android.galleryview`. *Specify* the android version in the **Minimum Required SDK**, **Target SDK**, and **Compile With** fields. In our case, the **Minimum Required SDK** is API 14: Android 4.0 (IceCreamSandwich), and **Target SDK** as well as **Compile With** is set to API 19:Android 4.4.2. Keep the **Theme** field as default, as shown in Figure 5.1:

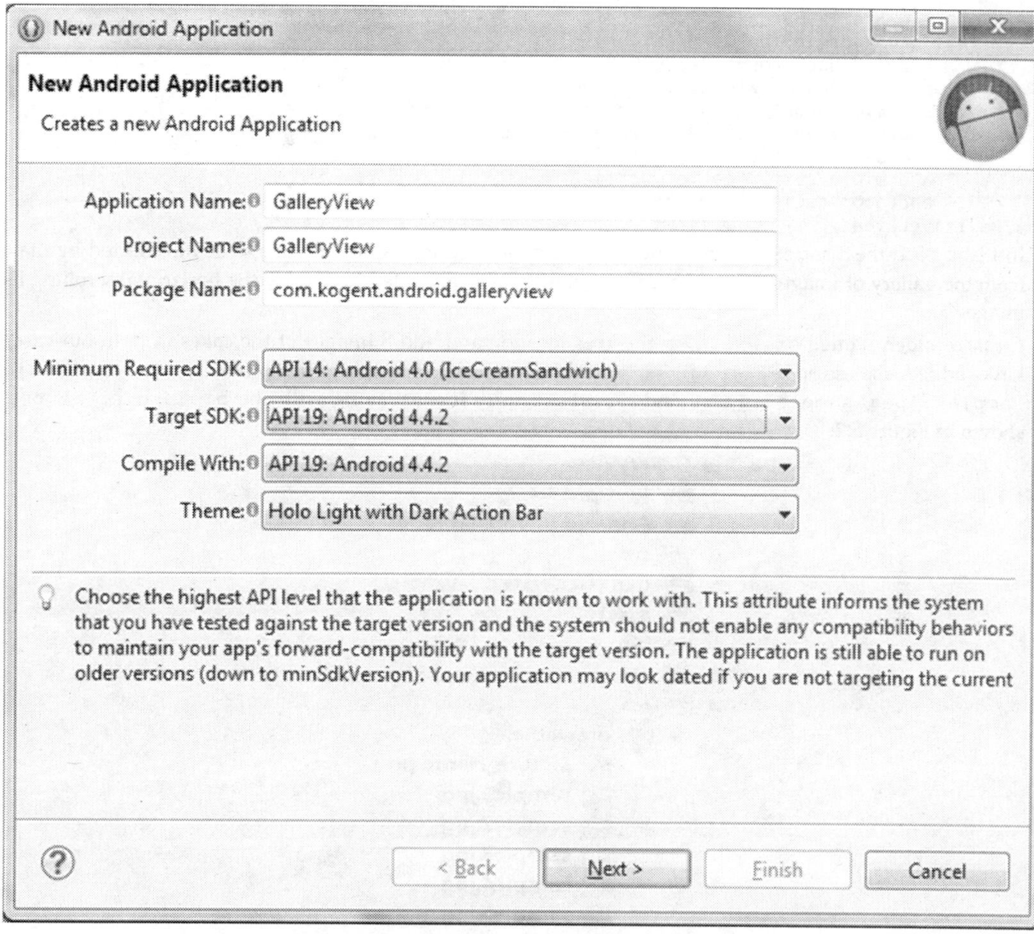

Figure 5.1: Displaying the New Android Application Wizard

4. *Click* the **Next** button. The **Configure Project** screen appears.
5. *Keep* the default settings and *click* the **Next** button.The **Configure launcher Icon** screen appears, which helps in configuring the attributes of the icon set.
6. *Keep* the default settings and click the **Next** button. The **Create Activity** screen appears, which helps in creating activity in Android application.
7. *Ensure* that the **Create Activity** check box is selected. *Select* the **Blank Activity** in the provided activities list.
8. *Click* the **Next** button. The **Blank Activity** screen appears.
9. *Enter* values in the **ActivityName** and **LayoutName** fields and in the **Navigation Type** combo box. In our case, we have specified as `MainActivity`, `activity_main`, and none, respectively.
10. *Replace* the code of the `activity_main.xml` file with the code shown in Listing 5.1:

Listing 5.1: Displaying the Code of the `activity_main.xml` File

```
<?xml version="1.0" encoding="utf-8"?>
<RelativeLayout xmlns:android="http://schemas.android.com/apk/res/android"
    android:layout_width="fill_parent"
    android:layout_height="fill_parent">
    <ImageSwitcher android:id="@+id/switcher"
        android:layout_width="fill_parent"
        android:layout_height="fill_parent"
        android:layout_alignParentTop="true"
```

```
        android:layout_alignParentLeft="true"/>
    <Gallery android:id="@+id/gallery"
        android:background="#55000000"
        android:layout_width="fill_parent"
        android:layout_height="50dp"
        android:layout_alignParentBottom="true"
        android:layout_alignParentLeft="true"
        android:gravity="center_vertical"
        android:spacing="16dp"/>
</RelativeLayout>
```

In Listing 5.1, the `ImageSwitcher` view has been defined to display the image being selected by the user from the gallery of images. Also, the Gallery view has been created to display the horizontal scrolling list of images.

11. *Create* a folder, named `drawable`, in the **\res** location and add 8 images of the cakes in it. In our case, we have added the `sample1.jpeg`, `sample2.jpeg`, `sample3.jpeg`, `sample4.jpeg`, `sample5.jpeg`, `sample6.jpeg`, `sample7.jpeg`, and `sample8.jpeg` images along with the `picture_frame.png`, as shown in Figure 5.2:

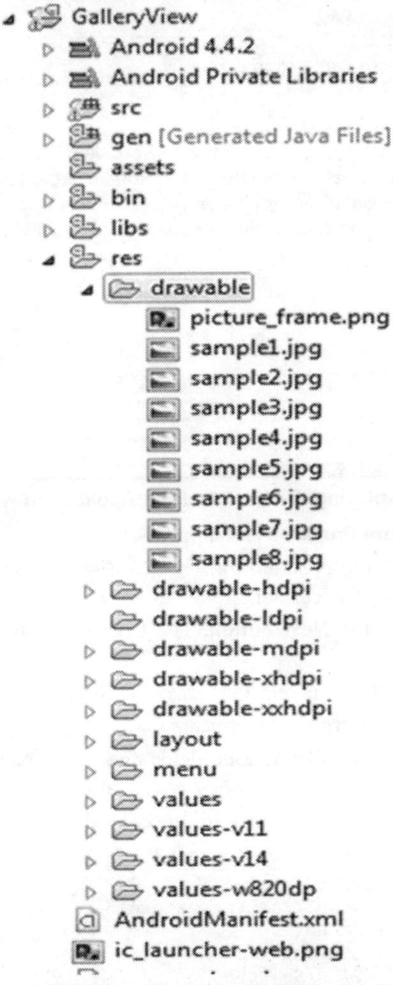

Figure 5.2: Showing the Image Samples Added to the GalleryView Application

Figure 5.2 shows the images that would be displayed in the Gallery view to the users.

NOTE

If you have images of different resolution, you can put these images in drawable–ldpi, drawable–mdpi, drawable–hdpi, drawable–xhdpi, or drawable–xxhdpi folder.

12. *Replace* the code shown in Listing 5.2 with the default code displayed in the `MainActivity` class:

Listing 5.2: Displaying the `MainActivity` Class of the `Gallery` Application

```
package com.kogent.android.galleryview;

import android.app.Activity;
import android.content.Context;
import android.os.Bundle;
import android.view.View;
import android.view.ViewGroup;
import android.view.Window;
import android.view.animation.AnimationUtils;
import android.widget.AdapterView;
import android.widget.BaseAdapter;
import android.widget.Gallery;
import android.widget.Gallery.LayoutParams;
import android.widget.ImageSwitcher;
import android.widget.ImageView;
import android.widget.Toast;
import android.widget.AdapterView.OnItemSelectedListener;
import android.widget.ViewSwitcher.ViewFactory;
public class MainActivity extends Activity implements
OnItemSelectedListener, ViewFactory {
private ImageSwitcher mSwitcher;
@Override
public void onCreate(Bundle savedInstanceState) {
super.onCreate(savedInstanceState);
requestWindowFeature(Window.FEATURE_NO_TITLE);
setContentView(R.layout.activity_main);
mSwitcher = (ImageSwitcher) findViewById(R.id.switcher);
mSwitcher.setFactory(this);
mSwitcher.setInAnimation(AnimationUtils.loadAnimation(this,android.R.anim.fade_in));
mSwitcher.setOutAnimation(AnimationUtils.loadAnimation(this,android.R.anim.fade_out));
Gallery g = (Gallery) findViewById(R.id.gallery);
g.setAdapter(new ImageAdapter(this));
g.setOnItemSelectedListener(this);
}
public void onItemSelected(AdapterView parent, View v, int position, long id) {
Toast.makeText(MainActivity.this, v +"  at location"+ position+1 ,
Toast.LENGTH_LONG).show();
mSwitcher.setImageResource(mImageIds[position]);
}
public void onNothingSelected(AdapterView parent) {
}
@Override
public View makeView() {
ImageView i = new ImageView(this);
i.setBackgroundColor(0xFF000000);
i.setScaleType(ImageView.ScaleType.FIT_CENTER);
i.setLayoutParams(new
ImageSwitcher.LayoutParams(LayoutParams.FILL_PARENT,LayoutParams.FILL_PARENT));
return i;
}
public class ImageAdapter extends BaseAdapter {
public ImageAdapter(Context c) {
mContext = c;
}
public int getCount() {
return mImageIds.length;
}
public Object getItem(int position) {
```

```
return position;
}
public long getItemId(int position) {
return position;
}
public View getView(int position, View convertView, ViewGroup parent) {
ImageView i = new ImageView(mContext);
i.setImageResource(mImageIds[position]);
i.setAdjustViewBounds(true);
i.setLayoutParams(new Gallery.LayoutParams(LayoutParams.WRAP_CONTENT,
LayoutParams.WRAP_CONTENT));
i.setBackgroundResource(R.drawable.picture_frame);
return i;
}
private Context mContext;
}
private Integer[] mImageIds = {
R.drawable.sample1, R.drawable.sample2,
R.drawable.sample3, R.drawable.sample4,
R.drawable.sample5, R.drawable.sample6,
R.drawable.sample7, R.drawable.sample8};
}
```

In Listing 5.2, the instance of the `ImageSwitcher` class (`mSwitcher`) has been created to load the switcher view defined in the layout (`activity_main.xml`) of the `GalleryView` application. Further, the in and out animations have been set for the `mSwitcher`. Next, the `ImageAdapter` class has been bound to the Gallery view defined in the `activity_main.xml` file. It has also been defined in Listing 5.2, which helps in retrieving the position of the item as well as the `ImageView` object. Moreover, the `onItemSelected()` listener has been defined for the gallery and would be triggered when the user clicks or selects an item from the gallery.

13. *Right-click* the `GalleryView` application and select **Run As→Android Application**. The output is displayed as shown in Figure 5.3:

Figure 5.3: Displaying the Added Images in the Gallery View

Now, select an image from the gallery; the image and the details of the selected image would be displayed as shown in Figure 5.4:

Figure 5.4: Showing the Images in the Gallery View

You can see the `Toast` notification in Figure 5.4, which displays the position of the image that has been selected by the user and the details of the `ImageView` used to display it.

Let us move ahead to learn how to display the images in the grid view.

Displaying Images in the Grid View

In the grid view, the images are displayed in the thumbnail view as a collection. Initially, in the `GalleryView` application, you have learned how to display images in the horizontal scrolling list form. Let us create an application to display those images in the grid view. Perform the following steps to create and run the `GridView` application:

1. *Create* the `GridView` application in the Eclipse IDE under the `com.kogent.android.gridview` package.
2. *Replace* the code of the `activity_main.xml` file, located in the **/res/layout** folder, with the code shown in Listing 5.3:

Listing 5.3: Code of the `activity_main.xml` File of the `GridView` Application

```
<?xml version="1.0" encoding="utf-8"?>
<GridView xmlns:android="http://schemas.android.com/apk/res/android"
    android:id="@+id/gridview"
    android:layout_width="fill_parent"
    android:layout_height="fill_parent"
    android:columnWidth="90dp"
    android:numColumns="auto_fit"
    android:verticalSpacing="10dp"
    android:horizontalSpacing="10dp"
    android:stretchMode="columnWidth"
    android:gravity="center"
/>
```

In Listing 5.3, the `<GridView>` element has been used to create a `GridView` to display the thumbnail of the images.

3. *Create* a folder, named **drawable**, in the **\res** location and add 8 images of the cakes in it. In our case, we have added the `sample1.jpeg`, `sample2.jpeg`, `sample3.jpeg`, `sample4.jpeg`, `sample5.jpeg`, `sample6.jpeg`, `sample7.jpeg`, and `sample8.jpeg` images along with the `picture_frame.png`.

NOTE

*If you have images of different resolution, you can put these images in **drawable–ldpi**, **drawable–mdpi**, **drawable–hdpi**, **drawable–xhdpi**, or **drawable–xxhdpi** folder.*

4. *Replace* the code shown in Listing 5.4 with the default code displayed in the `MainActivity` class:

Listing 5.4: Displaying the Code of the `MainActivity.java` File of the `GridView` Application

```
package com.kogent.android.gridview;

import android.app.Activity;
import android.os.Bundle;
import android.content.Context;
import android.view.View;
import android.view.ViewGroup;
import android.widget.BaseAdapter;
import android.widget.GridView;
import android.widget.ImageView;
import android.widget.AdapterView.OnItemClickListener;
import android.widget.AdapterView;
import android.widget.Toast;


public class MainActivity extends Activity {

  /** Called when the activity is first created. */
    @Override
    public void onCreate(Bundle savedInstanceState) {
        super.onCreate(savedInstanceState);
        setContentView(R.layout.activity_main);
        GridView gridview = (GridView) findViewById(R.id.gridview);
       gridview.setAdapter(new ImageAdapter(this));
        gridview.setOnItemClickListener(new OnItemClickListener() {
            public void onItemClick(AdapterView<?> parent, View v, int position,
         long id) {
                Toast.makeText(MainActivity.this, "" +
position,Toast.LENGTH_SHORT).show();
            }
        });
        registerForContextMenu(gridview);
    }
    public class ImageAdapter extends BaseAdapter {
        private Context mContext;

        public ImageAdapter(Context c) {
            mContext = c;
        }
        public int getCount() {
            return mThumbIds.length;
        }
        public Object getItem(int position) {
            return null;
        }
        public long getItemId(int position) {
            return 0;
        }
        // create a new ImageView
        public View getView(int position, View convertView, ViewGroup parent){
            ImageView imageView;
```

```
                if (convertView == null) {
                    imageView = new ImageView(mContext);
                    imageView.setLayoutParams(new GridView.LayoutParams(85, 85));
                    imageView.setScaleType(ImageView.ScaleType.CENTER_CROP);
                    imageView.setPadding(8, 8, 8, 8);
                } else {
                    imageView = (ImageView) convertView;
                }
                imageView.setImageResource(mThumbIds[position]);
                return imageView;
            }
            // references to our images
            private Integer[] mThumbIds = {
                    R.drawable.sample2, R.drawable.sample3,
                    R.drawable.sample4, R.drawable.sample5,
                    R.drawable.sample6, R.drawable.sample7,
                    R.drawable.sample8, R.drawable.sample1,
                    R.drawable.sample2, R.drawable.sample3,
                    R.drawable.sample4, R.drawable.sample5,
                    R.drawable.sample6, R.drawable.sample7,
                    R.drawable.sample8, R.drawable.sample1,
                    R.drawable.sample2, R.drawable.sample3,
                    R.drawable.sample4, R.drawable.sample5,
                    R.drawable.sample6, R.drawable.sample7,
                    R.drawable.sample8, R.drawable.sample1
            };
        }
}
```

In Listing 5.4, the instance of the `GridView` class is used to fetch the `GridView` view defined in the **layout** of the application. Further, the `ImageAdapter` class has been set as the adapter for the `GridView`. Moreover, the `mThumbIds` Integer type array has been created to define the images.

5. *Right-click* the `GridView` application and select **Run As→Android Application**. The output is displayed as shown in Figure 5.5:

Figure 5.5: Displaying the Images in the Grid View

It can be seen in the preceding figure that the images are displayed in the Grid view.

You have already learned how to use the `ImageSwitcher` view with the `Gallery` view. Let us now learn how to just display an image in the `ImageSwitcher` view that would change when a user clicks a button.

Using the `ImageSwitcher` View

The `ImageSwitcher` view allows you to switch from one image to another. The switching of the images can be due to the selection of an image in the Gallery view or on the button click. You have already learned how to change the image in the `ImageSwitcher` view by selecting an item from the Gallery view. In this section, you will learn how an image can be changed in the `ImageSwitcher` view, when a user clicks the button. Let us create an application, `ImageSwitcherDemo`, in which the next button is created to display the next image in the `ImageSwitcher` view. After displaying the last image, the `ImageSwitcher` view displays the first image again.

Perform the following steps to create the `ImageSwitcherDemo` application:

1. *Create* the `ImageSwitcherDemo` application, in the Eclipse IDE, under the `com.kogent.android.imageswitcherdemo` package.
2. *Replace* the code of the `activity_main.xml` file, located in the **\res\layout** folder, of the `ImageSwitcherDemo` application, with the code shown in Listing 5.5:

Listing 5.5: Code of the `activity_main.xml` File of the `ImageSwitcherDemo` Application

```
<RelativeLayout xmlns:android="http://schemas.android.com/apk/res/android"
    xmlns:tools="http://schemas.android.com/tools"
    android:layout_width="match_parent"
    android:layout_height="match_parent"
    tools:context=".MainActivity" >
    <Button
        android:id="@+id/btn_image"
        android:layout_width="wrap_content"
        android:layout_height="wrap_content"
        android:text="Change Image" />
    <ImageSwitcher
        android:id="@+id/switcher"
        android:layout_width="fill_parent"
        android:layout_height="fill_parent"
        android:layout_alignParentLeft="true"
        android:layout_below="@+id/btn_image" />
</RelativeLayout>
```

In Listing 5.5, the `Button` and `ImageSwitcher` views have been created.

3. *Create* a folder, **drawable**, in the **\res** location and add 8 images of the cakes in it. In our case, we have added the `sample1.jpeg`, `sample2.jpeg`, `sample3.jpeg`, `sample4.jpeg`, `sample5.jpeg`, `sample6.jpeg`, `sample7.jpeg`, and `sample8.jpeg` images.
4. *Replace* the code of the `MainActivity.java` file, located in the **\src\com\kogent\android\imageswitcherdemo** folder, with the code shown in Listing 5.6:

Listing 5.6: Code of the `MainActivity.java` File the `ImageSwitcherDemo` Application

```
package com.kogent.android.imageswitcherdemo;

import android.app.Activity;
import android.os.Bundle;
import android.view.View;
import android.view.animation.AnimationUtils;
import android.widget.Button;
import android.widget.ImageSwitcher;
import android.widget.ImageView;
import android.widget.Gallery.LayoutParams;
import android.widget.ViewSwitcher.ViewFactory;
import android.view.Menu;

public class MainActivity extends Activity implements ViewFactory
{
   private ImageSwitcher mSwitcher;
```

```
    private int position=0;
      Button btn_image;
    /** Called when the activity is first created. */
      @Override
      public void onCreate(Bundle savedInstanceState)
      {
           super.onCreate(savedInstanceState);
           setContentView(R.layout.activity_main);
           mSwitcher = (ImageSwitcher) findViewById(R.id.switcher);
           mSwitcher.setFactory(this);
  mSwitcher.setInAnimation(AnimationUtils.loadAnimation(this,android.R.anim.fade_in));
  mSwitcher.setOutAnimation(AnimationUtils.loadAnimation(this,android.R.anim.fade_out));
           mSwitcher.setImageResource(mImageIds[(position)]);
           btn_image = (Button) findViewById(R.id.btn_image);
           btn_image.setOnClickListener(new View.OnClickListener() {
            @Override
                    public void onClick(View v) {
                    position = position + 1;
                            if (position < 8)
                            {
                                     mSwitcher.setImageResource(mImageIds[(position)]);
                            }
                            else
                            {
                                     position = 0;
                                     mSwitcher.setImageResource(mImageIds[(position)]);

                            }
            }});
      }
    @Override
    public View makeView()
    {
          ImageView i = new ImageView(this);
          i.setBackgroundColor(0xFF000000);
          i.setScaleType(ImageView.ScaleType.FIT_CENTER);
          i.setLayoutParams(new
    ImageSwitcher.LayoutParams(LayoutParams.FILL_PARENT,LayoutParams.FILL_PARENT));
          return i;
    }
      private Integer[] mImageIds = {
              R.drawable.sample1, R.drawable.sample2,
              R.drawable.sample3, R.drawable.sample4,
              R.drawable.sample5, R.drawable.sample6,
              R.drawable.sample7, R.drawable.sample8
  };
  }
```

In Listing 5.6, the image resource for the `ImageSwitcher` view has been set on the click event of the button. Moreover, it has been checked that if the value of the `position` variable is less than 8, then the image resource of the specified location would be set for the `ImageSwitcher` view. Otherwise, the value of the `position` variable is set to zero and the image at the zero position is displayed in the `ImageSwitcher` view.

5. *Right-click* the `ImageSwitcherDemo` application and select `Run As→Android Application`. The output is displayed as shown in Figure 5.6:

Figure 5.6: Showing the Switching of Images

In Figure 5.6, the first image is being displayed, and when you click the `Change Image` button, the next image would be displayed in the `ImageSwitcher` view.

Let us now learn how to create context menu for the image.

Designing Context Menu for Image View

You may have noticed that when you touch an image for longer duration, the context menu for the image appears. This context menu provides various options, such as `Move`, `Edit`, or `Send`. Let us create an Android 4.4 application that displays an image, and when a user touches the image for longer duration, the context menu appears.

Perform the following steps to create and execute the `ImageMenus` application:

1. *Create* the `ImageMenus` application, in the Eclipse IDE, under the `com.kogent.android.imagemenus` package.
2. *Replace* the code of the `activity_main.xml` file of the `ImageMenus` application, located in the **/res/layout** folder, with the code shown in Listing 5.7:

Listing 5.7: Displaying the Code of the `activity_main.xml` File of the `ImageMenus` Application

```
<RelativeLayout xmlns:android="http://schemas.android.com/apk/res/android"
    xmlns:tools="http://schemas.android.com/tools"
    android:layout_width="match_parent"
    android:layout_height="match_parent"
    tools:context=".MainActivity" >
    <ImageView
        android:id="@+id/imageView"
        android:layout_width="fill_parent"
        android:layout_height="fill_parent"
        android:layout_alignParentLeft="true"
        android:layout_alignParentTop="true"
        android:contentDescription="@string/app_name" />
</RelativeLayout>
```

In Listing 5.7, the `<ImageView>` element has been used to display an image for which the context menu would be created.

3. *Create* a folder, named **drawable**, in the **\res** location and add an image in it. In our case, we have added the `sample1` image.

4. *Replace* the code of the `MainActivity.java` file, located in the **\src\com\kogent\android\imagemenus** folder, with the code shown in Listing 5.8:

Listing 5.8: Displaying the Code of the `MainActivity.java` File of the `ImageMenus` Application

```
package com.kogent.android.imagemenus;

import android.app.Activity;
import android.os.Bundle;
import android.view.ContextMenu;
import android.view.ContextMenu.ContextMenuInfo;
import android.view.MenuItem;
import android.view.View;
import android.widget.ImageView;
import android.widget.Toast;

public class MainActivity extends Activity {

   ImageView imageView;
     final static int EDIT_IMAGE=0,CHANGE_NAME=1, MOVE_IMAGE=2,
SEND_IMAGE=3;
   /** Called when the activity is first created. */
     @Override
     public void onCreate(Bundle savedInstanceState) {
          super.onCreate(savedInstanceState);
          setContentView(R.layout.activity_main);
          imageView = (ImageView) findViewById(R.id.imageView);
          imageView.setImageResource(R.drawable.sample1);
          imageView.setScaleType(ImageView.ScaleType.FIT_XY);
          registerForContextMenu(imageView);
     }
     @Override
     public void onCreateContextMenu(ContextMenu menu, View v, ContextMenuInfo    menuInfo)
     {
           super.onCreateContextMenu(menu, v, menuInfo);
           menu.add(0, EDIT_IMAGE, 0, "Edit");
           menu.add(0, CHANGE_NAME, 0, "Rename");
           menu.add(0, MOVE_IMAGE, 0, "Move");
           menu.add(0, SEND_IMAGE, 0, "Send");
     }
     @Override
     public boolean onContextItemSelected(MenuItem item)
     {
           switch(item.getItemId())
           {
               case EDIT_IMAGE:
                         editimage();
                         break;
               case CHANGE_NAME:
                         changename();
                         break;
               case MOVE_IMAGE:
                         moveImage();
                         break;
               case SEND_IMAGE:
                         sendImage();
                         break;
           }
           return true;
     }
   private void sendImage() {
           Toast.makeText(this, "You have clicked the Send option" ,
                   Toast.LENGTH_LONG).show();
   }
   private void moveImage() {
           Toast.makeText(this, "You have clicked the Move option",
```

```
                    Toast.LENGTH_LONG).show();
    }
    private void changename() {
        Toast.makeText(this, "You have clicked the Rename option" ,
                    Toast.LENGTH_LONG).show();
    }
    private void editimage() {
        Toast.makeText(this, "You have clicked the Edit option",
                    Toast.LENGTH_LONG).show();
    }
}
```

In Listing 5.8, the `registerForContextMenu()` method has been invoked by passing the `ImageView` instance as the argument. This method sets the context menu for the `View` that has been passed as an argument. Moreover, Listing 5.8 provides the implementation of the `onCreateContextMenu()` method that would be invoked to create the context menu. You can also find the implementation of the `onContextItemSelected()` method that would be invoked when an item from the context menu is to be selected.

5. *Right-click* the `ImageMenus` application and select `Run As→Android Application`. In our case, the `sample1` image would be displayed in the `ImageView` view.
6. *Touch* the image for longer duration, the context menu appears, as shown in Figure 5.7:

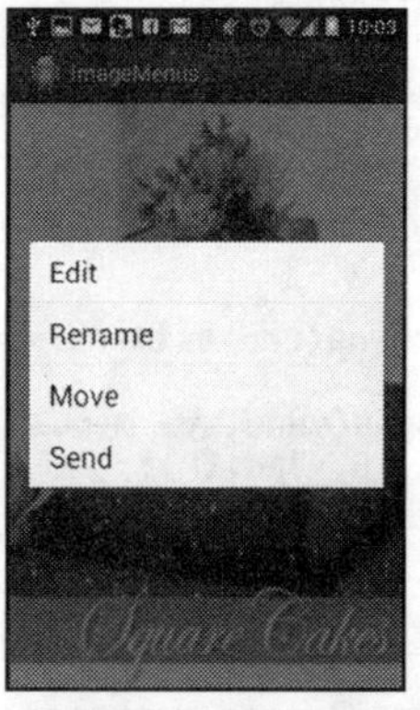

Figure 5.7: Showing the Context Menu of the Image

Whenever you click an option from the context menu, displayed in Figure 5.7, the relevant `Toast` notification would be displayed. For example, in our case, we have clicked the `Edit` option and the `Toast` notification displayed is shown in Figure 5.8:

Figure 5.8: Displaying the Toast Notification

Let us now create the `AnalogClock` and `DigitalClock` views.

Using the **AnalogClock** and **DigitalClock** Views

In Android-supported devices, there are two types of clock views, AnalogClock and DigitalClock. The AnalogClock view displays a clock with two hands, namely, minutes and hours. However, the DigitalClock view displays the clock in digital format. You can use the <AnalogClock> element in the layout (activity_main.xml) of the Android application to display the analog view of the clock. The <DigitalClock> element can be used in the activity_main.xml file to display the clock digitally. Apart from using these elements in the layout, you can also use the AnalogClock and DigitalClock classes and create the views programmatically.

Generally, it has been found in the Android user interface that views are placed within the layouts. For example, ListView, AnalogClock, and DigitalClock views are placed within the RelativeLayout element. Whenever an Activity is being created, the hierarchy of views is being loaded or created. Generally, in case of small screens, the users may navigate from one screen to another. For example, if the users want to see the AnalogClock and DigitalClock views, then they may click a button, and in the next window, the desired view may be displayed. However, in case of large screens, the DigitalClock and AnalogClock views are often displayed in two panes. In the left pane, the list may be displayed to the users to select the view to be displayed, and the appropriate view (DigitalClock or AnalogClock) can be displayed in the right pane. The simultaneous display of views in two panes reduces the back and forth navigation of the users.

The Android developers need to use the Fragment class to display the views in two panes for large screens. Let us create an Android 4.4 application in which the Analog Clock and Digital Clock would be displayed as the list items on the left pane. When the user selects an item from the list, the appropriate clock view would be displayed on the right pane. Perform the following steps to create and execute the ClockViews application:

1. *Create* the ClockViews application using the Eclipse IDE under the com.kogent.android.clockviews package.
2. Replace the code of the activity_main.xml file of the ClockViews application with the code shown in Listing 5.9:

Listing 5.9: Code of the activity_main.xml File in the ClockViews Application

```
<RelativeLayout xmlns:android="http://schemas.android.com/apk/res/android"
    xmlns:tools="http://schemas.android.com/tools"
    android:layout_width="match_parent"
    android:layout_height="match_parent"
    tools:context=".ClockFragment"
    android:background="@android:color/black">
    <ListView
        android:id="@+id/number_list"
        android:layout_width="250dip"
        android:layout_height="match_parent" />
    <fragment
        android:id="@+id/the_frag"
        android:layout_width="match_parent"
        android:layout_height="match_parent"
        android:layout_toRightOf="@+id/number_list"
        class="com.kogent.android.clockviews.ClockFragment" />
</RelativeLayout>
```

In Listing 5.9, a list view has been created by using the <ListView> element and a fragment class ClockFragment has been defined in the activity_main.xml file.

3. Add a new Java file, ClockFragment.java, in the **\src** location with the com.kogent.android.clockviews package, as shown in Listing 5.10:

Listing 5.10: Code of the `ClockFragment.java` File in the `ClockViews` Application

```
package com.kogent.android.clockviews;
import android.app.Fragment;
import android.content.Context;
import android.os.Bundle;
import android.view.LayoutInflater;
import android.view.View;
import android.view.ViewGroup;
import android.widget.AnalogClock;
import android.widget.DigitalClock;
import android.widget.RelativeLayout;
public class ClockFragment extends Fragment {
   private int index;
   public ClockFragment() {
   }
   public ClockFragment(int index) {
          this.index = index;
   }
          @Override
   public void onCreate(Bundle saved) {
          super.onCreate(saved);
          if (null != saved) {
                    index = saved.getInt("index");
                    }
          }
   @Override
   public void onSaveInstanceState(Bundle toSave) {
          toSave.putInt("index", index);
          }
   @Override
   public View onCreateView(LayoutInflater inflater, ViewGroup container, Bundle saved) {
          Context c = getActivity().getApplicationContext();
          RelativeLayout l = new RelativeLayout(c);
          if(index == 1)
          {
                    AnalogClock ac = new AnalogClock(c);
                    l.addView(ac);
          }
          else if (index == 2)
          {
                    DigitalClock dc = new DigitalClock(c);
                    dc.setTextSize((float) 30d);
                    l.addView(dc);
          }
          return l;
    }
}
```

In Listing 5.10, the parameterized constructor of the `ClockFragment` class has been created in which the parameter value is set for the `index` variable of the class. Further, the value of the `index` variable is being verified and accordingly the instance of the `AnalogClock` or `DigitalClock` class has been created. Finally, the instance of the class is added as a view to the layout.

4. *Replace* the code of the `MainActivity.java` file, located in the **/src/com/kogent/android/clockviews** folder, with the code shown in Listing 5.11:

Listing 5.11: Code of the `MainActivity.java` File in the `ClockViews` Application

```
package com.kogent.android.clockviews;
import android.app.Activity;
import android.app.Fragment;
import android.app.FragmentTransaction;
import android.os.Bundle;
import android.view.View;
import android.widget.AdapterView;
import android.widget.AdapterView.OnItemClickListener;
import android.widget.ArrayAdapter;
import android.widget.ListView;

public class MainActivity extends Activity implements OnItemClickListener {
  @Override
  public void onCreate(Bundle savedInstanceState) {
        super.onCreate(savedInstanceState);
        setContentView(R.layout.activity_main);
        ListView l = (ListView) findViewById(R.id.number_list);
        ArrayAdapter<String> numbers = new
 ArrayAdapter<String>(getApplicationContext(),android.R.layout.simple_list_item_1,
        new String [] {"Analog View", "Digital View"});
        l.setAdapter(numbers);
        l.setOnItemClickListener(this);
        }

  private void stackAFragment(int index) {
        Fragment f = new ClockFragment(index);
        FragmentTransaction ft = getFragmentManager().beginTransaction();
        ft.replace(R.id.the_frag, f);
        ft.setTransition(FragmentTransaction.TRANSIT_FRAGMENT_OPEN);
        ft.addToBackStack(null);
        ft.commit();
        }
  public void onItemClick(AdapterView<?> parent, View view, int position, long id)
  {
        stackAFragment(position + 1);
        }
}
```

In Listing 5.11, the instance of the `ArrayAdapter` class has been created and the two String type items have been added (Analog View and Digital View). Moreover, the parameterized constructor of the `ClockFragment` class has been invoked.

5. *Right-click* the `ClockViews` application and *select* `Run As→Android Application`. The output would be displayed, as shown in Figure 5.9:

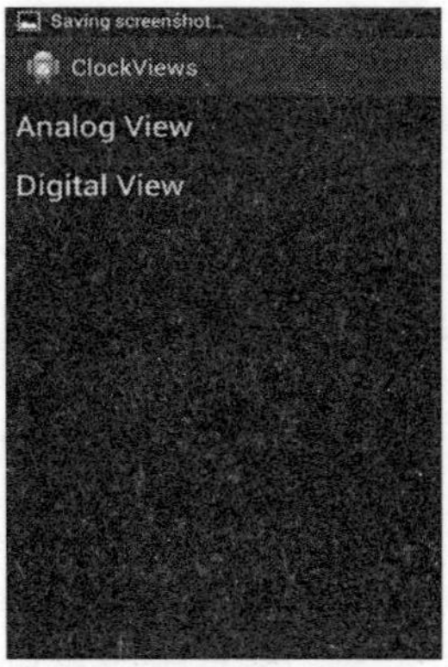

Figure 5.9: Showing the Main Interface of the ClockView Application

Now, click on the **Analog View** item; the analog clock view would be displayed, as shown in Figure 5.10:

Figure 5.10: Displaying the Analog Clock View

You can view the `DigitalClock` view by clicking the `DigitalView` item, as shown in Figure 5.11:

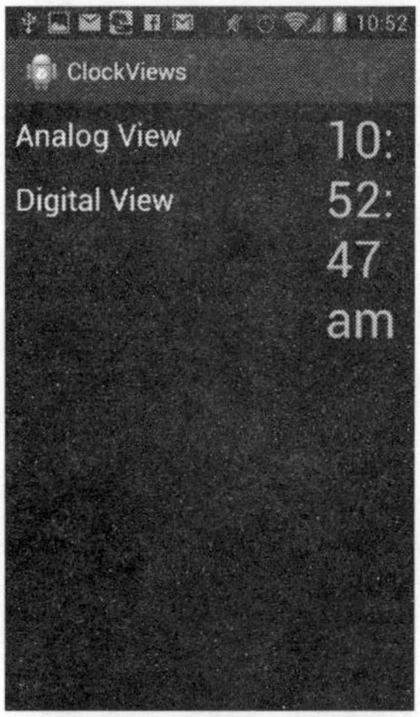

Figure 5.11: Displaying the Digital Clock View

Let us now learn how to embed Web browser in an activity of an Android application.

Embedding Web Browser in an Activity

You can embed a Web browser in your `Activity` class of the application by using Android's `WebView`. `WebView` is a class that allows you to programmatically load and display the content of a Web page in your Activity class. For instance if you want to display an image from a URL, you need to use the WebView class. Let's create an Android 4.4 application in which the image from a specific URL would be loaded and displayed using the WebView class.

Perform the following steps to create and run the `EmbedWeb` application:

1. *Create* the `EmbedWeb` application in the Eclipse IDE under the `com.kogent.android.embedweb` package.
2. *Replace* the code of the `activity_main.xml` file, located in the **/res/layout** folder, with the code shown in Listing 5.12:

Listing 5.12: Code of the `activity_main.xml` File in the `EmbedWeb` Application

```
<RelativeLayout xmlns:android="http://schemas.android.com/apk/res/android"
    xmlns:tools="http://schemas.android.com/tools"
    android:layout_width="match_parent"
    android:layout_height="match_parent"
    tools:context=".MainActivity" >
    <WebView
        android:id="@+id/webView"
        android:layout_width="match_parent"
        android:layout_height="match_parent" />
</RelativeLayout>
```

In Listing 5.12, the `<WebView>` element has been used to define the `WebView` within the `RelativeLayout`.

3. *Replace* the code of the `MainActivity.java` file, located in the **/src/com/kogent/android/embedweb** folder, with the code shown in Listing 5.13:

Listing 5.13: Code of the `MainActivity.java` File in the `EmbedWeb` Application

```
package com.kogent.android.embedweb;

import android.app.Activity;
import android.os.Bundle;
import android.webkit.WebView;

public class MainActivity extends Activity {

   /** Called when the activity is first created. */
    @Override

       public void onCreate(Bundle savedInstanceState) {
        super.onCreate(savedInstanceState);
        setContentView(R.layout.activity_main);
        WebView webView = (WebView) findViewById(R.id.webView);
        webView.getSettings().setJavaScriptEnabled(true);
        webView.loadUrl("https://www.google.co.in/?gfe_rd=cr&ei=6Jj8UuzgAq3M8gec1IHgA");
    }
}
```

In Listing 5.13, the instance of the `WebView` class has been created and the `setJavaScriptEnabled()` method has been invoked to enable the JavaScript settings. Finally, the `loadUrl()` method can be used to load the specified URL.

4. Add the `INTERNET` uses permission in the `AndroidManifest.xml` file, as shown in the following highlighted code snippet:

```
<application
        android:allowBackup="true"
        android:icon="@drawable/ic_launcher"
        android:label="@string/app_name"
        android:theme="@style/AppTheme" >
        <activity
            android:name="com.kogent.android.embedweb.MainActivity"
            android:label="@string/app_name" >
            <intent-filter>
                <action android:name="android.intent.action.MAIN" />

                <category android:name="android.intent.category.LAUNCHER" />
            </intent-filter>
        </activity>
    </application>

    <uses-permission android:name="android.permission.INTERNET" />
```

5. *Right-click* the `EmbedWeb` application and *select* Run As→Android Application. Figure 5.12 shows the output of the `EmbedWeb` application:

Figure 5.12: Showing the Embedding Web in an Application

Let us now learn about the different ways in which a user can be notified. For example, a user can be notified by creating a Toast notification or in the form of a dialog.

Notifying the User

Generally, in many situations, an event occurs in an application. For some events, the interaction of the user is not essential as the user is only required to be notified about the event. For example, consider a situation in which the user has clicked a button to save a file; now, when the saving process completes, the user needs to be notified that the file has been saved. It is also possible that an application is running in the background, in which case a notification should be displayed to the user so that the user can respond to the event according to his/her convenience. Moreover, if an operation is performed by an application, then the user should wait until the running process completes. In this case, the progress bar or the wheel should be displayed to the user. In all such cases, the following different notification techniques have been used:

- Toast notification
- Status bar notification
- Dialog notification

Let us learn how to create each of these notifications.

Creating the Toast Notification

The toast notification is a simple message that is displayed to the users on the surface of the window. This type of notification is displayed on the current activity to make it interactive with the users. For example, if an application has been created to rename or move a file, then once the task is completed, the user can be just prompted through a confirmation message. The `Toast` class can be used to create the message and display it to the users. You should note that the toast notification automatically fades in and fades out. Moreover, the events related to the user's interaction cannot be implemented during the toast notification. You can create the toast notification either from an `Activity` or a `Service`. In case of creating the toast notification from a service, the notification would be displayed in front of the current activity. In toast notification, you first need to instantiate the `Toast` object by using the `makeText()` method. You need to pass the following three arguments for the `makeText()` method:

- Application context
- Message to be displayed

- Duration for which the message needs to be displayed

While invoking the `makeText()` method, the initialized `Toast` object is being returned. Further, you can invoke the `show()` method to display the created toast notification. The following code snippet is used to create the `Toast` notification:

```
...
Context ctx = getApplicationContext();
String str = "This is the sample toast notification";
int duration = Toast.LENGTH_LONG;
Toast notify = Toast.makeText(ctx, str, duration);
notify.show();
...
```

In the preceding code snippet, the `ctx` instance has been created first to get the application context. Further, the message to be displayed has been defined and stored in the `str` variable. Moreover, the duration variable has been created to maintain the duration for which the `Toast` notification would be displayed. Next, the `makeText()` method has been invoked by passing the three arguments to initialize the notify variable. Finally, the `show()` method has been invoked on the notify variable.

Generally, the toast notification displays near the bottom of the screen, i.e., centered horizontally. The position of the toast notification can be changed by using the `setGravity()` method. The following code snippet shows the use of the `setGravity()` method:

```
notify.setGravity(Gravity.TOP(Gravity.RIGHT, 0, 0);
```

You should note that in the preceding code snippet, the value of the second parameter can be increased to nudge the position of the toast notification to the right.

Creating the Status Bar Notification

In the status bar notification, an icon is displayed in the system's status bar and the message is displayed in the notification window. The user can select the notification to display the details of the notification and to launch the activity associated with the notification. You should note that the sound alert or vibration can be configured during the notification.

Generally, the status bar notification is used in case of background service to alert the user about the event that has occurred, and the user is required to respond with respect to the event. You can create the status bar notification by using the two classes, `Notification` and `NotificationManager`. First of all, you need to create the instance of the `Notification` class to set the properties of the status bar notification, such as status bar icon, message to be displayed, and vibration to be set during the notification. The role of the `NotificationManager` class is to execute and manage all the status bar notifications. You should note that the `NotificationManager` class cannot be instantiated directly; instead, you need to get the reference through the `getSystemService()` method. The following code snippet can be used to create the status bar notification:

```
//Getting the reference to the NotificationManager
String str = Context.NOTIFICATION_SERVICE;
NotificationManager nm = (NotificationManager) getSystemService(str);

//Instantiating the Notification
int d_icon = R.drawable.android;
String msgText = "Welcome";
long duration = System.currentTimeMillis();
Notification notify = new Notification(d_icon, msg, duration);

//Setting the message and using PendingIntent
Context ctx = getApplicationContext();
String messageTitle = "Status bar notification";
String messageText = "This is a sample status bar notification";
Intent i = new Intent(this, MyIntent.class);
PendingIntent pi = PendingIntent.getActivity(this, 0, i, 0);
notify.setLatestEventInfo(ctx, messageTitle, messageText, pi);
```

```
//Passing the instance of the Notification Class to NotificationManager
private static final int HELLO_ID = 1;
nm.notify(HELLO_ID, notify);
```

In the preceding code snippet, first, the instance of the `NotificationManager` class has been retrieved by invoking the `getSystemService()` method. Next, the instance of the `Notification` class has been initialized. Further, the notification message has been set and the `PendingIntent` class has been used to retrieve the activity. Finally, the instance of the `Notification` class has been passed to the `NotificationManager` by using the `notify()` method.

Creating the Dialog Notification

The notification displayed in a small window in the form of a dialog is known as dialog notification. In case of the dialog notification, the focus of the current activity is lost and the user interaction is allowed. Generally, the dialog notification is displayed to show the progress bar or a message in which the confirmation from the user is essential. In other words, you can create a dialog box displaying the Yes, No, or Cancel buttons or displaying a progress bar.

Summary

This chapter has explained handling pictures and menus with views. Views are used to display various components, such as text box, buttons, and labels, to the users. You have learned that it is possible to display an image to the users through various views, such as `ImageView`, `Gallery`, and `ImageSwitcher`. All these views are provided by Android SDK. You have learned that a group of images can be displayed by using either Gallery view or Grid view. Images can be shown in the form of horizontal scrolling list in the Gallery View. On other hand, images can be shown as thumbnails by using the Grid view. After this, you have learned about the context menu, which appears when you tap an image for long period. You can use the context menu in your application by using the `ContextView` class.

The chapter has explained the analog and digital clock views, which can be implemented in your application by using the `AnalogClock` and `DigitalClock` classes of the `android.widget` package. Further, it has explained how to embed a Web browser in your application. You can embed a Web browser in your application by using the `WebView` class of the `android.webkit` package. You know that a specific URL can be loaded and displayed by using the `WebView` class.

Finally, you have learned how to notify a user about the ongoing events in your application. In this context, you know about the three notification techniques, namely, toast notification, status bar notification, and dialog notification. You have learned how to use these notification techniques in your application.

Quick Revise

Q1. In which of the following views, the images are displayed as thumbnails?

a. Grid View

b. Gallery View

c. ImageSwitcher View

d. Thumbnails View

Ans. The correct option is b.

Q2. Which of the following notifications would you use to configure sound alerts in an Android application?

a. Toast Notification

b. Status Bar Notification

c. Dialog Notification

d. Sound Notification

Ans. The correct option is b.

Q3. Which of the following file is not created by default in an Android application?

a. activity_main.xml

b. **strings.xml**

c. **AndroidManifest.xml**

d. **activity.xml**

Ans. The correct option is d.

Q4. Which of the following keywords is used to implement inheritance in an Android application?

a. **package**

b. **import**

c. **imports**

d. **extends**

Ans. The correct option is d.

Q5. In the grid view, the images are displayed in the thumbnail view as a __________.

a. **collection**

b. **horizontal list**

c. **scrolling list**

d. **none of these**

Ans. The correct option is a.

Q6. Which class would you use to allow a Web browser to be used in your Android application?

a. **WebBrowser**

b. **WebActivity**

c. **Toast**

d. **WebView**

Ans. The correct option is d.

Q7. You create an Android application project. Which of these classes is extended by default?

a. **Activity**

b. **Toast**

c. **ImageView**

d. **GridView**

Ans. The correct option is a.

Q8. In which of the following devices would you be able to implement the Android classes?

a. **Mobile devices**

b. **Laptops**

c. **Desktop PC'S**

d. **Super computers**

Ans. The correct option is a.

Q9. Which method is used to display the message in the toast notification?

a. **show()**

b. **makeText()**

c. **createText()**

d. **display()**

Ans. The correct option is b.

Q10. How can you create the status bar notification?

a. **Using Notification class**

b. **Using NotificationManager class**

c. **Both Notification and NotificationManager classes have to be used**

d. **Either of Notification or NotificationManager classes**

Ans. The correct option is c.

Q11. What is role of the ImageSwitcher view?

Ans. The ImageSwitcher view allows you to switch from one image to another. The switching of the images can be due to the selection of an image in the Gallery view or on the button click.

Q12. What are AnalogClock and DigitalClock views?

Ans. The AnalogClock view displays a clock with two hands, minutes and hours. However, the DigitalClock view displays the clock in the digital format.

Q13. How is a Web browser embedded in an activity class?

Ans. You can embed a Web browser in your activity class of the application by using the WebView, which allows you to programmatically load and display the content of a Web page in your activity class.

6

Storing the Data Persistently

If you need an information on:	See page:
Introducing the Data Storage Options	230
Using the Internal Storage	233
Using the External Storage	239
Using the SQLite Database	243
Working with Content Providers	262

Android allows a user to save the data persistently. For example, a user wants that the login id and password for an applicant should be saved persistently so that whenever he/she wants to login, the credentials should not be needed again. In such a case, the credentials should be saved persistently. Android provides various data storage options, such as shared preferences, internal storage, external storage, SQLite database, and network connection (Web). Using shared preferences mechanism, you can store primitive data through key-value pairs. Moreover, you can also store private data using internal and external storages. Android also allows you to store the data in the `SQLite` database in structured format. The data of an Android application can also be stored on the Web through your network server. The most amazing part is that the Android Software Development Kit (SDK) also allows the content providers to expose the private data to other applications. The content provider is a component that allows you to read or write the application data with respect to the restrictions that may have been imposed.

In this chapter, you learn how to save and retrieve data across multiple user session using the shared preferences mechanism. Next, the chapter explores the methods to use the internal storage for persistently storing the user data. You would also learn how to store the data on an external resource and retrieve the state of the external storage by using the `getExternalStorageState()` method. Toward the end of the chapter, you learn how to work with the `SQLite` database and content providers.

Introducing the Data Storage Options

Android platform provides multiple mechanisms for data persistence. These mechanisms depend on various factors, such as the amount of data to be stored, frequency of data accessibility, types of manipulations to be performed on the database, and the type of the application that needs to access the data. Let's now understand how the change in a factor can affect the selection of the mechanism. For example, if you want to store simple string or integer type values in your application, then the shared preference mechanism can be used. However, if you want to save your application data in files, then you can use internal or external storage mechanisms.

The different data storage options or mechanisms are as follows:

- The preferences
- The internal storage
- The external storage
- The SQLite database
- The content providers

Let us explore each of these options in detail.

Using Preferences

The simplest mechanism to store the user data for long term is the preferences system. In the Android platform, the activities and applications can store user preferences in the form of key/value pairs. When we say that the user preferences are being stored, it implies that the user-configuration details, such as the setting, user preference, sort order for a list, or the last website accessed by the user, are recorded. Note that the preferences can be stored either for a single activity or for multiple activities of an application.

You can access the user preferences by using the `getPreferences()`, `getSharedPreferences()`, or `getDefaultSharedPreferences()` method. The `getPreferences()` method is used within your `Activity` and allows you to access activity-specific preferences. The `getSharedPreferences()` method is also used within the `Activity` class or in other application context and allows you to access application-level preferences. The `getDefaultSharedPreferences()` method allows you to retrieve the shared preferences in relation to the overall Android preference framework.

The Android SDK provides the `SharedPreferences` class to facilitate you to save and fetch the persistent key/value pairs of primitive data types. The `SharedPreferences` class allows you to save the values of the following primitive data types:

- boolean
- float

- string
- int
- long

You should note that the data of any of the preceding data types would persist across a user's sessions even after the application has been killed. You can use either of the following methods to retrieve the instance of the `SharedPreferences` class:

- **The `getSharedPreferences()` method:** Allows you to work with multiple preferences files. Each file is identified through name, which is provided as the first parameter value.
- **The `getPreferences()` method:** Allows you to work with the single preferences file for your `Activity` class. You can avoid providing a name for the preference file as the single preference file would be your `Activity` class.

You can set the preferences in either of the following ways:

- Creating the `preferences.xml` file in the **/res/xml** folder
- Setting the preferences in the code

Let us create a simple Android application, `SharedPrefDemo`, in which the user needs to provide the login details, such as user name and password. Once the user enters these details, then the data is being maintained even after the application is closed. The data would be stored persistently using the `SharedPreferences` object. Perform the following steps to develop and execute the `SharedPrefDemo` application:

1. *Create* the `SharedPrefDemo` Android application using Eclipse under the `com.kogent.android.sharedprefdemo` package.
2. Replace the code of the `activity_main.xml` file, located in the **/res/layout** folder, with the code shown in Listing 6.1:

Listing 6.1: Displaying the Code of the `activity_main.xml` File of the `SharedPrefDemo` Application

```
<RelativeLayout xmlns:android="http://schemas.android.com/apk/res/android"
    xmlns:tools="http://schemas.android.com/tools"
    android:layout_width="match_parent"
    android:layout_height="match_parent"
    tools:context=".MainActivity" >

    <EditText
        android:id="@+id/upass"
        android:layout_width="fill_parent"
        android:layout_height="wrap_content"
        android:layout_alignParentLeft="true"
        android:layout_below="@+id/textView3"
        android:ems="10"
        android:inputType="textPassword"/>

    <TextView
        android:id="@+id/textView2"
        android:layout_width="fill_parent"
        android:layout_height="wrap_content"
        android:layout_alignParentLeft="true"
        android:layout_alignParentTop="true"
        android:text="Shared Preferences Application"
        android:textSize="30sp"/>
    <TextView
        android:id="@+id/textView1"
        android:layout_width="fill_parent"
        android:layout_height="wrap_content"
        android:layout_alignParentLeft="true"
        android:layout_below="@+id/textView2"
        android:layout_marginTop="18dp"
        android:text="User Name:" />
    <EditText
        android:id="@+id/uname"
```

```
        android:layout_width="fill_parent"
        android:layout_height="wrap_content"
        android:layout_alignParentLeft="true"
        android:layout_below="@+id/textView1"
        android:ems="10" >

        <requestFocus />
    </EditText>

    <TextView
        android:id="@+id/textView3"
        android:layout_width="fill_parent"
        android:layout_height="wrap_content"
        android:layout_alignParentLeft="true"
        android:layout_below="@+id/uname"
        android:layout_marginTop="18dp"
        android:text="User Password:" />
</RelativeLayout>
```

In Listing 6.1, two `TextView` views have been created for the user name and user password. Moreover, two `EditText` views have also been created to allow the user to enter name and password. These details provided by the user are being displayed again when the application is reloaded or re-executed.

3. Replace the code of the `MainActivity.java` file, located in the **/src/com/kogent/android/sharedprefdemo** folder, with the code shown in Listing 6.2:

Listing 6.2: Displaying the Code of the `MainActivity` Class in the `SharedPrefDemo` Application

```
package com.kogent.android.sharedprefdemo;

import android.app.Activity;
import android.content.SharedPreferences;
import android.os.Bundle;
import android.widget.EditText;

public class MainActivity extends Activity {
  public static final String User_Credentials = "User_Credentials";
  public static final String User_name = "User_name";
  public static final String User_pasword = "user_password";

  private EditText u_name;
  private EditText u_pass;
    public void onCreate(Bundle savedInstanceState) {
        super.onCreate(savedInstanceState);
        setContentView(R.layout.activity_main);
        u_name = (EditText) findViewById(R.id.uname);
        u_pass = (EditText) findViewById(R.id.upass);
       SharedPreferences settings = getSharedPreferences(User_Credentials, 0);
    String name = settings.getString(User_name, "");
    String password = settings.getString(User_pasword, "");
    u_name.setText(name);
    u_pass.setText(password);
    }
    protected void onStop(){
        super.onStop();
    SharedPreferences settings = getSharedPreferences(User_Credentials, 0);
    settings.edit()
      .putString(User_name, u_name.getText().toString())
      .putString(User_pasword, u_pass.getText().toString())
      .commit();
    }
}
```

In Listing 6.2, the settings instance has been created for the `SharedPreferences` class. When a user enters the values in the `EditText` views, the values are retrieved and set as string values for the `User_Credentials` key. For example, the user name is stored as `User_name` and the password as `User_password`. These values are stored when the `Activity` is stopped. Moreover, when the activity is being created, the values are retrieved from the `User_Credentials` key and set in the `EditText` views.

4. *Run* the `SharedPrefDemo` application and the output would be displayed as shown in Figure 6.1:

Figure 6.1: Showing User Name and Password

Now, when you enter the user name and password, as shown in Figure 6.2, then those details are displayed whenever you run the application:

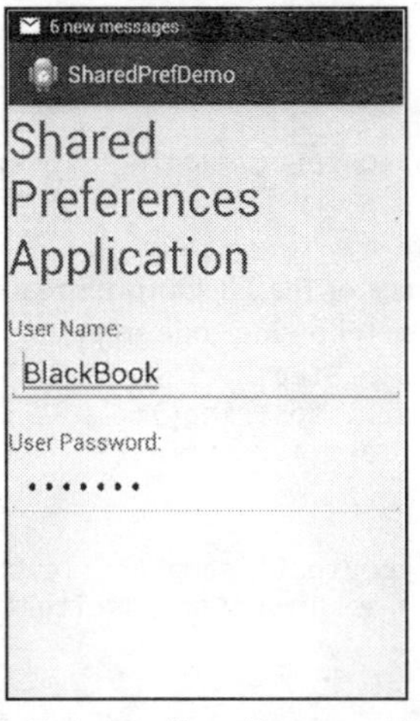

Figure 6.2: Entering User Name and Password

Note that after entering the details and closing the application, the same details are displayed on the re-execution of the application.

Let us now learn how to use the internal storage of the device to save the user data.

Using the Internal Storage

It is known that when storing the user data using the `SharedPreferences` object, the data is being stored in the key/value pairs. However, if a large amount of data needs to be stored, then you need to use the traditional mechanism of saving data using files. Imagine that you want to maintain a large amount of data, such as the details of books or products. For this, you need to create a text file to store the details, either internally within the device or externally on the Secure Digital (SD) card. In this section, you will learn how to store the data in the internal storage of an Android-supported device.

Let us first look at the methods that you can use in your application to store the data in the files.

Exploring the Methods Used for Internal Storage

You can store the data persistently in a file in the internal memory of the Android device by either creating a text file during the runtime or creating a static resource. Let us first explore how a text file can be created during the runtime of the application to store the data and saved in the internal memory of the device. Moreover, when you uninstall the application, the files (associated with the application) that have been saved on your device would also get removed automatically.

In this section, you will learn how to write the data to a file and how to read the data from an existing file.

Writing Data to Files

To create and save the data in a file, you first need to invoke the `openFileOutput()` method by passing two arguments, that is, name of the file and the operating mode. The following code snippet shows how you can use the `openFileOutput()` method:

```
//Using the openFileOutput method
FileOutputStream fOut = openFileOutput("sample_file.txt", MODE_WORLD_READABLE);
```

In the preceding code snippet, note that we have created an instance of the `FileOutputStream` class to capture the value returned by the `openFileOutput()` method. This implies that the return type of the `openFileOutput()` method is the `FileOutputStream` class. Moreover, we have passed the following two arguments to the `openFileOutput()` method:

- `sample_file.txt` – Represents the name of the file to be created to save the data
- `MODE_WORLD_READABLE` – Represents the operating mode of the file

Further, you need to write the data by invoking the `write()` method on the `FileOutputStream` object, as shown in the following code snippet:

```
String str = "Welcome Message";
FileOutputStream fOut = openFileOutput("sample_file.txt", MODE_WORLD_READABLE);
fOut.write(str.getBytes());
fOut.close();
```

Apart from writing data using the instance of the FileOutputStream class, you can also use the instance of the OutputStreamWriter class, as shown in the following code snippet:

```
String b_name = "Java 7 in Simple Steps"
String p_name = pub_Name.getText().toString();
String b_price = book_Price.getText().toString();
try
{
FileOutputStream fOut = openFileOutput("sample_file.txt", MODE_WORLD_READABLE);
   OutputStreamWriter outstr = new OutputStreamWriter(fOut);
   outstr.write(b_name);
   outstr.append(p_name);
   outstr.append(b_price);
```

After writing the data in the file, you need to close the stream by invoking the `close()` method.

Let us now look at the noteworthy operating modes that you can use to create the files that are meant to store the data. Table 6.1 describes the noteworthy operating modes:

Table 6.1: Noteworthy Operating Modes for the `openFileOutput()` Method

Name of the Operating Mode	Description
`MODE_PRIVATE`	Creates or replaces the file that would be private for your application.
`MODE_APPEND`	Allows you to write data to the end of the file, provided

Table 6.1: Noteworthy Operating Modes for the `openFileOutput()` Method	
Name of the Operating Mode	**Description**
	the file already exists. This operating mode is being used for the `openFileOutput(String, int)` method.
`MODE_WORLD_READABLE`	Al lows any application to read the created file.
`MODE_WORLD_WRITABLE`	Al lows any application to write the data to the created file

This was all about writing data to a file. Let's now learn about the methods that are used to read the data from a file.

Reading Data from a File

You need to invoke the `openFileInput()` method to read the data from a file. This method accepts the name of the file from where the content needs to be read, as an argument. The return type of the `openFileInput()` method is `FileInputStream`, as shown in the following code snippet:

```
//Using the openFileInput method
FileInputStream fInput = openFileInput("sample_file.txt);
```

After invoking the `openFileInput()` method, you can read the bytes from the file with the help of the `read()` method. Finally, you need to close the input stream by invoking the `close()` method.

Apart from the methods explored earlier in this section, the following are some noteworthy methods that you can use to store data persistently in a file:

- getFilesDir()
- getDir()
- deleteFile()
- fileList()

Let us now create an application in which the data provided by a user in the `EditText` views would be saved persistently in a file (internal storage).

Developing an Application to Save User Data Persistently in File

Imagine you want an Android application which would store the book details, provided by you, persistently in a file. In this section, we would be creating such an application, say, `PersistInternally`. In this application, you need to enter the name of the book, name of the publisher, and price of the book. After entering these details, when the user clicks the button, these details will be stored internally in a file. When the details are saved, a message is displayed, stating that the details entered by you have been saved and would display the location where the file has been saved.

Perform the following steps to create and run the `PersistInternally` application:

1. *Create* the Android application, `PersistInternally`, using Eclipse. The `MainActivity` class and the necessary XML files would be automatically created.
2. Replace the code of the `strings.xml` file in the **/res/values** folder, with the code shown in Listing 6.3:

Listing 6.3: Displaying the Code of the `strings.xml` File in the `PersistInternally` Application

```
<?xml version="1.0" encoding="utf-8"?>
<resources>
<string name="app_name">PersistInternally</string>
    <string name="action_settings">Settings</string>
    <string name="hello_world">Hello world!</string>
    <string name="hello">Hello World, PersistInternallyActivity!</string>
    <string name="title">Book Title:</string>
    <string name="publisherName">Publisher Name:</string>
    <string name="price">Price:</string>
    <string name="save">Save the Book Details</string>
</resources>
```

In Listing 6.3, some string text values are newly defined.

3. Replace the code of the `activity_main.xml` file, located in the **/res/layout** folder, with the code shown in Listing 6.4:

Listing 6.4: Displaying the Code of the `activity_main.xml` File in the `PersistInternally` Application

```
<RelativeLayout xmlns:android="http://schemas.android.com/apk/res/android"
    xmlns:tools="http://schemas.android.com/tools"
    android:layout_width="match_parent"
    android:layout_height="match_parent"
    tools:context=".MainActivity" >

    <TextView
        android:id="@+id/textView1"
        android:layout_width="fill_parent"
        android:layout_height="wrap_content"
        android:layout_alignParentLeft="true"
        android:layout_alignParentTop="true"
        android:text="@string/hello"
        android:textSize="20sp" />

    <TextView
        android:id="@+id/textView3"
        android:layout_width="wrap_content"
        android:layout_height="wrap_content"
        android:layout_alignParentLeft="true"
        android:layout_below="@+id/textView1"
        android:text="@string/title"
        android:textSize="20sp" />

    <EditText
        android:id="@+id/bookName"
        android:layout_width="fill_parent"
        android:layout_height="wrap_content"
        android:layout_alignParentLeft="true"
        android:layout_below="@+id/textView3"
        android:ems="10"
        android:textSize="20sp" />

    <TextView
        android:id="@+id/textView2"
        android:layout_width="wrap_content"
        android:layout_height="wrap_content"
        android:layout_alignParentLeft="true"
        android:layout_below="@+id/bookName"
        android:text="@string/publisherName"
        android:textSize="20sp" />

    <EditText
        android:id="@+id/pubName"
        android:layout_width="fill_parent"
        android:layout_height="wrap_content"
        android:layout_alignParentLeft="true"
        android:layout_below="@+id/textView2"
        android:ems="10"
        android:textSize="20sp" />

    <TextView
        android:id="@+id/textView4"
        android:layout_width="wrap_content"
        android:layout_height="wrap_content"
        android:layout_alignParentLeft="true"
        android:layout_below="@+id/pubName"
        android:text="@string/price"
        android:textSize="20sp" />

    <EditText
```

```
        android:id="@+id/bookPrice"
        android:layout_width="fill_parent"
        android:layout_height="wrap_content"
        android:layout_alignParentLeft="true"
        android:layout_below="@+id/textView4"
        android:ems="10"
        android:textSize="20sp" />

    <Button
        android:id="@+id/btnSave"
        android:layout_width="wrap_content"
        android:layout_height="wrap_content"
        android:layout_below="@+id/bookPrice"
        android:layout_centerHorizontal="true"
        android:text="@string/save"
        android:textSize="20sp" />
</RelativeLayout>
```

In Listing 6.4, the three `EditText` views have been created to accept the details from the user and three `TextView` views have been created as labels. Moreover, a button has been created whose id has been set as `btnSave`.

4. Replace the code of the `MainActivity.java` file, located in the **/src/com/kogent/android/persistinternally** folder, with the code shown in Listing 6.5:

Listing 6.5: Displaying the Code of the `MainActivity` Class of the `PersistInternally` Application

```
package com.kogent.android.persistinternally;

import android.app.Activity;
import android.os.Bundle;
import android.view.View;
import java.io.FileOutputStream;
import java.io.IOException;
import java.io.OutputStreamWriter;
import android.widget.Button;
import android.widget.EditText;
import android.widget.Toast;

public class MainActivity extends Activity {
    EditText book_Name, pub_Name, book_Price;
    Button btn_Save;
  /** Called when the activity is first created. */
    @Override
    public void onCreate(Bundle savedInstanceState) {
        super.onCreate(savedInstanceState);
        setContentView(R.layout.activity_main);
        book_Name = (EditText) findViewById(R.id.bookName);
        pub_Name = (EditText) findViewById(R.id.pubName);
        book_Price = (EditText) findViewById(R.id.bookPrice);
        btn_Save = (Button) findViewById(R.id.btnSave);
        btn_Save.setOnClickListener(new View.OnClickListener() {
@Override
public void onClick(View v) {
  String b_name = book_Name.getText().toString();
  String p_name = pub_Name.getText().toString();
  String b_price = book_Price.getText().toString();
  String str = "Book Name:" + b_name + " Publisher Name:" + p_name + " Price of tbook:" +
b_price;
  try
  {
        FileOutputStream fOut = openFileOutput("bookDetails.txt",
        MODE_WORLD_READABLE);
        OutputStreamWriter outstr = new OutputStreamWriter(fOut);
        outstr.write(str);
        outstr.flush();
```

```
            outstr.close();
            fout.close();
            Toast.makeText(getBaseContext(), "Book Details have been saved successfully" +
    getFilesDir(), Toast.LENGTH_LONG).show();
            book_Name.setText("");
            pub_Name.setText("");
            book_Price.setText("");
        }
        catch(IOException e)
        {
            e.printStackTrace();
        }
        }
        });
    }
}
```

In Listing 6.5, the values entered by the user in the `EditText` views have been stored in the variables and the `bookDetails.txt` file has been created. Next, the data entered by the user would be added in the `bookDetails.txt` file.

5. *Right-click* the `PersistInternally` application and select Run As→Android Application; the output would be displayed as shown in Figure 6.3:

Figure 6.3: Displaying the Entered Book Details in Application

Now, when the user enters the details in the `EditText` views and clicks the `Save the Book Details` button, the details are being saved in the `bookDetails.txt` file. After saving the user data, the message is displayed as shown in Figure 6.4:

Figure 6.4: Saving the Book Details Successfully

Let's now learn how to save files on the SD card or external storage.

Using the External Storage

In every Android-based device, you can save the data or files on an external storage, such as SD card. You have already learned how to save the files on the internal storage. While storing the files on the internal storage, you can set the operating mode of the file. However, in case of external storage, the files are in the `WORLD_READABLE` mode and the users can modify the file by transferring it to the computer. You should note that the external files can be removed if the user mounts the SD card on a computer.

Let us first explore the methods that would be used in creating the application that would store the files on an external storage and then develop the application.

Exploring the Methods Used for External Storage

Before saving the files on the external storage, you first need to validate whether or not the external storage is available in the device. You can check the availability of the external storage by using the `getExternalStorageState()` method. This method is a part of the `Environment` class, which provides the following noteworthy fields to depict the state of the external storage (media):

- **MEDIA_BAD_REMOVAL:** States that the external storage was removed before it was unmounted. The constant value of this field is `bad_removal`.
- **MEDIA_MOUNTED:** States that the external storage is available and you can either read or write data on it. The constant value of this field is mounted.
- **MEDIA_MOUNTED_READ_ONLY:** States that the external storage is available and you can only read the data from it. The constant value of this field is `mounted_ro`.
- **MEDIA_NOFS:** States that the external storage is available; however, it is either blank or the unsupported file system has been used. The constant value of this field is `nofs`.
- **MEDIA_REMOVED:** States that the external storage is not available. The constant value of this field is removed.
- **MEDIA_SHARED:** States that the external storage is available, but not mounted as the media would be shared through Universal Serial Bus (USB). The constant value of this field is shared.

Once you have checked whether the external storage media is in ready state, then you can get the absolute path of the external storage directory where you would be storing your files. To access the external storage directory, you need to invoke the `getExternalFilesDir()` method. This method returns the instance of the `File` type and accepts the type parameter, specifying the type of the directory that you want to retrieve, such as `DIRECTORY_PICTURES` or `DIRECTORY_MOVIES`. However, if you want to retrieve the root of the directory structure, then you should pass 'null' as the value of the argument. You should note that if you are using API Level 8 or higher, then you should use the `getExternalFilesDir()` method to access the directory structure of the external storage media. However, if you are using API Level 7 or lower, then you should use the `getExternalStorageDirectory()` method.

The following code snippet shows the use of the `getExternalStorageState()` and `getExternalFilesDir()` methods:

```
...
String reserve_state = Environment.getExternalStorageState();
if(Environment.MEDIA_MOUNTED.equals(reserve_state))
{
//Code to write data in the file on external storage
File sdcard = getExternalFilesDir(null);
File directory = new File (sdcard.getAbsolutePath() + "/MyFiles");
directory.mkdirs();
File file = new File(directory,"bookDetails.txt");
FileOutputStream fOut = new FileOutputStream(file);
OutputStreamWriter osw = new OutputStreamWriter(fOut);
osw.write("Welcome");
}
else if(Environment.MEDIA_MOUNTED_READ_ONLY.equals(reserve_state))
{
```

```
    //Code to read the data from a file available on the external storage media because
      the state of the media is read only
    }
...
```

After understanding how to save the data in a file on the external storage media, let us now create a simple application in which the book details provided by the user are saved in a file on the external storage media.

Developing Application to Save File in SD Card

In this section, you learn to create an Android application that saves details in a text file, which is externally saved on the space of an SD card. In this application, the text file name is `bookDetails.txt`, which will get stored in the SD card under the `MyFiles` folder. In the `bookDetails.txt` file, the book details provided by the user would be saved. However, before creating the application, you should be ensure that the running AVD device must be having sufficient space in the SD card:

Perform the following steps to create and run the `PersistExternally` application:

1. *Create* the Android application, `PersistExternally`, using Eclipse. The `MainActivity` class and the necessary XML files would be automatically created.
2. Replace the code of the `strings.xml` file in the **/res/values** folder, with the code shown in Listing 6.6:

Listing 6.6: Displaying the Code of the `strings.xml` File in the `PersistExternally` Application

```
<?xml version="1.0" encoding="utf-8"?>
<resources>
    <string name="app_name">PersistExternally</string>
    <string name="action_settings">Settings</string>
    <string name="hello_world">Hello world!</string>
    <string name="title">Book Title:</string>
    <string name="publisherName">Publisher Name:</string>
    <string name="price">Price:</string>
    <string name="save">Save the Book Details</string>
</resources>
```

In Listing 6.6, some string text values are newly defined.

3. Replace the code of the `activity_main.xml` file, located in the **/res/layout** folder, with the code shown in Listing 6.7:

Listing 6.7: Displaying the Code of the `activity_main.xml` File in the `PersistExternally` Application

```
<RelativeLayout xmlns:android="http://schemas.android.com/apk/res/android"
    xmlns:tools="http://schemas.android.com/tools"
    android:layout_width="match_parent"
    android:layout_height="match_parent"
    tools:context=".MainActivity" >

    <TextView
        android:id="@+id/textView1"
        android:layout_width="fill_parent"
        android:layout_height="wrap_content"
        android:layout_alignParentLeft="true"
        android:layout_alignParentTop="true"
        android:textSize="20sp" />

    <TextView
        android:id="@+id/textView3"
        android:layout_width="wrap_content"
        android:layout_height="wrap_content"
        android:layout_alignParentLeft="true"
        android:layout_below="@+id/textView1"
        android:text="@string/title"
        android:textSize="20sp" />

    <EditText
        android:id="@+id/bookName"
        android:layout_width="fill_parent"
        android:layout_height="wrap_content"
```

```
        android:layout_alignParentLeft="true"
        android:layout_below="@+id/textView3"
        android:ems="10"
        android:textSize="20sp" />

    <TextView
        android:id="@+id/textView2"
        android:layout_width="wrap_content"
        android:layout_height="wrap_content"
        android:layout_alignParentLeft="true"
        android:layout_below="@+id/bookName"
        android:text="@string/publisherName"
        android:textSize="20sp" />

    <EditText
        android:id="@+id/pubName"
        android:layout_width="fill_parent"
        android:layout_height="wrap_content"
        android:layout_alignParentLeft="true"
        android:layout_below="@+id/textView2"
        android:ems="10"
        android:textSize="20sp" />

    <TextView
        android:id="@+id/textView4"
        android:layout_width="wrap_content"
        android:layout_height="wrap_content"
        android:layout_alignParentLeft="true"
        android:layout_below="@+id/pubName"
        android:text="@string/price"
        android:textSize="20sp" />

    <EditText
        android:id="@+id/bookPrice"
        android:layout_width="fill_parent"
        android:layout_height="wrap_content"
        android:layout_alignParentLeft="true"
        android:layout_below="@+id/textView4"
        android:ems="10"
        android:textSize="20sp" />

    <Button
        android:id="@+id/btnSave"
        android:layout_width="wrap_content"
        android:layout_height="wrap_content"
        android:layout_below="@+id/bookPrice"
        android:layout_centerHorizontal="true"
        android:text="@string/save"
        android:textSize="20sp" />

</RelativeLayout>
```

In Listing 6.7, the three `EditText` views have been created to accept the details from the user and three `TextView` views have been created as labels. Moreover, a button has been created whose id has been set as `btnSave`.

4. Replace the code of the `MainActivity.java` file, located in the **/src/com/kogent/android/persistexternally** folder, with the code shown in Listing 6.8:

Listing 6.8: Displaying the Code of the `MainActivity` Class in the `PersistExternally` Application

```
package com.kogent.android.persistexternally;

import java.io.File;
import java.io.FileOutputStream;
import java.io.IOException;
import java.io.OutputStreamWriter;
```

```
import com.kogent.android.persistexternally.R;
import android.app.Activity;
import android.os.Bundle;
import android.view.View;
import android.widget.Button;
import android.widget.EditText;
import android.widget.Toast;

public class MainActivity extends Activity {
  EditText book_Name, pub_Name, book_Price;
  Button btn_Save;
  /** Called when the activity is first created. */
  @Override
  public void onCreate(Bundle savedInstanceState) {
  super.onCreate(savedInstanceState);
  setContentView(R.layout.activity_main);
  book_Name = (EditText) findViewById(R.id.bookName);
  pub_Name = (EditText) findViewById(R.id.pubName);
  book_Price = (EditText) findViewById(R.id.bookPrice);
  btn_Save = (Button) findViewById(R.id.btnSave);
  btn_Save.setOnClickListener(new View.OnClickListener() {
  @Override
  public void onClick(View v) {
  String b_name = book_Name.getText().toString();
  String p_name = pub_Name.getText().toString();
  String b_price = book_Price.getText().toString();
  String str = "Book Name:" + b_name + " Publisher Name:" + p_name + " Price of the
  book:" + b_price;
        try
        {
        File sdcard = getExternalFilesDir(null);
        File directory = new File (sdcard.getAbsolutePath() + "/MyFiles");
        directory.mkdirs();
        File file = new File(directory,"bookDetails.txt");
        FileOutputStream fOut = new FileOutputStream(file);
        OutputStreamWriter osw = new OutputStreamWriter(fOut);
        osw.write(str);
        osw.flush();
        osw.close();
        Toast.makeText(getBaseContext(), "Book Details have been saved successfully",
  Toast.LENGTH_LONG).show();
        book_Name.setText("");
        pub_Name.setText("");
        book_Price.setText("");
        }
        catch(IOException e)
        {
        e.printStackTrace();
        }
        }
        });
        }
  }
```

In Listing 6.8, the directory structure of the media is being fetched by using the `getExternalFilesDir()` method and the null argument has been passed to retrieve the root of the directory structure. Similar to the `MainActivity` class in the `PersistInternally` applications (Listing 6.5), the data of the `EditText` views has been retrieved and saved in the `bookDetails.txt` file, which has been saved in the `MyFiles` directory of the SD card.

5. *Provide* the writing access to the user on the external storage by providing the following code snippet in the `AndroidManifest.xml` file:

```
<uses-permission android:name="android.permission.WRITE_EXTERNAL_STORAGE"></uses-
permission>
```

6. *Right-click* the `PersistExternally` application and select `Run As→Android Application`. The output would be displayed (Figure 6.5). Enter the details of a book in the `EditText` views and click the `Save the Book Details` button. The message is displayed as shown in Figure 6.5:

Figure 6.5: Saving the Book Details Persisitently

Apart from storing the data persistently in files, you can also use tables of the database to store the user data.

Using the SQLite Database

Imagine you want to create an Android application that stores the data of all the employees of your organization. In such an application, huge amount of data needs to be stored and it is not feasible to store such data in text files or documents. For this, you need to create a database that can store the data in the form of a record. Android provides the support for the `SQLite` database, which can be accessed by developers while developing an application (or you can say within an application) and not beyond the application. When you work with the `SQLite` database, it is advisable to create the helper class for the database in which you can define few methods to perform the regular database operations. For example, whenever you need to update, insert, or delete a record from the database, you need to connect to the database, and when the database is no longer in use, you need to close the connection. Such implementations can be done in the methods defined in the database helper class.

Let's create the `EmployeeDatabaseApp` Android application in which you can add, update, or delete the details of an employee. Moreover, you can search the details of a specific employee on the basis of the employee id or you can fetch the records of all the employees from the database. Let's develop this application in the following modules:

- Database helper class
- Layout and code for the main activity class
- Layout and activity class to add a record
- Layout and activity class to search a record
- Layout and activity class to search all records
- Layout and activity class to update a record
- Layout and activity class to delete a record

Let us work on each of these modules.

Creating the Database Helper Class

For the `EmployeeDatabaseApp` application, you need to create a database helper class in which you would define various methods, such as `connect()`, `disconnect()`, `insertEmployee()`, `retrieveAllEmployees()`, `retrieveEmployee()`, `updateEmployee()`, and `deleteEmployee()`. In any activity class of the application, you can simply create an instance of the database helper class and invoke the desired method to perform a database operation. For example, if you are creating an activity class for inserting the employee record, then you can simply invoke the `insertEmployee()` method of the database helper class. You should first create the `EmployeeDatabaseApp` Android application using Eclipse. By default, the `MainActivity` class would be created as the main activity along with the required Android XML files. Perform the following steps to create the database helper class for the `EmployeeDatabaseApp` application:

1. *Right-click* the `EmployeeDatabaseApp` application and select **New→Class**, as shown in Figure 6.6:

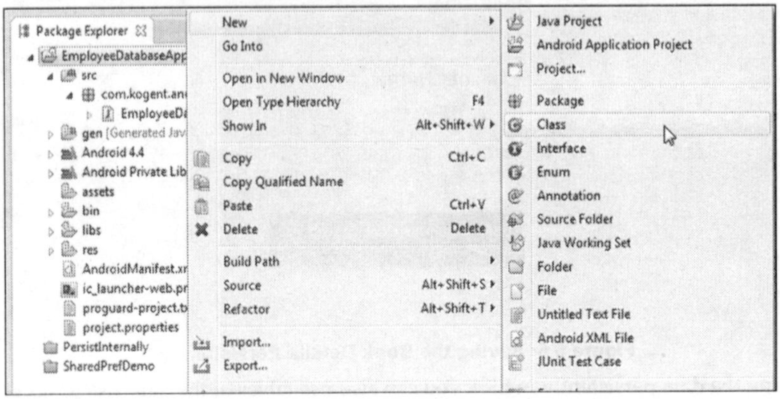

Figure 6.6: Adding a New Java Class

The **New Java Class** dialog box opens (Figure 6.7).

2. *Enter* the name of the package as `com.kogent.android.employeedatabaseapp` (Figure 6.7).
3. *Enter* the name of the class as `EmployeeDBHelper` in the **Name** text box (Figure 6.7).
4. *Click* the **Finish** button, as shown in Figure 6.7:

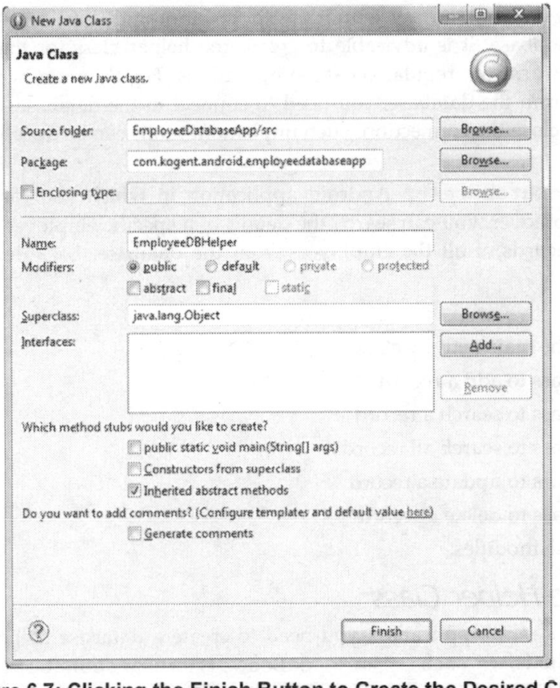

Figure 6.7: Clicking the Finish Button to Create the Desired Class

The `EmployeeDBHelper` class would be created and displayed in the **Package Explorer** view.

5. Replace the code of the `EmployeeDBHelper` class with the code shown in Listing 6.9:

Listing 6.9: Displaying the Code of the `EmployeeDBHelper` Class

```
package com.kogent.android.employeedatabaseapp;
import android.content.ContentValues;
import android.content.Context;
import android.database.Cursor;
import android.database.SQLException;
import android.database.sqlite.SQLiteDatabase;
import android.database.sqlite.SQLiteOpenHelper;
public class EmployeeDBHelper
{
public static final String EmpId = "EmpId";
public static final String EmpName = "EmpName";
public static final String EmpSal = "EmpSal";
private static final String databasename = "EmployeeDB";
private static final String tablename = "Employee";
private static final int databaseversion = 1;
private static final String create_table = "create table Employee (EmpId integer
   primary key autoincrement, " + "EmpName text not null, EmpSal integer not      null);";
private final Context ct;
private DatabaseHelper dbHelper;
private SQLiteDatabase database;
public EmployeeDBHelper(Context context)
{
   this.ct = context;
   dbHelper = new DatabaseHelper(ct);
}
private static class DatabaseHelper extends SQLiteOpenHelper
{
   DatabaseHelper(Context c)
   {
         super(c,databasename,null,databaseversion);
   }
   @Override
   public void onCreate(SQLiteDatabase database) {
         try
         {
                  database.execSQL(create_table);
         }
         catch(SQLException ex)
         {
                  ex.printStackTrace();
         }
   }
   @Override
   public void onUpgrade(SQLiteDatabase database, int arg1, int arg2) {
         database.execSQL("DROP TABLE IF EXISTS Employee");
         onCreate(database);
   }
}
   //Declaring the connect() method to connect to the database
public EmployeeDBHelper connect() throws SQLException
{
   database = dbHelper.getWritableDatabase();
   return this;
}
//Declaring the disconnect() method to close the database
public void disconnect()
{
   dbHelper.close();
}
//Declaring the insertEmployee() method to add the employee details into the     database
public long insertEmployee(String empname, int empsal)
```

```
{
   ContentValues cv = new ContentValues();
   cv.put(EmpName, empname);
   cv.put(EmpSal, empsal);
   this.connect();
   return database.insert(tablename, null, cv);
}
//Declaring the retrieveAllEmployees() method to retrieve the details of all the
   employees from the database
public Cursor retrieveAllEmployees()
{
   this.connect();
   return database.query(tablename, new String[] { EmpId, EmpName, EmpSal}, null,
         null, null, null, null);
}
//Declaring the retrieveEmployees() method to retrieve the details of an employee
   from the database
public Cursor retrieveEmployee(long id) throws SQLException
{
   this.connect();
   Cursor c = database.query(true, tablename, new String [] {EmpId, EmpName,
         EmpSal}, EmpId + "=" + id, null, null, null, null, null);
   if (c != null)
   {
         c.moveToFirst();
   }
   return c;
}
//Declaring the deleteEmployee() method to delete the details of an Employee
public boolean deleteEmployee(long id)
{
   this.connect();
   return database.delete(tablename, EmpId + "=" + id, null) > 0;
}
//Declaring the updateEmployee() method to update the details of an Employee
public boolean updateEmployee(long id, String empname, int empsal)
{
   this.connect();
   ContentValues cvalues = new ContentValues();
   cvalues.put(EmpName, empname);
   cvalues.put(EmpSal, empsal);
   return database.update(tablename, cvalues, EmpId + "=" + id, null) > 0;
}
}
```

In Listing 6.9, the queries for inserting, updating, deleting, and retrieving the records have been defined under the appropriate methods. Moreover, you can also find the query to create the `Employee` table which is used to maintain the employee records for the `EmployeeDatabaseApp` application.

Let us now create the `MainActivity` class from where the appropriate activity class would be invoked to perform the database operation.

Creating the Layout and Main Activity Class

When you create the `EmployeeDatabaseApp` application, the `MainActivity` class would have been created with the `activity_main.xml` file by default. The `MainActivity` class is the main class which would be invoked during the execution of the application. Perform the following steps to edit the `activity_main.xml` file and the `MainActivity` class:

1. *Open* the `activity_main.xml` file located in the **/res/layout** folder of the application.
2. *Replace* the code of the activity_main.xml file with the code shown in Listing 6.10:

Listing 6.10: Displaying the Code of the `activity_main.xml` File of the `EmployeeDatabaseApp` Application

```
<RelativeLayout xmlns:android="http://schemas.android.com/apk/res/android"
   xmlns:tools="http://schemas.android.com/tools"
```

```
    android:layout_width="match_parent"
    android:layout_height="match_parent"
    tools:context=".MainActivity" >

    <Button
        android:id="@+id/addEmp"
        android:layout_width="wrap_content"
        android:layout_height="wrap_content"
        android:layout_alignParentLeft="true"
        android:layout_alignParentTop="true"
        android:layout_alignRight="@+id/updateEmp"
        android:text="Add an Employee" />

    <Button
        android:id="@+id/updateEmp"
        android:layout_width="wrap_content"
        android:layout_height="wrap_content"
        android:layout_alignParentLeft="true"
        android:layout_below="@+id/addEmp"
        android:layout_marginTop="16dp"
        android:text="Update an Employee" />

    <Button
        android:id="@+id/deleteEmp"
        android:layout_width="match_parent"
        android:layout_height="wrap_content"
        android:layout_alignParentLeft="true"
        android:layout_alignRight="@+id/updateEmp"
        android:layout_below="@+id/updateEmp"
        android:layout_marginTop="30dp"
        android:text="Delete an Employee" />

    <Button
        android:id="@+id/selectEmp"
        android:layout_width="wrap_content"
        android:layout_height="wrap_content"
        android:layout_alignParentLeft="true"
        android:layout_alignRight="@+id/deleteEmp"
        android:layout_below="@+id/deleteEmp"
        android:layout_marginTop="23dp"
        android:text="Get an Employee" />

    <Button
        android:id="@+id/selectAllEmp"
        android:layout_width="wrap_content"
        android:layout_height="wrap_content"
        android:layout_alignParentLeft="true"
        android:layout_alignRight="@+id/selectEmp"
        android:layout_below="@+id/selectEmp"
        android:layout_marginTop="30dp"
        android:text="Get All Employees" />
</RelativeLayout>
```

In Listing 6.10, various buttons have been created for allowing a user to perform different database operations. For example, the **Add an Employee** button has been created to add the details of an employee in the `Employee` table.

3. Replace the code of the `MainActivity.java` file, located in the **/src/com/kogent/android/employeedatabaseapp** folder, with the code shown in Listing 6.11:

Listing 6.11: Displaying the Code of the `MainActivity` Class in the `EmployeeDatabaseApp` Application

```
package com.kogent.android.employeedatabaseapp;

import android.app.Activity;
import android.content.Intent;
import android.os.Bundle;
import android.view.View;
import android.view.View.OnClickListener;
import android.widget.Button;

public class MainActivity extends Activity implements OnClickListener
{
   Button add_emp, get_all_emp, get_emp, update_emp, delete_emp;
   /** Called when the activity is first created. */
     @Override
     public void onCreate(Bundle savedInstanceState) {
          super.onCreate(savedInstanceState);
          setContentView(R.layout.activity_main);
           add_emp = (Button) findViewById(R.id.addEmp);
           add_emp.setOnClickListener(this);
           get_all_emp = (Button) findViewById(R.id.selectAllEmp);
           get_all_emp.setOnClickListener(this);
           get_emp = (Button) findViewById(R.id.selectEmp);
           get_emp.setOnClickListener(this);
           update_emp = (Button) findViewById(R.id.updateEmp);
           update_emp.setOnClickListener(this);
           delete_emp = (Button) findViewById(R.id.deleteEmp);
           delete_emp.setOnClickListener(this);
     }
   public void onClick(View v) {
           if(v == findViewById(R.id.addEmp))
           {
                    Intent i = new Intent(this, AddEmployee.class);
                    startActivity(i);
           }
           if (v == findViewById(R.id.selectAllEmp))
           {
                    Intent i = new Intent(this, GetAllEmployees.class);
                    startActivity(i);
           }
           if (v == findViewById(R.id.selectEmp))
           {
                    Intent i = new Intent(this, GetEmployee.class);
                    startActivity(i);
           }
           if (v == findViewById(R.id.updateEmp))
           {
                    Intent i = new Intent(this, UpdateEmployee.class);
                    startActivity(i);
           }
           if (v == findViewById(R.id.deleteEmp))
           {
                    Intent i = new Intent(this, DeleteEmployee.class);
                    startActivity(i);
           }
     }
}
```

In Listing 6.11, the `OnClick` event has been set for the button designed in the `activity_main.xml` file. With the click of a button, the appropriate activity class would be invoked. For example, if a user clicks the **Add an Employee** button, whose id is `addEmp`, then the `AddEmployee` activity class would be invoked.

After adding the code in the `MainActivity` class file, you need to create various activity classes, such as `AddEmployee`, `GetAllEmployees`, `GetEmployee`, `UpdateEmployee`, and `DeleteEmployee`.

Creating the Layout and Activity for the Insert Operation

You need to create the layout and the activity class to insert an employee record in the `Employee` table. The layout shows the view that would be displayed to the user when the **Add an Employee** button (created in Listing 6.7) is clicked. In the `EmployeeDatabaseApp` application, to insert a record, a user needs to provide the name and salary of the employee in the `EditText` views. We would create the `addemployee` layout to accept the values to be added in the database. Moreover, we would create the `AddEmployee` activity class to invoke the `insertEmployee()` method of the `EmployeeDBHelper` database helper class. Perform the following steps to create the layout and activity for insert operation:

1. *Create* the Android XML file, `addemployee.xml`, in the **/res/layout** folder in the `EmployeeDatabaseApp` application. Listing 6.12 shows the code of the `addemployee.xml` file:

Listing 6.12: Displaying the Code of the `addemployee.xml` File in the `EmployeeDatabaseApp` Application

```
<?xml version="1.0" encoding="utf-8"?>
<LinearLayout xmlns:android="http://schemas.android.com/apk/res/android"
    android:layout_width="match_parent"
    android:layout_height="match_parent"
    android:orientation="vertical" >

    <TextView
        android:layout_width="wrap_content"
        android:layout_height="wrap_content"
        android:text="Enter the Name of the Employee:" />

    <EditText
        android:id="@+id/empname"
        android:layout_width="fill_parent"
        android:layout_height="wrap_content" />

    <TextView
        android:layout_width="wrap_content"
        android:layout_height="wrap_content"
        android:text="Enter the Salary of the Employee:" />

    <EditText
        android:id="@+id/empsal"
        android:layout_width="fill_parent"
        android:layout_height="wrap_content" />

    <Button
        android:id="@+id/addEmp"
        android:layout_width="wrap_content"
        android:layout_height="wrap_content"
        android:text="Add Employee" />

</LinearLayout>
```

In Listing 6.12, the layout containing two `EditText` views, two `TextViews`, and a `Button` has been designed.

2. *Create* a new Java class, named `AddEmployee`, in the **/src** folder and under the `com.kogent.android.employeedatabaseapp` package. Listing 6.13 shows the code of the `AddEmployee.java` file:

Listing 6.13: Displaying the Code of the `AddEmployee` Class in the `EmployeeDatabaseApp` Application

```
package com.kogent.android.employeedatabaseapp;
import android.app.Activity;
import android.os.Bundle;
import android.view.View;
import android.widget.Button;
import android.widget.EditText;
import android.widget.Toast;
public class AddEmployee extends Activity
{
   Button add_emp;
   EditText empname, empsal;
   @Override
     public void onCreate(Bundle savedInstanceState) {
          super.onCreate(savedInstanceState);
          setContentView(R.layout.addemployee);
          final EmployeeDBHelper empdbhelper = new EmployeeDBHelper(this);
         empname = (EditText) findViewById(R.id.empname);
          empsal = (EditText) findViewById(R.id.empsal);
          add_emp = (Button) findViewById(R.id.addEmp);
          add_emp.setOnClickListener(new View.OnClickListener()
          {
           @Override
           public void onClick(View v) {
  try{
  String name;
  int sal;
  name = empname.getText().toString();
  sal = (Integer.parseInt(empsal.getText().toString()));
  long id = empdbhelper.insertEmployee(name, sal);
   Toast.makeText(getBaseContext(), "Your record has been saved successfully with ID : " +
id,
           Toast.LENGTH_LONG).show();
                         }
                    catch(Exception e)
                    {
                              e.printStackTrace();
                    }
          }
     });
}
}
```

In Listing 6.13, the values entered by the user in the `EditText` views have been retrieved and passed to the `insertEmployee()` method of the database helper class. This method returns the long type value, i.e., the auto-generated employee id, which has been displayed using the `Toast` notification.

Similar to the insert operation, let us now create the layout and activity class to retrieve the details of a specific employee.

Creating the Layout and Activity to Search a Record

Similar to other databases, you can also search a specific record from the `SQLite` database. Imagine you need to view the details of an employee whose id is 1. In such a case, you first need to get the id of the employee (from the user) whose details need to be fetched from the database. Further, you need to query the database on the basis of the user data (employee id). Let us create the layout that would be displayed to the user to provide the employee id. Also, we would be creating the activity class in which the `retrieveEmployee()` method of the database helper class would be invoked.

Perform the following steps to create the layout and activity class to search a record from the database:

1. *Create* the Android XML file, `getemployee.xml`, in the **/res/layout** folder in the `EmployeeDatabaseApp` application. Listing 6.14 shows the code of the `getemployee.xml` file:

Listing 6.14: Displaying the Code of the `getemployee.xml` File in the `EmployeeDatabaseApp` Application

```
<?xml version="1.0" encoding="utf-8"?>
<LinearLayout xmlns:android="http://schemas.android.com/apk/res/android"
    android:layout_width="match_parent"
    android:layout_height="match_parent"
    android:orientation="vertical" >

    <TextView
        android:layout_width="wrap_content"
        android:layout_height="wrap_content"
        android:text="Enter the Employee id" />

    <EditText
        android:id="@+id/empid"
        android:layout_width="fill_parent"
        android:layout_height="wrap_content" />

    <Button
        android:id="@+id/btn_find"
        android:layout_width="wrap_content"
        android:layout_height="wrap_content"
        android:text="Find Employee" />

</LinearLayout>
```

In Listing 6.14, the `TextView`, `EditText`, and `Button` views have been created to accept the employee id from the user.

2. *Create* a new Java class, named `GetEmployee`, in the **/src** folder and under the `com.kogent.android.employeedatabaseapp` package. Listing 6.15 shows the code of the `GetEmployee.java` file:

Listing 6.15: Displaying the Code of the `GetEmployee.java` File in the `EmployeeDatabaseApp` Application

```
package com.kogent.android.employeedatabaseapp;

import android.app.Activity;
import android.database.Cursor;
import android.os.Bundle;
import android.view.View;
import android.widget.Button;
import android.widget.EditText;
import android.widget.Toast;

public class GetEmployee extends Activity
{
   Button find_emp;
   EditText empid;
   @Override
     public void onCreate(Bundle savedInstanceState) {
         super.onCreate(savedInstanceState);
         setContentView(R.layout.getemployee);
         final EmployeeDBHelper empdb = new EmployeeDBHelper(this);
         empid = (EditText) findViewById(R.id.empid);
```

```
        find_emp = (Button) findViewById(R.id.btn_find);
        find_emp.setOnClickListener(new View.OnClickListener()
        {
        @Override
        public void onClick(View v)
        {
                int emp_id = Integer.parseInt(empid.getText().toString());
                Cursor c = empdb.retrieveEmployee(emp_id);
                if(c.moveToFirst())
                {
                Toast.makeText(getBaseContext(), "Employee Id" + c.getString(0) +
                "\n Employee Name" + c.getString(1) + "  \n Employee Salary" +
                c.getString(2), Toast.LENGTH_LONG).show();
                }
                else
                {
                        Toast.makeText(getBaseContext(), "No Employee Record
                        Found", Toast.LENGTH_LONG).show();
                }
        }

      });
  }
  }
```

In Listing 6.15, the `retrieveEmployee()` method of the `EmployeeDBHelper` class has been invoked, which would return the `Cursor` type value. Further, the cursor has been iterated using the `moveToFirst()` method and the record fetched from the database would be displayed as the `Toast` notification to the users.

Apart from retrieving a single record from the database, you can also fetch all records from the `SQLite` database. Let us create the activity class to retrieve all employee records.

Creating the Activity Class to Fetch All Records

In the `EmployeeDBHelper` class, we have created the `retrieveAllEmployees()` method to fetch all employee records from the table. The `EmployeeDatabaseApp` application displays all the records, available in the table, one by one in the form of `Toast` notification to the users. As no user input is required to fetch all records from the database, you would be creating only the activity class `GetAllEmployees`.

Perform the following steps to create the `GetAllEmployees` activity class:

1. *Create* a new Java class, named `GetAllEmployees`, in the **/src** folder and under the `com.kogent.android.employeedatabaseapp` package. Listing 6.16 shows the code of the `GetAllEmployees.java` file:

Listing 6.16: Displaying the Code of the `GetAllEmployees.java` File in the `EmployeeDatabaseApp` Application

```
package com.kogent.android.employeedatabaseapp;

import android.app.Activity;
import android.database.Cursor;
import android.os.Bundle;
import android.widget.Toast;

public class GetAllEmployees extends Activity
{

  @Override
    public void onCreate(Bundle savedInstanceState) {
        super.onCreate(savedInstanceState);
        final EmployeeDBHelper emphelper = new EmployeeDBHelper(this);
        Cursor c = emphelper.retrieveAllEmployees();
```

```
            if(c.moveToFirst())
            {
             do
             {
                    Toast.makeText(this, "Employee Id:" + c.getString(0) + "\n" +
                    "Employee Name:" + c.getString(1) + "\n" + "Employee Salary:" +
                    c.getString(2), Toast.LENGTH_LONG).show();
             }
             while(c.moveToNext());
            }
            else
            {
             Toast.makeText(this, "No Records in the database",
             Toast.LENGTH_LONG).show();
            }
        }
    }
```

In Listing 6.16, the `retrieveAllEmployees()` method has been invoked, which returns the value of the `Cursor` type. The cursor is being iterated over the result obtained from the database to display the details of all the employees. You should note that the employee details have been displayed as `Toast` notification to the user, and if no record is available in the database, then **No Records in the database** message will be displayed.

Let us now design the layout for updating an employee record and create the activity class.

Creating the Layout and Activity for the Update Operation

A record can be updated in the table on the basis of a specific field. For example, if you want to update an employee record, you need to provide the id of the employee whose record needs to be updated in the database. Moreover, on the basis of the employee id, the details of that employee should be displayed to the users so that they can update the data. For this, we have created a layout, `updateemployee`, in which the user has to enter the id of the employee in the `EditText` view and the rest of the `EditText` views gets automatically filled up with the details of the employee, such as name and salary. Further, the user can edit the name or salary fields and click the `Update` button to make the updation in the database. The code to update the record would be provided in the activity class `UpdateEmployee`. Perform the following tasks to create the layout and activity class for the update database operation:

1. *Create* the Android XML file, `updateemployee.xml`, in the **/res/layout** folder in the `EmployeeDatabaseApp` application. Listing 6.17 shows the code of the `updateemployee.xml` file:

Listing 6.17: Displaying the Code of the `updateemployee.xml` File in the `EmployeeDatabaseApp` Application

```
<?xml version="1.0" encoding="utf-8"?>
<LinearLayout xmlns:android="http://schemas.android.com/apk/res/android"
    android:layout_width="match_parent"
    android:layout_height="match_parent"
    android:orientation="vertical" >
    <TextView
        android:layout_width="wrap_content"
        android:layout_height="wrap_content"
        android:text="Enter the Employee id" />
    <EditText
        android:id="@+id/empid"
        android:layout_width="fill_parent"
        android:layout_height="wrap_content" />
    <TextView
        android:layout_width="wrap_content"
        android:layout_height="wrap_content"
        android:text="Employee Name" />
    <EditText
        android:id="@+id/empname"
```

```
        android:layout_width="fill_parent"
        android:layout_height="wrap_content" />
    <TextView
        android:layout_width="wrap_content"
        android:layout_height="wrap_content"
        android:text="Employee Salary" />
    <EditText
        android:id="@+id/empsal"
        android:layout_width="fill_parent"
        android:layout_height="wrap_content" />
    <Button
        android:id="@+id/btn_update"
        android:layout_width="wrap_content"
        android:layout_height="wrap_content"
        android:text="Update" />

</LinearLayout>
```

In Listing 6.17, three `TextViews` and three `EditText` views along with a `Button` have been designed.

2. *Create* a new Java class, named `UpdateEmployee`, in the **/src** folder and under the `com.kogent.android.employeedatabaseapp` package. Listing 6.18 shows the code of the `UpdateEmployee.java` file:

Listing 6.18: Displaying the Code of the `UpdateEmployee.java` File in the `EmployeeDatabaseApp` Application

```
package com.kogent.android.employeedatabaseapp;

import android.app.Activity;
import android.database.Cursor;
import android.os.Bundle;
import android.text.Editable;
import android.text.TextWatcher;
import android.view.View;
import android.widget.Button;
import android.widget.EditText;
import android.widget.Toast;

public class UpdateEmployee extends Activity
{
   EditText empid, empname, empsal;
   Button update;
   @Override
     public void onCreate(Bundle savedInstanceState) {
          super.onCreate(savedInstanceState);
   setContentView(R.layout.updateemployee);
     final EmployeeDBHelper empdb = new EmployeeDBHelper(this);
     empid = (EditText) findViewById(R.id.empid);
     empname = (EditText) findViewById(R.id.empname);
     empsal = (EditText) findViewById(R.id.empsal);
     update = (Button) findViewById(R.id.btn_update);
     update.setOnClickListener(new View.OnClickListener()
     {
          @Override
          public void onClick(View v)
          {
                   int emp_id = Integer.parseInt(empid.getText().toString());
                   String empstr = empname.getText().toString();
                   int intsal = Integer.parseInt(empsal.getText().toString());
                   if (empdb.updateEmployee(emp_id, empstr, intsal))
```

Listing 6.19: Displaying the Code of the `deleteemployee.xml` File in the `EmployeeDatabaseApp` Application

```
<?xml version="1.0" encoding="utf-8"?>
<LinearLayout xmlns:android="http://schemas.android.com/apk/res/android"
    android:layout_width="match_parent"
    android:layout_height="match_parent"
    android:orientation="vertical" >
    <TextView
        android:layout_width="wrap_content"
        android:layout_height="wrap_content"
        android:text="Enter the Employee id" />
    <EditText
        android:id="@+id/empid"
        android:layout_width="fill_parent"
        android:layout_height="wrap_content" />
    <Button
        android:id="@+id/btn_delete"
        android:layout_width="wrap_content"
        android:layout_height="wrap_content"
        android:text="Delete Employee" />
</LinearLayout>
```

In Listing 6.19, the `TextView`, `EditText`, and `Button` views have been created. The user needs to provide the id in the `EditText` view, and when the `DeleteEmployee` button is clicked, the data of that employee would be deleted from the database.

2. *Create* the `DeleteEmployee` class, in the **/src** folder and under the `com.kogent.android.employeedatabaseapp` package, as the activity to implement the delete operation. Add the code shown in Listing 6.20 in the `DeleteEmployee.java` file:

Listing 6.20: Displaying the Code of the `DeleteEmployee.java` File in the `EmployeeDatabaseApp` Application

```
package com.kogent.android.employeedatabaseapp;

import android.app.Activity;
import android.os.Bundle;
import android.view.View;
import android.widget.Button;
import android.widget.EditText;
import android.widget.Toast;

public class DeleteEmployee extends Activity
{
  EditText empid;
  Button delete;
  @Override
    public void onCreate(Bundle savedInstanceState) {
        super.onCreate(savedInstanceState);
        setContentView(R.layout.deleteemployee);
        final EmployeeDBHelper empdbhelper = new EmployeeDBHelper(this);
         empid = (EditText) findViewById(R.id.empid);
        delete = (Button) findViewById(R.id.btn_delete);
        delete.setOnClickListener(new View.OnClickListener()
        {
         @Override
         public void onClick(View v) {
           int emp_id = Integer.parseInt(empid.getText().toString());
        if(empdbhelper.deleteEmployee(emp_id))
         Toast.makeText(getBaseContext(), "Your record has been deleted",
         Toast.LENGTH_LONG).show();
        else
         Toast.makeText(getBaseContext(), "Record does not exist",
         Toast.LENGTH_LONG).show();
```

```
                        {
                                Toast.makeText(getBaseContext(), "Record has been updated",
                        Toast.LENGTH_LONG).show();
                        }
                        else
                        {
                                Toast.makeText(getBaseContext(), "Record has not been update
                        Toast.LENGTH_LONG).show();
                        }

                }
        });
            empid.addTextChangedListener(new TextWatcher()
            {
                @Override
                public void afterTextChanged(Editable e){
                }
                @Override
                public void beforeTextChanged(CharSequence s, int start, int count,int
                after) {

                }
                @Override
                public void onTextChanged(CharSequence s, int start, int before,int count)
                {
                                empid.setEnabled(false);
                                int emp_id = Integer.parseInt(empid.getText().toString());
                        Cursor c = empdb.retrieveEmployee(emp_id);
                        if(c.moveToFirst())
                        {
                            empname.setText(c.getString(1));
                            empsal.setText(c.getString(2));
                        }
                        else
                        {
                                Toast.makeText(getBaseContext(), "No Employee Record
                                Found", Toast.LENGTH_LONG).show();
                        }
                }
            });
        }
        }
```

In Listing 6.18, the employee data from the database has been retrieved on the basis of the employee id provic by the user. This data is displayed in the `EditText` views so that the user can edit the data. Further, when user clicks the `Update` button, the values from the `EditText` views have been retrieved and updated in t database by invoking the `updateEmployee()` method.

Finally, let us understand the delete operation, i.e., to delete an employee record from the `Employee` table. Le us create the layout and activity class to delete a record.

Creating the Layout and Activity for the Delete Operation

Similar to other operations, let us design the `deleteemployee` layout in which the user needs to provide an employee id whose record needs to be deleted from the table. Perform the following steps to create the layout and the activity class to implement the delete operation:

1. *Create* the `deleteemployee.xml` file as the layout to implement the delete operation in the `EmployeeDatabaseApp` application. Add the code shown in Listing 6.19 in the `deleteemployee.xml` file:

```
        }
    });
    }
    }
```

In Listing 6.20, the `deleteEmployee()` method has been invoked by passing the employee id as an argument.

Finally, let us execute the `EmployeeDatabaseApp` application to perform all the database operations and see how the results are being displayed to the users.

Executing the Database Operations

You can execute the `EmployeeDatabaseApp` application by selecting the `Run As→Android Application` option, which appears during the right-click of the application.

Note that before executing the application, you should have configured all the activity classes in the `AndroidManifest.xml` file, as shown in the following code snippet:

```
    <application
            android:allowBackup="true"
            android:icon="@drawable/ic_launcher"
            android:label="@string/app_name"
            android:theme="@style/AppTheme" >
            <activity
                android:name="AddEmployee"
                android:label="Add Employee" >
            </activity>
            <activity
                android:name="DeleteEmployee"
                android:label="Delete Employee" >
            </activity>
            <activity
                android:name="EmployeeDBHelper"
                android:label="EmployeeDBHelper" >
            </activity>
            <activity
                android:name="GetAllEmployees"
                android:label="Get All Employee" >
            </activity>
            <activity
                android:name="GetEmployee"
                android:label="Get Employee" >
            </activity>
            <activity
                android:name="UpdateEmployee"
                android:label="Update Employee" >
            </activity>
            <activity
                android:name="com.kogent.android.employeedatabaseapp.MainActivity"
                android:label="@string/app_name" >
                <intent-filter>
                    <action android:name="android.intent.action.MAIN" />

                    <category android:name="android.intent.category.LAUNCHER" />
                </intent-filter>
            </activity>
        </application>
```

When you execute the application, the welcome screen is displayed, as shown in Figure 6.8:

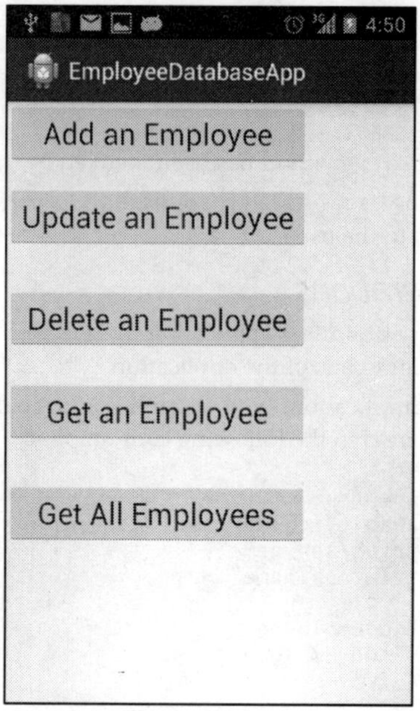

Figure 6.8: Displaying the Welcome Screen of the Application

Now, click the `Add an Employee` button to add the details of an employee in the database. When you click the button, the `addemployee` layout is displayed. You can enter the details of the employee to be added in the database, as shown in Figure 6.9:

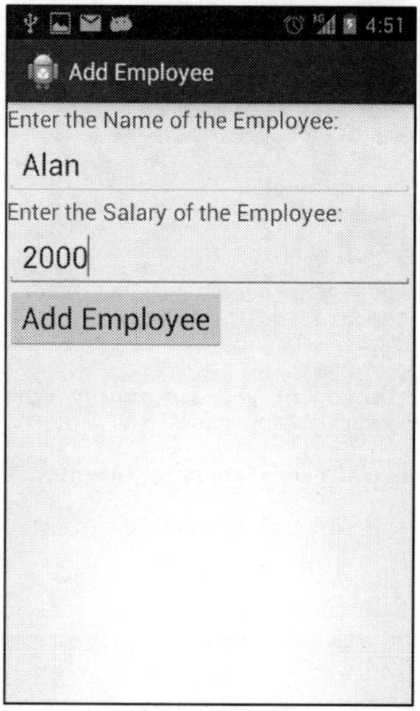

Figure 6.9: Adding a New Employee

After entering the details, when you click the **Add Employee** button, the message is displayed as shown in Figure 6.10:

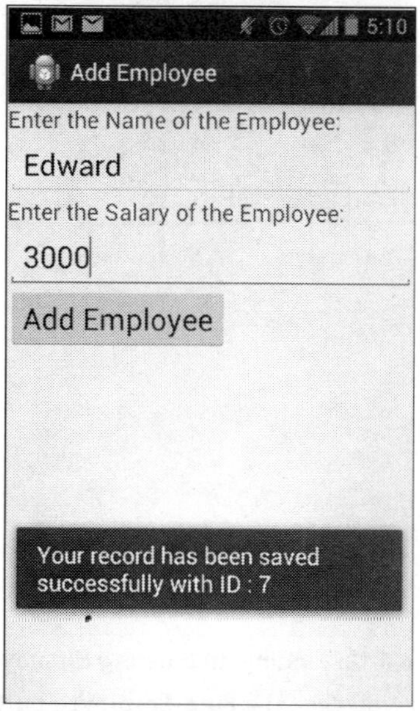

Figure 6.10: Saving the Employee Record

Next, let us see how the **Get All Employee** button (Figure 6.8) functions. When you click the button, the details of all the employees will be displayed one by one as the `Toast` notifications. For example, Figure 6.11 shows the details of an employee:

Figure 6.11: Getting the All Employee Details

Next, click the **Get an Employee** button (Figure 6.8); the `getemployee` layout is displayed in which you need to enter an employee id, as shown in Figure 6.12:

Figure 6.12: Finding an Existing Employee

After providing the employee id, when you click the **Find Employee** button, the details of that employee will be displayed, as shown in Figure 6.13:

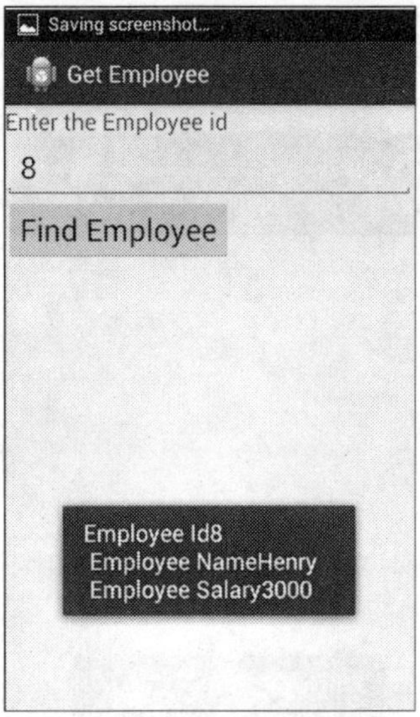

Figure 6.13: Displaying Successful Fetching of Employee Record

Let us now click the **Update an Employee** button (Figure 6.8), and the `updateemployee` layout will be displayed. When you enter the employee id, the remaining `EditText` views would be automatically filled up, as shown in Figure 6.14:

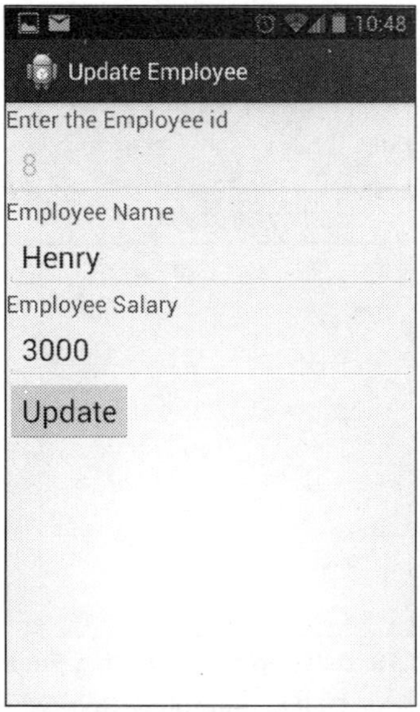

Figure 6.14: Updating the Record of an Existing Employee

Now, you can edit the name or salary of the employee and click the `Update` button. The details of the employee would be updated in the database and the message would be dispalyed as shown in Figure 6.15:

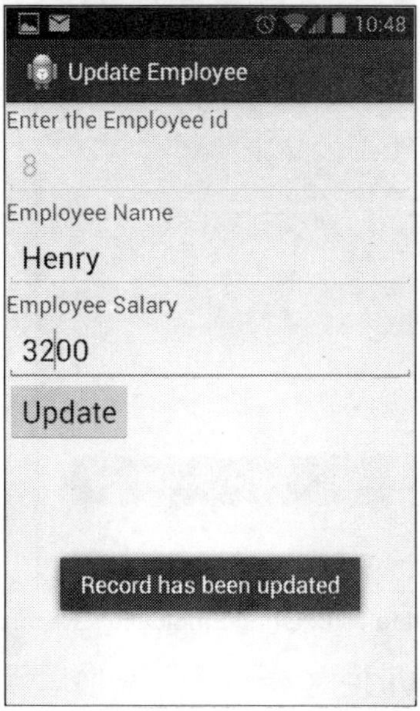

Figure 6.15: Udpating the Record Successfully

Finally, click the **Delete an Employee** button (Figure 6.8), and the `deleteemployee` layout would be displayed. You need to provide the employee id, as shown in Figure 6.16:

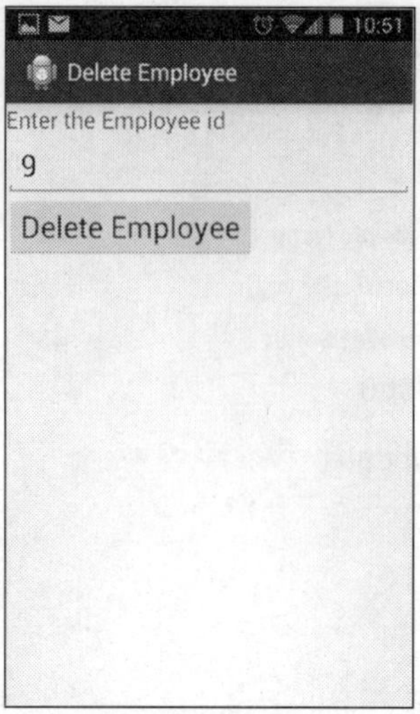

Figure 6.16: Deleting of an Existing Employee

After entering the employee id, click the **Delete Employee** button; the record would be deleted from the database and the message would be displayed as shown in Figure 6.17:

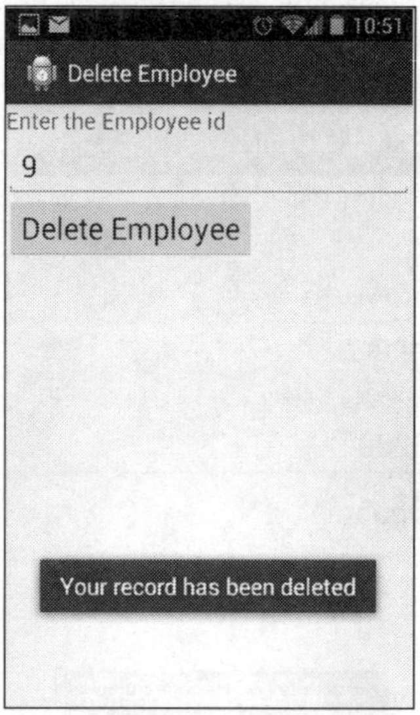

Figure 6.17: Deleting an Existing Employee's Record Successfully

Working with Content Providers

When the data of an application is persistently stored in the `SQLite` database, the data is accessible only within the package of the application. In other words, the data would not be shared with the other applications. If you want to share your data across multiple Android applications, then you should use content providers to persistently store and share the data. Note that the use of content providers is the only mechanism to share the data as there is no common location or storage from where all Android packages can access the data.

Each content provider may vary from one another in the manner the data is stored in them. However, the common interface of querying the provider and fetching the data is being followed for all content providers. You can query a content provider by using a query string in the form of a Uniform Resource Identifier (URI). The syntax of the query URI is as follows:

```
<standard_prefix>://<authority>/<data_path>/<id>
```

In the preceding syntax, we have:

- <standard_prefix>—Allows you to use content:// as the standard prefix for all content providers.
- <authority>—Represents the name of the content provider. For example, for the built-in Contacts content provider, the word contact is used as the authority. However, in case of third party content providers, you need to provide the fully qualified name, such as com.kogent.android need to be used depending upon the package of the content provider.
- <data_path>—States the type of data that would be requested from the content provider. For example, if you are working with the Contacts content provider, then you can use people as the data path as you need to work with the contact information stored in the provider.
- <id>—Represents the specific record to be requested. For example, if you want to fetch the details of the 2nd contact stored in the memory, then you can use 2 as the id in the query URI.

By default, there are multiple content providers in Android for various data types, such as images, audio, video, or any contact. The android.provider package lists various content providers that can be used. You can query the existing content providers according to the type of data held by them, provided you have specified the desired user permissions in the AndroidManifest XML file. However, if you want to make your own data for public use, then you either need to create your own content provider or add your data in the existing content provider. In this section, you first explore the android.provider package and would learn how to work with the existing content providers.

Exploring the android.provider Package

The android.provider package facilitates you with the classes that can be used to access the existing content providers. These classes contain various methods to add or retrive data from the content providers. Table 6.2 lists the noteworthy classes to access the existing content providers:

Table 6.2: Noteworthy Classes of the android.provider Package for Content Providers

Class	Description
AlarmClock	Serves as the provider that has an Intent action class to set an alarm in the clock application of the Android device.
CallLog	Serves as the provider containing the details of the missed and received calls.
ContactsContract	Serves as the provider to store the contact-related data in the three-tier data model database.
CalendarContract	Serves as the contract between the calendar provider and applications. The calendar database can be manipulated using this class.
MediaStore	Serves as the provider to store the meta-data of the media available in the internal and external storages of the Android device.
Settings	Serves as the provider to store global system-level preferences of the Android-based devices.
SyncStateContract	Serves as the provider contract to link the data with any array account containing data.
UserDictionary	Serves as the provider that contains some user-defined words that can be suggested to a user to input the text value.

To understand, let us select the `CalendarContract` class from the `android.provider` package as this class has been enhanced greatly in API 14.

In the APIs prior to Android 4.0 API (level 14), there was lack of support for the Android system's integrated calendar. Some unofficial APIs were used by developers to compensate the shortcoming of the calendar API. However, Google officially warned them not to use the third party APIs as this might break applications that were taking advantage. Google recognized the problem and released official APIs to interact with the core calendar application in Android 4. The class which does this in Android is called `CalendarContract`, which enables developer to read, write, and further manipulate the underneath database of calendar.

As mentioned earlier, the `CalendarContract` class is the class that provides the data model and event information. The table used to store the user data is defined by the subclasses of the `CalendarContract` class. Some of the subclasses of the `CalendarContract` class are as follows:

- **The `CalendarContract.Calendars`** – Refers to the table that stores basic calendar information such as name, sync information, and color.
- **The `CalendarContract.Events`** – Refers to the table that store events.
- **The `CalendarContract.Instances`** – Refers to the table that specifies the start and end of an event.
- **The `CalendarContract.Attendees`** – Refers to the table that stores the event attendee or guest information.
- **The `CalendarContract.Reminders`** – Refers to the table that holds the alert and notification data to the user.
- **The `CalendarContract.ExtendedProperties`** – Refers to the table that specifies opaque data fields accomplished by the sync adapter.

To access the read and write permissions for Android system calendar, you have to request them in the `AndroidManifest.xml` file.

For more understanding, let us make an Android application named `CalendarDemo` in Eclipse IDE. The steps for creating the `CalendarDemo` application are as follows:

1. *Create* the `CalendarDemo` Android application in Eclipse IDE with minimum SDK API level 14 under the `com.kogent.android.calendardemo` package.
2. In Package Explorer, *expand* the `CalendarDemo` project. *Write* the code for the `activity_main.xml` file in the **/res/layout** folder. Listing 6.21 shows the code for the `activity_main.xml` file:

Listing 6.21: Displaying the Code of the `activity_main.xml` File in the `CalendarDemo` Application

```
<?xml version="1.0" encoding="utf-8"?>
<LinearLayout xmlns:android="http://schemas.android.com/apk/res/android"
    android:layout_width="fill_parent"
    android:layout_height="fill_parent"
    android:orientation="vertical" >

    <TextView
        android:layout_width="fill_parent"
        android:layout_height="wrap_content"
        android:gravity="center"
        android:padding="10dip"
        android:text="Android 4.4.2 calendar" />
    <TextView
        android:id="@+id/stats"
        android:layout_width="fill_parent"
        android:layout_height="wrap_content"
        android:gravity="center"
        android:padding="10dip" />
    <LinearLayout
        android:layout_width="fill_parent"
        android:layout_height="wrap_content"
        android:gravity="center"
        android:orientation="horizontal" >
```

```
        <Button
            android:id="@+id/back"
            android:layout_width="wrap_content"
            android:layout_height="wrap_content"
            android:padding="10dip"
            android:text="Back" />

        <Button
            android:id="@+id/forward"
            android:layout_width="wrap_content"
            android:layout_height="wrap_content"
            android:padding="10dip"
            android:text="Forward" />
    </LinearLayout>
</LinearLayout>
```

In Listing 6.21, two `LinearLayouts` views are inserted with two `TextView` and two `Button` controls.

3. Now, let us write the code for the `MainActivity` class in the \src\`com\kogent\android\calendardemo` folder. Listing 6.22 shows the code of the `MainActivity` class:

Listing 6.22: Displaying the Code of the `MainActivity` Class in the `CalendarDemo` Application

```
package com.kogent.android.calendardemo;

import java.text.DateFormat;
import java.text.Format;
import android.os.Bundle;
import android.provider.CalendarContract;
import android.app.Activity;
import android.database.Cursor;
import android.view.Menu;
import android.view.View;
import android.view.View.OnClickListener;
import android.widget.Button;
import android.widget.TextView;

public class MainActivity extends Activity implements OnClickListener {
  private Cursor myCursor = null;
  private static final String[] CALEVENTS = new String[] {
             CalendarContract.Events.TITLE, CalendarContract.Events.DTSTART };

  @Override
  protected void onCreate(Bundle savedInstanceState) {
        super.onCreate(savedInstanceState);
        setContentView(R.layout.activity_main);
        myCursor = getContentResolver().query(
                    CalendarContract.Events.CONTENT_URI, CALEVENTS, null, null,
                    null);
        myCursor.moveToFirst();
        Button button = (Button) findViewById(R.id.forward);
        button.setOnClickListener(this);
        button = (Button) findViewById(R.id.back);
        button.setOnClickListener(this);
        onClick(findViewById(R.id.back));
  }

  @Override
  public void onClick(View v) {
        TextView textView = (TextView) findViewById(R.id.stats);
        String title = "N/A";
        Long start = 0L;
        switch (v.getId()) {
        case R.id.forward:
              if (!myCursor.isLast())
                    myCursor.moveToNext();
```

```
                break;
        case R.id.back:
                if (!myCursor.isFirst())
                        myCursor.moveToPrevious();
                break;
        }
        Format dateFormat = DateFormat.getDateInstance();
        Format timeFormat = DateFormat.getTimeInstance();
        try {
                title = myCursor.getString(0);
                start = myCursor.getLong(1);
        } catch (Exception e) {
                // ignore
        }
        textView.setText(title + " on " + dateFormat.format(start) + " at "
        + timeFormat.format(start));
    }
}
```

The `Cursor` class is used in Listing 6.22 for triggering database events.

4. *Request* for the read permission in the Android system calendar in the `AndroidManifest.xml` file. The following code snippet shows the request for the read permission:

```
<uses-permission android:name="android.permission.READ_CALENDAR"/>
```

5. The `CalendarDemo` application is now complete. Let us execute the application. Before the execution, remember that your AVD should target at API level 14. If not, do configure accordingly. When you execute the application, it will appear as shown in Figure 6.18:

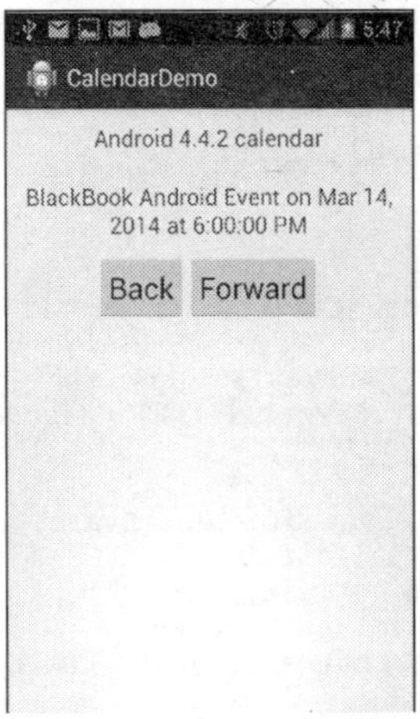

Figure 6.18: Displaying the Interface of Calendar Application

Since no event is added, the calendar shows the default UNIX date and time in Figure 6.18. By adding events in the calendar, we can navigate backward and forward in between the events. However, you have to register your email address to add the event with the calendar.

Creating User-Defined Content Provider

You can also create your own content providers in Android. For this, you have to extend a class from the `ContentProvider` base class and override the various methods defined in it. Let's create an Android application named `UserDefinedContentProvider` by performing the following steps:

1. *Create* the `UserDefinedContentProvider` Android application in the Eclipse IDE under the `com.kogent.android.userdefinedcontentprovider` package.
2. *Add* a new Java class named `Contentprovider.java`, in the **/src** folder under the `com.kogent.android.userdefinedcontentprovider` package, as shown in Listing 6.23:

Listing 6.23: Displaying the Code of the `Contentprovider.java` File in the `UserDefinedContentProvider` Application

```
package com.kogent.android.userdefinedcontentprovider;
import java.util.HashMap;
import android.content.ContentProvider;
import android.content.ContentUris;
import android.content.ContentValues;
import android.content.Context;
import android.content.UriMatcher;
import android.database.Cursor;
import android.database.SQLException;
import android.database.sqlite.SQLiteDatabase;
import android.database.sqlite.SQLiteOpenHelper;
import android.database.sqlite.SQLiteQueryBuilder;
import android.net.Uri;

public class Contentprovider extends ContentProvider {

   static final String PROVIDER_NAME =
   "com.kogent.android.userdefinedcontentprovider.Contentprovider";
   static final String URL = "content://" + PROVIDER_NAME + "/cte";
   static final Uri CONTENT_URI = Uri.parse(URL);

   static final String id = "id";
   static final String name = "name";
   static final int uriCode = 1;
   static final UriMatcher uriMatcher;
   private static HashMap<String, String> values;
   static {
         uriMatcher = new UriMatcher(UriMatcher.NO_MATCH);
         uriMatcher.addURI(PROVIDER_NAME, "cte", uriCode);
         uriMatcher.addURI(PROVIDER_NAME, "cte/*", uriCode);
   }

   @Override
   public int delete(Uri uri, String selection, String[] selectionArgs) {
         int count = 0;
         switch (uriMatcher.match(uri)) {
         case uriCode:
                count = db.delete(TABLE_NAME, selection, selectionArgs);
                break;
         default:
                throw new IllegalArgumentException("Unknown URI " + uri);
         }
         getContext().getContentResolver().notifyChange(uri, null);
         return count;
   }

   @Override
   public String getType(Uri uri) {
         switch (uriMatcher.match(uri)) {
         case uriCode:
                return "vnd.android.cursor.dir/cte";

         default:
                throw new IllegalArgumentException("Unsupported URI: " + uri);
         }
   }

   @Override
   public Uri insert(Uri uri, ContentValues values) {
         long rowID = db.insert(TABLE_NAME, "", values);
         if (rowID > 0) {
                Uri _uri = ContentUris.withAppendedId(CONTENT_URI, rowID);
                getContext().getContentResolver().notifyChange(_uri, null);
```

```
                return _uri;
        }
        throw new SQLException("Failed to add a record into " + uri);
}

@Override
public boolean onCreate() {
        Context context = getContext();
        DatabaseHelper dbHelper = new DatabaseHelper(context);
        db = dbHelper.getWritableDatabase();
        if (db != null) {
                return true;
        }
        return false;
}

@Override
public Cursor query(Uri uri, String[] projection, String selection,
                String[] selectionArgs, String sortOrder) {
        SQLiteQueryBuilder qb = new SQLiteQueryBuilder();
        qb.setTables(TABLE_NAME);

        switch (uriMatcher.match(uri)) {
        case uriCode:
                qb.setProjectionMap(values);
                break;
        default:
                throw new IllegalArgumentException("Unknown URI " + uri);
        }
        if (sortOrder == null || sortOrder == "") {
                sortOrder = name;
        }
        Cursor c = qb.query(db, projection, selection, selectionArgs, null,
                        null, sortOrder);
        c.setNotificationUri(getContext().getContentResolver(), uri);
        return c;
}

@Override
public int update(Uri uri, ContentValues values, String selection,
                String[] selectionArgs) {
        int count = 0;
        switch (uriMatcher.match(uri)) {
        case uriCode:
                count = db.update(TABLE_NAME, values, selection, selectionArgs);
                break;
        default:
                throw new IllegalArgumentException("Unknown URI " + uri);
        }
        getContext().getContentResolver().notifyChange(uri, null);
        return count;
}

private SQLiteDatabase db;
static final String DATABASE_NAME = "mydb";
static final String TABLE_NAME = "names";
static final int DATABASE_VERSION = 1;
static final String CREATE_DB_TABLE = " CREATE TABLE " + TABLE_NAME
                + " (id INTEGER PRIMARY KEY AUTOINCREMENT, "
                + " name TEXT NOT NULL);";

private static class DatabaseHelper extends SQLiteOpenHelper {
        DatabaseHelper(Context context) {
                super(context, DATABASE_NAME, null, DATABASE_VERSION);
        }
```

```
            @Override
            public void onCreate(SQLiteDatabase db) {
                    db.execSQL(CREATE_DB_TABLE);
            }

            @Override
            public void onUpgrade(SQLiteDatabase db, int oldVersion, int newVersion) {
                    db.execSQL("DROP TABLE IF EXISTS " + TABLE_NAME);
                    onCreate(db);
            }
    }
}
```

In Listing 6.23, the `Contentprovider` class extends the `ContentProvider` class and overrides the various methods of this class. The `getType()` method returns the `MIME` type of the data at the given `URI`. The `onCreate()` method is called when the provider is started. The `query()` method receives a request from a client. The result is returned as a `Cursor` object. The `insert()` method inserts a new record into the content provider. The `delete()` method that deletes an existing record from the content provider, and the `update()` method updates an existing record from the content provider.

3. Replace the code of the `strings.xml` file, located in the **/res/values** folder, with the code shown in Listing 6.24:

Listing 6.24: Displaying the Code of the `strings.xml` File in the `UserDefinedContentProvider` Application

```
<?xml version="1.0" encoding="utf-8"?>
<resources>

    <string name="app_name">UserDefinedContentProvider\n
android:authorities=\"com.kogent.android.userdefinedcontentprovider.Contentprovider\">\n&l
t;/provider></string>
    <string name="action_settings">Settings</string>
    <string name="hello_world">Hello world!</string>

</resources>
```

In Listing 6.24, android authority is configured to create a user defined content provider.

4. Replace the code of the `activity_main.xml` file, located in the /res/layout folder, with the code shown in Listing 6.25:

Listing 6.25: Displaying the Code of the `activity_main.xml` File in the `UserDefinedContentProvider` Application

```
<LinearLayout xmlns:android="http://schemas.android.com/apk/res/android"
    android:layout_width="fill_parent"
    android:layout_height="fill_parent"
    android:orientation="vertical" >
    <TextView
        android:layout_width="fill_parent"
        android:layout_height="wrap_content"
        android:text="Name" />
    <EditText
        android:id="@+id/txtName"
        android:layout_width="fill_parent"
        android:layout_height="wrap_content" />
    <Button
        android:id="@+id/btnAdd"
        android:layout_width="fill_parent"
        android:layout_height="wrap_content"
        android:onClick="onClickAddName"
        android:text="Add Name" />
</LinearLayout>
```

In Listing 6.25, a linear layout view is created with an `EditText` and a `Button` controls.

5. Replace the code of the MainActivity.java file, located in the **\src\com\kogent\android\userdefinedcontentprovider** folder, with the code shown in Listing 6.26:

Listing 6.26: Displaying the Code of the MainActivity.java File in the UserDefinedContentProvider Application

```
package com.kogent.android.userdefinedcontentprovider;

import android.os.Bundle;
import android.app.Activity;
import android.view.Menu;
import android.content.ContentValues;
import android.net.Uri;
import android.os.Bundle;
import android.view.Menu;
import android.view.View;
import android.widget.EditText;
import android.widget.Toast;
public class MainActivity extends Activity {
  @Override
  protected void onCreate(Bundle savedInstanceState) {
        super.onCreate(savedInstanceState);
        setContentView(R.layout.activity_main);
  }

  @Override
  public boolean onCreateOptionsMenu(Menu menu) {
        // Inflate the menu; this adds items to the action bar if it is present.
        getMenuInflater().inflate(R.menu.main, menu);
        return true;
  }

  public void onClickAddName(View view) {
          ContentValues values = new ContentValues();
          values.put(Contentprovider.name, ((EditText) findViewById(R.id.txtName))
            .getText().toString());
          Uri uri = getContentResolver().insert(Contentprovider.CONTENT_URI, values);
          Toast.makeText(getBaseContext(), "New record inserted", Toast.LENGTH_LONG)
            .show();
        }
}
```

In Listing 6.26, the MainActivity class is created. The onClickAddName() method is used to add new records.

6. Add the provider element in the AndroidManifest.xml file, as shown in the following code snippet:

```
<application
      android:allowBackup="true"
      android:icon="@drawable/ic_launcher"
      android:label="@string/app_name"
      android:theme="@style/AppTheme" >
      <activity
          android:name="com.kogent.blackbook.userdefinedcontentprovider.MainActivity"
          android:label="@string/app_name" >
          <intent-filter>
              <action android:name="android.intent.action.MAIN" />

              <category android:name="android.intent.category.LAUNCHER" />
          </intent-filter>
      </activity>
      <provider
               android:name=".contentprovider"
 android:authorities="com.kogent.blackbook.userdefinedcontentprovider.contentprovider"
        android:exported="true"
        android:grantUriPermissions="true"
       android:multiprocess="true" >
       </provider>
  </application>
```

The `UserDefinedContentProvider` application is now complete. Let us execute the application now. When you execute the application, it will appear as shown in Figure 6.19:

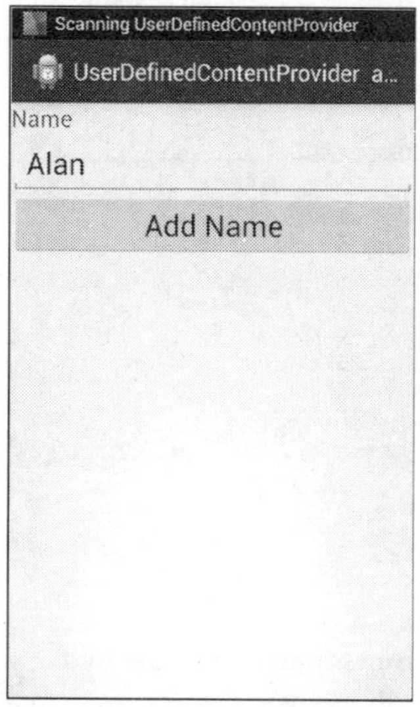

Figure 6.19: Displaying the Output of the UserDefinedContentProvider Application

Enter a name in the provide field and click the **Add Name** button. Then, the **New Record Inserted** message is displayed, as shown in Figure 6.20:

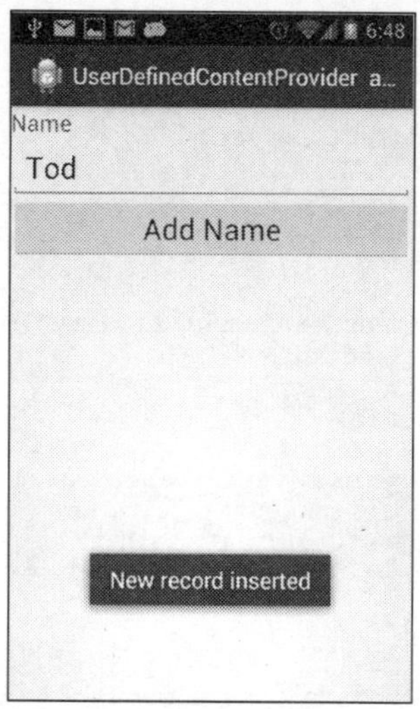

Figure 6.20: Adding New Record

Consuming User-Defined Content Provider

Now, let's learn how to consume the content provider, which is created in the earlier section. Let's create an Android application named `consumecontentprovider` by performing the following steps:

1. *Create* the `consumecontentprovider` Android application with the `MainActivity` class in the Eclipse IDE under the `com.kogent.android.consumecontentprovider` package.
2. Replace the code of the `activity_main.xml` file, located in the **/res/layout** folder, with the code shown in Listing 6.27:

Listing 6.27: Displaying the Code of the `activity_main.xml` File in the `consumecontentprovider` Application

```
<LinearLayout xmlns:android="http://schemas.android.com/apk/res/android"
    android:layout_width="fill_parent"
    android:layout_height="fill_parent"
    android:orientation="vertical" >
    <Button
        android:id="@+id/btnRetrieve"
        android:layout_width="fill_parent"
        android:layout_height="wrap_content"
        android:onClick="onClickDisplayNames"
        android:text="Display names" />
    <TextView
        android:id="@+id/res"
        android:layout_width="match_parent"
        android:layout_height="wrap_content"
        android:layout_marginLeft="20dp"
        android:clickable="false"
        android:ems="10" >
    </TextView>
</LinearLayout>
```

In Listing 6.27, a button and a textview are added.

3. Replace the code of the `MainActivity.java` file, located in the **\src\com\kogent\android\consumecontentprovider** folder, with the code shown in Listing 6.28:

Listing 6.28: Displaying the Code of the `MainActivity.java` File in the `consumecontentprovider` Application

```
package com.kogent.android.consumecontentprovider;
import android.net.Uri;
import android.os.Bundle;
import android.support.v4.app.FragmentActivity;
import android.support.v4.app.LoaderManager;
import android.support.v4.content.CursorLoader;
import android.support.v4.content.Loader;
import android.view.Menu;
import android.view.View;
import android.widget.TextView;
import android.database.Cursor;

public class MainActivity extends FragmentActivity implements
LoaderManager.LoaderCallbacks<Cursor> {
   TextView resultView=null;
      CursorLoader cursorLoader;
   @Override
   protected void onCreate(Bundle savedInstanceState) {
         super.onCreate(savedInstanceState);
         setContentView(R.layout.activity_main);
         resultView= (TextView) findViewById(R.id.res);
   }

   @Override
   public boolean onCreateOptionsMenu(Menu menu) {
         // Inflate the menu; this adds items to the action bar if it is present.
         getMenuInflater().inflate(R.menu.main, menu);
         return true;
   }

   public void onClickDisplayNames(View view) {
          getSupportLoaderManager().initLoader(1, null, this);
         }

   @Override
   public Loader<Cursor> onCreateLoader(int arg0, Bundle arg1) {
         cursorLoader= new CursorLoader(this,
```

```
  Uri.parse("content://com.kogent.android.userdefinedcontentprovider.Contentprovider/cte"),
  null, null, null, null);
            return cursorLoader;
    }

    @Override
    public void onLoadFinished(Loader<Cursor> arg0, Cursor cursor) {

          cursor.moveToFirst();
            StringBuilder res=new StringBuilder();
                  while (!cursor.isAfterLast()) {
                   res.append("\n"+cursor.getString(cursor.getColumnIndex("id"))+ "-"+
  cursor.getString(cursor.getColumnIndex("name")));
                      cursor.moveToNext();
                  }
                  resultView.setText(res);
          }


    @Override
    public void onLoaderReset(Loader<Cursor> arg0) {
          // TODO Auto-generated method stub

    }

    @Override
     public void onDestroy() {
            super.onDestroy();
       }

    }
```

In Listing 6.28, the `MainActivity` class extends the `FragmentActivity` class and implements the `LoadManager` interface. This class invokes the content provider created in the `contentprovider` in the `UserDefinedContentProvider` application. It should be noted that the Uri.parse ("content://com.kogent.android.userdefinedcontentprovider.Contentprovider/cte") method is used for external packages, which you need to refer to the content URI using the fully qualified
content URI. The `consumecontentprovider` application is now complete. Let us execute the application now. When you execute the application, it will appear as shown in Figure 6.21:

Figure 6.21: Displaying the Output of the `consumecontentprovider` Application

When you click the Display names button, a list of added names are displayed, as shown in Figure 6.22:

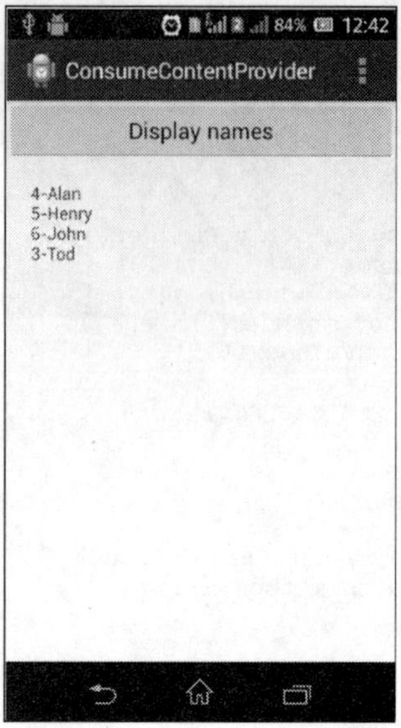

Figure 6.22: Displaying a List of Names

Summary

The chapter has provided the description of data storage options. It has explained the different data storage mechanisms in Android system, such as preferences, internal storage, external storage, the `SQLite` database, and content providers. The chapter has explained how the preference system is the simplest mechanism to store the user data for long term. In case of internal storage mechanism, you need to invoke the `openFileOutput()` and `openFileInput()` methods to write the data and read the data from a file, respectively. You have also learned that to save user data persistently, you are required to store the data internally in a text file or document. After this, you have learned about the external storage mechanism in which you can check the availability of free space by using the `getExternalStorageState()` method.

Further, the chapter has explained the `SQLite` database, which provides the best storage solution when you do not want to store your data in the form of text files or documents. You have also learned that the `SQLite` database can be accessed within the application and not beyond that application. The `SQLiteDatabase` and the `SQLiteOpenHelper` are the two classes of the `android.database.sqlite` package which are used to take the advantage of `SQLite` database.

You have learned that the data is accessible only within the package of the application if you have used `SQLite` database in that application. The chapter has discussed that content providers are used to persistently store and share the data across multiple Android applications. You can get various content providers from the `android.providers` package. On other hand, you can also create your own content provider for sharing data with other applications.

Quick Revise

Q1. Which of the following is the data storage option in an Android application?

- **a. The Preference**
- **b. The Internal Storage**
- **c. The External Storage**
- **d. The Activities**

Ans. The correct option is d.

Q2. **Which of the following data types is not supported by the SharedPreferences class?**

a. **int**

b. **float**

c. **long**

d. **DateTime**

Ans. The correct option is d.

Q3. **Which of the following methods can be used to view the Folders in an Android application?**

a. **getDir()**

b. **getFiles()**

c. **getFolders()**

d. **getDirs()**

Ans. The correct option is a.

Q4. **Which of the following fields indicate that the external storage is available but not mounted?**

a. **MEDIA_NOFS**

b. **MEDIA_SHARED**

c. **MEDIA_MOUNTED_READ-ONLY**

d. **MEDIA_BAD_REMOVAL**

Ans. The correct option is b.

Q5. **What is the return type of the getExternalStorageState() method which can be used to check the state of the external devices?**

a. **int**

b. **bool**

c. **Long**

d. **String**

Ans. The correct option is d.

Q6. **Which of these databases is inbuilt in the Android operating system?**

a. **SQL Server**

b. **SQLite**

c. **MySQL**

d. **MySQL Server**

Ans. The correct option is b.

Q7. **Which of the following classes serves as the provider used to store global system- level preferences of the Android-based devices?**

a. **Settings**

b. **SyncStateContract**

c. **UserDictionary**

d. **ContactsContract**

Ans. The correct option is a.

Q8. **Which of these methods can be used to view the user preferences in the context of the overall Android framework?**

a. **getPreferences(),**

b. **getSharedPreferences()**

c. **getDefaultSharedPreferences()**

d. **None of these**

Ans. The correct option is c.

Q9. You attempt to write some data in an Android-based device. In which of these folders will the file containing your data be created?

a. **MyFolders**

b. **MyFiles**

c. **Bluetooth**

d. **MyFile**

Ans. The correct option is b.

Q10. Which of these classes can provide the methods related to depicting the state of the media?

a. **Environment**

b. **Activity**

c. **FileInputStream**

d. **FileOutputStream**

Ans. The correct option is a.

Q11. Enlist some data storage mechanisms in Android development.

Ans. The different data storage mechanisms in Android development are as follows:

- The Preferences
- The internal storage
- The external storage
- The SQLite database
- The content providers

Q12. How is the user data stored for long term using preferences?

Ans. The simplest mechanism to store the user data for long term is the preferences system. In the Android platform, the activities and applications can store user preferences in the form of key/value pairs. When we say that the user preferences are being stored, it implies that the user-configuration details, such as the setting, user preference, sort order for a list, or the last website accessed by the user, are recorded. Note that the preferences can be stored either for a single activity or for multiple activities of an application.

Q13. Explain the role of the SharedPreferences class.

Ans. The Android SDK provides the SharedPreferences class to facilitate you to save and fetch the persistent key/value pairs of primitive data types. The SharedPreferences class allows you to save the values of various primitive data types, such as boolean and string. You can use either of the following methods to retrieve the instance of the SharedPreferences class:

- The getSharedPreferences() method: Allows you to work with multiple preferences files. Each file is identified through name, which is provided as the first parameter value.
- The getPreferences() method: Allows you to work with the single preferences file for your Activity class. You can avoid providing a name for the preference file as the single preference file would be your Activity class.

Q14. Create an Android application in which the shared preferences can be used across the multiple activities within an application.

Ans: Create the sharedpreferences application. Add the code of the activity_main.xml file in the/res/layout folder as follows:

```
<LinearLayout xmlns:android="http://schemas.android.com/apk/res/android"
    xmlns:tools="http://schemas.android.com/tools"
    android:layout_width="match_parent"
    android:layout_height="match_parent"
    tools:context=".SharedPreferences"
    android:orientation="vertical">

    <TextView
            android:layout_width="fill_parent"
```

```
            android:layout_height="35px"
            android:singleLine="true"
            android:layout_marginLeft="5px"
            android:layout_marginRight="5px"
            android:layout_marginTop="5px" />

    <EditText
        android:id="@+id/textbox"
        android:layout_width="wrap_content"
        android:layout_height="wrap_content"
        android:layout_alignBaseline="@+id/textView1"
        android:layout_alignBottom="@+id/textView1"
        android:layout_alignParentRight="true"
        android:ems="10" />


    <Button android:id="@+id/button"
            android:layout_width="wrap_content"
            android:layout_height="wrap_content"
            android:text="Save" />

    </LinearLayout>
```

Add the code of the secondactivity.xml file in the/res/layout folder as follows:

```
<?xml version="1.0" encoding="utf-8"?>
<LinearLayout xmlns:android="http://schemas.android.com/apk/res/android"
    android:layout_width="match_parent"
    android:layout_height="match_parent"
    android:orientation="vertical" >
        <TextView
            android:id="@+id/text"
            android:layout_width="fill_parent"
            android:layout_height="35px"
            android:singleLine="true"
            android:layout_marginLeft="5px"
            android:layout_marginRight="5px"
            android:layout_marginTop="5px" />

</LinearLayout>
```

Create the SecondActivity.java file as follows:

```
package com.kogent.sharedpreferences;

import android.app.Activity;
import android.os.Bundle;
import android.preference.PreferenceManager;
import android.widget.TextView;

public class SecondActivity extends Activity {

public void onCreate(Bundle savedInstanceState) {
          super.onCreate(savedInstanceState);
          setContentView(R.layout.secondactivity);
          TextView textView = (TextView) findViewById(R.id.text);
          android.content.SharedPreferences app_preferences =
PreferenceManager.getDefaultSharedPreferences(this);
          String text = app_preferences.getString("key", "null");
          textView.setText(text);
    }

}
```

At MainActivity class add following lines :

```
package com.kogent.sharedpreferences;

import android.app.Activity;
import android.content.Intent;
```

```
import android.os.Bundle;
import android.preference.PreferenceManager;
import android.view.View;
import android.view.View.OnClickListener;
import android.widget.Button;
import android.widget.EditText;

public class MainActivity extends Activity {

    private android.content.SharedPreferences score;
  @Override
  protected void onCreate(Bundle savedInstanceState) {
        super.onCreate(savedInstanceState);
        setContentView(R.layout.activity_main);
        Button button = (Button) findViewById(R.id.button);
       final EditText textbox = (EditText) findViewById(R.id.textbox);
       button.setOnClickListener(new OnClickListener(){

           public void onClick(View v) {
               android.content.SharedPreferences app_preferences =
                       PreferenceManager.getDefaultSharedPreferences(MainActivity.this);
               android.content.SharedPreferences.Editor editor = app_preferences.edit();
               String text = textbox.getText().toString();
               editor.putString("key", text);
               editor.commit();
               Intent myIntent = new Intent(MainActivity.this,SecondActivity.class);
               startActivity(myIntent);
           }

       });

  }

}
```

Add SecondActivity activity at androidmanifest.xml

```
<activity
            android:name="SecondActivity"
            android:label="Update " >
</activity>
```

7

Emailing and Networking in Android

If you need an information on:	See page:
Building an Application to Send Email	280
Networking in Android	283
Checking Network Availability	283

A consumer or a user, who is willing to buy a smartphone, would definitely look for the features of a smartphone, such as sending emails and accessing Web through it. In today's busy world, people want maximum works to be performed through their mobile phones, such as sending an image as an attachment or downloading an image from the Web. However, for sending, composing, replying, or forwarding an email, you need to configure an existing email account on your mobile phone. Presently, you are allowed to configure more than one email account, such as Gmail or Yahoo. Another way of communicating with the world is through wireless network available on the mobile phones.

This chapter explains how to send a simple text email to a specified list of email addresses. Then it explains the creation of an application for sending an attachment with the email. The chapter mainly discusses on networking, i.e., connecting to the Web or Internet through Android applications. Firstly, it explains the basic networking concepts and about their implementation in Android. Next, it discusses about accessing Web services using Hypertext Transfer Protocol (HTTP) by developing applications to download binary or text data and accessing Web services using the GET method. Next, you learn to consume JavaScript Object Notation (JSON) Web services and how to develop application connecting the client and server.

Building an Application to Send Email

Android provides a built-in Email application through which you can send or receive emails. You can develop an application which would invoke the built-in Email application to send the email to specific recipients. Similar to the invocation of the built-in Messaging application, you can instantiate the `Intent` object by using the `Intent.ACTION_SEND` value. Prior to the sending process, you should ensure that you have configured an email account using Post Office Protocol 3 (POP3) or Internet Message Access Protocol (IMAP). Let us create a simple email application in which the email addresses of the recipients and the message to be sent would be set by using the `putExtra()` method. Perform the following steps to create the `CustomEmail` Android 4.4 application:

1. *Create* the `CustomEmail` Android 4.4 application using Eclipse. By default, the `MainActivity` class along with the required Extensible Markup Language (*XML*) files, such as `AndroidManifest.xml` and `activity_main.xml` are created. Ensure the application is created within the `com.kogent.android.customemail` package.
2. *Replace* the code of the `activity_main.xml` file of the `CustomEmail` application with the code provided in Listing 7.1:

Listing 7.1: Displaying the Code of the `activity_main.xml` File of the `CustomEmail` Application

```
<RelativeLayout xmlns:android="http://schemas.android.com/apk/res/android"
    xmlns:tools = "http://schemas.android.com/tools"
    android:layout_width = "match_parent"
    android:layout_height = "match_parent"
    tools:context = ".MainActivity" >
    <TextView
        android:layout_width = "fill_parent"
        android:layout_height = "wrap_content"
        android:text = "Custom Email Activity" />
    <Button
        android:id = "@+id/buttonSendMail"
        android:layout_width = "fill_parent"
        android:layout_height="wrap_content"
        android:layout_marginTop="45dp"
        android:text="sendMail" />
</RelativeLayout>
```

In Listing 7.1, we have simply created a button whose id is `buttonSendMail`.

3. Replace the code of the `MainActivity.java` with the code provided in Listing 7.2:

Listing 7.2: Displaying the Code of the `MainActivity` Class of the `CustomEmail` Application

```
package com.kogent.android.customemail;

import android.app.Activity;
import android.content.Intent;
import android.net.Uri;
```

```
import android.os.Bundle;
import android.view.View;
import android.widget.Button;

public class MainActivity extends Activity
{
    Button buttonSendEmail;
      /** Called when the activity is first created. */
      @Override
      public void onCreate(Bundle savedInstanceState) {
           super.onCreate(savedInstanceState);
           setContentView(R.layout.activity_main);
           buttonSendEmail = (Button) findViewById(R.id.buttonSendMail);
           buttonSendEmail.setOnClickListener(new View.OnClickListener() {
            @Override
            public void onClick(View v) {
                    String[] emailReceivers = {"blackbookandroid@gmail.com"};
                    String[] emailcc = {"blackbookandroid@gmail.com"};
                    String[] emailbcc = {"blackbookandroid@gmail.com"};
                    sendEmail(emailReceivers, emailcc, emailbcc, "Welcome", "Welcome, to the
world to mailing!!");
            }
            });
      }
      private void sendEmail(String[] emailAdd, String[] ccopies, String[] bccReceivers,
String title, String emailMessage) {
            Intent mailIntent = new Intent(Intent.ACTION_SEND);
            mailIntent.setData(Uri.parse("mailto:"));
            String[] emailReceivers = emailAdd;
            String[] emailcc = ccopies;
            String[] emailbcc = bccReceivers;
            mailIntent.putExtra(Intent.EXTRA_EMAIL, emailReceivers);
            mailIntent.putExtra(Intent.EXTRA_CC, emailcc);
            mailIntent.putExtra(Intent.EXTRA_BCC, emailbcc);
            mailIntent.putExtra(Intent.EXTRA_SUBJECT, title);
            mailIntent.putExtra(Intent.EXTRA_TEXT, emailMessage);
            mailIntent.setType("message/rfc822");
            startActivity(Intent.createChooser(mailIntent, "Email"));
      }
}
```

In Listing 7.2, the `sendEmail()` method has been defined, which accepts the following five arguments:

- Email addresses to be added in the To: field
- Email addresses to be added in the Cc: field
- Email addresses to be added in the Bcc: field
- Subject of the email
- Body of the email

The values for these arguments have been set during the click event of the button. When the `sendEmail()` method is being invoked, the values of these arguments are being passed and set for the built-in email application. First of all, the instance of the `Intent` class, that is, `mailIntent`, has been created and initialized by using the `Intent.ACTION_SEND` value. Further, the data type of the `mailIntent` has been set by parsing the mailto: **Uniform Resource Identifier** (**URI**). Next, the email recipients to be added in the 'to', 'cc', and 'bcc' fields have been set by using the appropriate `Intent` type and its value. For example, the email recipients in the two fields have been set by using the `Intent.EXTRA_EMAIL` intent and its values are set by using the `emailReceivers` String array type. This array stores the email addresses of the recipients. Similarly, the other values have also been set along with the type of the `mailIntent` object as `message/rfc822`. Finally, the activity is started.

4. *Right-click* the **`CustomEmail`** application and select **`Run As→Android Application`** to run the application. Prior to the execution of the application, you should ensure that the Android 4.4 emulator is running.

Figure 7.1 shows the output of the `CustomEmail` application:

Figure 7.1: Showing the Output of the `CustomEmail` Application

Before running the application, ensure that an email account is configured on the emulator or the device on which you will be executing the application.

When you click the sendMail button (shown in Figure 7.1), the default email application would be displayed as shown in Figure 7.2:

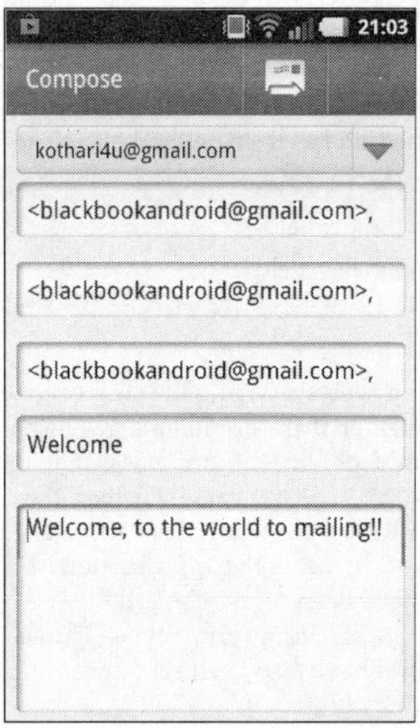

Figure 7.2: Showing the Default Email Application

When you click the **Send** button, the email would be sent to the one or more specified email recipients.

Networking in Android

Android-supported devices allow you to connect to Web using the HTTP protocol. You can access your email accounts, download Web pages, save pictures, and download text files from the Web using the HTTP protocol. Also, you can communicate through the SOAP or REST based services and client server socket programming.

This section first explores the fundamentals of networking, followed by the discussion on how to connect the Internet programmatically. In addition, the section also explains how to connect to Web services using the HTTP protocol. Then you would learn to access Web services using the GET and post method. Next, you would learn how to download an image and text file from the Web. Further, you would learn to develop Android applications consuming JSON services and implement sockets programming.

Getting an Overview of Networking Fundamentals

The Android Software Development Kit (**SDK**) provides packages to implement network capabilities in an application. Let us explore these networking packages and then use them to create the Android application. The Android SDK networking packages are as follows:

- **`java.net`**-Provides networking-related classes, such as `DatagramPacket`, `MulticastSocket`, `ServerSocket`, and `Socket`. The Java developers should be familiar with this package to create networking applications.
- **`java.io`**-Provides classes that are used to provide system input and output through files and data streams.
- **`java.nio`**-Provides classes representing buffers as the containers of data types.
- **`org.apache.*`**- Contains various packages that define perfect control and functionality for HTTP communications.
- **`android.net`**- Provides more network access sockets apart from the classes provided by the `java.net` package. Generally, the `URI` class of this package is being used to develop Android applications.
- **`android.net.http`**-Provides classes to work with Secure Sockets Layer (SSL) certificates.
- **`android.net.wifi`**-Provides classes to manage the Wifi functionality provided by Android-supported devices.
- **`android.telephony.gsm`**-Provides classes that are helpful in sending and managing text messages.

Checking Network Availability

Prior to creating an application to download text or image file, you need to check whether the network is available or not. You can use the following code snippet to check the network availability:

```
public static boolean isNetworkAvailable(Context context) {
  ConnectivityManager connectivity = (ConnectivityManager)
  context.getSystemService(Context.CONNECTIVITY_SERVICE);
  if (connectivity != null)  {
       NetworkInfo[] info = connectivity.getAllNetworkInfo();
       if (info != null)  {
                for (int i = 0; i < info.length; i++) {
                if (info[i].getState() == NetworkInfo.State.CONNECTED)  {
                          return true;
                }
       }
       }
  }
  return false;
  }
}
```

In the preceding code snippet, the `isNetworkAvailable()` method has been declared, which accepts the context of the application as argument. Within this method, the instance of the `ConnectivityManager` class has been created by initializing it with the `Context.CONNECTIVITY_SERVICE` value. Further, the information of all networks has been fetched and the `isNetworkAvailable()` method returns a `boolean` value.

According to the value returned by the `isNetworkAvailable()` method, further processing can be implemented.

Let us first understand how to communicate with the outside world.

Accessing Web Services Using HTTP Post

You can communicate with the outside world through HTTP, which is the protocol used to view and download Web pages from a Web server, download binary data, and more. The HTTP post method is used to send the request to the server that accepts a resource in the request. This resource is identified by the Request-URI in the Request-Line.

Let us first create a simple application in which you enter your name and the details are sent to the server. The server further sends the response displayed on the screen. In this example, the application communicates with the server using HTTP post method. Perform the following steps to create the Android 4.4 application:

1. *Create* the Android application project, named `WebServicesUsingHTTP`, using Eclipse. By default the Activity class, `MainActivity.java` and the XML resource file, `activity_main` are created. Ensure the package name is `com.kogent.android.WebServicesUsingHttp`.
2. *Replace* the code of the `activity_main.xml` file with the code shown in Listing 7.3:

Listing 7.3: Displaying the Code for Layout of the `WebServicesUsingHTTP` Application

```
<LinearLayout xmlns:android = "http://schemas.android.com/apk/res/android"
xmlns:tools = "http://schemas.android.com/tools"
android:layout_width = "fill_parent"
android:layout_height = "fill_parent"
android:paddingLeft = "16dp"
android:paddingRight = "16dp"
android:orientation = "vertical" >
<TextView
android:layout_width = "fill_parent"
android:layout_height ="wrap_content"
android:text = "HTTP Post Demo: Enter Your name " />
<EditText android:id = "@+id/name"
android:layout_width = "fill_parent"
android:layout_height = "wrap_content"/>
<Button android:text = "Get Server Response "
android:id = "@+id/save"
android:layout_width = "fill_parent"
android:layout_height = "wrap_content"
android:layout_gravity = "center"/>
<TextView android:id = "@+id/content"
android:layout_width = "fill_parent"
android:layout_height = "wrap_content"/>
</LinearLayout>
```

In Listing 7.3, the two `TextView`, an `EditText`, and the `Button` views are created.

3. *Replace* the code of the `MainActivity.java` file with the code shown in Listing 7.4:

Listing 7.4: Displaying the Code of the `MainActivity` Java File

```
package com.kogent.android.WebServicesUsingHttp;

import java.io.IOException;
import java.io.UnsupportedEncodingException;
import java.util.ArrayList;
import java.util.List;

import org.apache.http.NameValuePair;
import org.apache.http.client.ClientProtocolException;
import org.apache.http.client.HttpClient;
import org.apache.http.client.ResponseHandler;
import org.apache.http.client.entity.UrlEncodedFormEntity;
import org.apache.http.client.methods.HttpPost;
import org.apache.http.impl.client.BasicResponseHandler;
import org.apache.http.impl.client.DefaultHttpClient;
```

```
import org.apache.http.message.BasicNameValuePair;

import android.app.Activity;
import android.os.Bundle;
import android.os.StrictMode;
import android.view.View;
import android.widget.Button;
import android.widget.EditText;
import android.widget.TextView;

public class MainActivity extends Activity {
    EditText username;
      TextView content;
    @Override
    protected void onCreate(Bundle savedInstanceState) {
    super.onCreate(savedInstanceState);
    StrictMode.ThreadPolicy policy = new
StrictMode.ThreadPolicy.Builder().permitAll().build();
    StrictMode.setThreadPolicy(policy);
    setContentView(R.layout.activity_main);
    username= (EditText)findViewById(R.id.name);;
    Button savetext = (Button)findViewById(R.id.save);
    content   =  (TextView)findViewById(R.id.content);
    savetext.setOnClickListener(new Button.OnClickListener(){
    @Override
    public void onClick(View v) {
    String name = username.getText().toString();
    HttpClient client = new DefaultHttpClient();
    HttpPost post = new HttpPost("http://techoreo.com/post.php");
    List<NameValuePair> pairs = new ArrayList<NameValuePair>(1);
    pairs.add(new BasicNameValuePair("name", name));
    try {
    post.setEntity(new UrlEncodedFormEntity(pairs));
    } catch (UnsupportedEncodingException e) {
    // writing error to Log
    e.printStackTrace();
    }
    // Making HTTP Request
    try {
    String ServerResponse = "";
    ResponseHandler<String> responseHandler = new BasicResponseHandler();
    ServerResponse = client.execute(post, responseHandler);
// writing response to log
content.setText(ServerResponse);
} catch (ClientProtocolException e) {
// writing exception to log
e.printStackTrace();
} catch (IOException e) {
// writing exception to log
e.printStackTrace();
}
}
});
}
}
```

In Listing 7.4, the value entered in the `EditText` view, which is created in the `activity_main.xml` file, is retrieved and the HTTP request is made. The `BasicResponseHandler()` method is used to handle the response from the server.

4. *Add* the highlighted code shown in Listing 7.5 to the `AndroidManifest.xml` file of the `WebServicesUsingHTTP` application:

Listing 7.5: Displaying the Code of the `AndroidManifest.xml` File

```
<?xml version="1.0" encoding="utf-8"?>
<manifest xmlns:android="http://schemas.android.com/apk/res/android"
```

```
        package="com.kogent.android.WebServicesUsingHttp"
        android:versionCode="1"
        android:versionName="1.0" >
    <uses-sdk
            android:minSdkVersion="11"
            android:targetSdkVersion="19" />
    <uses-permission android:name="android.permission.INTERNET"/>
        <application
            android:allowBackup="true"
            android:icon="@drawable/ic_launcher"
            android:label="@string/app_name"
            android:theme="@style/AppTheme" >
            <activity
                android:name="com.kogent.android.WebServicesUsingHttp.MainActivity"
                android:label="@string/app_name" >
                <intent-filter>
                    <action android:name="android.intent.action.MAIN" />
                    <category android:name="android.intent.category.LAUNCHER" />
                </intent-filter>
            </activity>
        </application>
    </manifest>
```

In Listing 7.5, the code for the AndroidManifest.xml file is similar to any other manifest file except the user permission for Internet access is added.

5. *Right-click* the application and select Run As→Android Application.

Figure 7.3 shows the output of the code given in the WebServicesUsingHTTP application:

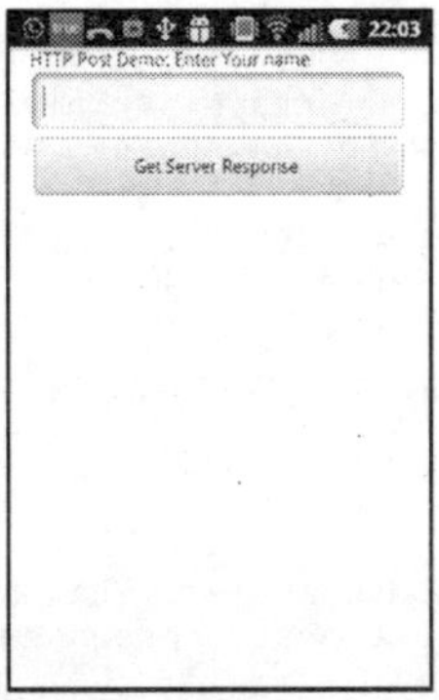

Figure 7.3: Output of the `WebServicesUsingHTTP` Application

Enter your name and click the **Get Server Response** button. The response from the server is displayed, as shown in Figure 7.4:

Figure 7.4: Displaying the Response from the Server

After understanding how to develop applications using the HTTP post method, let's learn to access Web services using the GET method.

Accessing Web Services Using the GET Method

In the previous section, you have learned to send the request to the server using the HTTP Post method. Sometimes, you need to download XML files and parse the content. In this section, let us develop an application and learn how to connect to a Web service using the HTTP GET method. Perform the following steps to create the application using the GET method:

1. *Create* the Android 4.4 application, named `HttpGetRequest`, using Eclipse. By default, the `MainActivity.java` source file and the required XML files, such as `activity_main.xml` and `AndroidManifest.xml`, are created. Ensure the package name is `com.kogent.android.httpgetrequest`.
2. *Replace* the code of the Android resource `activity_main.xml` file with the code shown in Listing 7.6:

Listing 7.6: Displaying the Code of the `activity_main.xml` File of the `HttpGetRequest` Application

```
<LinearLayout xmlns:android="http://schemas.android.com/apk/res/android"
    xmlns:tools="http://schemas.android.com/tools"
   android:layout_width="fill_parent"
    android:layout_height="fill_parent"
    android:paddingLeft="16dp"
    android:paddingRight="16dp"
    android:orientation="vertical" >
    <TextView
        android:layout_width="fill_parent"
        android:layout_height="wrap_content"
        android:text="HTTP GET Demo : Enter Your name " />
        <EditText android:id="@+id/name"
         android:layout_width="fill_parent"
        android:layout_height="wrap_content"/>
        <Button android:text="Get Server Response "
        android:id="@+id/save"
        android:layout_width="fill_parent"
        android:layout_height="wrap_content"
        android:layout_gravity="center"/>
           <TextView android:id="@+id/content"
        android:layout_width="fill_parent"
        android:layout_height="wrap_content"/>
</LinearLayout>
```

In Listing 7.6, two `TextView`, an `EditText`, and a `Button` views are created. Similar to the application `WebServicesUsingHTTP`, the resource XML file is created in which you need to enter the name and click the button to send and receive the response using the GET method.

3. *Replace* the code of the `MainActivity.java` file with the code shown in Listing 7.7:

Listing 7.7: Displaying the Code of the `MainActivity.java` File of the `HttpGetRequest` Application

```
package com.kogent.android.httpgetrequest;
import java.io.UnsupportedEncodingException;
import java.net.URLEncoder;
import org.apache.http.client.HttpClient;
import org.apache.http.client.ResponseHandler;
import org.apache.http.client.methods.HttpGet;
import org.apache.http.impl.client.BasicResponseHandler;
import org.apache.http.impl.client.DefaultHttpClient;
import android.os.Bundle;
import android.os.StrictMode;
import android.app.Activity;
import android.view.View;
import android.widget.Button;
import android.widget.EditText;
import android.widget.TextView;
public class MainActivity extends Activity {
  EditText username;
```

```
      TextView content;
    @Override
    protected void onCreate(Bundle savedInstanceState) {
          super.onCreate(savedInstanceState);
          setContentView(R.layout.activity_main);
    StrictMode.ThreadPolicy policy = new
StrictMode.ThreadPolicy.Builder().permitAll().build();
          StrictMode.setThreadPolicy(policy);
            username= (EditText)findViewById(R.id.name);;
            Button savetext=(Button)findViewById(R.id.save);
            content   =  (TextView)findViewById(R.id.content);
            savetext.setOnClickListener(new Button.OnClickListener(){
@Override
                    public void onClick(View v) {
                try{
                      String name  = URLEncoder.encode(username.getText().toString(),
"UTF-8");
                      HttpClient Client = new DefaultHttpClient();
                      String URL = "http://techoreo.com/get.php?name="+name;
                   try {
                                  String ServerData = "";
                                // Create Request to server and get response
                                HttpGet httpget = new HttpGet(URL);
                                 ResponseHandler<String> responseHandler = new
BasicResponseHandler();
                                 ServerData = Client.execute(httpget, responseHandler);
                                  // Show response on activity
                                 content.setText(ServerData);
                    }
                   catch(Exception ex) {
                             content.setText("Fail!" + ex.toString());
                      }
                }
              catch(UnsupportedEncodingException ex) {
                      content.setText("Fail");
                }
            }
        });
    }
}
```

In Listing 7.7, the `OnClickListener()` event is generated when a user clicks the button created in the layout XML file. The `HttpGet` class is used to create a request to the server and get response. Further, the response is displayed to the user.

4. *Modify* the highlighted code shown in Listing 7.8 in the `AndroidManifest` XML file for the `HttpGetRequest` application:

Listing 7.8: Showing the Code of the `AndroidManifest.xml` File of the `HttpGetRequest` Application

```
<?xml version="1.0" encoding="utf-8"?>
<manifest xmlns:android="http://schemas.android.com/apk/res/android"
    package="com.kogent.android.httpgetrequest"
    android:versionCode="1"
    android:versionName="1.0" >
    <uses-sdk
        android:minSdkVersion="11"
        android:targetSdkVersion="19" />
  <uses-permission android:name="android.permission.INTERNET"></uses-permission>
    <application
        android:allowBackup="true"
        android:icon="@drawable/ic_launcher"
        android:label="@string/app_name"
        android:theme="@style/AppTheme" >
        <activity
            android:name="com.kogent.android.httpgetrequest.MainActivity"
            android:label="@string/app_name" >
```

```
            <intent-filter>
                <action android:name="android.intent.action.MAIN" />
                <category android:name="android.intent.category.LAUNCHER" />
            </intent-filter>
        </activity>
    </application>
</manifest>
```

In Listing 7.8, the `<user-permission>` element is used to define the permission for the `INTERNET`. Also, the minimum SDK version has been changed to 11.

5. *Right-click* the application and select `Run As→Android Application` from the context menu. Figure 7.5 displays the output of the application:

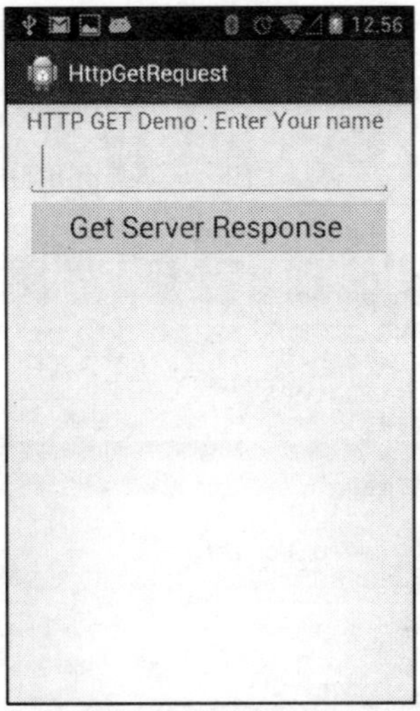

Figure 7.5: Displaying the Output of the Application

Now, enter your name and click the **Get Server Response** button; the response from the server will be displayed, as shown in Figure 7.6:

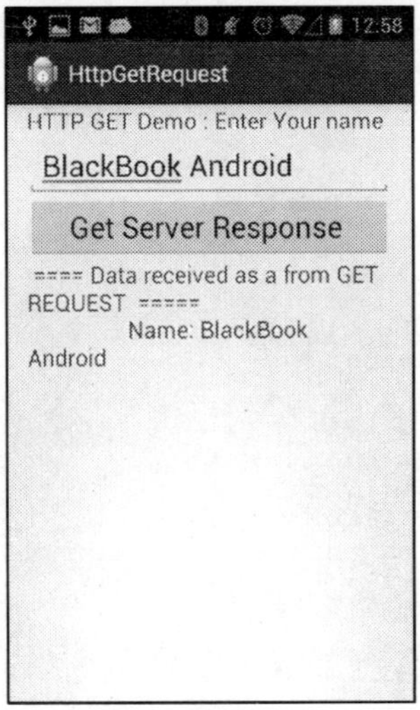

Figure 7.6: Displaying the Response Generated Using the GET Method

Let us now develop an application to download an image and text from Web.

Working with Binary Data and Text Files

You can create an Android application to download an image and text file from the Web. In this type of application, you first need to define the method to establish connection with the Web. Further, a method needs to be declared to decode the binary data of the image and then finally the image is being displayed on the ImageView view defined in the layout. To download the text file, you need to define a separate method. Perform the following steps to create the Android 4.4 application:

1. *Create* the Android 4.4 application, named ConnectWeb, using Eclipse. By default, the AndroidManifest.xml file is created. Ensure the package name is com.kogent.android.connectweb.
2. *Modify* the code of the AndroidManifest.xml file, as shown in the following code snippet:

```
<uses-permission android:name="android.permission.INTERNET" />
<uses-permission android:name="android.permission.WRITE_EXTERNAL_STORAGE" />
```

   Also, set the minimum sdk version as 9.
3. *Replace* the code of the activity_main.xml file of the application with the code shown in Listing 7.9:

Listing 7.9: Displaying the Code for Layout of the ConnectWeb Application

```
<ScrollView  xmlns:android="http://schemas.android.com/apk/res/android"
   android:layout_width="match_parent"
   android:layout_height="match_parent">
<LinearLayout  android:layout_width="fill_parent"
    android:layout_height="fill_parent"
    android:orientation="vertical" >
    <ImageView
        android:id="@+id/viewImage"
        android:layout_width="wrap_content"
        android:layout_height="wrap_content"
        android:layout_weight="0.46" />
   <TextView
        android:id="@+id/viewText"
        android:layout_width="wrap_content"
        android:layout_height="wrap_content"
        android:text="@string/hello_world"
        android:textSize="10dp" />
</LinearLayout>
</ScrollView>
```

In Listing 7.6, the <ImageView> element is used to display the image that would be downloaded from Web. Also, the <EditText> element has been used to display the text of the forum.

4. *Replace* the code of the MainActivity class with the code shown in Listing 7.10:

Listing 7.10: Displaying the MainActivity Class of the ConnectWeb Application

```
package com.kogent.android.connectweb;

import java.io.IOException;
import java.io.InputStream;
import java.io.InputStreamReader;
import java.net.HttpURLConnection;
import java.net.URL;
import java.net.URLConnection;
import android.app.Activity;
import android.graphics.Bitmap;
import android.graphics.BitmapFactory;
import android.os.Bundle;
import android.os.StrictMode;
import android.widget.EditText;
import android.widget.ImageView;
import android.widget.TextView;
import android.widget.Toast;

public class MainActivity extends Activity {
  ImageView iv;
```

```
    TextView edit;

    /** Called when the activity is first created. */
     @Override
     public void onCreate(Bundle savedInstanceState) {
         super.onCreate(savedInstanceState);
         StrictMode.ThreadPolicy policy = new
StrictMode.ThreadPolicy.Builder().permitAll().build();
         StrictMode.setThreadPolicy(policy);
         setContentView(R.layout.activity_main);
       //Code to download an image
         Bitmap b = WebImage("http://techoreo.com/android.jpg");
         iv = (ImageView) findViewById(R.id.viewImage);
         iv.setImageBitmap(b);
         String str = WebText("http://techoreo.com");
         edit = (TextView) findViewById(R.id.viewText);
         edit.setText(str);
     }

    private String WebText(String string) {
          int BUFFER_SIZE = 2000;
          InputStream is = null;
          try{
                  is = connect(string);
          }
          catch(Exception e) {
                  Toast.makeText(getBaseContext(), "Exception is:" +
e.getLocalizedMessage(), Toast.LENGTH_LONG).show();
                  e.printStackTrace();
                  return "";
          }
          InputStreamReader inputstr = new InputStreamReader(is);
          int characterReading;
          String s = " ";
          char[] inputBuffer = new char[BUFFER_SIZE];
          try {
                  while((characterReading = inputstr.read(inputBuffer))>0) {
                          String readstr = String.copyValueOf( inputBuffer, 0,
characterReading);
                          s += readstr;
                          inputBuffer = new char[BUFFER_SIZE];
                  }
          is.close();
          }
          catch(Exception e) {
                  Toast.makeText(this, "Exception is: " + e.getLocalizedMessage(),
Toast.LENGTH_LONG).show();
                  e.printStackTrace();
                  return "";
          }
          return s;
    }
    private Bitmap WebImage(String url) {
          //code to decode the input stream
          Bitmap bmp=null;
          InputStream is=null;
          try {
                  is = connect(url);
                  bmp = BitmapFactory.decodeStream(is);
                  System.out.println("Image Decoded");
                  is.close();
          }
          catch(Exception e) {
                  Toast.makeText(getBaseContext(), "Exception is::" +
e.getLocalizedMessage(), Toast.LENGTH_LONG).show();
          }
          return bmp;
    }
  private InputStream connect(String url) throws IOException{
          InputStream is = null;
          int res = -1;
                  URL u = new URL(url);
```

```
                URLConnection con = u.openConnection();
                if (!(con instanceof HttpURLConnection))
                        //throw new IOException("Not and HTTP Connection");
                Toast.makeText(getBaseContext(), "Not and HTTP Connection is::" ,
Toast.LENGTH_LONG).show();

                try {
                HttpURLConnection http = (HttpURLConnection) con;
                http.setAllowUserInteraction(false);
                http.setInstanceFollowRedirects(true);
                http.setRequestMethod("GET");
                http.connect();
                //System.out.println("Input Stream Connected");
  Toast.makeText(getBaseContext(), "Input Stream Connected" , Toast.LENGTH_LONG).show();
                res= http.getResponseCode();
                if(res == HttpURLConnection.HTTP_OK)
                        is = http.getInputStream();
        }
                        catch (IOException e) {
                                //throw new IOException("Error connecting");
                                e.printStackTrace();
                                Toast.makeText(getBaseContext(), "Error connecting" ,
Toast.LENGTH_LONG).show();
        }
        return is ;
    }
}
```

In Listing 7.10, the `WebText()` method has been declared to invoke the `connect()` method and set the downloaded text in the `EditText` view created in the layout of the application. In addition, the `WebImage()` method has been declared to invoke the `connect()` method and set the downloaded image in the `ImageView` view created in the layout of the application.

By default, the Android platform does not allow or recommends to perform background task or non UI related task on main UI thread. Therefore, the following code snippet is added in Listing 7.10 to force Android to perform the background task:

```
StrictMode.ThreadPolicy policy = new
StrictMode.ThreadPolicy.Builder().permitAll().build();
StrictMode.setThreadPolicy(policy);
```

5. *Right-click* the `ConnectWeb` application and select `Run As→Android Application`. The output would be displayed, as shown in Figure 7.7:

Figure 7.7: Displaying the Output of the `ConnectWeb` Application

NOTE

The `ConnectWeb` application is executed on the Tablet emulator to display each component of the application appropriately.

Let us now understand how the Web services are accessed using the GET method.

Consuming JSON Services

As mentioned in the introduction, an Android application would need to connect to the outside world to retrieve data such as live currency exchange rate or weather information. Your applications can easily connect to the outside world through Web services.

In early decades, XML Web services were primarily used for Web services as XML was the main medium for data exchange. However, using XML as the medium of data communication, the following problems were faced:

- XML documents are lengthy and heavy. The use of opening and closing tags to embed the information and the size of an XML document become very heavy. Downloading a heavy XML document implies that your device requires more bandwidth to download it, resulting into high cost.
- XML documents are difficult to process. These documents are parsed using either Document Object Model (DOM) or Simple APIs for XML (SAX), which are very expensive to be implemented on the mobile platform.

A more efficient mechanism to represent information is JSON. It is a text-based open standard to represent data and uses characters such as brackets, colon, and comma.

In this section, let's create an Android application, `ConsumingJsonWebService`, displaying the original JSON data and the parsed data. Perform the following steps to create the application:

1. *Create* the Android application project named `ConsumingJsonWebService`. By default, the `MainActivity.java` and `activity_main.xml` files are created in the application. Ensure the package name is `com.kogent.android.ConsumingJsonWebService`.
2. *Replace* the code of the XML resource file with the code shown in Listing 7.11:

Listing 7.11: Displaying the Code of the `activity_main.xml` File for `ConsumingJsonWebService` Application

```
<LinearLayout xmlns:android="http://schemas.android.com/apk/res/android"
xmlns:tools="http://schemas.android.com/tools"
android:layout_width="fill_parent"
android:layout_height="fill_parent"
android:paddingLeft="16dp"
android:paddingRight="16dp"
android:orientation="vertical" >
<Button android:text="Get Server Response "
android:id="@+id/save"
android:layout_width="fill_parent"
android:layout_height="wrap_content"
android:layout_gravity="center"/>
<TextView
android:layout_width="wrap_content"
android:layout_height="wrap_content"
android:text="Actual Received Json :" />
<TextView
android:id="@+id/actualparsedcontent"
android:layout_width="wrap_content"
android:layout_height="wrap_content"
android:text="" />
<TextView
android:layout_width="fill_parent"
android:layout_height="wrap_content"
android:text="Parsed Json :"/>
<TextView android:id="@+id/content"
android:layout_width="fill_parent"
android:layout_height="wrap_content"
android:text=""/>
</LinearLayout>
```

In Listing 7.11, four `TextViews` and a `Button` views are created. When you click the button, the original JSON data and the parsed data are displayed on the two `TextView` views.

3. *Replace* the code of the `MainActivity` class with the code shown in Listing 7.12:

Listing 7.12: Displaying the Code of the `MainActivity.java` File for the `ConsumingJsonWebService` Application

```
package com.kogent.android.ConsumingJsonWebService;
import java.io.BufferedReader;
import java.io.InputStreamReader;
import java.net.URL;
import java.net.URLConnection;
import org.json.JSONArray;
import org.json.JSONException;
import org.json.JSONObject;
import android.os.AsyncTask;
import android.os.Bundle;
import android.app.Activity;
import android.view.View;
import android.view.View.OnClickListener;
import android.widget.Button;
import android.widget.TextView;
public class MainActivity extends Activity {
@Override
protected void onCreate(Bundle savedInstanceState) {
super.onCreate(savedInstanceState);
setContentView(R.layout.activity_main);
final Button GetData = (Button) findViewById(R.id.save);
GetData.setOnClickListener(new OnClickListener() {
@Override
public void onClick(View arg0) {
// WebServer Request URL
String serverURL ="http://techoreo.com/restful.php";
// Use AsyncTask execute Method To Prevent ANR Problem
new backgroundtask().execute(serverURL);
}
});
}
private class backgroundtask  extends AsyncTask<String, Void, Void> {
        private String Content;
        private String Error = null;
        TextView jsonParsed = (TextView) findViewById(R.id.content);
        TextView actualjson = (TextView) findViewById(R.id.actualparsedcontent);
        protected void onPreExecute() {
        }
   protected Void doInBackground(String... urls) {
            BufferedReader reader=null;
                try {
                   // Defined URL  where to send data
                   URL url = new URL(urls[0]);
                  URLConnection conn = url.openConnection();
                  conn.setDoOutput(true);
                  reader = new BufferedReader(new
InputStreamReader(conn.getInputStream()));
                  StringBuilder sb = new StringBuilder();
                  String line = null;
                    // Read Server Response
                    while((line = reader.readLine()) != null) {
                                // Append server response in string
                                sb.append(line + "");
                        }
                    // Append Server Response To Content String
                   Content = sb.toString();
                }
                catch(Exception ex) {
```

```
                Error = ex.getMessage();
            }
            finally {
                try {
                    reader.close();
                }
                catch(Exception ex) {}
            }
        return null;
    }
    protected void onPostExecute(Void unused) {
        if (Error != null) {
            jsonParsed.setText("Output : "+Error);
        } else {
            actualjson.setText( Content );
            String OutputData = "";
            JSONObject jsonResponse;
            try {
                jsonResponse = new JSONObject(Content);
                JSONArray jsonMainNode = jsonResponse.optJSONArray("Android");
                int lengthJsonArr = jsonMainNode.length();
                for(int i=0; i <lengthJsonArr; i++){
                    JSONObject jsonChildNode = jsonMainNode.getJSONObject(i);
                    String name       = jsonChildNode.optString("name").toString();
                    String classname      =
jsonChildNode.optString("class").toString();
                    OutputData += " Name           : "+ name +"\n"
                        + "class          : "+ classname +"\n"
                        +"..................................    \n ";
                }
                jsonParsed.setText( OutputData );
            } catch (JSONException e) {
                e.printStackTrace();
            }
        }
    }
  }
}
```

In Listing 7.12, the data of the `content` and `actualparsedcontent` `TextViews` is retrieved and then the connection is established in the `doInBackground()` method. After the connection is established, the JSON response is displayed on the screen.

4. *Add* the following code in the `AndroidManifest.xml` file before the `<application>` element:

```
<uses-permission android:name="android.permission.INTERNET"/>
```

In the preceding code snippet, the user permission is given for the Internet access.

5. *Set* the minimum SDK version as `android:minSdkVersion = "9"` in the `AndroidManifest.xml` file.
6. *Right-click* the application and select `Run As→Android Application`. Figure 7.8 displays the output of the `ConsumingJsonWebService` application:

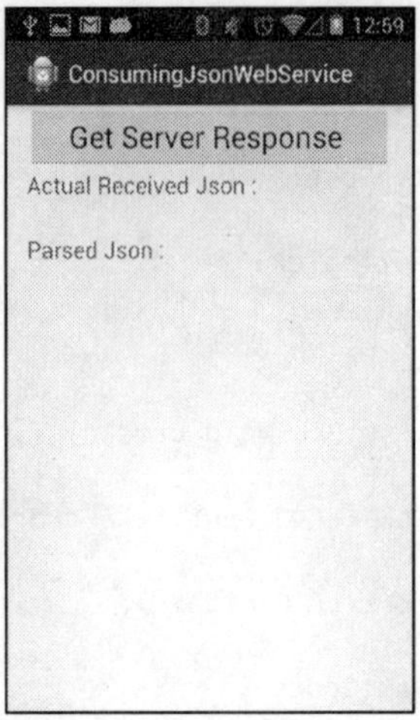

Figure 7.8: Displaying the Output of the `ConsumingJsonWebService` Application

7. *Click* the **Get Server Response** button to display the original JSON data and the parsed data, as shown in Figure 7.9:

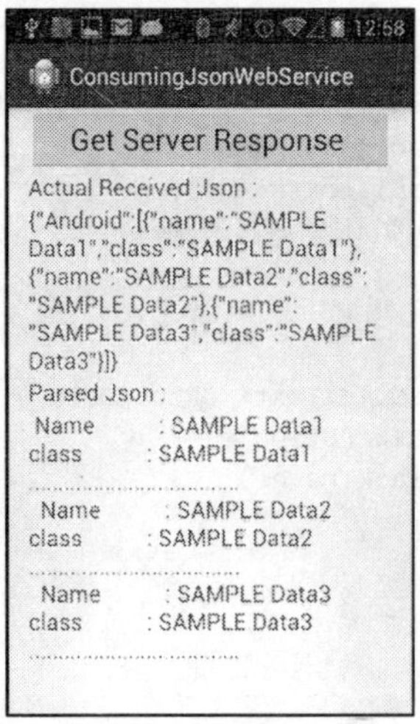

Figure 7.9: Displaying the Data Generated by the Server

Let us now learn about socket programming.

Sockets Programming

Till now, you have learned the use of HTTP to consume XML and JSON Web services. Generally, the Web services use HTTP for communication; however, they suffer from one disadvantage, that is, they are stateless. Each time you connect to a Web service using HTTP, a new connection is established and the Web server does not maintain a persistent connection with the clients.

Suppose your application connects to a Web service that books railway seats. When the seats are booked on the server by a client, the other clients are not aware of the current booking until the connection is established by them to the Web service again to book the seat. This regular pooling of clients incurs unnecessary bandwidth and makes your application inefficient. The efficient and ideal solution is to maintain individual connections to each client and send a message to each client whenever seats are booked by another client.

The technique of maintaining persistent connection with the server and notifying the server about the occurrence of changes is known as sockets programming. With the help of this programming, you can establish a connection between a client and a server.

Let us create an application implementing socket programming. You need to create a server socket and a client socket. The client will send the message to the server, which is displayed on the server. Perform the following steps to create the socket programming application:

1. *Create* an Android 4.4 application named `ServerSideSocket`. By default, the `MainActivity.java` and `activity_main.xml` files are created. Ensure the package name is `com.kogent.android.ServerSideSocket`.
2. *Replace* the code of the `MainActivity.java` file with the code shown in Listing 7.13:

Listing 7.13: Displaying the Code of the `MainActivity.java` File of the `ServerSideSocket` Application

```
package com.kogent.android.ServerSideSocket;

import java.io.BufferedReader;
import java.io.IOException;
import java.io.InputStreamReader;
import java.net.ServerSocket;
import java.net.Socket;

import android.os.Bundle;
import android.os.Handler;
import android.app.Activity;
import android.widget.TextView;

public class MainActivity extends Activity {
  private ServerSocket serverSocket;
  Handler updateConversationHandler;
  Thread serverThread = null;
private TextView ServerData;
public static final int SERVERPORT = 6000;
@Override
protected void onCreate(Bundle savedInstanceState) {
super.onCreate(savedInstanceState);
setContentView(R.layout.activity_main);
ServerData = (TextView) findViewById(R.id.text2);
updateConversationHandler = new Handler();
this.serverThread = new Thread(new ServerThread());
this.serverThread.start();
  }@Override
protected void onStop() {
super.onStop();
try {
serverSocket.close();
} catch (IOException e) {
e.printStackTrace();
}
}
class ServerThread implements Runnable {
public void run() {
Socket socket = null;
try {
serverSocket = new ServerSocket(SERVERPORT);
} catch (IOException e) {
e.printStackTrace();
}
while (!Thread.currentThread().isInterrupted()) {
try {
socket = serverSocket.accept();
BufferedReaderThread commThread = new BufferedReaderThread(socket);
new Thread(commThread).start();
} catch (IOException e) {
```

```
e.printStackTrace();
}
}
}
}

class BufferedReaderThread implements Runnable {
        private Socket clientSocket;
        private BufferedReader input;
        public BufferedReaderThread(Socket clientSocket) {
                this.clientSocket = clientSocket;
                try {
   this.input = new BufferedReader(new
InputStreamReader(this.clientSocket.getInputStream()));
                } catch (IOException e) {
                        e.printStackTrace();
                }
        }
        public void run() {
                while (!Thread.currentThread().isInterrupted()) {
                        try {
                                String read = input.readLine();
                                if(read !=null)
                                {
                        updateConversationHandler.post(new updateUIThread(read));
                                }
                        } catch (IOException e) {
                                e.printStackTrace();
                        }
                }
        }
   }
class updateUIThread implements Runnable {
private String msg;
public updateUIThread(String str) {
this.msg = str;
}
@Override
public void run() {
ServerData.setText(ServerData.getText().toString()+"Client Says: "+ msg + "\n");
}
}
}
```

In Listing 7.13, the instance of the `ServerSocket` class is created by passing Server port number as the argument. Next, the instance of the `BufferedReaderThread` class is created, which runs a thread.

3. *Replace* the code of the `activity_main.xml` file with the code shown in Listing 7.14:

Listing 7.14: Displaying the Code of the `activity_main.xml` File

```
<LinearLayout xmlns:android="http://schemas.android.com/apk/res/android"
    xmlns:tools="http://schemas.android.com/tools"
   android:layout_width="fill_parent"
    android:layout_height="fill_parent"
    android:paddingLeft="16dp"
    android:paddingRight="16dp"
    android:orientation="vertical">
<TextView
          android:id="@+id/ipaddess"
          android:layout_width="wrap_content"
          android:layout_height="wrap_content"
          android:text="At client Side you will need to IP address of this device . For
that go to Device settings and then wifi. Click on your wifi connection, there you will
find your ip address Kindly note this \n" >
</TextView>
<TextView
          android:id="@+id/text2"
```

```
        android:layout_width="wrap_content"
        android:layout_height="wrap_content"
        android:text="" >
</TextView>
</LinearLayout>
```

In Listing 7.14, two `TextView` views are created to display the welcome message and the message sent by the client.

4. *Add* the following code snippet before the `<application>` element:

```
<uses-permission android:name = "android.permission.INTERNET" />
<uses-permission android:name = "android.permission.ACCESS_NETWORK_STATE" />
<uses-permission android:name = "android.permission.ACCESS_WIFI_STATE" />
```

In the preceding code snippet, the required permissions such as Internet access, access to network state, and access to the WIFI are granted to the users accessing this application. Also, set the minimum SDK version using android:minSdkVersion = "9" in the `AndroidManifest.xml` file.

Now, let's create the client-side socket application.

5. *Create* the Android 4.4 application named `ClientSideSocket`. By default, the `MainActivity.java` and `activity_main.xml` files are created.
6. *Replace* the code of the `MainActivity.java` file with the code shown in Listing 7.15:

Listing 7.15: Displaying the Code of the `MainActivity.java` File of the `ClientSideSocket` Application

```
package com.kogent.android.ClientSideSocket;
import java.io.IOException;
import java.io.PrintWriter;
import java.net.Socket;
import java.net.UnknownHostException;
import android.os.Bundle;
import android.os.StrictMode;
import android.app.Activity;
import android.view.View;
import android.widget.Button;
import android.widget.EditText;

public class MainActivity extends Activity {
  private Socket client;
   private PrintWriter printwriter;
   private EditText textField;
   private Button button;
   private String message;
  @Override
  protected void onCreate(Bundle savedInstanceState) {
        super.onCreate(savedInstanceState);
        setContentView(R.layout.activity_main);
        StrictMode.ThreadPolicy policy = new
        StrictMode.ThreadPolicy.Builder().permitAll().build();
        StrictMode.setThreadPolicy(policy);
         textField = (EditText) findViewById(R.id.editText1); //reference to the text
        field
          button = (Button) findViewById(R.id.button1);   //reference to the send button
          //Button press event listener
          button.setOnClickListener(new View.OnClickListener() {
           public void onClick(View v) {
            message = textField.getText().toString(); //get the text message on the text
            field
            textField.setText("");      //Reset the text field to blank
            try {
             client = new Socket("192.168.0.102", 6000);  //connect to server
             printwriter = new PrintWriter(client.getOutputStream(),true);
             printwriter.write(message);  //write the message to output stream
             printwriter.flush();
             printwriter.close();
             client.close();   //closing the connection
            } catch (UnknownHostException e) {
```

```
                e.printStackTrace();
            } catch (IOException e) {
                e.printStackTrace();
            }
        }
    });
  }
}
```

In Listing 7.15, the connection with the server is established and the message sent by the client is displayed on the screen. In the code shown in Listing 7.15, you need to use your server mobile IP address instead of 192.168.0.102.

7. *Replace* the code of the `activity_main.xml` file with the code shown in Listing 7.16:

Listing 7.16: Displaying the Code of the `activity_main.xml` File of the `ClientSideSocket` Application

```
<LinearLayout xmlns:android="http://schemas.android.com/apk/res/android"
    xmlns:tools="http://schemas.android.com/tools"
  android:layout_width="fill_parent"
    android:layout_height="fill_parent"
    android:paddingLeft="16dp"
    android:paddingRight="16dp"
    android:orientation="vertical" >
<TextView
        android:layout_width="fill_parent"
        android:layout_height="wrap_content"
        android:text="Please ensure to enter your server ip inside the program before
running this program. Enter the text you want to send" />
<EditText android:id="@+id/editText1"
         android:layout_width="fill_parent"
        android:layout_height="wrap_content"/>
<Button android:text="Send to server"
        android:id="@+id/button1"
        android:layout_width="fill_parent"
        android:layout_height="wrap_content"
        android:layout_gravity="center"/>
</LinearLayout>
```

In Listing 7.16, a `TextView`, an `EditText` and a `Button` views are created. A user can enter the message to be displayed in the `EditText` view and click the button to send the message to the server. Further, the message is displayed on the server.

8. *Add* the following permissions in the `AndroidManifest.xml` file:

```
<uses-permission android:name = "android.permission.INTERNET" />
<uses-permission android:name = "android.permission.ACCESS_NETWORK_STATE" />
<uses-permission android:name = "android.permission.ACCESS_WIFI_STATE" />
```

In the preceding code snippet, the permissions for Internet, network state, and Wi-Fi state are defined. Also, change the minimum SDK version to 9.

When you run the `ServerSideSocket` application, the output is displayed, as shown in Figure 7.10:

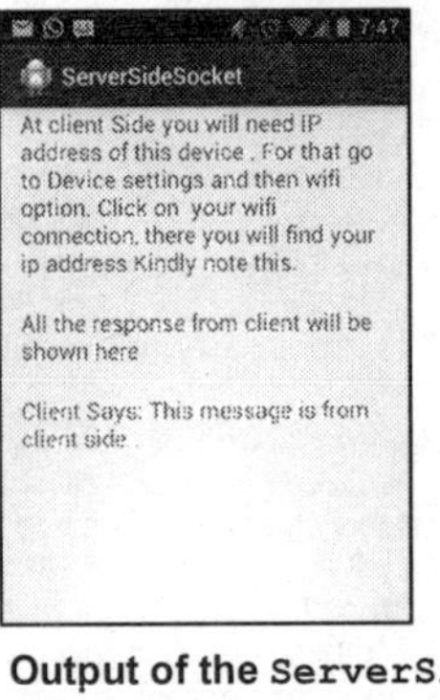

Figure 7.10: Showing the Output of the `ServerSideSocket` Application

Now, when you run the `ClientSideSocket` application, the output is displayed, as shown in Figure 7.11:

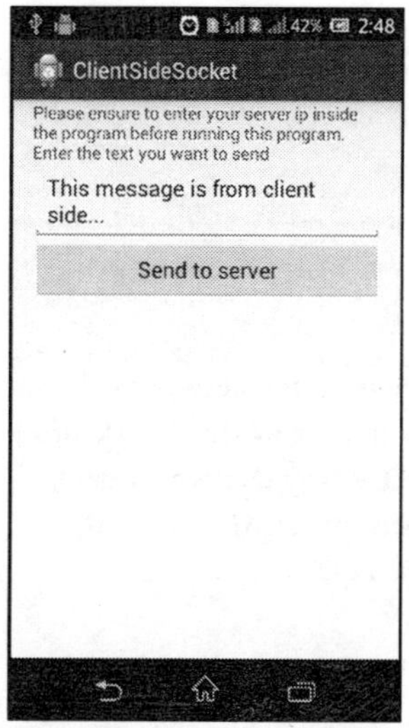

Figure 7.11: Showing the Output of the `ClientSideSocket` Application

Enter the message in the text box and click the **Send to server** button. The response will be displayed on the `ServerSideSocket` window.

Summary

In this chapter, you have learned to develop an Android application to send an email. You have also learned to establish network connectivity using HTTP and check whether or not the network connection is established. Later, in the chapter, you have learned to access Web services using HTTP by developing applications displaying the binary and text data. Also, you have learned to build application to access Web services using the GET method. Later on, the discussion moved on to the JSON services, which are used to send the data. Finally, the client and server application is developed to implement socket programming.

Quick Revise

Q1. Which of the following packages provide the Socket class?

a. **java.net**

b. **java.io**

c. **java.nio**

d. **org.apache**

Ans. The correct option is a.

Q2. Which of the following permission is required to allow users to access the Web services using HTTP?

a. **android.permission.INTERNET**

b. **android.permission.ACCESS_NETWORK_STATE**

c. **android.permission.ACCESS_WIFI_STATE**

d. **None of the above**

Ans. The correct option is a.

Q3. Which of the following packages provide classes to work with SSL certificates?

a. **android.net.http**

b. **java.net**

c. **java.nio**

d. **java.io**

Ans. The correct option is a.

Q4. To maintain the data persistently and display it to the clients, which of the following mechanisms should be used?

a. **Using `Http`**

b. **Using the `Get` method**

c. **Using Socket Programming**

d. **Using JSON**

Ans. The correct option is a.

Q5. Identify the correct code to retrieve all the network information.

a. **NetworkInfo[] info = connectivity.getAllNetworkInfo();**

b. **NetworkInfo[] info = connectivity.getNetworkInfo();**

c. **NetworkInfo[] info = connectivity.getAllNetwork();**

d. **NetworkInfo.State.CONNECTED**

Ans. The correct option is a.

Q6. Which member of the Intent class you would use to send an email?

a. **ACTION_SEND**

b. **EXTRA_SUBJECT**

c. **EXTRA_EMAIL**

d. **EXTRA_TEXT**

Ans. The correct option is a.

Q7. Which of the following classes is instantiated to provide the connection with the web for downloading an image?

a. **URL**

b. **URLConnection**

c. **HttpURLConnection**

d. **URI**

Ans. The correct option is b.

Q8. Which of the following android packages provide the classes for representing buffers as the containers of data types?

a. **java.nio**

b. **java.io**

c. **java.net**

d. **android.net**

Ans. The correct option is a.

Q9. Which of the following protocols can be used to connect to the web in Android-based devices?

a. **http**

b. **https**

c. **tcp**

d. **net.tcp**

Ans. The correct options are a and b.

Q10. Differentiate between the HTTP Post and HTTP Get methods.

Ans. In the HTTP get method, the request is sent from a specified resource and in the HTTP post method, the data is submitted to be processed to a specific resource.

8

Working with Location Services and Maps

If you need an information on:	See page:
Working with Google Maps	304
Working with Geocoding and Reverse Geocoding	322

The Map functionality has become a common feature in today's mobile or tablet devices. The Maps application in a device allows a user to navigate the locations of his/her choice, such as nearby restaurants, offices, institutes, and colleges. You can explore the places not only in your state, country, or city, but also globally across the world. The amazing part of the Map functionality in the devices is that it can help you to tell your current location. In Android-supported devices, you would find the Maps application by default. You can also create the Maps application to perform any desired operation. To create the Maps application, you need to use the Google Maps external library and access the appropriate class or methods.

The Map functionality also allows you to locate a location on the basis of its latitude and longitude. For example, if you know the latitude and longitude of Delhi, then you can navigate Delhi on the Map. Moreover, you can also navigate a location on map on the basis of the name of the location.

In this chapter, you will learn about the Google Maps external library, which allows you to work with the maps on a mobile device. Next, you learn how to add zoom control, change map type, navigate a specific location, and add markers on Map. Finally, the chapter helps you to understand as well as implement the geocoding and reverse geocoding concepts.

Working with Google Maps

Android-supported devices provide the capability of identifying a user location through cellular phone tower, built-in Global Positioning System (GPS) device, or Wi-Fi hotspot. Note that the user location is obtained on the basis of the location of device because it is assumed that wherever the user would go, the device would be at the same location. If you want to develop an application providing the location-based services, then you need to obtain the Maps key. In other words, to programmatically use the Google Maps Application Programming Interface (API), you first need to generate the Map key that can be used in your application. The location-based services provided by the Android-supported devices are very useful as they:

- Help in directing you to the places that you have never visited
- Provide the information about the places of your interest, which are near to your location

Let us now explore the Google Maps external library that you have to use to implement location-based services programmatically in your application.

Exploring Google Maps External Library

Google introduced the Google Maps Android API to allow developers to work with maps on the Android devices. The API consists of the following classes and elements:

- **GoogleMap**—Refers to the main class used to display map titles and map controls. You cannot directly create the instance of the GoogleMap class; instead, it is created after defining the MapView or MapFragment instances. A reference of the GoogleMap object is obtained by invoking the getMap() method of a MapView or MapFragment instance.
- **MapView**—Refers to the subclass of the View class, which provides a canvas to draw the map defined by the GoogleMap object.
- **MapFragment**—Refers to the subclass of the Fragment class, which allows you to place a map within the Fragment layout of the Activity class.
- **Marker**—Allows you to define markers on a map. You can add a marker by retrieving a reference to the GoogleMap object and then invoking the addMarker() method. While adding a marker, you should specify the longitude and latitude where the marker is to be placed.
- **UiSettings**—Refers to the class that allows you to control the interface and the elements appearing on the map. Using this class, you can enable or disable the zoom control on a map.

Creating an Application Using Google Maps Android API

The following tasks are performed for creating an application using the Google Maps API:

1. Create an android application
2. Add Google Play Services Library to the workspace

3. Obtain the Google Map API key
4. Create a layout with the Map fragment
5. Create the `Activity` class
6. Create the Manifest Extensible Markup Language (XML) file
7. Deploy and run the application

Let's learn in detail about each of these tasks.

Creating an Android Application

To create an android application, select `File→New→Android Application Project`. Enter the application name as `GoogleMap` and the package name as `com.kogent.android.googlemap`. Keep the remaining default selections, click the `Next` button, and finally the `Finish` button. The `GoogleMap` application is created.

Adding Google Play Services Library to the Workspace

To develop an application using the Google Play services, you should add the required APIs of the Google Play Services Library. First, you need to download the Google Play services from the SDK manager.

To install the Google Play Services SDK for application development, perform the following steps:

1. Launch the SDK manager in either of the following ways:
   a. In Eclipse (with ADT), select `Windows→SDK Manager`
   b. On Windows, double click the `SDKManager.exe` file located at the root of the Android SDK directory
2. Scroll to the bottom of the package list, expand `Extras`, select `Google Play Services`, and install the services, as shown in Figure 8.1:

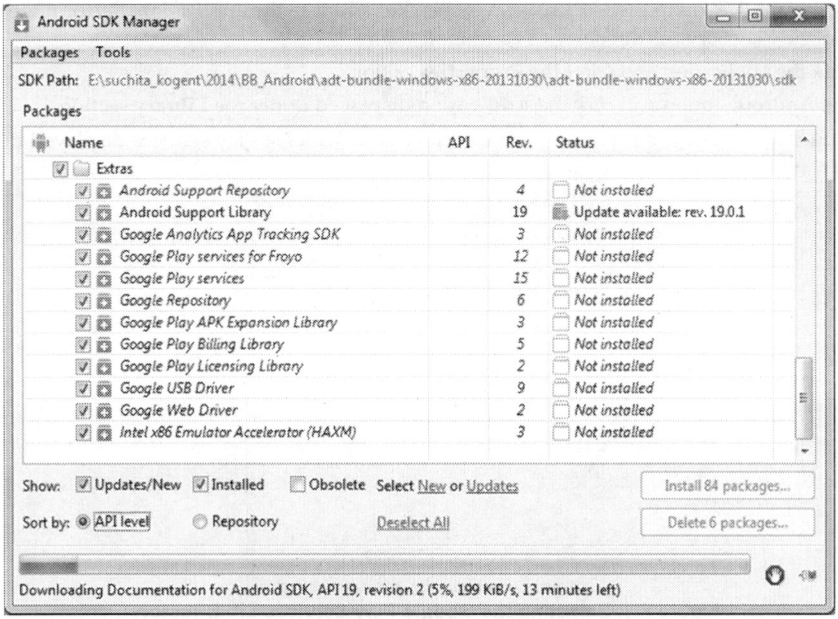

Figure 8.1: Installing the Google Play Services

The Google Play services are installed. Now, import the library into your current workspace. Select `File→Import` and select `Android→Existing Android Code Into Workspace` and browse to the location where the services were installed, that is, `<android-sdk>/extras/google/google_play_services/libproject/google-play-services_lib`, as shown in Figure 8.2:

Figure 8.2: Importing the Google Play Services in the Workspace

Ensure that you have checked the `Copy projects into workspace` checkbox. Also, deselect the checkboxes except the libproject. This will add the `google-play-services_lib` directory in the workspace, as shown in Figure 8.3:

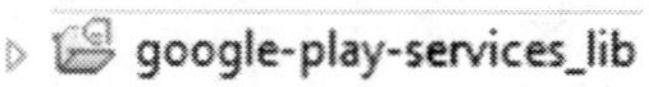

Figure 8.3: Adding the Google Play Services Directory in the Workspace

After adding the application in the workspace, you need to add it to the application. Perform the following steps to add the Google Play Services directory to your application:

1. *Right-click* the application and *select* the **Properties** option.
2. *Select* the **Android** option and *click* the **Add** button displayed under the **Library** section.
3. *Select* the `google-play-services_lib` directory of the Google Play services displayed in the dialog box, as shown in Figure 8.4:

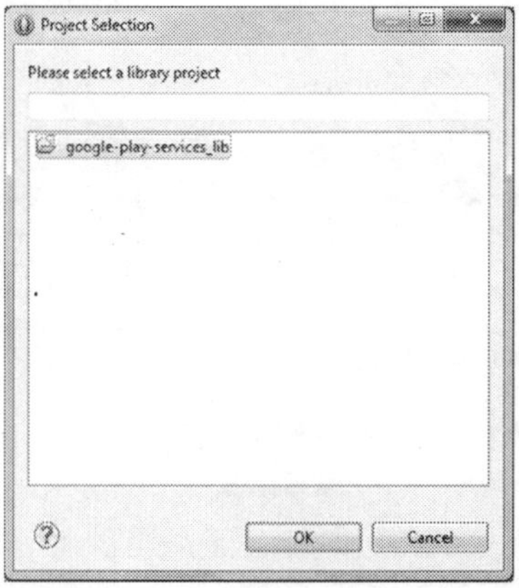

Figure 8.4: Selecting the Google Play Services Lib Directory

4. *Click* the **OK** button. The `google-play-services_lib` directory will be added to your application.

Obtaining the Google Map API Key

If you want to integrate Google Maps into your Android application, you need to get a free Google Maps API key. Note that when you apply for the key, you need to thoroughly read the Google's terms of use and accept it. Perform the following steps to register for Maps API key:

1. *Open* **Eclipse** to verify the existence of the debug certificate.

2. *Select* **Windows→Preferences** from the menu bar of the Eclipse development environment. The **Preferences** dialog box opens.
3. *Expand* the **Android** node and *select* the **Build** option, as shown in Figure 8.5:

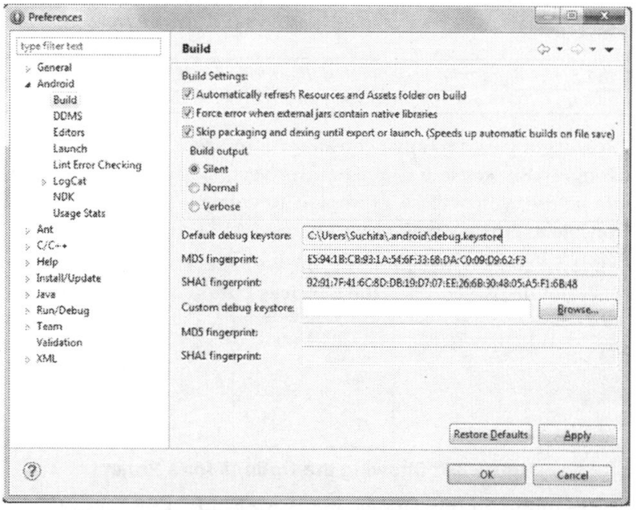

Figure 8.5: Showing the Default Debug Keystore

Note that in Figure 8.5, the filename of the debug certificate is `debug.keystore` and is located at the `C:\Users\<user_name>\.android` folder. This certificate would be used to extract the MD5 fingerprint using the `Keytool.exe` application. This application is available in the `bin` folder of the Java Runtime Environment (JRE) installation location. Perform the following steps to generate the key and get the certificate fingerprints:

1. *Execute* the following command from the `C:\Program Files\Java\<JDK_version_number>` location to extract the MD5 fingerprint:

```
keytool.exe -v -list -alias androiddebugkey -keystore
   "C:\Users\<user_name>\.android\debug.keystore" -storepass android -keypass android
```

For mac use the following command:

```
keytool -list -v -keystore ~/.android/debug.keystore -alias androiddebugkey -storepass
android -keypass android
```

The execution of the preceding command is shown in Figure 8.6:

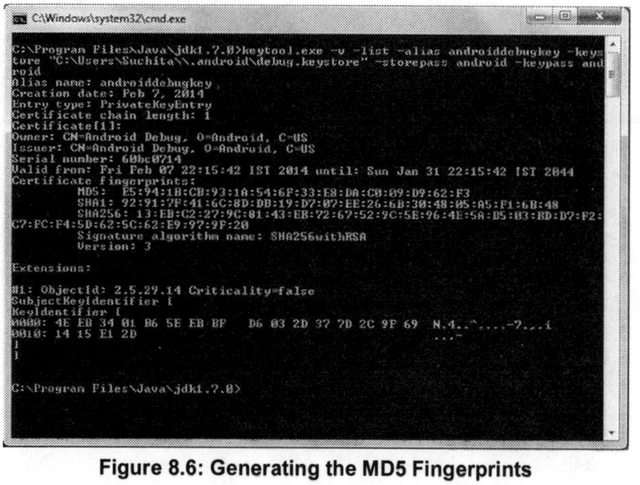

Figure 8.6: Generating the MD5 Fingerprints

NOTE
For best practices, always put your Java directory in the "C drive" instead of placing it in the "program files."

The MD5 fingerprint would be generated, which would be used to generate the Google Maps API.

NOTE
In case of JDK 1.7, by default, the SHA1 fingerprint is generated; therefore, for MD5 fingerprint, you need to use the –v option with the key tool. However, if you are using a lower version, then you can avoid using the –v option.

2. *Open* the "https://code.google.com/apis/console/?noredirect" URL in the Web browser. If you have already used the **GoogleAPIs** console to create a project, skip to the next step. If you have not used the Google APIs console before, you will be prompted to create a project. In such a case, click **Create Project** which causes the Console to create a new project named API Project.
3. In case you have already created the project, you will see a list of your existing projects and available services. If services are not displayed, click the **Services** button on the left, as shown in Figure 8.7:

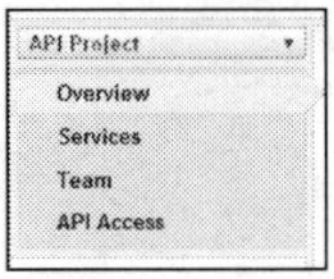

Figure 8.7: Showing the Options for a Project

4. *Scroll* the list of services until you find Google Maps Android API v2 and *click* the button to its right to turn it on, as shown in Figure 8.8:

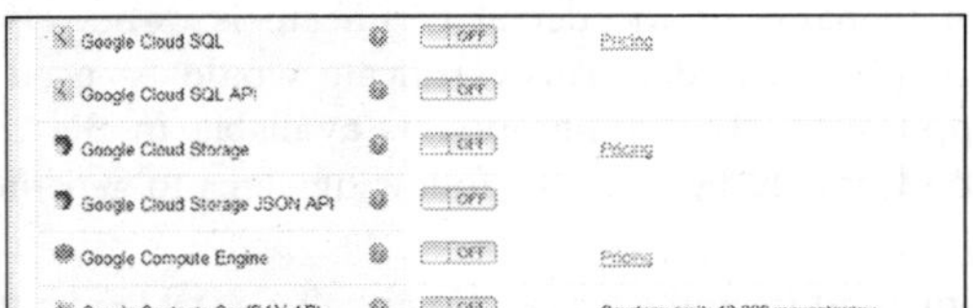

Figure 8.8: Displaying the List of Services

The terms of service agreement appears, as shown in Figure 8.9:

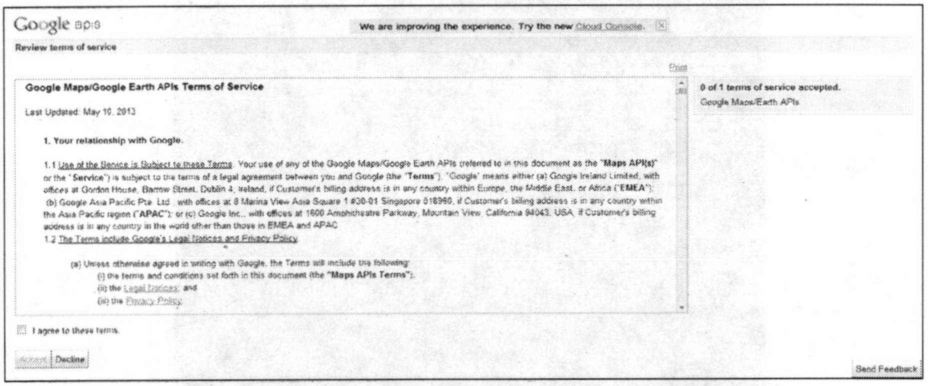

Figure 8.9: Showing the Terms of Service for Google Maps APIs

5. *Click* the **I agree to these terms** checkbox and click the **Accept** button shown in Figure 8.9. The required services will be accepted.

Now, perform the following steps to request a Maps API key:

1. *Navigate* to your project by clicking the "https://code.google.com/apis/console/?noredirect" URL.
2. *Click* the API Access in the left navigation bar shown in Figure 8.7. A new page appears, displaying the list of keys that you have previously created. To create a new key, click the **Create New Android Key**.
3. *Paste* the SHA-1 key generated in Figure 8.6 from your machine into the input field, followed by a semicolon and the full package name of your application, as shown in Figure 8.10:

Figure 8.10: Configuring Android Key for the Project

The server will add an entry to the page that contains the map key and will display as shown in Figure 8.11:

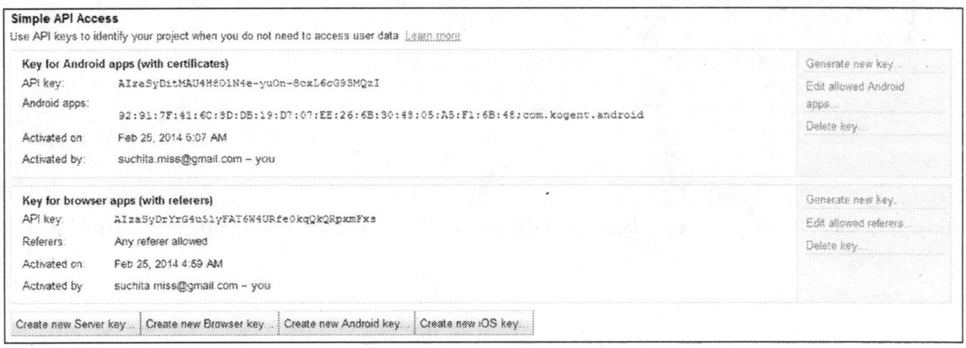

Figure 8.11: Displaying the Generated Key for Google Maps API

Once you have registered for the Google Maps API key, you can use that key to display the `Map` in your application.

Let's create the layout for the `GoogleMap` application.

Creating the Layout with Map Fragment

After creating the `GoogleMap` application, the XML file named `activity_main.xml` must be added. Also, the Activity class `MainActivity` must be added in the application.

You can embed maps into an activity as a fragment, as shown in Listing 8.1:

Listing 8.1: Displaying the Code of the Layout of the `GoogleMap` Application

```
<RelativeLayout xmlns:android="http://schemas.android.com/apk/res/android"
    xmlns:tools="http://schemas.android.com/tools"
    android:layout_width="match_parent"
    android:layout_height="match_parent"
    android:paddingBottom="@dimen/activity_vertical_margin"
    android:paddingLeft="@dimen/activity_horizontal_margin"
```

```
        android:paddingRight="@dimen/activity_horizontal_margin"
        android:paddingTop="@dimen/activity_vertical_margin"
        tools:context=".MainActivity" >
         <fragment
              android:id="@+id/map"
              android:layout_width="match_parent"
              android:layout_height="match_parent"
              android:name="com.google.android.gms.maps.MapFragment"/>
    </RelativeLayout>
```

In Listing 8.1, the `fragment` element is used in which the `com.google.android.gms.maps.MapFragment` activity class is called.

Let's now create the `Activity` class.

Creating the Activity Class

The `MainActivity.java` file is added in the `GoogleMap` Android application. *Replace* the code of the `MainActivity` class with the code shown in Listing 8.2:

Listing 8.2: Displaying the Code of the `MainActivity` Java File of the `GoogleMap` Application

```
package com.kogent.android.googlemap;

import android.os.Bundle;
import android.app.Activity;
import android.view.Menu;

public class MainActivity extends Activity {
    @Override
    protected void onCreate(Bundle savedInstanceState) {
        super.onCreate(savedInstanceState);
        setContentView(R.layout.activity_main);
    }
    @Override
    public boolean onCreateOptionsMenu(Menu menu) {
        // Inflate the menu; this adds items to the action bar if it is present.
        getMenuInflater().inflate(R.menu.main, menu);
        return true;
    }

}
```

In Listing 8.2, the `MainActivity` class extends the `Activity` class and implements the methods of the `Activity` class, such as `onCreate()`.

Creating the Manifest XML File

By default, the `AndroidManifest.xml` file is added in the `GoogleMap` application. In this file, you need to add the following elements:

- `<use-feature>`
- `<uses-permission>`
- `<meta-data>`

The highlighted code for each of these elements is shown in Listing 8.3:

Listing 8.3: Displaying the Code of the `AndroidManifest.xml` File of the `GoogleMap` Application

```
<?xml version="1.0" encoding="utf-8"?>
<manifest xmlns:android="http://schemas.android.com/apk/res/android"
    package="com.kogent.android"
    android:versionCode="1"
    android:versionName="1.0" >
<uses-sdk
        android:minSdkVersion="8"
        android:targetSdkVersion="19" />
<uses-permission android:name="android.permission.INTERNET" />
<uses-permission android:name="android.permission.ACCESS_NETWORK_STATE"/>
<uses-permission android:name="android.permission.WRITE_EXTERNAL_STORAGE"/>
```

```
<uses-permission
android:name="com.google.android.providers.gsf.permission.READ_GSERVICES"/>
<uses-permission android:name="android.permission.ACCESS_COARSE_LOCATION" />
<uses-permission android:name="android.permission.ACCESS_FINE_LOCATION" />
    <application
        android:allowBackup="true"
        android:icon="@drawable/ic_launcher"
        android:label="@string/app_name"
        android:theme="@style/AppTheme" >
        <activity
            android:name="com.kogent.android.MainActivity"
            android:label="@string/app_name" >
            <intent-filter>
                <action android:name="android.intent.action.MAIN" />

                <category android:name="android.intent.category.LAUNCHER" />
            </intent-filter>
        </activity>
         <meta-data
            android:name="com.google.android.maps.v2.API_KEY"
            android:value="AIzaSyDitMAU4H8OlN4e-yuOn-8oxL6cG93MQzI" />
         <meta-data android:name="com.google.android.gms.version"
             android:value="@integer/google_play_services_version" />
    </application>
</manifest>
```

In Listing 8.3, the `<uses-permission>` element is used to specify the permission for the Internet and the `<uses-library>` element has been used to specify the `com.google.android.maps` package.

Deploying and Running an Application

You can run the `GoogleMap` application on a real device by enabling the **Debugging Options** available under **Settings** of the Android device. The output displayed is shown in Figure 8.12:

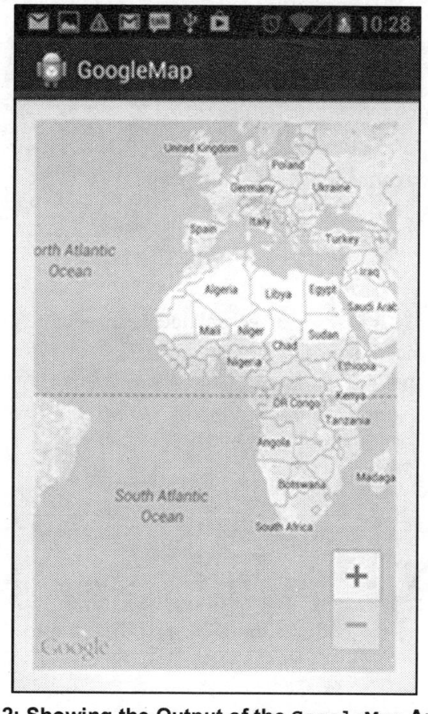

Figure 8.12: Showing the Output of the `GoogleMap` Application

NOTE

The applications based on Google Map API cannot be executed on the emulators; instead, you should configure the real device supporting Android 3.0 or greater.

Let us now learn how to disable the zoom control in the Google Map.

Disabling the Zoom Control Button

You have learned how to display the map; let us now understand how to disable the zoom control of the map's view. In other words, these zoom controls would allow you to zoom in or out a particular location.

You can disable the display of the zoom control button either programmatically or within the `map` element in the XML layout resources. Let us first understand to configure the controls programmatically.

Let us edit the code of the `MainActivity` class to disable the zoom control button. Listing 8.4 shows the edited code of the `MainActivity` class:

Listing 8.4: Displaying the Code to Disable the Zoom Control Button

```
package com.kogent.android;

import com.google.android.gms.maps.GoogleMap;
import com.google.android.gms.maps.MapFragment;
import com.google.android.gms.maps.UiSettings;

import android.os.Bundle;
import android.app.Activity;
import android.view.Menu;

public class MainActivity extends Activity {
    @Override
    protected void onCreate(Bundle savedInstanceState) {
        super.onCreate(savedInstanceState);
        setContentView(R.layout.main);
        GoogleMap map;
        map = ((MapFragment) getFragmentManager().findFragmentById(R.id.map)).getMap();
        UiSettings mapSettings;
    mapSettings = map.getUiSettings();
    mapSettings.setZoomControlsEnabled(false);
    }
    @Override
    public boolean onCreateOptionsMenu(Menu menu) {
        // Inflate the menu; this adds items to the action bar if it is present.
        getMenuInflater().inflate(R.menu.main, menu);
        return true;
    }
}
```

In Listing 8.4, a reference to the `UiSettings` object related to the `GoogleMap` object is retrieved. The reference of the map id is defined in the `activity_main.xml` file and stored in the `map` object. Further, the `setZoomControlsEnabled()` method has been invoked to set the zoom control buttons.

Also, add the following code snippet in the Android manifest XML file:

```
<uses-sdk
        android:minSdkVersion="11"
        android:targetSdkVersion="19" />
<permission
         android:name="com.kogent.android.permission.MAPS_RECEIVE"
         android:protectionLevel="signature"/>
  <uses-permission
         android:name="com.kogent.android.permission.MAPS_RECEIVE"/>
```

Alternatively, you can also change the code in the XML resource file to disable the zoom controls of the map view:

```
map:uiZoomControls="false"
```

Figure 8.13 shows the Map view after disabling the zoom control button:

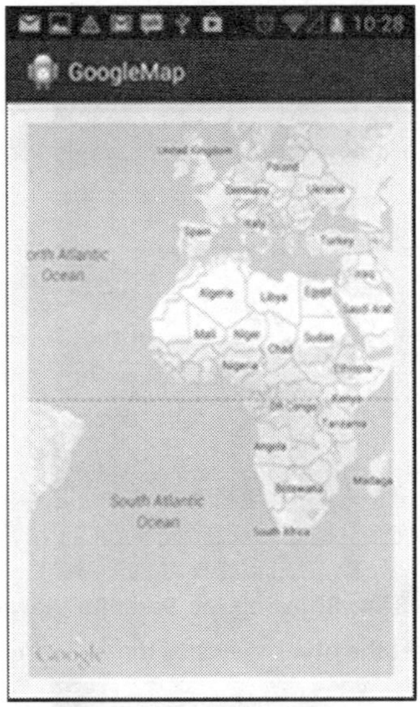

Figure 8.13: Showing the Map without Zoom Control

You can use the enable or disable the zoom control in the Map view.

By default, the Google Map is displayed in the map view. You can programmatically change the view of the map to the satellite or street views.

Changing the Map Type

Google Maps can be displayed in various views, such as satellite or terrain views. You can simply invoke the `setMapType()` method on the instance of the `GoogleMap` class. You need to pass either of the following values while calling the `setMapType()` method:

- **GoogleMap.MAP_TYPE_NONE** – Displays an empty grid with no mapping tiles displayed
- **GoogleMap.MAP_TYPE_NORMAL** – Displays the standard view comprising classic road map
- **GoogleMap.MAP_TYPE_SATELLITE** – Displays the statellite imagery of the map region
- **GoogleMap.MAP_TYPE_HYBRID** – Displays the statellite imagery with the road maps superimposed
- **GoogleMap.MAP_TYPE_TERRAIN** – Displays the topographical information such as contour lines and colors

The following code snippet shows how to set the satellite view of the map:

```
map.setMapType(GoogleMap.MAP_TYPE_SATELLITE);
```

In the preceding code snippet, the `GoogleMap.MAP_TYPE_SATELLITE` value is passed to the `setMapType()` method.

Alternatively, you can change the code of the XML resource file as follows to set the map type:

```
<?xml version="1.0" encoding="utf-8"?>
<fragment xmlns:android="http://schemas.android.com/apk/res/android"
          xmlns:map="http://schemas.android.com/apk/res-auto"
          android:id="@+id/map"
          android:layout_width="match_parent"
          android:layout_height="match_parent"
          map:mapType="hybrid"
          android:name="com.google.android.gms.maps.MapFragment"/>
```

In the preceding code snippet, the `xmlns` namespace is defined to access the `mapType` attribute of the map element.

Figure 8.14 shows the satellite view of the Google Maps:

Figure 8.14: Showing the Satellite View of Map

Similar to the Satellite view, you can set the other views of the map. Figure 8.15 shows the NONE map view:

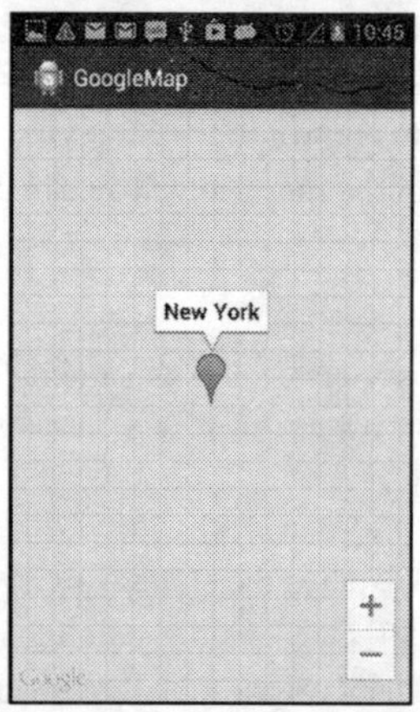

Figure 8.15 : Displaying the NONE Map Type

Figure 8.16 shows the NORMAL map view:

Figure 8.16: Displaying the NORMAL Map View

Figure 8.17 shows the HYBRID map view:

Figure 8.17: Displaying the HYBRID Map View

Figure 8.18 shows the TERRAIN map view:

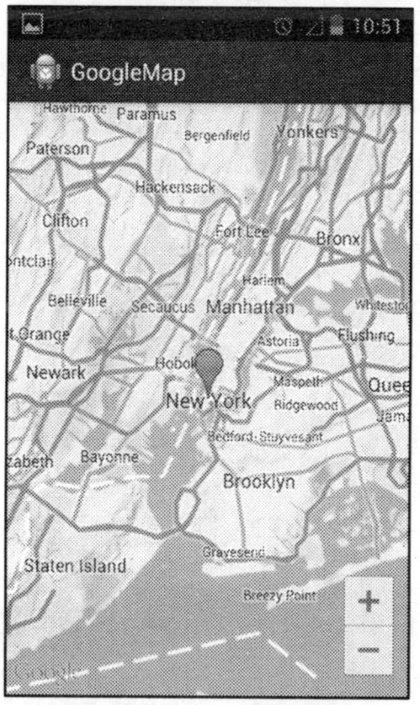

Figure 8.18: Displaying the TERRAIN Map View

Displaying the Specific Location and Adding Markers

You may notice that when the map is loaded for the first time, New York is displayed. However, you can also set the particular location in the map. To set the particular location, you need to specify the latitude and longitude of the specific location. Let us now edit the code of the `MainActivity` class to set the latitude and longitude of the location to be displayed on the map. Listing 8.5 shows the edited code of the `MainActivity` class:

Listing 8.5: Displaying the Code to View a Specific Location in the Map

```
package com.kogent.android.googlemap;
import android.os.Bundle;
import android.app.Activity;
import com.google.android.gms.maps.CameraUpdateFactory;
```

```
import com.google.android.gms.maps.GoogleMap;
import com.google.android.gms.maps.MapFragment;
import com.google.android.gms.maps.model.CameraPosition;
import com.google.android.gms.maps.model.LatLng;
import com.google.android.gms.maps.model.Marker;
import com.google.android.gms.maps.model.MarkerOptions;
import com.kogent.android.googlemapservice.R;
public class MainActivity extends Activity {
    static final LatLng locationinfo = new LatLng(40.7142700   , -74.0059700
);
      private GoogleMap mMap;
   @Override
   protected void onCreate(Bundle savedInstanceState) {
         super.onCreate(savedInstanceState);
         setContentView(R.layout.activity_main);
         try {
               if (mMap == null) {
                  mMap = ((MapFragment) getFragmentManager().
                   findFragmentById(R.id.the_map)).getMap();
               }
               mMap.setMapType(GoogleMap.MAP_TYPE_HYBRID);

            Marker TP = mMap.addMarker(new MarkerOptions().
            position(locationinfo).title("New York"));
            CameraPosition cameraPosition = new CameraPosition.Builder().target(
                              locationinfo).zoom(10).build();
            mMap.animateCamera(CameraUpdateFactory.newCameraPosition(cameraPosition));
         } catch (Exception e) {
            e.printStackTrace();
         }
      }
   }
```

Listing 8.5 shows the code to display the specific location along with its marker on the Google Maps.

Listing 8.6 shows the code of the `activity_main.xml` file:

Listing 8.6: Showing the Code of the `activity_main.xml` File to Add the Marker

```
<fragment xmlns:android="http://schemas.android.com/apk/res/android"
    xmlns:map="http://schemas.android.com/apk/res-auto"
    android:id="@+id/the_map"
    android:name="com.google.android.gms.maps.MapFragment"
    android:layout_width="match_parent"
    android:layout_height="match_parent" />
```

In Listing 8.6, the `MapFragment` is defined in the XML resource file.

Listing 8.7 shows the code of the `AndroidManifest.xml` file:

Listing 8.7: Showing the Code of the `AndroidManifest` XML File to Set Required Permissions

```
<?xml version="1.0" encoding="utf-8"?>
<manifest xmlns:android="http://schemas.android.com/apk/res/android"
    package="com.kogent.android"
    android:versionCode="1"
    android:versionName="1.0" >
<uses-sdk
        android:minSdkVersion="11"
        android:targetSdkVersion="19" />
<permission
         android:name="com.kogent.android.permission.MAPS_RECEIVE"
         android:protectionLevel="signature"/>
   <uses-permission
         android:name="com.kogent.android.permission.MAPS_RECEIVE"/>
<uses-permission android:name="android.permission.INTERNET" />
```

```
    <uses-permission android:name="android.permission.ACCESS_NETWORK_STATE"/>
    <uses-permission android:name="android.permission.WRITE_EXTERNAL_STORAGE"/>
    <uses-permission
    android:name="com.google.android.providers.gsf.permission.READ_GSERVICES"/>
    <uses-permission android:name="android.permission.ACCESS_COARSE_LOCATION" />
    <uses-permission android:name="android.permission.ACCESS_FINE_LOCATION" />
    <uses-feature
            android:glEsVersion="0x00020000"
            android:required="false"/>
        <application
            android:allowBackup="true"
            android:icon="@drawable/ic_launcher"
            android:label="@string/app_name"
            android:theme="@style/AppTheme" >
            <activity
                android:name="com.kogent.android.MainActivity"
                android:label="@string/app_name" >
                <intent-filter>
                    <action android:name="android.intent.action.MAIN" />
                    <category android:name="android.intent.category.LAUNCHER" />
                </intent-filter>
            </activity>
             <meta-data
                android:name="com.google.android.maps.v2.API_KEY"
                android:value="AIzaSyDitMAU4H8OlN4e-yuOn-8oxL6cG93MQzI" />
             <meta-data android:name="com.google.android.gms.version"
                 android:value="@integer/google_play_services_version" />
        </application>
    </manifest>
```

In Listing 8.7, the required permission is set and the details for metadata are defined using the `<meta-data>` element. Ensure that you have added the Google play services in the application else the application will result into errors.

The output of Listing 8.5 is shown in Figure 8.19:

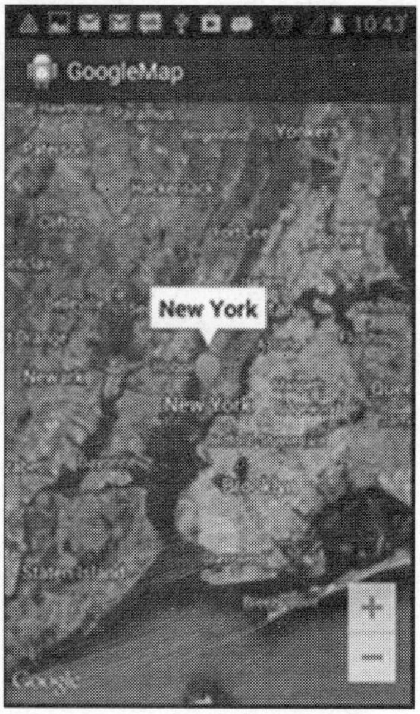

Figure 8.19: Showing Specific Locations in a Map

Handling Map Gestures Interaction

The Google Maps Android API allows you to set the responses to various gestures such as zooming, scrolling, tilting, or rotating the map. These user gestures change the area of the map to be displayed, the zoom level, and the angle of view.

Let us look at the code to set or manage the user gestures on map.

Map Zooming Gestures

The user gesture of zooming the map in or out can be enabled or disabled by using the `setZoomGesturesEnabled()` method on the instance of the `UiSettings` class. Consider the following code snippet to enable zoom gestures for our application:

```
UiSettings mapSettings;
mapSettings = map.getUiSettings();
mapSettings.setZoomGesturesEnabled(true);
```

You can also set the zooming gesture of map by setting the `map:uiZoomGestures` property to true or false.

Map Scrolling Gestures

The scrolling gesture allows a user to move around the map by dragging the map displayed on the screen through a single figure gesture. You can enable the scrolling gesture by using the `setScrollGesturesEnabled()` method, which accepts a `Boolean` value. This method is invoked on the instance of the `UiSettings` class. The following code snippet allows to manage the map scrolling gesture:

```
UiSettings mapSettings;
mapSettings = map.getUiSettings();
mapSettings.setScrollGesturesEnabled(true);
```

You can also configure the map scrolling gesture by setting the `map:uiScrollGestures` property in the resources XML file.

Map Tilting Gestures

A user tilts the angle of projection of the map by placing two fingers on the screen. Programatically, you can enable or disable the tilting gesture by invoking the `setTiltGesturesEnabled()` method, as shown in the following code snippet:

```
UiSettings mapSettings;
mapSettings = map.getUiSettings();
mapSettings.setTiltGesturesEnabled(true);
```

Alternatively, you may enable or disable the `map:uiTiltGestures` property in the resource XML layout.

Map Rotating Gestures

You can rotate the map by placing two fingers on the screen in a circular motion. Rotating the orientation of a map is possible only when the rotation gesture is enabled. Use the following code snippet to enable the rotation gestures:

```
UiSettings mapSettings;
mapSettings = map.getUiSettings();
mapSettings.setRotateGesturesEnabled(true);
```

Alternatively, you may enable or disable the `map:uiRotateGestures` property in the XML layout resource file.

Getting the Current Location of a User

Let us create an application displaying the current location of a user. *Create* the `GetCurrentLocation` Android application with the Activity class as `MainActivity.java` and the XML resource as `activity_main.xml`. Ensure the package name is `com.kogent.android.DialogFragment`.

After creating the application, ensure that the `google-play-services_lib` application available in your workspace is added to the `GetCurrentLocation` application.

Listing 8.8 shows the code of the `activity_main` XML file:

Listing 8.8: Displaying the Code of the `activity_main.xml` File of the `GetCurrentLocation` Application

```
<LinearLayout xmlns:android="http://schemas.android.com/apk/res/android"
    android:layout_width="fill_parent"
    android:layout_height="fill_parent"
    android:orientation="vertical" >

    <Button android:id="@+id/getLocation"
    android:layout_width="fill_parent"
    android:layout_height="wrap_content"
    android:text="Get location "/>

     <TextView
    android:id="@+id/locationLabel"
    android:layout_width="wrap_content"
    android:layout_height="wrap_content"/>

    <TextView
    android:id="@+id/addressLabel"
    android:layout_width="wrap_content"
    android:layout_height="wrap_content"/>

</LinearLayout>
```

In Listing 8.8 , two `TextViews`, namely, `locationLabel` and `addressLabel`, are created and a Button with id `getLocation` is also created. Set the string value for the `get_location` variable as "Get Location" in the `strings.xml` file located at the **/res/values** directory of the application.

Listing 8.9 shows the code of the `MainActivity.java` file:

Listing 8.9 : Displaying the Code for the Activity of the Application Getting the Location of a User

```
package com.kogent.android.DialogFragment;

import java.io.IOException;
import java.util.List;
import java.util.Locale;

import com.google.android.gms.common.ConnectionResult;
import com.google.android.gms.common.GooglePlayServicesClient;
import com.google.android.gms.location.LocationClient;

import android.content.Context;
import android.location.Address;
import android.location.Geocoder;
import android.location.Location;
import android.os.AsyncTask;
import android.os.Bundle;
import android.support.v4.app.FragmentActivity;

import android.util.Log;
import android.view.View;
import android.widget.Button;
import android.widget.TextView;
import android.widget.Toast;

public class MainActivity extends FragmentActivity implements
GooglePlayServicesClient.ConnectionCallbacks,
GooglePlayServicesClient.OnConnectionFailedListener {
  LocationClient mLocationClient;
  private TextView addressLabel;
  private TextView locationLabel;
  private Button getLocationBtn;
  @Override
  protected void onCreate(Bundle savedInstanceState) {
      super.onCreate(savedInstanceState);
        setContentView(R.layout.activity_main);
```

```
        locationLabel = (TextView) findViewById(R.id.locationLabel);
        addressLabel = (TextView) findViewById(R.id.addressLabel);
        getLocationBtn = (Button) findViewById(R.id.getLocation);

        mLocationClient = new LocationClient(this, this, this);

        getLocationBtn.setOnClickListener(new View.OnClickListener() {
                public void onClick(View view) {
                        // mLocationClient.connect();
        Location currentLocation = mLocationClient.getLastLocation();
        String msg = "Current Location: "
                        + Double.toString(currentLocation.getLatitude()) + ","
                        + Double.toString(currentLocation.getLongitude());

        // Display the current location in the UI

        locationLabel.setText(msg);
        Geocoder geocoder = new Geocoder(getApplicationContext(),
                        Locale.getDefault());
        List<Address> addresses = null;
        try {
                addresses = geocoder.getFromLocation(
                                currentLocation.getLatitude(),
                                currentLocation.getLongitude(), 1);
        } catch (IOException e1) {
                Log.e("LocationSampleActivity",
                                "IO Exception in getFromLocation()");
                e1.printStackTrace();
        } catch (IllegalArgumentException e2) {
                // Error message to post in the log
                String errorString = "Illegal arguments "
                                + Double.toString(currentLocation.getLatitude())
                                + " , "
                                + Double.toString(currentLocation.getLongitude())
                                + " passed to address service";
                Log.e("LocationSampleActivity", errorString);
                e2.printStackTrace();
        }
        // If the reverse geocode returned an address
        if (addresses != null && addresses.size() > 0) {
                // Get the first address
                Address address = addresses.get(0);
                /*
                 * Format the first line of address (if available), city,
                 * and country name.
                 */
                String addressText = String.format(
                                "%s, %s, %s",
                                // If there's a street address, add it
                                address.getMaxAddressLineIndex() > 0 ? address
                                                .getAddressLine(0) : "",
                                                // Locality is usually a city
                                                address.getLocality(),
                                                // The country of the address
                                                address.getCountryName());
                // Return the text
                        addressLabel.setText(addressText);
                }
        }
    });

  }// AsyncTask class

  @Override
  protected void onStart() {
```

```
        super.onStart();
        // Connect the client.
    mLocationClient.connect();
    locationLabel.setText("connected....");
    }

    @Override
    public void onConnectionFailed(ConnectionResult arg0) {
        // TODO Auto-generated method stub
    Toast.makeText(this, "Connection Failure :", Toast.LENGTH_SHORT).show();
    }

    @Override
    public void onConnected(Bundle arg0) {
        // TODO Auto-generated method stub
    Toast.makeText(this, "Connection Connected", Toast.LENGTH_SHORT).show();
    }

    @Override
    public void onDisconnected() {
        // TODO Auto-generated method stub
    Toast.makeText(this, "Connection Disconnecteded. Please re-connect.",
                    Toast.LENGTH_SHORT).show();
        }
    }
```

In Listing 8.9, firstly, the longitude and latitude of the current location are fetched using the `getLastLocation()`, `getLatitude()`, and `getLongitude()` methods. Next, the label is set to display the current location in the user interface of the map. This is done by using the `Geocoder` class. You will learn more about geocoding and reverse geocoding in the next section of the chapter.

Listing 8.10 shows the code of the `AndroidManifest.xml` file:

Listing 8.10: Displaying the Code of the `AndroidManifest.xml` File of the Application Getting the Location of a User

```
<?xml version="1.0" encoding="utf-8"?>
<manifest xmlns:android="http://schemas.android.com/apk/res/android"
    package="com.kogent.android.GetCurrentLocation"
    android:versionCode="1"
    android:versionName="1.0" >

    <uses-sdk
        android:minSdkVersion="8"
        android:targetSdkVersion="17" />

    <application
        android:allowBackup="true"
        android:icon="@drawable/ic_launcher"
        android:label="@string/app_name"
        android:theme="@style/AppTheme" >
        <activity
            android:name="com.kogent.android.DialogFragment.MainActivity"
            android:label="@string/app_name" >
            <intent-filter>
                <action android:name="android.intent.action.MAIN" />

                <category android:name="android.intent.category.LAUNCHER" />
            </intent-filter>
        </activity>
              <meta-data android:name="com.google.android.gms.version"
                       android:value="@integer/google_play_services_version" />

    </application>
   <uses-permission android:name="android.permission.ACCESS_COARSE_LOCATION"/>
      <uses-permission android:name="android.permission.INTERNET"/>
</manifest>
```

As already discussed in the chapter, the required permissions and metadata for the application are set in the `AndroidManifest.xml` file shown in Listing 8.10 .

Figure 8.20 shows the output of the `GetCurrentLocation` application:

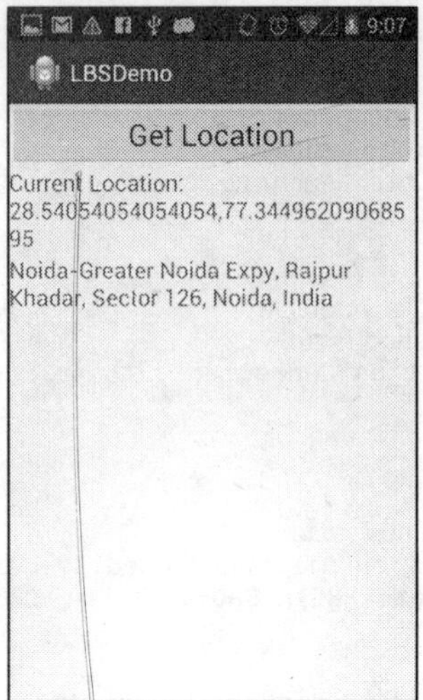

Figure 8.20: Showing the Output of the `GetCurrentLocation` Application

Let us now learn about geocoding and reverse geocoding in detail.

Working with Geocoding and Reverse Geocoding

The process of navigating the geographic location on the basis of the latitude, longitude, or location name is known as geocoding. In reverse, the process of finding location name and information on the basis of geographic location is known as reverse geocoding. The Android SDK provides the `Geocoder` class of the `android.location` package. This class allows you to implement geocoding and reverse geocoding. You can invoke the `getFromLocation()` or `getFromLocationName()` methods of the `Geocoder` class. For reverse geocoding, the `getFromLocation()` method is invoked. However, the geocoding is implemented by invoking the `getFromLocationName()` method. The following three parameters are passed as argument to the `getFromLocation()` method:

- Latitude
- Longitude
- Number of results to be returned

However, the `getFromLocationName()` method accepts the name of the location and the maximum number of results to be passed as argument. These methods return the list of `Address` class as the result of the query.

Let us create an application `GeoCodingApp` to define an activity class displaying the location name on the basis of latitude and longitude. Moreover, this activity class would also help to retrieve the latitude and longitude of your current location. Perform the following steps to create and execute the `GeoCodingApp` application:

1. *Create* the `GeoCodingApp` application using Google APIs Level 14. By default, the main activity class is the `MainActivity` class and the corresponding XML file is `activity_main.xml`. Other files such as `strings.xml` and `AndroidManifest.xml` will be automatically created. Ensure the package name is `com.kogent.android.geocodingapp`.
2. *Replace* the code of the `activity_main.xml` file to define the layout of the application with the code shown in Listing 8.11:

Listing 8.11: Displaying the Code of the Layout for the `GeoCodingApp` Application

```
<?xml version="1.0" encoding="utf-8"?>
<LinearLayout xmlns:android="http://schemas.android.com/apk/res/android"
  android:orientation="vertical" android:layout_width="fill_parent"
  android:layout_height="fill_parent">
<LinearLayout android:id="@+id/linearLayout1"
        android:layout_height="wrap_content" android:layout_width="match_parent"
        android:orientation="horizontal" android:layout_marginTop="40dip">
<TextView android:text="Latitude: " android:layout_height="wrap_content"
android:layout_width="wrap_content" android:id="@+id/TextView01"
  android:layout_marginLeft="10dip" android:layout_marginRight="5dip"
  android:textSize="20dip"></TextView>
<TextView android:text="unknown" android:layout_height="wrap_content"
android:layout_width="wrap_content" android:id="@+id/TextView02"
  android:textSize="20dip"></TextView>
</LinearLayout>
<LinearLayout android:id="@+id/linearLayout2"
android:layout_height="wrap_content" android:layout_width="match_parent">
<TextView android:text="Longitute: " android:layout_height="wrap_content"
android:layout_width="wrap_content" android:id="@+id/TextView03"
android:layout_marginLeft="10dip"      android:layout_marginRight="5dip"
android:textSize="20dip"></TextView>
<TextView android:text="unknown" android:layout_height="wrap_content"
android:layout_width="wrap_content" android:id="@+id/TextView04"
  android:textSize="20dip"></TextView>
</LinearLayout>
</LinearLayout>
```

3. *Replace* the code of the `MainActivity` class with the code shown in Listing 8.12:

Listing 8.12: Displaying the Code to Implement Reverse Geocoding

```
package com.kogent.android.geocodingapp;
import java.io.IOException;
import java.util.List;
import java.util.Locale;
import android.app.Activity;
import android.content.Context;
import android.location.Address;
import android.location.Criteria;
import android.location.Geocoder;
import android.location.Location;
import android.location.LocationListener;
import android.location.LocationManager;
import android.os.Bundle;
import android.widget.TextView;
import android.widget.Toast;
public class MainActivity extends Activity implements LocationListener {
```

```
    private TextView latituteField;
    private TextView longitudeField;
    private LocationManager locationManager;
    private String provider;
    /** Called when the activity is first created. */
    @Override
    public void onCreate(Bundle savedInstanceState) {
        super.onCreate(savedInstanceState);
        setContentView(R.layout.activity_main);
        latituteField = (TextView) findViewById(R.id.TextView02);
        longitudeField = (TextView) findViewById(R.id.TextView04);
        // Get the location manager
        locationManager = (LocationManager)
        getSystemService(Context.LOCATION_SERVICE);
        // Define the criteria how to select the location provider -> use
        // default
        Criteria criteria = new Criteria();
        provider = locationManager.getBestProvider(criteria, false);
        Location location = locationManager.getLastKnownLocation(provider);
        // Initialize the location fields
        if (location != null) {
        System.out.println("Provider " + provider + " has been selected.");
                int lat = (int) (location.getLatitude());
                int lng = (int) (location.getLongitude());
                latituteField.setText(String.valueOf(lat));
                longitudeField.setText(String.valueOf(lng));
        } else {
                latituteField.setText("Provider not available");
                longitudeField.setText("Provider not available");
        }
    }
    /* Request updates at startup */
    @Override
    protected void onResume() {
        super.onResume();
        locationManager.requestLocationUpdates(provider, 400, 1, this); }
    /* Remove the locationlistener updates when Activity is paused */
    @Override
    protected void onPause() {
        super.onPause();
        locationManager.removeUpdates(this);    }
    @Override
    public void onLocationChanged(Location location) {
```

```
        int lat = (int) (location.getLatitude());
        int lng = (int) (location.getLongitude());
    Geocoder gCoder = new Geocoder(getBaseContext(), Locale.getDefault());
        try
        {
                List<Address> add = gCoder.getFromLocation(lat, lng, 1);
                String stradd = "";
                if(add.size()>0)
                {
                        for(int i=0; i<add.get(0).getMaxAddressLineIndex(); i++)
                        stradd += add.get(0).getAddressLine(i) + "\n";  }
        Toast.makeText(getBaseContext(), stradd, Toast.LENGTH_LONG).show();     }
        catch(IOException e)
        {       e.printStackTrace();    }
        latituteField.setText(String.valueOf(lat));
        longitudeField.setText(String.valueOf(lng));    }
    @Override
    public void onStatusChanged(String provider, int status, Bundle extras) {
                }
    @Override
    public void onProviderEnabled(String provider) {
        Toast.makeText(this, "Enabled new provider " + provider,
                        Toast.LENGTH_SHORT).show();     }
    @Override
    public void onProviderDisabled(String provider) {
        Toast.makeText(this, "Disenabled provider " + provider,
                        Toast.LENGTH_SHORT).show();     }
}
```

In Listing 8.12, the `gCoder` instance of the `Geocoder` class has been created to retrieve the location name on the basis of the latitude and longitude of the current location of the user.

4. *Add* the following permissions in the `AndroidManifest.xml` file of the application:

```
<uses-permission android:name="android.permission.INTERNET"/>
<uses-permission android:name="android.permission.ACCESS_NETWORK_STATE"/>
<uses-permission android:name="android.permission.ACCESS_COARSE_LOCATION" />
<uses-permission android:name="android.permission.ACCESS_FINE_LOCATION" />
```

Note that the `<uses-permission>` element has been used to grant the following permissions to the user:

- INTERNET
- ACCESS_NETWORK_STATE
- ACCESS_COARSE_LOCATION
- ACCESS_FINE_LOCATION

5. *Execute* the `GeoCodingApp` application to run the `MainActivity` class. While executing the application, open the Dalvik Debug Monitor Server (DDMS) perspective and send the appropriate latitude and longitude values. You need to specify these values in the **Location Controls** section of the Emulator Control tab. In our case, we have specified 77 as longitude and 28 as latitude values. The name of the location would be displayed while executing the `MainActivity` class.

Figure 8.21 shows the output of Listing 8.12:

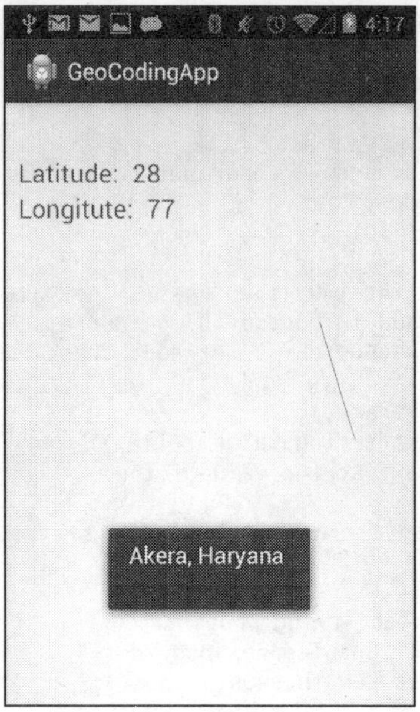

Figure 8.21: Showing Geocoding in a Map

In Figure 8.21, the name of the location displayed in our case is Akera, Haryana.

Let us now summarize the concepts explored in the chapter.

Summary

This chapter has briefly discussed about location services and maps. First, you have learned to work with Google Maps. The Google Maps APIs can be used in your application to take the benefits of maps or location-based services. You have also learned how to use the Google Maps APIs in which you are required to generate the `Map` key that can be used in your application. Using the `com.google.android.maps` package of the Google Maps external library just simplifies the task of adding mapping capabilities in your Android applications. You have also learned the steps to get a free Google Maps API key to integrate Google Maps into your Android application.

Emphasis is also laid on displaying various views in maps, such as satellite or terrain. You can simply invoke the various methods to handle map gestures. You have also learned that to change the map type, you need to invoke the appropriate field of the `GoogleMap` class. Next to this, you have learned that by specifying latitude and longitude of a specific location, you can set the particular location on the map. After this, you have learned to add markers to the map in your Android application. Finally, you have learned to implement geocoding and reverse geocoding in your Android application.

Quick Revise

Q1. Which of the following debug certificate is required to integrate Google Maps into your Android application?

- **a. debug.keystore**
- **b. default.keyset**
- **c. androidtool.cfg**
- **d. repositories.cfg**

Ans. The correct option is a.

Q2. **Which of the following certificate fingerprints is used to generate the Google Maps API?**

a. **SH1**

b. **SHA256**

c. **SHA**

d. **MD5**

Ans. The correct option is d.

Q3. **To use Google map in your Android 4 application, you have to set the add which of the following services?**

a. **Google Play Services**

b. **API 14**

c. **Google APIs (Google Inc.)**

d. **Google Maps API**

Ans. The correct option is a.

Q4. **Which of the following element is used to set the user permissions to add Google Maps functionality in your application?**

a. **<uses-sdk/>**

b. **<users-permission/>**

c. **<application/>**

d. **<activity/>**

Ans. The correct option is b.

Q5. **Which of the following values is used to display an empty grid with no mapping tiles?**

a. **GoogleMap.MAP_TYPE_NONE**

b. **GoogleMap.MAP_TYPE_SATELLITE**

c. **GoogleMap.MAP_TYPE_NORMAL**

d. **GoogleMap.MAP_TYPE_HYBRID**

Ans. The correct option is a.

Q6. **Which of the following methods enable or disable the zoom gestures of a Map-based application?**

a. **setZoomGesturesEnabled()**

b. **setScrollGesturesEnabled()**

c. **setTiltGesturesEnabled()**

d. **setRotateGesturesEnabled()**

Ans. The correct option is a.

Q7. **The method setBuiltInZoomControls() returns which of the following data type?**

a. **integer**

b. **float**

c. **char**

d. **boolean**

Ans. The correct option is d.

Q8. **To add marker to the map in your application, your class needs to extend which of the following classes?**

a. **MapView**

b. **Overlay**

c. **MapActivity**

d. **MapMode**

Ans. The correct option is b.

Q9. The process of navigating the geographic location on the basis of the latitude, longitude, or location name is known as:

a. **Geocoding**

b. **Reverse Geocoding**

c. **Georeferencing**

d. **Reverse Georeferencing**

Ans. The correct option is a.

Q10. Which of the following interface is implemented in reverse geocoding?

a. **Locator**

b. **Locator2**

c. **LocationListener**

d. **Lock**

Ans. The correct option is a.

9

Working with Graphics and Animation

If you need an information on:	See page:
Working with Graphics	330
Using the Drawable Object	336
Using the `ShapeDrawable` Object	340
Working with the NinePatchDrawable Graphics	343
Understanding the Concept of Hardware Acceleration	345
Working with Animations	346

The animation Application Programming Interface (API) was introduced in Android 3.0, and now there are slight changes in Android 4. The Android 4.0 API level 14 provides an improved version of the hardware-accelerated Two-Dimensional (2D) rendering pipeline. The Android framework contains two animation systems, namely, property animation and view animation. Both systems are equipped with all the tools that a developer expects. However, the property animation system is the preferred method to use since its tools are more flexible. Besides this, there is an additional class called `Drawable`, which also pertains to graphics and animations. An advantage of the `Drawable` animation is that it offers an elegant solution for the sequential frame animations. The `Drawable` class is a recommended class to use where you want to construct an application like an animation movie. The concept of hardware acceleration was also introduced in Android 3.0. However, in API 14 onward, hardware acceleration is on by default.

The rich graphics application can be built by using either XML file or Android code. However, the use of XML file is recommended as there is more readability, flexibility, and swapping of code.

In this chapter, you will learn how to work with graphics and animation. First, you will know about the use of graphics. You also learn that graphics can be created into either the `View` object or directly to the `Canvas` in an Android application. Next the chapter explains how to use the `SurfaceView` and `ShapeDrawable` classes. It also discusses the concept of nine patch drawable images. Then, you will learn about hardware acceleration. Finally, you will learn about the implementation of animation using the Animator class in an Android application.

Working with Graphics

The drawing of graphics plays a very important role in any application. You would find that drawing of different types of graphics has different techniques. For example, the drawing of graphics for a static application varies a lot from the drawing of graphics for an interactive game. The Android framework provides various `View` widgets that can be used to design the user interface of applications. The functionality of these widgets can be extended to modify their appearance and behavior.

In Android, you can create graphics into the `View` object or directly to the `Canvas`. In case of drawing graphics into a `View` object, the process of drawing the graphics is handled by the system's normal View hierarchy. However, while drawing the graphics on the `Canvas`, you need to invoke the `onDraw()` method and manage the drawing of the graphics on your own. Generally, the process of drawing into the `View` object is used when you need to draw simple graphics in an application. In other words, if you do not need to dynamically change the graphics and the graphics are not a part of the interactive game, then you can draw the graphics into the `View` object. However, if in an application, the graphics need to be redrawn regularly, then the graphics should be drawn to the `Canvas` on their own.

Let us learn how to create graphics directly to the `Canvas`.

Drawing Graphics to Canvas

You can draw specialized graphics and manage the animation of the graphics by using the `Canvas` in an application. The `Canvas` serves as a surface on which the graphics would be created and manages the invocation of the `onDraw()` method. Note that the graphics are drawn on `Bitmap` through the `Canvas`. When you draw the graphics within the `onDraw()` callback method, the `Canvas` is used to put the drawing calls. While working with the `SurfaceView` object, you can retrieve the `Canvas` by invoking the `lockCanvas()` method of the `SurfaceHolder` class.

If you want to define a new `Canvas`, then you should create a `Bitmap` by using the `createBitmap()` method and set up a new `Canvas` by passing the `Bitmap` object, as shown in the following code snippet:

```
Bitmap bmp = Bitmap. createBitmap(480, 800, Bitmap.Config.ARGB_8888);
Canvas can = new Canvas(bmp);
```

In the preceding code snippet, the `createBitmap()` method has been invoked, which accepts the following three arguments:

- Width of the `Bitmap`
- Height of the `Bitmap`

- Bitmap config to be created

After specifying the appropriate values for the preceding arguments, the Bitmap instance is passed as argument so that the Canvas would draw the defined Bitmap. You can now move your Bitmap to another Canvas by invoking the drawBitmap() method. This method accepts the following parameters:

- Instance of the Bitmap to be drawn
- The matrix used to transform the created Bitmap
- The paint that would be used to draw the Bitmap

Finally, you can draw the final graphics through a Canvas by using the View.onDraw() or SurfaceHolder.lockCanvas() method. The Canvas class provides different methods, such as drawArc(), drawBitmap(), drawCircle(), and drawRect(), to draw graphical objects, such as arc, bitmap, circle, oval, points, text, and path.

The two approaches to draw graphics with a Canvas are as follows:

- Using the View class
- Using the SurfaceView class

Let us explore each of these approaches in detail.

Drawing on the View Class

Generally, when a considerable amount of processing or frame-rate speed is not required in an application, you can create a custom View component and draw the graphics with Canvas in the View.onDraw() method. While drawing on the View, the Android framework would provide the Canvas on which you can put the drawing calls. Let us understand the process of drawing on the View. You need to extend your class with the View class first and then implement the onDraw() callback method. Now, when your View class is requested to draw the graphics on itself, then the onDraw() method would be invoked by the Android framework.

Note that only the onDraw() method is being invoked by the Android framework, and therefore, you need to explicitly invoke the invalidate() method to invalidate the View whenever the application is ready to draw the graphics. Within the View.onDraw() method, you can use the Canvas to draw the desired graphical shape by invoking the drawXXX() methods of the Canvas class.

Let us create a simple Android application, ViewGraphics, in which a blank screen is initially displayed to the users. Further, the users can touch the screen of the device to draw the desired graphics.

Perform the following steps to create and run the ViewGraphics application:

1. *Create* an Android application, ViewGraphics, in the Eclipse Integrated Development Environment (IDE) under the com.kogent.android.viewgraphics package. By default, the required Extensible Markup Language (**XML**) files, such as AndroidManifest.xml, activity_main.xml, and strings.xml, would be created. Moreover, the MainActivity class would also be created along with the ViewGraphics application.
2. *Replace* the code of the MainActivity.java file, located in the **/src/com/kogent/android/viewgraphics** folder, with the code shown in Listing 9.1:

Listing 9.1: Displaying the Code of the MainActivity.java File in the ViewGraphics Application

```
package com.kogent.android.viewgraphics;

import android.app.Activity;
import android.os.Bundle;
import android.view.Window;
import android.view.WindowManager;

public class MainActivity extends Activity {
  CreateView createView;
  /** Called when the activity is first created. */
    @Override
    public void onCreate(Bundle savedInstanceState) {
```

```
        super.onCreate(savedInstanceState);
       getWindow().setFlags(WindowManager.LayoutParams.FLAG_FULLSCREEN,
       WindowManager.LayoutParams.FLAG_FULLSCREEN);
        requestWindowFeature(Window.FEATURE_NO_TITLE);
        createView = new CreateView(this);
        setContentView(createView);
        createView.requestFocus();
    }
}
```

In Listing 9.1, the `MainActivity` class extends the `Activity` class and an instance of the `CreateView` class has been created. Note that we need to create the `CreateView` class. Within the `onCreate()` method of the `Activity` class, the full screen of the application has been set without the title bar. You would also find that the instance of the `CreateView` class has been passed through the `setContentView()` method of the `Activity` class.

3. *Create* a new Java class, named `CreateView`, in the **/src** folder and under the `com.kogent.android.viewgraphics` package, as shown in Listing 9.2:

Listing 9.2: Displaying the Code of the `CreateView.java` File in the `ViewGraphics` Application

```
package com.kogent.android.viewgraphics;
import java.util.ArrayList;
import java.util.List;
import android.content.Context;
import android.graphics.Canvas;
import android.graphics.Color;
import android.graphics.Paint;
import android.util.Log;
import android.view.MotionEvent;
import android.view.View;
import android.view.View.OnTouchListener;
public class CreateView extends View implements OnTouchListener
{
  private static final String TAG = "CreateView";
  List<Point> pts = new ArrayList<Point>();
  Paint p = new Paint();
  public CreateView(Context context) {
        super(context);
        setFocusable(true);
        setFocusableInTouchMode(true);
        this.setOnTouchListener(this);
        p.setColor(Color.RED);
        p.setAntiAlias(true);
        }
  @Override
  public void onDraw(Canvas c) {
        for (Point point : pts) {
               c.drawCircle(point.i, point.j, 5, p);
               }
        }
  public boolean onTouch(View view, MotionEvent event) {
        Point pt = new Point();
        pt.i = event.getX();
        pt.j = event.getY();
        pts.add(pt);
        invalidate();
        Log.d(TAG, "point: " + pt);
        return true;
        }
  }
```

```
class Point
{
   float i, j;
   @Override
   public String toString() {
         return i + ", " + j;
         }
}
```

In Listing 9.2, the instance of the `Canvas` class is passed as an argument to the `onDraw()` method. Note that the `drawCircle()` method has been invoked by using the `Canvas` object.

4. *Right-click* the `ViewGraphics` application and select `Run As→Android Application`. You would notice a blank screen as the output of the execution of the `ViewGraphics` application. Now, touch the screen and draw the desired graphics to view the results, as shown in Figure 9.1:

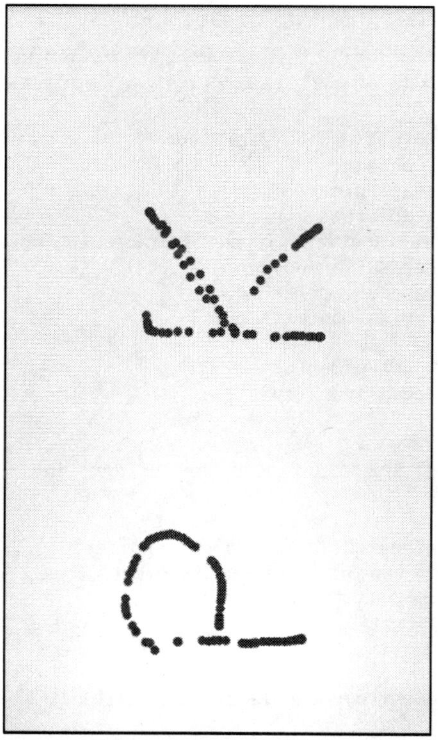

Figure 9.1: Displaying the Output of the `ViewGraphics` Application

After understanding how to draw on the `View`, let us explore how to draw on `SurfaceView`.

Drawing on the `SurfaceView` Class

Apart from extending your class from the `View` class, you can also use the `SurfaceView` class. This class is the subclass of the `View` class that provides a surface to draw the graphics, which is then provided to the secondary thread of the application. The advantage of defining the secondary thread of the application is that the application does not have to wait till the `View` hirerachy of the Android framework is requested to draw. However, the reference of the `SurfaceView` class is being passed to the secondary thread that can draw the graphics to its own `Canvas` and at its own speed.

To draw on the `SurfaceView` class, you need to ensure that your class extends the `SurfaceView` class and implements the `SurfaceHolder.Callback` interface. This interface is used to notify about the various events associated with the `Surface` object, such as surface created, modified, or destroyed. It is very essential that the notifications should be provided for these events so that you are aware when the drawing has started, when the modifications are required on a new surface, and finally when the drawing should stop.

Instead of defining the secondary thread as a separate class (i.e., separate file), you can define it within your `SurfaceView` class. Note that instead of working directly with the `Surface` object, you should manage it through `SurfaceHolder` interface. Therefore, after initializing the `SurfaceView` class, you can retrieve the `SurfaceHolder` interface by invoking the `getHolder()` method. Further, you should invoke the `addCallback()` method that notifies the `SurfaceHolder` to receive the callbacks. Finally, you should override all the `SurfaceHolder.Callback` methods within the `SurfaceView` class. Let us create an Android application, `CreateSurfaceView`, to understand how to draw on the `SurfaceView` class.

Perform the following steps to create and run the `CreateSurfaceView` application:

1. *Create* an Android application, `CreateSurfaceView`, in the Eclipse IDE under the `com.kogent.android.createsurfaceview` package.
2. *Create* a new Java class, named `CreateSurfaceView`, in the **/src** folder under the `com.kogent.android.createsurfaceview` package, as shown in Listing 9.3:

Listing 9.3: Displaying the Code of the `CreateSurfaceView.java` File in the `CreateSurfaceView` Application

```
package com.kogent.android.createsurfaceview;
import android.content.Context;
import android.view.SurfaceHolder;
import android.view.SurfaceView;
    public class CreateSurfaceView extends SurfaceView implements SurfaceHolder.Callback {
     private SurfaceHolder surfaceHolder;
     private SurfaceThread surfaceThread;
     public CreateSurfaceView(Context ctx) {
          super(ctx);
          surfaceHolder = getHolder();
          surfaceHolder.addCallback(this);
     }
     @Override
    public void surfaceChanged(SurfaceHolder sHolder, int format, int width, int height) {
     }
     @Override
     public void surfaceCreated(SurfaceHolder sHolder) {
           surfaceThread = new SurfaceThread(sHolder);
           surfaceThread.setRunning(true);
           surfaceThread.start();
     }
     @Override
     public void surfaceDestroyed(SurfaceHolder sHolder) {
          boolean retry = true;
          surfaceThread.setRunning(false);
          while (retry) {
               try {
                     surfaceThread.join();
                  retry = false;
               } catch (InterruptedException e) {
               }
          }
     }
}
```

In Listing 9.3, the `SurfaceHolder` interface is retrieved in the constructor of the class by invoking the `getHolder()` method. Next, the `addCallback()` method is invoked on the instance of the `SurfaceHolder` interface so that all the callback methods would be notified.

3. *Create* a new Java class, named `SurfaceThread`, in the **/src** folder under the `com.kogent.android.createsurfaceview` package, as shown in Listing 9.4:

Listing 9.4: Displaying the Code of the `SurfaceThread.java` File in the `CreateSurfaceView` Application

```
package com.kogent.android.createsurfaceview;
import android.graphics.Canvas;
import android.graphics.Color;
import android.graphics.Paint;
import android.view.SurfaceHolder;
public class SurfaceThread extends Thread {
    private SurfaceHolder surfaceHolder;
    private boolean running = true;
    int i = 0;
    public SurfaceThread(SurfaceHolder holder) {
        this.surfaceHolder = holder;    }
    @Override
    public void run() {
        while(running ) {
            Canvas canvas = null;
            try {
                canvas = surfaceHolder.lockCanvas();
                 synchronized (surfaceHolder) {
                    canvas.drawColor(Color.BLACK);
                    Paint paint = new Paint();
                    paint.setColor(Color.RED);
                    canvas.drawCircle(i++, 100, 50, paint);  }
            }
            finally {
                    if (canvas != null) {
                         surfaceHolder.unlockCanvasAndPost(canvas);
                         }
            }
        }
    }

    public void setRunning(boolean b) {
        running = b;
    }
}
```

In Listing 9.4, the `run()` method of the `SurfaceThread` class has been implemented to draw a circle of Red color which would keep on moving.

4. *Replace* the code of the `MainActivity.java` file, located in the **/src/com/kogent/android/createsurfaceview** folder, with the code shown in Listing 9.5:

Listing 9.5: Displaying the Code of the `MainActivity` Class to Draw on the `SurfaceView` Class

```
package com.kogent.android.createsurfaceview;
import android.app.Activity;
import android.os.Bundle;
public class MainActivity extends Activity {
   //CreateView createView;
   CreateSurfaceView createView;
   /** Called when the activity is first created. */
    @Override
    public void onCreate(Bundle savedInstanceState) {
            super.onCreate(savedInstanceState);
            // Set full screen view
//getWindow().setFlags(WindowManager.LayoutParams.FLAG_FULLSCREEN,WindowManager.LayoutPara
ms.FLAG_FULLSCREEN);
```

```
            //requestWindowFeature(Window.FEATURE_NO_TITLE);
            //createView = new CreateView(this);
            createView = new CreateSurfaceView(this);
            setContentView(createView);
            createView.requestFocus();    }}
```

In Listing 9.5, the instance of the `CreateSurfaceView` class has been set as the content view for the `MainActivity` class through the `setContentView()` method.

5. *Right-click* the `CreateSurfaceView` application and *select* `Run As→Android Application`. The output of the `CreateSurfaceView` application is displayed in Figure 9.2:

Figure 9.2: Displaying the Output of the `CreateSurfaceView` Application

Let us now learn how to use the `Drawable` object to draw the graphics.

Using the Drawable Object

In Android, the Two-Dimensional (2D) graphics library is used to draw various shapes and images. The `android.graphics.drawable` package provides the classes that can be used to draw 2D graphics. The `Drawable` class is an abstract class that defines the methods used to draw the graphics. This class is generally extended by the other drawable classes, such as `BitmapDrawable`, `ShapeDrawable`, `LayerDrawable`, and `PictureDrawable`. Further, you can extend any of these classes to create your own custom Drawable objects.

Apart from allowing you to draw the graphics, the `Drawable` class also provides the following methods to allow the client to interact with the drawn object:

- **The `setBounds(Rect)` method**—Refers to the method that is invoked to specify the `Drawable` class about the size and location at which it needs to be drawn. You can find the size of few drawable graphics by using the `getIntrinsicHeight()` or `getIntrinsicWidth()` method.
- **The `getPadding(Rect)` method**—Returns the padding details that are helpful in framing the content placed inside the `Drawable` class.
- **The `setState(int [])` method**—Allows the users to specify the state in which a drawable graphic would be drawn, such as focused, clicked, and selected.
- **The `setLevel(int)` method**—Allows the users to display the drawable graphics on the basis of current level, such as battery level or progress level.

You can define and instantiate the `Drawable` class in either of the following ways:

- Using an image that is stored as a resource in your Android project
- Using an XML file containing the `Drawable` properties

Let us learn how to define a `Drawable` object using the preceding approaches.

Referencing an Image File

In Android, the easiest approach to add graphics to an application is by using an image that is already added to the application. Generally, the Portable Network Graphics (PNG) or Joint Photographic Experts Group (JPG) files are supported. This approach is preferred when a user needs to use graphics as application icon, logo, or in games. For example, imagine you want to create a gaming application in which a car is moving, and when obstructed by an object, it reverses. In such an application, you would require the image of a car. Note that the resources, which are stored in the **/res/drawable** folder of the application, are automatically optimized with the help of the `aapt` tool. However, if you want to read an image in the form of a bit stream, then you need to store the images in the **/res/raw** folder of the application.

You can reference the image file (Drawable resource) either programmatically or in the XML file designed for the layout of the application. Let us create an Android application in which we would display an image (available in the **/res/drawable** folder of the application) on the screen using the `ImageView` class.

Perform the following steps to create and run the `DrawableImage` application:

1. *Create* an Android application, `DrawableImage`, in the Eclipse IDE under the `com.kogent.android.drawableimage` package.
2. *Create* the **drawable** folder in the **res** directory of the application. Copy the desired image that you want to display on the screen and then paste the image in the **/res/drawable** folder. In our case, we have pasted the `sample1.jpg` image in the **/res/drawable** folder on the `DrawableImage` application.
3. *Replace* the code of the `MainActivity.java` file, located in the **/src/com/kogent/android/drawableimage** folder, with the code shown in Listing 9.6:

Listing 9.6: Displaying the Code of the `MainActivity.java` File in the `DrawableImage` Application

```
package com.kogent.android.drawableimage;

import android.app.Activity;
import android.os.Bundle;
import android.widget.ImageView;
import android.widget.LinearLayout;

public class MainActivity extends Activity
{
    @Override
        public void onCreate(Bundle savedInstanceState) {
            super.onCreate(savedInstanceState);
            LinearLayout sampleLayout = new LinearLayout(this);
            ImageView imgView = new ImageView(this);
            imgView.setImageResource(R.drawable.sample1);
            imgView.setAdjustViewBounds(true);
            sampleLayout.addView(imgView);
            setContentView(sampleLayout);

        }
}
```

In Listing 9.6, the `sampleLayout` instance of the `LinearLayout` class has been created to display an image with the help of using the `ImageView` class. Further, a drawable image resource file has been provided by using the `setImageResource()` method and passing the `R.drawable.sample1` parameter in it. However, if the resource is not the Joint Photographic Experts Group (JPEG) image, then you need to use the following code snippet:

```
Resources resource = mContext.getResources();
Drawable sample = resources.getDrawable(R.drawable.sample1);
```

4. *Right-click* the `DrawableImage` application and select Run As→Android Application. The output of the `DrawableImage` application is displayed in Figure 9.3:

Figure 9.3: Displaying the Output of the `DrawableImage` Application

Let us now understand how to use the XML file to access the `Drawable` properties.

Defining Drawable in XML

You have already learned that you can reference the image available in the **/res/drawable** folder of your application. Apart from this, you can create the `Drawable` object by defining its properties in an XML file. For example, you can define the colors, which can be used for the views, in an XML file. Further, you can retrieve the appropriate color to be set for a View from the XML file.

Let us create an Android application in which you will create the `Drawable` object by creating an XML file. In this application, you need to create the `colors.xml` file and access the defined colors in it for the views in an `Activity` class.

Perform the following steps to create and run the `SampleDrawableXML` application:

1. *Create* an Android application, `SampleDrawableXML`, in the Eclipse IDE under the `com.kogent.android.sampledrawablexml` package.
2. *Create* the `colors.xml` file in the **/res/values** directory of the `SampleDrawableXML` application, as shown in Listing 9.7:

Listing 9.7: Displaying the Code of the `colors.xml` File in the `SampleDrawableXML` Application

```
<?xml version="1.0" encoding="utf-8"?>
<resources>
     <drawable name="red">#ff0000</drawable>
     <drawable name="blue">#0000ff</drawable>
     <drawable name="green">#00ff00</drawable>
</resources>
```

In Listing 9.7, we have defined three drawable resources, namely, red, blue, and green. For each resource, a specific color has been specified. Let us now create the `MainActivity` activity class to set these colors as background for the `TextView` element.

3. *Replace* the code of the `MainActivity.java` file, located in the **/src/com/kogent/android/sampledrawablexml** folder, with the code shown in Listing 9.8:

Listing 9.8: Displaying the Code of the `MainActivity` Activity Class in the `SampleDrawableXML` Application

```
package com.kogent.android.sampledrawablexml;

import android.app.Activity;
import android.graphics.drawable.ColorDrawable;
import android.os.Bundle;
import android.view.ViewGroup.LayoutParams;
import android.widget.LinearLayout;
import android.widget.TextView;

public class MainActivity extends Activity
{
    public void onCreate(Bundle savedInstanceState) {
          super.onCreate(savedInstanceState);
          LinearLayout sampleLayout = new LinearLayout(this);
          TextView tred = new TextView(this);
          TextView tblue = new TextView(this);
          TextView tgreen = new TextView(this);
          tred.setText("This is red");
          tblue.setText("This is blue");
          tgreen.setText("This is green");
   tred.setLayoutParams(new LayoutParams(LayoutParams.WRAP_CONTENT,
   LayoutParams.WRAP_CONTENT));
          tblue.setLayoutParams(new LayoutParams(LayoutParams.WRAP_CONTENT,
   LayoutParams.WRAP_CONTENT));
          tgreen.setLayoutParams(new LayoutParams(LayoutParams.WRAP_CONTENT,
   LayoutParams.WRAP_CONTENT));

          ColorDrawable red =
   (ColorDrawable)getResources().getDrawable(R.drawable.red);
          ColorDrawable green =
   (ColorDrawable)getResources().getDrawable(R.drawable.green);
          ColorDrawable blue =
   (ColorDrawable)getResources().getDrawable(R.drawable.blue);
          tred.setBackgroundDrawable(red);
          tblue.setBackgroundDrawable(blue);
          tgreen.setBackgroundDrawable(green);
          sampleLayout.addView(tred);
          sampleLayout.addView(tblue);
          sampleLayout.addView(tgreen);
          setContentView(sampleLayout);
    }
}
```

In Listing 9.8, the three instances of the `TextView` have been created, that is, tred, tblue, and tgreen. For each instance, the relevant text and layout params have been defined. Further, the three instances of the `ColorDrawable` class have been created to fetch the colors defined in the `colors.xml` file. You should note that the `ColorDrawable` class is the subclass of the `Drawable` class and the resource defined in the XML file has been retrieved by using the following code snippet:

```
getResources().getDrawable(R.drawable.red);
```

By using the preceding code snippet, all the three resources have been fetched and set as background for the `TextView` by invoking the `setBackgroundDrawable()` method.

4. *Right-click* the `SampleDrawableXML` application and select Run As→Android Application. The output of the `SampleDrawableXML` application is displayed in Figure 9.4:

Figure 9.4: Displaying the Output of the SampleDrawableXML Application

Let us now learn how to work with the ShapeDrawable object.

Using the ShapeDrawable Object

The ShapeDrawable class allows you to dynamically draw the 2-D graphics according to your requirements. Apart from drawing the primitive shapes, you can also apply the desired style to them. The ShapeDrawable class is the subclass of the Drawable class. Therefore, you can use the ShapeDrawable class wherever there is a need to use the Drawable object. Using the ShapeDrawable class, you can create the customized View that can be added to the layout of the application.

In this section, first you would learn how to create a shape in the XML file and then use that shape in the layout XML file of the application. Further, you would learn how to design a custom view using the View class and set that View for the layout of the Activity class. Let us create an Android application, ShapeDrawable, to learn the use of the ShapeDrawable class.

Perform the following steps to create and run the ShapeDrawable application:

1. *Create* an Android application, ShapeDrawable, in the Eclipse IDE under the com.kogent.android.shapedrawable package.
2. *Create* the custom_shape.xml file in the **/res/drawable** folder of the application, as shown in Listing 9.9:

Listing 9.9: Displaying the Code of the custom_shape.xml File in the ShapeDrawable Application

```
<?xml version="1.0" encoding="utf-8"?>
<shape                    xmlns:android="http://schemas.android.com/apk/res/android"
  android:shape="oval">
  <stroke android:width="10dip" android:color="#ffffff" />
  <solid android:color="#6000"/>
</shape>
```

In the preceding code snippet, we have created an oval shape and set the color for the stroke of the shape as white.

3. *Replace* the code of the activity_main.xml file, located in the **/res/layout** folder of the ShapeDrawable application with the code shown in Listing 9.10:

Listing 9.10: Displaying the Code of the `activity_main.xml` File in the `ShapeDrawable` Application

```
<?xml version="1.0" encoding="utf-8"?>
<RelativeLayout
    xmlns:android="http://schemas.android.com/apk/res/android"
    android:layout_height="fill_parent"
    android:layout_width="fill_parent">

<View android:id="@+id/myView"
    android:background="@drawable/custom_shape"
    android:layout_width="fill_parent"
    android:layout_height="fill_parent">
</View>
</RelativeLayout>
```

In Listing 9.10, the `custom_shape` XML file has been set as background for the `myView` View.

4. *Right-click* the `ShapeDrawable` application and select `Run As→Android Application`. The output of the `DrawableImage` application is displayed in Figure 9.5:

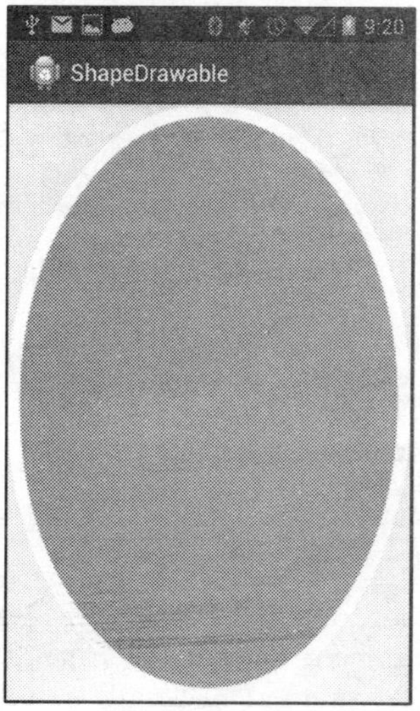

Figure 9.5: Drawing of a 2D Object Using the `ShapeDrawable` Class

Let us now create the customized shape using the `View` class and then set the `View` as the content view for the `Activity` class. Perform the following steps to learn how to create the custom `View` shape so that the View can be designed during the invocation of the `View.onDraw()` method:

1. *Create* an Android application, `CustomShapeDrawable`, in the Eclipse IDE under the `com.kogent.android.customshapedrawable` package.
2. *Create* a new Java class, `CustomShapeDrawable`, in the **/src** folder under the `com.kogent.android.customshapedrawable` folder, as shown in Listing 9.11:

Listing 9.11: Displaying the Code of the `CustomShapeDrawable.java` File in the `CustomShapeDrawable` Application

```
package com.kogent.android.customshapedrawable;
import android.content.Context;
import android.graphics.Canvas;
import android.graphics.drawable.ShapeDrawable;
import android.graphics.drawable.shapes.OvalShape;
import android.view.View;
public class CustomShapeDrawable extends View
{
    private ShapeDrawable sDrawable;
```

```
        public CustomShapeDrawable(Context ctx) {
                super(ctx);
                int i = 50;
                int j = 50;
                int width = 700;
                int height = 350;
                sDrawable = new ShapeDrawable(new OvalShape());
                sDrawable.getPaint().setColor(0xff0000ff);
                sDrawable.setBounds(i, j, i+width, j+height);
        }
        protected void onDraw(Canvas c) {
           sDrawable.draw(c);}
        }
```

In Listing 9.11, the `OvalShape` class is used to draw an oval by setting its color and bounds by invoking the `setColor()` and `setBounds()` methods.

3. *Replace* the code of the `MainActivity.java` file, located in the **/src/com/kogent/android/customshapedrawable** folder, with the code shown in Listing 9.12:

Listing 9.12: Displaying the Code of the `MainActivity.java` File in the `CustomShapeDrawable` Application

```
package com.kogent.android.customshapedrawable;

import android.app.Activity;
import android.os.Bundle;

public class MainActivity extends Activity {
   CustomShapeDrawable createView;

   /** Called when the activity is first created. */
   @Override
   public void onCreate(Bundle savedInstanceState) {
           super.onCreate(savedInstanceState);
           createView = new CustomShapeDrawable(this);
           setContentView(createView);
           createView.requestFocus();
   }
}
```

In Listing 9.12, the instance of the `CustomShapeDrawable` class has been created, which has been initialized by passing the this as argument. Further, the instance of the `CustomShapeDrawable` class has been set as the content view of the `MainActivity` class.

4. *Right-click* the `CustomShapeDrawable` application and select Run As→Android Application. The output of the `CustomShapeDrawable` application is displayed in Figure 9.6:

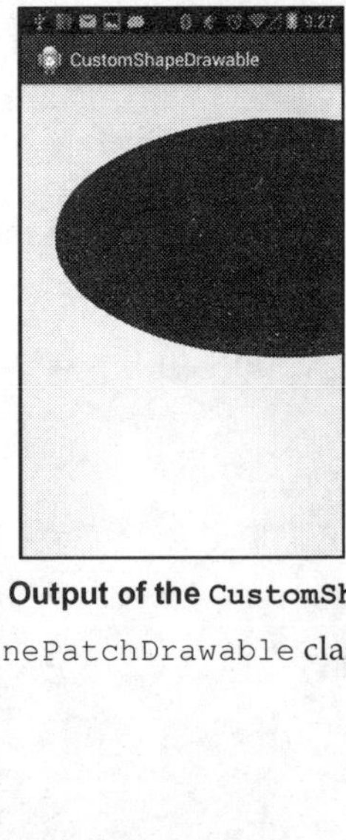

Figure 9.6: Displaying the Output of the `CustomShapeDrawable` Application

Let us now learn how to work with the `NinePatchDrawable` class.

Working with the NinePatchDrawable Graphics

The graphics that serve as the stretchable bitmap image is known as `NinePatchDrawable`. In other words, when you set the `NinePatchDrawable` image as background for a View, the Android automatically resizes it to fit the content of the View. For example, imagine you have set the `NinePatch` image as the background for a button. In such a case, if you set text of small size for the button, the image would automatically shrink according to the length of the text. However, if you try to set the large text for the button, then the image would automatically stretch to accommodate the text string.

The `NinePatch` drawable image is a PNG image that contains the extra border of width 1 pixel. Moreover, this type of image is always being saved with the .9.png extension and placed in the **/res/drawable** folder of the Android application. You can create the `NinePatch` image by using the Draw 9-patch tool provided in the tools directory of the Android 4.4.2 SDK.

Let's perform the following steps to create a nine-patch image:

1. *Navigate* to the **sdk/tools** folder in the Android SDK 4.4.2 bundle.
2. *Double-click* the `draw9patch.bat` file. It opens the **Draw 9-patch** editor.
3. *Select* the **File→Open 9-patch** option, as shown in Figure 9.7:

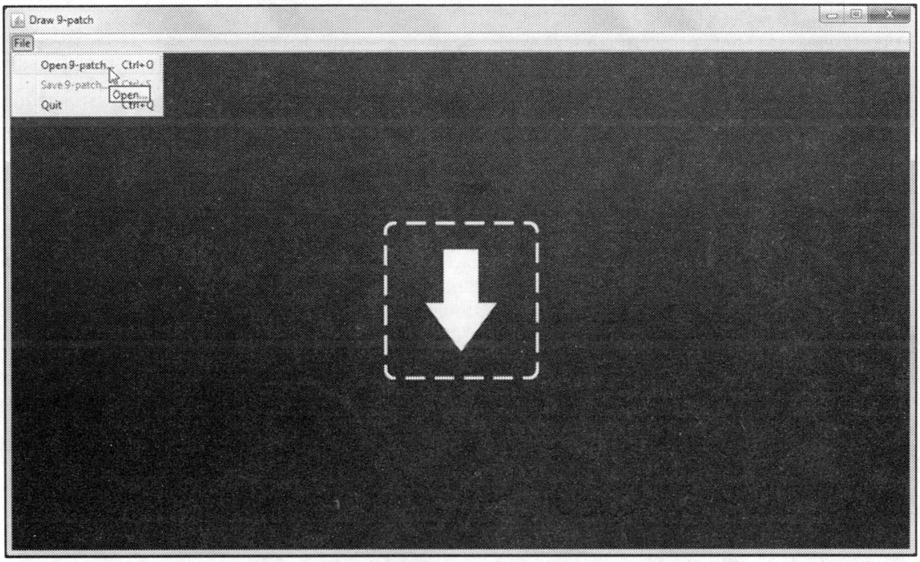

Figure 9.7: Displaying the Draw 9-patch Editor

4. *Navigate* and *open* a PNG file, which you want to create as a nine-patch image and click the **File→Save 9-patch** option. This step creates a nine-patch file, with the .9.png extension.

   Now, create an Android application, named `NinePatch`, to display the use of a nine-patch PNG format image file. Let's perform the following steps to create and run the `NinePatch` application:

5. *Create* an Android application, `NinePatch`, in the Eclipse IDE under the `com.kogent.android.ninepatch` package.
6. *Replace* the code of the `activity_main.xml` file, located in the **/res/layout** folder of the application, with the code shown in Listing 9.13:

Listing 9.13: Displaying the Code of the `activity_main.xml` File in the `NinePatch` Application

```
<?xml version="1.0" encoding="utf-8"?>
<ScrollView xmlns:android="http://schemas.android.com/apk/res/android"
    android:layout_width="fill_parent"
    android:layout_height="fill_parent">
<RelativeLayout
```

```
    android:layout_width="fill_parent"
    android:layout_height="fill_parent" >
    <Button
        android:id="@+id/small"
        android:layout_width="wrap_content"
        android:layout_height="wrap_content"
        android:layout_alignParentTop="true"
        android:layout_centerHorizontal="true"
        android:layout_marginTop="20dp"
        android:background="@drawable/nine_patch "
        android:text="Small"
        android:textSize="10sp" />

    <Button
        android:id="@+id/large"
        android:layout_width="wrap_content"
        android:layout_height="wrap_content"
        android:layout_alignLeft="@+id/small"
        android:layout_below="@+id/small"
        android:layout_marginTop="73dp"
        android:background="@drawable/nine_patch "
        android:text="Large Button"
        android:textSize="30sp" />
</RelativeLayout>
</ScrollView>
```

In Listing 9.13, the `btn_default_normal_red` `NinePatch` image has been set as background for both the buttons, that is, small and large.

7. *Create* a folder, named **drawable**, in the **/res** folder and place a nine-patch file in it. In our case, it is `nine_patch.9.png`.
8. Replace the code of the `MainActivity.java` file, located in the **/src/com/kogent/android/ninepatch** folder, with the code shown in Listing 9.14:

Listing 9.14: Displaying the Code of the `MainActivity.java` File in the `NinePatch` Application

```
package com.kogent.android.ninepatch;

import android.app.Activity;
import android.app.ActionBar;
import android.app.Fragment;
import android.os.Bundle;
import android.view.LayoutInflater;
import android.view.Menu;
import android.view.MenuItem;
import android.view.View;
import android.view.ViewGroup;
import android.os.Build;

public class MainActivity extends Activity {

  @Override
  protected void onCreate(Bundle savedInstanceState) {
        super.onCreate(savedInstanceState);
        setContentView(R.layout.activity_main);
  }
}
```

In Listing 9.14, the `nine_patch` XML file has been set as the layout of the `Activity` class.

9. *Right-click* the `NinePatch` application and select `Run As→Android Application`. The output of the `NinePatch` application is displayed in Figure 9.8:

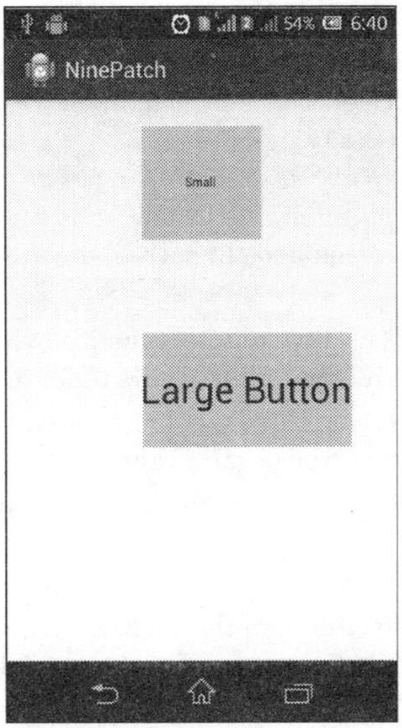

Figure 9.8: Displaying the Output of the NinePatch Application

Let us now learn about hardware acceleration.

Understanding the Concept of Hardware Acceleration

To provide hardware acceleration for an application is easy in Android 4. You just have to set either target SDK version or minimum SDK version to minimum the API level 14. All the drawing operations are performed on the View's canvas by using the Graphics Processing Units (GPUs). If you want to turn the hardware acceleration on, it is advisable to turn it on for the whole Android application. In other words, you can turn the hardware acceleration at four levels: Application, Activity, Window, and View.

You can add the following code snippet in the <application> tag of the Android manifest file to enable hardware acceleration at the application level:

```
<application android:hardwareAccelerated="true">
....
</application>
```

If you find that enabling of hardware acceleration for the whole application is not working properly, then you can enable or disable it for an activity. For example, let us disable the hardware acceleration for an activity and leave it enabled at the application level. The following code snippet is used to disable the hardware acceleration for an activity:

```
<application android:hardwareAccelerated="true">
   <activity ../>
   <activity android:hardwareAccelerated="false"/>
</application>
```

Let us now understand how to enable or disable hardware acceleration at the Window level. Generally, the hardware acceleration is enabled for a given Window when you need more fine-grained control. The following code snippet is used to enable the hardware acceleration for a specific window:

```
/** Called when the activity is first created. */
@Override
    public void onCreate(Bundle savedInstanceState) {
   getWindow().setFlags(WindowManager.LayoutParams.FLAG_HARDWARE_ACCELERATED,
   WindowManager.LayoutParams.FLAG_HARDWARE_ACCELERATED);
... }
```

In the preceding code snippet, the `FLAG_HARDWARE_ACCELERATED` field is used to enable the hardware acceleration. Finally, let's look at the code to enable or disable the hardware acceleration at the `View` level. In the following code snippet, the hardware acceleration is turned on for a `View` during runtime:

```
Button myButton = new Button(this);
myButton.setLayerType(View.LAYER_TYPE_SOFTWARE, null);
```

Now, imagine that for a `View` of an application, the hardware is being accelerated and you need to determine whether or not the `View` is hardware accelerated. In such a situation, you can invoke either of the following methods:

- `View.isHardwareAccelerated()`—Invoked to identify whether or not the `View` is attached to a hardware accelerated window. This method returns either the true or false value.
- `Canvas.isHardwareAccelerated()`—Invoked to identify whether or not the `Canvas` is hardware accelerated. This method returns either true or false value.

Let's now discuss about the different types of animations that can be implemented in the Android applications.

Working with Animations

In Android, you can apply animation effect to both the View and non-View objects. For example, you can scale or rotate a `View` and move a `View` across the screen. The Android 4.0 SDK or later allows you to implement either of the following animation systems:

- Property Animation
- View Animation
- Drawable Animation

Android 4.4.2 SDK provided the animation capabilities in the form of classes, interfaces, and methods abstracted within the `android.view.animation` package. The classes of this package allow you to implement various animation effects on the `Views`, such as move, rotate, or scale the Views. Moreover, you can also use the `AnimationSet` object to group multiple animations together. You can even automatically start the animation as soon as the container defines its child views by providing animations using the `LayoutAnimationController` class. You can also implement nonlinear behavior of animation by using `Bounce` or `AccelerateInterpolator`. The earlier animation system lacked some functionality that has been brought in the new package, that is, `android.animation`. One of the limitations of the earlier animation system is that you cannot animate the custom drawing, such as add translucency in the background color. This is because the earlier animation system allows you to manipulate only the `View` objects, such as `Button` or `TextView`. Although you could move, rotate, scale, or fade a `View` object, you could not animate the background color of the `View`. The introduction of property animation has overcome the preceding limitations. Let us now discuss all the three animation systems, namely, property, view, and drawable, in detail.

The Property Animation

The property animation allows you to animate the properties of a `View` object. Apart from animating the properties of Views, the property animation also allows you to animate the properties of custom Drawables. You can also specify the duration of the animation, which is 300 milliseconds by default. You can find most of the APIs required for property animation in the `android.animation` package. Moreover, the interpolators that have been defined in the `android.animation` package can also be used in the property animation.

Generally, the `Animator` class gives the fundamental structure of defining animations. However, you cannot directly use this class; instead, the other classes, such as `ValueAnimator`, `ObjectAnimator`, and `AnimatorSet`, extend this class to provide full animation support. The description of the subclasses of the `Animator` class is as follows:

- **The `ValueAnimator` Class**—Provides the timing engine for running the property animation and also estimates the animated values. These values are further set on the target objects. This class contains the following information:
  - Time-related details for each animation

- Whether or not to repeat the animation
- Details of the listener that would be notified about the update events

Note that the `ValueAnimator` class only calculates the animated values and does not set those values for the property of the object. Therefore, you need to set the appropriate listener to be notified about the update of these values.

- **The `ObjectAnimator` Class**-Extends the `ValueAnimator` class and sets the targeted object along with the property for animation. Whenever a new value for the animation is being computed, this class updates the property accordingly. The use of the `ObjectAnimator` class simplifies the task of animating values on target. Sometimes, it is possible that you need to directly use the `ValueAnimator` class because the `ObjectAnimator` class has some restrictions. An example of such a restriction is that the few accessor methods must be available on the target object.
- **The `AnimatorSet` Class**-Allows you to combine the related animations that can be executed together, in a sequence, or after the delay of the specified time duration.

After understanding about the classes, let us understand evaluators, which are useful in informing the property animation system about the process to evaluate the values for a specific property. The evaluators accept the start and end values from an `Animator` class, and the animated values of the property are evaluated on the basis of these values. The evaluators for the property animation system are as follows:

- **`IntEvaluator`**—Refers to the evaluator used to estimate the values for the `int` properties of animation.
- **`FloatEvaluator`**—Refers to the evaluator used to estimate the values for the `float` properties of animation.
- **`ArgbEvaluator`**—Refers to the evaluator used to estimate the values for the color properties depicted in hexadecimal.
- **`TypeEvaluator`**—Refers to the evaluator that is used to create the customized evaluator. Note that if the property that you are setting for animation is not of `int`, `float`, or `color` type, then the `TypeEvaluator` interface should be implemented to your class. You should also specify how to evaluate the animated values of the object's property. Moreover, you can also define the customized `TypeEvaluator` object by specifying its property as of the `int`, `float`, or `color` type.

An interpolator defines the rate at which an animation changes, while the `android.view.animation` package contains all types of interpolators. You can implement the appropriate interpolator to your `Activity` class according to your requirements. However, if none of the interpolators suits your requirements, then you should implement the `TimeInterpolator` interface, which would help you in creating the customized interpolator. The description of the interpolators is as follows:

- **`AccelerateDecelerateInterpolator`**-Refers to the interpolator whose rate of animation change is slow at start and end; however, the rate accelerates in between.
- **`AccelerateInterpolator`**-Refers to the interpolator whose rate of animation change is slow at start and then accelerates.
- **`AnticipateInterpolator`**-Refers to the interpolator whose animation change starts from the backward position and further flings forward.
- **`AnticipateOvershootInterpolator`**-Refers to the interpolator whose animation changes in the backward direction at the start and further flings forward. The basic difference between the `AnticipateInterpolator` and `AnticipateOvershootInterpolator` interpolators is that the `AnticipateOvershootInterpolator` interpolator overshoots the target value and at last returns to the final value.
- **`BounceInterpolator`**-Refers to the interpolator whose animation changes to bounce at last.
- **`CycleInterpolator`**-Refers to the interpolator whose animation repeats the number of cycles as specified by you.
- **`DecelerateInterpolator`**-Refers to the interpolator whose rate of animation change is fast at the start and then diminishes.

- **LinearInterpolator**-Refers to the interpolator whose rate of animation change remains stable throughout.
- **OvershootInterpolator**-Refers to the interpolator whose animation change flings forward and further overshoots the last value of animation and finally returns.
- **TimeInterpolator**-Refers to the interface that can be implemented to create the customized interpolator.

Let us now discuss each of the classes, such as `Animator`, `ValueAnimator`, and `ObjectAnimator`.

The `Animator` Class

The `Animator` class is extended by the other animation classes to implement its functionality. The attributes and the functionalities of the subclasses are similar to the `Animator` class. Note that the `Animator` class cannot be used directly; instead, few of the methods and properties of the subclasses, such as duration and listener functionality, are defined in the superclass. Let us understand how you can implement the listener functionality.

Generally, the listeners are being used to specify what action needs to be performed during the start or end of an animation. You need to implement the `AnimatorListener` interface to listen the animator lifecycle events. The following code snippet shows how to define the listeners for animation:

```
ValueAnimator vAnim;
….
….
vAnim.addListener(new Animator.AnimatorListener()) {
//Implement the onAnimationStart() method
public void onAnimationStart(Animator a) {
// provide the code to be executed when the animation starts    }
public void onAnimationEnd(Animator a) {
// provide the code to be executed when the animation ends      }
public void onAnimationCancel(Animator a) {
// provide the code to be executed when the animation s  }
public void onAnimationRepeat(Animator a) {
// provide the code to be executed when the animation starts    }
```

Let us now discuss the `ValueAnimator` class.

The `ValueAnimator` Class

The `ValueAnimator` class deals with the timing values of animated objects. It calculates the animated values and imposes them on the object to be animated. Also, if any animation repeats, it keeps the track of all the repetitions. In essence, all the timing values of the property animation are handled by the `ValueAnimator` class. This class resides in the `android.animation` package. The `ValueAnimator` class extends the `Animator` class and the `ValueAnimator` object can be achieved by using the factory methods such as `ofInt()`, `ofFloat()`, and `ofObject()`. The following code snippet shows how to get the animator value:

```
ValueAnimator vAnimation = ValueAnimator.ofInt(0, 5);
vAnimation.setDuration(2000);
vAnimation.start();
```

In the preceding code snippet, an object of `ValueAnimator` class is instantiated that animates between the value provided in the `ofInt()` method. The animation is started by using the `start()` method and takes place after each 2000 milliseconds, specified in the `setDuration()` method.

The `ObjectAnimator` Class

It is possible that the `ValueAnimator` class has least effect on the object since it does not deal directly with the object. Therefore, the `ObjectAnimator` class is a subclass of the `ValueAnimator` class that deals directly with the object.

You can instantiate the `ObjectAnimator` class similar to the `ValueAnimator` class although you have to specify the name and property of the object, including the two arguments that we have passed in the factory method of the `ValueAnimator` class. The following code snippet shows the way it can be done:

```
ObjectAnimator objAnimator = ObjectAnimator.ofInt(objName, objType, 0, 5);
objAnimator.setDuration(2000);
objAnimator.start();
```

The values function similar as they do in the `ValueAnimator` object arguments.

View Animation

The view animation is a tween animation of view. A tween animation can be understood as the animation that calculates almost all the parameters of an animation, such as the start and end points. Many other parameters of animation are also calculated by using the view animation. A sequence of transformations, such as position, size, and rotation, is applied on the `View` object by the tween animation. For example, you can rotate, move, grow, or shrink the texts in a `TextView` object. Similarly, much more can be achieved by applying creativity as `animation` package contains all the classes to satisfy the need of tween animation.

There are two ways in which you can use the tween animation. It can be used by either an XML file or by Android code. However, the use of a dedicated XML file gives you an edge over the hardcoded animation by Android code. Also, XML is more readable, reusable, and swappable.

Every aspect of a transformation (rotation, shrink, grow, etc.) is associated with animation instruction. A transformation may occur in series or it can be concurrent. A set of parameters is required for every single transformation.

From the XML code perspective, the animation XML file must reside in the **res/anim** directory of your project. There should be a single root element, such as `<translate>`, `<rotate>`, `<scale>`, `<alpha>`, `interpolator`, and `<set>` element, inside an XML animation file. However, the `<set>` element is different from other elements since it can occupy all of them. In Android system, all the animations are simultaneous by default. However, they can be made sequential by using the `startoffset` attribute, as shown in the following code snippet:

```
<?xml version="1.0" encoding="utf-8"?>
<set xmlns:android="http://schemas.android.com/apk/res/android"
    android:shareInterpolator="false" >
<translate
        android:interpolator="@android:anim/accelerate_decelerate_interpolator"
        android:fromXDelta="1.0"
        android:fromYDelta="2.0"
        android:toXDelta="2.0"
        android:toYDelta="1.0" />

    <rotate
        android:duration="300"
        android:fromDegrees="0"
        android:startOffset="500"
        android:toDegrees="90" />
</set>
```

Save this xml as the `animationdef.xml` file in the **res/anim** directory. The following code snippet will use this XML file as an `ImageView` object of layout:

```
ImageView testImage = (ImageView) findViewById(R.id.image);
Animation animation = AnimationUtils.loadAnimation(this, R.anim. animationdef);
testImage.startAnimation(animation);
```

Let us make a simple Android application, named `TestAnimation`, to practically understand the animation.

Perform the following steps to create and run the `TestAnimation` application:

1. *Create* an Android application, `TestAnimation`, in the Eclipse IDE under the `com.kogent.android.testanimation` package. It should be noted that this application must be developed using the minimum SDK Android level 14 APIs.
2. *Create* a folder named **anim** insider the **res** directory. In the **anim** folder, create a new XML file called `animationdef.xml`. This file contains definition of all the animations. Listing 9.15 shows the code for the `animationdef.xml` file:

Listing 9.15: Code of the `animationdef.xml` File in the `TestAnimation` Application

```
<?xml version="1.0" encoding="utf-8"?>

<set xmlns:android="http://schemas.android.com/apk/res/android"
    android:shareInterpolator="false" >

    <rotate
        android:fromDegrees="0"
        android:toDegrees="360"
        android:duration="6000"
        android:repeatCount="infinite" />
</set>
```

Since this application is intended to be a simple one, we are just rotating an object through this XML code. The preceding code conveys that an object rotated from 0^0 to 360^0 within a time duration of 6000 milliseconds (6 seconds) for one count and will keep rotating for infinite number of times.

3. *Create* a folder named **drawable** insider the **res** directory. In the **drawable** folder, add an image file, for instance `image.jpg`.
4. Replace the code of the `activity_main.xml` file, located in the **/res/layout** folder, with the code shown in Listing 9.16:

Listing 9.16: Code of the `activity_main.xml` File in the `TestAnimation` Application

```
<RelativeLayout xmlns:tools="http://schemas.android.com/tools"
    xmlns:android="http://schemas.android.com/apk/res/android"
    android:layout_width="match_parent"
    android:layout_height="match_parent">
    <ImageView
        android:id="@+id/image"
        android:layout_width="wrap_content"
        android:layout_height="wrap_content"
        android:layout_centerHorizontal="true"
        android:layout_centerVertical="true"
        android:contentDescription="@string/app_name"
        android:src="@drawable/image" />
  </RelativeLayout>
```

In Listing 9.16, an `ImageView` control is added to display an image.

5. *Replace* the code of the `MainActivity.java` file, located in the **/src/com/kogent/android/testanimation** folder, with the code shown in Listing 9.17:

Listing 9.17: Displaying the Code of the `MainActivity.java` File in the `TestAnimation` Application

```
package com.kogent.android.testanimation;

import android.app.Activity;
import android.os.Bundle;
import android.view.animation.Animation;
import android.view.animation.AnimationUtils;
import android.widget.ImageView;

public class MainActivity extends Activity {
  @Override
  protected void onCreate(Bundle savedInstanceState) {
        super.onCreate(savedInstanceState);
        setContentView(R.layout.activity_main);
        ImageView testImage = (ImageView) findViewById(R.id.image);
        Animation animation = AnimationUtils.loadAnimation(this,
                      R.anim.animationdef);
        testImage.startAnimation(animation);
  }
 }
```

6. Finally, *right-click* the `TestAnimation` application and select Run As→Android Application option. Figure 9.9 shows the output of the application:

Figure 9.9: Displaying the Output of the TestAnimation Application

After studying the View animation, let's have a look at the Drawable Animation.

Drawable Animation

The Drawable animations are achieved through the `AnimationDrawable` class of the `android.graphics.drawable` package. These animations are loaded sequentially in a pattern of one after the other to create an animation. The sequence of different images is used in `Drawable` animation that is executed sequentially to give a feel like animation movie.

An animation is composed of many frames and you can simply add the frames through Android code. However, a better way is to use a single XML file to list all the frames in your animation. This XML file must reside in the **res/drawable/** directory.

The root element in the Drawable Animation is `<animation-list>`. The frames are handled by its child element `<item>`. The following code snippet shows an example XML file for a `Drawable` animation:

```
<?xml version="1.0" encoding="utf-8"?>
<animation-list xmlns:android="http://schemas.android.com/apk/res/android" >
    <item
        android:drawable="@drawable/picture_frame1"
        android:duration="200"/>
    <item
        android:drawable="@drawable/picture_frame2"
        android:duration="200"/>
    <item
        android:drawable="@drawable/picture_frame3"
        android:duration="200"/>
</animation-list>
```

Save this XML file as `drawabledef.xml`. This animation makes infinite loop of frames by displaying them one after the other. Set the element `<android:oneshot="true">` to make this animation finite. The following code snippet shows the use of this element:

```
<animation-list xmlns:android="http://schemas.android.com/apk/res/android"
    android:oneshot="true">
```

The corresponding activity class snippet would be given as follows:

```
AnimationDrawable aDrawable;
  public void onCreate(Bundle savedInstanceState) {
        super.onCreate(savedInstanceState);
        setContentView(R.layout.activity_main);
        ImageView androidImage = (ImageView) findViewById(R.id.picture_frame);
        androidImage.setBackgroundResource(R.drawable.androiddef);
        aDrawable = (AnimationDrawable) androidImage.getBackground();
  }
  public boolean onTouchEvent(MotionEvent event) {
        if (event.getAction() == MotionEvent.ACTION_MOVE) {
              aDrawable.start();
              return true;
        }
        return super.onTouchEvent(event);
  }
```

Note that `start` method is being called on the `AnimationDrawable` class and not on the `onCreate` method. With this, we come to end of the chapter.

Summary

This chapter has broadly discussed about graphics and animation. Initially, you have learned the use of graphics. The Android framework lets you use the various View widgets for designing the user interface of applications. The functionality of these widgets can be extended to modify the appearance and behavior of the View widgets. You have also learned that graphics can be created into either the `View` object or directly to the `Canvas` in an Android application. The chapter has explained that while drawing the graphics on the `Canvas`, you have to invoke the `onDraw()` method. The graphics are drawn on the `Bitmap` using the `Canvas` class. On other hand, if you are drawing on the `View`, you are required to extend your class with the `View` class first and then implement the `onDraw()` callback method.

Further, you have that besides using the `Canvas` and `View` classes, you can also use the `SurfaceView` class. The `SurfaceView` class is a subclass of the `View` class that provides a surface to draw the graphics. To draw on the `SurfaceView` class, your class should extend the `SurfaceView` class and then implement the `SurfaceHolder.Callback` interface. After this, in case of 2D graphics, you have learned about the `android.graphics.drawable` package, which provides the classes to draw 2D graphics. You have also got acquainted with the power of XML when you come to know that you can define the properties of a `Drawable` object in an XML file. This XML file can be referenced for layouts.

In this chapter, you have also learned that the `ShapeDrawable` class can be used to dynamically draw the 2-D graphics according to your requirements. The chapter has discussed the concept of nine patch drawable images. The Nine Patch drawable image is a PNG image that contains the extra border of width 1-pixel and is always saved with the .9.png extension. Later in this chapter, you learned about the hardware acceleration, which provides the smooth graphics experience by using dedicated hardware called GPU. Finally, you have learned about the implementation of animation using the `Animator` class in your Android application.

Quick Revise

Q1. Which of the following is not the method of the Canvas class?

a. **drawArc()**

b. **drawBitmap()**

c. drawCircle()

d. draw()

Ans. The correct option is d.

Q2. What are the two approaches to draw graphics with a Canvas?

a. `View` class and `SurfaceView` class

b. `Canvas` and `Paint` Class

c. `Canvas` and `View` Class

d. `Canvas` and `SurfaceView` Class

Ans. The correct option is a.

Q3. Which of the following argument is not accepted by the `createBitmap()` method of the `Bitmap` class?

a. Width

b. Height

c. Bitmap config

d. Buffer

Ans. The correct option is d.

Q4. Which of the following methods is used to draw the final graphics using a `Canvas`?

a. Canvas.drawPicture()

b. Canvas.DrawRGB()

c. SurfaceHolder.lockCanvas()

d. SurfaceHolder.getSurfaceFrame()

Ans. The correct option is c.

Q5. Which of the following is an interface not a class related to surface?

a. Surface

b. SurfaceView

c. SurfaceConfig

d. SurfaceHolder

Ans. The correct option is d.

Q6. Which of the following methods of the `Drawable` class allows the client to interact with the drawn object?

a. getPadding()

b. getState()

c. copyBounds()

d. getLevel()

Ans. The correct option is a.

Q7. Which of the following ways defines and instantiates the `Drawable` class?

a. Using an XML file

b. Using a Java class

c. Using JUnit test case

d. Using a text file

Ans. The correct option is a.

Q8. **To provide hardware acceleration for an application, you must set either target SDK version or minimum SDK version to the minimum API level as ____________.**

a. **16**

b. **14**

c. **8**

d. **19**

Ans. The correct option is b.

Q9. **An image must be referenced only from which of the following folders?**

a. **bin**

b. **lib**

c. **res**

d. **drawable**

Ans. The correct option is d.

Q10. **Which of the following is a method of the `ColorDrawable` class?**

a. **getColor()**

b. **getBounds()**

c. **getPadding()**

d. **getOpacity()**

Ans. The correct option is a.

Q11. **Create an application that animates a suit of 10 images using the `ValueAnimator` class.**

Ans. Perform the following steps to create an application that animates a suit of 10 images using the `ValueAnimator` class:

1. *Create* an application `Value_Animator`.
2. *Add* an XML file, `activity_value_animator.xml`, in the **\res\layout** location as follows:

```
<?xml version="1.0" encoding="utf-8"?>
<ImageView xmlns:android="http://schemas.android.com/apk/res/android"
    android:id="@+id/aniImageView"
    android:layout_width="wrap_content"
    android:layout_height="wrap_content"
    android:layout_centerHorizontal="true"
    android:scaleType="fitCenter" />
```

3. Replace the code of the activity_main.xml file as follows:

```
<?xml version="1.0" encoding="utf-8"?>
<RelativeLayout xmlns:android="http://schemas.android.com/apk/res/android"
    android:id="@+id/main_layout"
    android:layout_width="fill_parent"
    android:gravity="center_horizontal"
    android:layout_height="fill_parent"
    android:background="@android:color/white" >

</RelativeLayout>
```

4. *Add* 11 images in the **/res/drawable** folder, namely, `images`, `images1`, `images2`, `images3`, `images4`, `images5`, `images6`, `images7`, `images8`, `images9`, and `images10`.
5. *Replace* the code of the Java file, `Value_Animator.java`, with the code shown as follows:

```
package com.kogent.android.value_animator;

import java.util.ArrayList;
import java.util.Random;
import java.util.Timer;
import java.util.TimerTask;
import android.os.Bundle;
```

```
import android.os.Handler;
import android.os.Message;
import android.animation.ValueAnimator;
import android.app.Activity;
import android.graphics.Rect;
import android.graphics.drawable.Drawable;
import android.util.DisplayMetrics;
import android.view.Display;
import android.view.LayoutInflater;
import android.view.View;
import android.view.animation.AccelerateInterpolator;
import android.widget.ImageView;
import android.widget.RelativeLayout;
import android.widget.RelativeLayout.LayoutParams;

public class MainActivity extends Activity {


  private int[] LEAVES = {
                R.drawable.images,
                R.drawable.images1,
                R.drawable.images2,
                R.drawable.images3,
                R.drawable.images4,
                R.drawable.images5,
                R.drawable.images6,
                R.drawable.images7,
                R.drawable.images8,
                R.drawable.images9,
                R.drawable.images10,
        };

  private Rect mDisplaySize = new Rect();

  private RelativeLayout mRootLayout;
  private ArrayList<View> mAllImageViews = new ArrayList<View>();

  private float mScale;
  public static final int MAX_DELAY = 6000;
  public static final int ANIM_DURATION = 10000;
  public static final int EMPTY_MESSAGE_WHAT = 0x001;

  @Override
  public void onCreate(Bundle savedInstanceState){
        super.onCreate(savedInstanceState);
        setContentView(R.layout.activity_main);

        Display display = getWindowManager().getDefaultDisplay();
        display.getRectSize(mDisplaySize);

        DisplayMetrics metrics = new DisplayMetrics();
        display.getMetrics(metrics);
        mScale = metrics.density;

        mRootLayout = (RelativeLayout) findViewById(R.id.main_layout);

        new Timer().schedule(new ExeTimerTask(), 0, 5000);
  }
```

```
    public void startAnimation(final ImageView aniView) {

            aniView.setPivotX(aniView.getWidth()/2);
            aniView.setPivotY(aniView.getHeight()/2);

            long delay = new Random().nextInt(MAX_DELAY);

            final ValueAnimator animator = ValueAnimator.ofFloat(0, 1);
            animator.setDuration(ANIM_DURATION);
            animator.setInterpolator(new AccelerateInterpolator());
            animator.setStartDelay(delay);

            animator.addUpdateListener(new ValueAnimator.AnimatorUpdateListener() {

                    int angle = 50 + (int)(Math.random() * 101);
                    int movex = new Random().nextInt(mDisplaySize.right);

                    @Override
                    public void onAnimationUpdate(ValueAnimator animation) {
                            float value = ((Float)
(animation.getAnimatedValue())).floatValue();

                            aniView.setRotation(angle*value);
                            aniView.setTranslationX((movex-40)*value);
                            aniView.setTranslationY((mDisplaySize.bottom +
(150*mScale))*value);
                    }
            });

            animator.start();
    }

    private Handler mHandler = new Handler() {
            @Override
            public void handleMessage(Message msg) {
                    super.handleMessage(msg);
                    int viewId = new Random().nextInt(LEAVES.length);
                    Drawable d = getResources().getDrawable(LEAVES[viewId]);
                    LayoutInflater inflate = LayoutInflater.from(MainActivity.this);
                    ImageView imageView = (ImageView)
inflate.inflate(R.layout.activity_value_animator, null);
                    imageView.setImageDrawable(d);
                    mRootLayout.addView(imageView);

                    mAllImageViews.add(imageView);

                    LayoutParams animationLayout = (LayoutParams)
imageView.getLayoutParams();
                    animationLayout.setMargins(0, (int)(-150*mScale), 0, 0);
                    animationLayout.width = (int) (60*mScale);
                    animationLayout.height = (int) (60*mScale);

                    startAnimation(imageView);
            }
    };

    private class ExeTimerTask extends TimerTask {
            @Override
            public void run() {
```

```
                // we don't really use the message 'what' but we have to specify
something.
                mHandler.sendEmptyMessage(EMPTY_MESSAGE_WHAT);
        }
    }
}
```

Q12. Create an Android application that animates a string, such as your name, using tween animation.

Ans. Perform the following steps to create an Android application that animates a string:

1. Create an application named `TweenAnimation` and replace the code of the `activity_main.xml` file in the **\res\layout** location as follows:

```
<LinearLayout xmlns:android="http://schemas.android.com/apk/res/android"
    xmlns:tools="http://schemas.android.com/tools"
    android:id="@+id/root"
    android:layout_width="fill_parent"
    android:layout_height="fill_parent"
    tools:context=".TweenAnimation" >
<TextView android:id="@+id/animatedText"
    android:layout_width="wrap_content"
    android:layout_height="wrap_content"
    android:text="@string/hello_world">
    </TextView>

</LinearLayout>
```

2. *Create* the **anim** folder in the **/res** location and add an XML file, `rotate.xml`, as follows:

```
<?xml version="1.0" encoding="utf-8"?>
<rotate xmlns:android="http://schemas.android.com/apk/res/android"
 android:fromDegrees="0" android:toDegrees="360" android:toYScale="0.0"
 android:pivotX="40%" android:pivotY="30%" android:duration="2000" />
```

3. *Replace* the code of the Java file, `MainActivity.java`, with the code given shown below:

```
package com.kogent.android.tweenanimation;
import android.app.Activity;
import android.os.Bundle;
import android.view.View;
import android.view.View.OnClickListener;
import android.view.animation.Animation;
import android.view.animation.AnimationUtils;
import android.widget.LinearLayout;
import android.widget.TextView;


public class MainActivity extends Activity {

  @Override
  protected void onCreate(Bundle savedInstanceState) {
        super.onCreate(savedInstanceState);
        setContentView(R.layout.activity_main);
        final Animation a = AnimationUtils.loadAnimation(this, R.anim.rotate);
       a.reset();
       final TextView rText = (TextView) findViewById(R.id.animatedText);

       LinearLayout layout = (LinearLayout) findViewById(R.id.root);
       layout.setOnClickListener(new OnClickListener() {
           @Override public void onClick(View v) {
               rText.startAnimation(a);
```

```
            }
        });

    }
}
```

Q13. Create an Android application that uses the `SurfaceAnimator` class to animate an object.

Ans. Perform the following steps to create an Android application using the `SurfaceAnimator` class:

1. *Create* an application named `SurfaceAnimator`.
2. *Replace* the code of the `activity_main.xml` file in the **\res\layout** location with the code given below:

```
<RelativeLayout xmlns:android="http://schemas.android.com/apk/res/android"
    xmlns:tools="http://schemas.android.com/tools"
    android:layout_width="match_parent"
    android:layout_height="match_parent">

    <TextView
        android:layout_width="wrap_content"
        android:layout_height="wrap_content"
        android:layout_centerHorizontal="true"
        android:layout_centerVertical="true"
        android:text="@string/hello_world" />

</RelativeLayout>
```

3. *Create* the **drawable** folder in the **/res** location and add a GIF file, `round.gif`, as follows:
4. *Replace* the code of the Java file, `MainActivity.java`, with the code given below:

```
package com.kogent.android.surfaceanimator;
import android.app.Activity;
import android.content.Context;
import android.graphics.Bitmap;
import android.graphics.BitmapFactory;
import android.graphics.Canvas;
import android.graphics.Color;
import android.os.Bundle;
import android.view.MotionEvent;
import android.view.SurfaceHolder;
import android.view.SurfaceView;
import android.view.View;
import android.view.View.OnTouchListener;
import android.app.Activity;
import android.view.Menu;

public class MainActivity extends Activity implements OnTouchListener {

   MineSurface ourSurfaceView;
    float x, y;

    protected void onCreate(Bundle b){
        super.onCreate(b);
        ourSurfaceView = new MineSurface(this);
        ourSurfaceView.setOnTouchListener(this);
        setContentView(ourSurfaceView);

    }

    protected void onPause(){
        super.onPause();
        ourSurfaceView.pause();

    }
    protected void onResume(){
```

```
            super.onResume();
            ourSurfaceView.resume();
        }

        public class MineSurface extends SurfaceView implements Runnable{
            SurfaceHolder ourHolder;
            Thread ourThread;
            boolean isRunning = false;
            Bitmap gball;

            public MineSurface(Context context){
                super(context);

                ourHolder = getHolder();
                gball = BitmapFactory.decodeResource(getResources(), R.drawable.round);

                x = 0;
                y = 0;

            }

            public void run(){
                while(isRunning){
                    if(!ourHolder.getSurface().isValid())
                        continue;
                    Canvas canvas = ourHolder.lockCanvas();
                    canvas.drawColor(Color.WHITE);
                    if(x != 0 && y != 0)
                        canvas.drawBitmap(gball, x - gball.getWidth()/2, y -
    gball.getHeight()/2, null);
                    ourHolder.unlockCanvasAndPost(canvas);

                }

            }
            public void pause(){
                isRunning = false;
                while(true){
                    try {
                        ourThread.join();
                    } catch (InterruptedException e) {
                        e.printStackTrace();
                    }

                    break;
                }
                ourThread = null;

            }
            public void resume(){
                isRunning = true;
                ourThread = new Thread(this);
                ourThread.start();
            }
        }
        public boolean onTouch(View view, MotionEvent event) {
                x = event.getX();
                y = event.getY();

            return true;
        }
    }
```

Q14. How is graphics drawn to `Canvas` in Android development?

Ans. To draw specialized graphics and manage the animation of the graphics, a `Canvas` is required in an application. The `Canvas` serves as a surface on which the graphics would be created and manages the invocation of the `onDraw()` method. Note that the graphics are drawn on the `Bitmap` through the `Canvas`. When you draw the graphics within the `onDraw()` callback method, the `Canvas` is used to put the drawing calls.

If you want to define a new `Canvas`, then you should create a `Bitmap` by using the `createBitmap()` and set up a new `Canvas` by passing the `Bitmap` object. After that, the `Bitmap` instance is passed as argument so that the `Canvas` would draw the defined `Bitmap`. Finally, you can draw the final graphics through a `Canvas` by using the `View.onDraw()` or `SurfaceHolder.lockCanvas()` method. Note that the `Canvas` class provides different methods, such as `drawArc()`, `drawBitmap()`, `drawCircle()`, and `drawRect()`, to draw graphical objects, such as arc, bitmap, circle, oval, points, text, and path.

Q15. Explain the role of the `ShapeDrawable` class.

Ans. The `ShapeDrawable` class allows you to dynamically draw the 2-D graphics according to your requirements. Apart from drawing the primitive shapes, you can also apply the desired style to them. The `ShapeDrawable` class is the subclass of the `Drawable` class. Therefore, you can use the `ShapeDrawable` class wherever there is a need to use the `Drawable` object. Using the `ShapeDrawable` class, you can create the customized View that can be added to the layout of the application.

10

Audio, Video, and Camera

If you need an information on:	*See page:*
Role of Media Playback	362
Using Media Player	362
Recording and Playing Sound	374
Creating a Sound Pool	380
Using Camera for Taking Pictures	382
Recording Video	386

Today, smartphones and tablets are everywhere and have become the most preferred choice of everyone due to various reasons. Some of these reasons are that these mobile devices are small, portable, Internet connected, and provide various facilities on a single touch. In addition, these devices contain the facility of media player, photo capturing camera, audio and video recording, etc. Android devices also provide such facilities as Android operating system has various media Application Programming Interfaces (APIs), which are used to play and record media files. These include audio files (for example, MP3s) and video files (for example, MP4).

Android APIs provide various classes and interfaces that handle media playing and media recording. Some of these are `MediaPlayer`, `AudioManager`, and `MediaRecorder`. `MediaPlayer` is the primary API for playing audio and video. It allows you to play media stored in application resources, local files, Content Providers, or streamed from a network Uniform Resource Locator (URL). The `AudioManager` class manages audio sources and audio output on a device. The `MediaRecorder` class allows recording of audio or video files that can be used in applications or can be stored in a media store.

In this chapter, you learn about audio, video, and camera handling by Android APIs. First, you learn about media playback and how it helps in controlling audio and video files, which are available from different locations. Next, you learn how to create a sound pool loaded with sound or audio files. You also learn how to record sound and create an audio file. Toward the end, you learn about the use of camera to capture still images and how to record videos using a media recorder.

Role of Media Playback

Android framework provides various APIs that allow you to add video, audio, and photo capabilities to your applications for playing and recording media. You can play audio or video files in your applications, which are stored in raw resources, file system, or from a data stream incoming from a network connection.

The Android framework provides the following classes to play audio and video files:

- `MediaPlayer`—Specifies the primary API for playing audio and video. This class allows you to play media stored in application resources, local files, Content Providers, or streamed from a network URL.
- `AudioManager`—Specifies the class that manages audio sources and audio output on a device.

Using Media Player

In Android, audio and video files and streams are managed by Media player as a state machine. The following transitions take place in this state machine:

1. Initialize the Media player with media to play
2. Prepare the Media player for playback
3. Start the playback
4. Use the pause or stop option for handling playback
5. The playback is complete

When you need to play a media resource, you need to create a new instance of the `MediaPlayer` class, initialize it with a media source, and prepare it for playback.

Media Formats Supported by Media Player

Android framework provides various network protocols that support audio and video playback.

The following network protocols are supported for audio and video playback:

- Real Time Streaming Protocol (RTSP) (Real-time Transport Protocol (RTP), Session Description Protocol (SDP))
- Hypertext Transfer Protocol (HTTP)/HTTPS progressive streaming
- TTP/HTTPS live streaming draft protocol

NOTE

The HTTPS protocol supports Android version from Android 3.1 onward and MPEG-2 TS media files only.

Table 10.1 lists the audio, video, and image file formats and codecs, which are supported by Android framework:

Table 10.1: Audio, Video, and Image File Formats and Codecs Supported by Android Framework

Audio Formats/Codecs	Image Formats/Codecs	Video Formats/Codecs
AAC LC/LTP HE-AACv1 (AAC+) HE-AACv2 (Enhanced AAC+) AMR-NB AMR-WB MP3 MIDI Ogg Vorbis PCM/WAVE FLAC	JPEG PNG WEBP GIF BMP	H.263 H.264 AVC MPEG-4 SP VP8

Preparing Audio for Playback

In Android development, there are many ways to play an audio content through Media player. They are listed as follows:

- To play audio content as an application resource by adding it to the **res/raw** folder of your resources hierarchy
- To play audio content from local files or content providers
- To play audio content by streaming it from a remote URL

You need to create an instance of the `MediaPlayer` class by using the `create()` method and then set the data source by following any of the following options:

- Specifying a Uniform Resource Identifier (URI) to a local file (using the file:// schema)
- Specifying a URI to an online audio resource (as a URL)
- Specifying a URI to a row within a content provider that returns an audio file

The following code snippet loads an audio resource from a package resource:

```
MediaPlayer resource_ player =MediaPlayer.create(this, R.raw.sample_audio);
```

The following code snippet loads an audio resource from a local file:

```
MediaPlayer local_file_player =
MediaPlayer.create(this,Uri.parse("file:///sdcard/samplefile.mp3"));
```

The following code snippet loads an audio resource from an online resource:

```
MediaPlayer url_player =
MediaPlayer.create(this,Uri.parse("http://site.com/audio/samplefile.mp3"));
```

The following code snippet loads an audio resource from a content provider:

```
MediaPlayer contentprovider_player = MediaPlayer.create(this,
Settings.System.DEFAULT_RINGTONE_URI);
```

You can also use the `setDataSource()` method on an existing `MediaPlayer` class instance to specify media data source, as shown in the following code snippet:

```
MediaPlayer mp= new MediaPlayer();
mp.setDataSource("/sdcard/myfavourite.mp3");
mp.prepare();
```

The `MediaPlayer` class supports various media sources, which include local resources, internal URIs, and external URLs (streaming). The following code snippet shows how the `MediaPlayer` class plays an audio file, which resides in the raw folder in your application:

```
MediaPlayer mp = MediaPlayer.create(context, R.raw.sound_file);
mp.start();
```

Now, let's consider the following code snippet that shows how to play an audio from a URI available locally in the system, which is obtained through a Content Resolver:

```
Uri sampleUri = ....;    // initialize Uri here
MediaPlayer mp = new MediaPlayer();
mp.setAudioStreamType(AudioManager.STREAM_MUSIC);
mp.setDataSource(getApplicationContext(), sampleUri);
mp.prepare();
mp.start();
```

However, the following code snippet shows how to play an audio from a remote URL through HTTP streaming:

```
String url = "http://........";                 //enter  your URL here
MediaPlayer mp = new MediaPlayer();
mp.setAudioStreamType(AudioManager.STREAM_MUSIC);
mp.setDataSource(url);
mp.prepare();                                  // can take more time for buffering
mp.start();
```

In both the code snippets, the `setDataSource()` method can throw exception if the file that you are referencing does not exist so that you must either catch or pass the `IllegalArgumentException` and `IOException` exception.

When you use the `MediaPlayer` class to play an audio or video through streaming, you must configure the following `uses-permissions` in the `AndroidManifest.xml` file of your application:

```
<uses-permission android:name="android.permission.INTERNET"/>
<uses-permission android:name="android.permission.READ_EXTERNAL_STORAGE" />
```

Preparing Video for Playback

When you need to play a video, you need to create a surface for it in order to show it. The following are the two ways in which you can play video content:

- Use the `VideoView` class to encapsulate the creation of a surface and to allocate and prepare video content using a media player, as shown in the following code snippet:

```
VideoView vwVideo = (VideoView) this.findViewById(R.id. vwVideo);
   MediaController  mc = new MediaController(this);
   vwVideo.setMediaController(mc);
   vwVideo.setVideoPath("/sdcard/sample_video.mp4");
   vwVideo.requestFocus();
   vwVideo.start();
```

- In the preceding code snippet, an instance of the `VideoView` class is created. It includes a surface on which the video is displayed. Then, an instance of the `MediaController` class is created, which provides a standard control with common media control buttons. The `VideoView` class provides the `setMediaController()` method to display your video content. Then, the `setVideoPath()` or `setVideoUri()` method is used to assign a video for playing. The following code line assigns a local file to play:

```
vwVideo.setVideoPath("/sdcard/sample_video.mp4");
```

However, the following code line assigns a URL of a remote video stream:

```
vwVideo.setVideoUri(my_favourite_streaming_source);
```

- Specify a user-defined surface and manipulate the underlying `MediaPlayer` class instance directly. To do this, you need to use the `MediaPlayer` class in order to create a surface to view the video content. Then, create an object of the `SurfaceView` object class, which is a wrapper around the `SurfaceHolder` object, which is again a wrapper around the Surface object that supports visual updates from background threads. After that, the `MediaPlayer` class uses the `SurfaceHolder` object to display the video content by using the `setDisplay()` method.

You can include a surface holder in the UI layout of your application by implementing the `SurfaceHolder.Callback` interface and using the `SurfaceView` class. Then, the `surfaceCreated` handler is fired and the `SurfaceHolder` object is provided to your media player with the help of the `setDataSource()` method. This method is used to specify the path, URL, or content provider URI of the video resource to play. After providing media file source, use the `prepare ()` method to initialize the media player for playback.

Creating Application to Play Audio and Video Using MediaPlayer

In this section, you learn to create an Android application that displays how to play audio and video content from different source locations using a media player. Let's create an application named `AudioVideoUsingMediaPlayer` to learn the use of `MediaPlayer`. Perform the following steps to create the `AudioVideoUsingMediaPlayer` application:

1. *Create* the `AudioVideoUsingMediaPlayer` application in the Eclipse Integrated Development Environment (IDE) under the `com.kogent.android.audiovideousingmediaplayer` package.
2. *Replace* the code of the `strings.xml` file in the **/res/values** folder, with the code shown in Listing 10.1:

Listing 10.1: Displaying the Code of the `strings.xml` File in the `AudioVideoUsingMediaPlayer` Application

```
<?xml version="1.0" encoding="utf-8"?>
<resources>
    <string name="app_name">AudioVideoUsingMediaPlayer</string>
    <string name="action_settings">Settings</string>
    <string name="hello_world">Hello world!</string>
     <string name="sdcard_audio">Play Audio from located at device </string>
    <string name="res_audio">Play Audio from Resources file </string>
    <string name="http_audio">Stream Audio</string>
     <string name="sdcard_video">Play Video from located at device </string>
<string name="res_video">Play Video from Resources file</string>
    <string name="http_video">Stream Video</string>
    </resources>
```

In Listing 10.1, some necessary strings that are required in the layout buttons of the application are set.

3. *Replace* the code of the `activity_main.xml` file in the **/res/layout** folder, with the code shown in Listing 10.2:

Listing 10.2: Displaying the Code of the `activity_main.xml` File in the `AudioVideoUsingMediaPlayer` Application

```
<?xml version="1.0" encoding="utf-8"?>
<LinearLayout xmlns:android="http://schemas.android.com/apk/res/android"
    android:orientation="vertical"
    android:layout_width="fill_parent"
    android:layout_height="fill_parent">
    <Button android:id="@+id/sdcardaudio"
        android:layout_height="wrap_content"
        android:layout_width="fill_parent"
        android:text="@string/sdcard_audio"/>
    <Button android:id="@+id/resaudio"
        android:layout_height="wrap_content"
        android:layout_width="fill_parent"
        android:text="@string/res_audio"/>
    <Button android:id="@+id/httpaudio"
        android:layout_height="wrap_content"
        android:layout_width="fill_parent"
        android:text="@string/http_audio"/>
     <Button android:id="@+id/sdcardvideo"
        android:layout_height="wrap_content"
        android:layout_width="fill_parent"
        android:text="@string/sdcard_video"/>
     <Button android:id="@+id/resvideo"
        android:layout_height="wrap_content"
        android:layout_width="fill_parent"
        android:text="@string/res_video"/>
     <Button android:id="@+id/httpvideo"
        android:layout_height="wrap_content"
        android:layout_width="fill_parent"
        android:text="@string/http_video"/>
/LinearLayout>
```

In Listing 10.2, six buttons are added with different strings, specified in the strings.xml.

4. Add an XML file named `mediaplayer.xml` in the **/res/layout** folder, as shown in Listing 10.3:

Listing 10.3: Displaying the Code of the `mediaplayer.xml` File in the `mediaplayer`_Application

```
<?xml version="1.0" encoding="utf-8"?>
<LinearLayout xmlns:android="http://schemas.android.com/apk/res/android"
    android:orientation="vertical"
    android:layout_width="fill_parent"
    android:layout_height="fill_parent">
    <SurfaceView android:id="@+id/surface"
        android:layout_width="fill_parent"
        android:layout_height="fill_parent"
        android:layout_gravity="center">
    </SurfaceView>
</LinearLayout>
```

In Listing 10.3, the UI layout of the application is specified and a surface view is created by using the `SurfaceView` element.

5. *Create* the raw folder in the **/res** location and add `sampleaudio.mp3` and `samplevideo.mp4` files in it.
6. *Create* a Java class, named `audioplayer`, in the **/src** location under the `com.kogent.android.AudioVideoUsingMediaplayer` package. Listing 10.4 shows the code of the `audioplayer.java` file:

Listing 10.4: Showing the Code of the `audioplayer.java` File in the `AudioVideoUsingMediaPlayer` Application

```
package com.kogent.android.audiovideousingmediaplayer;

import android.app.Activity;
import android.media.MediaPlayer;
import android.os.Bundle;
import android.util.Log;
import android.widget.TextView;

public class audioplayer extends Activity{

    private MediaPlayer mPlayer;
    private static final String MAINACTIVITY = "mainactivity";
    private static final int SDCARD_AUDIO = 1;
    private static final int HTTP_AUDIO = 2;
    private static final int RES_AUDIO = 3;
    private String path;
    private TextView tx;

    @Override
    public void onCreate(Bundle icicle) {
        super.onCreate(icicle);
        tx = new TextView(this);
        setContentView(tx);
        Bundle extras = getIntent().getExtras();
        playAudio(extras.getInt(MAINACTIVITY));
    }

    private void playAudio(Integer media) {
        try {
            switch (media) {
                case SDCARD_AUDIO:
                    path = "/sdcard/sample.mp3";
                    mPlayer = new MediaPlayer();
                    mPlayer.setDataSource(path);
                    mPlayer.prepare();
                    mPlayer.start();
                    break;
                case HTTP_AUDIO:
                 tx.setText("Please Wait...");
                    path = "http://www.techoreo.com/sample.mp3";
```

```
                    mPlayer = new MediaPlayer();
                    mPlayer.setDataSource(path);
                    mPlayer.prepare();
                    mPlayer.start();
                    break;
                case RES_AUDIO:
                    mPlayer = MediaPlayer.create(this, R.raw.sampleaudio);
                    mPlayer.start();
                    break;

            }
            tx.setText("Playing audio...");

        } catch (Exception e) {
            Log.e( "Exception: " , e.getMessage(), e);
        }
    }

    @Override
    protected void onDestroy() {
        super.onDestroy();
        if (mPlayer != null) {
            mPlayer.release();
            mPlayer = null;
        }
    }

    @Override
    protected void onPause() {
        super.onPause();

    }

    @Override
    protected void onStop() {
        super.onStop();

    }
}
```

In Listing 10.4, the `audioplayer` class is created to play audio content using the `MediaPlayer` class. An instance of this class is created in the `playAudio()` method. The `setDataSource()` method specifies an audio file resource, the `prepare()` method prepares the media player, and the `start()` method starts it. In the `onDestroy()` method, the `release()` method of the `MediaPlayer` class is used to free the associated resources.

7. Create a Java class, named `videoplayer`, in the **/src** location under the `com.kogent.android.AudioVideoUsingMediaplayer` package. Listing 10.5 shows the code of the `videoplayer.java` file:

Listing 10.5: Showing the Code of the `videoplayer.java` File in the `AudioVideoUsingMediaPlayer` Application

```
package com.kogent.android.audiovideousingmediaplayer;

import android.app.Activity;
import android.media.AudioManager;
import android.media.MediaPlayer;
import android.media.MediaPlayer.OnBufferingUpdateListener;
import android.media.MediaPlayer.OnCompletionListener;
import android.media.MediaPlayer.OnPreparedListener;
import android.media.MediaPlayer.OnVideoSizeChangedListener;
import android.os.Bundle;
import android.util.Log;
import android.view.SurfaceHolder;
```

```
import android.view.SurfaceView;
public class videoplayer extends Activity implements
OnCompletionListener,OnVideoSizeChangedListener,
OnPreparedListener,OnBufferingUpdateListener, SurfaceHolder.Callback {

    private int mWidth;
    private int mHeight;
    private MediaPlayer mPlayer;
    private SurfaceView mPreview;
    private SurfaceHolder surfaceholder;
    private String path;
    private Bundle extras;

    private static final String MAINACTIVITY = "mainactivity";

    private static final int SDCARD_VIDEO = 4;
    private static final int HTTP_VIDEO = 5;
    private static final int RESOURCES_VIDEO = 6;

    private boolean size = false;
    private boolean videoPlayed = false;

   @Override
    public void onCreate(Bundle icicle) {
        super.onCreate(icicle);
        setContentView(R.layout.mediaplayer);
        mPreview = (SurfaceView) findViewById(R.id.surface);
        surfaceholder = mPreview.getHolder();
        surfaceholder.addCallback(this);
        extras = getIntent().getExtras();
    }

    private void playVideo(Integer MAINACTIVITY) {
        reset();
        try {

            switch (MAINACTIVITY) {
                case SDCARD_VIDEO:
                 path = "/sdcard/sample.mp4";
                    // Create a new media player and set the listeners
                    mPlayer = new MediaPlayer();
                    mPlayer.setDataSource(path);
                    mPlayer.prepare();
                    mPlayer.setDisplay(surfaceholder);
                    mPlayer.setOnBufferingUpdateListener(this);
                    mPlayer.setOnCompletionListener(this);
                    mPlayer.setOnPreparedListener(this);
                    mPlayer.setOnVideoSizeChangedListener(this);
                    mPlayer.setAudioStreamType(AudioManager.STREAM_MUSIC);
                    break;
                case RESOURCES_VIDEO:
                    /* NOTE: Upload a video file to res/raw folder  */
                    mPlayer = MediaPlayer.create(this, R.raw.samplevideo);
                    mPlayer.start();
                    mPlayer.setDisplay(surfaceholder);
                    break;
                case HTTP_VIDEO:
                    path = "http://www.techoreo.com/sample.mp4";
                    mPlayer = new MediaPlayer();
                    mPlayer.setDataSource(path);
                    mPlayer.setDisplay(surfaceholder);
                    mPlayer.prepare();

                    mPlayer.setOnBufferingUpdateListener(this);
                    mPlayer.setOnCompletionListener(this);
```

```
                mPlayer.setOnPreparedListener(this);
                mPlayer.setOnVideoSizeChangedListener(this);
                mPlayer.setAudioStreamType(AudioManager.STREAM_MUSIC);
                break;
            }
        } catch (Exception error) {
            Log.e( "Exception ",  error.getMessage(), error);
        }
    }
    @Override
    public void onBufferingUpdate(MediaPlayer arg0, int percent) {
        Log.d("Buffering", "nBufferingUpdate" + percent);

    }

    public void onCompletion(MediaPlayer arg0) {
        Log.e("TAG", "onCompletion method");

    }

    public void onVideoSizeChanged(MediaPlayer mp, int width, int height) {
        mWidth = width;
        mHeight = height;
        prepareVideoPlayback();
    }

    public void onPrepared(MediaPlayer mediaplayer) {
        Log.d("", "onPrepared called");
        videoPlayed = true;
        if (videoPlayed && size) {
            prepareVideoPlayback();
        }
    }

    public void surfaceChanged(SurfaceHolder surfaceholder, int i, int j, int k) {
        Log.d("TAG", "surfaceChanged");

    }

    public void surfaceDestroyed(SurfaceHolder surfaceholder) {
        Log.d("TAG", "surfaceDestroyed");
    }

    public void surfaceCreated(SurfaceHolder holder) {
        Log.d("TAG", "surfaceCreated");
        playVideo(extras.getInt(MAINACTIVITY));
      //  mMediaPlayer.setDisplay(holder);

    }

    @Override
    protected void onPause() {
        super.onPause();
        releaseMediaPlayer();
        reset();
    }

    @Override
    protected void onDestroy() {
        super.onDestroy();
        releaseMediaPlayer();
        reset();
    }

    private void releaseMediaPlayer() {
```

```
            if (mPlayer != null) {
             mPlayer.release();
             mPlayer = null;
            }
        }

        private void reset() {
             mWidth = 0;
             mHeight = 0;
            videoPlayed = false;
            size = false;
        }

        private void prepareVideoPlayback() {
            Log.v("TAG", "prepareVideoPlayback");
            surfaceholder.setFixedSize(mWidth, mHeight);
            mPlayer.start();
        }
    }
```

In Listing 10.5, the `videoplayer` class is created to play video content using the `MediaPlayer` class. This class extends the `Activity` class and implements the `OnCompletionListener`, `OnVideoSizeChangedListener`, `OnPreparedListener`, `OnBufferingUpdateListener`, and `SurfaceHolder.Callback` interfaces. In the `onCreate()` method, the objects of the `SurfaceView` and `SurfaceHolder` classes are created to display the video content. An instance of the `MediaPlayer` class is created in the `playVideo()` method. The `setDataSource()` method specifies an video file resource, the `prepare()` method prepares the media player, and the `start()` method starts the player.

NOTE

You must be ensured that you have stored one audio file, named sample.mp3 and one video file, named sample.mp4, in the sdcard folder of your real mobile device.

8. Replace the code of the `MainActivity.java` file located in the **/src** folder, with the code shown in Listing 10.6:

Listing 10.6: Showing the Code of the `MainActivity.java` File in the `AudioVideoUsingMediaPlayer` Application

```
package com.kogent.android.audiovideousingmediaplayer;

import android.os.Bundle;
import android.app.Activity;
import android.content.Intent;
import android.view.Menu;
import android.view.View;
import android.widget.Button;
import android.view.View.OnClickListener;

public class MainActivity extends Activity {
  private Button sdcardvideo;
    private Button resvideo;
    private Button httpvideo;
    private Button sdcardaudio;
    private Button resaudio;
    private Button httpaudio;

    private static final String MAINACTIVITY = "mainactivity";
    private static final int SDCARD_AUDIO = 1;
    private static final int HTTP_AUDIO = 2;
    private static final int RES_AUDIO = 3;
    private static final int SDCARD_VIDEO = 4;
    private static final int HTTP_VIDEO = 5;
    private static final int RES_VIDEO = 6;
```

```
@Override
protected void onCreate(Bundle savedInstanceState) {
       super.onCreate(savedInstanceState);
       setContentView(R.layout.activity_main);
       sdcardaudio = (Button) findViewById(R.id.sdcardaudio);
       sdcardaudio.setOnClickListener(sdcardAudioListener);
      resaudio = (Button) findViewById(R.id.resaudio);
      resaudio.setOnClickListener(resAudioListener);
     httpaudio = (Button) findViewById(R.id.httpaudio);
      httpaudio.setOnClickListener(httpAudioListener);

      sdcardvideo = (Button) findViewById(R.id.sdcardvideo);
      sdcardvideo.setOnClickListener(sdcardVideoListener);
      resvideo = (Button) findViewById(R.id.resvideo);
      resvideo.setOnClickListener(resVideoListener);
      httpvideo = (Button) findViewById(R.id.httpvideo);
      httpvideo.setOnClickListener(httpVideoListener);

}
private OnClickListener sdcardAudioListener = new OnClickListener() {
       @Override
       public void onClick(View v) {
           Intent intent =
                   new Intent(MainActivity.this.getApplication(),
                           audioplayer.class);
           intent.putExtra(MAINACTIVITY, SDCARD_AUDIO);
           startActivity(intent);
       }

  };

  private OnClickListener resAudioListener = new OnClickListener() {
      public void onClick(View v) {
          Intent intent =
                  new Intent(MainActivity.this.getApplication(),
                          audioplayer.class);
          intent.putExtra(MAINACTIVITY, RES_AUDIO);
          startActivity(intent);
      }
  };

  private OnClickListener httpAudioListener = new OnClickListener() {
      public void onClick(View v) {
          Intent intent =
                  new Intent(MainActivity.this,
                          audioplayer.class);
          intent.putExtra(MAINACTIVITY, HTTP_AUDIO);
          startActivity(intent);
      }
  };

  private OnClickListener sdcardVideoListener = new OnClickListener() {
      public void onClick(View v) {
          Intent intent =
                  new Intent(MainActivity.this,
                          videoplayer.class);
          intent.putExtra(MAINACTIVITY, SDCARD_VIDEO);
          startActivity(intent);
      }
  };

  private OnClickListener resVideoListener = new OnClickListener() {
      public void onClick(View v) {
          Intent intent =
                  new Intent(MainActivity.this.getApplication(),
```

```
                                   videoplayer.class);
                intent.putExtra(MAINACTIVITY, RES_VIDEO);
                startActivity(intent);
            }
        };

        private OnClickListener httpVideoListener = new OnClickListener() {
            public void onClick(View v) {
                Intent intent =
                        new Intent(MainActivity.this,
                                   videoplayer.class);
                intent.putExtra(MAINACTIVITY, HTTP_VIDEO);
                startActivity(intent);
            }
        };
    }
```

In Listing 10.6, the `MainActivity` class is created to call the `audioplayer` and `videoplayer` classes. In this class, the code for six buttons is provided with the help the `OnClickListener` class.

9. Replace the highlighted code of the `AndroidManifest.xml` file, with the code shown in Listing 10.7:

Listing 10.7: Displaying the Code of the `AndroidManifest.xml` File in the `AudioVideoUsingMediaPlayer` Application

```
<?xml version="1.0" encoding="utf-8"?>
<manifest xmlns:android="http://schemas.android.com/apk/res/android"
    package="com.kogent.android.audiovideousingmediaplayer"
    android:versionCode="1"
    android:versionName="1.0" >

    <uses-sdk
        android:minSdkVersion="8"
        android:targetSdkVersion="17" />

    <application
        android:allowBackup="true"
        android:icon="@drawable/ic_launcher"
        android:label="@string/app_name"
        android:theme="@style/AppTheme" >
        <activity
            android:name="com.kogent.android.audiovideousingmediaplayer.MainActivity"
            android:label="@string/app_name" >
            <intent-filter>
                <action android:name="android.intent.action.MAIN" />

                <category android:name="android.intent.category.LAUNCHER" />
            </intent-filter>
        </activity>
        <activity
android:name="com.kogent.android.audiovideousinngmediaplayer.audioplayer"
android:label="audioplayer">
            <intent-filter>
                <category
android:name="com.kogent.android.audiovideousingmediaplayer.audioplayer" />
            </intent-filter>
        </activity>

        <activity android:name="com.kogent.android.audiovideousingmediaplayer.videoplayer"
android:label="videoplayer">
            <intent-filter>
                <category
android:name="com.kogent.android.audiovideousingmediaplayer.videoplayer" />
            </intent-filter>
        </activity>
    </application>
      <uses-permission android:name="android.permission.INTERNET"/>
```

```
        <uses-permission android:name="android.permission.READ_EXTERNAL_STORAGE" />
</manifest>
```

In Listing 10.7, all the activity classes are configured. In addition, `uses-permissions` are set to use the media content from the Internet.

10. Now, execute the `AudioVideoUsingMediaPlayer` application. Figure 10.1 shows the output of the `AudioVideoUsingMediaPlayer` application:

Figure 10.1: Showing the Output of the `AudioVideoUsingMediaPlayer` Application

If you click the **Play Audio from located at device** or **Play Video from located at device** button, the audio or video files are played, which are located locally on the device. If you click the **Play Audio from Resources file** button, then the resource files of the audio is played, as shown in Figure 10.2:

Figure 10.2: Playing Audio

Similarly, if you click the **Play Video from Resources file** button, then the resource files of the video is played, as shown in Figure 10.3:

Figure 10.3: Playing Video

Moreover, the **Stream Audio** or **Stream Video** button plays the audio or video file from streaming.

NOTE

Stream audio and video can take some time to play when you click their respective button in your application, because your application has to fetch these files from server.

Recording and Playing Sound

The Android operating system provides support for recording and playing of an audio. In addition, it also supports the encoding of a variety of audio file formats. For this, you have to use the `MediaRecorder` class, which enables you to record an audio or video file. The following code snippet shows how to configure a `MediaRecorder` to record an audio:

```
MediaRecorder audio_record = new MediaRecorder();
audio_record.setAudioSource(MediaRecorder.AudioSource.MIC);
audio_record.setOutputFormat(MediaRecorder.OutputFormat.THREE_GPP);
audio_record.setAudioEncoder(MediaRecorder.OutputFormat.AMR_NB);
audio_record.setOutputFile(outputFile);
audio_record.prepare();
audio_record.start();
```

In the preceding code snippet, an instance of the `MediaRecorder` class is created. Then, the `setAudioSource()` method is used to set a source of audio file for recording by passing the parameter of `MediaRecorder.AudioSource.MIC`. The `setOutputFormat()` and `setOutputFile()` methods are used to set an output file format and file name, respectively. The `setAudioEncoder()` method is used to specify the audio encoder. The `prepare()` and `start()` methods are used for preparing and starting audio recording. Moreover, the `stop()` and `release()` methods can be used to stop the process of audio recording and freeing the resources, respectively.

The `MediaRecorder` class is used to record audio or video files. To record an audio, the following settings must be configured in the `AndroidManifest.xml` file:

```
<uses-permission android:name="android.permission.WRITE_EXTERNAL_STORAGE" />
<uses-permission android:name="android.permission.RECORD_AUDIO" />
```

NOTE

The Android emulator does not provide the facility of audio, video, or image capturing; however, real devices have these capabilities.

Use of Media Store

When you create media files, they get stored in private application folders by default, which are not available to other applications. To make them visible to other applications, you need to insert them into a media store. In Android, you can insert a media file to a media store by using the `ContentValues` class. You need to create an object of the `ContentValues` class and add content in it by using the `put()` method, as shown in the following code snippet:

```
ContentValues content_values = new ContentValues(4);
        long current = System.currentTimeMillis();
        content_values.put(MediaStore.Audio.Media.TITLE, "audio" + "sample.3gp");
        content_values.put(MediaStore.Audio.Media.DATE_ADDED, (int) (current / 1000));
        content_values.put(MediaStore.Audio.Media.MIME_TYPE, "audio/3gpp");
        content_values.put(MediaStore.Audio.Media.DATA, outputFile);
```

It should be noted, that, you can specify the title, timestamp, and geocoding information for your new media file.

Now, you need to use the `ContentResolver` class that allows your application to add the media records in a media store, as shown in the following code snippet:

```
ContentResolver content_resolver = getContentResolver();
Uri base = MediaStore.Audio.Media.EXTERNAL_CONTENT_URI;
Uri sampleUri = content_resolver.insert(base, content_values);
```

After inserting the media file into a media store, you should announce its availability using a `Broadcast` Intent, as shown in the following code snippet:

```
sendBroadcast(new Intent(Intent.ACTION_MEDIA_SCANNER_SCAN_FILE, sampleUri));
```

Let's create an application to learn how to record an audio.

Audio Recording Application

In this section, you learn to create an Android application to learn how to record an audio and store it in a media store and then play it using a media player. Let's create an application, named `AudioRecorder`, to learn how to record and play audio content. Perform the following steps to create the `AudioRecorder` application:

1. *Create* the `AudioRecorder` application in the Eclipse IDE under the `com.kogent.android.audiorecoder` package.
2. *Replace* the code of the `activity_main.xml` file in the **/res/layout** folder, with the code shown in Listing 10.8:

Listing 10.8: Showing the Code of the `activity_main.xml` File in the `AudioRecorder` Application

```
<LinearLayout xmlns:android="http://schemas.android.com/apk/res/android"
    xmlns:tools="http://schemas.android.com/tools"
   android:layout_width="fill_parent"
    android:layout_height="fill_parent"
    android:paddingLeft="16dp"
    android:paddingRight="16dp"
    android:orientation="vertical" >

   <TextView
        android:layout_width="fill_parent"
        android:layout_height="wrap_content"
        android:text="Recording Demo : Please Press desired option  " />

   <Button android:id="@+id/button1"
        android:layout_height="wrap_content"
        android:layout_width="fill_parent"
        android:onClick="start"
        android:text="Start Recording"/>

   <Button android:id="@+id/button2"
        android:layout_height="wrap_content"
```

```
        android:layout_width="fill_parent"
        android:onClick="stop"
        android:text="Stop Recording"/>

    <Button android:id="@+id/button3"
        android:layout_height="wrap_content"
        android:layout_width="fill_parent"
        android:onClick="play"
        android:text="Play Recording"/>

    <Button android:id="@+id/button4"
        android:layout_height="wrap_content"
        android:layout_width="fill_parent"
        android:onClick="reset"
        android:text="Reset Recording"/>
</LinearLayout>
```

In Listing 10.8, a linear layout is set with four buttons and one text view.

3. *Replace* the code of the `MainActivity.java` file, with the code shown in Listing 10.9:

Listing 10.9: Displaying the Code of the `MainActivity.java` File in the `AudioRecorder` Application

```
package com.kogent.android.audiorecorder;

import java.io.IOException;

import android.media.MediaPlayer;
import android.media.MediaRecorder;
import android.net.Uri;
import android.os.Bundle;
import android.os.Environment;
import android.provider.MediaStore;
import android.app.Activity;
import android.content.ContentResolver;
import android.content.ContentValues;
import android.content.Intent;
import android.view.Menu;
import android.view.View;
import android.widget.Button;
import android.widget.Toast;

public class MainActivity extends Activity {

   private MediaRecorder mRecorder;
   private String outputFile = null;
   private Button start, stop, play, reset;
   MediaPlayer mPlayer;

   @Override
   protected void onCreate(Bundle savedInstanceState) {
         super.onCreate(savedInstanceState);
         setContentView(R.layout.activity_main);
         start = (Button) findViewById(R.id.button1);
         stop = (Button) findViewById(R.id.button2);
         play = (Button) findViewById(R.id.button3);
         reset = (Button) findViewById(R.id.button4);
         stop.setEnabled(false);
         play.setEnabled(false);
         reset.setEnabled(false);

   }

   public void start(View view) {
         outputFile = Environment.getExternalStorageDirectory()
                      .getAbsolutePath() + "/recording.3gp";
         try {
               mRecorder = new MediaRecorder();
```

```
                mRecorder.setAudioSource(MediaRecorder.AudioSource.MIC);
                mRecorder.setOutputFormat(MediaRecorder.OutputFormat.THREE_GPP);
                mRecorder.setAudioEncoder(MediaRecorder.OutputFormat.AMR_NB);
                mRecorder.setOutputFile(outputFile);
                mRecorder.prepare();
                mRecorder.start();
        } catch (IllegalStateException e) {
                e.printStackTrace();
        } catch (IOException e) {
                e.printStackTrace();
        }
        start.setEnabled(false);
        stop.setEnabled(true);
        Toast.makeText(getApplicationContext(), "Recording started",
                        Toast.LENGTH_LONG).show();

}

public void stop(View view) {
        try {
                mRecorder.stop();
                mRecorder.release();
                mRecorder = null;
        } catch (IllegalStateException e) {
                e.printStackTrace();
        }

        stop.setEnabled(false);
        play.setEnabled(true);
        reset.setEnabled(true);
        addToMediaLibrary();
        Toast.makeText(getApplicationContext(), "Audio recorded successfully",
                        Toast.LENGTH_LONG).show();
}

public void play(View view) throws IllegalArgumentException,
                SecurityException, IllegalStateException, IOException {

        mPlayer = new MediaPlayer();
        mPlayer.setDataSource(outputFile);
        mPlayer.prepare();
        mPlayer.start();
        Toast.makeText(getApplicationContext(), "Playing audio",
                        Toast.LENGTH_LONG).show();

}

public void reset(View view) {
        try {
                if (mPlayer != null) {
                        mPlayer.stop();
                        mPlayer.release();
                        mPlayer = null;
                }
        } catch (IllegalStateException e) {
                e.printStackTrace();
        }
        start.setEnabled(true);
        stop.setEnabled(false);
        play.setEnabled(false);
        reset.setEnabled(false);
        Toast.makeText(getApplicationContext(), "record audio again",
                        Toast.LENGTH_LONG).show();

}
```

```
            protected void addToMediaLibrary() {
        ContentResolver contentResolver = getContentResolver();
        Uri base = MediaStore.Audio.Media.EXTERNAL_CONTENT_URI;
      ContentValues contentValues = new ContentValues(4);
      long current = System.currentTimeMillis();
      contentValues.put(MediaStore.Audio.Media.TITLE, "audio" + "sample.3gp");
      contentValues.put(MediaStore.Audio.Media.DATE_ADDED, (int) (current / 1000));
      contentValues.put(MediaStore.Audio.Media.MIME_TYPE, "audio/3gpp");
      contentValues.put(MediaStore.Audio.Media.DATA, outputFile);
      Uri newUri = contentResolver.insert(base, contentValues);
      sendBroadcast(new Intent(Intent.ACTION_MEDIA_SCANNER_SCAN_FILE, newUri));
      Toast.makeText(this, "New File " + newUri, Toast.LENGTH_LONG).show();
    }

}
```

In Listing 10.9, an instance of the `MediaRecorder` class is created. In the `start()` method, the `setAudioSource()` method is used to set the audio source by using `MediaRecorder.AudioSource.MIC` parameter. Then, the `setOutputFormat()` and `setOutputFile()` methods are used to specify the output file format and output file name, respectively. The `setAudioEncoder()` method specifies audio encoder to encode the recorded audio. Then, the `prepare()` and `start()` methods start the media recorder to record an audio. In the `stop()` method, the `stop()` and `release()` methods of the `MediaRecorder` class are invoked. The `play()` method uses a media player to play the recorded sound. The `reset()` method again invokes the `stop()` and `release()` methods first and again prepares the `MediaRecorder` class to launch. There is one more method, that is, `addRecordingToMediaLibrary()`, which adds the recorded sound in a media store.

4. *Replace* the code of the `AndroidManifest.xml` file, with the code shown in Listing 10.10:

Listing 10.10: Displaying the Code of the `AndroidManifest.xml` File in the `AudioRecorder` Application

```
<?xml version="1.0" encoding="utf-8"?>
<manifest xmlns:android="http://schemas.android.com/apk/res/android"
    package="com.kogent.android.audiorecorder"
    android:versionCode="1"
    android:versionName="1.0" >

    <uses-sdk
        android:minSdkVersion="8"
        android:targetSdkVersion="17" />

    <application
        android:allowBackup="true"
        android:icon="@drawable/ic_launcher"
        android:label="@string/app_name"
        android:theme="@style/AppTheme" >
        <activity
            android:name="com.kogent.android.audiorecorder.MainActivity"
            android:label="@string/app_name" >
            <intent-filter>
                <action android:name="android.intent.action.MAIN" />

                <category android:name="android.intent.category.LAUNCHER" />
            </intent-filter>
        </activity>
    </application>
   <uses-permission android:name="android.permission.WRITE_EXTERNAL_STORAGE"/>
    <uses-permission android:name="android.permission.RECORD_AUDIO" />

</manifest>
```

In Listing 10.10, the `uses-permissions` are configured to record an audio and store it to an external storage.

5. *Execute* the `AudioRecorder` application. Figure 10.4 shows the output of the `AudioRecorder` application:

Figure 10.4: Showing the Output of the `AudioRecorder` Application

When you click the **Start Recording** button, the recording of sound will be started, as shown in Figure 10.5:

Figure 10.5: Recording an Audio

If you click the **Stop Recording** button, the recording will be stopped and the recorded audio will be stored in a media store, as shown in Figure 10.6:

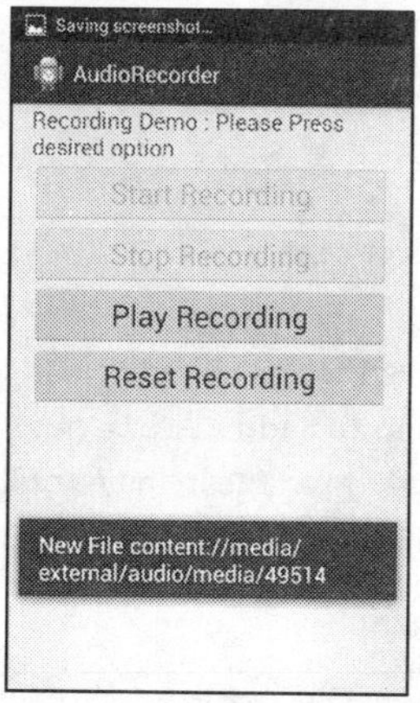

Figure 10.6: Saving Newly Recorded Audio

Moreover, you can use the **Play Recoding** button to play the recorded audio file, and the **Reset Recording** button to restart the media recorder to record a new audio.

Creating a Sound Pool

Android framework allows you to create a sound pool, which is a collection of audio files that can be loaded into the memory from a resource inside the Android Application Package (APK) or from a file in the file system. To create a sound pool, you need to use the `SoundPool` class to manage and play audio resources for the applications. The `SoundPool` class helps in managing audio when your application requires low audio latency and playing multiple audio streams simultaneously. The audio files added to the `SoundPool` are decompressed and decoded into raw 16-bit PCM streams, allowing you to package compressed audio resources without suffering from latency and CPU effects of decompression during playback.

The following code snippet shows how to create an instance of the `SoundPool` class and load it with sample audio files:

```
int maximum_streams = 10;
SoundPool sp = new SoundPool(maximum_streams, AudioManager.STREAM_MUSIC, 0);
int sample1 = sp.load(this, R.raw.sample1, 0);
int sample2 = sp.load(this, R.raw.sample2, 0);
int sample3 = sp.load(this, R.raw.sample3, 0);
```

In the preceding code snippet, you can see how you can specify the maximum number of concurrent streams to play, allowing it to minimize the effect of the audio mixing by automatically stopping the oldest and lowest priority stream within the pool when the limit is reached. It should be noted that when creating a new `SoundPool`, you should specify the target stream as `STREAM_MUSIC` and the maximum number of simultaneous streams that can be played concurrently. Then, the `load()` method of the `SoundPool` class is used to load audio resources from an Asset File Descriptor, package resource, file path, or file descriptor.

Let's create an application named `SoundPool` to learn the use of the `SoundPool` class. Perform the following steps to create the `SoundPool` application:

1. *Create* the `SoundPool` application in the Eclipse IDE under the `com.kogent.android.soundpool` package.
2. *Replace* the code of the `activity_main.xml` file located in the **/res/layout** folder, with the code shown in Listing 10.11:

Listing 10.11: Displaying the Code of the `activity_main.xml` File in the `SoundPool` Application

```
<LinearLayout xmlns:android="http://schemas.android.com/apk/res/android"
android:layout_width="fill_parent"
android:layout_height="fill_parent"
android:orientation="vertical" >

    <TextView android:text="Click on the screen to start playing"
        android:layout_width="wrap_content"
        android:layout_height="wrap_content">
    </TextView>
     <Button android:id="@+id/Start_Play"
   android:layout_width="fill_parent"
   android:layout_height="wrap_content"
   android:text="Start Play"/>
</LinearLayout>
```

   In Listing 10.11, a linear layout is created with a text view and a button.

3. *Create* the raw folder in the **/res** location and add `sample.mp3` file in it.
4. *Replace* the code of the `MainActivity.java` file in the **/src** folder, with the code shown in Listing 10.12:

Listing 10.12: Showing the Code of the `MainActivity.java` File in the `SoundPool` Application

```
package com.kogent.android.soundpool;
import android.media.AudioManager;
import android.media.SoundPool;
import android.media.SoundPool.OnLoadCompleteListener;
import android.os.Bundle;
```

```
import android.app.Activity;
import android.util.Log;
import android.view.Menu;
import android.view.MotionEvent;
import android.view.View;
import android.view.View.OnTouchListener;
import android.widget.Button;

public class MainActivity extends Activity {

   private SoundPool mSoundPool;
   private int soundinfo;
   boolean loaded = false;
   Button PlayButton;

   @Override
   public void onCreate(Bundle savedInstanceState) {
         super.onCreate(savedInstanceState);
         setContentView(R.layout.activity_main);

         mSoundPool = new SoundPool(2, AudioManager.STREAM_MUSIC, 0);
         mSoundPool.setOnLoadCompleteListener(new OnLoadCompleteListener() {
                 @Override
                 public void onLoadComplete(SoundPool soundPool, int sampleId,
                               int status) {
                       loaded = true;
                 }
         });
         soundinfo = mSoundPool.load(this, R.raw.sample, 1);
         PlayButton = (Button) findViewById(R.id.Start_Play);
         PlayButton.setOnClickListener(new View.OnClickListener() {
                 public void onClick(View view) {
                       startPlay();
                 }
         });
   }

   protected void startPlay() {
         AudioManager audio_Manager = (AudioManager) getSystemService(AUDIO_SERVICE);
         float volume = ((float) (audio_Manager
                       .getStreamVolume(AudioManager.STREAM_MUSIC)))
                       / ((float) (audio_Manager
                                   .getStreamMaxVolume(AudioManager.STREAM_MUSIC)));
         if (loaded) {
                 mSoundPool.play(soundinfo, volume, volume, 1, 0, 1f);
                 Log.e("Test", "Played sound");
         }
   }
}
```

In Listing 10.12, an instance of the `SoundPool` is created and loaded with a sample audio file. This loaded audio file is played on the click event of a button. The click event invokes the `startPlay()` method, in which an instance of the `AudioManager` class is created using the `getSystemService()` method. This method takes a parameter of an audio service. The `getStreamVolume()` and `getStreamMaxVolume()` methods are used to specify the volume level on which a recorded audio will be played from the created sound pool.

5. *Execute* the `SoundPool` application. Figure 10.7 shows the output of the `SoundPool` application:

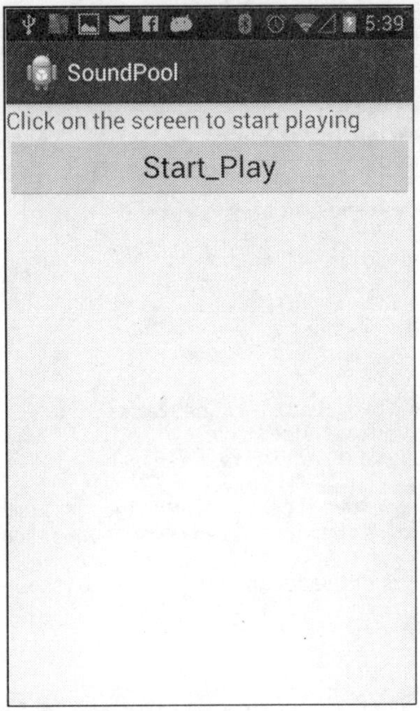

Figure 10.7: Showing the Output of the `SoundPool` Application

When you click button on the screen, the sample provided in the application will be played.

Using Camera for Taking Pictures

In Android applications, you need to use the `Camera` class to capture images. It also allows you to adjust camera settings and specify image preferences. The `open()` method of the `Camera` class provides the access of the camera as follows:

```
Camera cam = Camera.open();
```

And when you have done all the tasks related to camera, you need to free it by calling the `release()` method. It should be noted that to access the camera hardware directly, you need to add the following CAMERA `uses-permission` to your application in the `AndroidManifest.xml` file:

```
<uses-permission android:name="android.permission.CAMERA"/>
```

You might have noticed that when you use your mobile device to capture an image, first you see the preview of the event that you have captured. This is because it is not possible to take a picture using the `Camera` class without displaying a preview. Therefore, when you need to implement your own camera in an application, you also need to display a preview of what is being captured by the camera. The camera preview is displayed by using the `SurfaceHolder` interface for which you must include a surface view within your UI layout to view the live camera stream within your application. The `Callback()` method of the `SurfaceHolder` interface allows the construction of a valid surface for capturing images. Then, the `setPreviewDisplay()` method of `Camera` class displays the preview of the image captured. Moreover, the `startPreview()` and `stopPreview()` methods are used to begin the streaming and end the streaming, respectively.

After configuring camera settings and activating a preview, you can take a picture by invoking the `takePicture()` method of the `Camera` class and passing it in a `ShutterCallback` object. Two objects of the `PictureCallback` class are created for the RAW and JPEG-encoded images.

Let's create an application, named `CaptureImage`, to learn the use of Camera to capture still images. Perform the following steps to create the `CaptureImage` application:

1. *Create* the `CaptureImage` application in the Eclipse IDE under the `com.kogent.android.captureimage` package.

2. *Add* an XML file named `control.xml` in the **/res/layout** folder, as shown in Listing 10.13:

Listing 10.13: Displaying the Code of the `control.xml` File in the `CaptureImage` Application

```
<?xml version="1.0" encoding="utf-8"?>
<LinearLayout xmlns:android="http://schemas.android.com/apk/res/android"
    android:orientation="vertical"
    android:layout_width="fill_parent"
    android:layout_height="fill_parent"
    android:gravity="bottom"
    >
<Button
android:id="@+id/clickimage"
    android:layout_width="wrap_content"
    android:layout_height="wrap_content"
  android:text=" * Click Picture "
  android:layout_gravity="center"
  android:layout_margin="10px"
    />
</LinearLayout>
```

In Listing 10.13, a linear layout is set and a button is added.

3. Replace the code of the `activity_main.xml` file in the **/res/layout** folder, with the code shown in Listing 10.14:

Listing 10.14: Showing the Code of the `activity_main.xml` File in the `CaptureImage` Application

```
<?xml version="1.0" encoding="utf-8"?>
<LinearLayout xmlns:android="http://schemas.android.com/apk/res/android"
    android:orientation="vertical"
    android:layout_width="fill_parent"
    android:layout_height="fill_parent"
    >
<SurfaceView

  android:id="@+id/camerapreview"
    android:layout_width="fill_parent"
    android:layout_height="wrap_content"
    />
</LinearLayout>
```

In Listing 10.14, a linear layout is set and a surface view is added.

4. Replace the code of the `MainActivity.java` file in the **/src** folder, as shown in Listing 10.15:

Listing 10.15: Displaying the Code of the `MainActivity.java` File in the `CaptureImage` Application

```
package com.kogent.android.captureimage;

import java.io.File;
import java.io.FileNotFoundException;
import java.io.FileOutputStream;
import java.io.IOException;
import android.app.Activity;
import android.content.pm.ActivityInfo;
import android.graphics.PixelFormat;
import android.view.SurfaceHolder;
import android.view.SurfaceView;
import android.os.Bundle;
import android.os.Environment;
import android.util.Log;
import android.hardware.Camera;
import android.hardware.Camera.PictureCallback;
import android.hardware.Camera.ShutterCallback;
import android.view.LayoutInflater;
import android.view.View;
import android.view.ViewGroup.LayoutParams;
import android.widget.Button;
import android.widget.Toast;
```

```
public class MainActivity extends Activity implements SurfaceHolder.Callback{
   Camera devicecamera;
   SurfaceView mySurfaceView;
   SurfaceHolder holder;
   LayoutInflater layoutInflater = null;

    @Override
    public void onCreate(Bundle savedInstanceState) {
        super.onCreate(savedInstanceState);
        setContentView(R.layout.activity_main);
        setRequestedOrientation(ActivityInfo.SCREEN_ORIENTATION_LANDSCAPE);
        getWindow().setFormat(PixelFormat.UNKNOWN);
        mySurfaceView = (SurfaceView)findViewById(R.id.camerapreview);
        holder = mySurfaceView.getHolder();
        holder.addCallback(this);
        layoutInflater = LayoutInflater.from(getBaseContext());
        View view = layoutInflater.inflate(R.layout.control, null);
        LayoutParams layoutparams
         = new LayoutParams(LayoutParams.MATCH_PARENT,
         LayoutParams.MATCH_PARENT);
        this.addContentView(view, layoutparams );
        Button buttonTakePicture = (Button)findViewById(R.id.clickimage);
        buttonTakePicture.setOnClickListener(new Button.OnClickListener(){
                @Override
                public void onClick(View arg0) {
                        devicecamera.takePicture(mShutterCallback,
                                        mPictureCallback, mPictureCallback_JPG);
                }});
    }

    ShutterCallback mShutterCallback = new ShutterCallback(){
        @Override
        public void onShutter() {
        }};

   PictureCallback mPictureCallback = new PictureCallback(){
        @Override
        public void onPictureTaken(byte[] arg0, Camera arg1) {
        }};

   PictureCallback mPictureCallback_JPG = new PictureCallback(){
        @Override
        public void onPictureTaken(byte[] arg0, Camera arg1) {
                File sdDir =new File(
   Environment.getExternalStoragePublicDirectory(Environment.DIRECTORY_PICTURES),"CaptureI
   mage");
                 if (!sdDir.exists())
                    if (!sdDir.mkdirs()) {
                        Log.d("MyCameraApp", "failed to create directory");
                        return;
                    }
                 File Image=new File (sdDir.getPath()+"/newimage.png");
        try {
                FileOutputStream fos = new FileOutputStream(Image);
                fos.write(arg0);
                fos.close();
                Toast.makeText(getApplicationContext(), "Image saved successfully",
                            Toast.LENGTH_LONG).show();
            } catch (FileNotFoundException e) {
            } catch (IOException e) {
            }
   }};

   @Override
   public void surfaceChanged(SurfaceHolder holder, int format, int width,
```

```
                int height) {
        try {
                devicecamera.setPreviewDisplay(holder);
                devicecamera.startPreview();
        } catch (IOException e) {
                e.printStackTrace();
        }
    }
    @Override
    public void surfaceCreated(SurfaceHolder holder) {
        devicecamera = Camera.open();
    }

    @Override
    public void surfaceDestroyed(SurfaceHolder holder) {
        devicecamera.stopPreview();
        devicecamera.release();
    }
}
```

In Listing 10.15, the `MainActivity` class implements the `SurfaceHolder.Callback` interface. Then, the instances of the `Camera`, `SurfaceView`, `SurfaceHolder`, and `LayoutInflater` classes are created. These instances are initialized in the `onCreate()` method. Then the objects of the `ShutterCallback` and `PictureCallback` classes are created and initialized. In the `surfaceCreated()` method, a camera is opened. The provided button can be clicked to take picture in the `onClick()` method and the `takePicture()` method of the `Camera` is invoked. If any surface change takes place, the `startPreview()` or `stopPreview()` method will be invoked accordingly. Moreover, the `stopPreview()` and `release()` methods of the `Camera` are invoked in the `surfaceDestroyed()` method.

5. *Replace* the code of the `AndroidManifest.xml` file, with the code shown in Listing 10.16:

Listing 10.16: Showing the Code of the `AndroidManifest.xml` File in the `CaptureImage` Application

```
<?xml version="1.0" encoding="utf-8"?>
<manifest xmlns:android="http://schemas.android.com/apk/res/android"
    package="com.kogent.android.captureimage"
    android:versionCode="1"
    android:versionName="1.0" >

    <uses-sdk
        android:minSdkVersion="8"
        android:targetSdkVersion="17" />

    <application
        android:allowBackup="true"
        android:icon="@drawable/ic_launcher"
        android:label="@string/app_name"
        android:theme="@style/AppTheme" >
        <activity
            android:name="com.kogent.android.captureimage.MainActivity"
            android:label="@string/app_name" >
            <intent-filter>
                <action android:name="android.intent.action.MAIN" />

                <category android:name="android.intent.category.LAUNCHER" />
            </intent-filter>
        </activity>

    </application>
    <uses-permission android:name="android.permission.CAMERA" />
    <uses-permission android:name="android.permission.WRITE_EXTERNAL_STORAGE" />

</manifest>
```

In Listing 10.16, `CAMERA` and `WRITE_EXTERNAL_STORAGE` uses permissions are configured.

6. *Execute* the `CaptureImage` application. Figure 10.8 shows the output of the `CaptureImage` application:

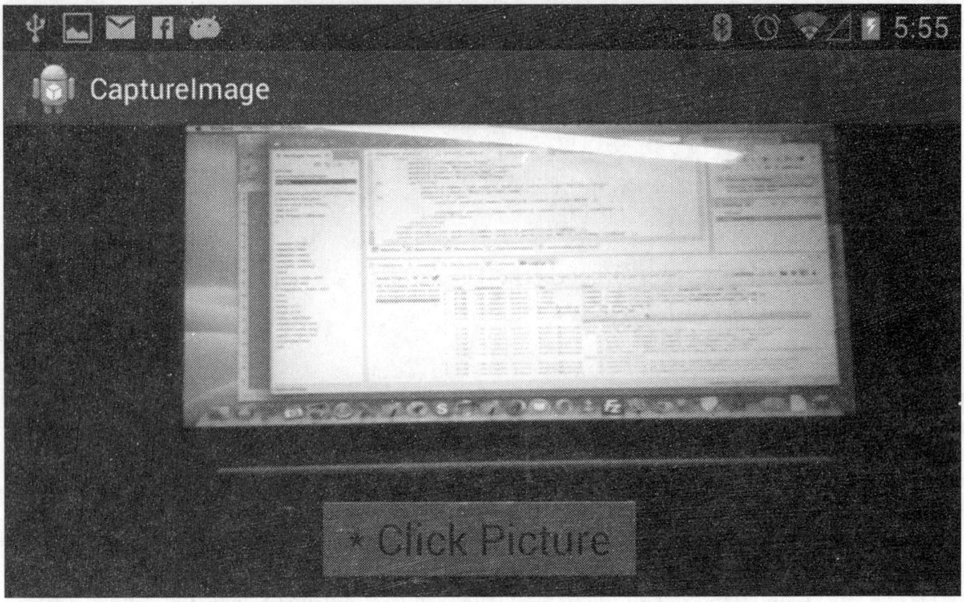

Figure 10.8: Displaying the Output of the `CaptureImage` Application

Recording Video

Android provides two options for recording video within your application. These options are as follows:

- **Using Intents to Record Video**—Specifies the technique in which intents are used to launch the video camera application. You need to initiate video recording by using the `MediaStore.ACTION_VIDEO_CAPTURE` action Intent. The following code snippet shows how to use the video capture action to record a new video:

```
private static final int RECORD_VIDEO = 0;
private void startRecording() {
Intent intentobj = new Intent(MediaStore.ACTION_VIDEO_CAPTURE);
startActivityForResult(intentobj, RECORD_VIDEO);
}
@Override
protected void onActivityResult(int request_code,
int result_code, Intent data) {
if (request_code == RECORD_VIDEO) {
VideoView videovw = (VideoView)findViewById(R.id.videovw);
videovw.setVideoURI(data.getData());
videovw.start()
}
}
```

- **Using the `MediaRecorder` Class**—Specifies the technique in which you use the `MediaRecorder` class to record the audio or video files. To record any media in Android, your application must configure the `CAMERA`, `RECORD_AUDIO`, and `RECORD_VIDEO` uses permissions in the `AndroidManifest.xml` file as follows:

```
<uses-permission android:name="android.permission.RECORD_AUDIO"/>
<uses-permission android:name="android.permission.RECORD_VIDEO"/>
<uses-permission android:name="android.permission.CAMERA"/>
```

The `MediaRecorder` class allows you to specify the audio and video input sources by using the `setAudioSource()` and `setVideoSource()` methods. After selecting your input sources, you need to specify the recording profile by using the `setProfile()` method. A profile is created by using the `CamcorderProfile` class's `get()` method. Then, use the `setOutputFile()` method to assign a file to store the recorded media before allocating a preview surface and calling the `prepare()` method.

The following code snippet shows how to configure a `MediaRecorder` to record audio and video from the microphone and camera:

```
MediaRecorder mediaRecorder = new MediaRecorder();
mediaRecorder.setAudioSource(MediaRecorder.AudioSource.DEFAULT);
mediaRecorder.setVideoSource(MediaRecorder.VideoSource.DEFAULT);
CamcorderProfile camcorderProfile_HQ =
CamcorderProfile.get(CamcorderProfile.QUALITY_HIGH);
mediaRecorder.setProfile(camcorderProfile_HQ);
mediaRecorder.setOutputFile("/sdcard/myvideo.mp4");
```

When recording video, it is considered a good practice to display a preview of the recorded video. For this, you need to invoke the `setPreviewDisplay()` method of the `MediaRecorder` class. Moreover, the `prepare()` method starts live video preview stream, and the `start()` and `stop()` methods control the recording through media recorder.

NOTE

Sometime the `setPreviewDisplay()` method of the `MediaRecorder` class does not give the desired result; instead of you need to use the `setPreviewDisplay()` method of the `Camera` class for taking a live preview.

Creating Video Recording Application

In this section, you learn to create an Android application that allows you record a video using a camera. Let's create an application, named `VideoRecording`, to learn the use of Camera for recording a video. Perform the following steps to create the `VideoRecording` application:

1. *Create* the `VideoRecording` application in the Eclipse IDE under the `com.kogent.android.videorecording` package.
2. *Replace* the code of the `activity_main.xml` file in the **/res/layout** folder, with the code shown in Listing 10.17:

Listing 10.17: Showing the Code of the `activity_main.xml` File in the `VideoRecording` Application

```
<?xml version="1.0" encoding="utf-8"?>
<LinearLayout xmlns:android="http://schemas.android.com/apk/res/android"
    android:orientation="vertical"
    android:layout_width="fill_parent"
    android:layout_height="fill_parent">

    <LinearLayout
        android:orientation="horizontal"
        android:layout_width="fill_parent"
        android:layout_height="fill_parent">

        <SurfaceView
                android:id="@+id/camera_preview"
                android:layout_width="320px"
                android:layout_height="480px"/>

            <LinearLayout
                android:orientation="vertical"
              android:layout_width="wrap_content"
              android:layout_height="fill_parent"
              android:layout_weight="0.5"
              android:gravity="bottom">

                <Button
```

```
                android:id="@+id/record"
                android:layout_width="fill_parent"
                android:layout_height="wrap_content"
                android:text="REC"
                android:onClick="record"
                android:textSize="12dp"/>

                 <Button
                  android:id="@+id/stop"
                  android:layout_height="wrap_content"
                  android:layout_width="fill_parent"
                  android:onClick="stop"
                  android:text="Stop Recording"/>


  </LinearLayout>

    </LinearLayout>

  </LinearLayout>
```

In Listing 10.17, three linear layouts are used, where one is parent and other two are its child. The top most linear layout is vertically set. The second is contained in it and horizontally set, containing a surface view. Another linear layout is again vertically set in the top most linear layout, containing two buttons.

3. *Replace* the code of the `MainActivity.java` file in the **/src** folder, as shown in Listing 10.18:

Listing 10.18: Displaying the Code of the `MainActivity.java` File in the `VideoRecording` Application

```
package com.kogent.android.videorecording;

import java.io.IOException;
import android.os.Bundle;
import android.app.Activity;
import android.media.CamcorderProfile;
import android.media.MediaRecorder;
import android.view.SurfaceHolder;
import android.view.SurfaceView;
import android.view.View;
import android.widget.Button;
import android.widget.Toast;

public class MainActivity extends Activity implements SurfaceHolder.Callback{

   Button mRecord, mStop, mCapture;
   MediaRecorder mediaRecorder;
   SurfaceHolder surfaceHolder;
   SurfaceView myVideoView;

   @Override
   public void onCreate(Bundle savedInstanceState) {
         super.onCreate(savedInstanceState);
         setContentView(R.layout.activity_main);
         SetupView();

         mRecord = (Button)findViewById(R.id.record);
         mRecord.setEnabled(true);
         mStop = (Button)findViewById(R.id.stop);
         mStop.setEnabled(false);


   }
   private void SetupView(){
         SurfaceView myVideoView = (SurfaceView)findViewById(R.id.camera_preview);
         surfaceHolder = myVideoView.getHolder();
         surfaceHolder.addCallback(this);
   }
```

```
    public void record(View view) {
          try {
                  mediaRecorder = new MediaRecorder();
                  mediaRecorder.setAudioSource(MediaRecorder.AudioSource.DEFAULT);
                  mediaRecorder.setVideoSource(MediaRecorder.VideoSource.DEFAULT);
                  CamcorderProfile camcorderProfile_HQ =
                  CamcorderProfile.get(CamcorderProfile.QUALITY_HIGH);
                  mediaRecorder.setProfile(camcorderProfile_HQ);
                  mediaRecorder.setOutputFile("/sdcard/myvideo.mp4");
                  mediaRecorder.setMaxDuration(60000); // Set max duration 60 sec.
                  mediaRecorder.setMaxFileSize(5000000); // Set max file size 5M
                  mediaRecorder.setPreviewDisplay(surfaceHolder.getSurface());
                  prepareMediaRecorder();
                  mediaRecorder.start();
                  mRecord.setEnabled(false);
                  mStop.setEnabled(true);
                  Toast.makeText(getApplicationContext(), "Recording started",
                  Toast.LENGTH_LONG).show();
          } catch (IllegalStateException e) {

                  e.printStackTrace();
          }
    }
    public void stop(View view) {
          mediaRecorder.stop();
          mediaRecorder.release();
          mRecord.setEnabled(true);
          mStop.setEnabled(false);
          Toast.makeText(getApplicationContext(), "Video recorded successfully",
                          Toast.LENGTH_LONG).show();
    }


    private void prepareMediaRecorder(){

          try {
                  mediaRecorder.prepare();
          } catch (IllegalStateException e) {

                  e.printStackTrace();
          } catch (IOException e) {

                  e.printStackTrace();
          }
    }
    @Override
    public void surfaceChanged(SurfaceHolder holder, int format, int width,
                  int height) {

    }

    @Override
    public void surfaceCreated(SurfaceHolder holder) {

    }

    @Override
    public void surfaceDestroyed(SurfaceHolder holder) {
          }

}
```

In Listing 10.18, the `MainActivity` class implements the `SurfaceHolder.Callback` interface. Then, the instances of the `Button`, `MediaRecorder`, `SurfaceView`, and `SurfaceHolder` classes are created. In the `onCreate()` method, three buttons are initialized. In the `SetupView()` method, the surface of the application is created by using the `SurfaceView` and `SurfaceHolder` classes. In the `record()` method, the `MediaRecorder` class is initialized, its `setAudioSource()` and `setVideoSource()` methods are used to specify the audio and video sources. The `setProfile()` method is used to set `CamcorderProfile`. The `setOutputFile()` method is used to specify the output file name and location, the `setMaxDuration()` method specifies the maximum duration of video recording, and the `setMaxFileSize()` method specifies the maximum file size of video recording. The `prepareMediaRecorder()` and `start()` methods prepare and start the video recording process. In the `stop()` method, the `stop()` and `release()` methods of the `MediaRecorder` class are invoked to stop the process of video recording. It should be noted that the `prepareMediaRecorder()` method also handles any exception, `IllegalStateException` or `IOException`, which can be raised while preparing a media by invoking the `prepare()` method.

4. *Replace* the code of the `AndroidManifest.xml` file, with the code shown in Listing 10.19:

Listing 10.19: Displaying the Code of the `AndroidManifest.xml` File in the `VideoRecording` Application

```
<?xml version="1.0" encoding="utf-8"?>
<manifest xmlns:android="http://schemas.android.com/apk/res/android"
    package="com.kogent.android.videorecording"
    android:versionCode="1"
    android:versionName="1.0" >

    <uses-sdk
        android:minSdkVersion="8"
        android:targetSdkVersion="17" />
    <application
        android:allowBackup="true"
        android:icon="@drawable/ic_launcher"
        android:label="@string/app_name"
        android:theme="@style/AppTheme" >
        <activity
            android:name="com.kogent.android.videorecording.MainActivity"
            android:label="@string/app_name" >
            <intent-filter>
                <action android:name="android.intent.action.MAIN" />

                <category android:name="android.intent.category.LAUNCHER" />
            </intent-filter>
        </activity>

    </application>

   <uses-feature android:name="android.hardware.camera.autofocus"/>
   <uses-permission android:name="android.permission.CAMERA"/>
   <uses-permission android:name="android.permission.VIBRATE"/>
        <uses-permission android:name="android.permission.RECORD_AUDIO"/>
    <uses-permission android:name="android.permission.RECORD_VIDEO"/>
    <uses-permission android:name="android.permission.WRITE_EXTERNAL_STORAGE"/>
    <uses-permission android:name="android.permission.READ_EXTERNAL_STORAGE"/>
</manifest>
```

In Listing 10.19, various uses-permissions, which include `CAMERA`, `VIBRATE`, `RECORD_AUDIO`, `WRITE_EXTERNAL_STORAGE`, and `READ_EXTERNAL_STORAGE` are configured. In addition the `uses-feature`, i.e. of `hardware.camera.autofocus` is configured.

5. *Execute* the `VideoRecording` application. Figure 10.9 shows the output of the `VideoRecording` application:

Figure 10.9: Showing the Output of the `VideoRecording` Application

Summary

In this chapter, you have learned about audio, video, and camera handling by Android APIs. First, you have learned about media playback and how it helps in controlling audio and video files, which are available from different locations. Next, you have learned how to create a sound pool loaded with sound or audio files. You have also learned how to record sound and create an audio file. Finally, the chapter has discussed the use of camera to capture still images and record videos.

Quick Revise

Q1. Which of the following code snippet shows that an application is requesting network access in order to stream audio or video for `MediaPlayer`?

- a. **<uses-permission android:name="android.permission.INTERNET" />**
- b. **<uses-permission android:name="android.permission.RECORD_AUDIO"/>**
- c. **<uses-permission android:name="android.permission.RECORD_VIDEO"/>**
- d. **<uses-permission android:name="android.permission.CAMERA"/>**

Ans. The correct option is a.

Q2. Which of the following class manages audio sources and audio output on a device?

- a. **MediaPlayer**
- b. **MediaRecorder**
- c. **AudioManager**
- d. **Intent**

Ans. The correct option is c.

Q3. Which of the following is not a valid video format or video codec?

a. **H.263**

b. **MPEG-4 SP**

c. **VP8**

d. **JPEG**

Ans. The correct option is d.

Q4. The __ class is a wrapper around the `SurfaceHolder` object.

a. **SurfaceView**

b. **MediaController**

c. **VideoView**

d. **MediaPlayer**

Ans. The correct option is a.

Q5. Which of the following method of the `MediaPlayer` class uses the `SurfaceHolder` object to display video content?

a. **create()**

b. **setDisplay()**

c. **prepare()**

d. **start()**

Ans. The correct option is b.

Q6. Which of the following method of the `Camera` class displays the preview of the image captured?

a. **setPreviewDisplay()**

b. **startPreview()**

c. **takePicture()**

d. **stopPreview()**

Ans. The correct option is a.

Q7. Which of the following method helps in creating a profile settings from a `CamcorderProfile` object for recording?

a. **get()**

b. **setOutputFile()**

c. **setProfile()**

d. **prepare()**

Ans. The correct option is c.

Q8. `MediaPlayer` allows you to play media stored in __.

a. **Application resources and local files**

b. **Streamed from a network URL**

c. **Content Providers**

d. **All the above**

Ans. The correct option is d.

Q9. Which of the following is not a valid audio file format or codec?

a. **MP3**

b. **MIDI**

c. **MPEG-4 SP**

d. **Ogg**

Ans. The correct option is c.

Q10. In which of the following option you need to add audio content in the res/raw folder of your resources hierarchy?

a. When you need to play audio content from local files

b. When you need to play audio content as an application resource

c. When you need to play audio content by streaming it from a remote URL

d. When you need to play audio content from content providers

Ans. The correct option is b.

Q11. How is the data source set by using the `MediaPlayer` class?

Ans. You need to create an instance of the `MediaPlayer` class by using the `create()` method and then set the data source by following any of the following option:

- Specifying a URI to a local file (using the file:// schema)
- Specifying a URI to an online audio resource (as a URL)
- Specifying a URI to a row within a content provider that returns an audio file

Q12. How is the `VideoView` class used to allocate and prepare video content using a media player?

Ans. The following code snippet shows the use of the `VideoView` class to encapsulate the creation of a surface and allocate and prepare video content using a media player:

```
VideoView vv = (VideoView)this.findViewById(R.id.vv);
        MediaController  mc = new MediaController(this);
        vv.setMediaController(mc);
        vv.setVideoPath("/sdcard/sample_video.mp4");
        vv.requestFocus();
        vv.start();
```

Q13. Write the code that displays how to use Intent to record videos in Android development.

Ans. To record video, you can create an instance of the Intent class by using the `MediaStore.ACTION_VIDEO_CAPTURE` action Intent.

The following code snippet shows how to use the video capture action to record a new video:

```
private static final int RECORD_VIDEO = 0;
private void startRecording() {
Intent intentobj = new Intent(MediaStore.ACTION_VIDEO_CAPTURE);
startActivityForResult(intentobj, RECORD_VIDEO);
}
@Override
protected void onActivityResult(int request_code,
int result_code, Intent data) {
if (request_code == RECORD_VIDEO) {
VideoView videovw = (VideoView)findViewById(R.id.videovw);
videovw.setVideoURI(data.getData());
videovw.start()
}
}
```

Q14. What is sound pool? How is it created in Android applications?

Ans. Android framework allows you to create a sound pool, which is a collection of audio files that can be loaded into the memory from a resource inside the APK or from a file in the file system. To create a sound pool, you need to use the SoundPool class to manage and play audio resources for applications. The SoundPool class helps in managing audio when your application requires low audio latency and can play multiple audio streams simultaneously. The audio files added to the SoundPool are decompressed and decoded into raw 16-bit PCM streams, allowing you to package compressed audio resources without suffering from the latency and CPU effects of decompression during playback. The following code snippet shows how to create an instance of the SoundPool class and load it with sample audio files:

```
int max_num = 10;
SoundPool sp = new SoundPool(max_num, AudioManager.STREAM_MUSIC, 0);
int track1 = sp.load(this, R.raw.track1, 0);
int track2 = sp.load(this, R.raw.track2, 0);
int track3 = sp.load(this, R.raw.track3, 0);
```

Q15. What type of settings must be configured in order to record a media in Android applications?

Ans. To record any media in Android, your application must configure the `CAMERA`, `RECORD_AUDIO`, and `RECORD_VIDEO` uses-permissions in the `AndroidManifest.xml` file as follows:

```
<uses-permission android:name="android.permission.RECORD_AUDIO"/>
<uses-permission android:name="android.permission.RECORD_VIDEO"/>
<uses-permission android:name="android.permission.CAMERA"/>
```

11

Threads and Services

If you need an information on:	See page:
Introducing Threads	396
Introducing Services	401

In day-to-day access to mobile phones, you must have run multiple applications. While listening to music, you must have downloaded e-mails. This act of doing more than one activity at a time is known as multitasking; this is possible if multiple processes are running and each process of a component is different. Sometimes, if two applications need to use the same resources, the current running thread is to be blocked so that the resource can be used by another application.

In this chapter, you will learn about threads and services. You will learn how multiple threads can run asynchronously and a single thread can also run by blocking the current running thread. Next, you will learn about the different types of services, such as start service, bound service, and intent service. You will also develop an application to create bound service and use the service through another application.

Introducing Threads

During the launching of an application, the system creates a thread of execution for the application, which is known as "main thread". This thread plays an important role as it is responsible for dispatching events to appropriate User Interface (UI) widgets. With the help of this thread, your application interacts with the components from the Android UI toolkit. This main thread is also known as UI thread.

An application can contain multiple components, but the system does not create a separate thread for each instance of a component. Instead, all the components running in the same process are instantiated in the UI thread and the system calls to each component are passed from the single thread. As a result, the methods that respond to the system callbacks always run in the UI thread of the process.

The performance of the single thread is down when your application is performing intensive work in response to user interactions. Note that if all the operations are happening in the UI thread, performing long operations such as accessing a network or querying a database will block the entire UI. When a thread is blocked, no event will be passed and the application will appear hanging to the users. In such cases, generally, android kills the application itself if the application is in the specified state for more than 4 seconds. This is known as ANR message.

Worker Threads

As discussed in the previous section, it is important for your application to respond and that you do not block the UI thread. If you need to perform operations which are not instant, then it is ideal to do them as separate threads.

The syntax of creating a thread is similar to the one in Java, as shown in the code snippet below:

```
Thread thread = new Thread() {
@Override
public void run() {
//Code to implement the run method
}
```

In the preceding code snippet, the instance of the `Thread` class is created.

Let's create an application, named `Thread`, demonstrating normal thread in Android. Perform the following steps to create the application:

1. *Create* the `Thread` Android application using Eclipse Integrated Development Environment (IDE). By default, the `MainActivity.java` and `activity_main.xml` files are created. Ensure that you developed the Activity class in the `com.kogent.android.thread` package.
2. *Replace* the code of the `MainActivity.java` file with the code shown in Listing 11.1:

Listing 11.1: Displaying the Code for the `MainActivity.java` File for the `Thread` Application

```
package com.kogent.android.thread;
import android.os.Bundle;
import android.app.Activity;
import android.view.Menu;
import android.view.View;
import android.widget.Toast;

public class MainActivity extends Activity {
   @Override
```

```
    protected void onCreate(Bundle savedInstanceState) {
            super.onCreate(savedInstanceState);
            setContentView(R.layout.activity_main);
    }

   public void start(View view) {
            Thread thread = new Thread() {
                    @Override
                    public void run() {
                            // Block this thread for 10 seconds.
                            try {
                                    Thread.sleep(10000);
                            } catch (InterruptedException e) {
                            }
                            // After completing task go to UI Thread for onscreen update
                            runOnUiThread(new Runnable() {
                                    @Override
                                    public void run() {

   Toast.makeText(getApplicationContext(),"Executed after 10 seconds ", Toast.LENGTH_LONG)
     .show();

   }

   });
                    }
            };
     // Don't forget to start the thread.
            thread.start();

    }
   }
```

In Listing 11.1, the `thread` instance of the `Thread` class is created. On execution, the `Toast` message will appear on the screen, displaying the users that the thread is running after 10 seconds.

3. *Replace* the code of the `activity_main.xml` file with the code shown in Listing 11.2:

Listing 11.2: Displaying the Code of the XML Android Resource File of the `Thread` Application

```
<LinearLayout xmlns:android="http://schemas.android.com/apk/res/android"
    xmlns:tools="http://schemas.android.com/tools"
   android:layout_width="fill_parent"
    android:layout_height="fill_parent"
    android:paddingLeft="16dp"
    android:paddingRight="16dp"
    android:orientation="vertical" >

<TextView
        android:layout_width="wrap_content"
        android:layout_height="wrap_content"
        android:text="Thread Example" />

<Button android:id="@+id/button1"
        android:layout_height="wrap_content"
        android:layout_width="fill_parent"
        android:onClick="start"
        android:text="Click Here to get response after 10 sec"/>

</LinearLayout>
```

In Listing 11.2, a `TextView` and a `Button` are created. On clicking the Button, the `MainActivity` class that displays the `Toast` message to the users is called.

4. *Right-click* the application and select `Run As→Android Application` to view the output of the application. Ensure that before running the application, the Android Virtual Device (AVD) is running.
5. *Click* the button and the output will be displayed as shown in Figure 11.1:

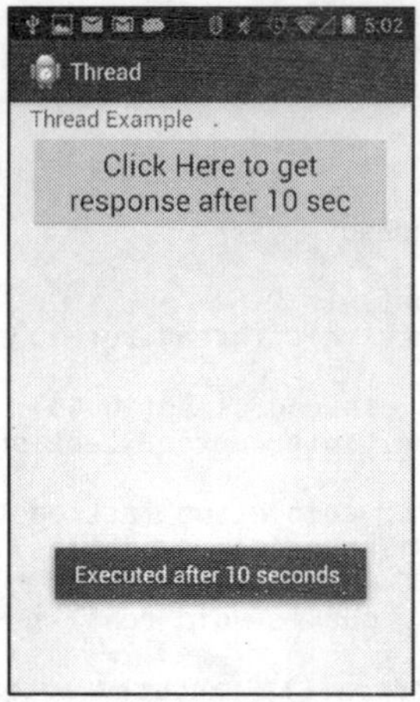

Figure 11.1: Showing the Output of the `Thread` Application

Instead of using the UI thread, you can run a component of an application as a background thread.

Using AsyncTask

`AsyncTask` also creates a new thread but the thread is created on behalf of the Android platform. To use the `AsyncTask`, ensure that you extend your class with the `AsyncTask` subclass and implement the `doInBackground()` callback method that runs in a pool of background threads. To update your UI, you should implement the `onPostExecute()` method. This method passes the result from the `doInBackground()` method and runs in the UI thread so that the UI can be updated safely. Then, you can execute the task by invoking the `execute()` method from the UI thread. Similar to the `onPostExecute()` method, the `onProgressUpdate()` method is also used to send information to the main thread.

Let's create an Android application by implementing the `AsyncTask` subclass. Perform the following steps to create the Android 4.4 application:

1. *Create* the Android application named `AsyncTaskExample` by using Eclipse IDE. By default, the `MainActivity` and `activity_main.xml` files are created. Ensure the package name is `com.kogent.android.asynctaskexample`.
2. *Replace* the code of the `MainActivity.java` file with the code shown in Listing 11.3:

Listing 11.3: Displaying the Code for the `MainActivity.java` File of the `AsyncTaskExample` Application

```
package com.kogent.android.asynctaskexample;
import java.io.IOException;
import java.io.UnsupportedEncodingException;
import java.net.URL;

import java.net.URLConnection;
import java.util.ArrayList;
import java.util.List;

import org.apache.http.NameValuePair;
import org.apache.http.client.ClientProtocolException;
import org.apache.http.client.HttpClient;
import org.apache.http.client.ResponseHandler;

import org.apache.http.client.entity.UrlEncodedFormEntity;
import org.apache.http.client.methods.HttpPost;
import org.apache.http.impl.client.BasicResponseHandler;

import org.apache.http.impl.client.DefaultHttpClient;
import org.apache.http.message.BasicNameValuePair;
import android.os.AsyncTask;
```

```
import android.os.Bundle;

import android.os.StrictMode;
import android.app.Activity;
import android.util.Log;

import android.view.Menu;
import android.view.View;
import android.widget.Button;

import android.widget.EditText;
import android.widget.TextView;
public class MainActivity extends Activity {

   EditText username;
     TextView content;
     String ServeResponse = "";
   @Override

protected void onCreate(Bundle savedInstanceState) {
         super.onCreate(savedInstanceState);
         setContentView(R.layout.activity_main);
         username= (EditText)findViewById(R.id.name);;
           Button savetext = (Button)findViewById(R.id.save);
           content   =  (TextView)findViewById(R.id.content);

savetext.setOnClickListener(new Button.OnClickListener(){
                 @Override
                 public void onClick(View v) {
                // WebServer Request URL
                String post = "http://techoreo.com/post.php";
                // Use AsyncTask execute Method To Prevent ANR Problem
                new backgroundtask().execute(post);
            }
        });
    }
private class backgroundtask  extends AsyncTask<String, Void, Void> {
   protected void onPreExecute() {
         // Things to be done before execution of running into background .
   }
   @Override
   protected Void doInBackground(String... params) {
         // TODO Auto-generated method stub
         String name = username.getText().toString();
         HttpClient client = new DefaultHttpClient();
         HttpPost post = new HttpPost(params[0]);
         List<NameValuePair> pairs = new ArrayList<NameValuePair>(1);
         pairs.add(new BasicNameValuePair("name", name));
         try {
                 post.setEntity(new UrlEncodedFormEntity(pairs));
         } catch (UnsupportedEncodingException e) {
                 // writing error to Log

   e.printStackTrace();
         }
         // Making HTTP Request
         try {
                 ResponseHandler<String> responseHandler = new BasicResponseHandler();
                 ServeResponse = client.execute(post, responseHandler);
                 Log.e("Test::::::::", ServeResponse);
                 // writing response to log

} catch (ClientProtocolException e) {
                 // writing exception to log
                 e.printStackTrace();
```

```
            } catch (IOException e) {
                    // writing exception to log

                    e.printStackTrace();
        }
            return null;
        }
    protected void onPostExecute(Void unused) {
            content.setText(ServeResponse);
        }
    }}
```

In Listing 11.3, the `backgroundtask()` method extends the `AsyncTask` subclass, and the `onPostExecute()`, `doInBackground()`, and `onPreExecute()` methods are implemented. The `doInBackground()` method executes automatically on a worker thread and the `onPreExecute()`, `onPostExecute()`, and `onProgressUpdate()` methods are all invoked on the UI thread. The values returned by the `doInBackground()` method is passed to the `onPostExecute()` method.

To better understand the code given in Listing 11.3, recall the `WebServicesUsingHTTP` application created in *Chapter 7, Working with Location Services and Maps* of the book. In this application, we had used the following code:

```
StrictMode.ThreadPolicy policy = new
StrictMode.ThreadPolicy.Builder().permitAll().build();
StrictMode.setThreadPolicy(policy);
```

The mechanism used in the preceding code is not the ethical way. The better way to implement is shown in the `Activity` class created in Listing 11.3.

3. *Replace* the code of the `activity_main.xml` file with the code shown in Listing 11.4:

Listing 11.4: Displaying the Code for the XML Resource File of the `AsyncTaskExample` Application

```
<LinearLayout xmlns:android="http://schemas.android.com/apk/res/android"
    xmlns:tools="http://schemas.android.com/tools"
   android:layout_width="fill_parent"
   android:layout_height="fill_parent"
   android:paddingLeft="16dp"
   android:paddingRight="16dp"
   android:orientation="vertical" >

<TextView
   android:layout_width="fill_parent"
   android:layout_height="wrap_content"
   android:text="HTTP Post Demo : Enter Your name " />

<EditText android:id="@+id/name"
   android:layout_width="fill_parent"
   android:layout_height="wrap_content"/>

<Button android:text="Get Server Response "
   android:id="@+id/save"
   android:layout_width="fill_parent"
   android:layout_height="wrap_content"
   android:layout_gravity="center" />

<TextView android:id="@+id/content"
   android:layout_width="fill_parent"
   android:layout_height="wrap_content"/>

</LinearLayout>
```

In Listing 11.4, the two `TextView`, an `EditText`, and a `Button` are created.

4. *Add* the required permissions in the `AndroidManifest.xml` file by using the following code snippet:

```
<uses-permission android:name="android.permission.INTERNET" />
```

In the preceding code snippet, the required permissions are set for accessing the Internet in the application.

5. *Right-click* the `AsyncTaskExample` application and select `Run As→Android Application`. Figure 11.2 shows the output of the application:

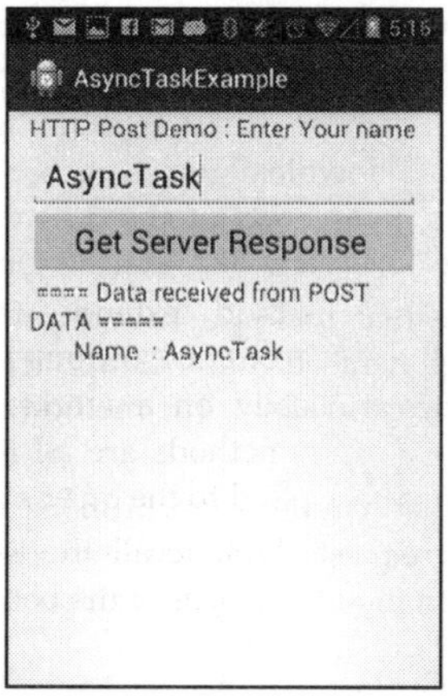

Figure 11.2: Showing the Output of the `AsyncTaskExample` Application

6. *Enter* your name in the text box and click the **Get Server Response** button. The response will be generated and displayed on the window.

Introducing Services

The component of an application that runs in background and having no UI is called a service. A service is basically intended for an application, not for a user; thereby, the user cannot directly interact with it. However, a service greatly enhances the application's functionality to provide high-end experience to the user. A component of another application can start a service and it will continue to run in the background even if the user closes the application. Moreover, a component can bind to a service for communication purposes and even perform Interprocess Communication (IPC).

The methodology of a service lies in its capability to get attached with an application component to communicate with it. The attached component can stimulate a service to perform various tasks for it, such as play music, download data, network management, and many others, all from the background.

Exploring Services Essentials

You can make your application with or without using services. However, services provide an excellent mechanism for handling data in background. As a result, this sustains the concept of multitasking in Android system. Let's start learning from when to use a service in your application, followed by service types.

Using Services in an Application

An application is not necessarily bound to use services. It depends on the nature of the application whether it needs inclusion of services or not. Your application requires the services functionality if it exhibits either of the following properties:

- The applications possess long running processes. The termination of such processes result into the loss of data even on the restart of the application. For example, downloading process in the application.
- An application with long running processes that are not meant for interaction with the user.
- The applications that require interprocess communication.
- The application that can share data with other application irrespective of any user interference.
- The applications that usually download or upload the data and require location information.

A service can be introduced to your application in any of the types such as started or bounded. Let's see the types of service.

Exploring Services Types

As discussed earlier in the chapter, a service can be of different types such as start, bound, or intent. A service can be of started type in your application that runs for longer period in background. The description of different types of services is as follows:

- **Start Service—** Refers to a service that can run for a longer period and ends on completion of the task. For example, if your application allows data download, then one of the components of your application starts a service for download, which ends on completion of the download. A service is started by invoking the `startService()` method. Such type of services once started cannot be controlled in between.
- **Bound Service—** Refers to a service that makes a bound among components. The existence of bound service takes place only when components of another application are bound. As soon as the binding between them breaks, the bound service also stops. The method `bindService()` is required to implement bound service in your application.
- **Intent Service—** Refers to a service that handles asynchronous requests. The `IntentService` is the base class for the Services. The client sends requests through the `startService(Intent)` method, followed by starting the service, then handling each intent using the worker thread, and finally stops the service when it runs out of work.

Let's now understand the service lifecycle.

Understanding the Lifecycle of a Service

Prior to understanding the details, let's know how a service starts and ends in Android system. A service is defined in the `AndroidManifest.xml` file using the `<service>` tag. You are also required to have permissions regarding the services in the `AndroidManifest.xml` file.

On completion of all the permissions and declarations in the `AndroidManifest.xml` file, you can start service using the `Context.startService()` method. Note that only a single call to this method is required to start the service. If a service is active at present, there would be no impact of recalling this method again. In fact, no other instance of this method will be created. To stop the service, you can call either the `Context.stopService()` method or the `stopSelf()` method.

An application can connect with a service using the `Context.bindService()` method. The same application can be disconnected with a service using the `Context.unbindService()` method. Figure 11.3 shows the life cycle of a service:

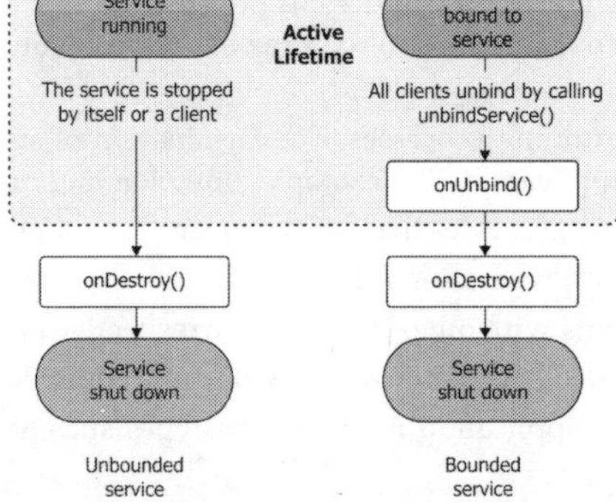

Figure 11.3: Representing the Life Cycle of a Service

In Figure 11.3, initially the call to a service is made using the `startService()` method, then the `onCreate()` method is invoked. Further, the `onStartCommand()` method is called. Lastly, the service is stopped by itself using the `onDestroy()` method or by a client. This lifecycle is followed in the unbound service. In case of the bounded service, firstly the `onCreate()` method is invoked followed by the invocation of the `onBind()` method. Then, all clients unbind services by calling the `onUnbind()` method. Finally, the `onDestroy()` method is invoked to shut down the service. This process is followed in the bounded service.

Exploring the `Service` Class

The `Service` class extends three classes and implements two interfaces. Therefore, there are more than 150 methods to handle the services with versatility. The upcoming section provides introduction to the `Service` class and then the example to create a service. Let's start from the insight of the `Service` class.

Introducing the `Service` Class

The `Service` class is an abstract class, which lies in the `android.app` package. This class inherits the method from three classes and two interfaces. The three classes are `java.lang.Object`, `android.content.Context`, and `android.content.ContextWrapper`. The two interfaces are `android.content.ComponentCallbacks`, and `android.content.ComponentCallbacks2`. Figure 11.4 shows the service class and its associated classes:

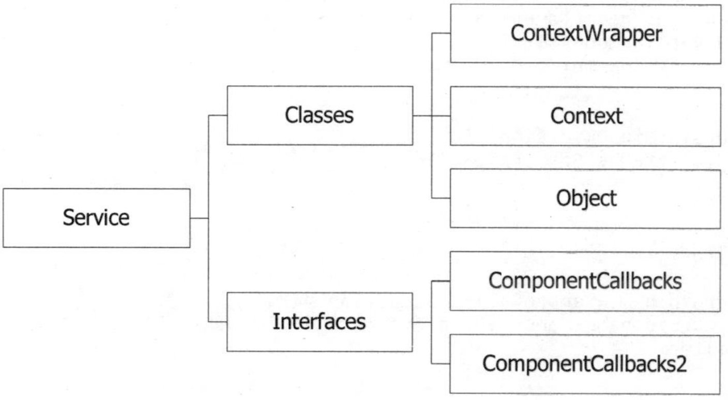

Figure 11.4: Displaying the Classes and Interfaces Used by the `Service` Class

The `Service` class has its own methods and it also inherit methods from the aforementioned classes and interfaces. The `Service` class has approximately 150 methods. Availability of so many methods makes this class robust and enough powerful to deal with any kind of application.

After being conversant with all the aspects of services, let's now create a service.

Creating a Service

The two main tasks for creating a service are to extend your class with the `Service` class and register this service class in the `AndroidManifest.xml` file. Since the `Service` class is an abstract class, it overrides the `onBind()` method by default. To handle a service, the most important callback methods to override are `onStartCommand()`, `onBind()`, `onCreate()`, and `onDestroy()`. The following code snippet shows that our `ServiceDemo` class extends to the `Service` class:

```
public class ServiceDemo extends Service {
   @Override
   public void onCreate() {
         super.onCreate();

}
   @Override
```

```
    public int onStartCommand(Intent intent, int flags, int startId) {
          // Starts the service
          return super.onStartCommand(intent, flags, startId);

  }
    @Override
    public IBinder onBind(Intent intent) {
          // binds the service with other components
          return null;

    }
    @Override
    public void onDestroy() {
          // Destroys the service
          super.onDestroy();

  }
  }
```

The class that extends to the `Service` class needs to be registered in the `AndroidManifest.xml` file. The `<service>` element inside the `<application>` element is used to define a service. Note that the activity class is different from a service class. However, the service class serves as a component of the activity class. The following code snippet shows the registration of a service inside the `AndroidManifest.xml` file:

```
<?xml version="1.0" encoding="utf-8"?>
<manifest xmlns:android="http://schemas.android.com/apk/res/android"
    package="com.kogent.android"
    android:versionCode="1"
    android:versionName="1.0" >

<uses-sdk
        android:minSdkVersion="14"
        android:targetSdkVersion="14" />

<application>
<activity>
<intent-filter>

<action android:name="android.intent.action.MAIN" />
<category android:name="android.intent.category.LAUNCHER" />
</intent-filter>

</activity>
<service android:name="ServiceDemo" />
</application>

</manifest>
```

In the preceding code snippet, our service class `ServiceDemo` is specified by the `android:name` attribute of the `<service>` element inside the `<application>` element. After getting the overview of the technical aspects of a service, let's now create a simple application called `ServiceAppProject`. Create an Android 4.4 project named `ServiceAppProject` under the `com.kogent.android.serviceappproject` package using the Eclipse IDE. Set API level 14 against the minimum required SDK, target SDK, and compile the application. Assign `MainActivity` and `activity_main.xml` as the activity name and layout name, respectively.

Let's now focus on the coding part of the application. The steps to prepare an application inside the Eclipse IDE are as follows:

1. *Expand* the `ServiceAppProject` application inside the Package Explorer.
2. *Open* the `activity_main.xml` file that lies in the **res/layout** directory. *Replace* the code of the `activity_main.xml` file with the code shown in Listing 11.5:

Listing 11.5: Displaying the Code in the `activity_main` XML File of the `ServiceAppProject` Application

```
<RelativeLayout xmlns:android="http://schemas.android.com/apk/res/android"
    xmlns:tools="http://schemas.android.com/tools"
    android:layout_width="match_parent"
    android:layout_height="match_parent"
    tools:context=".MainActivity" >

<Button
  android:id="@+id/start"
  android:layout_width="wrap_content"
  android:layout_height="wrap_content"
  android:layout_alignParentLeft="true"
  android:text="Start Service" />

<Button
  android:id="@+id/stop"
  android:layout_width="wrap_content"
  android:layout_height="wrap_content"
  android:layout_alignParentRight="true"
  android:text="Stop Service" />

</RelativeLayout>
```

In Listing 11.5, we have created two buttons with ids `start` and `stop`, respectively. We will use these buttons to start and stop the service.

3. *Create* a new Java class `ServiceDemo.java` in the `com.kogent.android.serviceappproject` package of the `ServiceAppProject` application. This is our service class that contains the code for a service. Listing 11.6 shows the code for the `ServiceDemo.java` file:

Listing 11.6: Displaying the Code for the `ServiceDemo.java` File

```
package com.kogent.android.serviceappproject;
import android.app.Service;
import android.content.Intent;
import android.os.IBinder;
import android.widget.Toast;
public class ServiceDemo extends Service {
   // This method can be invoked only once no other instance is created
   // After invoking this method, the service continues
   @Override
   public void onCreate() {
          super.onCreate();
          Toast.makeText(this, "Service has been created", Toast.LENGTH_LONG).show();
   }
   // This method starts functioning after the onCreate method.
   // This method can be invoked multiple times to starts the service
   @Override
   public int onStartCommand(Intent intent, int flags, int startId) {
          Toast.makeText(this, "Task is in progress", Toast.LENGTH_LONG).show();
          return super.onStartCommand(intent, flags, startId);
   }
   // Service is not binded with other component, so null is being returned
   @Override
   public IBinder onBind(Intent intent) {
          return null;
   }
   // To kill the service
   @Override
   public void onDestroy() {
          super.onDestroy();
          Toast.makeText(this, "Service has been destroyed", Toast.LENGTH_LONG).show();
   }
}
```

In the preceding code of the `ServiceDemo.java` class, you can analyze that we have used only four methods. The description of each method is given in comments.

A toast notification is used for every method, which shows the method which is being used by the service at runtime.

4. *Open* the `MainActivity` activity class of the `com.kogent.android.serviceappproject` package and add the code given in Listing 11.7:

Listing 11.7: Showing the Code for the `MainActivity` Class of the `ServiceAppProject` Application

```
package com.kogent.android.serviceappproject;
import android.app.Activity;
import android.content.Intent;

import android.os.Bundle;
import android.view.View;
import android.view.View.OnClickListener;

public class MainActivity extends Activity implements OnClickListener {
Intent myItent;
   /** Called when the activity is first created. */

   @Override

   public void onCreate(Bundle savedInstanceState) {
          super.onCreate(savedInstanceState);
          setContentView(R.layout.activity_main);

findViewById(R.id.start).setOnClickListener(this);
          findViewById(R.id.stop).setOnClickListener(this);

}
   @Override
   public void onClick(View v) {
          switch (v.getId()) {

case R.id.start:
                 myItent = new Intent(this, ServiceDemo.class);
                 startService(myItent);
                 break;

case R.id.stop:
                 myItent = new Intent(this, ServiceDemo.class);

stopService(myItent);
                 break;
          }

   }

}
```

The preceding code of the `MainActivity` class contains the intents to start and stop the service. We are almost done with the coding of the `ServiceAppProject` application. Before running this application, first we are required to register it inside the `AndroidManifest.xml` file.

5. *Open* the `AndroidManifest.xml` file of the `ServiceAppProject` application. *Add* the highlighted code given in Listing 11.8 in the `AndroidManifest` file:

Listing 11.8: Showing the Code of the `AndroidManifest.xml` File of the `ServiceAppProject` Application

```
<?xml version="1.0" encoding="utf-8"?>

<manifest xmlns:android="http://schemas.android.com/apk/res/android"
    package="com.kogent.android.serviceappproject"

android:versionCode="1"
```

```
    android:versionName="1.0" >
    <uses-sdk

  android:minSdkVersion="8"
        android:targetSdkVersion="19" />

 <application
        android:allowBackup="true"
        android:icon="@drawable/ic_launcher"

 android:label="@string/app_name"
        android:theme="@style/AppTheme" >


 <activity
            android:name="com.kogent.android.serviceappproject.MainActivity"
            android:label="@string/app_name" >
            <intent-filter>


 <action android:name="android.intent.action.MAIN" />
                <category android:name="android.intent.category.LAUNCHER" />
            </intent-filter>

 </activity>
                <service android:name="ServiceDemo" >
        </service>
            </application>

</manifest>
```

In Listing 11.8, we have registered the `ServiceDemo` class since it contains the service. The `<service>` element inside the `<application>` element is used to define the service.

Finally, we are ready with our service. In Eclipse, right-click on the `ServiceAppProject` application inside the Package Explorer and click `Run As→Android Application`.

Figure 11.5 shows the `ServiceAppProject` application's interface on successful running:

Figure 11.5: Showing the Output of the `ServiceAppProject` Application

On clicking the **Start Service** button, the `onCreate()` method is invoked first. The toast notification appears as you click or tap on the **Start Service** button. Figure 11.6 shows the appearing of the toast notification after clicking the **Start Service** button:

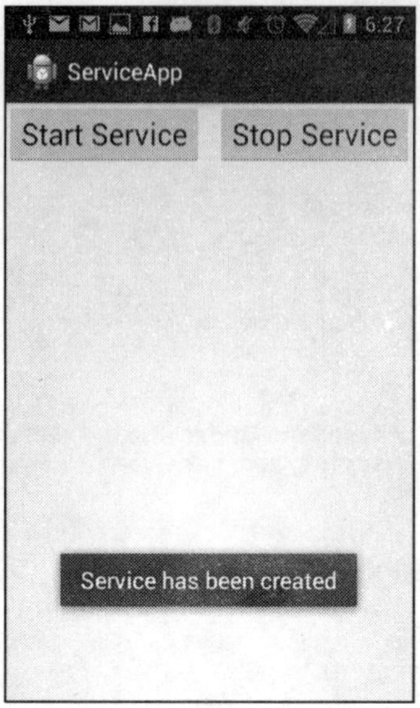

Figure 11.6: Displaying the Creation of the Message Service

After the creation of service, the control transfers to the onStartCommand() method. This method triggers two notifications back to back after clicking the **Start Service** button. The first toast notification is related to the creation of the service, which we have already shown in Figure 11.6. Figure 11.7 shows the toast notification immediately after the toast notification of Figure 11.6:

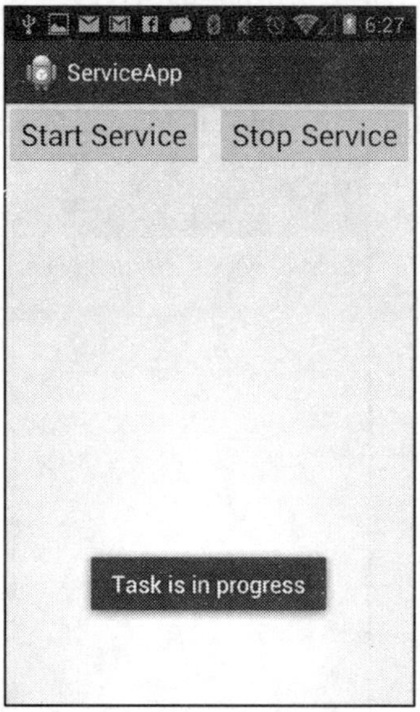

Figure 11.7: Displaying the Message When a Task is Currently in Process

Now the control is held with the `onStartCommand()` method, so the service is in continuation. If you click the **Start Service** button on this stage, there will be no impact on the current service state. It is mentioned earlier that no new instance of the application is created; therefore, the `onCreate()` method has no impact on the current service. To stop this service, you have to destroy it. The method `onDestroy()` is used to kill the service. The impact of the **Stop Service** button is shown in Figure 11.8:

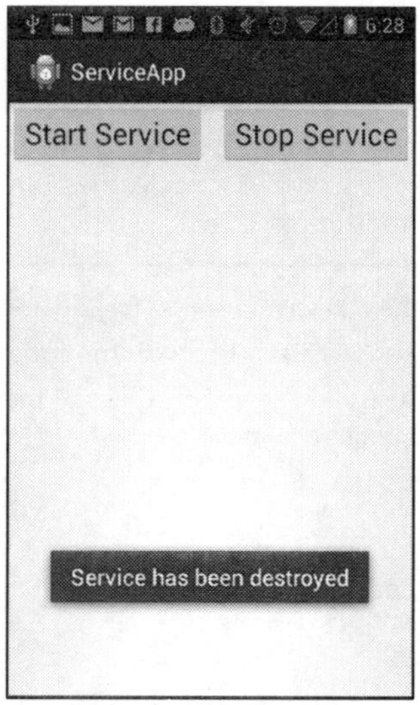

Figure 11.8: Displaying the Message When the Service Stops

On clicking or tapping on the **Stop Service** button, the service which was in progress earlier is stopped.

The `ServiceAppProject` application is simple although it explains the functionality of a service in excellent way. For example, in Listing 11.6, if you shuffle the sequence of methods, even then there will be no difference in the functionality of the `ServiceAppProject` application. The methods will be called in the same sequence as they were called earlier before shuffling. In other words, the `onCreate()` method is the first method that is being called on the creation of a service and the `onDestroy()` method is the last method being used to kill a service.

Creating a Bound Service

A bound service works as a server in a client-server interface. A bound service binds the components of an application, such as activities to the service, send requests, and receive responses. It becomes active only when it is servicing another application component and does not run in the background.

To create a bound service, you need to implement the `Service` class and implement the `onBind()` callback method. This method returns an `IBinder` object used by the client (application consuming the bound service) to interact with the service.

To consume the bound service, you must implement the `ServiceConnection` class used to manage the connection with the service. The application using the bound service can invoke the `bindService()` method, which returns the service immediately without a value. While establishing the connection, the `onServiceConnected()` method is invoked on the instance of the `ServiceConnection` class to pass the instance of the `IBinder` interface that can be used to connect with the service.

To create the bound service, you should define the `IBinder` object, providing an interface to allow clients to interact with the service. The following are the ways to define the interface:

- **Extending the `Binder` class—** Use this technique only if your service is used locally instead of across processes. Extending your service with the `Binder` class allows the consumer of the service to access the public methods directly.
- **Using a Messenger—** Use this technique if you need your service to communicate with remote processes. In this case, you can provide the interface for your service to perform interprocess communication. In this technique, a queue is created for all the client's requests in a single thread.
- **Using Android Interface Definition Language (AIDL) —** Use this technique to handle multiple requests simultaneously. The previous technique, *Using a Messenger*, is also based on Android Interface Definition Language (AIDL); however, in the former a queue of all client's requests is created in a single thread.

Let's create an application `BoundService` in which we define a bound service that adds the two numbers. Then, we create the `ConsumeBoundService` application which uses the bound service to perform the additional task. Perform the following steps to create the service:

1. *Create* the Android application named `BoundService` by using Eclipse. By default, the `MainActivity.java` and `activity_main.xml` files are created. Ensure the package name is `com.kogent.android.boundservice`.
2. To create the Java class named `BoundService.java`, *right-click* the `BoundService` application and *select* `New→Class`. *Enter* the name of the class as `BoundService` and *click* the `Finish` button.
3. *Replace* the code of the `BoundService.java` file with the code shown in Listing 11.9:

Listing 11.9: Displaying the Code of the `BoundService` Class of the `BoundService` Application

```
package com.kogent.android.boundservice;

import android.app.Service;
import android.content.Intent;
import android.os.IBinder;
import android.os.RemoteException;
public class BoundService extends Service{
@Override
public IBinder onBind(Intent intent) {
        // TODO Auto-generated method stub
        return mBinder;

}
@Override
public void onCreate() {
        super.onCreate();

}
@Override
public void onDestroy() {
        super.onDestroy();
  }
@Override
public int onStartCommand(Intent intent, int flags, int startId) {
        super.onStartCommand(intent, flags, startId);
        return Service.BIND_AUTO_CREATE;

  }
private final ISum.Stub mBinder = new ISum.Stub() {
        @Override
        public long add(long a, long b) throws RemoteException {
                // TODO Auto-generated method stub
                return (a + b);

}
  };
}
```

In Listing 11.9, the Java source file extends the `Service` class. The `onStartCommand()` method of the `Service` class is overridden in the source file.

NOTE

Some errors may be displayed in the BoundService Java source file. These errors will be resolved after creating the AIDL file.

4. *Add* the AIDL file to the `BoundService` Android application. *Right-click* the application and *select* the `New→File` option.
5. *Select* the package `com.kogent.android.boundservice` under the **src** directory of the application and enter the name of the file as `ISum.aidl`.
6. *Add* the code shown in Listing 11.10 in the `ISum.aidl` file:

Listing 11.10: Displaying the Code of the `ISum.aidl` File

```
package com.kogent.android.boundservice;
interface ISum {
long add(long a, long b);
}
```

In Listing 11.10, the `ISum` interface containing the `add()` method is created, which accepts two parameters, `a` and `b`. Wait for a few seconds to resolve the errors of the `BoundService` Java source file.

7. *Modify* the highlighted code, shown in Listing 11.11, in the `AndroidManifest.xml` file:

Listing 11.11: Showing the Code of the `AndroidManifest.xml` File of the `BoundService` Application

```
<?xml version="1.0" encoding="utf-8"?>
<manifest xmlns:android="http://schemas.android.com/apk/res/android"
    package="com.kogent.android.boundservice"
    android:versionCode="1"
    android:versionName="1.0" >
    <uses-sdk
        android:minSdkVersion="8"
        android:targetSdkVersion="17" />
    <application
        android:allowBackup="true"
        android:icon="@drawable/ic_launcher"
        android:label="@string/app_name"
        android:theme="@style/AppTheme" >
        <activity
            android:name="com.kogent.android.boundservice.MainActivity"
            android:label="@string/app_name" >
            <intent-filter>
                <action android:name="android.intent.action.MAIN" />
                <category android:name="android.intent.category.DEFAULT" />
            </intent-filter>
        </activity>
        <service android:name="BoundService">
            <intent-filter>
                <action android:name="com.kogent.android.boundservice.ISum" />
            </intent-filter>
        </service>
    </application>
</manifest>
```

In Listing 11.11, the `<service>` element is added for the `BoundService` application and the intent filter is `com.kogent.android.boundservice.ISum`. To specify the intent filter, the `<intent-filter>` element is used.

8. *Replace* the code of the `activity_main.xml` file, with the code shown in Listing 11.12:

Listing 11.12: Code of the `activity_main.xml` File of the `BoundService` Application

```
<RelativeLayout xmlns:android="http://schemas.android.com/apk/res/android"
xmlns:tools="http://schemas.android.com/tools"
android:layout_width="match_parent"
android:layout_height="match_parent"
android:paddingBottom="@dimen/activity_vertical_margin"
android:paddingLeft="@dimen/activity_horizontal_margin"
android:paddingRight="@dimen/activity_horizontal_margin"
android:paddingTop="@dimen/activity_vertical_margin"
tools:context=".MainActivity" >
<TextView
android:layout_width="wrap_content"
android:layout_height="wrap_content"
android:text = "This is an example of Service. As soon as you see this message your
service got started. Even if you close this program and run Consumeboundservice you will
be able to see results of addition." />
</RelativeLayout>
```

In Listing 11.12, a message to be displayed to the users is set in the `activity_main.xml` file of the application. While executing the `BoundService` application, you will see the message and even after closing the application, the service will run in the background of your device.

Let's now create the application named `ConsumeBoundService` to use the bound service created earlier. Perform the following steps to create the application:

1. *Create* a new application named `ConsumeBoundService` by selecting `File→New→Android Application Project`. By default, the `activity_main.xml`, `MainActivity.java`, and `AndroidManifest.xml` files are created. *Ensure* that the package name should be `com.kogent.android.consumeboundservice`.
2. *Replace* the code of the `MainActivity.java` file with the code shown in Listing 11.13:

Listing 11.13: Showing the Code for the `MainActivity.java` File of the `ConsumeBoundService` Application

```
package com.kogent.android.consumeboundservice;

import android.app.Activity;
import android.app.Service;
import android.content.ComponentName;
import android.content.Intent;
import android.content.ServiceConnection;
import android.os.Bundle;
import android.os.IBinder;
import android.os.RemoteException;
import android.util.Log;
import android.view.View;
import android.view.View.OnClickListener;
import android.widget.Button;
import android.widget.EditText;
import android.widget.TextView;

import com.kogent.android.boundservice.ISum;

public class MainActivity extends Activity implements OnClickListener {
   EditText mFirst, mSecond;
   Button mAdd;
   TextView mResult;
   private ISum mService;
   /** Called when the activity is first created. */
   private ServiceConnection mServiceConnection = new ServiceConnection() {
         @Override
         public void onServiceDisconnected(ComponentName name) {
                  // TODO Auto-generated method stub
                  mService = null;
                  Log.d("IRemote", "Service disconnected");
         }
         @Override
         public void onServiceConnected(ComponentName name, IBinder service) {
                  // TODO Auto-generated method stub
                  mService = ISum.Stub.asInterface((IBinder) service);
                  Log.d("IRemote", "Service connected");
         }
   };
   @Override
   public void onCreate(Bundle savedInstanceState) {
         super.onCreate(savedInstanceState);
         setContentView(R.layout.activity_main);
         mFirst = (EditText) findViewById(R.id.firstValue);
         mSecond = (EditText) findViewById(R.id.secondValue);
         mResult = (TextView) findViewById(R.id.resultText);
         mAdd = (Button) findViewById(R.id.add);
         mAdd.setOnClickListener(this);
         //Starting the service
         if(mService == null) {
```

```
                Intent it = new Intent();
                it.setAction("com.kogent.android.boundservice.ISum");
                //binding to remote service
                bindService(it, mServiceConnection, Service.BIND_AUTO_CREATE);
        }
    }
    @Override
    public void onClick(View v) {
        // TODO Auto-generated method stub
        switch(v.getId()){
        case R.id.add: {
        long a = Long.parseLong(mFirst.getText().toString());
        long b = Long.parseLong(mSecond.getText().toString());
        try {
                mResult.setText("Result For addition    " +mService.add(a, b));
        } catch (RemoteException e) {
        // TODO Auto-generated catch block
        e.printStackTrace();
        }
        }
        break;
    }}
}
```

In Listing 11.13, the `ServiceConnection` is established and the service is bound using the `bindService()` method. Also, the service is started using the `setAction()` method.

3. *Replace* the code of the `activity_main.xml` file with the code shown in Listing 11.14:

Listing 11.14: Displaying the Code of the `activity_main.xml` File of the `ConsumeBoundService` Application

```
<LinearLayout xmlns:android="http://schemas.android.com/apk/res/android"
    xmlns:tools="http://schemas.android.com/tools"
   android:layout_width="fill_parent"
    android:layout_height="fill_parent"
    android:paddingLeft="16dp"
    android:paddingRight="16dp"
    android:orientation="vertical" >
<EditText android:id="@+id/firstValue"
  android:layout_width="fill_parent"
  android:layout_height="wrap_content"
  android:hint="Enter a numeric value"/>
<EditText android:id="@+id/secondValue"
  android:layout_width="fill_parent"
  android:layout_height="wrap_content"
  android:hint="Enter a numeric value"/>
<Button android:id="@+id/add"
  android:layout_width="fill_parent"
  android:layout_height="wrap_content"
  android:text="Add" />
<TextView android:id="@+id/resultText"
  android:layout_width="fill_parent"
  android:layout_height="wrap_content"/>
</LinearLayout>
```

In Listing 11.14, two `EditText` views, a `Button` view, and a `TextView` are created.

4. *Create* the `com.kogent.android.boundservice` package by right-clicking the project and selecting `New→Package`. *Enter* the name of the package and click the `Finish` button
5. *Create* the new file under the `com.kogent.android.boundservice` package by right-clicking the package and selecting the `New→File` option. *Enter* the name of the file as `ISum.aidl` and *click* the `Finish` button.
6. *Add* the code shown in Listing 11.10 in the `ISum.aidl` file.
7. *Right-click* the `BoundService` application and *select* `Run As→Android Application`. *Ensure* that the appropriate emulator or device is running.

8. *Right-click* the `ConsumeBoundService` application and select `Run As→Android Application`.
9. *Enter* the two numeric digits for addition and click the **Add** button. Figure 11.9 shows the output of the `ConsumeBoundService` application:

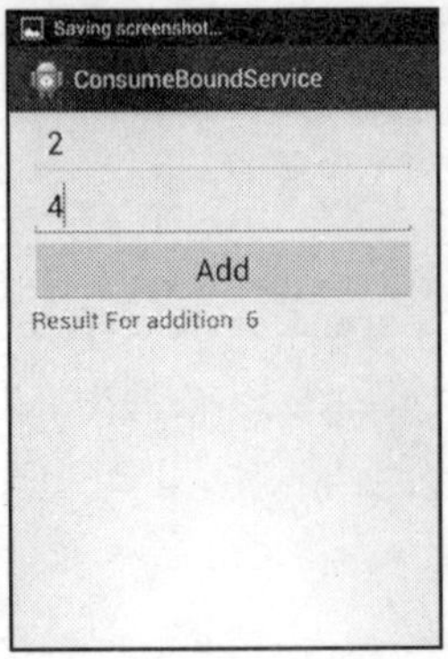

Figure 11.9: Showing the Output of the `ConsumeBoundService` Application

Summary

In this chapter, you have learned about threads and how to develop the applications in which UI threads are defined and implement the `AsyncTask` subclass to perform the tasks asynchronously.

This chapter has explained the impacts of services on an Android application. Typically, a service runs in the background of an application and provides interaction between Android application components, such as activity, intents, and broadcast receivers. In this chapter, you have learned that a service is used to enhance the application productivity and functionality. You come to know when your application needs to employ services. After this, you have learned about the different forms of a service. Regarding forms, a service can be a started service, a bound service, or a combination of both. It entirely depends on your application that which type of service is applicable to your application.

Next, the chapter has discussed the lifecycle of a service, wherein you have learned about the methods which are essential to start and end a service. Then you get acquainted with the `Service` class and its associated classes and interfaces. Having support of several classes equip this class with hundreds of methods. Therefore, the `Service` class is enough robust and powerful to deal with any kind of application.

A simple service application has been created in this chapter. The service application we have made is very simple and very capable to make you comfortable with the concept of services. After this, you have learned the use of `onCreate()`, `onStartCommand()`, and `onDestroy()` methods. You have also executed the application and got its output through the toast notification.

Finally, you have created the bound service to add two numbers and another application, using the service, prompted the users to enter two numbers.

Quick Revise

Q1. Which of the following statement best describes a service?

a. It's a foreground service

b. It's a background service

c. It's just like an Activity

d. It has a user interface

Ans. The correct option is d.

Q2. Which of the following property of an Android application forces to employ services?

a. The applications which possess short period processes

b. The applications that are meant for frequent user interactions

c. **The applications that require interprocess communication**

d. **The applications that neither download and nor upload the data**

Ans. The correct option is b.

Q3. Which of the following service represents communication between the components of two different applications?

a. **Start service**

b. **Bound service**

c. **Both start and bound services**

d. **Neither start nor bound service**

Ans. The correct option is b.

Q4. Which of the following method is called very first on execution of a service?

a. **onStart()**

b. **onStartCommand()**

c. **onCreate()**

d. **onBind()**

Ans. The correct option is c.

Q5. The number of interface(s) implemented by the Service class is/are:

a. **1**

b. **2**

c. **3**

d. **4**

Ans. The correct option is d.

Q6. Which of the following method is called just before the onDestroy() method?

a. **onCreate()**

b. **onBind()**

c. **onStart()**

d. **onStartCommand()**

Ans. The correct option is b.

Q7. Which of the following method is deprecated in API level 5 of Android system?

a. **onStartCommand()**

b. **onCreate()**

c. **onStart()**

d. **onBind()**

Ans. The correct option is a.

Q8. The number of classes to whom a Service class can extends is:

a. **2**

b. **3**

c. **4**

d. **5**

Ans. The correct option is a.

Q9. Which of the following class comprises the onCreate() method?

a. **Service**

b. **Context**

c. **ContextWrapper**

d. **Object**

Ans. The correct option is a.

Q10. A <service> element is declared inside which of the following element in the Androidmanifest.xml file?

a. **Inside <Intent> element**

b. **Inside <uses-sdk> element**

c. **Inside <application> element**

d. **Inside <activity> element**

Ans. The correct option is c.

Q11. Write the code to start a new thread.

```
public void start(View view) {
        Thread thread = new Thread() {
              @Override
              public void run() {
//Write the code for the task to be implemented in the run method
                    // After completing task go to UI Thread for onscreen update
                    runOnUiThread(new Runnable() {
                          @Override
                          public void run() {
//Write the required code
                          }
                    });
              }
        };
  // Don't forget to start the thread.
        thread.start();
  }
```

12

Bluetooth, NFC, and Wi-Fi

If you need an information on:	*See page:*
Working with Bluetooth	418
Creating an Application Using Bluetooth Functionality	422
Connecting the Devices Using Bluetooth for Data Transfer	428
Working with Bluetooth Low Energy	433
Working with NFC	434
Working with Wi-Fi	439

Nowadays, the most important task performed through mobile devices is transferring pictures, audios, and videos from one device to another. This can be achieved by connecting your device with a laptop through a charging cable. However, connecting two Android mobile devices for data transfer requires the wireless technology. The wireless technology allows users to transfer data within a specified range. In this chapter, you will learn about various wireless technologies such as Bluetooth, Near Field Communication (NFC), and Wi-Fi.

The range and speed within which the data can be transferred from one device to another varies for different technologies. This chapter explores the classes, interfaces, methods, constants, and fields required to implement each of these wireless technologies in an application. The data transfer is possible only if both the sending and receiving devices have the wireless technology through which the data is being transferred.

Working with Bluetooth

Bluetooth is a wireless technology standard that allows you to exchange data from one or more devices. In an Android platform, you can use the `android.bluetooth` package to implement the Bluetooth functionality in an application. In this section, you will learn to use the Bluetooth Application Programming Interface (API) to search for other Bluetooth devices, enable or disable Bluetooth device, and get the local Bluetooth device adapter.

You will learn to implement Classic Bluetooth and Bluetooth Low Energy (BLE). Generally, Android developers use the Classic Bluetooth to perform battery-intensive tasks. Some of these tasks are streaming and communicating between two or more Android devices. Android 4.3 introduced APIs for BLE. BLE is developed to reduce power consumption and cost of the devices while establishing the same communication range as done by the Classic Bluetooth devices. You will find the BLE devices in health care applications, sporting and fitness, and proximity sensing.

Let's first explore the Android Bluetooth APIs to learn how to perform the preceding listed tasks.

Exploring the Android Bluetooth APIs

The `android.bluetooth` package provides the classes and interfaces to implement the Bluetooth functionality on the applications, such as scanning for devices, pairing with the devices, and transferring data between devices. The Bluetooth API supports for both the Classic and BLE.

Let's now look at the interfaces and classes of the `android.bluetooth` package.

Table 12.1 lists the interfaces of the `android.bluetooth` package:

Table 12.1: Interfaces of the Android Bluetooth Package

Interfaces	Description
`BluetoothAdapter.LeScanCallback`	Refers to the interface used to send the LE scan results. This interface provides the onLeScan() method that accepts an instance of the remote device, a Received Signal Strength Indicator (RSSI) value for the remote device, and the scanned record of the byte[] type.
`BluetoothProfile`	Refers to the interface that must be implemented for the Bluetooth profiles.
`BluetoothProfile.ServiceListener`	Refers to the interface notifying the BluetoothProfile clients about their connection or disconnection with the service.

Table 12.2 describes the classes of the `android.bluetooth` package:

Table 12.2: Classes of the Android Bluetooth Package

Classes	Description
`BluetoothA2dp`	Specifies the public APIs to manage the Bluetooth A2DP profile.
`BluetoothAdapter`	Depicts the local Bluetooth device adapter. This class is the

Table 12.2: Classes of the Android Bluetooth Package

Classes	Description
	entry level for all Bluetooth interactions. With the help of this class, you can perform various Bluetooth device tasks, such as: • Identify the other Bluetooth devices • Fetch the results from the paired devices • Create an instance of a Bluetooth device with the help of the Media Access Control (MAC) address • Create an instance of the Bluetooth server socket to listen the notifications from other devices
`BluetoothAssignedNumbers`	Represents the number assigned to Bluetooth devices.
`BluetoothClass`	Refers to the class describing the general features and functionalities of a device.
`BluetoothClass.Device`	Refers to the class that defines the constants of the devices.
`BluetoothClass.Device.Major`	Refers to the class that defines the major constants of the devices.
`BluetoothClass.Service`	Refers to the class that defines all the constants of the `Service` class.
`BluetoothDevice`	Refers to the class that depicts the remote Bluetooth device. The instance of this class requests a connection with a remote Bluetooth device with the help of `BluetoothSocket` class. Through this class, you can fetch the required information, such as the name of the device.
`BluetoothGatt`	Defines the public APIs for the Bluetooth Generic Attribute (GATT) profile.
`BluetoothGattCallbacks`	Defines the abstract class used to implement the callback methods of the `BluetoothGatt` class.
`BluetoothGattCharacteristic`	Refers to the class that depicts the functionalities required to construct a GATT service, `BluetoothGattService`.
`BluetoothGattDescriptor`	Refers to the class that depicts the additional information and attributes of a GATT characteristic.
`BluetoothGattServer`	Defines the methods, fields, and attributes for the Bluetooth GATT profile server role.
`BluetoothGattServerCallback`	Refers to the abstract class implementing the callback methods of the `BluetoothGattServer` class.
`BluetoothGattService`	Refers to the class depicting the collection of Bluetooth GATT characteristics and referenced services.
`BluetoothHeadset`	Provides the methods and fields to control the Bluetooth Headset service.
`BluetoothHealth`	Provides the methods and fields for Bluetooth Health profile.
`BluetoothHealthAppConfiguration`	Provides the configuration details for the Bluetooth Health application, which is used along with the `BluetoothHealth` class.

Table 12.2: Classes of the Android Bluetooth Package

Classes	Description
BluetoothHealthCallback	Refers to the abstract class used to implement the callback methods of the BluetoothHealth class.
BluetoothManager	Refers to the high-level manager used to fetch an instance of the BluetoothAdapter class and handle the Bluetooth management.
BluetoothServerSocket	Allows you to create an instance of the Bluetooth listening socket.
BluetoothSocket	Allows you to create an instance of the connected Bluetooth socket. The instance of this class allows an application to transfer data to other Bluetooth devices through InputStream and OutputStream objects.

Permissions Required to Access Bluetooth

To access the functionalities of a Bluetooth in your application, use the BLUETOOTH permission in the AndroidManifest.xml file. By setting this permission, you will be able to request a connection, accept a connection, and transfer the data to other device.

To discover a device or modify Bluetooth settings, you should also define the BLUETOOTH_ADMIN permission in the AndroidManifest.xml file. By setting this permission, your application can discover local Bluetooth devices. Ensure that if you are setting the BLUETOOTH_ADMIN permission, you must also have the BLUETOOTH permission.

Use the following code snippet in the AndroidManifest.xml file:

```
<uses-permission android:name = "android.permission.BLUETOOTH"/>
<uses-permission android:name = "android.permission.BLUETOOTH_ADMIN"/>
```

Setting Up the Bluetooth for an Application

To use the Bluetooth in your application, you need to ensure that your device supports the Bluetooth functionality. If the device does not support the Bluetooth functionality, then disable the Bluetooth features in your application. If the device supports the Bluetooth but it is disabled, then request the user to enable Bluetooth without exiting the application. For this, you need to first retrieve the BluetoothAdapter object and then enable it.

To get the BluetoothAdapter object, use the getDefaultAdapter() method, which returns the adapter of the Bluetooth device. After retrieving the adapter, your application can interact with the Bluetooth functionality using the object of the BluetoothAdapter class. If the object returns null, the device does not support Bluetooth. Use the following code snippet to get the BluetoothAdapter object:

```
BluetoothAdapter mAdapter;
mAdapter = BluetoothAdapter.getDefaultAdapter();
if (mAdapter == null) {
textview1.append("Device not supported \n");
}
```

In the preceding code, the object mAdapter is created of the BluetoothAdapter class. The getDefaultAdapter() method is used to retrieve the adapter. Let's now learn to enable the Bluetooth.

The next step is to ensure that the Bluetooth is enabled. Invoke the isEnabled() method to ensure whether the Bluetooth is currently enable or not. If this method returns false, the Bluetooth is disabled. You can enable the Bluetooth by calling the startActivityForResult() method using the ACTION_REQUEST_ENABLE action Intent, as shown in the following code snippet:

```
private static final int REQUEST_ENABLE_BT = 0;
...
if (!mAdapter.isEnabled()) {
Intent enableBluetooth = new Intent(
```

```
BluetoothAdapter.ACTION_REQUEST_ENABLE);
startActivityForResult(enableBluetooth, REQUEST_ENABLE_BT);
```

On the execution of the preceding code, a dialog box appears, requesting the user to enable the Bluetooth service on the device. If the user clicks the Yes button, the Bluetooth service is enabled and the focus will be back to the application.

In the preceding code snippet, the `REQUEST_ENABLE_BT` is a constant value initialized as zero and is passed to the `startActivityForResult()` method. If the Bluetooth is enabled on your device, your activity receives the `RESULT_OK` result code. However, in case of an error, the result code sent to the activity is `RESULT_CANCELED`.

Once the Bluetooth functionality is enabled on a device, you need to find the available devices.

Identifying the Bluetooth-Enabled Devices

Using the `BluetoothAdapter` object, you can locate the remote Bluetooth devices. There are two ways to identify the devices, which are as follows:

- Device discovery
- Querying the list of paired devices

Device discovery is the process used to scan the local area of the Bluetooth-enabled devices and further request specific information about each device. However, the Bluetooth-enabled device will respond to the scanning process only if the device is currently enabled for discovery. If the device is discoverable, the required information will be shared by the device. This information can then be used to initiate a connection to the discovered device.

After establishing connection with the remote device, the user is requested to pair the device. Once the devices are paired, the basic information of the device is saved. You can retrieve the required information about the device using the Bluetooth APIs.

NOTE

In case of pairing, the two devices are aware of each other's existence and contain the shared key to be used for authentication purposes and are capable of maintaining an encrypted connection with each other. However, in case of connected, the two devices share an RFCOMM channel to transfer data with each other.

Before discovering the devices, you first need to query the set of paired devices.

Querying the Paired Devices

The Android Bluetooth API provides the `getBondedDevices()` method, which returns the set of Bluetooth devices depicting the paired devices. Use the following code to query all the paired devices and display their names using a `TextView` view:

```
if (mAdapter.isEnabled()) {
Set<BluetoothDevice> devices = mAdapter.getBondedDevices();
  for (BluetoothDevice device : devices) {
  textview1.append("\n  Found device:: " + device.getName()     + "Add: " +
device.getAddress()+"\n");
}
```

In the preceding code, the list of paired devices is retrieved by the `getBondedDevices()` method and stored in the `devices` object created using the `Set` interface. Each element of the `Set` interface will store the details of a paired device. The list of the paired devices is appended in the `TextView` view.

Discovering Devices

To start the process of discovering devices, invoke the `startDiscovery()` method. The process of identifying the Bluetooth-enabled devices is asynchronous and will return a `Boolean` value, specifying whether or not the discovery process has successfully started.

During the process of discovering devices, register a `BroadcastReceiver` object for your application. To identify whether a new device is discovered or not, the `ACTION_FOUND` intent is used. Use the following code to identify and register the broadcast when the devices are discovered:

```
private final BroadcastReceiver mBroadcastReceiver = new BroadcastReceiver() {
@Override
public void onReceive(Context context, Intent intent) {
String action = intent.getAction();
  if (BluetoothDevice.ACTION_FOUND.equals(action)) {
  BluetoothDevice bluetoothdevice =
intent.getParcelableExtra(BluetoothDevice.EXTRA_DEVICE);
  if (bluetoothdevice.getBondState() != BluetoothDevice.BOND_BONDED) {
  textview1.append("\n Device Name :  " + bluetoothdevice.getName() + "\n"
  + "Device Address " + bluetoothdevice.getAddress()+"\n");
  }
}
}
};
```

Let's create an application implementing the Bluetooth functionalities.

Creating an Application Using Bluetooth Functionality

In this section, you'll develop an application enabling the Bluetooth service, making your device discoverable, listing the paired devices, listing the new devices, and disabling the Bluetooth service. Let's create the `BluetoothDiscoveryAndPair` application to implement these functionalities:

1. *Create* an Android application named `BluetoothDiscoveryAndPair` and change the package name to `com.kogent.android.bluetoothdiscoveryandpair`. By default, the `MainActivity.java` and `activity_main.xml` files will be created.
2. *Replace* the code of the `MainActivity.java` source file with the code shown in Listing 12.1:

Listing 12.1: Displaying the Code of the `MainActivity.java` File

```
package com.kogent.android.bluetoothdiscoveryandpair;
import java.util.Set;
import android.os.Bundle;
import android.app.Activity;
import android.bluetooth.BluetoothAdapter;
import android.bluetooth.BluetoothDevice;
import android.content.BroadcastReceiver;
import android.content.Context;
import android.content.Intent;
import android.content.IntentFilter;
import android.view.View;
import android.widget.TextView;
import android.widget.Toast;
public class MainActivity extends Activity {
  private static final int REQUEST_ENABLE_BT = 0;
  private static final int REQUEST_DISCOVERABLE_BT = 0;
  TextView textview1;
  BluetoothAdapter mAdapter;
  @Override
  protected void onCreate(Bundle savedInstanceState) {
        super.onCreate(savedInstanceState);
        setContentView(R.layout.activity_main);
        textview1 = (TextView) findViewById(R.id.textview1);
        mAdapter = BluetoothAdapter.getDefaultAdapter();
        if (mAdapter == null) {
              textview1.append("Device not supported \n");
        } else if (mAdapter.isEnabled()) {
```

```
                String Deviceaddress = mAdapter.getAddress();
                String Devicename = mAdapter.getName();
textview1.append("\n This Device Name : " + Devicename + "\n Address " +
Deviceaddress + "\n");
        }
        IntentFilter filter = new IntentFilter(BluetoothDevice.ACTION_FOUND);
        this.registerReceiver(mBroadcastReceiver, filter);
    }
    public void turnOn(View view) {
        if (!mAdapter.isEnabled()) {
                Intent enableBluetooth = new Intent(
                BluetoothAdapter.ACTION_REQUEST_ENABLE);
                startActivityForResult(enableBluetooth, REQUEST_ENABLE_BT);
        }
    }
    public void discoverable(View view) {
        if (!mAdapter.isDiscovering()) {
    Toast.makeText(getApplicationContext(), "Making your device discoverable",
Toast.LENGTH_LONG);
                Intent enableBluetooth = new Intent(
                BluetoothAdapter.ACTION_REQUEST_DISCOVERABLE);
                startActivityForResult(enableBluetooth, REQUEST_DISCOVERABLE_BT);
        }
    }
    public void TurnOf(View view) {
        mAdapter.disable();
        Toast.makeText(getApplicationContext(), "Turning Bluetooth Off",
Toast.LENGTH_LONG);
    }
    public void paired(View view) {
        textview1.append("\nPaired Devices are: \n");
        GetBondedDevices();
    }
    public void newdevice(View view) {
        textview1.append("\n New Devices are: \n");
        mAdapter.startDiscovery();
}
    private void GetBondedDevices() {
        if (mAdapter == null) {
                textview1.append("\n Bluetooth NOT supported. Aborting.");
                return;
        } else {
                if (mAdapter.isEnabled()) {
                        Set<BluetoothDevice> devices = mAdapter.getBondedDevices();
                        for (BluetoothDevice device : devices) {
                                textview1.append("\n  Found device:: " +
device.getName()
                                                + "Add: " +
device.getAddress()+"\n");
```

```
                        }
                } else {
                        Intent enableBluetooth = new Intent(
                        BluetoothAdapter.ACTION_REQUEST_ENABLE);
                        startActivityForResult(enableBluetooth, REQUEST_ENABLE_BT);
                }
        }
  }
private final BroadcastReceiver mBroadcastReceiver = new BroadcastReceiver() {
        @Override
        public void onReceive(Context context, Intent intent) {
                String action = intent.getAction();
                if (BluetoothDevice.ACTION_FOUND.equals(action)) {
        BluetoothDevice bluetoothdevice =
intent.getParcelableExtra(BluetoothDevice.EXTRA_DEVICE);
                        if (bluetoothdevice.getBondState() !=
BluetoothDevice.BOND_BONDED) {
                        textview1.append("\n Device Name :  " +
bluetoothdevice.getName() + "\n"
                                + "Device Address " +
bluetoothdevice.getAddress()+"\n");
                        }
                }
        }
  };
  @Override
  protected void onDestroy() {
        super.onDestroy();
        // Unregister broadcast listeners
        this.unregisterReceiver(mBroadcastReceiver);
  }
}
```

In Listing 12.1, the `BluetoothAdapter` object is fetched and the required functionalities are included on the click event of the buttons.

3. *Replace* the code of the `activity_main.xml` file with the code shown in Listing 12.2:

Listing 12.2: Displaying the Code for the `activity_main.xml` File of the `BluetoothDiscoveryAndPair` Application

```
<LinearLayout
  xmlns:android="http://schemas.android.com/apk/res/android"
  xmlns:tools="http://schemas.android.com/tools"
  android:layout_width = "fill_parent"
  android:layout_height = "fill_parent"
  android:paddingLeft = "16dp"
  android:paddingRight = "16dp"
  android:orientation = "vertical" >

<Button
  android:id = "@+id/turn_on"
  android:layout_height = "wrap_content"
  android:layout_width = "fill_parent"
  android:onClick = "turnOn"
  android:text = "Turn On Bluetooth"/>
```

```
<Button
  android:id = "@+id/discoverable"
  android:layout_height = "wrap_content"
  android:layout_width = "fill_parent"
  android:onClick = "discoverable"
  android:text = "Make Your Device Discoverable"/>

<Button
  android:id = "@+id/turn_off"
  android:layout_height = "wrap_content"
  android:layout_width = "fill_parent"
  android:onClick = "TurnOf"
  android:text = "Turn Off Bluetooth"/>

<Button
  android:id = "@+id/paired"
  android:layout_height = "wrap_content"
  android:layout_width = "fill_parent"
  android:onClick = "paired"
  android:text = "List of Paired Devices"/>

<Button
  android:id = "@+id/new_device"
  android:layout_height = "wrap_content"
  android:layout_width = "fill_parent"
  android:onClick = "newdevice"
  android:text = "List of New Devices"/>

<ScrollView
  android:id = "@+id/textAreaScroller"
  android:layout_width = "fill_parent"
  android:layout_height = "fill_parent"
  android:layout_below = "@+id/button4" >

<TextView
  android:id = "@+id/textView1"
  android:layout_width = "wrap_content"
  android:layout_height = "wrap_content"
  android:layout_alignParentLeft = "true"
  android:layout_marginLeft = "18dp"
  android:text = "Showing Paired Devices:" />
</ScrollView>
</LinearLayout>
```

In Listing 12.2, five buttons are created and a `TextView` view is defined to display the list of the paired devices.

4. *Add* the following permission in the `AndroidManifest.xml` file:

```
<uses-permission android:name="android.permission.BLUETOOTH"/>
<uses-permission android:name="android.permission.BLUETOOTH_ADMIN"/>
```

5. *Right-click* the `BluetoothDiscoveryAndPair` application and select `Run As→Android Application`. Figure 12.1 shows the output of the application:

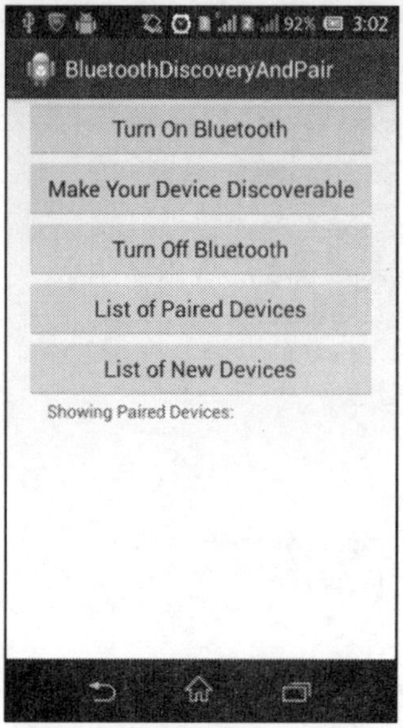

Figure 12.1: Showing the Output of the Application

6. *Click* the **Turn On Bluetooth** button (Figure 12.1); the dialog box appears as shown in Figure 12.2:

Figure 12.2: Showing the Dialog Box to Turn On Bluetooth

Click the **Allow** button to enable the Bluetooth on your device.

7. *Click* the **Make Your Device Discoverable** button to make your device discoverable. The dialog box appears as shown in Figure 12.3:

Figure 12.3: Displaying the Dialog Box to Make Your Device Visible

Click the **Yes** button and your device will be visible for data transfer through Bluetooth.

8. *Click* the **List of Paired Devices** button on the application to display the list of the paired devices, as shown in Figure 12.4:

Figure 12.4: Showing the List of Paired Devices

9. *Click* the **List of New Devices** button to display the list of new devices, as shown in Figure 12.5:

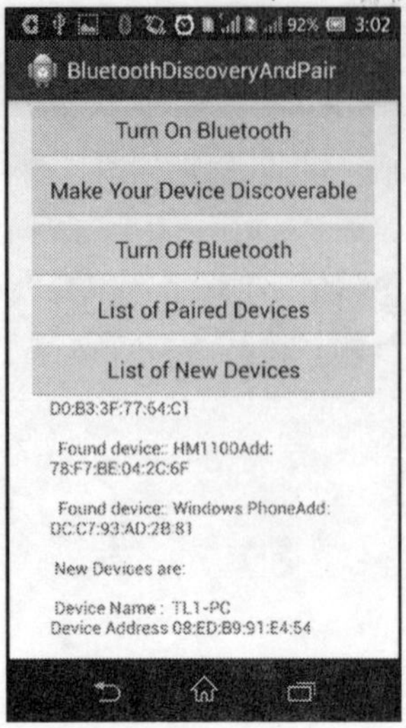

Figure 12.5: Displaying the List of New Devices

10. *Click* the **Turn Off Bluetooth** button to disable the Bluetooth services on your device.

Let's now learn to connect two devices to transfer the data between them.

Connecting the Devices Using Bluetooth for Data Transfer

In this section, you will learn to establish a connection between your applications running on two devices. For this, you need to develop the client and server applications. Among the two devices, one device should open a server socket and other should start the connection. The two devices are said to be connected to each other only if they have a connected `BluetoothSocket` socket on a single `RFCOMM` channel. After establishing the connection, each device can obtain input and output streams and start the data transferring process. The client and the server, each retrieve the `BluetoothSocket` object in different ways. The server will receive the socket when an incoming connection is accepted, whereas the client will receive it when it opens an RFCOMM channel to the server.

To learn how to send data from one device to another, let's create the applications named `BluetoothClient` and `BluetoothServer`.

Connecting as a Server

Perform the following steps to create the application named `BluetoothServer`:

1. *Create* the Bluetooth server named `BluetoothServer` and ensure that the package is `com.kogent.android.bluetoothserver`. By default, the `MainActivity.java` and `activity_main.xml` files are created.
2. *Replace* the code of the `MainActivity.java` of the `BluetoothServer` application with the code shown in Listing 12.3:

Listing 12.3: Showing the Code of the Java Source File of the `BluetoothServer` Application

```
package com.kogent.android.bluetoothserver;
import android.os.Bundle;
import android.app.Activity;
import android.view.View;
import java.io.DataInputStream;
import java.io.DataOutputStream;
import java.io.IOException;
import java.util.UUID;

import android.bluetooth.BluetoothAdapter;
```

```
import android.bluetooth.BluetoothServerSocket;
import android.bluetooth.BluetoothSocket;
import android.widget.TextView;
import android.widget.Toast;

public class MainActivity extends Activity {

   String dataReceived = null;
   BluetoothAdapter bluetoothAdapter = null;
   public void onCreate(Bundle savedInstanceState) {
          super.onCreate(savedInstanceState);
          setContentView(R.layout.activity_main);
   }
   public void Connect(View view) {
          bluetoothAdapter = BluetoothAdapter.getDefaultAdapter();
          Thread thread = new Thread() {
                  @Override
                  public void run() {
                          BluetoothServerSocket bluetoothServerSocket;
                          BluetoothSocket socket = null;
                          try {
bluetoothServerSocket =
bluetoothAdapter.listenUsingRfcommWithServiceRecord("helloService",
                                  UUID.fromString("00000101-0000-1000-8000-
00805E9B34FB "));
                          socket = bluetoothServerSocket.accept(); // block for
connect
                          dataReceived = "Accept connection";
DataInputStream inputStream = new DataInputStream(socket.getInputStream());
DataOutputStream outputStream = new DataOutputStream(socket.getOutputStream());
                          dataReceived = inputStream.readUTF(); // Read from client
                          outputStream.writeUTF("Echo " + dataReceived); // Send  to
client
                          runOnUiThread(new Runnable() {
                                  @Override
                                  public void run() {
TextView chat = (TextView) findViewById(R.id.Chat);
Toast.makeText(getApplicationContext(), " Chat Received from Client ",
Toast.LENGTH_LONG).show();
chat.append("\n Chat Received from Client:    " + dataReceived+"\n");
                                  }
                          });
                          bluetoothServerSocket.close();
                          socket.close();
                  } catch (IOException e) {
                          // TODO Auto-generated catch block
                          e.printStackTrace();
                  }
          }
   };
   // Don't forget to start the thread.
          thread.start();
   }
}
```

In Listing 12.3, the instance of the `BluetoothSocket` is created and the `getRemoteDevice()` method is used to retrieve the `BluetoothDevice` instance by passing the server MAC address. The `createRfcommSocketToServiceRecord()` function is used to get the Bluetooth server socket instance. Next, the `connect()` function is called to connect to the server. Also, the `DataInputStream` and `DataOutputStream` objects are used to read data from the server and write data to the server.

3. *Replace* the code of the `activity_main.xml` file with the code shown in Listing 12.4:

Listing 12.4: Displaying the Code for the XML Resource File

```
<?xml version="1.0" encoding="utf-8"?>
<LinearLayout xmlns:android="http://schemas.android.com/apk/res/android"
```

```
        android:layout_width="fill_parent"
        android:layout_height="fill_parent"
        android:orientation="vertical">

    <TextView
            android:layout_width="wrap_content"
            android:layout_height="wrap_content"
            android:gravity="center"
            android:text="Press Connect to Start Server"/>

    <Button
            android:id="@+id/Connect"
            android:layout_width="fill_parent"
            android:layout_height="wrap_content"
            android:onClick="Connect"
            android:text="Connect"/>

    <TextView
            android:id="@+id/Chat"
            android:layout_width="wrap_content"
            android:layout_height="wrap_content"
            android:gravity="center"/>
    </LinearLayout>
```

In Listing 12.4, two `TextView` and a `Button` views are added as the graphical layout of the application.

4. *Add* the required permissions in the `AndroidManifest.xml` file, as shown in the code below:

```
<uses-permission android:name="android.permission.BLUETOOTH" />
 <uses-permission android:name="android.permission.BLUETOOTH_ADMIN"/>
```

5. *Right-click* the application and select `Run As→Android Application`. Figure 12.6 shows the output of the `BluetoothServer` application:

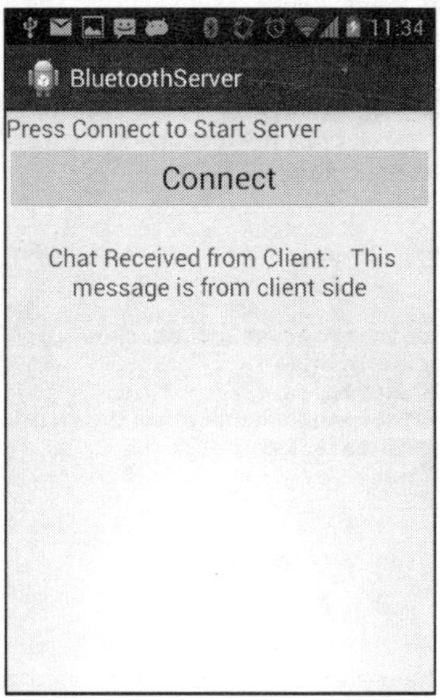

Figure 12.6: Showing the Output of the BluetoothServer Application

Connecting as a Client

Perform the following steps to create the client-side Bluetooth application:

1. *Create* the `BluetoothClient` application in which the `MainActivity.java` and `activity_main.xml` files are created by default. Ensure that the package is `com.kogent.android.bluetoothclient`.
2. *Replace* the code of the `MainActivity.java` file with the code shown in Listing 12.5:

Listing 12.5: Displaying the Code for the `MainActivity.java` File of the `BluetoothClient` Application

```
package com.kogent.android.bluetoothclient;
import android.os.Bundle;
import android.app.Activity;
import android.util.Log;
import android.view.View;
import java.io.DataInputStream;
import java.io.DataOutputStream;
import java.util.UUID;
import android.bluetooth.BluetoothAdapter;
import android.bluetooth.BluetoothDevice;
import android.bluetooth.BluetoothSocket;
import android.widget.EditText;
import android.widget.TextView;
import android.widget.Toast;
public class MainActivity extends Activity {
   String returnAcknowledgement = null;
   BluetoothAdapter mBluetoothAdapter = null;
   EditText textToSend;
   public void onCreate(Bundle savedInstanceState) {
         super.onCreate(savedInstanceState);
         setContentView(R.layout.activity_main);
   }
   public void Connect(View view) {
         textToSend = (EditText) findViewById(R.id.Text);
         mBluetoothAdapter = BluetoothAdapter.getDefaultAdapter();
         Thread thread = new Thread() {
                 @Override
                 public void run() {
                         BluetoothSocket bluetoothSocket = null;
                         // Client knows the server MAC address F0:08:F1:4E:60:FC
         BluetoothDevice bluetoothDevice =
mBluetoothAdapter.getRemoteDevice("F0:08:F1:4E:60:FC");
                         try {
                                 // UUID string name used by server
bluetoothSocket =
bluetoothDevice.createRfcommSocketToServiceRecord(UUID.fromString("00000101-0000-
1000-8000-00805E9B34FB "));
                                 // Cancel, discovery slows connection
                                 mBluetoothAdapter.cancelDiscovery();
                                 bluetoothSocket.connect();
                                 DataInputStream inputstream = new DataInputStream(
                                                 bluetoothSocket.getInputStream());
                                 DataOutputStream outputstream = new
DataOutputStream(
                                                 bluetoothSocket.getOutputStream());
                                 //Send to server
                                 outputstream.writeUTF(textToSend.getText().toString());
                                 //Read from server
                                 returnAcknowledgement = inputstream.readUTF();
                                 runOnUiThread(new Runnable() {
                                         @Override
                                         public void run() {
                                                 Toast.makeText(getApplicationContext(),
                                                                 "Executed after 10
seconds ",
   Toast.LENGTH_LONG).show();
                                                 TextView chat = (TextView)
findViewById(R.id.ReceivedFromServer);
chat.append("\n ECHO Received from
Client:    "
                         +
returnAcknowledgement + "\n");
                                         }
```

```
                        });
                } catch (Exception e) {
                        Log.e("DEBUG_TAG", "" + e.getStackTrace());
                }
            }
        };
        // Don't forget to start the thread.
        thread.start();
    }
}
```

In Listing 12.5, the `getRemoteDevice()` method is invoked by passing the MAC address of the server. Also, the `createRfcommSocketToServiceRecord()` method is used to fetch the `BluetoothSocket`. The `connect()` method is invoked to connect to the server socket. Further, the data is read from the server and written to the server.

3. *Replace* the code of the `activity_main.xml` file with the code shown in Listing 12.6:

Listing 12.6: Showing the Code for the Activity XML Resource File for the Client Application

```
<?xml version="1.0" encoding="utf-8"?>
<LinearLayout xmlns:android = "http://schemas.android.com/apk/res/android"
        android:layout_width = "fill_parent"
        android:layout_height = "fill_parent"
        android:orientation = "vertical" >

<TextView
        android:layout_width="wrap_content"
        android:layout_height="wrap_content"
        android:gravity="center"
        android:text="This Program have some requirement \n
        1. The server Android Device should be paired with client Android device  \n
        2. Server Bluetooth Mac ID should be entered in the program before running
i.e. in format F0:08:F1:4E:60:FC \n
        Press Enter the Text and press Send \n" />

<EditText
        android:id = "@+id/Text"
        android:layout_width = "fill_parent"
        android:layout_height = "wrap_content"
        android:textSize = "18sp"/>

<Button
        android:id="@+id/Connect"
        android:layout_width="fill_parent"
        android:layout_height="wrap_content"
        android:onClick="Connect"
        android:text="Send To server" />
<TextView
        android:id = "@+id/ReceivedFromServer"
        android:layout_width = "wrap_content"
        android:layout_height = "wrap_content"
        android:gravity = "center"/>

</LinearLayout>
```

In Listing 12.6, two `TextView`, an `EditText`, and a `Button` views are created. Also, add the required permissions to the `AndroidManifest.xml` file.

4. *Right-click* the `BluetoothClient` application and select `Run As→Android Application`. Figure 12.7 shows the output of the `BluetoothClient` application:

Figure 12.7: Showing the Output of the `BluetoothClient` Application

The basic requirements of the `BluetoothClient` application are:

1. The server Android device should be paired with the client Android device.
2. The server Bluetooth Mac ID should be entered in the application before execution. Ensure that the Mac ID is in the format F0:08:F1:4E:60:FC.

NOTE

You learned how to get MAC address of a Bluetooth device in the `BluetoothDiscoveryAndPair` application.

In Figure 12.7, when you enter text in the textbox and click the **Send to server** button, the output is sent to the server and the required message is displayed on the server.

Working with Bluetooth Low Energy

As discussed in the chapter, the Android 4.3 platform provides APIs that can be used to develop applications for the BLE devices. Some key BLE terms and concepts are as follows:

- **Generic Attribute Profile (GATT)**— Refers to a general specification used to send and receive data in the form of attributes over a BLE link.
- **Attribute Protocol (ATT)** — Is optimized to run on BLE devices and consumes fewer bytes. A unique identification number is assigned to each attribute and formatted as characteristics and services.
- **Characteristic**— Contains a single value and descriptors explaining the characteristic value. In other words, you can say that a characteristic is a type that is analogous to a class.
- **Descriptor**— Explains a characteristic value. For example, a descriptor specifies a human-readable description.
- **Service**— Refers to a collection of characteristics. To better understand, consider the example of a service called "Heart Rate Monitor," including the characteristics such as measuring the heart rate.

Similar to the implementation of Bluetooth, you need to set the permissions for BLE. Use the following permissions in the `AndroidManifest.xml` file:

```
<uses-permission android:name = "android.permission.BLUETOOTH"/>
<uses-permission android:name = "android.permission.BLUETOOTH_ADMIN"/>
```

To ensure the availability of your application to BLE-enabled devices, use the following permission in the manifest file:

```
<uses-feature android:name= "android.hardware.bluetooth_le" android:required=
"true"/>
```

Now, let's understand how to set up BLE. First, you need to ensure that BLE is supported on your device. Next, you need to enable Bluetooth. Let's discuss these steps in detail:

- **Get the BluetoothAdapter—** Use the following code snippet to get the adapter:

```
//Initializing Bluetooth adapter
final BluetoothManager bManager = (BluetoothManager)
getSystemService(Context.BLUETOOTH_SERVICE);
bManager = bManager.getAdapter();
```

- **Enable Bluetooth—** Use the following code snippet to ensure whether or not the Bluetooth is enabled in the BLE-supported devices:

```
private BluetoothAdapter bAdapter;
if (bAdapter = null || !bAdapter.isEnabled()) {
Intent enableIntent = new Intent(BluetoothAdapter.ACTION_REQUEST_ENABLE);
startActivityForResult(enableIntent, REQUEST_ENABLE_BT);
}
```

After getting the understanding of the Bluetooth functionalities, let's learn about NFC.

Working with NFC

NFC, as the name suggests, is a wireless communication done within the distance of 4 cm or less to establish connection between two or more devices. NFC allows you to share small chunks of data between two Android-supporting devices or between NFC tag and an Android-powered device.

Tags can be of different types, such as simple tags or complex tags. Simple tags provide read and write semantics to make the card read only. The complex tags provide math operations and cryptographic hardware to validate the access to an area. The data stored in the tags are written in various formats and are developed using the Android framework APIs around the NFC standard called NFC Data Exchange Format (NDEF).

Android device supporting NFC can perform the following three main modes of operations:

- **Reader/Writer mode—** Allows NFC device to read or write NFC tags
- **P2P mode—** Allows NFC device to transfer data with other NFC through Android Beam
- **Card Emulation mode—** Allows NFC device to act as an NFC card, which can be accessed by an external NFC reader

Exploring the Basics of NFC

In this section, you will learn to read data from an NFC tag and beam NDEF message from one NFC-supported device to the other. An application can read data from an NFC tag with the help of the tag dispatch system. This system first analyzes the identified NFC tags and then categorizes the tags appropriately followed by the execution of the application that requires the categorized data. You need to declare an intent filter in the application that needs to read the scanned data of the NFC tags.

To transfer the data between two Android devices through NFC, tap the devices physically together. This transfer of data is possible because of the Android Beam feature that pushes an NDEF message to the device. The data transfer through NFC is easier compared to the data transfer through other wireless technologies, such as Bluetooth, because you do not need to manually pair the devices. The NFC connection starts automatically when two or more devices are within the range of 4 cm. You can use the Android Beam feature through the NFC APIs to transfer data or messages between devices.

The Tag Dispatch System

When the screen is unlocked and the NFC is enabled in the **Settings** menu, the Android device can identify the NFC tags. When the device locates an NFC tag, the most appropriate activity manages the intent without prompting the users to select an action. As the devices read the NFC tags within a short range of distance, it is possible that the manual selection of an activity by a user would break the connection. Therefore, while developing an application, you should ensure that your activity manages the NFC tag, preventing the user to view the **Activity Chooser** dialog box.

To implement this, Android provides a special tag dispatch system that reads and parses the scanned NFC tags. Finally, send the scanned messages to the applications that are interested in such data. This is achieved through the following steps:

1. *Parse* the NFC tags and identify the Multi-Purpose Internet Mail Extensions (MIME) type or Uniform Resource Identifier (URI)
2. *Hide* the details of the MIME type or URI in an intent
3. *Start* the activity that is dependent on the intent

Let's first understand how NFC tags are mapped to the MIME types or URIs.

Mapping the NFC Tags to the MIME Types or URIs

The NFC tags are available in various forms according to the NDEF standard defined by the NFC forum. The NFC data is hidden inside the `NdefMessage` message that comprises one or more records, `NdefRecord`. You should create well-formed NDEF records according to the specifications required for the type of message you want to create. Android also supports various types of tags that do not contain NDEF data. You can use such tags through the classes defined in the `android.nfc.tech` package.

When the Android Beam-supported device reads an NFC tag containing the NDEF-formatted data, the device parses the message and identifies the MIME type or URI. For this, firstly, the `NdefRecord` is read, which resides within the `NdefMessage` message to identify the mechanism to be used to interpret the entire NDEF message. The `NdefRecord` record contains the following details:

- **3-bit type name format**— Specifies how to interpret the value of the variable length type field. Some of the TNF are `TNF_ABSOLUTE_URI`, `TNF_EMPTY`, `TNF_EXTERNAL_TYPE`, `TNF_MIME_MEDIA`, `TNF_UNCHANGED`, and `TNF_WELL_KNOWN`.
- **Variable length type**— Specifies the type of record. Ensure that if you use `TNF_WELL_KNOW` as TNF, then the value of the variable length type field should contain the Record Type Definition (RTD). Various valid RTDs are `RTD_ALTERNATIVE_CARRIER`, `RTD_HANDOVER_CARRIER`, `RTD_HANDOVER_REQUEST`, `RTD_HANDOVER_SELECT`, `RTD_SMART_POSTER`, `RTD_TEXT`, and `RTD_URI`.
- **Variable length id**— Specifies a unique identifier for the record. It is not essential to use this field; however, in case of uniquely identifying a tag, define the ID for it.
- **Variable length payload**— Defines the actual data to be read or written.

The tag dispatch system uses the TNF and type fields to map the MIME type or URI to the `NdefMessage` message. If the mapping is done successfully, the details of the TNF and type fields are encapsulated in the `ACTION_NDEF_DISCOVERED` intent along with the actual payload. If the system is unable to map the type, it encapsulates the details in the `ACTION_TECH_DISCOVERED` intent.

Table 12.3 presents the mapping of the TNFs with the intents:

Table 12.3: Supported TNFs and Their Mapping

TNF	Mapping
`TNF_ABSOULTE_URI`	Maps to the URI dependent on the type field
`TNF_EMPTY`	Falls back to the `ACTION_TECH_DISCOVERED` intent
`TNF_EXTERNAL_TYPE`	Maps to the URI dependent on the type field
`TNF_MIME_MEDIA`	Maps to the MIME type dependent on the type field
`TNF_UNCHANGED`	Falls back to the `ACTION_TECH_DISCOVERED` intent
`TNF_UNKNOWN`	Falls back to the `ACTION_TECH_DISCOVERED` intent
`TNF_WELL_KNOWN`	Maps to the `MIME` type or `URI` based on the `RTD` defined in the `type` field

Dispatching NFC Tags to an Application

When the NFC tag and its information are encapsulated in intent, the tag dispatch system sends the intent to an application for filtering the intent. As discussed earlier in the chapter, if more than one application can handle the intent, the **Activity Chooser** is displayed to the user to select the most appropriate activity. The three intents defined by the tag dispatch system are as follows:

- **ACTION_NDEF_DISCOVERED**– Starts an activity if the tag containing the NDEF payload is scanned and is of the defined type. This intent is the highest priority intent and allows the tag dispatch system to start the appropriate activity with this intent prior to any other intent.
- **ACTION_TECH_DISCOVERED**– Starts an activity if no activity is registered to handle the `ACTION_NDEF_DISCOVERED` intent.
- **ACTION_TAG_DISCOVERED**– Starts an activity if no activities are registered to handle the `ACTION_NDEF_DISCOVERED` and `ACTION_TECH_DISCOVERED` intents.

Setting NFC Access Permission in the Android Manifest

Similar to what you have done for Bluetooth, you need to set the following permission in the Android Manifest XML file to allow the access of the NFC hardware:

```
<uses-permission android:name = "android.permission.NFC" />
```

You should also specify the minimum Software Development Kit (SDK) version for your application as 10. This is because the API level 9 only supports limited tag dispatch APIs. Use the following code to set the SDK:

```
<uses-sdk android:minSdkVersion = "10"/>
```

You should also use the `<uses-feature/>` element to ensure that your application shows up in Google Play only for devices that have NFC hardware. Use the following code to implement the functionality:

```
<uses-feature android:name = "android.hardware.nfc" android:required = "true" />
```

Defining Filters for NFC Intents

When the NFC tag to be handled is scanned, your application can filter for one, two, or all three of the NFC intents in the Android manifest. Generally, you need to filter the `ACTION_NDEF_DISCOVERED` intent when your application starts. When no application filter is defined for the `ACTION_NDEF_DISCOVERED` intent, the `ACTION_TECH_DISCOVERED` intent is a fallback to the `ACTION_NDEF_DISCOVERED` intent.

To better understand, consider the example to filter the `ACTION_NDEF_DISCOVERED` intent for the URI http://oracle.com/index.html. Use the following code in the Android Manifest XML file:

```
<intent-filter>
<action android:name = "android.nfc.action.NDEF_DISCOVERED" />
<category android:name = "android.intent.category.DEFAULT"/>
<data android:scheme = "http"
   android:host = "oracle.com"
   android:pathPrefix = "/index.html" />
</intent-filter>
```

For the `ACTION_TAG_DISCOVERED` intent, you can define the intent filter using the following code:

```
<intent-filter>
<action android:name = "android.nfc.action.TAG_DISCOVERED"/>
</intent-filter>
```

Let's now create an application transferring messages between two Android-powered devices using NFC.

Developing an Application Using NFC

Let's create an application named `NFC` containing the `MainActivity.java` and `activity_main.xml` files. *Ensure* that the package name under which the `MainActivity` Java source file is defined is `com.kogent.android.nfc`.

Replace the code of the `MainActivity.java` file with the code shown in Listing 12.7:

Listing 12.7: Showing the Code to Implement the NFC Functionality

```
package com.kogent.android.nfc;
import java.nio.charset.Charset;
import android.nfc.NdefMessage;
import android.nfc.NdefRecord;
import android.nfc.NfcAdapter;
import android.nfc.NfcAdapter.CreateNdefMessageCallback;
import android.nfc.NfcAdapter.OnNdefPushCompleteCallback;
```

```
import android.nfc.NfcEvent;
import android.os.Bundle;
import android.os.Handler;
import android.os.Message;
import android.os.Parcelable;
import android.provider.Settings;
import android.app.Activity;
import android.content.Intent;
import android.text.format.Time;
import android.view.Menu;
import android.view.MenuInflater;
import android.view.MenuItem;
import android.widget.TextView;
import android.widget.Toast;

public class MainActivity extends Activity implements
        CreateNdefMessageCallback, OnNdefPushCompleteCallback {
    NfcAdapter adapter;
    TextView textView;
    private static final int MESSAGE_INFORMATION = 1;

    @Override
    protected void onCreate(Bundle savedInstanceState) {
        super.onCreate(savedInstanceState);
        setContentView(R.layout.activity_main);
        textView = (TextView) findViewById(R.id.textView1);
        adapter = NfcAdapter.getDefaultAdapter(this);
        if (adapter == null) {
            textView = (TextView) findViewById(R.id.textView1);
            textView.setText("NFC Device Not available ");
        }
        adapter.setNdefPushMessageCallback(this, this);
        adapter.setOnNdefPushCompleteCallback(this, this);
    }
    @Override
    public void onNdefPushComplete(NfcEvent event) {
        handler.obtainMessage(MESSAGE_INFORMATION).sendToTarget();
    }
    @Override
    public NdefMessage createNdefMessage(NfcEvent event) {
        String sendToDevice = ("This is a sample text send from device 1");
        NdefMessage msg = new NdefMessage(new NdefRecord[] { ndefRecord(
                "application/com.kogent.android.nfc",
sendToDevice.getBytes()) });
        return msg;
    }
    private final Handler handler = new Handler() {
        @Override
        public void handleMessage(Message msg) {
            switch (msg.what) {
            case MESSAGE_INFORMATION:
                Toast.makeText(getApplicationContext(), "Message
sent!",Toast.LENGTH_LONG).show();
                break;
            }
        }
    };
    @Override
    public void onResume() {
        super.onResume();
        // Check to see that the Activity started due to an Android Beam
        if (NfcAdapter.ACTION_NDEF_DISCOVERED.equals(getIntent().getAction())) {
            processIntent(getIntent());
        }
    }
```

```
    @Override
    public void onNewIntent(Intent intent) {
          setIntent(intent);
    }

    void processIntent(Intent intent) {
          Parcelable[] message =
intent.getParcelableArrayExtra(NfcAdapter.EXTRA_NDEF_MESSAGES);
          // only one message sent during the beam
          NdefMessage ndefMessage = (NdefMessage) message[0];
          // record 0 contains the MIME type, record 1 is the AAR, if present
          textView.setText(new String("Text Received from device 1:
"+ndefMessage.getRecords()[0].getPayload()));
    }

    public NdefRecord ndefRecord(String mimeType, byte[] payload) {
          byte[] mimeBytes = mimeType.getBytes(Charset.forName("US-ASCII"));
          NdefRecord ndefRecord = new NdefRecord(NdefRecord.TNF_MIME_MEDIA,
                        mimeBytes, new byte[0], payload);
          return ndefRecord;
    }
}
```

In Listing 12.7, `NdefRecord` record is created in the `ndefRecord()` method that creates the `MIME` type record. The `NdefMessage` message is created using the `createNdefMessage()` method. This message is pushed to the other device through the `onNdefPushComplete()` method.

Replace the code of the `activity_main.xml` file of the `NFC` application with the code shown in Listing 12.8:

Listing 12.8: Showing the Code to Design the Layout for the `NFC` Application

```
<?xml version="1.0" encoding="utf-8"?>
<LinearLayout xmlns:android="http://schemas.android.com/apk/res/android"
    android:layout_width="fill_parent"
    android:layout_height="fill_parent"
    android:orientation="vertical" >
   <TextView
    android:id="@+id/textView1"
    android:layout_width="fill_parent"
    android:layout_height="wrap_content"
    android:text="Ensure that Android Beam is enabled by turning it on in
        the system Settings (select the setting icon above), then place this device
up
        against another Android device that supports Android Beam to send a
        message"
    android:padding="10dp"
    android:textSize="18sp"
    />
</LinearLayout>
```

In Listing 12.8, a `TextView` view is created to display the instructions of enabling Android Beam to the users.

Modify the highlighted code shown in Listing 12.9 in the Android Manifest XML file of the `NFC` application:

Listing 12.9: Showing the Code for the `NFC` Manifest File

```
<?xml version="1.0" encoding="utf-8"?>
<manifest xmlns:android="http://schemas.android.com/apk/res/android"
    package="com.kogent.android.nfc"
    android:versionCode="1"
    android:versionName="1.0" >

    <uses-sdk
        android:minSdkVersion="14"
        android:targetSdkVersion="17" />

    <application
        android:allowBackup="true"
```

```
        android:icon="@drawable/ic_launcher"
        android:label="@string/app_name"
        android:theme="@style/AppTheme" >
        <activity
            android:name="com.kogent.android.nfc.MainActivity"
            android:label="@string/app_name" >
            <intent-filter>
                <action android:name="android.intent.action.MAIN" />
                <category android:name="android.intent.category.LAUNCHER" />
            </intent-filter>
            <intent-filter>
                <action android:name="android.nfc.action.NDEF_DISCOVERED" />
                <category android:name="android.intent.category.DEFAULT" />
                <data android:mimeType="application/com.kogent.android.nfc" />
            </intent-filter>
        </activity>
    </application>
<uses-permission android:name="android.permission.NFC" />
</manifest>
```

In Listing 12.9, the intent filter is defined for the `NDEF_DISCOVERED` intent.

Right-click the `NFC` application and select `Run As→Android Application`. Figure 12.8 shows the output of the `NFC` application:

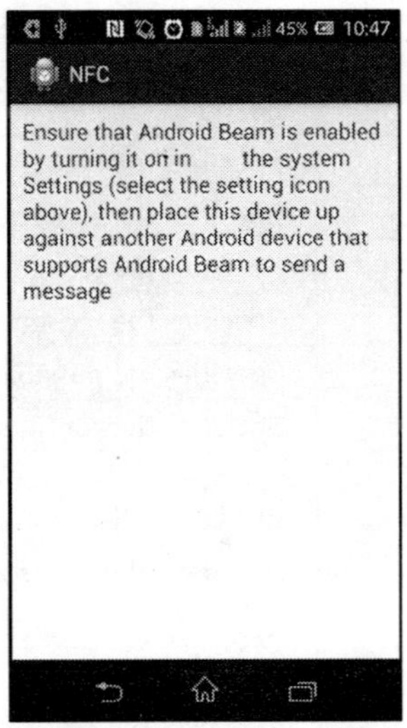

Figure 12.8: Displaying the Output of the NFC Application

Ensure that you have enabled the Android Beam by selecting the NFC option available under the `Settings` option on the device on which you are running the NFC application. Also, enable the Android Beam functionality on the other device. Tapping the two devices together will transfer the message from one device to another through the NFC.

Another way to transfer the data is Wi-Fi, which is discussed in detail in the next section.

Working with Wi-Fi

Similar to Bluetooth, the Android devices allow users to transfer data through Wi-Fi. Wi-Fi is a popular wireless technology used to exchange data or connect to the Internet wirelessly within the range of 20 meters. Android provides the APIs to discover and connect to the devices when each device supports Wi-Fi. The `android.net.wifi` package provides classes to manage the Wi-Fi functionality on the devices.

Let's first explore the APIs to be used to implement Wi-Fi functionality and then create an application using Wi-Fi.

Exploring the Wi-Fi APIs

The Android SDK provides the classes and methods within the `android.net.wifi` package. To implement the Wi-Fi functionality such as transferring data or retrieving the list of the Wi-Fi enabled devices, you should extend your class through the `BroadcastReceiver` class. Then, you should implement the functionality within the `onReceive()` method. Let's explore such classes and methods in this section.

Before exploring the Wi-Fi APIs, you should know about the permissions to be set in the Android Manifest file of the application to use the Wi-Fi function. The Wi-Fi APIs may require the following permissions:

- `ACCESS_WIFI_STATE`
- `CHANGE_WIFI_STATE`
- `CHANGE_WIFI_MULTICAST_STATE`

You need to use the following code in the Android Manifest XML file:

```
<uses-feature android:name = "android.hardware.wifi"/>
```

Table 12.4 presents the classes that can be used to implement Wi-Fi functionality in an application:

Table 12.4: Classes Defined in the `android.net.wifi` Package

Classes	Description
`ScanResult`	Describes the details of a detected access point
`WifiConfiguration`	Specifies the configured Wi-Fi network
`WifiConfiguration.AuthAlgorithm`	Specifies the authentication algorithm recognized as IEEE 802.11
`WifiConfiguration.GroupCipher`	Specifies the recognized group ciphers
`WifiConfiguration.KeyMgmt`	Specifies the recognized key management schemes
`WifiConfiguration.PairwiseCipher`	Specifies the recognized pairwise ciphers for WPA
`WifiConfiguration.Protocol`	Specifies the recognized security protocols
`WifiConfiguration.Status`	Specifies the possible status of a network configuration
`WifiEnterpriseConfig`	Specifies the configuration details for Wi-Fi
`WifiEnterpriseConfig.Eap`	Specifies the extensible authentication protocol method used in a Wi-Fi network
`WifiEnterpriseConfig.Phase2`	Specified the inner authentication method used in a Wi-Fi network
`WifiInfo`	Specifies whether or not a Wi-Fi connection is active
`WifiManager`	Provides the main API for handling and implementing all the Wi-Fi connectivity in an application
`WifiManager.MulticastLock`	Allows an application to receive Wi-Fi multicast packets of data
`WifiManager.WifiLock`	Allows an application to keep the Wi-Fi radio awake
`WpsInfo`	Specifies a class representing Wi-Fi-protected setup

From Table 12.4, it can be concluded that the `WifiManager` class plays an important role in implementing the Wi-Fi functionality in an application. This class allows to fetch the list of the configured networks, display any sort of change in the state of Wi-Fi networks, and enable or disable the Wi-Fi connectivity. Table 12.5 lists the important constants available in the `WifiManager` class:

Table 12.5: Noteworthy Constants Required for Implementing Wi-Fi Functionality through the `WifiManager` Class

Constants	Description
`ACTION_PICK_WIFI_NETWORK`	Allows to select a Wi-Fi network to establish a connection
`ACTION_REQUEST_SCAN_ALWAYS_AVAILABLE`	Allows a user to enable scans even if the Wi-Fi is disabled
`ERROR_AUTHENTICATING`	Depicts the error code if there exists a problem in authentication
`EXTRA_BSSID`	Refers to the lookup key that gives the Basic Service Set Identification (BSSID) of the access point to which the connection is established
`EXTRA_NETWORK_INFO`	Refers to the lookup key for the NetworkInfo object related with the Wi-Fi network
`WIFI_STATE_DISABLED`	Specifies that the Wi-Fi is disabled
`WIFI_STATE_DISABLING`	Specifies that the Wi-Fi is in the process of disabling
`WIFI_ENABLED`	Specifies that the Wi-Fi is enabled
`WIFI_STATE_ENABLING`	Specifies that the Wi-Fi is in the process of enabling
`WIFI_MODE_SCAN_ONLY`	Locks the Wi-Fi mode; the Wi-Fi will be activated, but will perform only the scanning process and reporting of the scanning results

Table 12.6 presents the important methods of the `WifiManager` class:

Table 12.6: Noteworthy Methods Required for Implementing Wi-Fi Functionality through the `WifiManager` Class

Method	Description
`addNetwork(WifiConfiguration conf)`	Adds the network description to a list of configured networks
`disableNetwork(int netId)`	Disables the configured network based on the passed argument
`enableNetwork(int netId, boolean disable)`	Enables the network by disabling the previously configured networks
`getScanResults()`	Returns the results of the last access point scanned
`getWifiState()`	Returns the Wi-Fi-enabled state of a device
`isWifiEnabled()`	Verifies whether Wi-Fi is enabled or disabled
`startScan()`	Starts the process of scanning the access points
`setWifiEnabled(boolean enable)`	Enables or disables the Wi-Fi network
`updateNetwork(WifiConfiguration conf)`	Updates the description of an already configured network

Let's now create an application implementing Wi-Fi functionalities.

Creating an Application Using Wi-Fi

In this section, you will create a `Wifi` application in which the Wi-Fi feature is enabled and disabled on the device. Also, the list of the Wi-Fi-enabled devices will be displayed on the click of a button. Create the Android application project named `Wifi`, and the following files will be added by default:

- `MainActivity.java`

- activity_main.xml
- AndroidManifest.xml

Ensure that the package name used for the Wifi application is com.kogent.android.wifi.

Replace the code of the MainActivity.java file with the code shown in Listing 12.10:

Listing 12.10: Displaying the Code to Implement the Wi-Fi Functionality

```
package com.kogent.android.wifi;

import java.util.List;

import android.os.Bundle;
import android.app.Activity;
import android.view.View;

import android.content.BroadcastReceiver;
import android.content.Context;
import android.content.Intent;
import android.content.IntentFilter;
import android.net.wifi.ScanResult;
import android.net.wifi.WifiManager;
import android.widget.ArrayAdapter;
import android.widget.ListView;
import android.widget.Toast;

public class MainActivity extends Activity {

    WifiManager wifimanager;
    WifiScanReceiver wifiscanReciever;
    String wifilist[];
    ListView listView;

    public void onCreate(Bundle savedInstanceState) {
       super.onCreate(savedInstanceState);
       setContentView(R.layout.activity_main);
       listView = (ListView)findViewById(R.id.listView1);
       wifiscanReciever = new WifiScanReceiver();
    }

    protected void onPause() {
       unregisterReceiver(wifiscanReciever);
       super.onPause();
    }

    protected void onResume() {
       registerReceiver(wifiscanReciever, new IntentFilter(
       WifiManager.SCAN_RESULTS_AVAILABLE_ACTION));
       super.onResume();
    }

    public void enable(View view) {
          wifimanager = (WifiManager) getSystemService(Context.WIFI_SERVICE);
          wifimanager.setWifiEnabled(true);
          Toast.makeText(getApplicationContext(), "Enabling Wifi",
Toast.LENGTH_LONG).show();
          }

    public void disable(View view) {
          wifimanager = (WifiManager) getSystemService(Context.WIFI_SERVICE);
          wifimanager.setWifiEnabled(false);
          Toast.makeText(getApplicationContext(), "Disabling Wifi",
Toast.LENGTH_LONG).show();
          }
```

```
    public void getlist(View view) {
      wifimanager = (WifiManager) getSystemService(Context.WIFI_SERVICE);
      wifimanager.startScan();
      Toast.makeText(getApplicationContext(), "Scanning  wifi please wait ...",
    Toast.LENGTH_LONG).show();
    }
          class WifiScanReceiver extends BroadcastReceiver {
             public void onReceive(Context c, Intent intent) {
                List<ScanResult> wifiList = wifimanager.getScanResults();
                wifilist = new String[wifiList.size()];
                for(int i = 0; i < wifiList.size(); i++){
                        wifilist[i] = ((wifiList.get(i)).toString()+"\n");
                }
                listView.setAdapter(new ArrayAdapter<String>(getApplicationContext(),
                android.R.layout.simple_list_item_1,wifilist));
             }
          }
      }
```

In Listing 12.10, the instance of the `WifiManager` class is created to manage the enable and disable of the Wi-Fi on the device on which the application will run. To scan the list of the available Wi-Fi devices, use the `WifiScanReceiver` class. The `enable()` and `disable()` methods allow the application to enable and disable the Wi-Fi, respectively. In Listing 12.10, the `WifiScanReceiver` class is extended to the `BroadcastReceiver` class.

Replace the code of the `activity_main.xml` file with the code shown in Listing 12.11:

Listing 12.11: Displaying the Code of the Interface of the Application Implementing Wi-Fi

```
    <?xml version="1.0" encoding="utf-8"?>
    <LinearLayout xmlns:android="http://schemas.android.com/apk/res/android"
        android:layout_width="fill_parent"
        android:layout_height="fill_parent"
        android:orientation="vertical" >

    <Button android:id="@+id/enable_wifi"
            android:layout_height="wrap_content"
            android:layout_width="fill_parent"
            android:onClick="enable"
            android:text="Enable Wifi"/>

    <Button android:id="@+id/enable_wifi"
            android:layout_height="wrap_content"
            android:layout_width="fill_parent"
            android:onClick="disable"
            android:text="Disble Wifi"/>

    <Button android:id="@+id/get_list"
            android:layout_height="wrap_content"
            android:layout_width="fill_parent"
            android:onClick="getlist"
            android:text="Get List of Wifi available"/>

    <ListView
          android:id="@+id/listView1"
          android:layout_width="match_parent"
          android:layout_height="wrap_content"
          android:background="@android:color/background_dark"
          android:listSelector="@android:color/darker_gray" >

    </ListView>
    </LinearLayout>
```

In Listing 12.11, three `Button` views and a `ListView` view are created.

Replace the code in the Android Manifest XML file of the `Wifi` application shown in Listing 12.12:

Listing 12.12: Displaying the Code of the Android Manifest XML File

```
<?xml version="1.0" encoding="utf-8"?>
<manifest xmlns:android="http://schemas.android.com/apk/res/android"
    package="com.kogent.android.wifi"
    android:versionCode="1"
    android:versionName="1.0" >

    <uses-sdk
        android:minSdkVersion="8"
        android:targetSdkVersion="17" />

    <application
        android:allowBackup="true"
        android:icon="@drawable/ic_launcher"
        android:label="@string/app_name"
        android:theme="@style/AppTheme" >
        <activity
            android:name="com.kogent.android.wifi.MainActivity"
            android:label="@string/app_name" >
            <intent-filter>
                <action android:name="android.intent.action.MAIN" />
                <category android:name="android.intent.category.LAUNCHER" />
            </intent-filter>
        </activity>
    </application>
   <uses-permission android:name="android.permission.ACCESS_WIFI_STATE" />
   <uses-permission android:name="android.permission.CHANGE_WIFI_STATE" />
</manifest>
```

In Listing 12.12, the `ACCESS_WIFI_STATE` and `CHANGE_WIFI_STATE` permissions are configured.

Right-click the `Wifi` application and *select* `Run As→Android Application`. Figure 12.9 shows the output of the `Wifi` application:

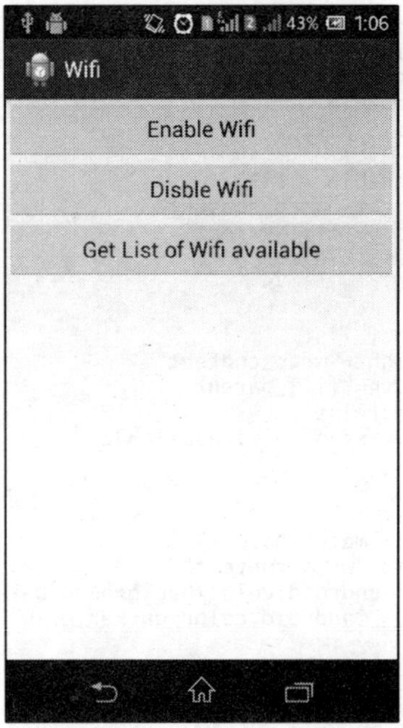

Figure 12.9: Showing the Output of the `Wifi` Application

Click the **Enable Wifi** button shown in Figure 12.9. The Toast message is displayed, as shown in Figure 12.10:

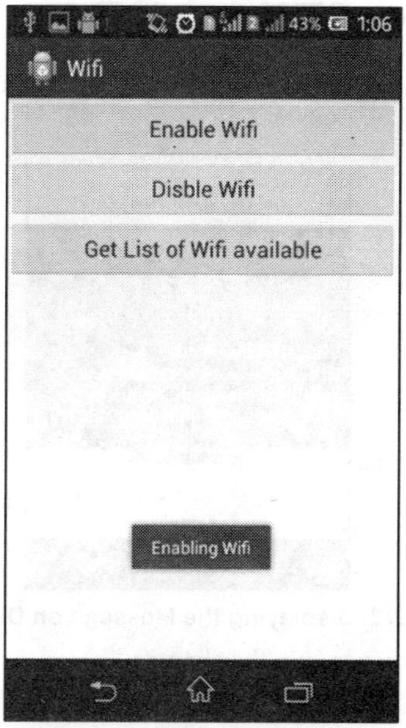

Figure 12.10: Displaying the Message Displayed on Enabling Wifi

Click the `Get List of Wifi available` button. During the scanning process, the Toast message is displayed as shown in Figure 12.11:

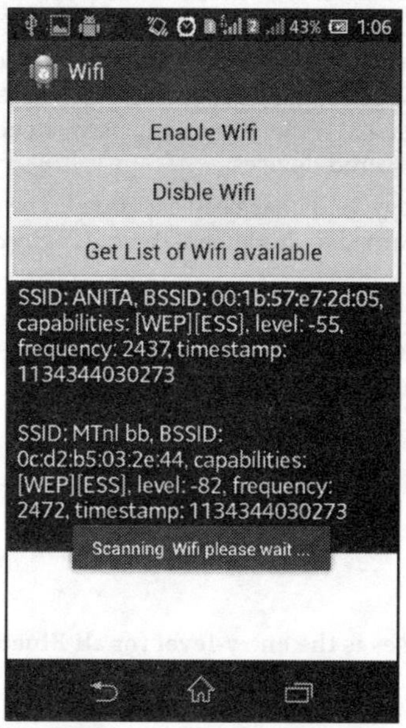

Figure 12.11: Displaying the Message on Scanning the Wifi-Enabled Devices

The list of the Wifi devices will be displayed to the users. *Click* the `Disable Wifi` button; the Toast message displayed is shown in Figure 12.12:

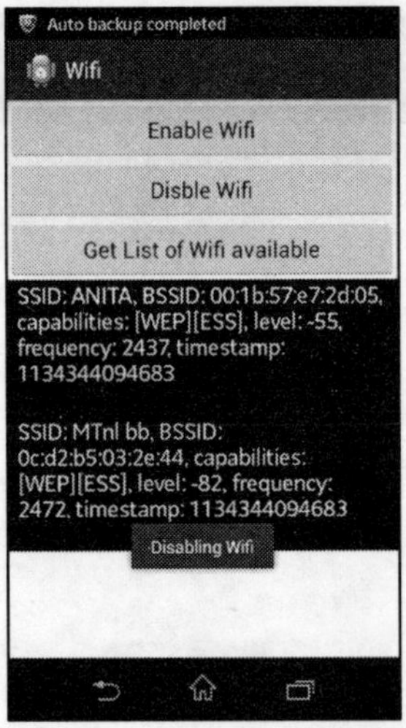

Figure 12.12: Displaying the Message on Disabling Wifi

Let's now summarize the key points covered in the chapter.

Summary

This chapter has broadly discussed about Bluetooth and BLE APIs used to get the default Bluetooth adapter, enable or disable the Bluetooth feature, list the paired devices, and prompt the users to make the device discoverable. Later, you have learned to create client and server sockets to transfer data from one device to another through Bluetooth. Apart from exploring the Bluetooth Android APIs, you also learned about implementing NFC functionality. The chapter has explained the process followed by the tag dispatch system to read, scan, parse, and push the NDEF data using Android Beam. It has also explored to define the filters for the NFC intents in the Android Manifest XML file. Then, you have developed the application to transfer the data using NFC between two Android-powered devices.

Toward the end, the wireless technology Wi-Fi has been explained. The classes, methods, and constants of the Wi-FI APIs were discussed. You have also learned to implement these APIs by creating an application using Wi-Fi.

Quick Revise

Q1. Which of the following interfaces notifies the BluetoothProfile clients about their connection or disconnection with the service?

a. **LeScanCallback**

b. **BluetoothProfile**

c. **ServiceListener**

d. **BluetoothAdapter**

Ans. The correct option is b.

Q2. Which of the following classes is the entry-level for all Bluetooth interaction?

a. **BluetoothAdapter**

b. **BluetoothA2dp**

c. **BluetoothClass**

d. **BluetoothDevice**

Ans. The correct option is a.

Q3. Write the code to get the default Bluetooth adapter.

Ans.

```
BluetoothAdapter mAdapter;
mAdapter = BluetoothAdapter.getDefaultAdapter();
if (mAdapter == null) {
//Code to be implemented
}
```

Q4. In case of an error in implementing the Bluetooth functionality, the result code is sent to which of the following activities?

a. REQUEST_ENABLE_BT

b. RESULT_CANCELED

c. RESULT_OK

d. ACTION_REQUEST_ENABLE

Ans. The correct option is b.

Q5. Which of the following methods returns the set of Bluetooth devices depicting the paired devices?

a. getName()

b. getAddress()

c. getBondedDevices()

d. None of these

Ans. The correct option is c.

Q6. Write the code to query the paired devices.

Ans.

```
if (mAdapter.isEnabled()) {
Set<BluetoothDevice> devices = mAdapter.getBondedDevices();
  for (BluetoothDevice device : devices) {
//Code to be implemented
}
```

Q7. Which of the following methods is used to get the Bluetooth server socket instance?

a. createRfcommSocketToServiceRecord()

b. connect()

c. getRemoteDevice()

d. getBondedDevices()

Ans. The correct option is a.

Q8. Which of the following explains the characteristic value of a Bluetooth device?

a. Descriptor

b. Characteristic

c. Service

d. ATT

Ans. The correct option is a.

Q9. Which of the following modes allows the NFC device to transfer data with other NFC through Android Beam?

a. Reader/Writer mode

b. P2P mode

c. Card emulation mode

d. None of these

Ans. The correct option is b.

Q10. Which of the following intents starts an activity if no activity is registered to handle the `ACTION_NDEF_DISCOVERED` intent?

a. **ACTION_NDEF_DISCOVERED**

b. **ACTION_TECH_DISCOVERED**

c. **ACTION_TAG_DISCOVERED**

d. **None of these**

Ans. The correct option is b.

Q11. Write the permissions to be set in the Android Manifest file to access NFC.

Ans. <uses-permission android:name = "android.permission.NFC" />

Q12. Which of the following classes of the Wi-Fi package specifies the configuration details for Wi-Fi?

a. **WifiEnterpriseConfig**

b. **WifiEnterpriseConfig.Eap**

c. **WifiEnterpriseConfig.Phase2**

d. **WifiInfo**

Ans. The correct option is a.

Q13. Which of the following methods returns the Wi-Fi-enabled state of a device?

a. **addNetwork()**

b. **getWifiState()**

c. **isWifiEnabled()**

d. **getScanResults()**

Ans. The correct option is b.

13

Telephony and SMS

If you need an information on:	See page:
Handling Telephony	450
Handling SMS	460
Sending SMS Using Intent	463

In the present era, when a customer goes to purchase a mobile phone, the basic feature that he/she would be demanding is telephony and messaging capabilities. The basic applications in all mobile phones are making an outgoing call, receiving an incoming call, and sending Short Message Service (SMS) text. All users, irrespective of their age group, are aware with how to make and receive calls and send or receive SMS. Android-supported devices also provide the built-in telephony and SMS applications with the help of which the users can make and receive calls and send and receive SMS.

Android Application Programming Interfaces (APIs) provide various classes that handle telephony and messaging features in mobile devices. Some of these are `TelephonyManager`, `PhoneStateListener`, and `SmsManager`. The `TelephonyManager` class provides direct access to various types of phone properties, such as phone type, network-related details, Subscriber Identity Module (SIM) details, or data state details. The `PhoneStateListener` class is a listener class that helps in monitoring the changes in different telephony states on mobile devices, such as available service state or signal strength. The `SmsManager` class is used to send text messages.

In this chapter, you learn how to develop Android applications that handle telephony and SMS. First, you learn about the use of the `TelephonyManager` class to create Android applications, which include how to display phone information, outgoing call application, and incoming call application. Then, you learn how to handle SMS text messaging using different classes, such as `SmsManager` and `Intent`.

Let's start with handling telephony in Android.

Handling Telephony

In Android development, the `TelephonyManager` class is used to manage the telephony services on the mobile devices. It provides various methods to determine mobile-device-related information, such as phone type, network operator, and call states. To instantiate the `TelephonyManager` class, you require the `getSystemService()` method that takes a parameter of telephone service context, as shown in the following code snippet:

```
TelephonyManager  telman=(TelephonyManager)getSystemService(Context.TELEPHONY_SERVICE);
```

The `TelephonyManager` class allows direct access to various types of phone properties, such as device, network, SIM, and data state details, as shown in the following code snippet:

```
TelephonyManager  telman=(TelephonyManager)getSystemService(Context.TELEPHONY_SERVICE);

String IMEI_no = telman.getDeviceId();
String SIM_serial_no = telman.getSimSerialNumber();
String network_country_ISO = telman.getNetworkCountryIso();
String SIM_country_ISO = telman.getSimCountryIso();
String software_version = telman.getDeviceSoftwareVersion();
String voice_mail_number = telman.getVoiceMailNumber();
```

The `TelephonyManager` class also allows you to know the phone type, which can be either Global System for Mobile Communications (GSM) or Code Division Multiple Access (CDMA) or Session Initiation Protocol (SIP), as shown in the following code snippet:

```
//Get the phone type
   String strphoneType="";
   int phoneType=telman.getPhoneType();
   switch (phoneType)
       {
         case (TelephonyManager.PHONE_TYPE_CDMA):
         strphoneType="CDMA";
         break;
         case (TelephonyManager.PHONE_TYPE_GSM):
         strphoneType="GSM";
         break;
         case (TelephonyManager.PHONE_TYPE_NONE):
         strphoneType="NONE";
         break;
       }
```

Table 13.1 presents some noteworthy methods of the `TelephonyManager` class:

Table 13.1: Noteworthy Methods of the `TelephonyManager` Class

Method	Description
`getAllCellInfo()`	Specifies a method that returns a list of cell information from all radios on the device
`getCallState()`	Specifies a method that returns a number, which indicates the call state on the device
`getCellLocation()`	Specifies a method that returns an object of `CellLocation`, which indicates the current location of the device
`getDataActivity()`	Specifies a method that returns a number, which indicates the type of activity on a data connection
`getDataState()`	Specifies a method that returns a number, which indicates the current data connection state
`getDeviceId()`	Specifies a method that returns a string, which indicates the unique device ID; for example, the International Mobile Station Equipment Identity (IMEI) for GSM and the Mobile Equipment IDentifier (MEID) or Electronic Serial Number (ESN) for CDMA phones
`getDeviceSoftwareVersion()`	Specifies a method that returns a string, which indicates the software version number for the device
`getMmsUAProfUrl()`	Specifies a method that returns a string, which indicates the Multimedia Messaging Service (MMS) user agent profile Uniform Resource Locator (URL)
`getMmsUserAgent()`	Specifies a method that returns a string, which indicates the MMS user agent
`getNetworkCountryIso()`	Specifies a method that returns a string, which indicates the International Organization for Standardization (ISO) country code
`getNetworkOperator()`	Specifies a method that returns a string, which indicates the numeric name of the current registered operator
`getNetworkOperatorName()`	Specifies a method that returns a string, which indicates the alphabetic name of the current registered operator
`getNetworkType()`	Specifies a method that returns a number, which indicates the network type for the current data connection
`getPhoneType()`	Specifies a method that returns a number, which indicates the phone type of the device
`getSimCountryIso()`	Specifies a method that returns a string, which indicates the ISO country code
`getSimOperator()`	Specifies a method that returns a string, which indicates the Mobile Country Code + Mobile Network Code (MCC+MNC) of the provider of the SIM
`getSimOperatorName()`	Specifies a method that returns a string, which indicates the Service Provider Name (SPN)
`getSimSerialNumber()`	Specifies a method that returns a string, which indicates the serial number of the SIM
`getSimState()`	Specifies a method that returns a number, which indicates the state of SIM card inserted in the device
`getSubscriberId()`	Specifies a method that returns a string, which indicates the unique subscriber ID
`getVoiceMailAlphaTag()`	Specifies a method that returns a string, which indicates the alphabetic identifier associated with the voice mail number
`getVoiceMailNumber()`	Specifies a method that returns a string, which indicates the voice mail number
`isNetworkRoaming()`	Specifies a method that returns a boolean value to determine whether the device is having roaming on the current network

Table 13.1: Noteworthy Methods of the TelephonyManager Class	
Method	**Description**
`listen(PhoneStateListener listener, int events)`	Specifies a method that returns a listener object that receives notifications when changes take place in specified telephony states

The `TelephonyManager` class also provides the various constant values listed in Table 13.2:

Table 13.2: Noteworthy Constant Values of the TelephonyManager Class	
Constant	**Description**
`ACTION_PHONE_STATE_CHANGED`	Specifies a string value, which indicates that the call state on the device has changed
`ACTION_RESPOND_VIA_MESSAGE`	Specifies a string value, which indicates that a user has opted to give response through message during an incoming call
`CALL_STATE_IDLE`	Specifies a number that indicates the call state as idle
`CALL_STATE_OFFHOOK`	Specifies a number that indicates the call state as off hook
`CALL_STATE_RINGING`	Specifies a number that indicates the call state as ringing
`DATA_CONNECTED`	Specifies a number that indicates the data connection state is connected
`DATA_CONNECTING`	Specifies a number that indicates the data connection state is currently setting up a data connection
`DATA_DISCONNECTED`	Specifies a number that indicates the data connection state is disconnected
`DATA_SUSPENDED`	Specifies a number that indicates the data connection state is suspended
`NETWORK_TYPE_CDMA`	Specifies a number that indicates the current network is CDMA, either IS95A or IS95B
`NETWORK_TYPE_GPRS`	Specifies a number that indicates the current network is GPRS
`NETWORK_TYPE_HSDPA`	Specifies a number that indicates the current network is HSDPA
`NETWORK_TYPE_HSPA`	Specifies a number that indicates the current network is HSPA
`NETWORK_TYPE_HSUPA`	Specifies a number that indicates the current network is HSUPA
`NETWORK_TYPE_UNKNOWN`	Specifies a number that indicates the network type is unknown
`PHONE_TYPE_CDMA`	Specifies a number that indicates the phone type is CDMA
`PHONE_TYPE_GSM`	Specifies a number that indicates the phone type is GSM
`PHONE_TYPE_NONE`	Specifies a number that indicates the phone type is none
`PHONE_TYPE_SIP`	Specifies a number that indicates the phone type is SIP
`SIM_STATE_ABSENT`	Specifies a number that indicates the SIM card state as not available
`SIM_STATE_NETWORK_LOCKED`	Specifies a number that indicates the SIM card state as locked and requires a network PIN to unlock
`SIM_STATE_PIN_REQUIRED`	Specifies a number that indicates the SIM card state as locked and requires the user's SIM PIN to unlock
`SIM_STATE_PUK_REQUIRED`	Specifies a number that indicates the SIM card state as locked and requires the user's SIM PUK to unlock
`SIM_STATE_READY`	Specifies a number that indicates the SIM card state as ready

Table 13.2: Noteworthy Constant Values of the `TelephonyManager` Class

Constant	Description
SIM_STATE_UNKNOWN	Specifies a number that indicates the SIM card state as unknown

It should be noted that some telephony information is permission protected. Therefore, to access such telephony information, you should also configure the `READ_PHONE_STATE` uses permission in the `AndroidManifest.xml` file, as shown in the following code snippet:

```
<uses-permission android:name="android.permission.READ_PHONE_STATE"/>
```

Displaying Phone Information Application

In this section, you learn to create an Android application that will display your phone details. Let's create an application named `PhoneInformation` to learn how to display phone details.

Perform the following steps to create the `PhoneInformation` application:

1. *Create* the `PhoneInformation` application in the Eclipse IDE under the `com.kogent.android.phoneinformation` package.
2. *Replace* the code of the `activity_main.xml` file in the **/res/layout** folder, with the code shown in Listing 13.1:

Listing 13.1: Showing the Code of the `activity_main.xml` File in the `PhoneInformation` Application

```
<LinearLayout xmlns:android="http://schemas.android.com/apk/res/android"
    xmlns:tools="http://schemas.android.com/tools"
   android:layout_width="fill_parent"
    android:layout_height="fill_parent"
    android:paddingLeft="16dp"
    android:paddingRight="16dp"
    android:orientation="vertical" >

   <TextView
        android:id="@+id/textView"
        android:layout_width="fill_parent"
        android:layout_height="wrap_content"
        android:text="This application gives you information about call state of your
phone. Call from other phone to this phone and see the result on toast message" />

</LinearLayout>
```

In Listing 13.1, a relative layout is created with a text view.

3. *Replace* the code of the `MainActivity.java` file located in the **/src** folder, with the code shown in Listing 13.2:

Listing 13.2: Showing the Code of the `MainActivity.java` File in the `PhoneInformation` Application

```
package com.kogent.android.phoneinformation;

import android.os.Bundle;
import android.app.Activity;
import android.content.Context;
import android.telephony.TelephonyManager;
import android.widget.TextView;

public class MainActivity extends Activity {
     TextView textView;
     String sPhoneTrasmitionType;
      @Override
      protected void onCreate(Bundle savedInstanceState) {
          super.onCreate(savedInstanceState);
          setContentView(R.layout.activity_main);

          textView=(TextView)findViewById(R.id.textView);
```

```
        TelephonyManager
telephonymanager=(TelephonyManager)getSystemService(Context.TELEPHONY_SERVICE);

        textView.append("\n DeviceId= "+telephonymanager.getDeviceId());
        textView.append("\n NetworkRoaming= "+telephonymanager.isNetworkRoaming());
        textView.append("\n SimSerialNumber= "+telephonymanager.getSimSerialNumber());
        textView.append("\n NetworkCountryIs=
"+telephonymanager.getNetworkCountryIso());
        textView.append("\n SimCountryIso= "+telephonymanager.getSimCountryIso());
        textView.append("\n DeviceSoftwareVersion=
"+telephonymanager.getDeviceSoftwareVersion());
        textView.append("\n CellLocation= "+telephonymanager.getCellLocation());
        int iPhoneTrasmitionType=telephonymanager.getPhoneType();

             switch (iPhoneTrasmitionType)
        {
              case (TelephonyManager.PHONE_TYPE_CDMA):
                   sPhoneTrasmitionType="CDMA";
                         break;
              case (TelephonyManager.PHONE_TYPE_GSM):
                   sPhoneTrasmitionType="GSM";
                         break;
              case (TelephonyManager.PHONE_TYPE_NONE):
                   sPhoneTrasmitionType="NONE";
                         break;
        }

             textView.append("\n PhoneTrasmitionType= "+sPhoneTrasmitionType);

    }

}
```

In Listing 13.2, the MainActivity class contains the onCreate() method in which the TelephonyManager class is initialized using the getSystemService() method. Then, the getDeviceId(), getSimSerialNumber(), getNetworkCountryIso(), getSimCountryIso(), getDeviceSoftwareVersion(), and getCellLocation() methods are used to get the IMEI number, SIM serial number, ISO network of country, ISE SIM of country, software version of device, and cell location, respectively. The getPhoneType() method is invoked to get the phone type. In addition, the isNetworkRoaming() method is used to determine whether the phone is in roaming or not. Finally, all the phone-related information is displayed on a text view.

4. *Replace* the code of the `AndroidManifest.xml` file, with the code shown in Listing 13.3:

Listing 13.3: Showing the Code of the `AndroidManifest.xml` File in the `PhoneInformation` Application

```
<?xml version="1.0" encoding="utf-8"?>
<manifest xmlns:android="http://schemas.android.com/apk/res/android"
    package="com.kogent.android.phoneinformation"
    android:versionCode="1"
    android:versionName="1.0" >

    <uses-sdk
        android:minSdkVersion="8"
        android:targetSdkVersion="17" />

    <application
        android:allowBackup="true"
        android:icon="@drawable/ic_launcher"
        android:label="@string/app_name"
        android:theme="@style/AppTheme" >
        <activity
            android:name="com.kogent.android.phoneinformation.MainActivity"
            android:label="@string/app_name" >
            <intent-filter>
                <action android:name="android.intent.action.MAIN" />

                <category android:name="android.intent.category.LAUNCHER" />
```

```
            </intent-filter>
        </activity>
    </application>
<uses-permission android:name="android.permission.READ_PHONE_STATE"/>
<uses-permission android:name="android.permission.ACCESS_COARSE_LOCATION"/>

</manifest>
```

In Listing 13.3, besides the default configuration, the `READ_PHONE_STATE` and `ACCESS_COARSE_LOCATION` uses permissions are also configured.

5. *Execute* the `PhoneInformation` application. Figure 13.1 shows the output of the `PhoneInformation` application:

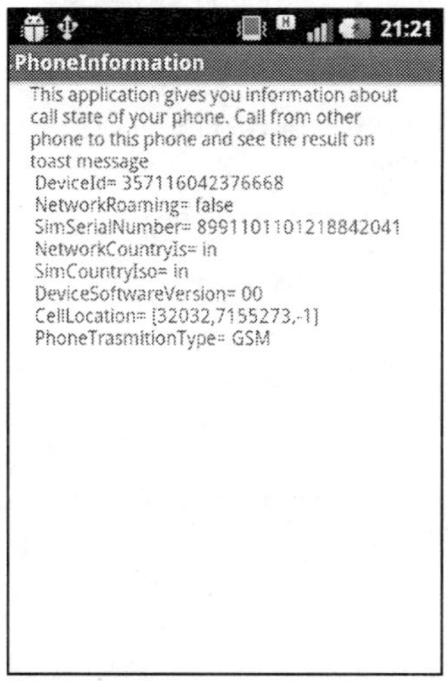

Figure 13.1: Showing the Output of the `PhoneInformation` Application

Let's learn about receiving incoming phone calls.

Receiving Phone Calls Application

The `TelephonyManager` class also provides the `listen()` method (Table 13.1), which takes two parameters, one of the `PhoneStateListener` object and the other of an event number. The `PhoneStateListener` object is a listener object, which helps in monitoring the changes in different telephony states on mobile devices, such as service state, signal strength, or message waiting indicator. Let's create an application, named `IncomingCall`, to display how to receive incoming phone calls.

Perform the following steps to create the `IncomingCall` application:

1. *Create* the `IncomingCall` application in the Eclipse IDE under the `com.kogent.android.incomingcall` package.
2. *Replace* the code of the `MainActivity.java` file located in the **/src** folder, with the code shown in Listing 13.4:

Listing 13.4: Displaying the Code of the `MainActivity.java` File in the `IncomingCall` Application

```
package com.kogent.android.incomingcall;

import android.os.Bundle;
import android.app.Activity;
import android.content.Context;
import android.telephony.PhoneStateListener;
import android.telephony.TelephonyManager;
import android.widget.Toast;

public class MainActivity extends Activity {
```

```
    @Override
    protected void onCreate(Bundle savedInstanceState) {
     super.onCreate(savedInstanceState);
     setContentView(R.layout.activity_main);
     TelephonyManager TelephonyMgr = (TelephonyManager)
getSystemService(Context.TELEPHONY_SERVICE);
     TelephonyMgr.listen(new TeleListener(),
        PhoneStateListener.LISTEN_CALL_STATE);
    }
    class TeleListener extends PhoneStateListener {
     public void onCallStateChanged(int state, String incomingNumber) {
      super.onCallStateChanged(state, incomingNumber);
      switch (state) {
      case TelephonyManager.CALL_STATE_IDLE:
       // CALL_STATE_IDLE;
       Toast.makeText(getApplicationContext(), "CALL_STATE_IDLE",
         Toast.LENGTH_LONG).show();
       break;
      case TelephonyManager.CALL_STATE_OFFHOOK:
       // CALL_STATE_OFFHOOK;
       Toast.makeText(getApplicationContext(), "CALL_STATE_OFFHOOK",
         Toast.LENGTH_LONG).show();
       break;
      case TelephonyManager.CALL_STATE_RINGING:
       // CALL_STATE_RINGING
       Toast.makeText(getApplicationContext(), incomingNumber,
         Toast.LENGTH_LONG).show();
       Toast.makeText(getApplicationContext(), "CALL_STATE_RINGING",
         Toast.LENGTH_LONG).show();
       break;
      default:
       break;
      }
     }

    }
   }
```

In Listing 13.4, the `MainActivity` class contains the `onCreate()` method in which the `TelephonyManager` class is initialized using the `getSystemService()` method. Then, the `listen()` method is used to determine the changes in the specified telephony states. For this a new class, `TeleListener` is created, which extends the `PhoneStateListener` class. In this class, the `onCallStateChanged()` method is used to display the call state, which can be `ideal`, `offhook`, or `ringing`.

3. Replace the code of the `AndroidManifest.xml` file, with the code shown in Listing 13.5:

Listing 13.5: Displaying the Code of the `AndroidManifest.xml` File in the `IncomingCall` Application

```
<?xml version="1.0" encoding="utf-8"?>
<manifest xmlns:android="http://schemas.android.com/apk/res/android"
    package="com.kogent.android.incomingcall"
    android:versionCode="1"
    android:versionName="1.0" >

    <uses-sdk
        android:minSdkVersion="8"
        android:targetSdkVersion="17" />

    <application
        android:allowBackup="true"
        android:icon="@drawable/ic_launcher"
        android:label="@string/app_name"
        android:theme="@style/AppTheme" >
        <activity
            android:name="com.kogent.android.incomingcall.MainActivity"
```

```
                android:label="@string/app_name" >
                <intent-filter>
                    <action android:name="android.intent.action.MAIN" />

                    <category android:name="android.intent.category.LAUNCHER" />
                </intent-filter>
            </activity>
        </application>
    <uses-permission android:name="android.permission.READ_PHONE_STATE"/>
    </manifest>
```

In Listing 13.5, besides the default configuration, the `READ_PHONE_STATE` uses permission is also configured.

4. Execute the `IncomingCall` application. Figure 13.2 shows the output of the `IncomingCall` application:

Figure 13.2: Showing the Output of the IncomingCall Application

Making Outgoing Phone Calls Application

To create an Android application that makes an outgoing call, the system telephony stack is used. This is a simple technique which allows you to use the existing telephony stack by using the Intent.ACTION_CALL action, as shown in the following code snippet:

```
Intent phone_call_intent = new Intent(Intent.ACTION_CALL);
phone_call_intent.setData(Uri.parse("tel:123456"));
startActivity(phone_call_intent);
```

The preceding code allows your application to initiate a call and allows the system to manage dialing, connection, and voice handling. You have to use the `Intent.ACTION_CALL` intent and specify a number that has to be dialed using a tel: schema.

It should be noted that you should also configure the `CALL_PHONE` uses permission in the `AndroidManifest.xml` file, as shown in the following code snippet:

```
<uses-permission android:name="android.permission.CALL_PHONE"/>
```

Let's create an application named `OutgoingCall` to show how to make an outgoing call. Perform the following steps to create the `OutgoingCall` application:

1. *Create* the `OutgoingCall` application in the Eclipse IDE under the `com.kogent.android.outgoingcall` package.
2. *Replace* the code of the `activity_main.xml` file in the **/res/layout** folder, with the code shown in Listing 13.6:

Listing 13.6: Displaying the Code of the `activity_main.xml` File in the `OutgoingCall` Application

```
<?xml version="1.0" encoding="utf-8"?>
<LinearLayout xmlns:android="http://schemas.android.com/apk/res/android"
    android:layout_width="fill_parent"
    android:layout_height="fill_parent"
    android:orientation="vertical" >

    <Button
        android:id="@+id/button"
        android:layout_width="fill_parent"
        android:layout_height="wrap_content"
        android:text="Call +919971101299" />

</LinearLayout>
```

In Listing 13.6, a linear layout is set with a button in it.

3. *Replace* the code of the `MainActivity.java` file in the **/src** folder, with the code shown in Listing 13.7:

Listing 13.7: Showing the Code of the `MainActivity.java` File in the `OutgoingCall` Application

```
package com.kogent.android.outgoingcall;

import android.os.Bundle;
import android.app.Activity;
import android.content.Context;
import android.content.Intent;
import android.net.Uri;
import android.view.View;
import android.view.View.OnClickListener;
import android.widget.Button;
public class MainActivity extends Activity {

   final Context context = this;
   private Button button;

   public void onCreate(Bundle savedInstanceState) {

         super.onCreate(savedInstanceState);
         setContentView(R.layout.activity_main);
         button = (Button) findViewById(R.id.button);
         button.setOnClickListener(new OnClickListener() {

                @Override
                public void onClick(View view) {

                        Intent diallerIntent = new Intent(Intent.ACTION_CALL);
                        diallerIntent.setData(Uri.parse("tel:+919971101299"));
                        startActivity(diallerIntent);

                }

         });

   }

}
```

In Listing 13.7, the `MainActivity` class contains the `onCreate()` method in which the `TelephonyManager` class is initialized using the `getSystemService()` method. A button is initialized to make an outgoing call. On the click event of the button, an `Intent` object is created and the `setData()` method is used to parse a telephone number.

4. *Replace* the code of the `AndroidManifest.xml` file with the code shown in Listing 13.8:

Listing 13.8: Showing the Code of the `AndroidManifest.xml` File in the `OutgoingCall` Application

```
<?xml version="1.0" encoding="utf-8"?>
```

```
<manifest xmlns:android="http://schemas.android.com/apk/res/android"
    package="com.kogent.android.outgoingcall"
    android:versionCode="1"
    android:versionName="1.0" >

    <uses-sdk
        android:minSdkVersion="8"
        android:targetSdkVersion="17" />

    <application
        android:allowBackup="true"
        android:icon="@drawable/ic_launcher"
        android:label="@string/app_name"
        android:theme="@style/AppTheme" >
        <activity
            android:name="com.kogent.android.outgoingcall.MainActivity"
            android:label="@string/app_name" >
            <intent-filter>
                <action android:name="android.intent.action.MAIN" />

                <category android:name="android.intent.category.LAUNCHER" />
            </intent-filter>
        </activity>
    </application>
   <uses-permission android:name="android.permission.CALL_PHONE" />
    <uses-permission android:name="android.permission.READ_PHONE_STATE" />
</manifest>
```

In Listing 13.8, besides the default configuration, the `CALL_PHONE` and `READ_PHONE_STATE` uses permissions are also configured.

5. *Execute* the `OutgoingCall` application. Figure 13.3 shows the output of the `OutgoingCall` application:

Figure 13.3: Showing the Output of the `OutgoingCall` Application

When you click the given button, the application makes an outgoing call, as shown in Figure 13.4:

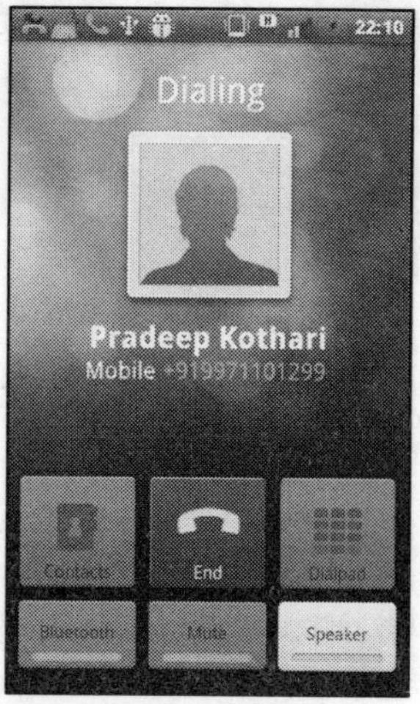

Figure 13.4: Outgoing Call

Handling SMS

In Android development, there are two techniques to send SMS on mobile devices. These techniques are as follows:

- Using the `SmsManager` Class: Allows you to programmatically send an SMS
- Creating `Intent` object: Allows you to use the built-in messaging application to send an SMS

Let's start with an explanation on the `SmsManager` class. The `SmsManager` class allows you to programmatically send an SMS. You should invoke the `getDefault()` method of the class instead of directly instantiating the class. The invocation of the `getDefault()` method returns the `SmsManager` object, which can be used to invoke the `sendTextMessage()` method. When this method is invoked, the SMS is sent to the specified recipient. This method accepts the following arguments:

- `destinationAddress`: Represents the phone number of the recipient to whom the SMS needs to be sent.
- `serviceCenterAddress`: Represents the address of the service center to be used to send the SMS. You can specify the value of this argument as null if you want to use the default SMSC.
- `message`: Represents the body of the message to be sent.
- `sentIntent`: Represents the `PendingIntent` to be invoked after sending the message.
- `deliveryIntent`: Represents the `PendingIntent` to be invoked after the message has been delivered.

The following code snippet shows the use of the `SmsManager` class to send text messages:

```
SmsManager sms_manager = SmsManager.getDefault();
sms_manager.sendDataMessage(destination_address, sc_address, destination_port, data,
sent_intent, delivery_intent);
```

It should be noted that you should also configure the `SEND_SMS` uses permission in the `AndroidManifest.xml` file, as shown in the following code snippet:

```
<uses-permission android:name="android.permission.SEND_SMS" />
```

Sending SMS Using SmsManager

In this section, you learn to create an Android application that allows users to send SMS. This application will use the `SmsManager` class in order to send SMS. Let's create an application, named `SendSMS`, to send SMS using the `SmsManager` class. Perform the following steps to create the `SendSMS` application:

1. *Create* the `SendSMS` application in the Eclipse IDE under the `com.kogent.android.SendSms` package.
2. *Replace* the code of the `strings.xml` file in the **/res/values** folder, with the code shown in Listing 13.9:

Listing 13.9: Showing the Code of the `strings.xml` File in the `SendSMS` Application

```
<?xml version="1.0" encoding="utf-8"?>
<resources>

    <string name="app_name">SendSMS</string>
    <string name="action_settings">Settings</string>
    <string name="hello_world">Hello world!</string>
     <string name="phone_label">Enter Phone Number:</string>
    <string name="sms_label">Enter SMS Message:</string>
    <string name="send_sms_label">Send SMS</string>

</resources>
```

In Listing 13.9, some necessary strings are set, which are required in the layout text views and buttons of the application.

3. *Replace* the code of the `activity_main.xml` file in the **/res/layout** folder, as shown in Listing 13.10:

Listing 13.10: Showing the Code of the `activity_main.xml` File in the `SendSMS` Application

```
<LinearLayout xmlns:android="http://schemas.android.com/apk/res/android"

android:layout_width="fill_parent"
android:layout_height="fill_parent"
android:orientation="vertical" >

    <TextView
    android:layout_width="wrap_content"
    android:layout_height="wrap_content"
    android:text="@string/phone_label" />

    <EditText
    android:id="@+id/PhoneNo"
    android:layout_width="fill_parent"
    android:layout_height="wrap_content"
    android:inputType="phone"/>

    <TextView
    android:layout_width="wrap_content"
    android:layout_height="wrap_content"
    android:text="@string/sms_label" />

    <EditText
    android:id="@+id/SMS"
    android:layout_width="fill_parent"
    android:layout_height="wrap_content"
    android:inputType="textMultiLine"/>

    <Button android:id="@+id/SendSMS"
    android:layout_width="fill_parent"
    android:layout_height="wrap_content"
    android:text="@string/send_sms_label"/>

</LinearLayout>
```

In Listing 13.10, a linear layout is set with two text views, two edit views, and one button.

4. *Replace* the code of the `MainActivity.java` file in the **/src** folder, with the code shown in Listing 13.11:

Listing 13.11: Displaying the Code of the `MainActivity.java` File in the `SendSMS` Application

```
package com.kogent.android.SendSms;

import android.os.Bundle;
import android.app.Activity;
import android.telephony.SmsManager;
import android.util.Log;
import android.view.View;
import android.widget.Button;
import android.widget.EditText;
```

```
import android.widget.Toast;
import com.kogent.android.SendSms.R;

public class MainActivity extends Activity {

      Button sendButton;
      EditText ReciverPhoneNumber;
      EditText textMessage;

      @Override
      protected void onCreate(Bundle savedInstanceState) {
         super.onCreate(savedInstanceState);
         setContentView(R.layout.activity_main);

         ReciverPhoneNumber = (EditText) findViewById(R.id.PhoneNo);
         textMessage = (EditText) findViewById(R.id.SMS);
         sendButton = (Button) findViewById(R.id.SendSMS);

         sendButton.setOnClickListener(new View.OnClickListener() {
            public void onClick(View view) {
               sendMessage();
            }
         });

      }
      protected void sendMessage() {
         Log.i("Send SMS", "");

         String phoneNuber = ReciverPhoneNumber.getText().toString();
         String ReceipentMessage = textMessage.getText().toString();

         try {
            SmsManager smsOperation = SmsManager.getDefault();
            smsOperation.sendTextMessage(phoneNuber, null, ReceipentMessage, null, null);
            Toast.makeText(getApplicationContext(), "SMS Sent Sucessfully
",Toast.LENGTH_LONG).show();
         } catch (Exception e) {
            e.printStackTrace();
            Toast.makeText(getApplicationContext(),"Message Not Delivered
.",Toast.LENGTH_LONG).show();

         }
      }

   }
```

In Listing 13.11, the code is provided for two `EditText` and one `Button` controls. The `EditText` controls are used to accept a phone number and the message string, the button is used to send the message. The `SmsManager` class is instantiated by invoking the `getDefault()` method, and its `sendTextMessage()` method is invoked by passing the phone number of the recipient and the message to be delivered.

5. *Replace* the code of the `AndroidManifest.xml` file, with the code shown in Listing 13.12:

Listing 13.12: Showing the Code of the `AndroidManifest.xml` File in the `SendSMS` Application

```
<?xml version="1.0" encoding="utf-8"?>

<manifest xmlns:android="http://schemas.android.com/apk/res/android"
    package="com.kogent.android.SendSms"
    android:versionCode="1"
    android:versionName="1.0" >

    <uses-sdk
        android:minSdkVersion="8"
        android:targetSdkVersion="17" />
```

```
        <application
            android:allowBackup="true"
            android:icon="@drawable/ic_launcher"
            android:label="@string/app_name"
            android:theme="@style/AppTheme" >
            <activity
                android:name="com.kogent.android.SendSms.MainActivity"
                android:label="@string/app_name" >
                <intent-filter>
                    <action android:name="android.intent.action.MAIN" />

                    <category android:name="android.intent.category.LAUNCHER" />
                </intent-filter>

    </activity>
        </application>
     <uses-permission android:name="android.permission.SEND_SMS" />
    </manifest>
```

In Listing 13.12, besides the default configuration, the `SEND_SMS` uses permission is also configured.

6. *Execute* the `SendSMS` application. Figure 13.5 shows the output of the `SendSMS` application:

Figure 13.5: Showing the Output of the `SendSMS` Application

Let's now learn to create Android application using the `Intent` object.

Sending SMS Using Intent

Earlier, you have learned how to use the `SmsManager` class to send SMS from your Android application without invoking the built-in messaging application. While programmatically sending SMS, you also need to track or monitor the status of the SMS whether or not it has been delivered to the recipient. For this, you can create an `Intent` object and set its type as `vnd.android-dir/mms-sms`, as shown in the following code snippet:

```
Intent sms_intent = new Intent(Intent.ACTION_VIEW);
  // prompts only sms-mms clients
  sms_intent.setType("vnd.android-dir/mms-sms");
  // extra fields for number and message respectively
  sms_intent.putExtra("address", txtphoneNo.getText().toString());
  sms_intent.putExtra("sms_body", txtMessage.getText().toString());
  startActivity(sms_intent);
```

Let's create an application named `SendSMSIntent` to learn the sending of SMS using the `Intent` object. Perform the following steps to create the `SendSMSIntent` application:

1. *Create* the `SendSMSIntent` application in the Eclipse IDE under the `com.kogent.android.SendSmsIntent` package.
2. *Replace* the code of the `strings.xml` file in the **/res/values** folder with the code shown in Listing 13.13:

Listing 13.13: Displaying the Code of the `strings.xml` File in the `SendSMSIntent` Application

```
<?xml version="1.0" encoding="utf-8"?>

<resources>
    <string name="app_name">SendSMSIntent</string>
    <string name="action_settings">Settings</string>
    <string name="hello_world">Hello world!</string>
     <string name="phone_label">Enter Phone Number:</string>
    <string name="sms_label">Enter SMS Message:</string>
    <string name="send_sms_label">Send SMS</string>
</resources>
```

In Listing 13.13, some necessary strings are set, which are required in the layout text views and buttons of the application.

3. *Replace* the code of the `activity_main.xml` file, in the **/res/layout** folder, as shown in Listing 13.14:

Listing 13.14: Displaying the Code of the `activity_main.xml` File in the `SendSMSIntent` Application

```
<LinearLayout xmlns:android="http://schemas.android.com/apk/res/android"
android:layout_width="fill_parent"
android:layout_height="fill_parent"
android:orientation="vertical" >

   <TextView
   android:id="@+id/textViewPhoneNo"
   android:layout_width="wrap_content"
   android:layout_height="wrap_content"
   android:text="@string/phone_label" />

   <EditText
   android:id="@+id/editTextPhoneNo"
   android:layout_width="fill_parent"
   android:layout_height="wrap_content"
   android:inputType="phone"/>

   <TextView
   android:id="@+id/textViewMessage"
   android:layout_width="wrap_content"
   android:layout_height="wrap_content"
   android:text="@string/sms_label" />

   <EditText
   android:id="@+id/editTextSMS"
   android:layout_width="fill_parent"
   android:layout_height="wrap_content"
   android:inputType="textMultiLine"/>

   <Button android:id="@+id/btnSendSMS"
   android:layout_width="fill_parent"
   android:layout_height="wrap_content"
   android:text="@string/send_sms_label"/>

</LinearLayout>
```

In Listing 13.14, a linear layout is set with two text views, two edit views, and one button.

4. Replace the code of the `MainActivity.java` file in the **/src** folder, as shown in Listing 13.15:

Listing 13.15: Displaying the Code of the `MainActivity.java` File in the `SendSMSIntent` Application

```
package com.kogent.android.SendSmsIntent;

import android.os.Bundle;
import android.app.Activity;
import android.content.Intent;
import android.view.View;
import android.widget.Button;
import android.widget.EditText;
import android.widget.Toast;
import com.kogent.android.SendSmsIntent.R;

public class MainActivity extends Activity {

      Button sendBtn;
      EditText txtphoneNo;
      EditText txtMessage;

      @Override
      protected void onCreate(Bundle savedInstanceState) {
         super.onCreate(savedInstanceState);
         setContentView(R.layout.activity_main);

         sendBtn = (Button) findViewById(R.id.btnSendSMS);
         txtphoneNo = (EditText) findViewById(R.id.editTextPhoneNo);
         txtMessage = (EditText) findViewById(R.id.editTextSMS);

         sendBtn.setOnClickListener(new View.OnClickListener() {
            public void onClick(View view) {
               sendSMSMessage();
            }
         });

      }

 protected void sendSMSMessage() {

            Intent smsVIntent = new Intent(Intent.ACTION_VIEW);
                // prompts only sms-mms clients
                smsVIntent.setType("vnd.android-dir/mms-sms");

                // extra fields for number and message respectively
                smsVIntent.putExtra("address", txtphoneNo.getText().toString());
                smsVIntent.putExtra("sms_body", txtMessage.getText().toString());
                try{
                        startActivity(smsVIntent);
                } catch (Exception ex) {
                        Toast.makeText(MainActivity.this, "Your sms has failed...",
                                 Toast.LENGTH_LONG).show();
                        ex.printStackTrace();
                }
      }
   }
```

In Listing 13.15, the code is provided for two `EditText` and one `Button` controls. The `EditText` controls are used to accept a phone number and the message string, and the `Button` control is used to send the message. Next, an instance of the `Intent` class is created using the `Intent.ACTION_VIEW` action. Then, the `setType("vnd.android-dir/mms-sms")` method is used to prompt for SMS or MMS client. The `putExtra()` method is used to provide extra information, such as phone number of the recipient, and the body of the message is set. Finally, the `startActivity(smsVIntent)` method is invoked to start the functionality of the defined activity.

5. *Replace* the code of the `AndroidManifest.xml` file, with the code shown in Listing 13.16:

Listing 13.16: Displaying the Code of the `AndroidManifest.xml` File in the `SendSMSIntent` Application

```
<?xml version="1.0" encoding="utf-8"?>
<manifest xmlns:android="http://schemas.android.com/apk/res/android"

 package="com.kogent.android.SendSmsIntent"
    android:versionCode="1"
    android:versionName="1.0" >
    <uses-sdk
        android:minSdkVersion="8"
        android:targetSdkVersion="17" />
    <application
        android:allowBackup="true"
        android:icon="@drawable/ic_launcher"
        android:label="@string/app_name"
        android:theme="@style/AppTheme" >

<activity
            android:name="com.kogent.android.SendSmsIntent.MainActivity"
            android:label="@string/app_name" >
            <intent-filter>
                <action android:name="android.intent.action.MAIN" />
                <category android:name="android.intent.category.LAUNCHER" />
            </intent-filter>
        </activity>
    </application>

<uses-permission android:name="android.permission.SEND_SMS" />
</manifest>
```

In Listing 13.16, besides the default configuration, the SEND_SMS uses permission is also configured.

6. *Execute* the `SendSMSIntent` application. Figure 13.6 shows the output of the `SendSMSIntent` application:

Figure 13.6: Showing the Output of the `SendSMSIntent` Application

Enter a phone number and a message in the provided fields and *click* the **Send SMS** button; you see the screen as shown in Figure 13.7:

Figure 13.7: Messaging Screen

You can send as many messages as you want to send, as shown in Figure 13.8:

Figure 13.8: Sending Messages

With this, the discussion on sending SMS in Android ends. Let us now understand how to receive SMS.

Receiving SMS Using the BroadcastReceiver Object

Apart from sending the SMS programmatically, you can also develop an Android application to intercept the incoming SMS. You can use the `BroadcastReceiver` object to receive the SMS within your Android application. You first need to add the `<receiver>` element in the `AndroidManifest.xml` file. This element allows the application to intercept the incoming messages through the `SmsReceiver` class. The following code snippet shows how to extend a class by the `BroadcastReceiver` class:

```
public class ReceiveSMS extends BroadcastReceiver

{
   @Override
  public void onReceive(Context ctx, Intent intent) {
         Bundle b = intent.getExtras();
         SmsMessage[] sms = null;
```

```
                String str="";
                if(b != null)
                {
                        //Fetch the body of the message received
                        Object[] pdus = (Object[]) b.get("pdus");
                        sms = new SmsMessage[pdus.length];
                        for(int x=0;x<sms.length; x++)
                        {
                                sms[x] = SmsMessage.createFromPdu((byte[])pdus[x]);
                                str += "SMS has been received from: " +
                                        sms[x].getOriginatingAddress();
                                str += "Body of the message is";
                                str += sms[x].getMessageBody().toString();
                                str +="\n";
                        }
                        Toast.makeText(ctx, str, Toast.LENGTH_LONG).show();

        }
          }
        }
```

In the preceding code snippet, the `sms` array instance of the `SmsMessage` type has been created and the length of the array has been initialized according to the length of the `pdus` object. Note that the `ReceiveSMS` is the `BroadcastReceiver` class that allows your Android application to receive the messages sent by the other applications.

It is also necessary to configure the `ReceiveSMS` class in the `AndroidManifest.xml` file and specify it as the SMS receiver class, as shown in the following code snippet:

```
<receiver android:name=".ReceiveSMS">
<intent-filter>
<action android:name="android.provider.Telephony.SMS_RECEIVED"/>
</intent-filter>
</receiver>
```

In the preceding code snippet, the `ReceiveSMS` class has been configured as a broadcast receiver.

Role of Default SMS Providers

With Android API level 19, a new feature is added, which is called as default SMS app. According to this feature only one application, among multiple, in your mobile can receive the new `SMS_DELIVER_ACTION` intent, which the system broadcasts when a new SMS message arrives. A mobile user has to select an application as the default SMS application to receive SMS messages in system settings. Similarly, one default application can receive the `WAP_PUSH_DELIVER_ACTION` intent when a new MMS arrives. It should be noted that the application that is specified as default SMS app by receiving the `SMS_DELIVER_ACTION` intent can only be able to write to the SMS provider. A SMS provider is defined by the `android.provider.Telephony` class, which provides data related to SMS and MMS messages in phones. Moreover, if other applications are required to read new messages, they need to use the `SMS_DELIVER_ACTION SMS_RECEIVED_ACTION` intent.

To configure an application as default SMS app in system settings, you have to do the following changes in the application:

- Include an intent filter for the `android.provider.Telephony.SMS_DELIVER` action in a broadcast receiver. In addition, add the `BROADCAST_SMS` permission in the broadcast receiver to directly receive incoming SMS messages, as shown in the following code snippet of Android manifest file:

```
<manifest>
...
<application>

<!-- BroadcastReceiver that listens for incoming SMS messages -->
    <receiver android:name=".SmsReceiver"
            android:permission="android.permission.BROADCAST_SMS">
        <intent-filter>
            <action android:name="android.provider.Telephony.SMS_DELIVER" />
        </intent-filter>
    </receiver>
```

```
</application>

</manifest>
```

- Include an intent filter for the `android.provider.Telephony.WAP_PUSH_DELIVER` action along with the `application/vnd.wap.mms-message` MIME type in a broadcast receiver. In addition, add the `BROADCAST_WAP_PUSH` permission in the broadcast receiver to directly receive incoming MMS messages, as shown in the following code snippet of Android manifest file:

```
<manifest>
...

<application>
    <!-- BroadcastReceiver that listens for incoming MMS messages -->
    <receiver android:name=".MmsReceiver"
        android:permission="android.permission.BROADCAST_WAP_PUSH">
        <intent-filter>
            <action android:name="android.provider.Telephony.WAP_PUSH_DELIVER" />
            <data android:mimeType="application/vnd.wap.mms-message" />
        </intent-filter>
    </receiver>

</application>

</manifest>
```

- Include an intent filter for the `android.intent.action.SENDTO` action with the sms:, smsto:, mms:, and mmsto schemas, in the activity of your application to deliver messages. The following code snippet of Android manifest file allows your application to receive intents from other applications that want to deliver a message:

```
<manifest>
...
<application>
    <!-- Activity that allows the user to send new SMS/MMS messages -->
    <activity android:name=".UserSmsActivity" >
        <intent-filter>
            <action android:name="android.intent.action.SEND" />
            <action android:name="android.intent.action.SENDTO" />
            <category android:name="android.intent.category.DEFAULT" />
            <category android:name="android.intent.category.BROWSABLE" />
            <data android:scheme="sms" />
            <data android:scheme="smsto" />
            <data android:scheme="mms" />
            <data android:scheme="mmsto" />
        </intent-filter>
    </activity>

</application>

</manifest>
```

- Include an intent filter for the `android.intent.action.RESPOND_VIA_MESSAGE` action with the sms:, smsto:, mms:, and mmsto schemas in a service. In addition, add the `SEND_RESPOND_VIA_MESSAGE` permission in the service to allow users to respond to incoming phone calls with an immediate text message using your application, as shown in the following code snippet of Android manifest file:

```
<manifest>
...
<application>
    <!-- Service that delivers messages from the phone "quick response" -->
    <service android:name=".UserSmsSendService"
             android:permission="android.permission.SEND_RESPOND_VIA_MESSAGE"
             android:exported="true" >
        <intent-filter>
            <action android:name="android.intent.action.RESPOND_VIA_MESSAGE" />
            <category android:name="android.intent.category.DEFAULT" />
            <data android:scheme="sms" />
            <data android:scheme="smsto" />
            <data android:scheme="mms" />
            <data android:scheme="mmsto" />
        </intent-filter>
```

```
        </service>
    </application>
    </manifest>
```

With this, we come to the end of the chapter. Let's now summarize the main topics of the chapter.

Summary

In this chapter, you have learned about telephony and SMS text messaging in Android development. The chapter has explained the `TelephonyManager` class, which provides direct access to various types of phone properties, such as phone type, network-related details, and SIM details. You also learn about the `PhoneStateListener` class, which is a listener class that helps in monitoring the changes in different telephony states on mobile devices. Using these classes, different applications are created, which include how to display phone information, outgoing call application, and incoming call application. Then, the chapter has explained how to handle SMS text messaging using different classes, such as `SmsManager` and `Intent`. The Intent object allows you to use the built-in messaging application to send an SMS, while the `SmsManager` class allows you to programmatically send an SMS.

Quick Revise

Q1. Which of the following code snippet instantiates the TelephonyManager class?

- **a. TelephonyManager telman=(TelephonyManager)getSystemService();**
- **b. TelephonyManager telman=(TelephonyManager)getSystem(Context.TELEPHONY_SERVICE);**
- **c. TelephonyManager telman=(TelephonyManager)getSystemService(Context.TELEPHONY_SERVICE);**
- **d. TelephonyManager telman=getSystemService(Context.TELEPHONY_SERVICE);**

Ans. The correct option is c.

Q2. Which of the following class allows direct access to network-related details on mobile devices?

- **a. TelephonyManager**
- **b. SmsManager**
- **c. Intent**
- **d. PhoneStateListener**

Ans. The correct option is a.

Q3. Which of the following is not a valid phone type?

- **a. GSM**
- **b. CDMA**
- **c. SIP**
- **d. MEID**

Ans. The correct option is d.

Q4. Which of the following method returns a number that indicates the call state on the device?

- **a. getAllCellInfo()**
- **b. getCallState()**
- **c. getCellLocation()**
- **d. getDataState()**

Ans. The correct option is b.

Q5. Which of the following method returns the IMEI number in case of GSM and the MEID or ESN number in case of CDMA phones?

a. **getDeviceId()**

b. **getDeviceSoftwareVersion()**

c. **getNetworkType()**

d. **getPhoneType()**

Ans. The correct option is a.

Q6. Which of the following method returns a string that indicates mobile network code of the provider of the SIM?

a. **getNetworkOperator()**

b. **getSimOperator()**

c. **getSimOperatorName()**

d. **getNetworkOperatorName()**

Ans. The correct option is b.

Q7. The __ constant specifies that the data connection state is connected.

a. **DATA_CONNECTING**

b. **DATA_DISCONNECTED**

c. **DATA_CONNECTED**

d. **DATA_SUSPENDED**

Ans. The correct option is c.

Q8. Which of the following uses permission must be configured in the AndroidManifest.xml file to access telephony information?

a. **CALL_PHONE**

b. **SEND_SMS**

c. **READ_PHONE_STATE**

d. **None of these**

Ans. The correct option is c.

Q9. Which of the following method returns an object of the SmsManager class?

a. **setType()**

b. **putExtra()**

c. **sendTextMessage()**

d. **getDefault()**

Ans. The correct option is d.

Q10. Which of the following class is used to receive the SMS within your Android application?

a. **BroadcastReceiver**

b. **SmsManager**

c. **Intent**

d. **TelephonyManager**

Ans. The correct option is a.

Q11. What is the role of the TelephonyManager class?

Ans. The TelephonyManager class is used to manage the telephony services on the mobile devices. It provides various methods to determine mobile device-related information, such as phone type, network operator, and call states. To instantiate the TelephonyManager class, you require the getSystemService() method that takes a parameter of telephone service context, as shown in the following code snippet:

```
TelephonyManager  telman=(TelephonyManager)getSystemService(Context.TELEPHONY_SERVICE);
```

The TelephonyManager class allows direct access to various types of phone properties, such as device, network, SIM, and data state details.

Q12. What is the role of the PhoneStateListener class?

Ans. The PhoneStateListener class is a listener object, which helps in monitoring the changes in different telephony states on mobile devices, such as service state, signal strength, or message waiting indicator.

Q13. Which uses permission must be configured in the AndroidManifest.xml file to create an Android application that makes an outgoing call using the system telephony stack?

Ans. The CALL_PHONE uses-permission must be configured in the AndroidManifest.xml file to create an Android application that makes an outgoing call, as shown in the following code snippet:

```
<uses-permission android:name="android.permission.CALL_PHONE"/>
```

Q14. Explain the SmsManager class in Android development.

Ans. The SmsManager class allows you to programmatically send an SMS. You should invoke the getDefault() method of the class instead of directly instantiating the class. The invocation of the getDefault() method returns the SmsManager object, which can be used to invoke the sendTextMessage() method. When this method is invoked, the SMS is sent to the specified recipient. The following code snippet shows the use of the SmsManager class to send text messages:

```
SmsManager sms_manager = SmsManager.getDefault();
Sms_manager.sendDataMessage(destinationAddress, scAddress, destinationPort, data,
sentIntent, deliveryIntent);
```

Q15. Why the <receiver> element must be configured in the manifest file while developing an Android application to receive SMS text messages?

Ans. The <receiver> element in the AndroidManifest.xml file allows the application to intercept the incoming messages through the SmsReceiver class. Therefore, it must be configured in the manifest file while developing an Android application to receive SMS text messages.

14

Hardware Sensors

If you need an information on:	*See page:*
Introducing Sensors	474
Understanding the Sensor Coordinate System	479
Using Sensors	479

Presently, Android devices have built-in hardware sensors, such as accelerometers, gyroscopes, and barometers. These sensors help the devices in calculating the movement, direction, and various environmental conditions. These sensors play an important role in gaming applications such as car racing. In such applications, you require high precision and accurate values to monitor three-dimensional or positioning of an object. Such information can be fetched using hardware sensors of the Android devices. Also, in a gaming application, you need to track the readings from a device's gravity sensor to get the required information about the complex user gestures and motions, such as tilting or shaking the device. Similarly, in a weather application, Android developers use the temperature and humidity sensor to estimate the dew point.

In this chapter, you will learn to use various types of sensors in an application. You will explore the Application Programming Interfaces (APIs) of the hardware sensors and work with the `SensorManager` class. The chapter will also help you in developing an application displaying the accurate position based on the movement of the Android device. Toward the end, the chapter explains how to develop an application that displays different images on shaking the mobile device.

Introducing Sensors

The Android platform provides support for three broad categories of sensors, namely, motion sensors, environmental sensors, and position sensors. The motion sensor estimates the acceleration forces and rotational forces along the x-, y-, and z-axes. Some examples of motion sensors are accelerometers, gravity sensors, and rotational vector sensors. The environmental sensor estimates the environmental parameters such as humidity and air temperature. Some examples of environmental sensors are barometers and thermometers. The sensors of the third category include orientation sensors and magnetometers.

The Android SDK provides the sensor framework to retrieve the sensor available on the device and fetch the required sensor data. This framework provides classes and interfaces that are used to perform various sensor-related tasks. You can perform the following tasks:

- Identify the sensors available on the Android-powered device
- Identify the features or characteristics of a sensor, such as its range, vendor, power requirements, and screen resolution
- Fetch raw sensor data and specify the minimum rate to acquire sensor data
- Register and unregister sensor event listeners monitoring sensor changes

The Android sensor framework allows to access many types of sensors. Apart from the categorization of sensors done earlier, the sensors are broadly categorized as hardware based and software-based. The physical components available in a handset or tablet device are known as hardware-based sensors. You can estimate specific environmental properties to fetch the data directly. Some examples of environmental properties are acceleration, geomagnetic field, or angular changes. Software-based sensors fetch their data from hardware-based sensors and are known as virtual sensors or synthetic sensors. Some examples of software-based sensors are linear acceleration sensor and gravity sensor.

Table 14.1 presents the sensors supported by the Android platform:

Table 14.1: Sensors Provided by Android

Sensor	Type	Description	Common Uses
TYPE_ACCELEROMETER	Hardware sensor	Calculates the acceleration force in m/s^2 on the basis of three physical axes, that is, x, y, and z, including the force of gravity	Detecting motion on shaking or tilting of the Android phone
`TYPE_AMBIENT_TEMPERATURE`	Hardware sensor	Estimates the room temperature in degrees Celsius (°C).	Monitoring air temperature
`TYPE_GRAVITY`	Hardware or software sensor	Estimates the force of gravity in m/s^2 that is used on a device on the x, y, and	Detecting motion on shaking or tilting of the Android phone

Table 14.1: Sensors Provided by Android			
Sensor	**Type**	**Description**	**Common Uses**
		z physical axes.	
TYPE_GYROSCOPE	Hardware sensor	Estimates the rate of rotation of a device around the x-, y-, and z-axes.	Detecting rotation on spinning or turning of the Android phone
TYPE_LIGHT	Hardware sensor	Estimates the ambient light illumination	Controlling screen brightness
TYPE_LINEAR_ACCELERATION	Software or hardware sensor	Estimates the acceleration force in m/s^2 on the basis of the x-, y-, and z-axes, excluding the force of gravity	Monitoring acceleration along a single axis
TYPE_MAGNETIC_FIELD	Hardware sensor	Estimates the geomagnetic field for the x-, y-, and z-axes	Creating a compass
TYPE_ORIENTATION	Software sensor	Estimates the degree of rotation using the gravity sensor and geomagnetic field sensor	Determining device position
TYPE_PRESSURE	Hardware sensor	Estimates the ambient air pressure in hPa or mbar	Monitoring air pressure changes
TYPE_PROXIMITY	Hardware sensor	Estimates the proximity of an object in cm with respect to view screen of a device.	Position of a device during a call
TYPE_RELATIVE_HUMIDITY	Hardware sensor	Estimates the relative ambient humidity in percent	Monitoring dew point
TYPE_ROTATION_VECTOR	Software or hardware sensor	Estimates the device orientation by specifying the three elements of device rotation	Detecting the motion and rotation of devices
TYPE_TEMPERATURE	Hardware sensor	Estimates the temperature of the device in degrees Celsius (°C)	Monitoring temperatures

Exploring the Sensor Framework

The Android SDK provides the Sensor framework in the form of `android.hardware` package providing the classes and interfaces, as presented in Table 14.2:

Table 14.2: Classes and Interfaces of the `android.hardware` Package	
Classes/Interfaces	**Description**
SensorManager	Allows you to create an instance of the sensor service. This class provides different methods to use and list sensors, register and unregister sensor event listeners, and acquire details of device orientation.
Sensor	Allows you to create an instance of a specific sensor. This class provides different methods, allowing you to identify sensor's capabilities.
SensorEvent	Allows to create an instance of the sensor event object. This object provides information about a sensor event, such as raw sensor data, type of sensor resulting to event occurrence, accuracy of data, and timestamp for the event.
SensorEventListener	Allows to create two callback methods, receiving sensor events when either the sensor values or sensor accuracy changes.

Among the classes and interfaces listed in Table 14.2, the `Sensor` and `SensorManager` are noteworthy. Table 14.3 describes the important methods of the `Sensor` class:

Table 14.3: Noteworthy Methods of the `Sensor` Class

Methods	Description
`getMaximumRange()`	Returns the maximum range of the sensor in the sensor's unit
`getMinDelay()`	Returns the minimum duration between two events in microseconds, provided the sensor returns a value when the measuring of data changes
`getName()`	Returns the name of the sensor
`getPower()`	Returns the power in mA used by the sensor in the running mode
`getResolution()`	Returns the resolution of the sensor in the sensor's unit
`getType()`	Returns the generic type of this sensor
`getVendor()`	Returns the string for this sensor
`getVersion()`	Returns the version of the sensor's module

Next, Table 14.4 describes the important methods of the `SensorManager` class:

Table 14.4: Noteworthy Methods of the SensorManager class

Methods	Description
`cancelTriggerSensor()`	Cancels trigger events received for a trigger sensor
`flush()`	Flushes the batch First In First Out (FIFO) of all sensors defined for this listener
`getAltitude()`	Estimates the altitude in meters from the atmospheric pressure and the pressure at sea level
`getAngleChange()`	Refers to the helper function used to estimate the change of angle between two rotation matrices
`getDefaultSensor()`	Refers to the function to retrieve the default sensor for a specific type
`getInclination()`	Estimates the geomagnetic angle in radians from the inclination matrix returned by the getRotationMatrix() method
`getOrientation()`	Estimates the orientation of a device on the basis of the rotation matrix
`getSensorList()`	Refers to the method used to fetch the list of available sensors of a specific type
`remapCoordinateSystem()`	Changes the rotation matrix expressed in a different coordinate system
`requestTriggerSensor()`	Requests the receiving trigger events for a trigger sensor
`unregisterListener()`	Unregisters a listener for a sensor

With the help of the classes, interfaces, and methods discussed in Tables 14.2--14.4, you can perform the following tasks:

- Identify sensor and sensor capabilities
- Monitor the sensor events

Let's discuss each of them in detail.

Identifying Sensors and Sensor Capabilities

The APIs for the Android sensor framework provides various functions to identify the sensor type at runtime and identify the features of each sensor, such as range, resolution, and power requirements. To locate the sensors available on a device, first get a reference to the sensor service by invoking the `getSystemService()` method on the instance of the `SensorManager` class and passing the `SENSOR_SERVICE` argument, as shown in the following code snippet:

```
private SensorManager mSensor;
...
mSensor = (SensorManager) getSystemService(Context.SENSOR_SERVICE);
```

Next, you need to retrieve the list of every sensor available on a device by invoking the `getSensorList()` method and using the `TYPE_ALL` constant. Consider the following code snippet:

```
List<Sensor> devices = mSensor.getSensorList(Sensor.TYPE_ALL);
```

To display the list of all the sensors of a specific type, you can use another constant, such as `TYPE_GYROSCOPE`, `TYPE_LINEAR_ACCELERATION`, or `TYPE_GRAVITY`.

To check the availability of a sensor on a device, use the `getDefaultSensor()` method and pass the constant type of specific sensor. If there are more than one sensor of a specific type, one of the sensors should be assigned as the default sensor. If the device does not support the default sensor of a specific type, the method returns null. For example, the following code snippet ensures whether or not the accelerometer is available on a device:

```
private SensorManager mSensor;
...
mSensor = (SensorManager) getSystemService(Context.SENSOR_SERVICE);
if(mSensor.getDefaultSensor(Sensor. TYPE_ACCELEROMETER) != null) {
// Add the code for the operation to be performed if the sensor is available on the device
}
else {
//Add the code for the operation to be performed if the sensor is not available on the
device
}
```

Apart from listing the sensors available on a device, use the public methods of the `Sensor` class to identify the features or characteristics of each sensor. For example, to obtain the sensor's resolution, use the `getResolution()` method, and to obtain maximum range of measurement, use the `getMaximumRange()` method. In addition, the `getPower()` method is used to obtain the power details of a sensor.

Monitoring Sensor Events

To manage the raw sensor data, use two callback methods provided by the `SensorEventListener` interface: `onAccuracyChanged()` and `onSensorChanged()`. These methods are invoked when the following events occur:

- **A sensor's Accuracy Changes**—The system calls the `onAccuracyChanged()` method, returning the reference to the `Sensor` object. This object is used to return the accuracy of the sensor. Accuracy can be depicted by either of the following status constants:
  - `SENSOR_STATUS_ACCURACY_LOW`
  - `SENSOR_STATUS_ACCURACY_MEDIUM`
  - `SENSOR_STATUS_ACCURACY_HIGH`
  - `SENSOR_STATUS_ACCURACY_UNRELIABLE`
- **A Sensor Reports a New Value**—The system calls the `onSensorChanged()` method, returning the `SensorEvent` object. This object contains the details of the new sensor data, including:
  - Data accuracy
  - Sensor used to generate the data
  - Timestamp at which the data was generated
  - New data recorded by the sensor

Let's look at the code snippet using the `onSensorChanged()` method to monitor data from the light sensor. Using the following code snippet, you can display the raw sensor data in a `TextView` view defined in the main.xml file as `sensordata`:

```
public class MainActivity extends Activity implements  SensorEventListener {
private SensorManager mSensor;
private Sensor mLight;
@Override
public final void onCreate(Bundle savedInstanceState) {
super.onCreate(savedInstanceState);
setContentView(R.layout.main);
mSensor = (SensorManager) getSystemService(Context.SENSOR_SERVICE);
mLight = mSensor.getDefaultSensor(Sensor.TYPE_LIGHT);
```

```
}
@Override
public final void onAccuracyChanged(Sensor s, int accurate) {
//Code to perform the operation when sensor accuracy changes
}
@Override
public final void onSensorChanged(SensorEvent ev) {
float light = ev.values[0];
}
@Override
protected void onResume() {
super.onResume();
mSensor.registerListener(this, mLight, SensorManager.SENSOR_DELAY_NORMAL);
}
@Override
protected void onPause() {
super.onPause();
mSensor.unregisteredListener(this);
}
```

In the preceding code snippet, the default data delay `SENSOR_DELAY_NORMAL` is mentioned when the `registerListener()` method is called. The data delay manages the time duration at which the sensor events are passed to the application through the `onSensorChanged()` callback method.

Let's learn to manage various sensor configurations.

Managing Various Sensor Configurations

The Android platform does not provide a standard sensor configuration for devices. In other words, the device vendors can add any sensor capability into the Android-powered devices. Therefore, devices can include various sensors in a wide range of configurations. For example, the Motorola Xoom device has a pressure sensor; however, the Samsung Nexus S does not support the pressure sensor. Similarly, the Xoom and Nexus S devices support gyroscopes; however, the HTC Nexus One does not. If your application is dependent on a sensor of a specific vendor, you need to ensure that the sensor is available on a device so that the application can run successfully. The options to ensure that the specific sensor is available on a device are as follows:

- Identify sensors at runtime
- Use Google Play filters to target devices

Let's discuss each of these options in detail.

Identifying Sensors at Runtime

The sensor framework allows you to identify the sensor at runtime if an application uses a particular sensor and is not dependent on it. You can also enable or disable the application features as per the requirements. Use the following code to check whether or not there is a temperature sensor on a device:

```
private SensorManager mSensor;
...
mSensor = (SensorManager) getSystemService(Context.SENSOR_SERVICE);
if(mSensor.getDefaultSensor(Sensor.TYPE_TEMPERATURE) != null) {
//Code to be implemented if there is a temperature sensor
}
else {
//Code to be implemented if there is not a temperature sensor
}
```

Using Google Play Filters

You should use the `<uses-feature>` element in the Android Manifest file to publish your application on Google Play. The use of this element will filter your application from devices unsupported to a specific type of sensor configuration for the application. The `<uses-feature>` element has several hardware descriptors that allow you to filter applications on the basis of the availability of a specific sensor. Use the following code snippet in the `AndroidManifest.xml` file that filters the applications that do not have gyroscope sensor:

```
<uses-feature android:name = "android.hardware.sensor.gyroscope" android:required =
"true"/>
```

After adding the element and descriptor, shown in the preceding code, your application will be available on Google Play only if the device has gyroscope. You should specify `android:required = yes` only if your application is dependent on a specific sensor. However, if an application uses a sensor for a specific feature and executes without the use of sensor, display the names of sensors in the `<uses-feature>` element but specify the value of the descriptor to `android:required = "false"`.

Understanding the Sensor Coordinate System

Generally, the sensor framework provides three-axes coordinate system to express data values. The coordinate system for a device is generally defined relative to the screen size of the device, provided the device is in its default orientation. In this orientation, the X-axis is horizontal and indicates toward the right direction, the Y-axis is vertical and indicates the upward direction, and the Z-axis points toward the outside of the screen face. In this system, coordinates behind the screen have negative Z values. This type of coordinate system is supported by the following sensors:

- Acceleration sensor
- Gravity sensor
- Gyroscope
- Linear acceleration sensor
- Geomagnetic field sensor

In this type of coordinate system, the axes do not swap when the orientation of the device screen changes, that is, the sensor's coordinate system never changes on the movement of the device. The behavior of this sensor coordinate system is similar to the OpenGL coordinate system.

NOTE

An application should not assume that the default orientation of a device is portrait. The default orientation for various tablet devices is landscape and the sensor coordinate system is based on the default orientation of a device.

Using Sensors

Let's create an application displaying the values of X, Y, and Z coordinates on the movement of a device. We will accomplish this by using the accelerometer sensor of a device. Perform the following steps to create the `Accelerometer` application:

1. *Create* the `Accelerometer` Android application using Eclipse. By default, the `MainActivity.java` and `activity_main.xml` files are created. *Ensure* that the package name is `com.kogent.android.accelerometer`.
2. *Replace* the code of the `MainActivity.java` file with the code shown in Listing 14.1:

Listing 14.1: Displaying the Code for the MainActivity.java File of the `Accelerometer` Application

```
package com.kogent.android.accelerometer;

import android.app.Activity;
import android.content.Context;
import android.hardware.Sensor;
import android.hardware.SensorEvent;
import android.hardware.SensorEventListener;
import android.hardware.SensorManager;
import android.os.Bundle;
import android.util.Log;
import android.widget.TextView;

public class MainActivity extends Activity implements SensorEventListener {
   private SensorManager sensorManager;
     private Sensor accelerometer, gyroscope;
     @Override
     public void onCreate(Bundle savedInstanceState) {
          super.onCreate(savedInstanceState);
          setContentView(R.layout.activity_main);
```

```
        sensorManager = (SensorManager) getSystemService(Context.SENSOR_SERVICE);
        accelerometer = sensorManager.getDefaultSensor(Sensor.TYPE_ACCELEROMETER);
        sensorManager.registerListener(this, accelerometer ,
SensorManager.SENSOR_DELAY_NORMAL);
    }
    protected void onResume() {
        super.onResume();
        sensorManager.registerListener(this, accelerometer,
SensorManager.SENSOR_DELAY_NORMAL);
    }
    protected void onPause() {
        super.onPause();
        sensorManager.unregisterListener(this);
    }
   @Override
   public void onAccuracyChanged(Sensor sensor, int accuracy) {
         // can be safely ignored for this demo
         Log.d("tag", "onAccuracyChanged: " + sensor.getName() + ", accuracy: " +
accuracy);
   }
   @Override
   public void onSensorChanged(SensorEvent sensorevent) {
         TextView Xaxis= (TextView)findViewById(R.id.xaxis);
         TextView Yaxis= (TextView)findViewById(R.id.yaxis);
         TextView Zaxis= (TextView)findViewById(R.id.zaxis);
         float x = sensorevent.values[0];
         float y = sensorevent.values[1];
         float z = sensorevent.values[2];
         // display values using TextView
         Xaxis.setText("X_axis    " +Float.toString(x));
         Yaxis.setText("Y_axis    " +Float.toString(y));
         Zaxis.setText("Z_axis   " +Float.toString(z));
   }
}
```

In Listing 14.1, the `onSensorChanged()` method is implemented, which sets the values of the three axes X, Y, and Z. Also, the instance of the `SensorManager` class is created and set the type as `TYPE_ACCELEROMETER`. The `registerListener()` method is invoked on the instance of the `SensorManager` class. The arguments passed to this method are the type of the sensor, that is, `accelerometer`, and the time duration is `SENSOR_DELAY_NORMAL`.

3. *Replace* the code of the `activity_main.xml` file with the code shown in Listing 14.2:

Listing 14.2: Displaying the Code of the `activity_main.xml` File of the `Accelerometer` Application

```
<?xml version="1.0" encoding="utf-8"?>
<LinearLayout xmlns:android="http://schemas.android.com/apk/res/android"
    android:layout_width="fill_parent"
    android:layout_height="fill_parent"
    android:orientation="vertical" >
    <TextView
        android:id="@+id/xaxis"
        android:layout_width="wrap_content"
        android:layout_height="wrap_content"
        android:gravity="center" />
    <TextView
        android:id="@+id/yaxis"
        android:layout_width="wrap_content"
        android:layout_height="wrap_content"
        android:gravity="center" />
    <TextView
        android:id="@+id/zaxis"
        android:layout_width="wrap_content"
        android:layout_height="wrap_content"
        android:gravity="center" />
</LinearLayout>
```

In Listing 14.2, the three `TextViews`, that is, `xaxis`, `yaxis`, and `zaxis`, are created to display the values of the three coordinates on the motion of an Android device.

4. *Modify* the SDK version in the Android application by using the following code snippet:

```
<uses-sdk
        android:minSdkVersion="8"
        android:targetSdkVersion="17" />
```

5. *Right-click* the application and select `Run As→Android Application`. Figure 14.1 shows the output of the `Accelerometer` application:

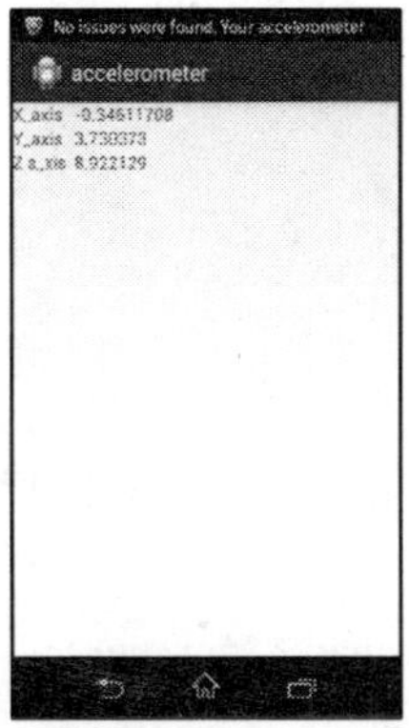

Figure 14.1: Showing the Output of the `Accelerometer` Application

Let's now create the application displaying different images on shaking the Android mobile device. Perform the following steps to create the `ChangeFlag` application:

1. *Create* the `ChangeFlag` Android application. By default, the `MainActivity.java` and the `activity_main.xml` files are created. Also, the `AndroidManifest.xml` file is created.
2. *Replace* the code of the `MainActivity` file with the code shown in Listing 14.3:

Listing 14.3: Displaying the Code of the `MainActivity` Java File of the `ChangeFlag` Application

```
package com.kogent.android.ChangeFlag;

import android.app.Activity;
import android.content.Context;
import android.hardware.Sensor;
import android.hardware.SensorManager;
import android.os.Bundle;
import android.widget.ImageView;
import android.widget.TextView;

public class MainActivity extends Activity {
  private SensorManager sManager;
  private ShakeListen sListener;
  private int[] v = { R.drawable.afghanistan, R.drawable.albania,
              R.drawable.algeria, R.drawable.andorra, R.drawable.angola,
              R.drawable.antigua_and_barbuda, R.drawable.argentina,
              R.drawable.armenia, R.drawable.australia, R.drawable.austria };
  private String[] v2 = { "AFGHANISTAN", "ALBANIA", "ALGERIA", "ANDORRA",
              "ANGOLA", "ANTIGUA AND BARBUDA", "ARGENTINA", "ARMENIA",
              "AUSTRALIA", "AUSTRIA" };
  private ImageView imageView;
  private TextView textView;
  @Override
  protected void onCreate(Bundle savedInstanceState) {
        super.onCreate(savedInstanceState);
        setContentView(R.layout.activity_main);
        imageView = (ImageView) findViewById(R.id.image);
        textView = (TextView) findViewById(R.id.text);
```

```
            sManager = (SensorManager) getSystemService(Context.SENSOR_SERVICE);
            sListener = new ShakeListen();
            sListener.setOnShakeListener(new ShakeListen.CheckShake() {
                    public void onShake() {
                            try {
                                    Double random = Math.random();
                                    random = random * 10;
                                    Integer i = random.intValue();
                                    imageView.setBackgroundResource(v[i]);
                                    textView.setText(v2[i]);
                            } catch (Exception e) {
                                    e.printStackTrace();
                            }
                    }
            });
    }
    @Override
    protected void onResume() {
            super.onResume();
            sManager.registerListener(sListener,
                            sManager.getDefaultSensor(Sensor.TYPE_ACCELEROMETER),
                            SensorManager.SENSOR_DELAY_UI);
    }
    @Override
    protected void onPause() {
            sManager.unregisterListener(sListener);
            super.onPause();
    }
}
```

In Listing 14.3, the instance of the `SensorManager` class, `sManager`, is created. The `ShakeListener` interface is used to handle the event of the Android-powered device. The `v2` array is created to maintain the images of the flags of different countries. The `setOnShakeListener()` method is invoked on the instance of the `ShakeListener` class to handle the motion event of the Android device.

3. *Replace* the code of the `activity_main.xml` file with the code shown in Listing 14.4:

Listing 14.4: Displaying the Code of the `activity_main.xml` File of the `ChangeFlag` Application

```
<RelativeLayout xmlns:android="http://schemas.android.com/apk/res/android"
    xmlns:tools="http://schemas.android.com/tools"
    android:layout_width="match_parent"
    android:layout_height="match_parent"
    tools:context=".MainActivity" >
<ImageView
        android:id="@+id/image"
        android:layout_width="wrap_content"
        android:layout_height="wrap_content"
        android:layout_centerHorizontal="true"
        android:layout_centerVertical="true" />
<TextView
        android:id="@+id/text"
        android:layout_width="wrap_content"
        android:layout_height="wrap_content"
        android:layout_below="@id/image"
        android:layout_centerHorizontal="true"
        android:layout_marginTop="15dp"
        android:text="Shake device for fun!!!" />
</RelativeLayout>
```

In Listing 14.4, the `ImageView` view is created to display the images of the flags of different countries, and the text "Shake device for fun" is displayed.

4. *Create* a Java class, named `ShakeListen`, within the `com.kogent.android.ChangeFlag` package, as shown in Listing 14.5:

Listing 14.5: Displaying the Code of the `ShakeListen` Java File

```
package com.kogent.android.ChangeFlag;
import android.hardware.Sensor;
import android.hardware.SensorEvent;
import android.hardware.SensorEventListener;
import android.hardware.SensorManager;
public class ShakeListen implements SensorEventListener {
  private static final int min_value = 10;
  private static final int directions = 3;
  private static final int pause = 200;
  private static final int duration = 400;
  private long firstTime = 0;
  private long lastTime;
  private int directionCount = 0;
  private float xAxis = 0;
  private float yAxis = 0;
  private float zAxis = 0;
  private CheckShake shakeListener;
  public interface CheckShake {
        void onShake();
  }
  public void setOnShakeListener(CheckShake listener) {
        shakeListener = listener;
  }
  @Override
  public void onSensorChanged(SensorEvent sensor) {
        float x = sensor.values[SensorManager.DATA_X];
        float y = sensor.values[SensorManager.DATA_Y];
        float z = sensor.values[SensorManager.DATA_Z];
        float finalMove = Math.abs(x + y + z - xAxis - yAxis - zAxis);
        if (finalMove > min_value) {
                long current = System.currentTimeMillis();
                if (firstTime == 0) {
                        firstTime = current;
                        lastTime = current;
                }
                long lastVal = current - lastTime;
                if (lastVal < pause) {
                        lastTime = current;
                        directionCount++;
                        xAxis = x;
                        yAxis = y;
                        zAxis = z;
                        if (directionCount >= directions) {
                                long totalDur = current - firstTime;
                                if (totalDur < duration) {
                                        shakeListener.onShake();
                                        resetValues();
                                }
                        }
                } else {
                        resetValues();
                }
        }
  }
  private void resetValues() {
        firstTime = 0;
        directionCount = 0;
        lastTime = 0;
        xAxis = 0;
        yAxis = 0;
        zAxis = 0;
  }
  @Override
  public void onAccuracyChanged(Sensor s, int acc) {
}
}
```

In Listing 14.5, the `setOnShakeListener()` and `onSensorChanged()` methods are implemented to handle the sensor events.

5. *Replace* the code of the `AndroidManifest.xml` file of the `ChangeFlag` application with the code shown in Listing 14.6:

Listing 14.6: Displaying the Code of the `AndroidManifest.xml` File of the `ChangeFlag` Application

```
<?xml version="1.0" encoding="utf-8"?>
<manifest xmlns:android="http://schemas.android.com/apk/res/android"
    package="com.kogent.android.ChangeFlag"
    android:versionCode="1"
    android:versionName="1.0" >
<uses-sdk android:minSdkVersion="8"
        android:targetSdkVersion="17" />
<application android:allowBackup="true"
        android:icon="@drawable/ic_launcher"
        android:label="@string/app_name"
        android:theme="@style/AppTheme" >
<activity android:name="com.kogent.android.ChangeFlag.MainActivity"
            android:label="@string/app_name"
            android:screenOrientation="portrait" >
            <intent-filter>
                <action android:name="android.intent.action.MAIN" />
                <category android:name="android.intent.category.LAUNCHER" />
            </intent-filter>
        </activity>
    </application>
</manifest>
```

Listing 14.6 shows the code to be modified in the `AndroidManifest.xml` file. You need to change the minimum SDK version as 8 and `targetSdkVersion` as 17. You also need to set the `screenOrientation` attribute for the `MainActivity` of the `ChangeFlag` application.

6. *Right-click* the `ChangeFlag` application and select `Run As→Android Application`. Figure 14.2 shows the output of the `ChangeFlag` application:

Figure 14.2: Showing the Output of the `ChangeFlag` Application

7. *Shake* the Android device and the images will be displayed as shown in Figure 14.3:

Figure 14.3: Showing the Images Displayed after Shaking of the Device

Summary

In the chapter, you have learned about the different types of sensors, such as accelerometer and gravity. You have also explored the classes, interfaces, and methods of the `Sensor` and `SensorManager` classes. The chapter has helped you in understanding how to manage various sensor configurations by identifying sensors at runtime and using sensors at runtime. You have also learned about the sensor coordinate system comprising the x-, y-, and z-axes.

Quick Revise

Q1. Which of the following Sensor calculates the acceleration force in m/s2 on the basis of three physical axes, x, y, and z, including the force of gravity?

- **a. TYPE_ACCELEROMETER**
- **b. TYPE_AMBIENT_TEMPERATURE**
- **c. TYPE_GRAVITY**
- **d. TYPE_GYROSCOPE**

Ans. The correct option is a.

Q2. Which of the following classes provides the different methods to use and list sensors?

- **a. SensorManager**
- **b. Sensor**
- **c. SensorEvent**
- **d. SensorEventListener**

Ans. The correct option is a.

Q3. Which of the following methods estimates the geomagnetic angle in radians from the inclination matrix returned by the getRotationMatrix() method?

- **a. getAngleChange()**
- **b. getDefaultSensor()**

c. **getInclination()**

d. **getOrientation()**

Ans. The correct option is b.

Q4. Write the code to create an instance of the SensorManager class and pass the SENSOR_SERVICE argument.

```
private SensorManager mSensor;
...
mSensor = (SensorManager) getSystemService(Context.SENSOR_SERVICE);
```

Q5. Which of the following sensors estimates the force of gravity in m/s2 that is used on a device on the x, y, and z physical axes?

a. **TYPE_ACCELEROMETER**

b. **TYPE_AMBIENT_TEMPERATURE**

c. **TYPE_GRAVITY**

d. **TYPE_GYROSCOPE**

Ans. The correct option is c.

Q6. Which of the following methods requests the receiving trigger events for a trigger sensor?

a. **getSensorList()**

b. **remapCoordinateSystem()**

c. **requestTriggerSensor()**

d. **unregisterListener()**

Ans. The correct option is c.

Q7. Write the code to check whether or not there is proximity sensor.

Ans.

```
private SensorManager mSensor;
...
mSensor = (SensorManager) getSystemService(Context.SENSOR_SERVICE);
if(mSensor.getDefaultSensor(Sensor.PROXIMITY) != null) {
//Code to be implemented if there is a temperature sensor
}
else {
//Code to be implemented if there is not a temperature sensor
}
```

Q8. Write the code to display the list of sensors available on a device.

Ans.

```
List<Sensor> devices = mSensor.getSensorList(Sensor.TYPE_ALL)
```

Q9. Write the code to filter the applications that do not have accelerometer sensor.

```
<uses-feature android:name = "android.hardware.sensor.accelerometer" android:required =
"true"/>
```

Q10. Which of the following methods returns the reference to the Sensor object that changed and the new accuracy of the sensor?

a. **onAccuracyChanged()**

b. **getResolution()**

c. **onSensorChanged()**

d. **getMaximumRange()**

Ans. The correct option is a.

15

Widgets and Live Wallpapers in Android

If you need an information on:	*See page:*
Home Screen Widgets	488
Collection View Widgets	494
Live Wallpaper	497

Nowadays, you can see that some small gadgets are working all the time on the home screen of your device. These gadgets are small applications or shortcuts of large applications, which are known as widgets. Technically, a widget is a self-contained code that displays a program. Some common examples of such widgets are bookmark, today agenda, digital clock, or picture frame. In Android, widgets are introduced with version 1.5, and now they have become an essential aspect of the home screen of mobile devices. After that, with Android 3.0, a new style of widget called collection views widget is introduced, which displays collections of data as lists, grids, or stacks. Android Application Programming Interfaces (APIs) allow you to create your own widgets with the help of various classes and interfaces. Some examples of these are `AppWidgetProvider` and `AppWidgetManager`. The `AppWidgetProvider` class provides a widget on the basis of broadcast events, while the `AppWidgetManager` class is used to update widgets and provide details related to them.

Another exciting feature that helps in decorating the home screen of your mobile devices is live wallpaper. Live wallpapers are special applications that provide animated and interactive backgrounds on the home screens.

In this chapter, you learn to create your own widgets and live wallpapers programs in Android. The chapter also discusses how to create resource layout of such widgets, how to use various classes to code the functioning of widgets, and how to configure widgets in Android manifest. Next, the chapter explains about the collection view widgets, which display various widgets in the form of list, grid, or stack. It discusses about live wallpapers and how to create an Android application to display a user-defined wall paper on the home screen of mobile device.

Home Screen Widgets

Widgets are one of the exciting features of the home screen of Android-based mobile devices. These widgets are also known as App Widgets. They are small application views that can be embedded in other applications. The application that holds one or more widgets is called as an App Widget host. Generally, the host application is the home screen of mobile devices.

Technically, widgets act as broadcast receivers; they use remote views to update a view hierarchy, which is hosted in another application. Generally, this host application is the home screen of mobile devices.

To create a user-defined widget in an application, the following components are required:

1. An Extensible Markup Language (XML) layout resource that specifies a User Interface (UI). For example, the following code snippet in an XML layout resource can display an analog clock:

```
<AnalogClock
        android:id="@+id/Clock"
        android:layout_width="wrap_content"
        android:layout_height="wrap_content"
        android:dial="@drawable/widgetdial"
        android:hand_hour="@drawable/widgethour"
        android:hand_minute="@drawable/widgetminute"/>
```

2. An XML file that describes the metadata associated with your widget. This XML file is created in the **/res/xml** folder of your project. The metadata is defined by using the `appwidget-provider` tag, which describes widget-related attributes. These attributes are listed in Table 15.1:

Table 15.1: Attributes of the appwidget-provider Tag

Attribute	Description
`initialLayout`	Specifies the layout resource used in constructing the widget's UI.
`minWidth/minHeight`	Specify the minimum width and minimum height of the widget, respectively.
`resizeMode`	Specifies the direction in which a widget can be resized using a combination of horizontal and vertical directions.
`label`	Specifies the title used in a widget in the App Widget picker.
`updatePeriodMillis`	Specifies the minimum period in which a widget should be updated.
`configure`	Specifies that you are using an Activity to be launched when your widget is added to the home screen. This Activity class is optionally used to specify widget settings and user preferences.

Table 15.1: Attributes of the appwidget-provider Tag	
Attribute	**Description**
`icon`	Specifies the icon of your widget.
`previewImage`	Specifies a preview of the widget.

The following code snippet shows the use of the `appwidget-provider` tag:

```
<appwidget-provider
    xmlns:android="http://schemas.android.com/apk/res/android"
    android:minWidth="146dip"
     android:updatePeriodMillis="0"
    android:minHeight="146dip"
    android:initialLayout="@layout/clock_widget"/>
```

3. A broadcast receiver class that extends the `AppWidgetProvider` class to control the widget. The `AppWidgetProvider` class encapsulates the `Intent` class, which provides you with event handlers for the update, delete, enable, and disable events. A widget uses intent filters to listen widget updates using the `AppWidget.ACTION_APPWIDGET_UPDATE`, `DELETED`, `ENABLED`, and `DISABLED` actions. The following code snippet shows how to create a broadcast receiver class extending the `AppWidgetProvider` class :

```
public class SampleAppWidget extends AppWidgetProvider {
public void onUpdate(Context con,
AppWidgetManager appWidgetManager,
int[] appWidgetIds) {
...
...
}
public void onDeleted(Context con, int[] appWidgetIds) {
...
...
super.onDeleted(con, appWidgetIds);
}
public void onDisabled(Context con) {
...
...
super.onDisabled(con);
}
public void onEnabled(Context con) {
...
...
super.onEnabled(con);
}
}
```

In the preceding code snippet, `SampleAppWidget` is a broadcast receiver class that extends the `AppWidgetProvider` class. The `AppWidgetProvider` class provides a widget on the basis of broadcast events. These broadcast events are generated whenever the widget is updated, enabled, disabled, or deleted.

Adding the Broadcast Receiver Class to an Android Manifest

After creating a broadcast receiver class, you need to add your widget in the `AndroidManifest.xml` file by using the receiver tag. This tag contains the `intent-filter` and `meta-data` tags. The `intent-filter` tag specifies an intent filter for the `android.appwidget.action.APPWIDGET_UPDATE` action. The `metadata` tag provides the reference of the XML file, which contains the `appwidget-provider` tag declaration. The following code snippet shows how to use the receiver tag in the `AndroidManifest.xml` file:

```
<receiver android:name="com.kogent.android.ClockWidget.clockWidget" android:label="Custom
Clock">
          <intent-filter>
               <action android:name="android.appwidget.action.APPWIDGET_UPDATE" />
          </intent-filter>
          <meta-data android:name="android.appwidget.provider"
android:resource="@xml/clock_widget" />
     </receiver>
```

Using the RemoteViews and AppWidgetManager Classes

RemoteViews is a class that acts as a proxy to a view hierarchy, which is hosted by another application. This class allows you to modify the views of a widget. The following code snippet creates an instance of the RemoteViews class:

```
RemoteViews views = new RemoteViews(context.getPackageName(),R.layout.mywidget_layout);
```

In the preceding code snippet, a new object of the RemoteViews class is created by passing the name of an application's package and the layout resource that have to be modified. Then, you can use various methods of this class to access the various properties of the views, as shown in the following code snippet:

```
// Set the image level for an ImageView.
views.setInt(R.id.mywidget_imageview, "setImageLevel", 1);
// Show the cursor of a TextView.
views.setBoolean(R.id.mywidget_textview, "setCursorVisible", true);
// Assign a bitmap to an ImageButton.
views.setBitmap(R.id.mywidget_imagebutton, "setImageBitmap", myBitmapImg);
```

Then, apply the changes made to the remote views of a widget by using the updateAppWidget() method of the AppWidgetManager class. This class is used to update widgets and provide details related to them. The updateAppWidget() method takes the parameters of identifiers of widgets and the remote views that have to be applied to update the widget, as shown in the following code snippet:

```
appWidgetManager.updateAppWidget(appWidgetId, views);
```

You can also update a widget directly from a service, activity, or broadcast receiver by getting a reference of the AppWidgetManager class by invoking its getInstance() method. The following code snippet shows how to invoke the its getInstance() method():

```
AppWidgetManager appWidgetManager = AppWidgetManager.getInstance(context);
```

Creating a Customized Clock Widget

In this section, you learn to create an Android application that will display a customized clock in the widgets section. Let's create an application, named ClockWidget, to learn how to display a clock widget.

Perform the following steps to create the ClockWidget application:

1. *Create* the ClockWidget application in the Eclipse IDE under the com.kogent.android.ClockWidget package.
2. *Create* a new folder, named **drawable**, in the **/res** location, and add four image files, that is, icon.png, widgetdial.png, widgethour.png, and widgetminute.png, in it.
3. *Create* a new XML file, named clock_widget.xml, in the **/res/layout** folder, as shown in Listing 15.1:

Listing 15.1: Displaying the Code of the clock_widget.xml File in the ClockWidget Application

```
<?xml version="1.0" encoding="utf-8"?>
<LinearLayout xmlns:android="http://schemas.android.com/apk/res/android"
    android:layout_width="fill_parent"
    android:layout_height="fill_parent"
    android:orientation="vertical"
    android:id="@+id/ClockWidget" >

  <AnalogClock
      android:id="@+id/Clock"
      android:layout_width="wrap_content"
      android:layout_height="wrap_content"
      android:dial="@drawable/widgetdial"
      android:hand_hour="@drawable/widgethour"
      android:hand_minute="@drawable/widgetminute"/>

</LinearLayout>
```

In Listing 15.1, a linear layout is set in which an analog clock is inserted by using the AnalogClock element.

4. Replace the code of the activity_main.xml file located in the **/res/layout** folder, with the code shown in Listing 15.2:

Listing 15.2: Displaying the Code of the `activity_main.xml` File in the `ClockWidget` Application

```
<?xml version="1.0" encoding="utf-8"?>
<LinearLayout xmlns:android="http://schemas.android.com/apk/res/android"
     android:layout_width="fill_parent"
      android:layout_height="fill_parent"
      android:orientation="vertical" >

   <TextView
       android:layout_width="fill_parent"
       android:layout_height="wrap_content"
       android:text="Clock Widget with Alarm is successfully installed in your widget
section .Close this program and go to Widget Section to get custom clock \n" />

</LinearLayout>
```

In Listing 15.2, a linear layout is set in which a text view is added to display a message on the screen.

5. *Create* a new folder, named **xml**, in the **/res** location, and create a new XML file `clock_widget.xml` in it. Listing 15.3 shows the code of the `clock_widget.xml` file:

Listing 15.3: Displaying the Code of the `clock_widget.xml` File in the XML Folder

```
<?xml version="1.0" encoding="utf-8"?>
<appwidget-provider
    xmlns:android="http://schemas.android.com/apk/res/android"
    android:minWidth="146dip"
     android:updatePeriodMillis="0"
    android:minHeight="146dip"
    android:initialLayout="@layout/clock_widget"/>
```

In Listing 15.3, the `appwidget-provider` element is used to specify the metadata of the widget created by you. This metadata defines various attributes of your widget, such as its size, layout, and update period rate.

6. *Create* a new Java class file, named `clockWidget.java`, in the **/src** folder under the `com.kogent.android.ClockWidget` package, as shown in Listing 15.4:

Listing 15.4: Displaying the Code of the `clockWidget.java` File in the `ClockWidget` Application

```
package com.kogent.android.ClockWidget;

import android.app.PendingIntent;
import android.appwidget.AppWidgetManager;
import android.appwidget.AppWidgetProvider;
import android.content.ComponentName;
import android.content.Context;
import android.content.Intent;
import android.content.pm.ActivityInfo;
import android.content.pm.PackageManager;
import android.content.pm.PackageManager.NameNotFoundException;
import android.util.Log;
import android.widget.RemoteViews;

public class clockWidget extends AppWidgetProvider {
  public void onReceive(Context context, Intent intent) {
        String action = intent.getAction();
        if (AppWidgetManager.ACTION_APPWIDGET_UPDATE.equals(action)) {

               RemoteViews views = new RemoteViews(context.getPackageName(),
                           R.layout.clock_widget);
               PackageManager packageManager = context.getPackageManager();
               boolean clockFound = false;
               Intent alarmWidget = new
```

```
Intent(Intent.ACTION_MAIN).addCategory(Intent.CATEGORY_LAUNCHER);
                String vendorClock[][] = {
                        {"HTC Alarm Clock", "com.htc.android.worldclock",

"com.htc.android.worldclock.WorldClockTabControl" },
                        {"Standar Alarm Clock", "com.android.deskclock",
"com.android.deskclock.AlarmClock"},
                        {"Moto Blur Alarm Clock", "com.motorola.blur.alarmclock",
"com.motorola.blur.alarmclock.AlarmClock"},
                        {"Samsung Galaxy Clock",
"com.sec.android.app.clockpackage","com.sec.android.app.clockpackage.ClockPackage"},
                        { "Sony Ericsson Xperia Z", "com.sonyericsson.organizer",
"com.sonyericsson.organizer.Organizer_WorldClock" },
                        {"Standar Alarm Clock2", "com.google.android.deskclock",
"com.android.deskclock.AlarmClock"},
                        {"Froyo Nexus Alarm Clock", "com.google.android.deskclock",
"com.android.deskclock.DeskClock"}
                };

                for(int i=0; i<vendorClock.length; i++) {
                    String OEM = vendorClock[i][0];
                    String packageName = vendorClock[i][1];
                    String classInfo = vendorClock[i][2];
                    try {
                        ComponentName componentName = new ComponentName(packageName,
classInfo);
                        ActivityInfo aInfo =
packageManager.getActivityInfo(componentName, PackageManager.GET_META_DATA);
                        alarmWidget.setComponent(componentName);
                        Log.e("OEM Name ", OEM + " --> " + packageName + "/" +
classInfo);
                        clockFound = true;
                    } catch (NameNotFoundException e) {
                        Log.e(" OEM Does not exists   ",OEM );
                    }
                }
                if (clockFound) {
                        PendingIntent pendingIntent = PendingIntent.getActivity(context,
0,
                                alarmWidget, 0);
                        views.setOnClickPendingIntent(R.id.Clock, pendingIntent);
                }

                AppWidgetManager
                        .getInstance(context)
                        .updateAppWidget(

  intent.getIntArrayExtra(AppWidgetManager.EXTRA_APPWIDGET_IDS),
                                views);
        }
    }
}
```

In Listing 15.4, a class named `clockWidget` extends the `AppWidgetProvider` class that is created. The code of this class acts as a broadcast receiver that actually handles the `AppWidget` requests. The `AppWidgetProvider` class is a helper class that helps your widget in managing all the broadcast events occurred. The `AppWidgetManager` class is used to provide the details of the widget used in your application. The `RemoteViews` class is used as a proxy, which allows you to change a property on a view running within another application.

7. *Replace* the code of the `MainActivity.java` file, located in the **/src/com/kogent/android/ClockWidget** folder, with the code shown in Listing 15.5:

Listing 15.5: Displaying the Code of the `MainActivity.java` File in the `ClockWidget` Application

```
package com.kogent.android.ClockWidget;
import android.os.Bundle;
import android.app.Activity;
public class MainActivity extends Activity {
   @Override
   protected void onCreate(Bundle savedInstanceState) {
         super.onCreate(savedInstanceState);
         setContentView(R.layout.activity_main);
   }
}
```

In Listing 15.5, the `MainActivity` class extends the `Activity` class in order to display a message on the screen, which guides the user about the actual functioning of the application.

8. *Replace* the code of the `AndroidManifest.xml` file with the code shown in Listing 15.6:

Listing 15.6: Displaying the Code of the `AndroidManifest.xml` File in the `ClockWidget` Application

```
<?xml version="1.0" encoding="utf-8"?>
<manifest xmlns:android="http://schemas.android.com/apk/res/android"
    package="com.kogent.android.ClockWidget"
    android:versionCode="1"
    android:versionName="1.0" >
    <uses-sdk
        android:minSdkVersion="8"
        android:targetSdkVersion="17" />

    <application
        android:allowBackup="true"
        android:icon="@drawable/ic_launcher"
        android:label="@string/app_name"
        android:theme="@style/AppTheme" >
        <activity
            android:name="com.kogent.android.ClockWidget.MainActivity"
            android:label="@string/app_name" >
            <intent-filter>
                <action android:name="android.intent.action.MAIN" />
                <category android:name="android.intent.category.LAUNCHER" />
            </intent-filter>
        </activity>
        <receiver android:name="com.kogent.android.ClockWidget.clockWidget"
android:label="Custom Clock">
            <intent-filter>
                <action android:name="android.appwidget.action.APPWIDGET_UPDATE" />
            </intent-filter>
            <meta-data android:name="android.appwidget.provider"
android:resource="@xml/clock_widget" />
        </receiver>
    </application>
<uses-permission android:name="com.android.alarm.permission.SET_ALARM"/>
</manifest>
```

In Listing 15.6, the receiver tag is used to add your widget to the application manifest. The `intent-filter` and `metadata` tags are used to specify a broadcast receiver as an App Widget. The `intent-filter` tag is used to provide the reference of the `android.appwidget.action.APPWIDGET_UPDATE` action, and the `metadata` tag is used to give the reference of the `appwidget-provider` meta data XML resource. Moreover, the `SET_ALARM` uses permission is configured to use an alarm.

9. *Execute* the `ClockWidget` application. Figure 15.1 shows the output of the `ClockWidget` application:

Figure 15.1: Displaying the Output of the `ClockWidget` Application

Now, when you see the widgets section, you see the Custom Clock icon. If you drag and drop this Custom Clock icon on the home screen of your mobile device, you see a clock symbol, as shown in Figure 15.2:

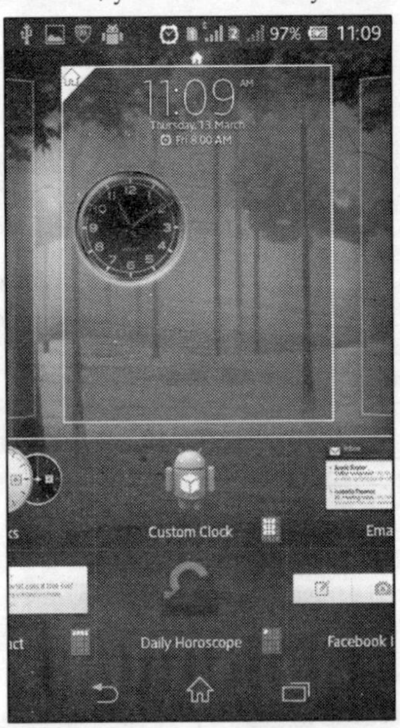

Figure 15.2: Displaying Custom Clock

Collection View Widgets

Collection view widget is a new style of widget that displays collections of data in the form of a list, grid, or stack. It is introduced with Android 3.0 (API level 11). Collection view widgets are available in the following views:

- **StackView**— Specifies a flip-card style that displays its child views as a stack. The stack can automatically rotate through its collection from the topmost item to the back.
- **ListView**— Specifies a list style in which each item is displayed as a row on a vertical list.
- **GridView**— Specifies a two-dimensional matrix style in which each item is displayed within a cell.

Collection view widgets are generally used to create dynamic widgets. They are implemented in the same way as we create App Widgets. Here, we use the `AppWidgetProviderInfo` class is used configure widget settings, the `BroadcastReceivers` class is used to define their behavior, and the `RemoteViews` class are used to modify their views at run time. In addition, they require the following components:

- Additional layout resource to specify the UI of each item displayed within the widget.
- A class that implements the `RemoteViewsFactory` interface, which acts as a store of remote views for your widget to provide the views that will be displayed within your collection view.
- A `RemoteViewsService` class is used to manage the `RemoteViewsFactory` interface.

Collection View Widget Layouts

Collection view widgets require two layout definitions, one for the stack, list, or grid view, and another for the layout to be used by each item within the stack, list, or grid.

The following code snippet shows how to define a widget layout for a stack widget

```
<StackView
android:id="@+id/widget_stack_view"
android:layout_width="match_parent"
android:layout_height="match_parent"
/>
```

The following code snippet shows how a layout resource is used to describe the UI of each item displayed by the stack view widget:

```
<?xml version="1.0" encoding="utf-8"?>
<RelativeLayout
xmlns:android="http://schemas.android.com/apk/res/android"
android:layout_width="match_parent"
android:layout_height="match_parent"
android:background="#FF555222"
android:padding="4dp">
<TextView
android:id="@+id/widgetText"
android:layout_width="fill_parent"
android:layout_height="wrap_content"
android:layout_alignParentBottom="true"
android:gravity="center_horizontal"
android:text="@string/widgetText"
/>
<TextView
android:id="@+id/widget_TitleText"
android:layout_width="match_parent"
android:layout_height="match_parent"
android:layout_above="@id/widgetText"
android:textSize="20sp"
android:gravity="center"
android:text="---"
/>
</RelativeLayout>
```

Creating the Remote Views Service Class

`RemoteViewsService` is a class that is used as a wrapper to manage the `RemoteViewsFactory` interface. This interface is used as a store to supply views that are displayed within the collection view widget. The following code snippet shows how to create a remote views service class that extends the `RemoteViewsService`:

```
public class SampleRemoteViewsService extends RemoteViewsService {
public RemoteViewsFactory onGetViewFactory(Intent objIntent) {
```

```
return new SampleRemoteViewsFactory(getApplicationContext(),objIntent);
}
}
```

You also need to configure a remote views service class in the `AndroidManifest.xml` file of the Android application by using the service tag and specifying the `android.permission.BIND_REMOTEVIEWS` permission, as shown in the following code snippet:

```
<service android:name=".SampleRemoteViewsService"
android:permission="android.permission.BIND_REMOTEVIEWS">
</service>
```

Creating a Remote Views Factory Interface

The `RemoteViewsFactory` interface acts as a wrapper around the `Adapter` class. It is used to create views that will be displayed in the collection view widget. You need to create a class that extends the `RemoteViewsFactory` class and uses a static array List to populate various views. The following code snippet shows how a class implements the `RemoteViewsFactory` interface:

```
class SampleRemoteViewsFactory implements RemoteViewsFactory {
private ArrayList<String> sample_widget_text = new ArrayList<String>();
private Context context;
private Intent intent;
private int widgetId;
public SampleRemoteViewsFactory(Context context, Intent intent) {
this.context = context;
this.intent = intent;
widgetId = intent.getIntExtra(AppWidgetManager.EXTRA_APPWIDGET_ID,
AppWidgetManager.INVALID_APPWIDGET_ID);
}
public void onCreate() {
sample_widget_text.add("Enjoy");
sample_widget_text.add("Android");
sample_widget_text.add("Learning");
}
public void onDataSetChanged() {
}
public int getCount() {
return sample_widget_text.size();
}
public boolean hasStableIds() {
return false;
}
public long getItemId(int index) {
return index;
}
public int getViewTypeCount() {
return 1;
}
public RemoteViews getLoadingView() {
return null;
}
public RemoteViews getViewAt(int index) {
RemoteViews rv = new RemoteViews(context.getPackageName(),
R.layout.my_stack_widget_item_layout);
rv.setTextViewText(R.id.widget_title_text,
sample_widget_text.get(index));
rv.setTextViewText(R.id.widget_text, "View Number: " +
String.valueOf(index));
Intent fillInIntent = new Intent();
fillInIntent.putExtra(Intent.EXTRA_TEXT, sample_widget_text.get(index));
rv.setOnClickFillInIntent(R.id.widget_title_text, fillInIntent);
```

```
return rv;
}
public void onDestroy() {
sample_widget_text.clear();
}
}
```

Populating Collection View Widgets

After creating a class that implements the `RemoteViewsFactory` interface, you need to bind the list, grid, or stack view within your widget layout using the `RemoteViewsService` class. For this, you need the `RemoteView` class instance and the `setRemoteAdapter()` method to bind the `RemoteViewsService` class to the particular list, grid, or stack view within the widget layout. The `RemoteViewService` class is specified as shown in the following code snippet:

```
Intent intent = new Intent(context, SampleRemoteViewsService.class);
```

After completing the binding process, you have to use the `updateAppWidget()` method of the `AppWidgetManager` class to apply the binding to the specified widget.

Live Wallpaper

Live wallpapers are special applications that are developed to provide animated and interactive backgrounds on the home screens of mobile devices. This feature of mobile devices was introduced in Android 2.1 (API level 7). Live wallpapers use a surface view to provide a dynamic display that can be interacted with in real time. You can also create your own live wallpaper by having the following three components:

- **XML Resource**— Specifies the metadata associated with your live wallpaper. This metadata includes the information, such as its author, description, and a thumbnail, used to represent it.
- **WallpaperService Implementation**— Specifies a class that wraps, instantiate, and manage your wallpaper service engine.
- **Engine Implementation**— Specifies a class that is returned through the Wallpaper Service class. The Engine class is used to define the UI and interactive behavior of your live wallpaper.

Creating Live Wallpaper Resource and Service

The live wallpaper resource is defined in an XML file, which is stored in the **res/xml** folder. It is defined with the help of the `wallpaper` tag. This tag has various attributes, such as author name, description, and thumbnail, to display in the live wallpaper gallery. The following code snippet shows the use of the `wallpaper` tag:

```
<wallpaper xmlns:android="http://schemas.android.com/apk/res/android"
android:author="@string/author"
android:description="@string/description"
android:thumbnail="@drawable/wallpaper_image"
/>
```

Next, you need to create a class that extends the `WallpaperService` class to create a wrapper service. This wrapper service instantiates and manages the `WallpaperService.Engine` class. An instance of the `WallpaperService.Engine` class is returned by the `onCreateEngine()` handler method. The following code snippet shows how to create a class that extends the `WallpaperService` class:

```
public class MyLiveWallpaper extends WallpaperService {
public Engine onCreateEngine() {
return new MyLiveWallpaperEngine();
}
}
```

In the preceding code snippet, a class named `MyLiveWallpaper` is created by extending the `WallpaperService` class. In this class, an instance of the `Engine` class is returned by the `onCreateEngine()` method.

The `WallpaperService.Engine` class is used to specify the behavior of the live wallpaper. This `Engine` class includes a surface view on which you draw your live Wallpaper and handlers, which notify about the touch events. A surface view is a drawing canvas that supports updates from background threads so that the view appears dynamic and interactive.

Configuring Wallpaper Service

After creating a wallpaper service class by using the Wallpaper Service class, you have to add it to the `AndroidManifest.xml` file of your application by using the `service` tag. The following code snippet shows the use of the `service` tag:

```
<service android:label="@string/liveWallpaper"
         android:name=".livewallpaper"
         android:permission="android.permission.BIND_WALLPAPER">
         <intent-filter>
                <action android:name="android.service.wallpaper.WallpaperService"
/>
         </intent-filter>
    <meta-data android:name="android.service.wallpaper"
         android:resource="@xml/livewallpaper" />
</service>
```

In the preceding code snippet, the service tag includes the `android.permission.BIND_WALLPAPER` permission to use a wallpaper service class. The intent-filter tag is required to listen for the `android.service.wallpaper.WallpaperService` action, and the `metadata` tag is required to specify the name and resource of the `android.service.wallpaper` package.

Creating Live Wallpaper Application

In this section, you learn to create an Android application, `LiveWallpaperService`, to see a live wallpaper of blackbook style on your mobile devices. Let's create the `LiveWallpaperService` application to see this live wallpaper. In this application, a different theme is used, which is available in API 16. Therefore, you must install Android API 16 on your system before executing this application.

Perform the following steps to create the `LiveWallpaperService` application:

1. *Create* the `LiveWallpaperService` application in the Eclipse IDE under the `com.kogent.android.livewallpaperservice` package.
2. Replace the code of the `strings.xml` file located in the **/res/values** folder, with the code shown in \Listing 15.7:

Listing 15.7: Displaying the Code of the `strings.xml` File in the `LiveWallpaperService` Application

```
<?xml version="1.0" encoding="utf-8"?>
<resources>

    <string name="app_name">LiveWallpaperService</string>
    <string name="hello_world">Hello world!</string>
    <string name="action_settings">Settings</string>
     <string name="liveWallpaper">Black Book Wallpaper</string>

</resources>
```

In Listing 15.7, a new string is added to display the text as "Black Book Wallpaper."

3. *Create* a new folder named **drawable** in the **/res** location, and add three image files, that is, `android_logo.jpeg`, `ios_logo.jpg`, and `ic_launcher.png`, in it.
4. *Create* a new folder named **xml** in the **/res** location, and create a new XML file `livewallpaper.xml` **in it.** Listing 15.8 shows the code of the `livewallpaper.xml` file:

Listing 15.8: Displaying the Code of the `livewallpaper.xml` File in the `LiveWallpaperService` Application

```
<?xml version="1.0" encoding="utf-8"?>
<wallpaper xmlns:android="http://schemas.android.com/apk/res/android"
  android:thumbnail="@drawable/ic_launcher" />
```

In Listing 15.8, the wallpaper tag is used to define thumbnail to display in the Live Wallpaper gallery.

5. *Replace* the code of the `activity_main.xml` file located in the **/res/layout** folder with the code shown in Listing 15.9:

Listing 15.9: Displaying the Code of the `activity_main.xml` File in the `LiveWallpaperService` Application

```
<?xml version="1.0" encoding="utf-8"?>
<LinearLayout xmlns:android="http://schemas.android.com/apk/res/android"
     android:layout_width="fill_parent"
      android:layout_height="fill_parent"
      android:orientation="vertical" >

   <TextView
      android:layout_width="fill_parent"
      android:layout_height="wrap_content"
      android:text="This is an example of Livewallpaper. To see the livewallpaper close
this application and longpress any of your homescreen you will get option to go to
Livewallpaper section from there. Select Blackbook Wallpaper to view output of this
example" />

</LinearLayout>
```

In Listing 15.9, a linear layout is set with a text view to display message on the screen.

6. *Create* a new Java class named `livewallpaper.java` in the **/src** folder under the `com.kogent.android.livewallpaperservice` package, as shown in Listing 15.10:

Listing 15.10: Displaying the Code of the `livewallpaper.java` File in the `LiveWallpaperService` Application

```
package com.kogent.android.livewallpaperservice;

import android.graphics.Bitmap;
import android.graphics.BitmapFactory;
import android.graphics.Canvas;
import android.graphics.Color;
import android.os.Handler;
import android.service.wallpaper.WallpaperService;
import android.view.SurfaceHolder;

public class livewallpaper extends WallpaperService {
   private Handler handler = null;
   int x, y;
   public Bitmap android, ios;

   private class liveWallpaperEngine extends Engine {

          private final Runnable runnable = new Runnable() {
                 /**
                  * {@inheritDoc}
                  */
                 public void run() {
                        draw();
                 }
          };
          private boolean visible;

          private void draw() {
                 final SurfaceHolder holder = getSurfaceHolder();
                 android = BitmapFactory.decodeResource(getResources(),
                               R.drawable.android_logo);
                 ios = BitmapFactory.decodeResource(getResources(),
                               R.drawable.ios_logo);
                 Canvas canvas = null;
                 try {
                        canvas = holder.lockCanvas();
                        canvas.drawColor(Color.WHITE);
                        if (canvas != null) {
```

```
                        canvas.drawBitmap(ios, x, y + 320, null);
                        canvas.drawBitmap(android, x, y, null);
                        int width = canvas.getWidth();

                        if (x > width + 110) {
                            x = -100;
                        }
                        x = x + 5;
                    }
                } finally {
                    if (canvas != null)
                        holder.unlockCanvasAndPost(canvas);
                }

                handler.removeCallbacks(runnable);
                if (visible) {
                    handler.postDelayed(runnable, 5);
                }
            }

            public void onDestroy() {
                super.onDestroy();
                handler.removeCallbacks(runnable);
            }

            public void onVisibilityChanged(boolean visible) {
                super.onVisibilityChanged(visible);

                this.visible = visible;

                if (visible) {
                    draw();
                } else {
                    handler.removeCallbacks(runnable);
                }
            }
        }
        public livewallpaper() {
            handler = new Handler();
            x = -100; // initialize x position
            y = 0; // initialize y position
        }

        public Engine onCreateEngine() {
            return new liveWallpaperEngine();
        }
    }
```

In Listing 15.10, a class named `livewallpaper` extends the `WallpaperService` class. The `WallpaperService` class is used to create a wrapper service that manages the `Engine` class. The `onCreateEngine()` method is used to return a new instance of the `liveWallpaperEngine` class. The `Engine` class of the `WallpaperService` class is used to describe the behavior of the live wallpaper. The `draw()` method is used to create a surface view using the `SurfaceHolder` interface on which your live wallpaper is drawn.

7. *Replace* the code of the `MainActivity.java` file located in the **/src/com/kogent/android/livewallpaperservice** folder with the code shown in Listing 15.11:

Listing 15.11: Displaying the Code of the `MainActivity.java` File in the `LiveWallpaperService` Application

```
package com.kogent.android.livewallpaperservice;
import android.app.Activity;
import android.os.Bundle;
public class MainActivity extends Activity {
  @Override
  protected void onCreate(Bundle savedInstanceState) {
        super.onCreate(savedInstanceState);
        setContentView(R.layout.activity_main);
        }
  }
```

In Listing 15.11, the `MainActivity` class extends the `Activity` class in order to display a message on the screen, which guides the user about the actual functioning of the application.

8. *Replace* the code of the `AndroidManifest.xml` file with the code shown in Listing 15.12:

Listing 15.12: Displaying the Code of the `AndroidManifest.xml` File in the `LiveWallpaperService` Application

```
<?xml version="1.0" encoding="utf-8"?>
<manifest xmlns:android="http://schemas.android.com/apk/res/android"
    package="com.kogent.android.livewallpaperservice"
    android:versionCode="1"
    android:versionName="1.0" >
    <uses-sdk
        android:minSdkVersion="8"
        android:targetSdkVersion="16" />
    <application
        android:allowBackup="true"
        android:icon="@drawable/ic_launcher"
        android:label="@string/app_name"
        android:theme="@style/AppTheme" >
        <activity
            android:name="com.kogent.android.livewallpaperservice.MainActivity"
            android:label="@string/app_name" >
            <intent-filter>
                <action android:name="android.intent.action.MAIN" />
                <category android:name="android.intent.category.LAUNCHER" />
            </intent-filter>
        </activity>
        <service android:label="@string/liveWallpaper"
                 android:name=".livewallpaper"
                 android:permission="android.permission.BIND_WALLPAPER">
                 <intent-filter>
                         <action android:name="android.service.wallpaper.WallpaperService"
/>
                 </intent-filter>
            <meta-data android:name="android.service.wallpaper"
                 android:resource="@xml/livewallpaper" />
         </service>
    </application>
  <uses-feature android:name="android.software.live_wallpaper" />
</manifest>
```

In Listing 15.12, the `service` tag is used to add your wallpaper service to the application manifest. The `intent-filter` tag is used to listen for the `android.service.wallpaper.WallpaperService` action, and the metadata tag is used to specify `android.service.wallpaper` as the `name` attribute and associates it with the `livewallpaper.xml` file. In addition, the `android.software.live_wallpaper` uses feature is configured.

9. *Click* the **Apply** and **OK** buttons in the **Properties for LiveWallpaperService** dialog box.

10. *Execute* the `LiveWallpaperService` application. Figure 15.3 shows the output of the `LiveWallpaperService` application:

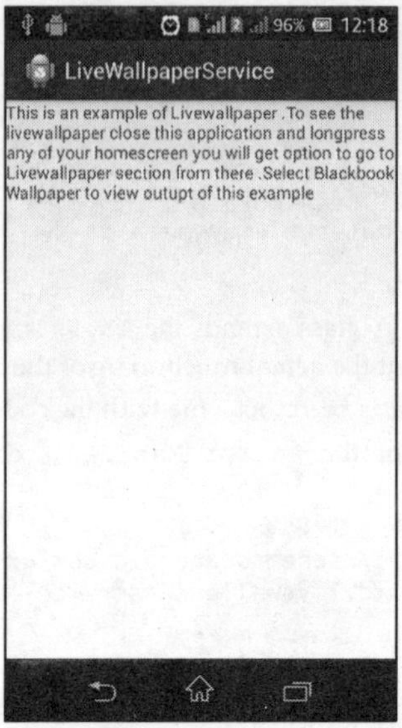

Figure 15.3: Displaying the Output of the `LiveWallpaperService` Application

Now, when you see the live wallpapers section in your mobile device, you find a new live wallpaper option named Black Book Wallpaper, as shown in Figure 15.4:

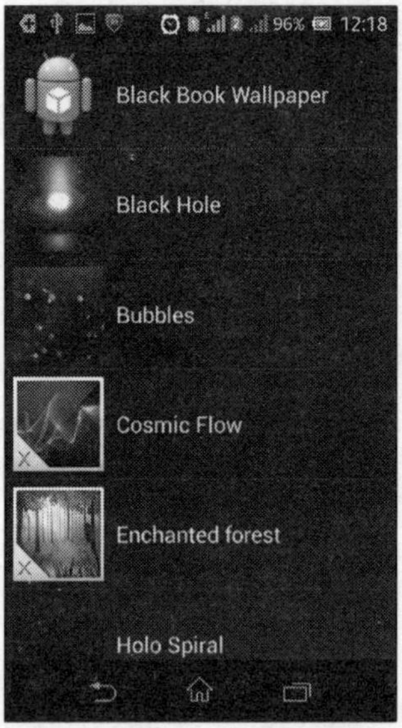

Figure 15.4: Displaying the Black Book Wallpaper Option

Select the **Black Book Wallpaper** option to see the customized live wallpaper, as shown in Figure 15.5:

Figure 15.5: Displaying Customized Live Wallpaper

With this, we come to the end of the chapter. Let's now summarize the main topics of the chapter.

Summary

In this chapter, you have learned about widgets and live wallpapers in Android. Widgets are small applications or shortcuts of large applications, while the live wallpapers are special applications that provide animated and interactive backgrounds on the home screens. First, you have learned about widgets, how to create their resource layout, how to use various classes to code the functioning of widgets, and then how to configure widgets in Android manifest. In the chapter, we have also given an Android application to display a clock widget. Next, you have learned about the collection view widgets, which display various widgets in the form of list, grid, or stack. Then, you have learned how to create your own Android application to display live wallpaper.

Quick Revise

Q1. Which version of Android introduced App Widgets?

- **a. Version 1.5**
- **b. Version 4.4.2**
- **c. Version 2.1**
- **d. Version 4.0**

Ans. The correct option is a.

Q2. Which class provides a widget on the basis of broadcast events?

- **a. AppWidgetManager**
- **b. AppWidgetProvider**
- **c. RemoteViews**
- **d. None of these**

Ans. The correct option is b.

Q3. A widget uses __ to listen widget updates using the AppWidget.ACTION_APPWIDGET_UPDATE, DELETED, ENABLED, and DISABLED actions.

- **a. event handlers**
- **b. intents**

c. **metadata**

d. **intent filters**

Ans. The correct option is d.

Q4. Which tag is used to configure a broadcast receiver class in the Android manifest of an application?

a. **Intent-filter**

b. **Receiver**

c. **Metadata**

d. **Service**

Ans. The correct option is b.

Q5. Which of the following attribute of the appwidget-provider tag specifies the direction in which a widget can be resized, using a combination of horizontal and vertical directions?

a. **Configure**

b. **Label**

c. **ResizeMode**

d. **minWidth/minHeight**

Ans. The correct option is c.

Q6. __ is a class that acts as a proxy to a view hierarchy, which is hosted by another application.

a. **AppWidgetManager**

b. **AppWidgetProvider**

c. **RemoteViews**

d. **None of these**

Ans. The correct option is c.

Q7. Which of the following method is used to update a widget directly from a service, activity, or broadcast receiver by getting a reference of the AppWidgetManager class?

a. **updateAppWidget()**

b. **getInstance()**

c. **getPackageName()**

d. **getIntArrayExtra()**

Ans. The correct option is b.

Q8. Which of the attributes are of the wallpaper tag?

a. **author**

b. **description**

c. **thumbnail**

d. **All the above**

Ans. The correct option is d.

Q9. An instance of the Wallpaper Service Engine class is returned by the __ handler method.

a. **onCreate()**

b. **getInstance()**

c. **onCreateEngine()**

d. **None of these**

Ans. The correct option is c.

Q10. Which tag is used to configure a wallpaper service class in the Android manifest of an application?

a. **Intent-filter**

b. **Receiver**

c. **Metadata**

d. **Service**

Ans. The correct option is d.

Q11. Define widget.

Ans. A widget is a self-contained code that displays a program. Some common examples of widget are bookmark, today agenda, digital clock, or picture frame. In Android, widgets are introduced with version 1.5. These widgets are also known as App Widgets. They are small application views that can be embedded in other applications. The application that holds one or more widgets is called as an App Widget host. Technically, widgets act as broadcast receivers; they use remote views to update a view hierarchy, which is hosted in another application.

Q12. How is the metadata of a widget defined in the XML file?

Ans. An XML file that describes the metadata of a widget is created in the res/xml folder of your project. The metadata is defined by using the appwidget-provider tag, which describes widget-related attributes such as its initial layout and update rate. The following code snippet shows the use of the appwidget-provider tag:

```
<appwidget-provider
    xmlns:android="http://schemas.android.com/apk/res/android"
    android:minWidth="146dip"
     android:updatePeriodMillis="0"
    android:minHeight="146dip"
    android:initialLayout="@layout/clock_widget"/>
```

Q13. Explain the use of the RemoteViews class.

Ans. RemoteViews is a class that acts as a proxy to a view hierarchy, which is hosted by another application. This class allows you to modify the views of a widget. The following code snippet creates an instance of the RemoteViews class:

```
RemoteViews views = new RemoteViews(context.getPackageName(),R.layout.mywidget_layout);
```

In the preceding code snippet, a new object of the RemoteViews class is created by passing the name of an application's package and the layout resource that have to be modified. Then, you can use various methods of this class to access the various properties of the views, as shown in the following code snippet:

```
// Set the image level for an ImageView.
views.setInt(R.id.mywidget_imageview, "setImageLevel", 1);
// Show the cursor of a TextView.
views.setBoolean(R.id.mywidget_textview, "setCursorVisible", true);
// Assign a bitmap to an ImageButton.
views.setBitmap(R.id.mywidget_imagebutton, "setImageBitmap", myBitmapImg);
```

Q14. How is the resource of a live wallpaper defined?

Ans. The live wallpaper resource is defined in an XML file, which is stored in the res/xml folder. It is defined with the help of the wallpaper tag. This tag has various attributes, such as author name, description, and thumbnail, to display in the live wallpaper gallery. The following code snippet shows the use of the wallpaper tag:

```
<wallpaper xmlns:android="http://schemas.android.com/apk/res/android"
android:author="@string/author"
android:description="@string/description"
android:thumbnail="@drawable/wallpaper_image"
/>
```

Q15. How is the service tag used to configure a wallpaper service class in the Android manifest of an application?

Ans. A wallpaper service class is configured by using the service tag in the AndroidManifest.xml file of your application. The following code snippet shows the use of the service tag:

```
        <service android:label="@string/liveWallpaper"
                 android:name=".livewallpaper"
                 android:permission="android.permission.BIND_WALLPAPER">
                 <intent-filter>
                         <action android:name="android.service.wallpaper.WallpaperService"
```

```
/>
                </intent-filter>
            <meta-data android:name="android.service.wallpaper"
                android:resource="@xml/livewallpaper" />
        </service>
```

In the preceding code snippet, the service tag includes the android.permission.BIND_WALLPAPER permission to use a wallpaper service class. The intent-filter tag is required to listen for the android.service.wallpaper.WallpaperService action, and the meta-data tag is required to specify the name and resource of the android.service.wallpaper package.

16

Working with NDK

If you need an information on:	See page:
Introducing NDK	508
Installing the NDK	509
Building the Basic NDK Application	519

For building Android applications, developers are provided with two development packages, namely, Software Development Kit (SDK) and Native Development Kit (NDK). The Android SDK contains modular packages that can be downloaded separately using the Android SDK manager. For example, when a new version of Android platform is available, the SDK manager is used to download the Application Programming Interfaces (APIs). On the other hand, NDK is a set of tools used to develop the components of your application using C/C++ programming languages.

So far, you have developed various Android applications using Java and its object-oriented programming features. However, the Java programming language has various limitations, such as memory management and performance. These limitations can be overcome by programming directly into Android native interface. The Android platform provides support for native development in C/C++ programming languages. In the previous chapters, you have developed the applications using Android Software Development Kit (Android SDK) that supports Java. Now, you will learn to develop native applications using NDK.

This chapter firstly explains when to use the NDK and then explores its benefits. Next, it explains how to download, install, and configure NDK in the Android Eclipse. Finally, you learn to develop basic NDK application.

Introducing NDK

NDK is a toolset that allows you to implement the components of your application using the native-code language such as C and C++. It is useful for some specific type of applications in which you need to reuse the existing code libraries written using C/C++. Prior to downloading the NDK, you, as a developer, should understand that NDK is beneficial for some applications only, while it increases the complexity in some other applications. Generally, you should use the NDK for the applications that are Central Processing Unit (CPU) intensive and do not allocate much memory such as signal processing.

Let's now understand when to use NDK.

When to Use NDK?

The conditions specifying when to use NDK are as follows:

- NDK should be used to develop applications whose performance needs to be improved. For example, to develop the application to sort large volumes of data, NDK should be used.
- If your application requires the platform-dependent features that are not supported by the standard Java class library.
- If you have a library written in C/C++ language and want to access the library in the Java code of your application through **Java Native Interface (JNI)**, then use NDK.
- NDK should be used to implement a part of code in a lower level language, such as assembly.

Benefits of NDK

NDK allows you to use native methods to:

- Create, inspect, and update Java objects, such as arrays and strings
- Invoke Java methods
- Implement the catch and throw exceptions
- Load classes and fetch the class details
- Perform runtime type checking

Communication between Java and Native Code

The Android Virtual Machine (VM) allows the source code of an application to invoke the methods to be implemented in the native code through JNI. In other words, you can declare one or more methods using the `native` keyword specifying that they can be implemented through native code. For example, let's create the `loadFile()` method using the following code snippet:

```
native byte[] loadFile(String filePath);
```

You should create a native shared library providing the implementation of the native methods to be packaged into the application's Android application Package Kit (APK). You should name this library according to the standard Unix convention, such as `lib.so` or `libFileLoading.so`. Then you should ensure that your application explicitly loads the library. To load the native shared library in your application, use the following code snippet:

```
static {System.loadLibrary("FileLoading"); }
```

Ensure that while loading the library, you do not use the prefix `lib` and suffix `.so`.

Let's now learn to install the NDK on your system.

Installing the NDK

To install the NDK, perform the following steps:

1. Install Eclipse and Android SDK
2. Install C/C++ support on Eclipse
3. Install the NDK plugin through Android Development Tool (**ADT**)
4. Install Cygwin
5. Install the Android NDK
6. Configure Eclipse for NDK
7. Set the Environment variable

In chapter 1 of this book, you have learned to install Eclipse and Android SDK. Let's perform the remaining steps to install NDK on your system.

Installing C/C++ Support on Eclipse

At times, the Eclipse version that you have downloaded/installed on your computer may not have C/C++ support. Therefore, you need to install C/C++ support on Eclipse. Perform the following steps to install C/C++ on Eclipse:

1. *Select* **Help→Install New Software**. The **Install** dialog box appears.
2. *Enter* the http://download.eclipse.org/releases/juno/201209280900 or http://download.eclipse.org.releases/galileo **Uniform Resource Locator** (**URL**) in the **Work with** text field. The list of the available software appears.
3. *Select* the **C/C++ Development Tools** checkbox under the **Programming Languages** node, as shown in Figure 16.1:

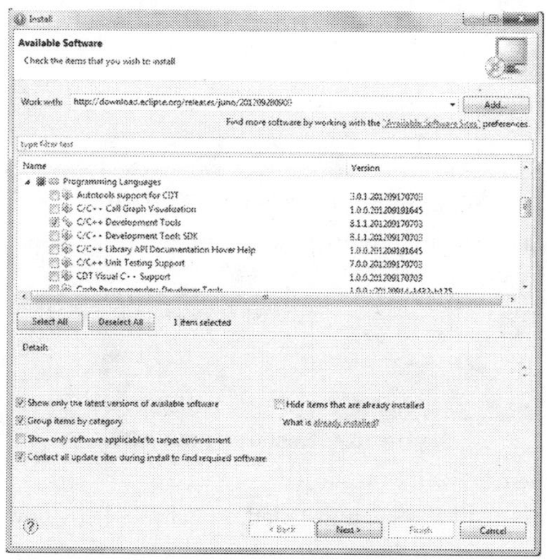

Figure 16.1: Selecting the C/C++ Development Tools Option

4. *Click* the **Next** button. The **Review License** page is displayed.
5. *Select* the I accept the terms of the license agreement radio button.
6. *Click* the **Finish** button, as shown in Figure 16.2:

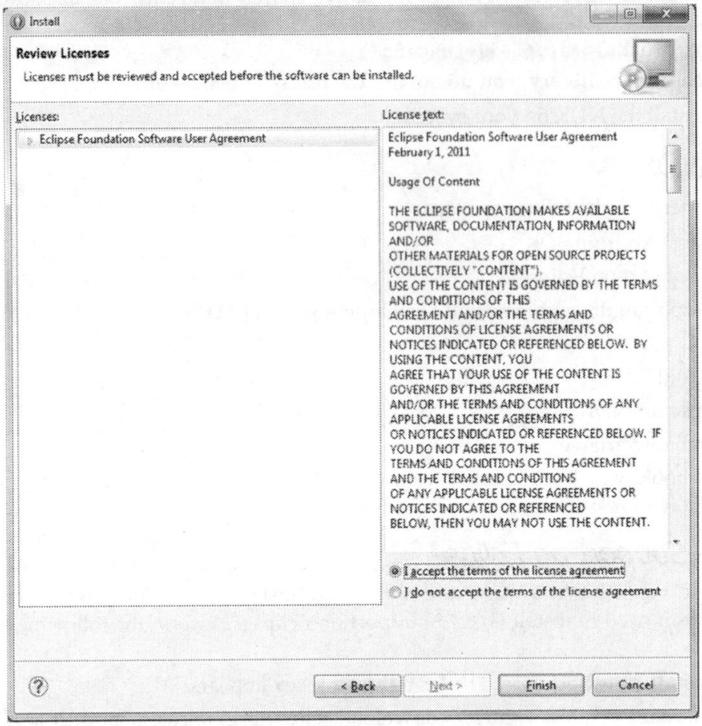

Figure 16.2: Accepting the License

The process of installing the software begins, as shown in Figure 16.3:

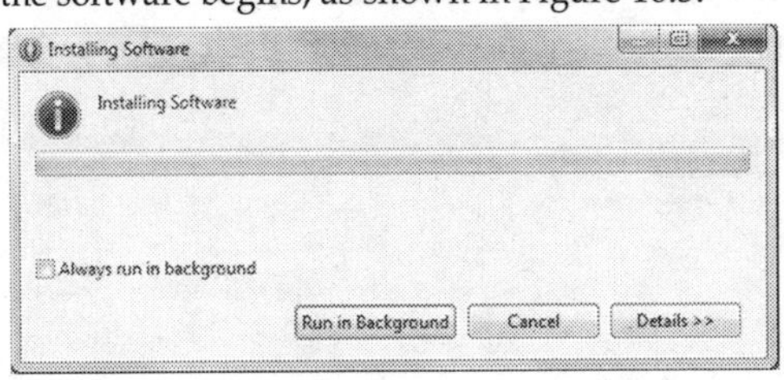

Figure 16.3: Installing the Software

After the software is installed, you are prompted to restart the ADT, as shown in Figure 16.4:

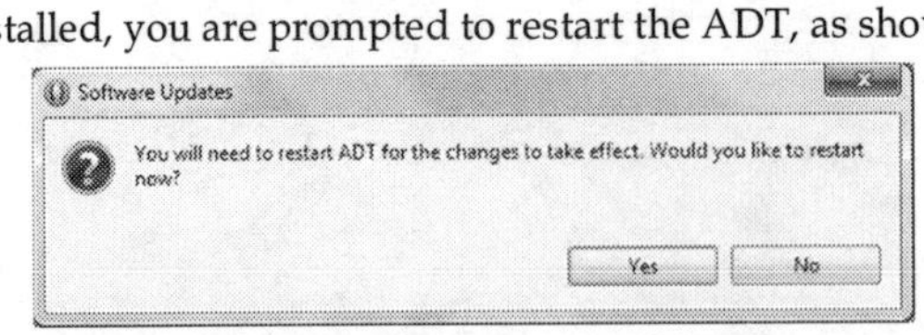

Figure 16.4: Restarting the ADT

7. *Click* the **Yes** button and the ADT will be restarted.

With this, the C/C++ support must have been installed on Eclipse. Let's now learn to install the NDK plugin through ADT.

Installing NDK Plugin through ADT

Now you need to install the NDK plugin in Eclipse. Perform the following steps to do so:

1. *Select* **Help→Install New Software** in Eclipse. The **Install** dialog box appears.
2. *Enter* the http://dl-ssl.google.com/android/eclipse URL and *select* the **Android Native Development Tools** option under the **NDK Plugins** node.
3. *Click* the **Next** button, as shown in Figure 16.5:

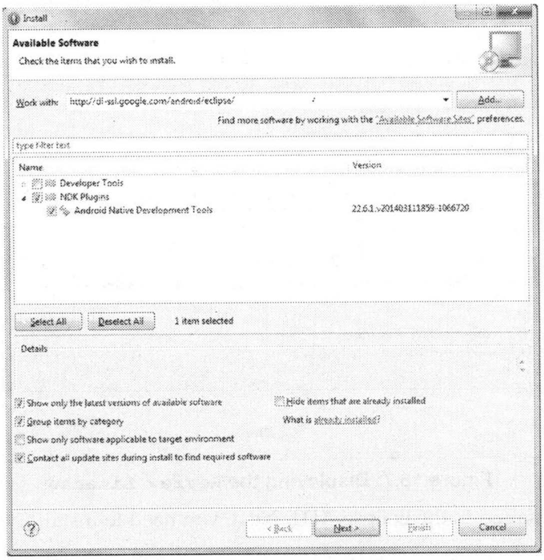

Figure 16.5: Selecting the Option to Install the Android Native Development Tools

The **Android Native Development Tools** option is displayed.

4. *Click* the **Next** button, as shown in Figure 16.6:

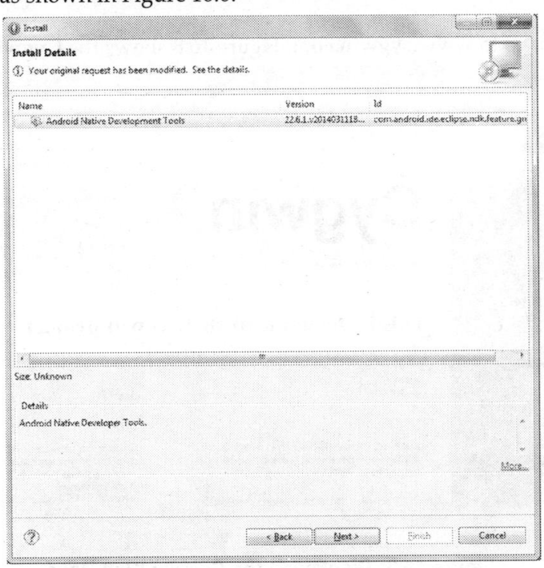

Figure 16.6: Displaying the Install Details

The **Review License** is displayed.

5. *Select* the **I accept the terms of the license agreement** radio button and *click* the **Finish** button, as shown in Figure 16.7:

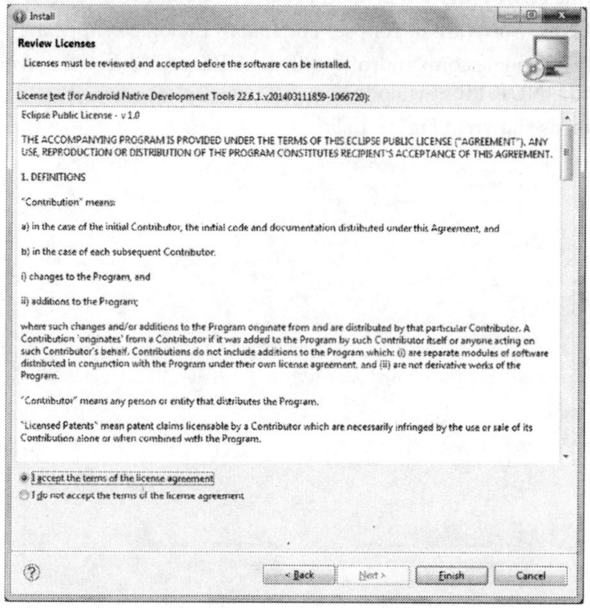

Figure 16.7: Displaying the `Review License`

The NDK plugin will be installed in the Eclipse ADT. Next, you need to install Cygwin.

Installing Cygwin

The Android platform is Linux based; therefore, when you build the native code for it, you will require some Unix tools. For Windows, you need to download Cygwin 1.7.x and above. Perform the following steps to install Cygwin:

1. To download Cygwin, go to **www.cygwin.com**. Figure 16.8 shows the **Cygwin** page on the Web browser:

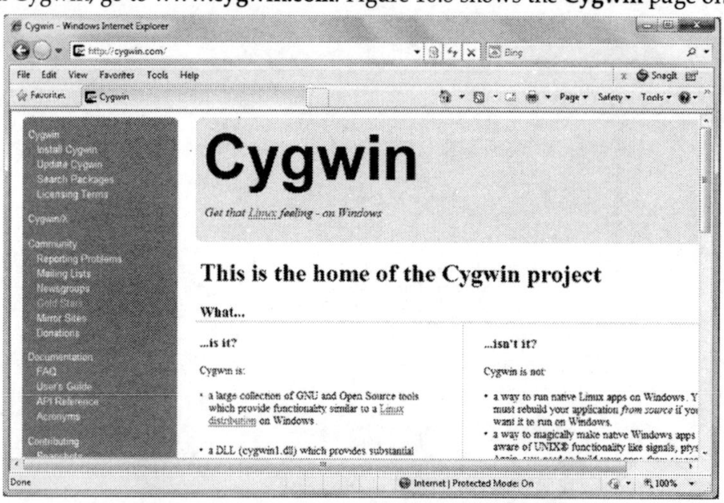

Figure 16.8: Displaying the Cygwin Web Page

2. *Click* the **Install Cygwin** button to install Cygwin. The **Security Warning** dialog box will be displayed, as shown in Figure 16.9:

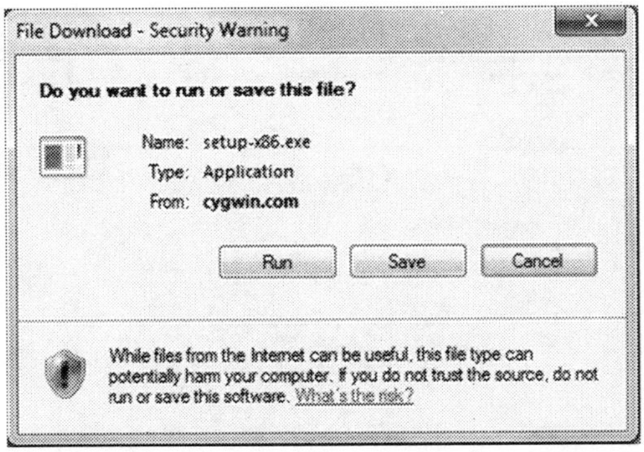

Figure 16.9: Displaying the Security Warning Dialog Box

3. *Click* the **Run** button. The **Cygwin Setup** dialog box opens.
4. *Click* the **Next** button, as shown in Figure 16.10:

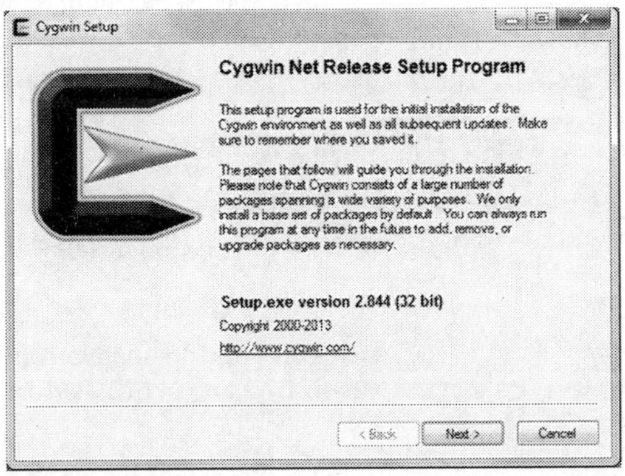

Figure 16.10: Showing the Cygwin Setup Dialog Box

The **Choose Installation Type** dialog box appears.

By default, the **Install from Internet** option is selected.

5. *Click* the **Next** button, as shown in Figure 16.11:

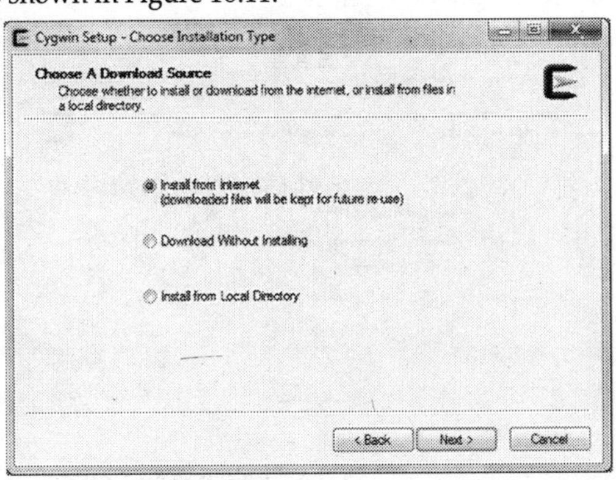

Figure 16.11: Showing the Choose Installation Type Dialog Box

The **Choose Installation Directory** dialog box appears.

By default, the root directory is `C:\cygwin`.

6. *Click* the **Next** button, as shown in Figure 16.12:

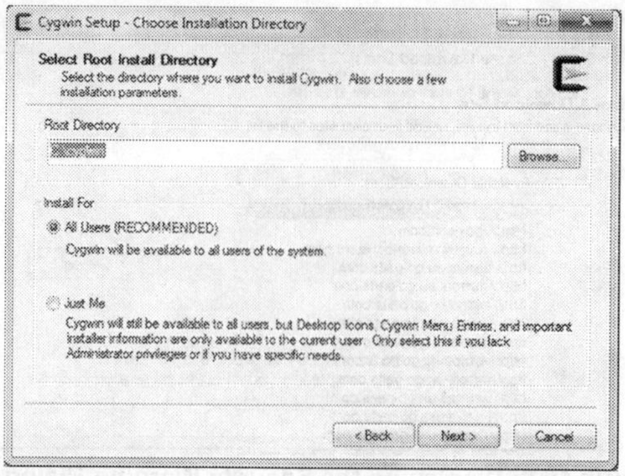

Figure 16.12: Displaying the `Choose Installation Directory` Dialog Box

The **Select Local Package Directory** dialog box appears.

By default, the local package directory is `Desktop` of the user account on which you are working.

7. *Click* the **Next** button, as shown in Figure 16.13:

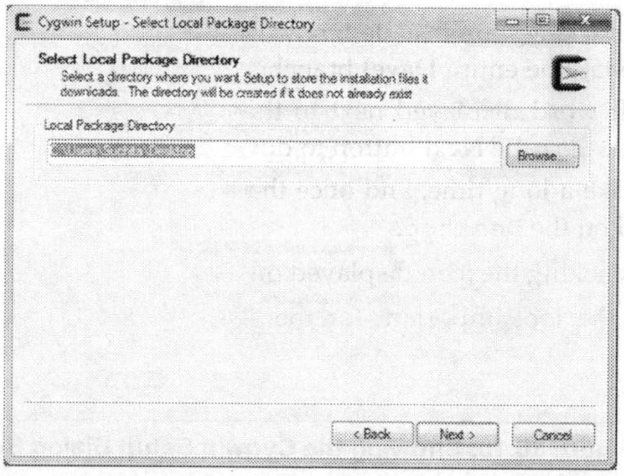

Figure 16.13: Displaying the `Select Local Package Directory` Dialog Box

The **Select Connection Type** dialog box appears.

By default, the **Direct Connection** option is selected.

8. *Click* the **Next** button, as shown in Figure 16.14:

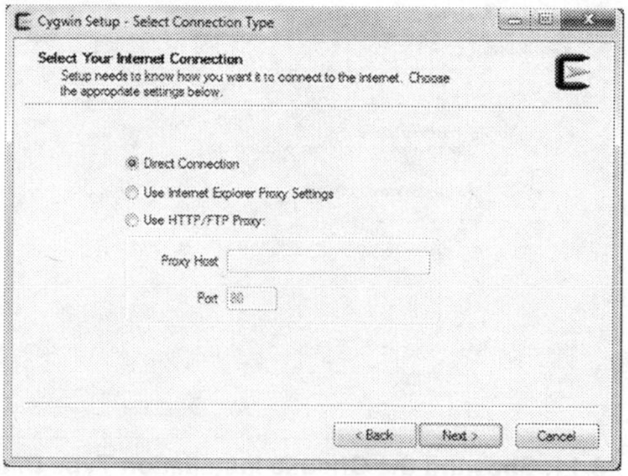

Figure 16.14: Showing the `Select Connection Type` Dialog Box

The **Choose Download Site(s)** dialog box appears.

9. *Select* the mirror from where you want to download the required libraries. *Click* the **Next** button, as shown in Figure 16.15:

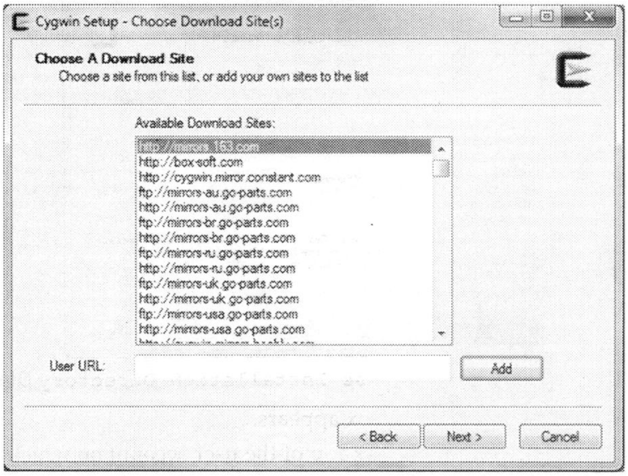

Figure 16.15: Showing the `Choose Download Site(s)` Dialog Box

By default, only the base packages are installed; however, we require the development packages. Instead of selecting the packages, install the entire **Devel** branch.

10. *Click* once on the **Default** word displayed next to the root **Devel** node and wait for few seconds till the **Default** changes to **Install**. *Click* the **Next** button to download the packages and install the environment.

The installation process will take a long time, and once the installation is complete, *click* the **Finish** button. The `Cygwin` icon will be displayed on the `Desktop`.

Now *open* `Cygwin` by double-clicking the icon displayed on the `Desktop`. The **Cygwin** console will start up.

To ensure the availability of the tool important for the Android NDK, type the `make -v` command in the console.

Installing Android NDK

Next, you need to download Android NDK on your system. Download the Android NDK from the following website:

- https://developer.android.com/tools/sdk/ndk/index.html

Figure 16.16 shows the Web page to download NDK:

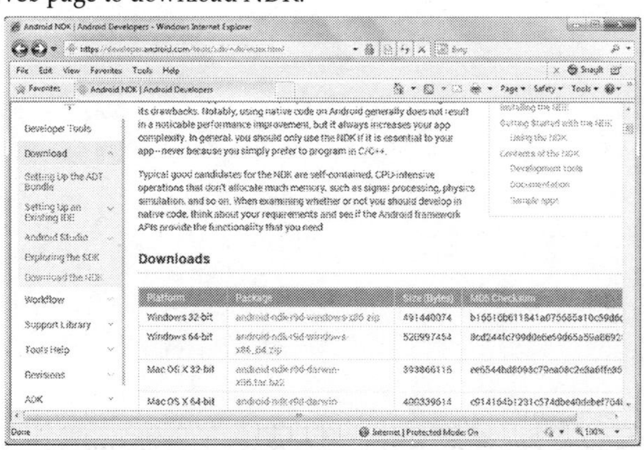

Figure 16.16: Showing the Android Official Page to Download NDK

Download the NDK zip file according to the system platform on which you are working. In our case, we download NDK for Windows 32-bit. While downloading, you need to accept the license, as shown in Figure 16.17:

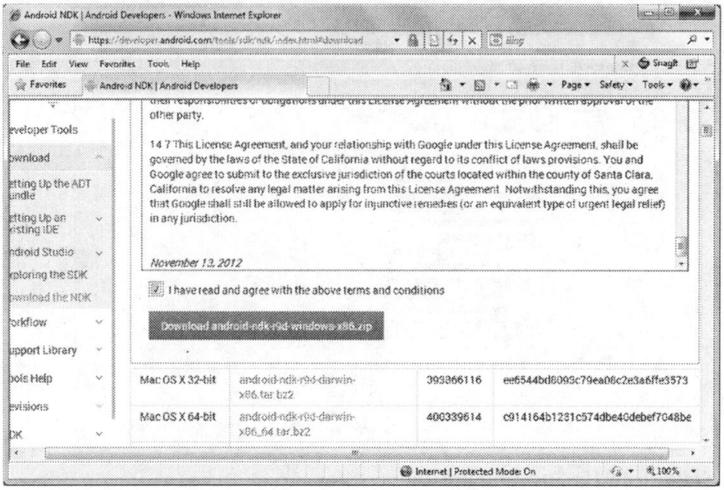

Figure 16.17: Showing the License Agreement Page for Downloading NDK

Extract the downloaded package in the **Cygwin** folder installed in the previous section. Ensure that there are no spaces in the path where you have downloaded Cygwin. In our case, we have downloaded the Cygwin and extracted to **C:\Cygwin**. Therefore, the path for extracting the NDK will be **C:\Cygwin\android-ndk-r9**.

Now, to build your first NDK application, you need to configure Eclipse for NDK programming.

Configuring Eclipse for NDK Programming

After downloading the NDK, you need to configure it in Eclipse. Perform the following steps to configure Eclipse for NDK:

1. To configure Eclipse for NDK, navigate **Windows→Preferences**, as shown in Figure 16.18:

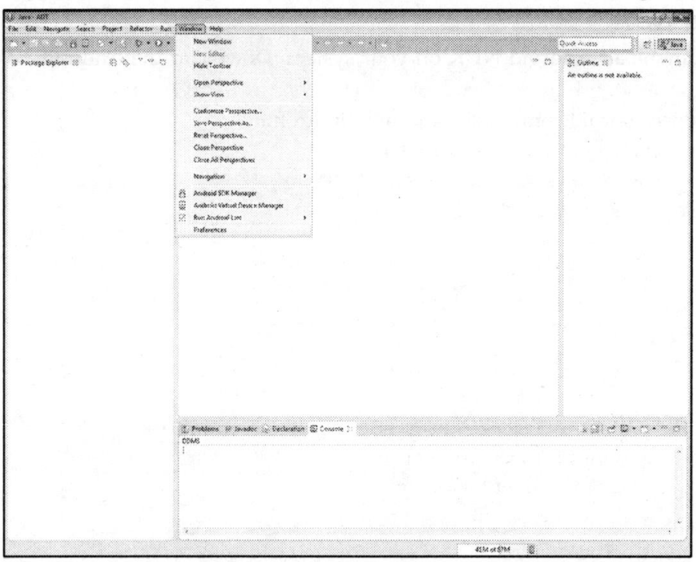

Figure 16.18: Selecting the Preferences Option from the Windows Menu

The **Preferences** dialog box appears.

2. *Select* the **NDK** option below the Android node to configure the folder in which NDK is installed, as shown in Figure 16.19:

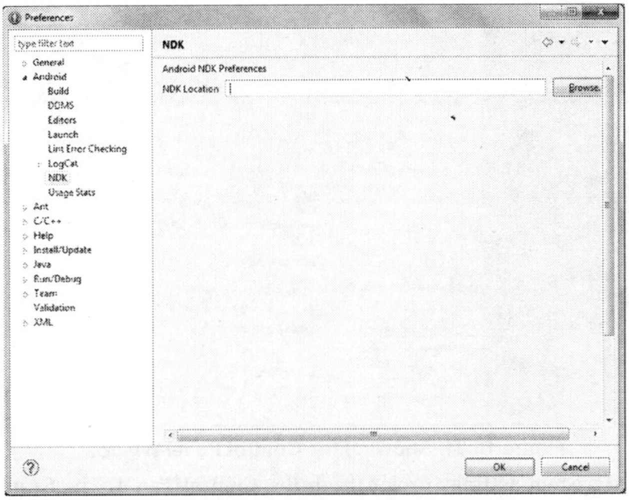

Figure 16.19: Selecting the NDK Option

3. *Click* the **Browse** button to navigate the path where NDK is installed and *click* the **OK** button, as shown in Figure 16.20:

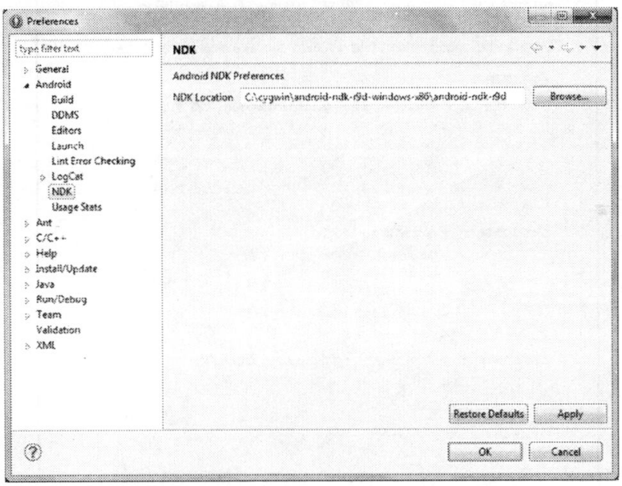

Figure 16.20: Navigating the NDK Path

The NDK will be configured.

Now, you need to configure the environment variable.

Setting the Environment Variable

After installing all the required software, you need to configure the PATH environment variable. Perform the following steps to set the environment variable:

1. *Right-click* **Computer** and select **Properties** from the context menu. The **Control Panel** window opens, as shown in Figure 16.21:

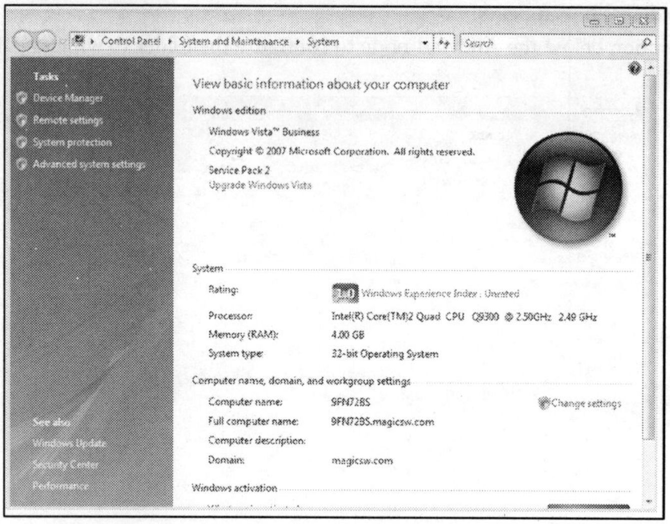

Figure 16.21: Showing the Control Panel Window

2. *Select* the **Advanced system settings** option from the **Control Panel**. The **System Properties** dialog box opens, as shown in Figure 16.22:

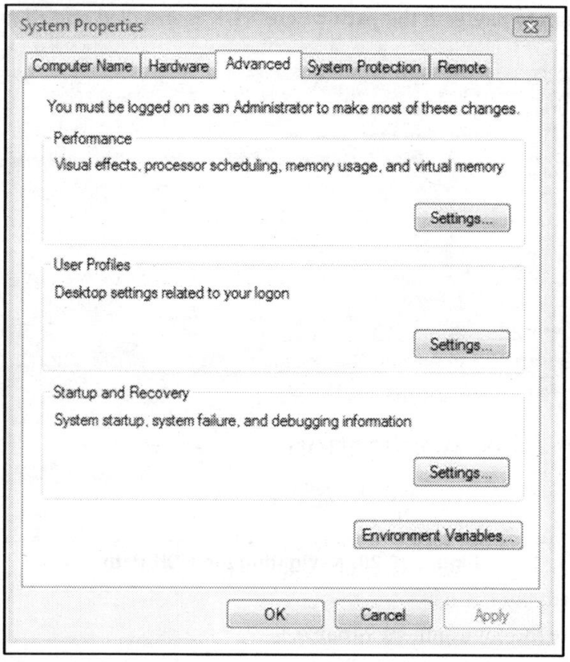

Figure 16.22: Showing the System Properties Dialog Box

3. *Click* the **Environment Variables** button from the **System Properties** dialog box. The **Environment Variables** dialog box opens, as shown in Figure 16.23:

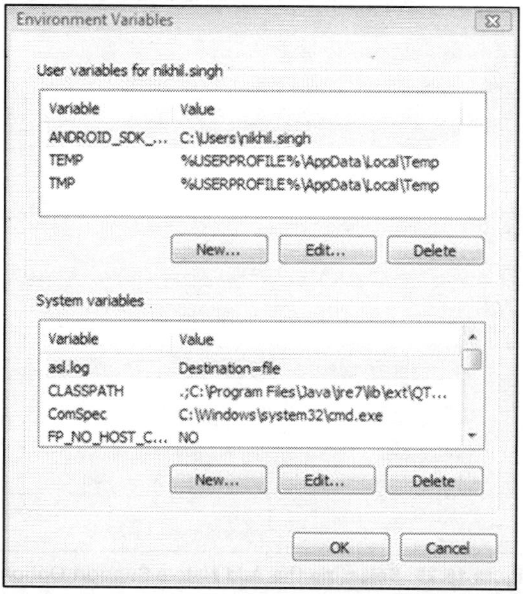

Figure 16.23: Showing the Environment Variables Dialog Box

4. *Select* the **Path** variables from the **System variables** section. The **Edit User Variable** dialog box opens.
5. *Add* the location **C:\cygwin\android-ndk-r9d** for the Android NDK and the location C:\cygwin\bin for the Cygwin in the **Variable value** text box of the **Edit User Variable** dialog box, as shown in Figure 16.24:

Figure 16.24: Adding the Location of Android NDK and Cygwin

With this, the environment variable for the Android NDK is configured.

Building the Basic NDK Application

After performing all the preliminary steps to install and configure Android NDK and C/C++ support in the Eclipse, you can develop the basic NDK application. Create the basic `Helloworld` Android application by performing the steps discussed in *Chapter 1, Getting an Overview of Android,* of the book. Ensure that the package name is `com.kogent.android.helloworld`. Now, you need to add the native support to the `Helloworld` application. Perform the following steps to add the native support in the NDK application:

1. *Right-click* the `Helloworld` application and *select* the **Android Tools→Add Native Support** option from the context menu, as shown in Figure 16.25:

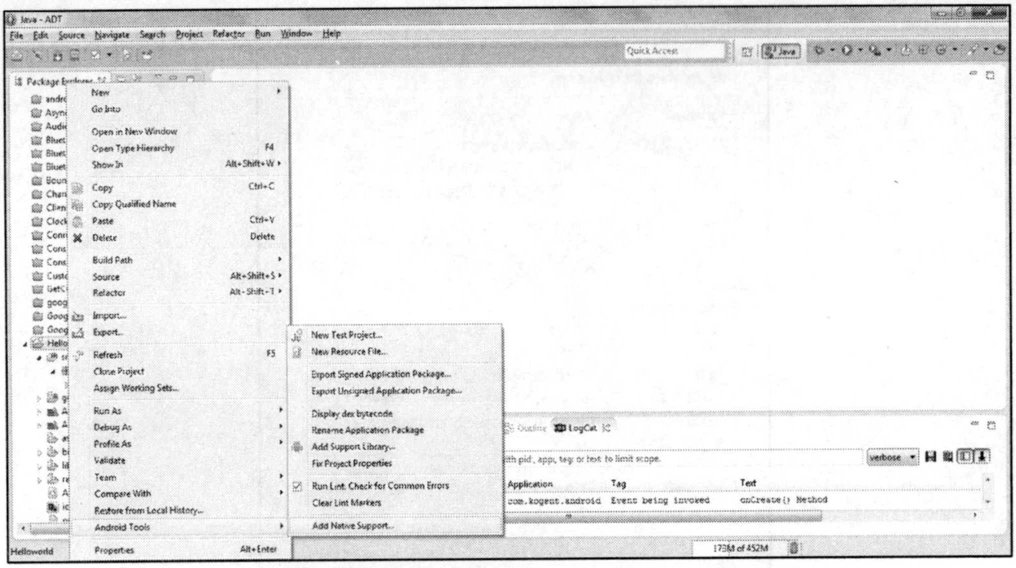

Figure 16.25: Selecting the Add Native Support Option

The **Add Android Native Support** dialog box opens.

2. *Select* the default library name and *click* the **Finish** button, as shown in Figure 16.26:

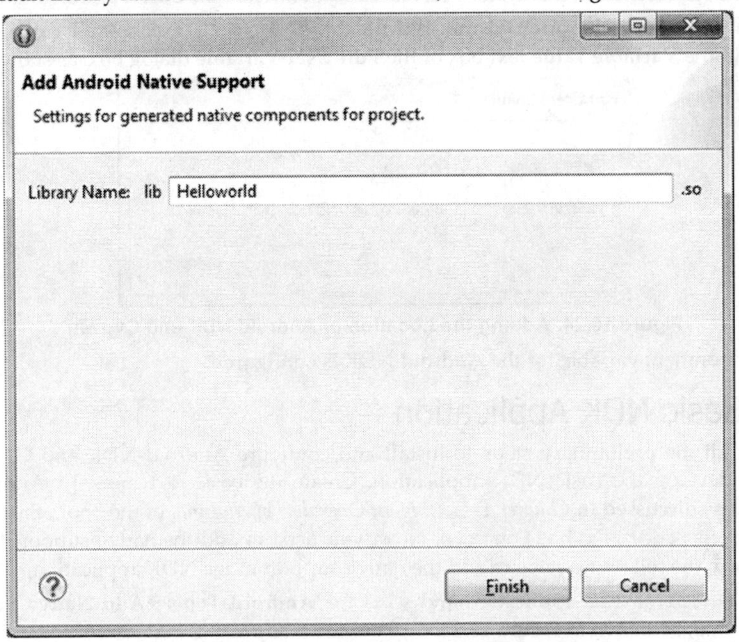

Figure 16.26: Displaying the Default Library Name

The C/C++ perspective opens in the **Eclipse** and the **jni** folder is added to the `Helloworld` application, as shown in Figure 16.27:

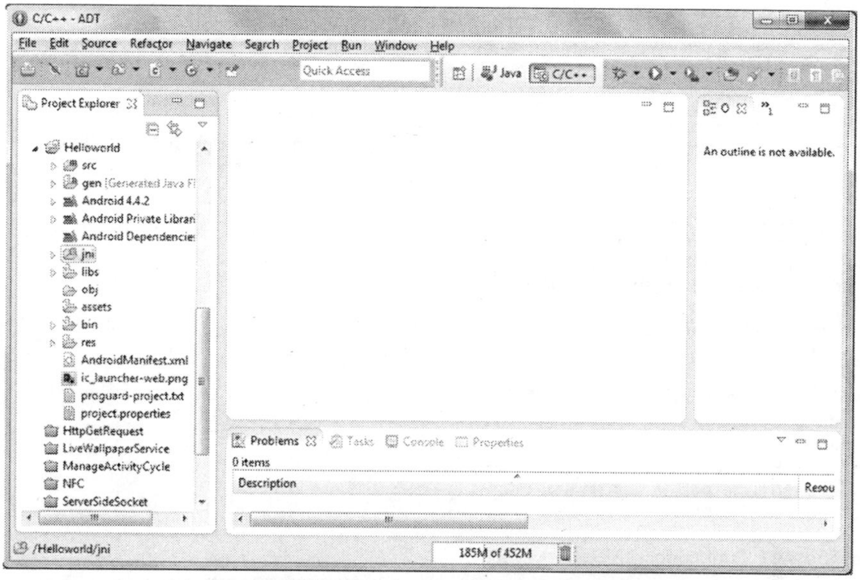

Figure 16.27: Showing the C/C++ Perspective

Within the **jni** folder, you will find the `Helloworld.cpp` and `android.mk` files. You need to create a C source file, named `Helloworld.c`.

3. *Right-Click* the **jni** folder and *select* **New→Source File** option. The **New Source File** dialog box opens.
4. *Enter* the name of the file as `Helloworld.c` file and *select* Template as **Default C source template**.
5. *Click* the **Finish** button, as shown in Figure 16.28:

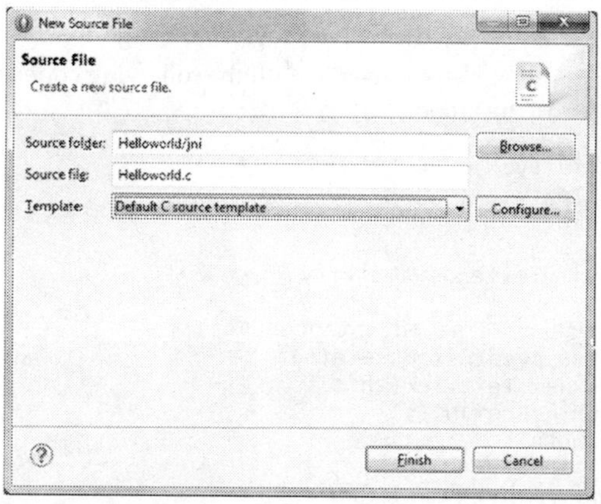

Figure 16.28: Showing the New Source File Dialog Box

6. *Edit* the code of the `Android.mk` file, as shown in the following code snippet:

```
LOCAL_PATH := $(call my-dir)

include $(CLEAR_VARS)

LOCAL_MODULE    := Helloworld
LOCAL_SRC_FILES := Helloworld.c

include $(BUILD_SHARED_LIBRARY)
```

In the preceding code snippet, the name of the source file has been changed to `Helloworld.c`.

7. *Replace* the code of the `Helloworld.c` file with the following code snippet:

```
#include <string.h>
#include <jni.h>

jstring
Java_com_kogent_android_helloworld_MainActivity_stringFromJNI( JNIEnv* env,
                                                  jobject thiz )
{
#if defined(__arm__)
  #if defined(__ARM_ARCH_7A__)
    #if defined(__ARM_NEON__)
      #define ABI "armeabi-v7a/NEON"
    #else
      #define ABI "armeabi-v7a"
    #endif
  #else
   #define ABI "armeabi"
  #endif
#elif defined(__i386__)
   #define ABI "x86"
#elif defined(__mips__)
   #define ABI "mips"
#else
   #define ABI "unknown"
#endif
    return (*env)->NewStringUTF(env, "Hello from JNI !  Compiled with ABI " ABI ".");
}
```

In the preceding code, the `NewStringUTF()` method is used to display the welcome message.

NOTE

You will find some errors in the Helloworld.c file, which will be resolved after adding the C/C++ support to the application, discussed later in this section.

Finally, you need to communicate with the native program through the `MainActivity` source file.

8. *Replace* the code of the `MainActivity` source file with the following code:

```
package com.kogent.android.helloworld;

import android.app.Activity;
import android.widget.TextView;
import android.os.Bundle;

public class MainActivity extends Activity {
  @Override
  public void onCreate(Bundle savedInstanceState) {
         super.onCreate(savedInstanceState);
         TextView tv = new TextView(this);
         tv.setText(stringFromJNI());
         setContentView(tv);
  }
  public native String stringFromJNI();
  public native String unimplementedStringFromJNI();
  static {
         System.loadLibrary("Helloworld");
  }
}
```

In the preceding code snippet, the library is loaded using the `System.loadLibrary()` function. In our case, the library name is Helloworld; therefore, we used the `System.loadLibrary("Helloworld")` method. The required string will be returned by the `stringFromJNI()` method.

Now, let's perform the following steps to add the C/C++ support to the `Helloworld` application.

9. *Right-click* the `Helloworld` application and *select* the **Properties** option. The **Properties for Helloworld** dialog box opens.

10. *Select* the **Paths and Symbols** option from the **C/C++ General** node, as shown in Figure 16.29:

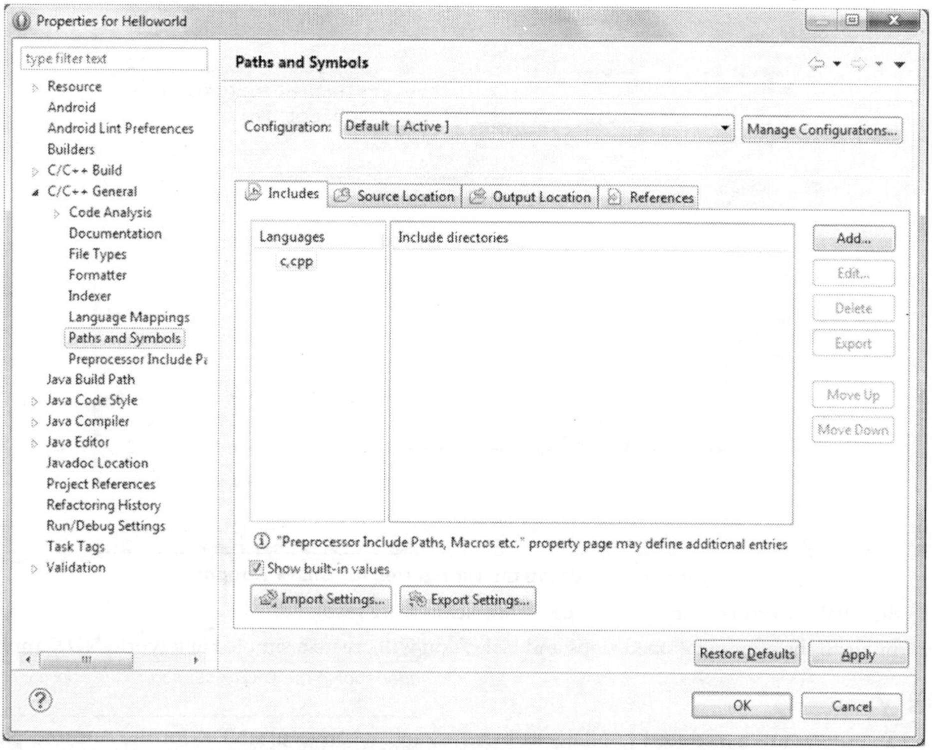

Figure 16.29: Selecting the Paths and Symbols Option

11. *Click* the **Add** button to include the required support for C/C++. The **Add directory path** dialog box opens.
12. *Click* the **File system** button to navigate to the C:\cygwin\android-ndk-r9d-windows-x86\android-ndk-r9d\platforms\android-4\arch-arm\usr\include path, as shown in Figure 16.30:

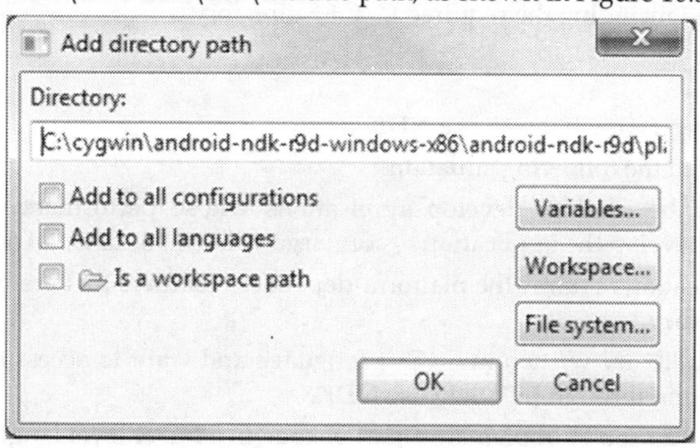

Figure 16.30: Showing the Add directory path Dialog Box

13. *Click* the **OK** button. The selected directory will be added in the **Properties for Helloworld** dialog box, as shown in Figure 16.31:

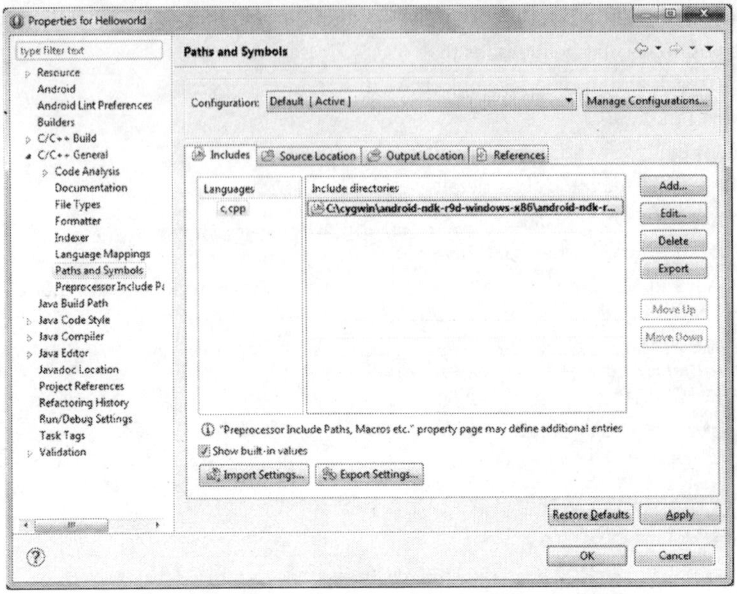

Figure 16.31: Adding the Directories for C/C++ Support

You will find that the errors of the `Helloworld` application are resolved.

By performing all the aforementioned steps and tasks, you will create a simple Helloworld NDK application.

Summary

In this chapter, you are introduced to NDK, its benefits, and when to use NDK for the Android platform. The chapter has helped you to communicate between Java and native code. Next, it has explained the journey of installing NDK by performing a series of tasks such as adding C/C++ support on Eclipse, installing NDK plugin through ADT, installing Cygwin, installing Android NDK, configuring Eclipse for NDK programming, and finally setting the PATH environment variable. You have also developed a basic Helloworld NDK application by adding native support and including the required C/C++ directory.

Quick Revise

Q1. List the points specifying when to use NDK.

Ans. NDK can be used in the following situations:

- NDK should be used to develop applications whose performance needs to be improved. For example, to develop the application to sort large volumes of data, NDK should be used.
- If your application requires the platform-dependent features that are not supported by the standard Java class library.
- If you have a library written in C/C++ language and want to access the library in the Java code of your application through JNI, then use NDK.
- NDK should be used to implement a part of code in a lower level language, such as assembly.

Q2. Write a short note on NDK.

Ans. NDK is a toolset that allows you to implement the components of your application using the native-code language such as C and C++. NDK is useful for some specific type of applications in which you need to reuse the existing code libraries written using C/C++. Prior to downloading the NDK, you, as a developer, should understand that NDK is beneficial for some applications only, while it increases the complexity for some other applications. Generally, you should use the NDK for the applications that are CPU intensive and do not allocate much memory, such as signal processing.

Q3. List the benefits of NDK.

Ans. NDK allows you to use native methods to:

- Create, inspect, and update Java objects, such as arrays and strings
- Invoke Java methods
- Implement the catch and throw exceptions
- Load classes and fetch the class details
- Perform runtime type checking

Q4. Explain the communication between Java and Native Code.

Ans. The Android Virtual Machine (VM) allows the source code of an application to invoke the methods to be implemented in the native code through the Java Native Interface (JNI). In other words, you can declare one or more methods using the native keyword specifying that they can be implemented through native code. For example, let's create the `loadFile()` method using the following code snippet:

```
native byte[] loadFile(String filePath);
```

You should create a native shared library providing the implementation of the native methods to be packaged into the application's APK. You should name this library according to the standard Unix convention, such as lib.so or `libFileLoading.so`. Then you should ensure that your application explicitly loads the library. To load the native shared library in your application, use the following code snippet:

```
static {System.loadLibrary("FileLoading"); }
```

Ensure that while loading the library, you do not use the prefix lib and suffix .so.

Q5. List the broad-level steps to install NDK for your application.

Ans. The broad-level steps to install NDK are as follows:

- Installing C/C++ support on Eclipse
- Installing NDK plugin through ADT
- Installing Cygwin
- Installing Android NDK
- Configuring Eclipse for NDK programming
- Setting the Environment variable

Q6. Which of the following languages are used for NDK programming?

a. Java

b. C \ C++

c. ASP.NET

d. C#

Ans. The correct option is b.

Q7. Which of the following programming language should be used for real-time application development?

a. Java

b. C

c. C++

d. C#

Ans. The correct option is b & c.

Q8. List the steps to convert the Android project to the native application.

Ans. Perform the following steps to convert the Android project to the native application:

1. *Create* the Android Application Project.
2. *Right-click* the project and select Android Tools→Add Native Support. The Add Android Native Support dialog box opens.

3. *Select* the default name of the library and click the Finish button to add the native support to the application.

Q9. While configuring the Eclipse for NDK programming, explain how to configure the PATH variable.

Ans. To configure the Eclipse for NDK programming, you need to add the bin path of the Cygwin and the root directory of the Android NDK package in the PATH environment variable.

Q10. Which of the following file appears in the jni folder after adding the native support to the application?

a. android.mk

b. MainActivity

c. AndroidManifest.xml

d. activity_main

Ans. The correct option is a.

17

Publishing, Monetizing, and Distributing Android Applications

If you need an information on:	*See page:*
Signing the Android Application	528
Versioning the Android Application	535
Publishing the Android Application	536
Monetizing Applications	541

Publishing is the last phase of development of an Android application. However, there are some important steps, such as development, debugging and testing, that you need to follow before publishing or releasing the Android application. In other words, the Android application is first developed, debugged, tested, and finally released. Note that you cannot publish your application directly. You need to sign it with a private key and then you can publish it.

The process of publishing completes in two steps. In the first step, the application is prepared for release, and in the second step, the application is released for users.

In the preparing phase, you configure, build, and test the release version of your application. The configuration involves the cleaning of code and elimination of garbage values. The building process comprises the development of project using Java Development Kit (JDK) and Software Development Kit (SDK). Finally, you test your application on at least one real device related to your target Application Program Interface (API). As soon you complete these steps, your application is ready to release. You can release your application through a marketplace, such as Google Play, through email, or using Web hosting.

This chapter explains how to sign the Android application. Then, it discusses about monetizing application.

Signing the Android Application

To make an Android application trustworthy for users as well as Google community, you need to sign it before release. A digital certificate is required for all the installed applications, and the developer who has made those applications must have the private key of that certificate. The certificate is used as an identity of the application developer. However, certificate does not impose any restriction on the installation of applications by users. Fortunately, Google has not appointed any authority to sign the certificate and thereby Android applications can use self-signed certificates. Some of the points that should be kept in mind regarding the signing of Android applications are as follows:

- The applications are required to be signed properly. Any unsigned application installation will be rejected by the emulator or any device. Eclipse IDE assigns a special debug key (generated by Android SDK) automatically to your applications. However, when you release your application to end users, you cannot use the debug key generated by Android SDK to sign the application. You must have a suitable private key to sign the application before releasing.
- A self-signed certificate can be used to sign your application, eliminating the need of any authority to sign it. The Android system tests the expiry date of the application's signer certificate at the time of installation. If the signer certificate expires after the installation, it will not affect the functioning of the application.

Standard tools such as keytool and jarsigner are used to generate keys and sign your application, respectively. After the successful signing of an application, the zipalign tool is used for final optimization of .apk files.

Exploring the Strategies for Signing the Application

The most important point you should consider while signing the Android application is that you must use the same certificate for all of your applications. Some of the reasons highlighting the need of using the same certificate are as follows:

- To let the users upgrade the new versions of your application seamlessly, use the same certificate (the one used at the time of installation) at the time of release of your application. On other hand, if you change the certificate, then the user has to install the full upgraded version again. In addition, if your certificate is changed, then you have to assign different package to your application. In essence, using the same certificate implies much lesser data download, thereby providing convenience to the users.
- Using the same certificate for your applications ensures that there is only one process assigned for all your applications in Android system. This approach sustains the modularity concept as you can deploy your application in different modules and release separate updates for each of the modules. This is also beneficial from the user's point of view, as the user can download the update only for the desired module.
- Preference to same certificate also provides reliable exposure of data to other applications that are signed with a specified certificate. Your application is secured for any kind of data sharing with a third-party application.

We have understood the advantages of using the same certificate. Now, let's see how to set the validity period of the key that is used to sign your application and update. The following points regarding the validity period of the key must be noted:

- Always set the lifespan of the key equal to or more than 99 years (Maximum permissible limit) if you are going to support a single application. If the lifespan of the key expires, the user will be unable to upgrade any new version of your application.
- If you are going to publish multiple applications using the same key, then ensure that your key's validity must surpass the lifespan of all the available versions of all the applications in a suite.
- Finally, if you plan to publish your application on Google Play, then your key must expire after October 22, 2033, as Google Play wants the users to get seamless upgrades of an application on the availability of new versions.

Obtaining the Appropriate Private Key

To obtain a private key, the first step involves the interaction between the keytool and jarsigner utilities of JDK and the Android SDK build tools. This interaction can be performed in two ways. The first way is to set the `JAVA_HOME` variable in Environment Variables of Windows in a computer system. In this variable, you have to provide the path up to the JDK directory. The second way is to set the path of the standard commands, keytool and jarsigner, as `PATH` variable in the environment variables.

By using the `keytool` command and passing the options listed in Table 16.1, we can generate a self-signed key with the keytool command. For example:

The following command is used to generate a private key:

```
keytool -genkey -v -keystore your-key-name.keystore
-alias alias-key-name -keyalg RSA -keysize 2048 -validity 10000
```

The options given in the preceding command are described in Table 16.1:

Table 16.1: The Keytool Options with Their Use

Keytool Option	Use
-genkey	Generates public and private keys (key pair).
-v	Displays verbose output.
-alias	Displays an alias for the key. It uses the first eight characters of the alias.
-keyalg <alg>	Displays the key encryption algorithm used for generating the key. In our case, we have used the RSA algorithm.
-keypass <password>	Displays the password for the key. Note that we are not using this option in the preceding keytools command. If we use this option, the password remains in shell history and an intruder can read it; however, if this option is excluded from the command, the `keytool` command will prompt you to enter the password after the execution of command.
-keysize<size>	Displays the size (bits) of the generated key. The `keytool` command uses a key size that is of 1024 bits by default, if this option is excluded from the command. However, using a key size of 2048 bit or higher is recommended.
-validity	Displays the lifespan (in days) of the key. It should be equal to or more than 10000.
-keystore <keystore-name>.keystore	Displays the name of the `keystore` in which the key lies.
-storepass<password>	Displays the password for the `keystore`.

Table 16.1: The Keytool Options with Their Use	
Keytool Option	**Use**
	Note that we are not using this option in the preceding `keytool` command. If we use this option, the password remains in shell history and an intruder can read it; however, if we exclude this option from the command, the `keytool` command will prompt you to enter the password after the execution of command.

For the sake of practice, let's suppose we want to store the private key named `TabLayout` in the **D:\apk** directory. For this, we can use the keytool command as follows:

```
    keytool -genkey -v -keystore D:\apk\TabLayout.keystore -alias TabLayout -keyalg RSA       -
keysize 2048 -validity 10000
```

The preceding command depicts that on execution, the keytool command will generate a `Tablayout.keystore` private key whose size will be 2048 bits with a validity of 10000 days.

On executing the preceding command on the command prompt, you are asked to provide the following details, as shown in Figure 17.1:

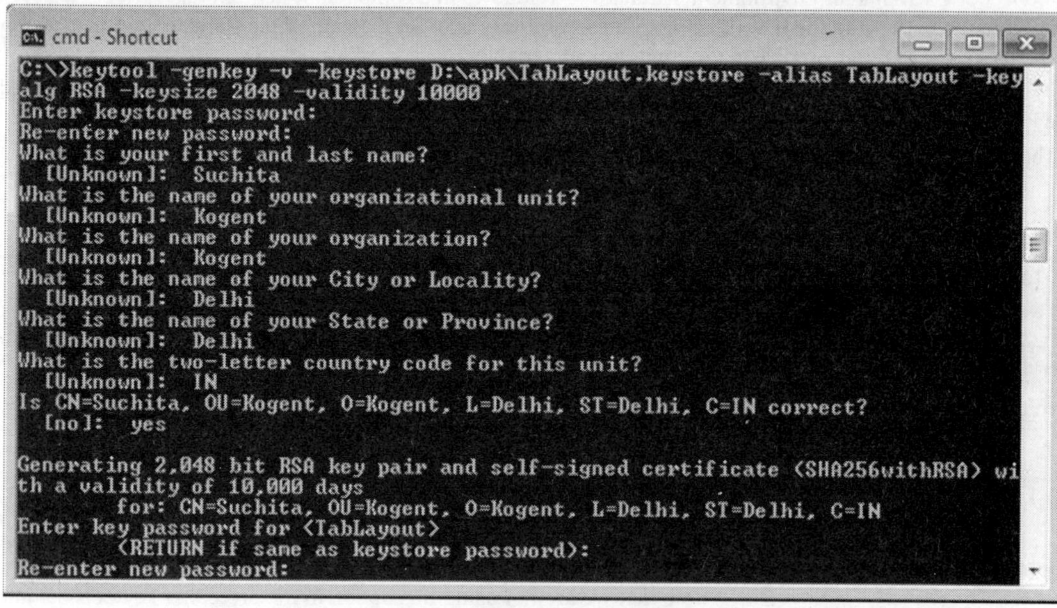

Figure 17.1: Executing the Command for Private Key

These details include the password for keystore, name, organizational unit, organization, city or locality, state or province, and two letter country code. After this, you are asked about the correctness of details that you have entered. Enter 'yes,' and then again you are prompted for the password; re-enter that password again. Note that this password should match with the password you have provided in the very first step. After providing the password, your key named `TabLayout.keystore` will be generated in the directory **D:\apk**. Figure 17.2 shows the generation of the key:

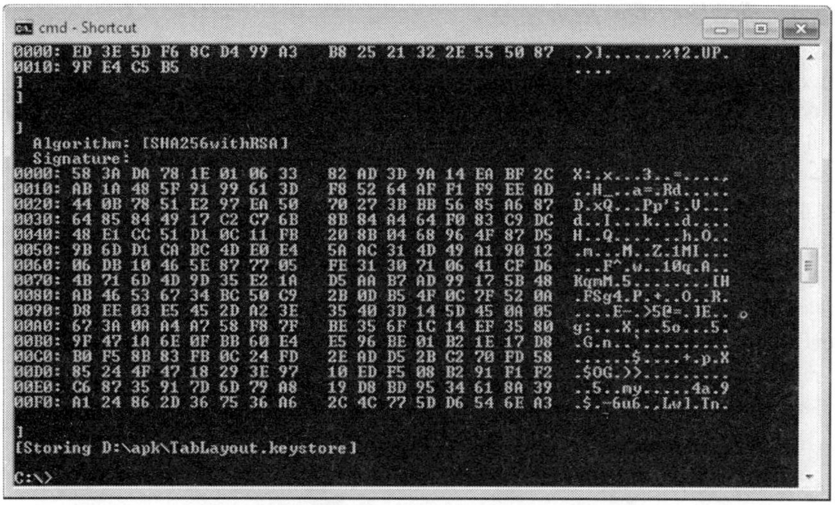

Figure 17.2: Showing the Generated Private Key

The private key thus generated should be saved carefully for future references.

Since you have already created the private key called `TabLayout.keystore`, you can use it to sign as many applications as you wish. To sign an application, the following `jarsigner` command is used:

```
jarsigner -verbose  -keystore YourPrivateKey.keystore YourAppName.apk YourAppAlias
```

Let's now learn how to sign an application called `TabLayout`. The signing is done by using the following command:

```
jarsigner -verbose  -keystore D:\apk\TabLayout.keystore D:\apk\TabLayout.apk TabLayout
```

Note that we have placed both apk file and private key in the same directory. You can place them in different directories also. However, you have to specify their full qualified path in the `jarsigner` command. The execution of the `jarsigner` command after entering the password is shown in Figure 17.3:

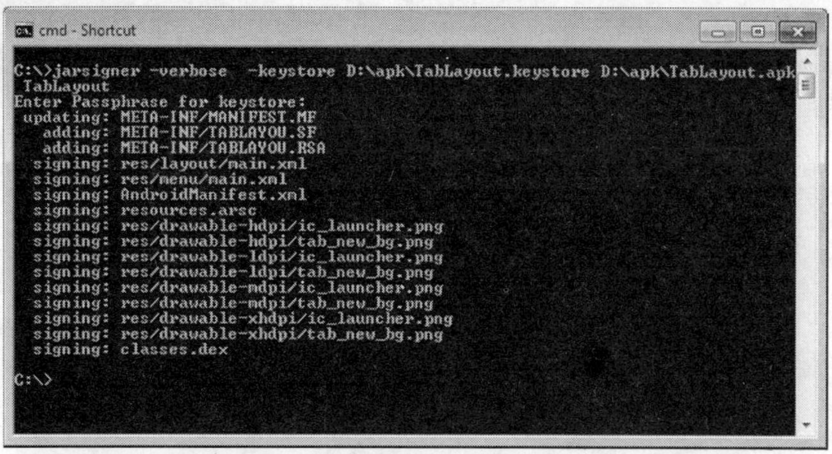

Figure 17.3: Signing the TabLayout Application with the Private Key

Your application is now signed up. You can verify it by executing the following command:

```
jarsigner -verify yoursignedapp.apk
```

Let's now learn how to prepare the application for release.

Preparing the Application for Release

Your application must be signed properly before release. When you release your application, users download and install it on their Android-powered devices. The tasks that are required to be accomplished to prepare your application for release are as follows:

- There should not be any unwanted or garbage code, such as log calls and `android:debuggable` attribute in the `AndroidManifest.xml` file.
- Provide proper versioning to your application in the `AndroidManifest.xml` file.
- Sign your application properly.
- Test your application on a real device for which your application is intended.
- All application resources, such as multimedia and graphics, must be updated and included.
- Prepare an End User License Agreement (EULA) to protect your intellectual property.
- Prepare remote servers and services on which your application relies.

After the completion of all the preceding tasks, your application is ready for release with signed APK.

Let's now learn how to align the APK package.

Aligning the APK Package

Aligning refers to the process of optimizing the Android Application Package (APK). This alignment enhances interaction between Android system and your application. Moreover, there is less consumption of system Random Access Memory (RAM) using the `zipalign` utility. The aligning procedure is accomplished by using `zipalign`, which is an archive alignment tool. The command line tool used to align the `.apk` file is as follows:

```
zipalign -v 4 your_app_name-unaligned.apk your_app_name.apk
```

The command used to align an application called `TabLayout` is as follows:

```
zipalign -v 4 D:\apk\TabLayout.apk D:\apk\TabLayout_signed.apk
```

The preceding command will align your `apk` file. Figure 17.4 shows the `command-line` tool upon execution:

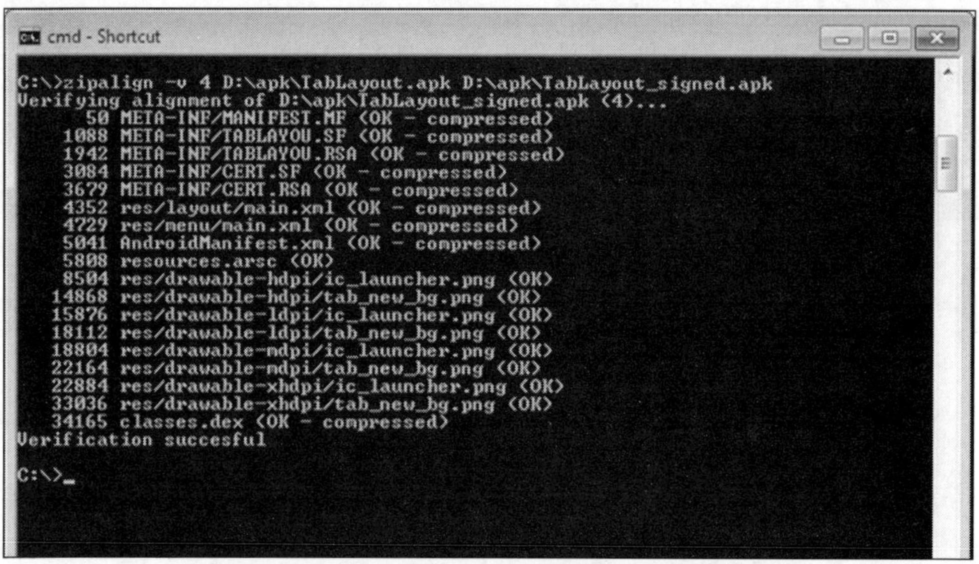

Figure 17.4: Aligning the Package Using the Command-Line Tool

From the preceding command, we can see that the -v flag is the verbose output, and `Tablayout.apk` is the apk file to be aligned. The `TabLayout_signed.apk` is the aligned file.

Signing and Aligning APK Using the Eclipse IDE

Once you have the private key, you can sign and align your application by using the Eclipse IDE in a much easier way. Note that you cannot publish your application using the debug.keystore key. A suitable signed key should be created by setting the keytool and jarsigner commands as `PATH` variable in the environment variable. The steps to sign and align APK using the Eclipse IDE are as follows:

1. In the **Package Explorer**, *right-click* on the project you want to export and *click* the **Export** option. The **Export** window appears (Figure 17.5).
2. *Expand* the **Android** directory and *select* **Export Android Application** (Figure 17.5).
3. *Click* the **Next** button, as shown in Figure 17.5:

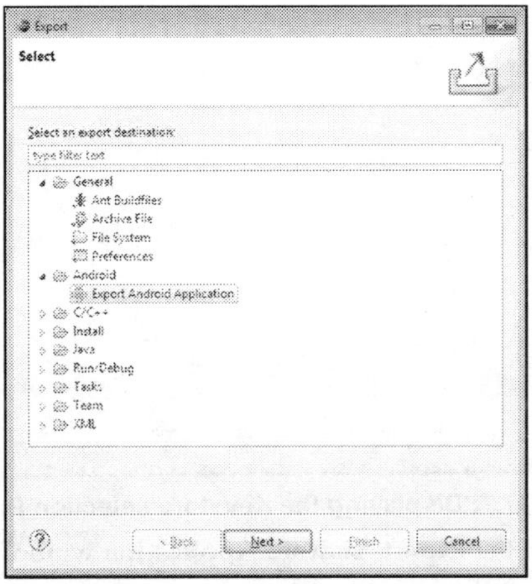

Figure 17.5: Displaying the Export Wizard of the Eclipse IDE

NOTE

Another way to open the Export wizard is, right-click the project in the Package Explorer and select the Android Tools→Export Signed Application Package option.

The **Project Checks** page of the **Export Android Application** window appears (Figure 17.6). The project that you have selected to export will appear automatically in the **Project** text box (Figure 17.6). If any error is found at this step, then the project cannot be exported. Now, *click* the **Next** button, as shown in Figure 17.6:

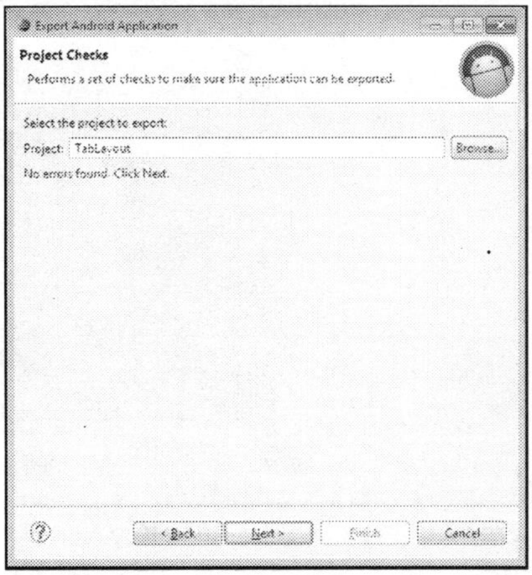

Figure 17.6: Exporting the Android Application

The **Keystore** selection page of the **Export Android Application** window appears (Figure 17.7).

4. *Enter* the location and password of the private key in the **Location** and **Password** text boxes, respectively (Figure 17.7).
5. *Click* the **Next** button, as shown in Figure 17.7:

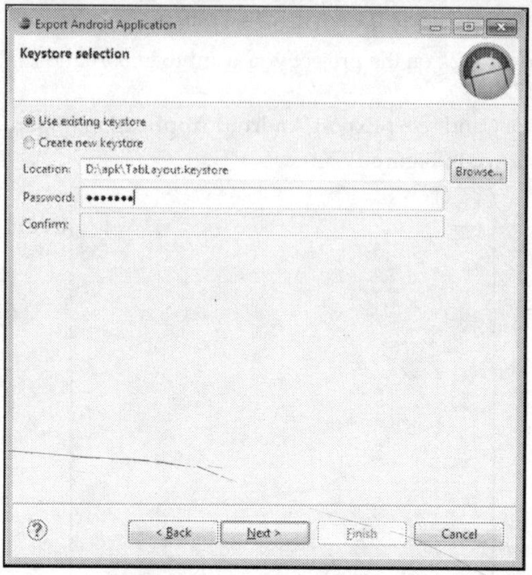

Figure 17.7: Displaying the Keystore selection Page

The **Key alias selection** page of the **Export Android Application** window appears (Figure 17.8).

6. *Select* the **Alias** name from the drop-down list of the **Alias** text box and *enter* the same password that you have entered in the **password** text box in the preceding step (Figure 17.8).
7. *Click* the **Next** button, as shown in Figure 17.8:

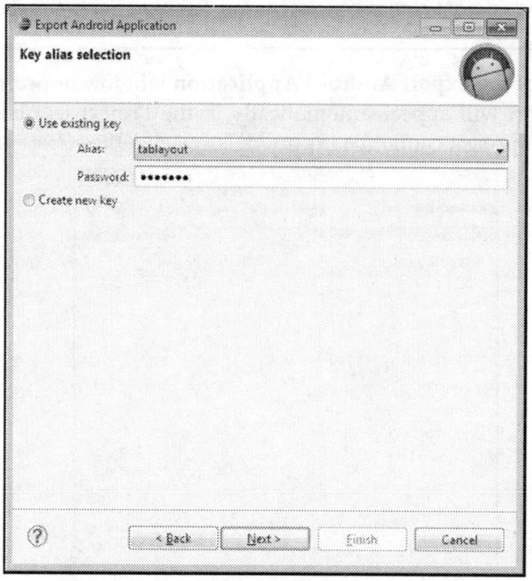

Figure 17.8: Selecting the Alias Key Name

The Destination and key/certificate checks page of the Export Android Application window appears (Figure 17.9).

8. *Select* the destination where you want to save your application (Figure 17.9).
9. *Click* the **Finish** button, as shown in Figure 17.9:

Figure 17.9: Providing the Destination of the .apk file

The signed and aligned application will be generated at the specified location.

In this way, you can easily sign and align the Android application using Eclipse IDE.

Let's now learn about versioning of the Android application.

Versioning the Android Application

Versioning tells the users about the version of application they are using. It is an upgrade and maintenance strategy, which is provided to user from time to time. The following points portray the essentials behind versioning of an application:

- Users want to know the application version that they are using and the upgrades available for that version.
- The compatibility issues are heavily dependent on the versioning of your application.
- When you release your application through a service, it prompts for application version so that it can be displayed to the user at the time of download.

There is no restriction imposed on the application version by Android system. In fact, it is your (or developer) responsibility to tell the user whether your application is compatible to their device or not. In other words, it is your duty to inform users about any version restrictions in your application.

Setting the Application Version

There are two attributes to set the application version: `android:versionCode` and `android:versionName`. The description of these two attributes is as follows:

- `android:versionCode`: This attribute is an integer value and as the attribute name implies; it represents the version of the application code. The integer value is assessed programmatically by all the services that require information about the version. In best practices, you should increment the version code so that the services can identify the new release. However, the version code is not basically visible to the users. The version, which is displayed to the user, is set by the `android:versionName` attribute, which is discussed next.
- `android:versionName`: This is the string value, which is visible to the user. This attribute is completely intended for users as it displays the version name, and it does not have any impact on the program.

An example of the `AndroidManifest.xml` file, which shows these two attributes, is as follows:

```
<?xml version="1.0" encoding="utf-8"?>
<manifest xmlns:android="http://schemas.android.com/apk/res/android"
    package="com.kogent.android"
    android:versionCode="1"
    android:versionName="1.2" >
    <uses-sdk
        .
      />
    <application
        .
        .
    </application>
</manifest>
```

Specifying API Requirements of an Android Application

There can be certain compatibility issues if user's device does not support the API you have used in your application. Therefore, you must specify the API level used in your application to the users. This can be accomplished by using the `<uses-sdk>` element in your `AndroidManifest.xml` file. An example of the `AndroidManifest.xml` file is as follows:

```
<?xml version="1.0" encoding="utf-8"?>
<manifest xmlns:android="http://schemas.android.com/apk/res/android"
    package="com.kogent.android"
    android:versionCode="1"
    android:versionName="1.2" >
    <uses-sdk
        android:minSdkVersion="14"
        android:targetSdkVersion="19" />
    <application
        .>
  .
    </application>
</manifest>
```

The attributes used to specify the API used along with their description are as follows:

- `android:minSdkVersion`: This attribute is used to express the minimum version Android platform to which the application is intended. The identifier used for this attribute is the API level. For example, you can set the `android:minSdkVersion` attribute as API level 10, which is intended for Android version 2.3.3.
- `android:targetSdkVersion`: This attribute informs the Android version for which the application is primarily made.
- `android:maxSdkVersion`: This is an optional attribute that specifies a number representing the maximum API Level on which the application is designed to run. The use of this attribute is not recommended, as it as it blocks the deployment of your application on a new version of the Android platform.

If your `AndroidManifest.xml` file does not include these attributes, then the Android system assumes that your application is compatible with all available Android platforms. However, if the value of the `android:minSdkVersion` attribute is greater than the `android:targetSdkVersion` attribute, then the system aborts installation.

After learning about versioning of the Android application, let's learn how to publish the Android application in an application market.

Publishing the Android Application

Publishing is the last phase of the development process of an Android application, wherein you expose the application to the market, thereby letting the users download it.

As you know, Google Play is the Google's Android application marketplace from where you can upload and download the applications. It is recommended that you should release your application on Google Play. However, there are also other ways to release your application, such as sending applications to the users directly through email or making it available on your website for download. Figure 17.10 shows the publishing process of Android applications:

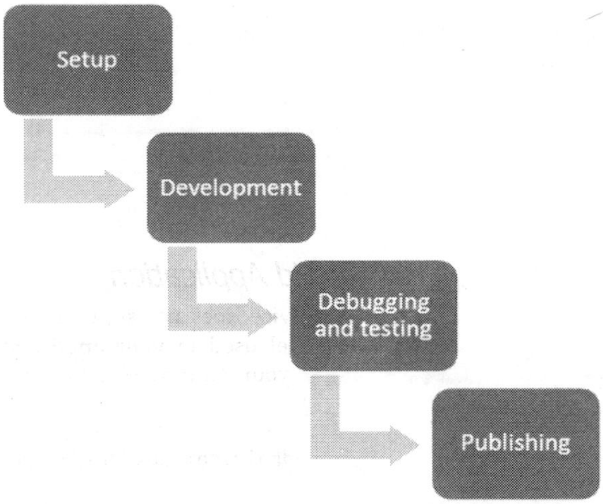

Figure 17.10: Dispaying the Publishing Process of the Android Application

Generally, publishing of application is a combination of two tasks, that is, preparing application for release and releasing application to users. You have already learned about preparing an application for release. Let's now learn about releasing an application to users.

As described earlier, you can release your application to users in several ways, such as through Google Play, email, and letting them download the application from your website.

Let's now discuss each of the ways mentioned in the preceding paragraph one by one.

Releasing Applications on Google Play

Google Play is one of the best ways to release an application as it is Google's premier marketplace. Here, you can publicize, sell, and distribute your Android applications across the world. Google Play offers you tools to track your sales, identify market trends, and a wider array of other developer friendly tools. The steps to publish your application on Google Play are as follows:

- To make your application popular, you can add advertising material to your application, such as screenshots and videos.
- You can configure the various Google play settings, such as pricing of your application, and the countries in which you want to publish your application. When the configuration is complete, you can upload your advertising material as a draft (unpublished) application.
- Finally, you can publish your application by just clicking the **Publish** button on the developer console. After some time, your application will be available across the world for downloading.

Google Play acts similar to a store that allows you to sell and distribute your application instead of allowing a merchant to sell it on your behalf. It provides all the tools and mechanisms required to handle application distribution, updates, sales, and promotion. To publish your application on Google Play, you need to create a developer account at https://play.google.com/apps/publish/signup, as shown in Figure 17.11:

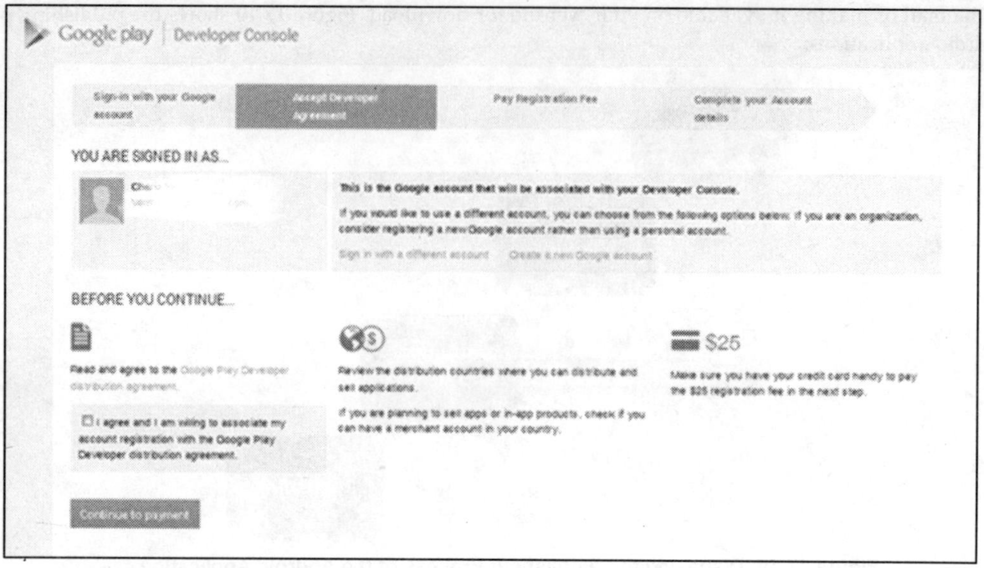

Figure 17.11: Displaying Google Play Developer Console

You will be asked to provide a Developer Name and your company name, which will be used within Google Play to identify the developer of your applications. After creating your Android developer profile, you have to pay $25 as subscription fee, so that you are allowed to upload your application.

Once you completed the payment procedure, you can access the applications dashboard as shown in Figure 17.12:

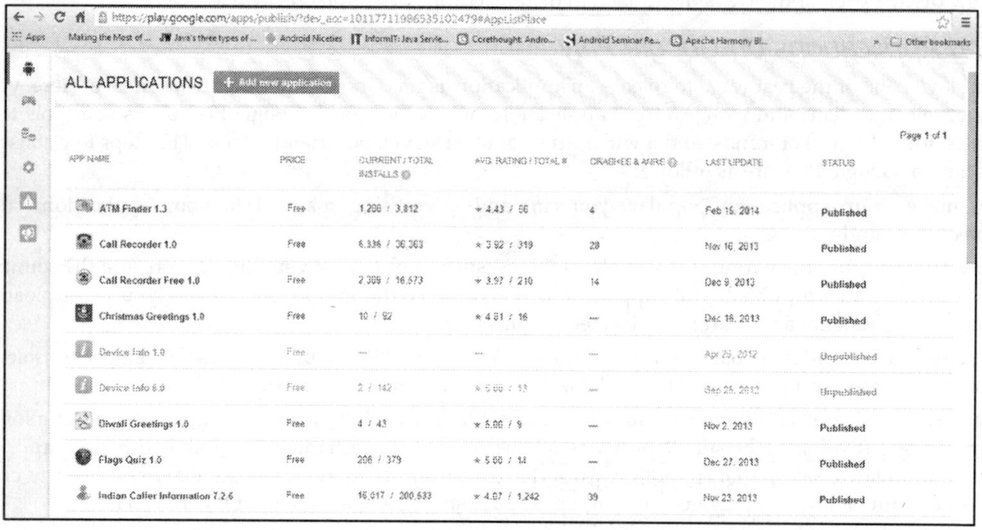

Figure 17.12: Displaying Dashboard for Uploading Applications

In Figure 17.12, you can see a list of applications that are uploaded at Google play store. You need to click the Add new application button to add a new application. You need to provide the name of your application. For example, you see the `ACCELEROMETER DEMO` application, as shown in Figure 17.13:

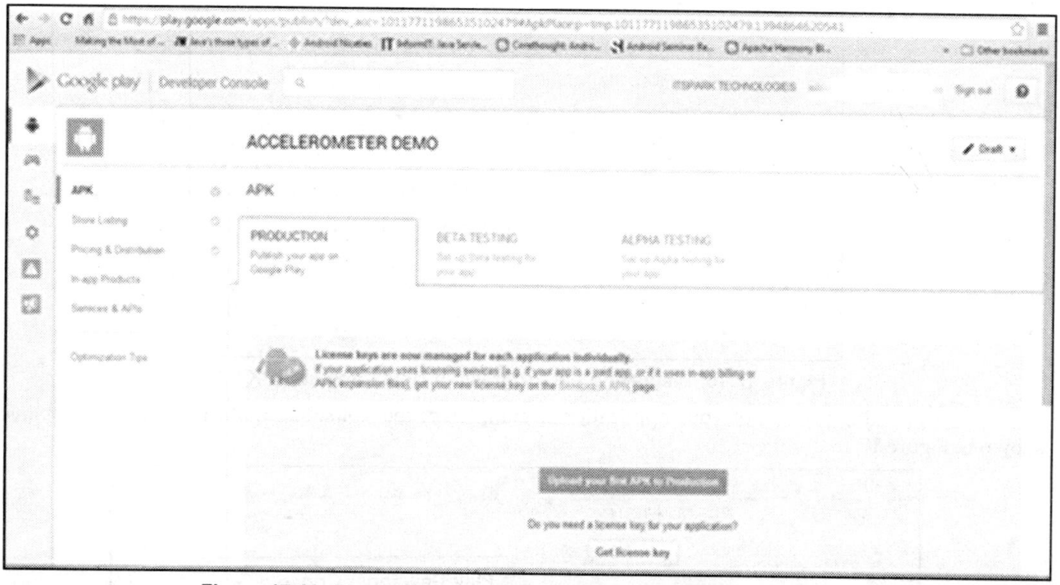

Figure 17.13: Displaying the ACCELEROMETER DEMO Application

You need to select the **PRODUCTION** tab to make your application publicly available at Google store. The **BETA TESTING** and **ALPHA TESTING** options are used to test the applications on a variety of devices before their actual launching. Then, click the **Upload your first APK to Production** button, which displays the **UPLOAD NEW APK TO PRODUCTION** dialog box to browse the application related files, as shown in Figure 17.14:

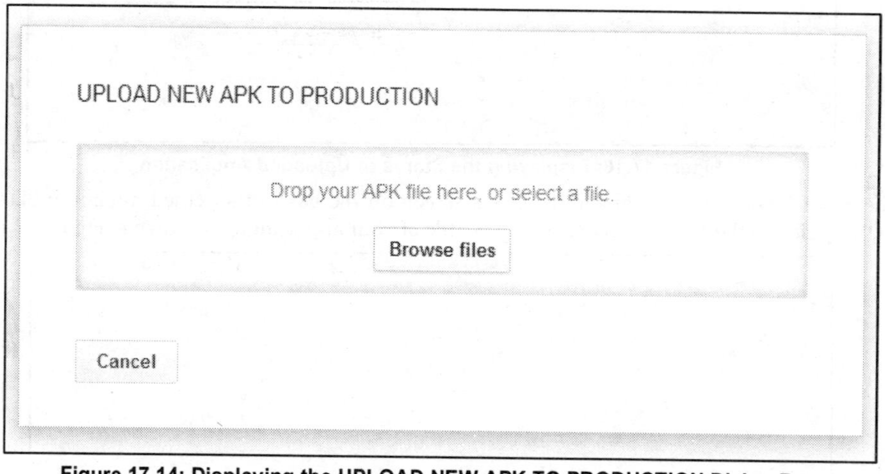

Figure 17.14: Displaying the UPLOAD NEW APK TO PRODUCTION Dialog Box

You need to drop your apk in the provided area or browse its location to access it. For instance, the `AccelerometerDemo.apk` is provided in our case, as shown in Figure 17.15:

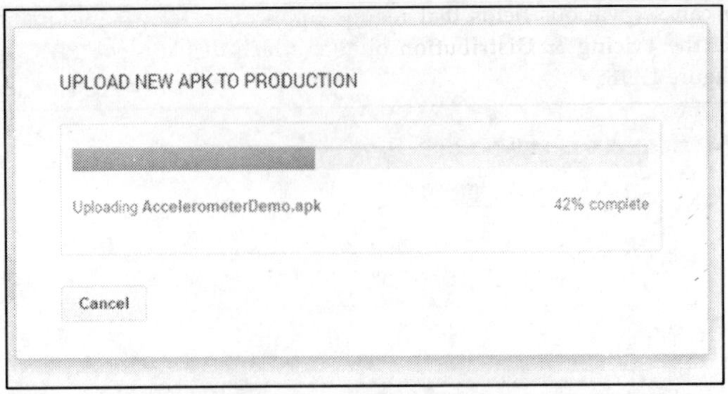

Figure 17.15: Displaying the Progress of Uploading an APK File

When the uploading process of your application is completed, the uploaded application will be displayed, as shown in Figure 17.16:

Figure 17.16: Displaying the Status of Uploaded Application

Select the **Store Listing** option, which displays a screen on the basis of specified minimum SDK version and target SDK version in the `AndroidManifest.xml` file of your application, as shown in Figure 17.17:

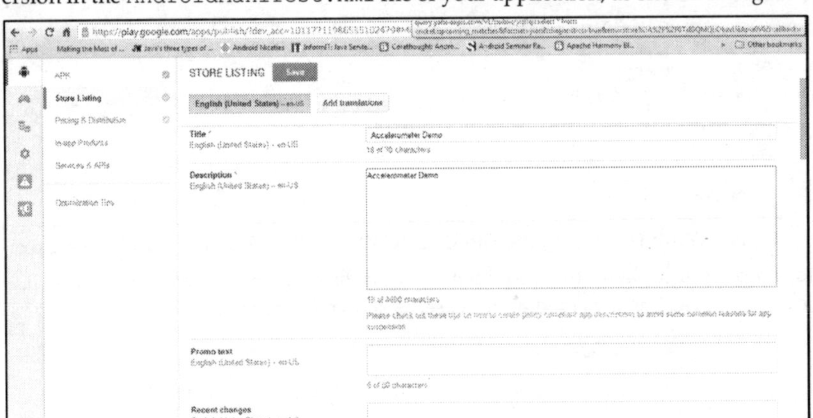

Figure 17.17: Displaying the STORE LISTING Screen

In Figure 17.17, you can see various fields that require application related information, such as `Title` and `Description`. Select the **Pricing & Distribution** option, which displays the **PRICING & DISTRIBUTION** screen, as shown in Figure 17.18:

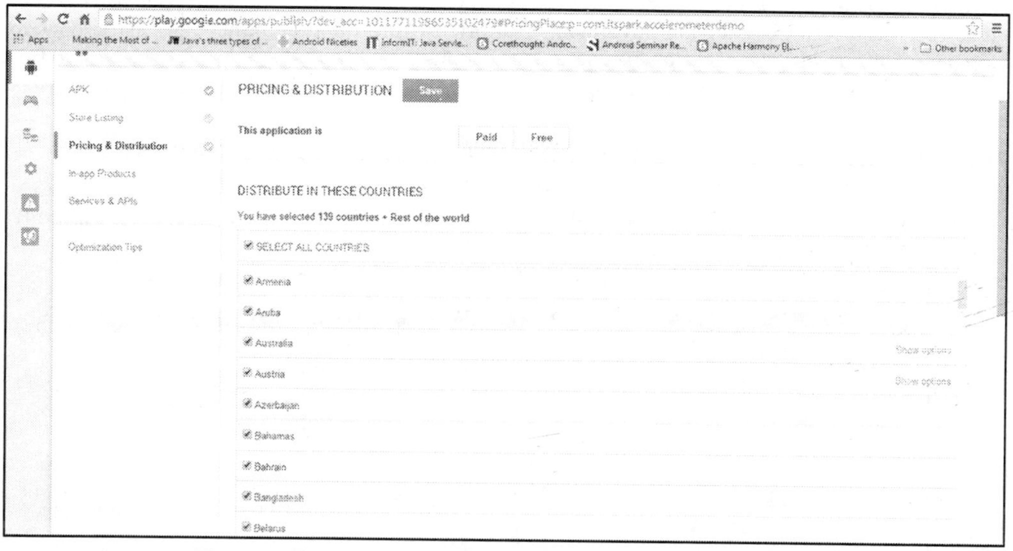

Figure 17.18: Displaying the PRICING & DISTRIBUTION Screen

In Figure 17.18, you see the **PRICING & DISTRIBUTION** screen, which allows you to specify the names of various countries in which you want to see your application and also allows the price of your application. Now, click the **Save** button to save the specified changes.

Releasing Applications through Email

Releasing application to users through email is the simplest and fastest way to publish your application. Just prepare your application and release it through the email. However, publishing in this way is inefficient as someone can pirate your application and also dispose it to unauthorized publishing.

Releasing Applications through a Website

This is the third way in which you can host your prepared application for release. When a user downloads the application, the Android system automatically recognizes it and then installs it. Releasing through website seems to be a better choice; however, it is not considered an efficient way to release an application because you cannot properly monetize and track all the transactions of your applications. Ultimately, your application is vulnerable to unauthorized installation.

Monetizing Applications

Android enables you to monetize your applications using various mechanisms. One of the common options is again of Google Play. It provides you the following options:

- **Paid Application**—Specifies the option that demands fee from users before downloading and installing your application.
- **Free Applications with In-App Billing (IAB)**—Specifies the option that allows users to download and install your application free, but charge its upgrades and other value-adds.
- **Advertising-Supported Application**—Specifies the option that allows its users to download and install your application free, but monetize it by displaying advertising.

Monetizing an Application through Advertising Platform

Google allows you to monetize an application using their advertising platform or any other company advertisement platform. For this you need to integrate the advertising platform with your bank account. In this section you learn how to integrate advertising platform with admob account. Let's learn how to use the advertising platform of `AdMob` to monetize your applications. For this, first, you need to set an Android Eclipse application with required SDKs from the respective advertisement network and embed the respective layout and code in the application.

Perform the following steps to integrate Google Ad network or admob in your Android application:

1. *Open* the http://www.admob.com website in your Web browser.
2. *Create* a login ID and sign in with the created account in the **AdMob** website, as shown in Figure 17.19:

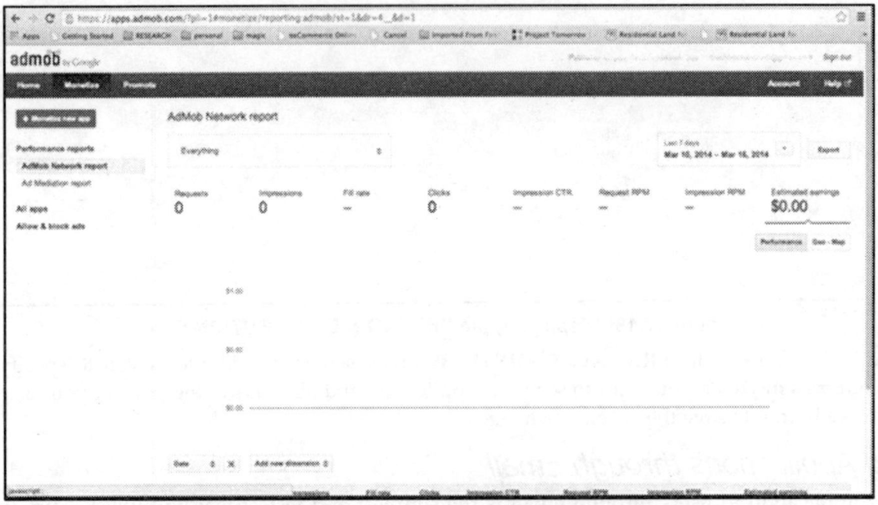

Figure 17.19: Displaying the AdMob Website after Sign In

3. *Select* the **Monetize** tab, which displays the **Monetize a new app** screen, as shown in Figure 17.20:

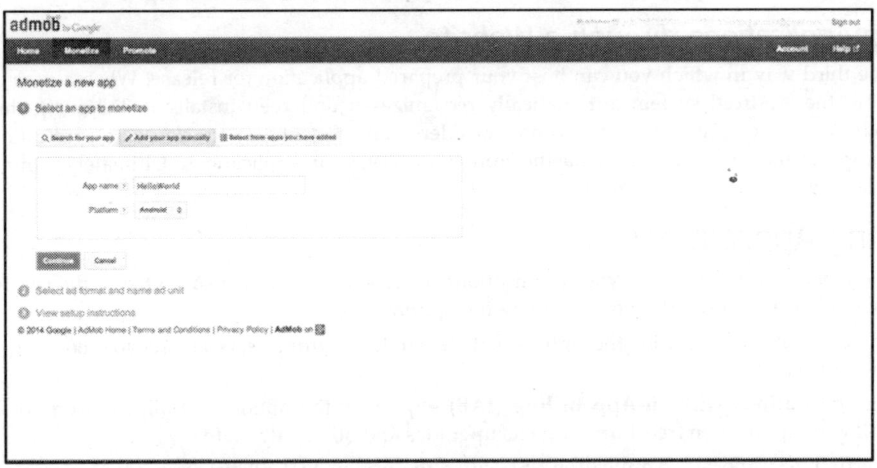

Figure 17.20: Displaying the Monetize a new app Screen

In Figure 17.20, you can see that there are three sections to monetize an application, which are as follows:

- **Select a New App**—In this section, you have to enter your application name and its platform for execution (Figure 17.20).

- **Select ad Format and Name Ad Unit**—In this section, you have to provide banner or interstitial related details, such as Text ad style and Ad unit name, as shown in Figure 17.21:

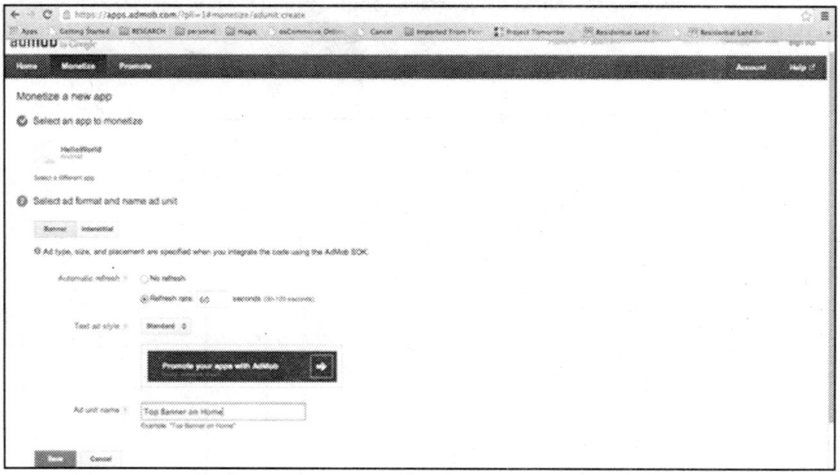

Figure 17.21: Displaying the Select Ad Format and Name Ad Unit Section

- **View Setup Instructions**—In this section, you can view instructions that guide you how to integrate the Google AdMob SDK, as shown in Figure 17.22:

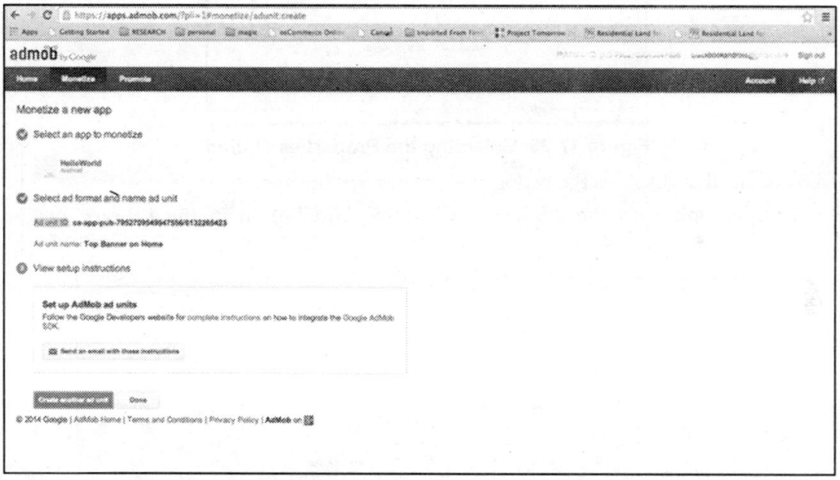

Figure 17.22: Displaying the View setup instructions Section

After providing all details related to monetize an application on the **Monetize a new app** screen, you get a unique Ad unit ID, which is required to add in your application.

Integrating the Google AdMob SDK with an Application

In this section you learn to integrate the Google AdMob SDK within an application. This process includes the four basic steps:

1. *Add* the reference of the Google Play services library project in your **Eclipse** workspace.
2. *Add* a `meta-data` tag in the `AndroidManifest.xml` file of your application.
3. *Use* an <Activity> tag to declare com.google.android.gms.ads.AdActivity in the AndroidManifest.xml file.
4. *Set up* network permissions in the `AndroidManifest.xml` file, as shown in the following code snippet:

Let's perform the following steps to integrate the Google AdMob SDK within an application:

1. *Open* Eclipse IDE and import the **google-play-services_lib** project. It should be noted that the **google-play-services_lib** project is located in the **\sdk\extras\google\google_play_services\libproject** folder of the ADT bundle of Android SDK 4.4.2.
2. *Right-click* the name of your application in the **Package Explorer** and select the **Properties** option, as shown in Figure 17.23:

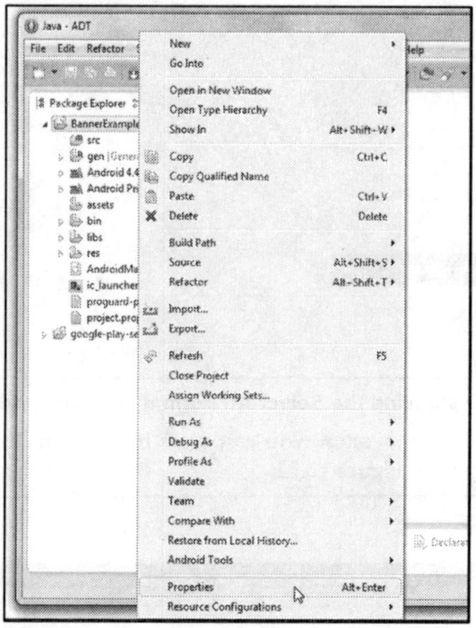

Figure 17.23: Selecting the Properties Option

A dialog box opens that displays the properties of your application.

3. *Select* the **Android** option in the left pane. *Click* the **Add** button in the **Library** section, as shown in Figure 17.24:

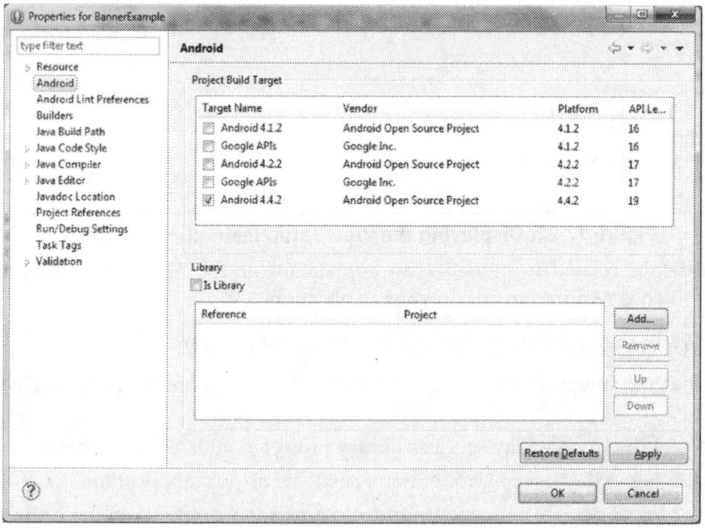

Figure 17.24: Displaying the Properties Dialog Box of an Application

The **Project Selection** dialog box displays.

4. *Select* the **google-play-services_lib** project in the available list and *click* the **OK** button, as shown in Figure 17.25:

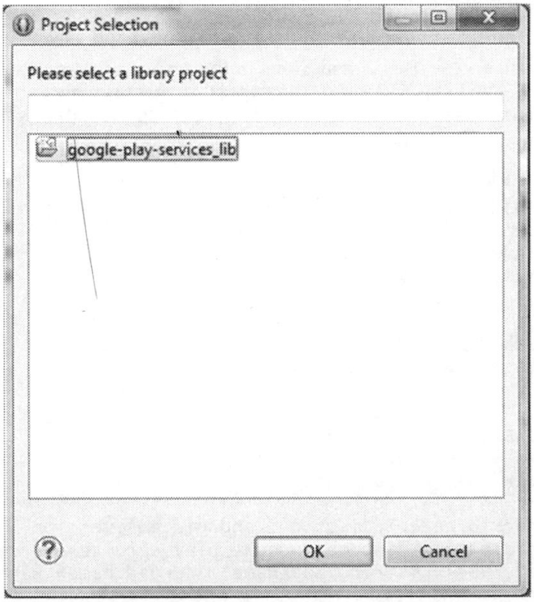

Figure 17.25: Displaying the Project Selection Dialog Box

You can see that the reference of the **google-play-services_lib** project is added in the **Library** section of the **Properties** dialog box, as shown in Figure 17.26:

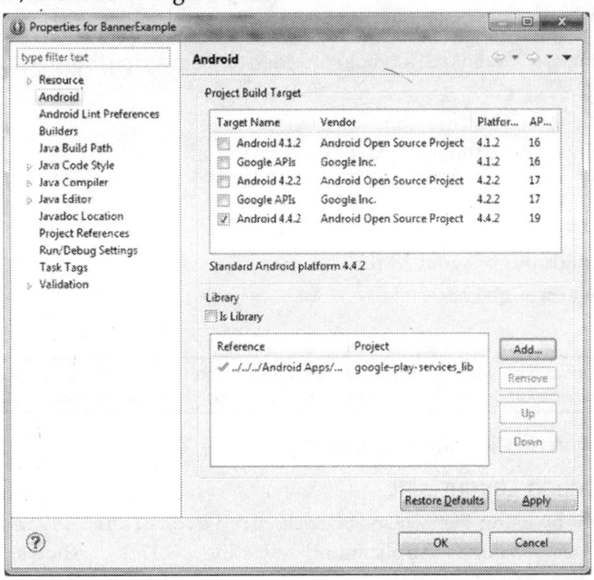

Figure 17.26: Displaying Added Reference of the google-play-services_lib Project

5. *Click* the **Apply** and **OK** button to complete the task.
6. *Add* the following `meta-data` tag in the `Android.Manifest.xml` file:

```
<meta-data android:name="com.google.android.gms.version"
android:value="@integer/google_play_services_version"/>
```

7. *Add* the following `activity` tag in the `Android.Manifest.xml` file:

```
<activity android:name="com.google.android.gms.ads.AdActivity"
  android:configChanges="keyboard|keyboardHidden|orientation|screenLayout|uiMode|screenSize|smallestScreenSize"/>
```

8. *Add* the following network access uses permissions in the `Android.Manifest.xml` file:

```
<uses-permission android:name="android.permission.INTERNET"/>
<uses-permission android:name="android.permission.ACCESS_NETWORK_STATE"/>
```

The complete code of the `AndroidManifest.xml` file is given in Listing 17.1:

Listing 17.1: Displaying the Code of the `AndroidManifest.xml` File

```
<manifest xmlns:android="http://schemas.android.com/apk/res/android"
    package="com.kogent.android.bannerexample"
    android:versionCode="1"
    android:versionName="1.0" >

    <uses-sdk
        android:minSdkVersion="14"
        android:targetSdkVersion="19" />

    <application
        android:allowBackup="true"
        android:icon="@drawable/ic_launcher"
        android:label="@string/app_name"
        android:theme="@style/AppTheme" >
       <meta-data android:name="com.google.android.gms.version"
               android:value="@integer/google_play_services_version"/>
    <activity android:label="@string/app_name" android:name="BannerExample">
      <intent-filter>
        <action android:name="android.intent.action.MAIN"/>
        <category android:name="android.intent.category.LAUNCHER"/>
      </intent-filter>
    </activity>
    <activity android:name="com.google.android.gms.ads.AdActivity"

android:configChanges="keyboard|keyboardHidden|orientation|screenLayout|uiMode|screenSize|
smallestScreenSize"/>

  </application>
  <uses-permission android:name="android.permission.INTERNET"/>
  <uses-permission android:name="android.permission.ACCESS_NETWORK_STATE"/>
</manifest>
```

Now, add advertisement by using any of the following option:

- Adding advertisement through layout XML
- Adding advertisement through code

NOTE

To use any of these options, you must first create a Google Checkout Merchant Account from your Android publisher account. Then, you need to set a price for your application or monetize your application using in-app advertising.

Let's learn about these options in the following sections.

Adding Advertisement through Layout XML

You can add advertisement by using the `com.google.android.gms.ads.AdView` view in an XML file in the /res/layout folder of your application. Listing 17.2 shows the use of the `com.google.android.gms.ads.AdView` view:

Listing 17.2: Displaying the Code of the `activity_main.xml` File

```
<?xml version="1.0" encoding="utf-8"?>
<LinearLayout xmlns:android="http://schemas.android.com/apk/res/android"
    xmlns:ads="http://schemas.android.com/apk/res-auto"
```

```
        android:layout_width="match_parent"
        android:layout_height="match_parent"
        android:orientation="vertical" >
    <TextView
            android:layout_width="match_parent"
            android:layout_height="wrap_content"
            android:text="Admob example " />
    <com.google.android.gms.ads.AdView
            android:id="@+id/adView"
            android:layout_width="match_parent"
            android:layout_height="wrap_content"
            ads:adSize="BANNER"
            ads:adUnitId="ca-app-pub-7952709549947556/2899597426" />
    </LinearLayout>
```

Adding Advertisement through Code

Another way to add advertisement in application is to write the code in the `MainActivity` class of the application. The following code snippet shows how to add advertisement in an application through code:

```
public class MainActivity extends Activity {
   private static final String AD_UNIT_ID_TEXT = "ca-app-pub-7952709549947556/8806530223";

   @Override
   public void onCreate(Bundle savedInstanceState) {
          super.onCreate(savedInstanceState);
          setContentView(R.layout.activity_main);
          AdView adView = (AdView) this.findViewById(R.id.adView);
       AdRequest adRequest = new AdRequest.Builder()
           .addTestDevice(AdRequest.DEVICE_ID_EMULATOR)
           .addTestDevice(AD_UNIT_ID_TEXT)
           .build();
       adView.loadAd(adRequest);
   }
}
```

With this, we come to the end of the chapter. Let's now summarize the main topics of the chapter.

Summary

The chapter has explained the publishing phase of the Android application. In the process of development of an Android application, the development is the first phase, which is followed by debugging, testing, and publishing. You have noticed that signing of the Android application is a compulsion before publishing or exposing the application to users. This chapter has also discussed about the `debug` key. You cannot sign an Android application using a `debug` key. You must have a private self-signed key to sign all your Android applications. An application signed without a private key is rejected by the Android system. The chapter has explained the importance of using same sign key. Further, you have learned about the signing strategies that are required to be followed before signing an Android application.

Next, the chapter has discussed how to obtain a private key by using `command-line` tool along with various options. Further, it has explained aligning of the `.apk` file. Aligning refers to the process of optimizing the APK. This alignment enhances interaction between Android system and your application. You have also learned how to sign and align the Android application using Eclipse IDE. Further, you have learned about the versioning of Android application. Versioning tells the users about the version of application they are using. Then, the chapter has discussed how to publish the Android application by using various means, such as Google Play, website, and email. Toward the end, the chapter has discussed how to monetize Android applications.

Quick Revise

Q1. Which of the following is not a good strategy to sign an Android application?

- **a. Use the same private key for signing all your applications**
- **b. Always use a different key for signing all your applications**
- **c. Lifespan of the private key should be more than 25 years**

d. **Private key's validity must surpass the lifespan of all the available versions of applications in a suit**

Ans. The correct option is b.

Q2. **Using same private key to sign all your applications serves which of the following purpose?**

a. **There are many processes for all your applications**

b. **The user gets a new application on each update**

c. **User has to install the full upgraded version**

d. **User can download the update only for desired module**

Ans. The correct option is d.

Q3. **To publish your application on Google Play, your private key must expire after which of the following date?**

a. **October 22, 2033**

b. **October 23, 2033**

c. **October 24, 2033**

d. **October 25, 2033**

Ans. The correct option is a.

Q4. **Which of the following tools is used to generate private key for signing Android applications?**

a. **Keyset**

b. **Keystore**

c. **Keyalg**

d. **Keytool**

Ans. The correct option is d.

Q5. **Which of the following tools is used for signing Android applications?**

a. **Jarsigner**

b. **Jar**

c. **xjc**

d. **extcheck**

Ans. The correct option is a.

Q6. **Which of the following is the minimum recommended size by Google for private key?**

a. **256 bit**

b. **512 bit**

c. **1024 bit**

d. **2048 bit**

Ans. The correct option is d.

Q7. **Which of the following is the minimum recommended validity by Google for private key?**

a. **6000 days**

b. **8000 days**

c. **10000 days**

d. **12000 days**

Ans. The correct option is c.

Q8. **Which of the following is not required in a signed `AndroidManifest.xml` file when preparing Android application?**

a. **Log calls**

b. **Version name**

c. **Version code**

d. **False value of the android:debuggable attribute**

Ans. The correct option is a.

Q9. Which of the following is the correct syntax of aligning an APK package?

a. **zipalign -v 4 app1.apk app2.apk**

b. **zipalign -v 5 app1.apk app2.apk**

c. **zipalign -v 6 app1.apk app2.apk**

d. **zipalign -v 7 app1.apk app2.apk**

Ans. The correct option is a.

Q10. Which of the following attributes display the Android application version to the user?

a. **android:versionCode**

b. **android:minSdkVersion**

c. **android:targetSdkVersion**

d. **android:versionName**

Ans. The correct option is d.

Q11. Why is it necessary to sign all Android applications of a suite with a single certificate?

Ans. The most important point you should consider while signing the Android application is that you must use the same certificate for all of your applications. The needs of using the same certificate are as follows:

- To let the users upgrade the new versions of your application seamlessly, use the same certificate (the one used at the time of installation) at the time of release of your application. On other hand, if you change the certificate, then the user has to install the full upgraded version again. In addition, if your certificate is changed, then you have to assign different packages to your application. In essence, using the same certificate implies much lesser data download, thereby providing convenience to the users.
- Using the same certificate for your applications ensures that there is only one process assigned for all your applications in Android system. This approach sustains the modularity concept as you can deploy your application in different modules and release separate updates for each of the modules. This is also beneficial from the user's point of view as a user can download the update only for the desired module.
- Preference to same certificate also provides reliable exposure of data to other applications that are signed with a specified certificate. Your application is secured for any kind of data sharing with the third-party application.

Q12. How will you generate a private key for signing an Android application?

Ans. To obtain a private key, the first step involves the interaction between the keytool and jarsigner utilities of JDK and the Android SDK build tools. This interaction can be performed in two ways. The first way is to set the `JAVA_HOME` as the environment variable in which you have to provide the path up to the `JDK` directory. The second way is to set the path of the keytool and jarsigner commands as the `PATH` variable in the environment variables.

By using the `keytool` command, we can generate a self-signed key with `Keytool`, as shown in the following syntax:

```
keytool -genkey -v -keystore your-key-name.keystore
-alias alias-key-name -keyalg RSA -keysize 2048 -validity 10000
```

Q13. How will you prepare the APK package?

Ans. When you release your application, users download it and install it on their Android-powered devices. The tasks that are required to be accomplished to prepare your application for release are as follows:

- There should not be any unwanted or garbage code, such as log calls and android:debuggable attribute, in the AndroidManifest.xml file.
- Provide proper versioning to your application in the AndroidManifest.xml file.
- Sign your application properly.
- Test your application on a real device for which your application is intended.
- All application resources, such as multimedia and graphics, must be updated and included.

- ❑ Prepare an End User License Agreement (EULA) to protect your intellectual property.
- ❑ Prepare remote servers and services on which your application relies.

Q14. How will you align the APK package? Write its command.

Ans. Aligning optimizes the Android Application Package (APK) by enhancing interaction between Android system and your application. Moreover, there is less consumption of system RAM using the `zipalign` utility. The aligning procedure is accomplished by using the `zipalign` utility, which is an archive alignment tool. The `command-line` tool used to align the `.apk` file is as follows:

```
zipalign -v 4 your_app_name-unaligned.apk your_app_name.apk
```

Q15. What is the importance of versioning the Android application?

Ans. Versioning tells the users about the version of application they are using. It is an upgrade and maintenance strategy, which is provided to user from time to time. The following points portray the essentials behind versioning of an application:

- ❑ Users want to know the application version that they are using and the upgrades available for that version.
- ❑ The compatibility issues are heavily dependent on the versioning of your application.
- ❑ When you release your application through a service, it prompts for application version so that it can be displayed to the user at the time of download.

Q16. What is publishing?

Ans. Publishing refers to the last phase of the development process of an Android application, wherein you expose the application to the market, thereby letting the users download it.

Q17. What is Google Play?

Ans. Google Play refers to the Google's premier market place to release Android applications. Here, you can publicize, sell, and distribute your Android applications across the world.

Glossary

Android SDK

Android SDK includes a compiler, debugger, a device emulator, and its own virtual machine to run Android programs.

Application framework

Application framework is of utmost importance for developer as the blocks inside this layer directly communicate with Android applications.

Application layer

Application layer is the place where your application is finally deployed over a device.

Activity

The screen of an application with which a user interacts is provided by an application component called activity.

Services

An application component in the working process that does not use UI is called a service.

Content providers

Accessing of contents from the central data warehouse is managed by a content provider.

Broadcast Receivers

Many system-generated notifications, such as battery low, downloading starts, or file received, are broadcasted by broadcast receivers.

DDMS perspective

The DDMS perspective in Eclipse provides you the full functionality of the DDMS features inside the Eclipse IDE.

ImageSwitcher

The ImageSwitcher view allows you to switch from one image to another.

Fragment

The Fragment class is used to display the views in two panes for large screens.

WebView

WebView is a class that allows you to programmatically load and display the content of a Web page in your Activity class.

Toast notification

The toast notification is a simple message that is displayed to the users on the surface of the window.

Dialog notification

The notification displayed in a small window in the form of a dialog is known as dialog notification.

SharedPreferences

The SharedPreferences class to facilitate you to save and fetch the persistent key/value pairs of primitive data types.

android.provider

The android.provider package facilitates you with the classes that can be used to access the existing content providers.

Socket programming

The technique of maintaining persistent connection with the server and notifying the server about the occurrence of changes is known as sockets programming.

GoogleMap

GoogleMap refers to the main class used to display map titles and map controls.

MapView

MapView refers to the subclass of the View class, which provides a canvas to draw the map defined by the GoogleMap object.

MapFragment

MapFragment refers to the subclass of the Fragment class, which allows you to place a map within the Fragment layout of the Activity class.

Marker

Marker allows you to define markers on a map.

UiSettings

UiSettings refers to the class that allows you to control the interface and the elements appearing on the map.

Geocoder

The Geocoder class allows you to implement geocoding and reverse geocoding.

SurfaceView

The SurfaceView class is the subclass of the View class that provides a surface to draw the graphics, which is then provided to the secondary thread of the application.

SurfaceHolder.Callback

The SurfaceHolder.Callback interface is used to notify about the various events associated with the Surface object.

Drawable

The Drawable class is an abstract class that defines the methods used to draw the graphics.

ShapeDrawable

The ShapeDrawable class allows you to dynamically draw the 2-D graphics according to your requirements.

NinePatchDrawable

The graphics that serve as the stretchable bitmap image is known as NinePatchDrawable.

Property animation

The property animation allows you to animate the properties of a View object.

ValueAnimator

The ValueAnimator class provides the timing engine for running the property animation and also estimates the animated values.

ObjectAnimator

The ObjectAnimator class extends the ValueAnimator class and sets the targeted object along with the property for animation.

AnimatorSet

The AnimatorSet class allows you to combine the related animations that can be executed together, in a sequence, or after the delay of the specified time duration.

ObjectAnimator

The ObjectAnimator class is a subclass of the ValueAnimator class that deals directly with the object.

Drawable animation

The Drawable animations are achieved through the AnimationDrawable class of the android.graphics.drawable package.

MediaPlayer

MediaPlayer specifies the primary API for playing audio and video.

VideoView

The VideoView class encapsulates the creation of a surface and allocates and prepares video content using a media player.

MediaRecorder

The MediaRecorder class specifies the technique in which you use the MediaRecorder class to record the audio or video files.

AsyncTask

AsyncTask also creates a new thread but the thread is created on behalf of the Android platform.

Start Service

Start Service refers to a service that can run for a longer period and ends on completion of the task.

Bound Service

Bound service refers to a service that makes a bound among components.

Intent Service

Intent service refers to a service that handles asynchronous requests.

Bluetooth

Bluetooth is a wireless technology standard that allows you to exchange data from one or more devices.

android.bluetooth

The android.bluetooth package provides the classes and interfaces to implement the Bluetooth functionality on the applications, such as scanning for devices, pairing with the devices, and transferring data between devices.

GATT

GATT refers to a general specification used to send and receive data in the form of attributes over a BLE link.

ATT

ATT is optimized to run on BLE devices and consumes fewer bytes.

Characteristic

Characteristic contains a single value and descriptors explaining the characteristic value.

Descriptor

A descriptor explains a characteristic value.

NdefMessage

The NdefMessage comprises one or more records.

Wi-Fi

Wi-Fi is a popular wireless technology used to exchange data or connect to the Internet wirelessly within the range of 20 meters.

TelephonyManager

The TelephonyManager class provides direct access to various types of phone properties, such as phone type, network-related details, Subscriber Identity Module (SIM) details, or data state details.

PhoneStateListener

The PhoneStateListener class is a listener class that helps in monitoring the changes in different telephony states on mobile devices, such as available service state or signal strength. The SmsManager class is used to send text messages.

AppWidgetProviÞr

The AppWidgetProvider class provides a widget on the basis of broadcast events.

AppWidgetManager

The AppWidgetManager class is used to update widgets and provide details related to them.

RemoteViews

RemoteViews is a class that acts as a proxy to a view hierarchy, which is hosted by another application.

RemoteViewsSe0072vice

`RemoteViewsService` is a class that is used as a wrapper to manage the `RemoteViewsFactory` interface.

RemoteViewsFactory

The `RemoteViewsFactory` interface acts as a wrapper around the `Adapter` class.

Index

<

<action>, 72, 109, 113

<activity>, 71, 82, 90, 130, 138, 139, 404, 416

<application>, 71, 90, 130, 295, 299, 345, 404, 407, 416, 468, 469

<category>, 72

<intent-filter>, 72, 82, 104, 109, 113, 121, 133, 138, 157, 223, 257, 270, 286, 289, 311, 317, 321, 372, 378, 385, 390, 404, 407, 411, 436, 439, 444, 454, 457, 459, 463, 466, 468, 469, 484, 489, 493, 498, 501, 505, 546

<manifest>, 71, 468, 469

<use-feature>, 310

<uses-feature>, 478, 479

<uses-permission>, 310, 311, 325

<uses-sdk>, 71, 416, 536

A

AccelerateDecelerateInterpolator, 347

AccelerateInterpolator, 346, 347, 355, 356

ACCESS_WIFI_STATE, 299, 300, 301, 440, 444

ACTION_HEADSET_PLUG, 108

ACTION_NDEF_DISCOVERED, 435, 436, 437, 448

ACTION_TAG_DISCOVERED, 436, 448

ACTION_TECH_DISCOVERED, 435, 436, 448

ActivityGroup , 80, 130

addCallback(), 334

admob, 542

AIDL, 409, 410

AlertDialog, 92, 93, 96, 97, 99, 102, 129, 130, 131, 203, 204

AnalogClock, 205, 206, 218, 219, 220, 226, 228, 488, 490

Android architecture, 52, 54, 75, 76, 77

android.appwidget.action.APPWIDGET_UPDATE, 489, 493

android.bluetooth, 418, 422, 428, 429, 430, 431

android.content.ComponentCallbacks, 403

android.content.ComponentCallbacks2, 403

android.content.Context, 150, 184, 209, 212, 220, 245, 267, 319, 323, 332, 334, 341, 358, 403, 422, 442, 453, 455, 458, 479, 481, 491

android.content.ContextWrapper, 403

android.graphics.drawable, 336, 339, 341, 351, 352, 355

android.hardware, 383, 390, 433, 436, 440, 475, 478, 479, 481, 483, 486

android.intent.action.MAIN, 82, 106, 109, 121, 133, 138, 157, 223, 257, 270, 286, 289, 311, 317, 321, 372, 378, 385, 390, 404, 407, 411, 439, 444, 454, 457, 459, 463, 466, 484, 493, 501, 546

android.intent.action.RESPOND_VIA_MESSAGE, 469

android.intent.action.SENDTO, 107, 469

android.intent.action.VIEW, 106, 109, 134

android.net, 85, 117, 127, 134, 267, 270, 272, 280, 283, 301, 302, 376, 439, 440, 442, 458

android.net.http, 283, 301

android.net.wifi, 283, 439, 440, 442

android.nfc.tech, 435

android.provider, 85, 263, 264, 265, 274, 311, 317, 376, 437, 468, 469

android.provider.Telephony.SMS_DELIVER, 468

android.provider.Telephony.WAP_PUSH_DELIVER, 469

android.telephony.gsm, 283

android.view.animation, 209, 214, 346, 347, 350, 355, 357

android:targetSdkVersion, 121, 133, 138, 157, 286, 288, 310, 312, 316, 321, 372, 378, 385, 390, 404, 407, 411, 438, 444, 454, 456, 459, 462, 466, 481, 484, 493, 501, 536, 546, 549

android:versionCode, 121, 133, 138, 157, 286, 288, 310, 316, 321, 372, 378, 385, 390, 404, 406, 411, 438, 444, 454, 456, 459, 462, 466, 484, 493, 501, 535, 536, 546, 549

android:versionName, 121, 133, 138, 157, 286, 288, 310, 316, 321, 372, 378, 385, 390, 404, 407, 411, 438, 444, 454, 456, 459, 462, 466, 484, 493, 501, 535, 536, 546, 549

AnimationDrawable, 351, 352

Animator, 330, 346, 347, 348, 349, 352, 354, 355, 356, 358

AnimatorListener, 348

AnimatorSet, 346, 347

AnticipateInterpolator, 347

AnticipateOvershootInterpolator, 347

Apache ant, 74

appwidget-provider, 488, 489, 491, 493, 504, 505

AppWidget.ACTION_APPWIDGET_UPDATE, 489, 503

AppWidgetManager, 488, 489, 490, 491, 492, 496, 497, 503, 504

AppWidgetProvider, 488, 489, 491, 492, 495, 503, 504

ArgbEvaluator, 347

AsyncTask, 294, 319, 320, 398, 399, 400, 401, 414

Attribute Protocol (ATT), 433

AudioManager, 362, 364, 367, 368, 369, 380, 381, 391, 393

B

Binder, 404, 405, 409, 410, 412

BitmapDrawable, 336

BluetoothAdapter, 418, 420, 421, 422, 423, 424, 428, 429, 431, 434, 446, 447

BluetoothAdapter.LeScanCallback, 418

BluetoothGatt, 419

BluetoothGattService, 419

BluetoothHealth, 419, 420

BluetoothProfile, 418, 446

BluetoothProfile.ServiceListener, 418

BluetoothSocket, 419, 420, 428, 429, 431, 432

BounceInterpolator, 347

bound service, 396, 402, 403, 409, 410, 412, 414, 415

Broadcast receivers, 76

BROADCAST_SMS, 468

BroadcastReceiver, 421, 422, 423, 424, 440, 442, 443, 467, 468, 469, 471, 495

C

CalendarContract.Attendees, 264

CalendarContract.Calendars, 264

CalendarContract.Events, 264, 265

CalendarContract.ExtendedProperties, 264

CalendarContract.Instances, 264

CalendarContract.Reminders, 264

CamcorderProfile, 387, 388, 389, 390, 392

Camera, 315, 316, 361, 363, 365, 367, 369, 371, 373, 375, 377, 379, 381, 382, 383, 384, 385, 387, 389, 391, 392, 393

Canvas, 330, 331, 332, 333, 335, 341, 342, 346, 352, 353, 358, 359, 360, 499, 500

Canvas.isHardwareAccelerated(), 346

CHANGE_WIFI_MULTICAST_STATE, 440

CHANGE_WIFI_STATE, 440, 444

Characteristic, 3, 419, 433, 447

ContentProvider, 266, 267, 269, 270, 271, 273

ContentValues, 245, 246, 267, 268, 270, 375, 376, 378

Context.startActivity(), 105

create(), 92, 93, 97, 130, 204, 363, 392, 393

createBitmap(), 330, 353, 360

createRfcommSocketToServiceRecord(), 429, 432, 447

CycleInterpolator, 347

D

Dalvik virtual machine, 5, 53, 75, 77

DatePickerDialog, 92, 94, 95, 96, 98, 103, 104, 129

DDMS perspective, 63

DecelerateInterpolator, 347

Descriptor, 380, 419, 433, 447

Dialog Notification, 226

DigitalClock, 205, 206, 218, 219, 220, 222, 226, 228

doInBackground() , 295, 398, 400

Drawable, 329, 330, 336, 337, 338, 339, 340, 341, 342, 343, 346, 351, 352, 353, 354, 355, 356, 360

Drawable animation, 330, 351

drawBitmap(), 331, 352, 360

F

FileOutputStream, 234, 237, 239, 241, 242, 276, 383, 384

FLAG_HARDWARE_ACCELERATED, 345, 346

FloatEvaluator, 347

FragmentManager, 123, 125, 126, 131, 188, 190, 192, 193, 221, 312, 316

Fragments, 79, 81, 83, 85, 87, 89, 91, 93, 95, 97, 99, 101, 103, 105, 107, 109, 111, 113, 115, 117, 119, 121, 123, 125, 126, 127, 129, 131, 133, 135, 187, 191, 192, 193

G

Generic Attribute Profile (GATT), 433

geocoding, 304, 321, 322, 323, 326, 328, 375

getData(), 85, 106, 107, 116, 386, 393

getDefaultAdapter(), 420, 422, 429, 431, 447

getDefaultSensor(), 476, 477, 485

getExternalStorageState(), 230, 239, 274, 275

getHolder(), 334, 359, 368, 384, 388

getIntrinsicHeight(), 336

getMaximumRange(), 476, 477, 486

getPadding(Rect), 336

getPreferences(), 230, 231, 275, 276

getResolution(), 476, 477, 486

getSensorList(), 476, 477, 486

getSystemService(), 225, 226, 381, 450, 454, 456, 458, 470, 471, 476

Google play, 317, 537, 538

GoogleMap, 304, 305, 309, 310, 311, 312, 313, 316, 326, 327

GoogleMap.MAP_TYPE_HYBRID, 313, 316, 327

GoogleMap.MAP_TYPE_SATELLITE, 313, 327

GoogleMap.MAP_TYPE_TERRAIN, 313

GridView, 206, 211, 212, 213, 227, 495

Gyroscope, 479

H

Hardware Acceleration, 329, 345

HttpGet, 287, 288

I

IBinder, 404, 405, 409, 410, 412

ImageSwitcher, 206, 207, 208, 209, 210, 214, 215, 216, 226, 228

ImageView, 97, 98, 101, 206, 209, 210, 211, 212, 213, 214, 215, 216, 217, 218, 226, 227, 290, 291, 292, 337, 349, 350, 352, 354, 355, 356, 481, 482, 490, 505

Intent, 76, 79, 81, 82, 83, 85, 87, 89, 91, 93, 95, 97, 99, 101, 103, 105, 106, 107, 108, 109, 110, 111, 113, 114, 115, 116, 117, 118, 119, 120, 121, 122, 123, 125, 126, 127, 128, 129, 130, 131, 132, 133, 134, 137, 138, 156, 157, 187, 225, 226, 248, 263, 277, 278, 280, 281, 302, 366, 368, 370, 371, 372, 375, 376, 378, 386, 391, 393, 402, 404, 405, 406, 410, 412, 413, 416, 420, 422, 423,

424, 434, 436, 437, 438, 442, 443, 449, 450, 457, 458, 460, 463, 464, 465, 466, 467, 470, 471, 472, 489, 491, 492, 495, 496, 497, 504

intent service, 396

Intent.ACTION_CALL, 457, 458

Intent.ACTION_SEND, 108, 280, 281

IntentFilter, 109, 422, 423, 442

IntEvaluator, 347

J

jarsigner, 528, 529, 531, 533, 549

java.io, 237, 241, 283, 284, 287, 290, 294, 297, 299, 301, 302, 319, 323, 376, 383, 388, 398, 428, 431

java.net, 283, 287, 290, 294, 297, 299, 301, 302, 398

java.nio, 283, 301, 302, 436

JSON services, 283, 301

K

keytool, 307, 528, 529, 530, 533, 549

L

LayerDrawable, 336

LayoutInflater, 125, 152, 188, 190, 220, 344, 355, 356, 383, 384, 385

LinearInterpolator, 348

Linux kernel, 50, 52, 53, 75, 76

ListView, 154, 174, 175, 179, 187, 188, 189, 200, 201, 219, 221, 442, 443, 495

lockCanvas(), 330, 331, 335, 353, 359, 360, 499

M

main thread, 396, 398

Map, 267, 268, 303, 304, 305, 306, 307, 308, 309, 310, 311, 312, 313, 314, 315, 316, 317, 318, 319, 321, 323, 325, 326, 327, 400, 435

MapFragment, 304, 310, 312, 313, 316

MapView, 304, 327

Marker, 304, 315, 316

MediaController, 364, 392, 393

MediaPlayer, 362, 363, 364, 365, 366, 367, 368, 369, 370, 372, 373, 376, 377, 391, 392, 393

MediaRecorder. MediaPlayer, 362

MediaRecorder.AudioSource.MIC, 374, 377, 378

MediaStore.ACTION_VIDEO_CAPTURE, 386, 393

N

native code, 2, 508, 512, 524, 525

NdefMessage, 435, 436, 437, 438

NdefRecord, 435, 436, 437, 438

NDK, 507, 508, 509, 510, 511, 512, 513, 515, 516, 517, 519, 521, 523, 524, 525, 526

Near Field Communication, 418

NinePatch, 329, 342, 343, 344, 345

NinePatchDrawable, 329, 342, 343

NotificationManager, 225, 226, 227

O

ObjectAnimator, 346, 347, 348

onAccuracyChanged(), 477, 486

onActivityCreated(), 124

onAttach(), 124

onBind(), 403, 409, 415

OnBufferingUpdateListener, 367, 368, 370

OnClickListener(), 93, 94, 97, 98, 111, 119, 127, 131, 132, 134, 138, 161, 162, 164, 165, 166, 167, 168, 169, 170, 171, 183, 186, 199, 202, 203, 215, 237, 242, 250, 252, 254, 256, 278, 281, 285, 288, 294, 299, 320, 357, 371, 372, 381, 384, 399, 458, 462, 465

OnCompletionListener, 367, 368, 370

onCreate(), 72, 80, 82, 87, 88, 89, 90, 105, 124, 180, 268, 269, 310, 332, 370, 385, 389, 403, 405, 407, 408, 409, 410, 414, 415, 454, 456, 458, 496, 504

onCreateView(), 124, 188

OnDateSetListener(), 94, 98

onLeScan(), 418

onPostExecute(), 398, 400

OnPreparedListener, 367, 368, 369, 370
onProgressUpdate() , 398, 400
onSensorChanged(), 477, 478, 480, 484, 486
onStartCommand(), 403, 408, 410, 414, 415
OnTimeSetListener(), 95, 98
onTouchEvent(), 85
OnVideoSizeChangedListener, 367, 368, 369, 370
openFileOutput(), 234, 235, 274
OpenGL, 53, 76, 77, 479
OutputStreamWriter, 234, 237, 239, 241, 242
OvershootInterpolator, 347, 348

P

PhoneStateListener, 450, 455, 456, 470, 472
PictureCallback, 382, 383, 384, 385
PictureDrawable, 336
prepare(), 363, 364, 365, 366, 367, 368, 370, 374, 377, 378, 387, 389, 390, 392
ProcessDialog, 92
publishing, 528, 537, 541, 547, 550
putExtra(), 280, 465, 471

R

READ_PHONE_STATE, 453, 455, 457, 459, 471
registerListener(), 476, 478, 480, 486
RemoteViews, 490, 491, 492, 495, 496, 497, 503, 504, 505
RemoteViewService, 497
RemoteViewsFactory, 495, 496, 497
reverse geocoding, 304, 321, 322, 326, 328
RFCOMM, 421, 428

S

SEND_SMS, 460, 463, 466, 471
sendBroadcast(), 105
sendOrderedBroadcast(), 105
sendStickyBroadcast(), 105
Sensor, 473, 474, 475, 476, 477, 478, 479, 480, 481, 482, 483, 484, 485, 486
SensorEvent, 475, 477, 478, 479, 480, 483, 485
SensorEventListener, 475, 477, 479, 483, 485
SensorManager, 474, 475, 476, 477, 478, 479, 480, 481, 482, 483, 485, 486
ServerSocket, 283, 297, 298, 420, 429
Service, 55, 77, 105, 184, 224, 225, 226, 283, 284, 285, 286, 287, 293, 294, 295, 296, 303, 304, 305, 306, 307, 308, 309, 311, 313, 315, 317, 319, 321, 323, 324, 325, 327, 381, 395, 397, 399, 400, 401, 402, 403, 404, 405, 406, 407, 408, 409, 410, 411, 412, 413, 414, 415, 418, 419, 429, 431, 432, 433, 434, 441, 442, 443, 446, 447, 450, 451, 454, 456, 458, 469, 470, 471, 472, 476, 477, 478, 480, 482, 486, 495, 496, 497, 498, 499, 500, 501, 502, 504, 505, 506
setAudioEncoder(), 374, 378
setBounds(Rect), 336
setContentView(View), 80, 130
setDataSource(), 363, 364, 367, 370
setLevel(int), 336
setMapType(), 313
setMediaController(), 364
setMessage(), 93
setOnShakeListener(), 482, 484
setOutputFile(), 374, 378, 387, 390, 392
setOutputFormat(), 374, 378
setRemoteAdapter(), 497
setScrollGesturesEnabled(), 318, 327
setState(int []), 336
setVideoUri(), 364
setZoomGesturesEnabled(), 318, 327
ShakeListener, 482, 483, 484
ShapeDrawable, 329, 330, 336, 340, 341, 342, 352, 360
SharedPreferences, 230, 231, 232, 233, 275, 276, 277, 278
show(), 36, 93, 94, 95, 97, 98, 131, 152, 163, 164, 165, 166, 167, 168, 169, 170, 171, 172, 173, 176, 177, 179, 185, 186, 188, 190, 195, 197, 203, 204, 209, 212, 217, 218, 225, 227, 238, 242, 250, 252, 253, 255, 256, 270, 291, 292, 321, 325, 377, 378, 384, 389, 397, 405, 429, 431, 437, 442, 443, 456, 462, 465, 468

ShutterCallback, 382, 383, 384, 385
SMS_DELIVER_ACTION, 468
SMS_RECEIVED_ACTION, 468
SmsManager, 450, 460, 461, 462, 463, 470, 471, 472
SQLite, 53, 75, 76, 77, 229, 230, 243, 245, 250, 252, 262, 267, 268, 269, 274, 275, 276
StackView, 495
start service, 396, 402
startActivity(Intent), 82
startActivityForResult(), 85, 105, 115, 116, 420, 421
SurfaceHolder, 330, 331, 333, 334, 335, 352, 353, 358, 359, 360, 364, 367, 368, 369, 370, 382, 383, 384, 385, 388, 389, 390, 392, 499, 500
SurfaceHolder.Callback, 333, 334, 352, 364, 368, 370, 384, 385, 388, 389
SurfaceView, 330, 331, 333, 334, 335, 336, 352, 353, 358, 359, 364, 366, 368, 370, 383, 384, 385, 387, 388, 389, 390, 392

T

Tag Dispatch System, 434
TelephonyManager, 450, 451, 452, 453, 454, 455, 456, 458, 470, 471, 472
Thread, 63, 285, 288, 291, 292, 297, 298, 299, 334, 335, 359, 395, 396, 397, 398, 399, 400, 401, 403, 405, 407, 409, 411, 413, 415, 416, 429, 431
TimeInterpolator, 347, 348
TimePickerDialog, 92, 94, 95, 96, 98, 129
Toast notification, 206, 211, 218, 224, 225, 250, 252, 253, 259
TYPE_ACCELEROMETER, 474, 477, 480, 482, 485, 486
TypeEvaluator, 347

U

UiSettings, 304, 312, 318
updateAppWidget(), 490, 497, 504

V

ValueAnimator, 346, 347, 348, 349, 354, 355, 356
VideoView, 364, 386, 388, 392, 393
View animation, 351
View.isHardwareAccelerated(), 346

W

WebView, 222, 223, 226, 227, 228
WifiManager, 440, 441, 442, 443
windowIsFloating , 80, 130

Z

zipalign, 528, 532, 549, 550

Online Resource Available with the Book

The Online Resources available with **Android Application Development Black Book** contain elements specifically selected to enhance the usefulness of this book. The following elements are available on the **http://www.dreamtechpress.com** website:

- **Bonus chapters**—Three advance level chapters are provided on the website as bonus chapters.
- **Code from the book**—All executable applications provided in the book are provided on the website, so that you can run them without manually coding them line by line. You can find the code for these applications in Java on the website.

System Requirements

- Windows XP/Visa/2000/2003/7
- JDK 1.6 or 1.7
- Eclipse IDE
- Android SDK

Hardware Requirements

- PC: P4/AMD 64
- Processor: 1 GHz CPU (recommended)
- Hard disk: 5 GB of disk space
- Memory: 1 GB of RAM minimum (2GB recommended)

To access the Online Resources

1. Visit *http://www.dreamtechpress.com/TitlePage.aspx?x=978-93-5119-409-5*
2. Click the Companion Content tab.
3. Enter the Download code: AAD-4095-BB-464.
4. Click the Download button.